WITHDRAWN

WITHDRAWN

THE STATE OF THE MASSES

THE STATE OF THE MASSES

Richard F. Hamilton
James D. Wright

ALDINE
Publishing Company

New York

ABOUT THE AUTHORS

Richard F. Hamilton is Professor of Sociology, McGill University. In addition to authoring many articles, he has written several books including: *Who Voted For Hitler?, Restraining Myths, Class Politics in the United States,* and *Affluence and the French Worker in the Fourth Republic.*

James D. Wright is Professor of Sociology, University of Massachusetts and Director of the Social and Demographic Research Institute. He is the author of many ground-breaking books including: *Victims of the Environment, The Handbook of Survey Research,* and *Under the Gun: Weapons, Crime, and Violence in America.* He is currently completing *Armed and Considered Dangerous* with Peter H. Rossi.

Aldine Publishing Company
200 Saw Mill River Road
Hawthorne, New York 10532

Library of Congress Cataloging-in-Publication Data

Hamilton, Richard F.
   The state of the masses.

   Bibliography: p.
   Includes index.
   1. United States—Social conditions—1970-
2. Public opinion—United States.   I. Wright, James D.
II. Title.
HN59.H244   1986   973.92   85-20127
ISBN 0-202-30324-1 (lib. bdg.)
ISBN 0-202-30325-X (pbk.)

Printed in the United States
10 9 8 7 6 5 4 3 2 1

To Irene and Chris,
with Gratitude and Affection

CONTENTS

PREFACE

We have borrowed the title. It comes from a book by Emil Lederer, one first published in 1940. The title, we thought, contains a useful idea, that is, the need for a summary portrait, for a picture of the social conditions, outlooks, and leading motives found within "the masses." Although we do not agree with the fundamentals of the portrait Lederer provided, we do, obviously, like and appreciate the essential idea.

The word "masses," in most formulations, is accompanied by rather unsavory predicates. "The masses" are said to lack intelligence, character, and constancy of purpose. They are gullible, easily led, subject to manipulation, and are moved either by zealous demagogues or by scheming "elites." On the side of the angels today, tomorrow the masses could easily be in the sway of a self-declared people's tribune. The alternative reading sees them caught up by the latest mass media offering. Here the complaint is about their inactivity, their torpor. They are immobilized, transfixed, refusing to work toward the "higher synthesis" that some astute analyst has discovered to be close at hand.

An obvious correlate to this deprecation of "the masses" is the claim that some other segment of the population is behaving in an opposite way, showing intelligence, self-sacrifice, and responsibility. The most frequent references are to traditional upper classes (or elites), to those doing what they can to channel unpredictable mass demands, or to *engagé* intellectuals, to those who, out of a generous, public-spirited concern, offer guidance and direction to the masses.

We do not accept—at least not as *a priori* stipulations—the elements of the above depiction. We did not wish to prejudge any of the empirical questions involved in the drawing of a social portrait. From the outset, therefore, we sought to remain open to other readings. Following the basic Cartesian principle—skepticism—we were willing to entertain opposite hypotheses, such as the possibility of reasonable "masses" and the possibility of gullible or manipulated elites and/or intellectuals.

In keeping with that skepticism, our use of the term "masses" differs from that found in most discussions of "the mass society." Throughout the book

ix

we are referring either to the population of the United States in its entirety or, more frequently, to the nation's adult population. Our discussion, therefore, embraces all segments, manual, nonmanual, and farm. The upper-middle-class "masses" appear there along with the working-class "masses." Also included is a tiny segment, a minuscule portion of the whole, but still a large absolute number, the hundreds of thousands who form the upper-class "masses." It also includes a somewhat larger collectivity, the "masses" of intellectuals.

One can, in most seasons, find many competing depictions of "the state of the masses." This work deals with some that were current in the 1970's. As of this writing, some five years into the 1980's, most of those depictions no longer have any popular resonance. A famous work by Charles Reich, a "smash" best-seller in the early 1970's, is now no more than a nostalgic memory for some. For others, for those too young to have experienced the event, even recognition of the name is a rarity. This raises a simple question: why have we taken up such "ancient" concerns?

A first reason is that of historical interest: we were interested in establishing, as best we could, what actually happened. If one were to depend on the claims made in the course of that decade, an array of contradictions would be an early discovery. Against the claims of Charles Reich, for example, are those put forward by Richard Scammon and Ben Wattenberg. A principal task, therefore, has been that of assessment, to ascertain which of the claims have proved valid. Another possibility, of course, is that both contradictory claims are mistaken; they might both involve a misreading of the state of human affairs at the time.

A second reason for this exploration is to see if the experience of the 1970's does not contain some more general lessons. Several of the major claims reviewed and discussed here reflect (or are derived from) one or another general theoretical orientation. Our review and assessment, therefore, will have implications for those general theories. Our task, therefore, goes beyond mere scorekeeping. We wish to see if the lessons contained in that experience can guide us in our understanding of the human condition at other times and in other places. Part of our effort, as will be seen, is to spell out a more adequate theory, one that, we hope, will be more realistic and have more general application.

A third consideration that has motivated us is a concern with the sociology of knowledge. In some instances, as will be shown, a viewpoint gained wide currency (we cannot be sure of acceptance) although based on the most casual of all possible "research" methods. One viewpoint, another that gained wide currency, achieved that following even though it stood in sharp opposition to a very extensive body of research findings. One of our tasks, therefore, has been to explain or account for the development of these otherwise unexpected "understandings" of things and for their popular resonance.

People are trained (in a Pavlovian sense) to see things in given ways. They learn basic paradigms—schemes allowing them to categorize and simplify a wide range of otherwise troublesome experience. People are also trained, in the same way, to approve or disapprove of data sources or research styles. Some of this training takes the form of common sense guidelines, as for example, when people reject all content provided by a "fast talker." Other people, some of them fast talkers, operate with a similar casual "methodological" guideline. Leading intellectual journals rarely mention "statistics" or "polls" or "surveys" without some accompanying terms of denigration. That reaction, we feel, is as unthinking as the former procedure. On the whole, we think, the rejection of the "fast talker" has more justification—the aim is to protect relatively defenseless populations from the detrimental effects of various merchandisers, the sellers of dubious commercial, political, or cultural "goods." That intellectuals should defend prejudicial procedure is, we feel, something of a disgrace.

C. Wright Mills offered the following advice to sociologists: "First, one tries to get it straight, to make an adequate statement. . . . " That is our major aim, both with respect to the factual or empirical questions raised about the 1970's and with respect to the general theoretical concerns. The human condition might be improved, we feel, if one can "get it straight." Demagogic misleads would thereby be discouraged. One would have an realistic estimate of the magnitude or seriousness of any given problem. One would not be worrying about the wrong things. Effort would not be diverted from real problems to those that were simply made up.

Mills added a proviso with regard to the "adequate statement." "If it is gloomy," he said, "too bad; if it leads to hope, fine." Some social commentators, however, reverse the priorities. The adequate statement, in their view, is one that fits the requirements of their theory. For them, if it is gloomy, it is an inadequate statement. That procedure, we feel, is one with no intellectual merit whatsoever. If the aim is to impose appropriate readings on a recalcitrant world, we feel the best advice is to give up the social science pretense entirely. One should openly declare that the effort is basically a matter of belief, a "defense of the faith." Those *believers* might simplify matters for all parties concerned by developing a set of "adequate statements," a confession, that could be recited at meetings of the sodality. The *faithful* could gather together and chant "I believe in a seditious and discontented working class." Or perhaps, to lend a certain mystery, it might be rendered as: *Credo in plebem seditiosam et turbulentam.*

One final point. Although a given theory, claim, or position may at a given time appear to be "dead," that is, without any current interest, none is so far removed that it will not sometime later resurface as new, profound, and "meaningful" intellectual coinage. Nietzsche spoke of *le retour éternel.* If he is correct, rather than seeing the disappearance as mere historical fact (as something people once believed, a topic now of interest only to intellectual historians), our review, we feel, might help our understanding of the process, of the cycle of ideas. It is for this reason that we ask the additional question:

why was it believed? It might help one to understand and better appreciate Theory Q when it makes its appearance the next time around.

Many people have helped us with the creation of this book. Persons deserving special thanks, for their reading of manuscript chapters and extremely generous provision of comment, are Norval D. Glenn, Paul C. Glick, and George Strauss. Another who provided aid that went far beyond any "call of duty" was Edward J. Withers.

For their assistance in one form or another, we wish to thank all of the following: Chandler Davidson, William Domhoff, Paul Eberts, Robert Faulkner, William Form, Naomi Gerstel, Carl Hamilton, William Kornblum, Theodore Marmor, James N. Morgan, Al Nash, Maurice Pinard, Jerome M. Rosow, Pepper Schwartz, Melvin Seeman, Lou Sieberlich, Rollin Simonds, George Snider, David N. Solomon, Curt Tausky, Laurie Tough, and Axel van den Berg. We also acknowledge the assistance of Matthew Wright, Julie Lam, and Derek Wright in preparing the name index.

Special thanks are also due Ms. Eleanor Weber-Burdin and Ms. Marianne Geronimo for their capable assistance with the computer work and data analysis.

All responsibility for this text, of course, for the findings as presented here and for the interpretations, is ours alone.

The survey data analyzed here were obtained through the auspices of the Inter-University Consortium for Political and Social Research (University of Michigan) and the Roper Public Opinion Research Center (University of Connecticut). We extend our gratitude to both organizations, and to the original investigators, for making the information available. Through the efforts of these data archives, scholars are given ready access to high-quality "state-of-the-art" information on the consciousness and conditions of the American population, and all serious students of American social and political life are therefore enormously in their debt.

This research was generously supported by the Social Sciences and Humanities Research Council of Canada (Grant #410–78–0343). We thank the Council and the ultimate sponsors, the people of Canada, for their support. Additional support was also provided through Faculty Research Grants from the University of Massachusetts, for which we are also grateful.

Richard F. Hamilton
James D. Wright

1

CLAIMING THE MASSES: SOME CONFLICTING PORTRAITS

INTRODUCTION

This book is concerned with the outlooks, desires, satisfactions, and sorrows of the American people. More specifically, it reviews and presents evidence bearing on various accounts and claims made about the American population during the course of the 1970's. These accounts purport to describe majority characteristics or tendencies. But in many instances, there is more than mere description at work; there is an effort to *claim* the majority, declaring it to be an advocate, supporter, or agency of some specific political direction or program. The purpose here is to evaluate the plausibility of these claims on the basis of the best existing evidence and studies produced in the decade.

Most of the accounts we consider assume, in one way or another, the existence of widespread dismay, anxiety, or disenchantment. Most, that is, postulate a rampant malaise, a vast and ever-increasing sense that there are fundamental problems with contemporary American life. In most accounts, this sense of strain or malaise is said to constitute a continuous pressure to change the way society presently works. Some see the pressure as involving a demand for progressive, even radical, change, where others see the strain as creating a reactive demand, one frequently characterized by the term "backlash."

It is obviously worth knowing whether society is moving in a leftward or rightward direction, or not moving at all. It is also helpful to know the sources of that change or stability. One cannot object to largely speculative accounts of the society and its dynamics, such as those reviewed and analyzed here, but speculation is only a first step. A crucial second step is to test the various accounts against evidence to see which contain valid insights and which are mere fancy. Such is the purpose of this work.

All the accounts reviewed here claim to have some empirical basis. It will nevertheless be seen that some of them make diametrically opposed claims and therefore cannot be equally valid. If some of these claims are true, then others, of necessity, must be false. The overriding concern of this volume is to determine which is which.

1

The remainder of the present chapter describes the various claims and viewpoints to be assessed. We begin with a recounting of the 1970 work by Charles Reich, *The Greening of America,* and of some similar works of social criticism. As we shall see, most of the key themes of this work contrast pointedly with another influential volume published in the same year, *The Real Majority,* by Scammon and Wattenberg, which we also review. A third tradition discussed here involves a group of workplace critics, as exemplified in works such as *False Promises* by Stanley Aronowitz (1973) or *Labor and Monopoly Capital* by Harry Braverman (1974). We contrast the claims of this tradition with the writings on work and its discontents that emerge in the professional social science literature. Finally, we recount the central themes of what has come to be known as the theory of postindustrialism, as set forth in works such as Daniel Bell's *The Coming of Post-Industrial Society* (1973) or Ronald Inglehart's *The Silent Revolution* (1977a), and contrast them with what may be seen as the antithesis of the theory of postindustrialism; namely, what we call "the theory of the little man's revolt."

The works to be considered here are not all of the same character. Some are essentially speculative, even polemical, and virtually devoid of empirical evidence; others present reams of data from many sources. Some, such as Reich, are best-selling popularizations and have been read by millions of people; others are technical academic works of the sort seldom read by more than a few thousand people. As a generalization, it may be said that readership declines as complexity and evidentiary contents increase; the most data-laden sources, in short, have few readers. This in turn produces a considerable imbalance in impact: the sweeping and provocative speculation comes to be widely known and will, in some cases, attract avid followers, while the scientific evidence bearing on the veracity of that speculation is buried in out-of-the-way, inaccessible scholarly journals. This is one of several reasons why the assertions of the speculative literature tend to retain popular currency long after they have been dismissed by specialists in the field. One auxiliary purpose of the present work is to bridge the gap between popularizations and scholarly treatments of the nature and direction of American society, to bring the best available research evidence to bear on some of the more common assertions and claims.

The remainder of this chapter involves a brief intellectual history of the 1970's: it provides a statement about the repertory of claims to be discussed in later chapters. Chapter 2 begins our assessment of the evidence on which these claims are based. Essentially, it investigates and comments upon the quality of the evidence assembled by the authors themselves. Beginning, then, with Chapter 3, we present additional evidence from other sources bearing on these same claims.

As will be seen, the findings do not fully support any of the positions described in this chapter. None of the viewpoints we consider, that is, provides a fully acceptable account of the outlooks and conditions of the American majority. Our effort, however, is not entirely negative. In the end, we reject many of the claims commonly made about the American population, but we have also tried to provide an intellectual framework that gives a closer "fit" to the evidence, the elements of which are presented and discussed as appropriate throughout the text, beginning with the opening pages of Chapter 3. One final task, undertaken in the concluding chapter, is to consider some reasons for these distorted claims and to say something about the reasons for their initial popularity.

THE GREENING OF AMERICA AND THE COMING OF CONSCIOUSNESS III

One of the most widely read and discussed accounts of American Society produced in the 1970's was Charles Reich's *The Greening of America*. Today, fifteen years later, it is difficult to appreciate the initial impact of this book. Indeed, a contemporary reader would doubtlessly find much of it either *passé* or bizarre. Still, it was certainly among the best-sellers of the decade, was adopted as required reading in many college and university courses in the early 1970's, and was reviewed upon publication in every major literary-political journal and magazine. To indicate something of its impact, the 1972 Democratic presidential candidate, George McGovern, read the book and found it to be "one of the most gripping, penetrating, and revealing analyses of American society I have yet seen."[1]

Intellectual interest in the Reichian theses was sufficiently widespread to spawn a secondary publication, a collection of critical reactions and commentary edited by Philip Nobile and published under the title *The Con III Controversy* (1971). This reader on *The Greening of America* contains pieces by "more than thirty of America's most important social critics" (from the flyleaf). Many of them were openly hostile to Reich's book. Malcolm Muggeridge, for example, found it "intrinsically silly," and Stewart Alsop characterized it as "astonishingly empty of real content" and as having "obvious Fascist overtones." But most of the commentary was laudatory. Karl Meyer was struck by "the appalling accuracy of his description of present-day America," John Kenneth Galbraith pronounced it "an enormously interesting book," and Ralph Gleason was moved to remark, "Reich is . . . more important than Marcuse."[2]

[1] It is sometimes wondered whether the works of American intellectuals have impact on the operation of the larger society; the supposition is that they usually do not. In this case, however, we have a candidate for President of the United States among the readership, pronouncing himself to have been greatly informed by the work in question. (Reich's is not the only work reviewed in this chapter to have had an apparent impact on leading national politicians. As discussed later, a 1969 article by Pete Hamill, "The Revolt of the White Lower-Middle Class," was circulated in the highest levels of the Nixon Administration and was taken quite seriously by them.)

[2] Reich was a professor at Yale University when the book was published, and Nobile's reader (1971) contains, along with various critical commentaries, the following snippet from the Yale Course Description Guide:

The essential themes of the book can be readily summarized. On the second page, Reich announces that "there is a revolution coming"—"the revolution of the new generation." Indeed, Reich's revolution is said to be presently under way. "It is now spreading with amazing rapidity, and already our laws, institutions and social structure are changing in consequence."

The revolution Reich depicts will bring a new and better world, a world qualitatively different from the one we now inhabit. "It promises a higher reason, a more human community, and a new and liberated individual." Continuing, "its ultimate creation will be a new and enduring wholeness and beauty—a renewed relationship of man to himself, to other men, to society, to nature, and to the land." Further, he argues, this revolution "is both necessary and inevitable, and in time it will include not only youth, but all the people in America" (p. 2).

As is perhaps already obvious, a key premise is that the young people of today (or of 1970)—"the new generation," as Reich refers to them—are much different from all other generations that have preceded them. Virtually alone in history, the new generation is seen as somehow having been liberated from the conventions of the past. They have become the bearers of a whole new consciousness, which Reich calls Consciousness III, and it is the diffusion of this consciousness and its eventual dominance that constitutes the revolution of which he is speaking. In this sense, it could be said that the "greening of America" will have been complete, the revolution accomplished, once all or most of the society has come around to thinking in ways that the youth of the late 1960's thought. And it is this precise development that Reich sees to be both "necessary and inevitable."[3]

> "Perhaps the most cogent comment to be made about Mr. Reich's course is that he thinks kids are neat and what can be bad about someone telling you how the system and the older generation have warped and destroyed things for us?" (p. 46).

[3]Reich, of course, was not the only critic of the day arguing for the imminence of the youth revolution. Another work from the same era, arguing many of the same themes, was Theodore Roszak's *The Making of a Counter-Culture* (1969); this too had a sizable initial impact. Some mention must also be made of the all-time best-seller in the *genre*, Alvin Toffler's *Future Shock* (1971), which, according to the *New York Times*, was the fifth best-selling work of nonfiction published in the decade, with total sales in excess of five million volumes.

The role of the young people of today in forging a new and better tomorrow is an insistent theme in the Roszak volume, no less than in Reich's:

> The struggle of the generations is one of the obvious constants of human affairs. One stands in peril of some presumption, therefore, to suggest that the rivalry between young and adult . . . during the current decade is uniquely critical. And yet it is necessary to risk such presumption if one is not to lose sight of our most important contemporary source of radical dissent and cultural innovation. For better or for worse, most of what is presently happening that is new, provocative, and engaging in politics, education, the arts, social relations . . . is

Revolutions of any sort seldom arise among a contented or satisfied population, and thus Reich's announcement of the imminent revolution is necessarily accompanied by a depiction of present conditions that emphasizes alienation, hostility, and discontent. His catalog of the alienations of the times begins on page 4 and is stressed consistently throughout. As Reich tells the story, there is scarcely an aspect of society that is not condemned by "most of us." Under the subheading "disorder, corruption, hypocrisy, war," Reich recounts "the disintegration of the social fabric, and the resulting atmosphere of anxiety and terror in which we all live." "Disorder, corruption, hypocrisy, war" is, moreover, only the first of seven major indictments. Elsewhere on the list of particulars are "uncontrolled technology and the destruction of the environment," a "decline of democracy and liberty," "the artificiality of work and culture," the "absence of community," and "the loss of self." In short, his is a theory of total decline; virtually everything in the society and culture has turned sour, and it is the bitter and sweeping hatred of things as they are that, in the first instance, makes his revolution "inevitable."

That most Americans or all of us are in the throes of massive dissatisfaction with who we are and how we live is a consistent and explicit theme. "Work and living," we are told on page 6, "have become more and more pointless and empty." On the next page, we learn that "for most Americans, work is mindless, exhausting, boring, servile, and hateful, something to be endured, while 'life' is confined to 'time off'." The dread "commercialism" also makes an appearance. "Our culture has been reduced to the grossly commercial; all cultural values are for sale, and those that fail to make a profit are not preserved. Our life activities have become plastic, vicarious, and false to our genuine needs."

Reich's depiction is truly relentless. "America is one vast, terrifying anti-community. The great organizations to which most people give their working day, and the apartments and suburbs to which they return at night, are equally places of loneliness and isolation. Modern living has obliterated place, locality, and neighborhood. . . . The family, the most basic social system, has been ruthlessly stripped to its functional essentials. Friendship has been coated over with a layer of impenetrable artificiality . . . " (Reich, p. 7). And these are just the epiphenomena. The genuine crisis in our culture is "the loss of self. . . . Of all the forms of impoverishment that can be seen or felt in America, loss of self, or death in life, is surely the most devastating." It is this loss of self, "even more than the draft and the Vietnam War," that is "the source of discontent and rage in the new generation." The individual is, Reich says, "systematically stripped of his imagination, his creativity, his

_____
the creation either of youth who are profoundly, even fanatically alienated, from the parental generation, or of those who address themselves primarily to the young (Roszak, p. 1).

heritage, his dreams, and his personal uniqueness, in order to style him into a productive unit for a mass, technological society."

The preponderance of flatly declarative sentences in the passages quoted above is worth a brief note. Reich does not say, for example, that America *may have become* "one vast, terrifying anti-community," but that it *is* such a community. Nor does he say that work *may be* mindless and hateful for *some* Americans, or even for *many* Americans; rather, that it *is* mindless and hateful for *most*. The presentation is clearly not offered as hypothetical possibility, but as accomplished fact. The serious analytic question, then, is whether the facts are as Reich depicts them.

What, then, is the evidentiary basis to what is obviously being presented as a descriptive account? How, for example, did Reich find out about the feelings most Americans have toward their work? Or their communities? What evidence does he give to support his depiction of total decline? In fact, he gives none. The entire thesis is offered as a self-evident proposition, and one will find, in the whole of his 433 pages, not even a passing effort to demonstrate that any of it is true.

By Reich's own admission, "much of the book was written in the Stiles-Morse dining halls at Yale" (Reich, p. 433). This and other comments throughout the book suggest that much of its content derives from his conversations with Yale undergraduates. But his formulations are not of the form, "most undergraduates at Yale are" such and such, or even that "undergraduates at Yale tell me" such and such. His claims, rather, are about "most Americans" or "all of us." So far as can be told, however, no one in Dayton or Des Moines or Newark or Mobile was contacted about any of this; no national survey was done; no poll results were consulted. Indeed, judging just by what appears in the book, there was no effort to examine serious evidence of any kind. And yet, assisted by no empirical methodology whatever, Reich claims, purely through an act of intellectual will, to have penetrated the inner depths of the consciousness and conditions of the American millions. Our point, of course, is not that Reich's image of the general decline is false, only that there is nothing in the book itself to convince anyone that it is true. In the absence of supporting evidence, the assertions quoted above are plausible surmises that could, in principle, be true or false. Deciding on their truth or falsity, however, is not a simple matter of assertion or faith.[4]

----

[4]The matters touched on in Reich's book—community, selfhood, family, work, and so on—have all been extensively studied and researched for decades. To take just one example, to be discussed in greater depth later, the social-scientific concern with work discontent extends back at least forty years and consists of more than 3000 separate studies, and much the same is true of other areas of social life discussed in Reich's book. Reich shows no awareness anywhere in the volume that this research literature even exists, much less that he has read any of it or tried to incorporate its findings into his own analysis.

Having announced the arrival of a total decline, Reich next queries, "What has caused the American system to go wrong in such an organic way? The first crucial fact is the existence of a universal sense of powerlessness" (Reich, 1971: p. 8) "Unreality," in turn, "is the true source of powerlessness. What we do not understand, we cannot control" (Reich, p. 13). We become alienated from our labor because we do not understand how our work fits into the larger productive process; we thus "lose control" over the products of our work. We become alienated from modern society as a whole because it is based on an ever more complex technology whose workings we cannot possibly understand; we thus lose control of society and its direction. The technology that should liberate us comes instead to dominate us.

Similar themes can be found in Roszak's *The Making of a Counter-Culture* (1969); here, too, technology is, ultimately, an oppressive force:

> In the Technocracy, nothing is any longer small or simple or readily apparent to the non-technical man. Instead, the scale and intricacy of all human activities— political, economic, cultural—transcends the competence of the amateurish citizen and inexorably demands the attention of specially trained experts . . . . Thus, even before the general public has become fully aware of new developments, the technocracy has doped them out and laid its plans for adopting or rejecting, promoting or disparaging.
> Within such a society, the citizen, confronted by bewildering bigness and complexity, finds it necessary to defer on all matters to those who know better . . . (Roszak, pp. 6–7).

One can readily agree with the first element of the Reich-Roszak position; namely, that in a modern society, most people do not understand most of the technologies on which their lives depend. There are, for example, probably not more than a few hundred people in the whole of the society who understand the physics on which the semiconductor industry is based. This aside, it is hard to see how people are somehow "oppressed" by hand-held calculators. Very few people even understand in detail how the modern automobile works, most of all now that automobiles routinely contain pieces of semiconductor technology. Yet "it," the automobile, takes us to the beach, to work, to shopping and leisure activities, and it is hard to see how "it" dominates "us." It is a safe bet that there were more people who understood the mechanics of the horse and carriage than there are who today understand just how a car works. As a mode of family transportation, the horse and carriage was, nonetheless, far and away the more oppressive technology.

The point can be readily generalized. In every society that has evolved beyond flint tools and cave dwellings, there is much that is not understood, indeed, cannot be understood by all people in all details. Lack of knowledge about, and thus control over, many or all of the important technologies is not some new development; it is, rather, true in varying degrees of all civilizations—indeed, it is in part implied in the very *concept* of civilization. A society so crude and simple as to lie within the ready grasp of all its members would surely be very primitive.

In the final analysis, then, the cause of the total decline of society and culture is nothing less than the division of labor in modern society, a concept to which Reich is relentlessly hostile. Now many might suppose, not unrealistically, that a fine-grained division of labor is essential to sustain the productivity on which contemporary standards of living are based, but this is not Reich's supposition. To the contrary, "machines can produce enough food and shelter for all" (Reich, p. 383). As for humans, "each person should pursue several careers, either simultaneously or successively during his life. This is not only feasible today, it is necessary and essential" (Reich, p. 405)[5]

Reich is inconsistent. He is hostile to technology and to the dehumanization that results from it, and yet he looks to machines to produce the goods and services his revolutionary society would otherwise have to do without. This, it will be noted, is a rather idyllic solution to the problem of productivity. Who, after all, will develop the science that underlies these marvelous machines? Who will build, install, and repair them? Who will explain to successive generations how they work? These questions become all the more cogent in the hypothetical Reichian society where there are no specialists, where every person rotates through several careers in the course of one's life. Just how many people in the society can we expect to master advanced computer design and programming, or solid state electronics, or the genetics of plant hybridization, or any of the other present-day technologies that make our standard of living possible? Does it not seem more plausible that as technology advances to the point where "machines can produce enough food and shelter for all" (Reich, p. 383), the need for advanced specialization would increase, not disappear?

[5]Reich's postulation of the division of labor as the ultimate source of alienation in the modern world, and of the end of divided labor as the solution to alienation is, of course, borrowed wholesale from the formulations of Marx and Engels in *The German Ideology* (New York: International Publishers, 1947, p. 22):

> . . . as soon as labour is distributed, each man has a particular, exclusive sphere of activity, which is forced upon him and from which he cannot escape. He is a hunter, a fisherman, a shepherd, or a critical critic, and must remain so if he does not want to lose his means of livelihood; while in communist society, where nobody has one exclusive sphere of activity but each can become accomplished in any branch he wishes, society regulates the general production and thus makes it possible for me to do one thing to-day and another to-morrow, to hunt in the morning, fish in the afternoon, rear cattle in the evening, criticize after dinner, just as I have a mind, without ever becoming hunter, fisherman, shepherd or critic.

The notion that "divided labor" is inherently "alienated labor" is also argued in Braverman's *Labor and Monopoly Capital* (1974, pp. 75–83 *et passim*), and, more recently, in a work by Dan Clawson, *Bureaucracy and the Labor Process* (Chapter 1 *et passim*). And for the leading original source on the subject, see Adam Smith, 1937 (original, 1776), especially his Book I, Chapter I, "On the Division of Labour." Smith, of course, makes a markedly different evaluation, seeing in the division of labor the principal source of economic development, and, accordingly, *the* first decisive step toward a solution to the problem of human want.

This, of course, is one of the problems one encounters in fantasizing about possible future societies after conversations with students at Yale. In a society composed entirely of persons whose talents rival those of the typical Yale student, many things would be feasible. But there is no known society that has this composition. For persons with IQ's in the range of 120 and up, rotation through multiple careers in the course of one's life is obviously possible. But what of those persons with IQ's of 80 or less (who are, by definition, exactly as numerous)? How many careers will they be expected to master?

The best-known and most widely cited aspect of *The Greening of America* is its discussion of the three levels of consciousness—Consciousness I, Consciousness II, and Consciousness III—these being, respectively, the prevailing modes of thought, belief, and value of the past, the present, and the future. Consciousness I, Reich says, is the consciousness of "the American farmer, small businessman, and worker who is trying to get ahead." It stresses individualism, hard work, self-denial, and the conquest of nature, and is thus very similar to Max Weber's notion of the Protestant Ethic (or, more recently, Daniel Yankelovich's "ethic of self-denial" [1981]). Consciousness II is the predominant consciousness of twentieth century industrial society, the consciousness "that created the Corporate State" and that embodies "the values of an organizational society." It stresses conformity to external dictates, technology, organization, planning, and reform. "Throughout all of Consciousness II runs the theme that society will function best if it is planned, organized, rationalized, administered" (Reich, p. 74). Consciousness II is thus the consciousness of the bureaucracy; "Consciousness II believes in *control*" (Reich's emphasis). And finally, there is Consciousness III, the consciousness of the "new generation" and thus the consciousness to be ushered in under the ascendancy of the coming revolution. "Beginning with a few individuals in the mid-nineteen-sixties, and gathering numbers ever more rapidly thereafter, Consciousness III has sprouted up, astonishingly and miraculously, out of the stony soil of the American Corporate State" (Reich, p. 233).

No secondary account of Consciousness III and its bearers can adequately capture the effusiveness of Reich's celebration of it.[6] Here, we simply note that it is the antithesis of Consciousnesses I and II. It is, first of all, intensely individualistic, but not in the grubby get ahead sense in which Conscious-

---

[6]There is, for example, his several-pages-long encomium to blue jeans, which, he says, are more "authentic" than conventional garb because "jeans express the shape of the legs" and therefore "authentically" reflect the body beneath. Then there is his discussion of bell-bottomed trousers, which, he says, "have to be worn to be understood." Bell-bottoms, continuing, "express the body, as jeans do, but they say much more. They give the ankles a special freedom, as if to invite dancing right on the street . . . " (Reich, p. 255). Somehow, "Freedom for Ankles" seems rather an unlikely political slogan, to say the very least. (Nowhere in the discussion, incidentally, does Reich mention that bell-bottom trousers originated as the uniform of issue for American sailors—a rather militaristic origin for such a liberating concept.)

ness I is individualistic. Rather, it declares that "the individual self is the only true reality." Consciousness III thus rejects the material values of other Consciousnesses. For the "III's," as Reich refers to them, "the prospect of a dreary corporate job, a ranch house life, or a miserable death in war is utterly intolerable" (Reich, p. 236). The authentic III "must live on a modest scale to retain the freedom that his commitment demands." The III's, likewise, "reject the whole concept of excellence and comparative merit." Their view is that "the goals of status, a position in the hierarchy, security, money, possessions, power, respect, and honor are not merely wrong, they are *unreal*" (p. 257); that is, they are inauthentic, nothing a true III could be concerned with.

Thus, "the foundation of Consciousness III is liberation"—liberation from all the conventions of the past, liberation from materialism and social striving, from competition and the ethic of success. And it is this consciousness, these "do your own thing" values, that will mark the society of the future. "Today we are witnesses to a great moment in history: a turn from the pessimism that has closed in on modern industrial society; the rebirth of a future; the rebirth of people in a sterile land" (Reich, p. 279). We stand, even now, at the edge of the Great Transformation—"*only Consciousness III can make possible the continued survival of man as a species in this age of technology*" (Reich, p. 383).

The focus on the self and its realization is, of course, not unique to *The Greening of America*, this being one of the prominent themes in another work to be discussed below, Inglehart's *The Silent Revolution*. It is also a key element in Abraham Maslow's (1954) work on need hierarchies. (Maslow is, in some respects, the originator of the self-actualization concept in its modern form, and his theory, too, is considered in more depth later.) To anticipate somewhat, Inglehart's version of the point is that "the values of Western publics have been shifting from an overwhelming emphasis on material well-being and physical security toward greater emphasis on the quality of life" (Inglehart, 1977a, p. 3). And later, "when at least minimal economic and physical security are present, the needs for love, belonging, and esteem become increasingly important; and later, a set of goals related to intellectual and aesthetic satisfaction loom large" (Inglehart, 1977a, p. 22).

Another work to mention in this connection is by Daniel Yankelovitch, *The New Morality* (1974). Based on a series of surveys of youth conducted in the late 1960's and early 1970's Yankelovitch argues that there have been "vast changes in the complexion and outlook of an entire generation of young people" (p. 3). The "new values," another catchphrase, include "new moral norms" in the areas of sexuality, religion, patriotism, and authority, "new social values" concerning the work ethic, marriage, family, and materialism, and a new emphasis on the "concept of self-fulfillment." Consistent with a central Reichian theme, Yankelovitch remarks, "we are amazed by the rapidity with which this process [of value change] is taking place" (p. 11).

Yankelovich's most recent book, *New Rules* (1981), continues the theme of the earlier work, except that by 1981 (as Yankelovich depicts it), the "new values" had left the campuses and had begun to spread to the whole of society: the "ethic of self-denial" is being replaced by an "ethic of self-fulfillment." Constraints of space preclude a detailed exegesis of the Yankelovich volume; see Wright and Rossi (1982) for a critical discussion of the work.

Judged in the light of the ensuing decade, it is clear that *The Greening of America* and many similar works of "criticism" produced in the late 1960's and early 1970's were not so much analyses as rhapsodies—very *un*critical celebrations of fads, trends, and developments that have proven to be rather ephemeral and short-lived. To be sure, Consciousness III has had, and continues to have, some effects on the operation of the larger society. There is, for example, the effort to humanize the workplace (about which we have more to say later), which is clearly an expression of Consciousness III values. The small-is-beautiful ideology and its variations (for example, the continuing suspicion in many quarters of high-technology solutions to problems, the widespread hostility to nuclear power, the concept of "limits to growth") are, perhaps, the major remaining repositories of this consciousness, and these are not by any stretch of the imagination trivial or passing forces on the contemporary political scene. But they are obviously not the dominant force; like all other ideologies, these compete more or less favorably, winning some battles and losing others, enthusiastically supported here but opposed intensely over there. Consciousness III in all its forms, in short, is just one ideology among many, each competing against the others for adherents and popular support. The argument that it will "inevitably" be victorious, that it is the universal and sweeping wave of the future, has become rather muted.

Still, one need not share in Reich's rhapsodies to understand that he has formulated some interesting hypotheses, which, if proved true, would amount to genuine and important insights. For example, he depicts the present as one of seething dissatisfaction, and it is obviously worth knowing whether this depiction is true. He claims that a whole new package of values very different from the values of the past has arisen in modern industrial society, and that the young are the vanguard of a "New Morality," and it is also obviously worth knowing whether any of this is true. He argues that the masses, being incapable of comprehending modern society, have become deeply alienated from it. It would be useful to know whether this is true, too. Certainly, when the book first appeared, it was taken *very* seriously by a large number of commentators, politicians, and social critics, and even though the luster of the work has since faded, it is worth asking whether the initial enthusiasm for Reich's analysis of modern American life was justified.

"THE REAL MAJORITY": THE DIALECTICAL NEGATION
OF CONSCIOUSNESS III

An alternate and wholly different line of intellectual analysis on who the American people are and how they are changing appeared almost simultaneously with *The Greening of America*; it is the well-known work of Scammon and Wattenberg, *The Real Majority* (also published in 1970). The work, one could say with very little distortion, offers a "dialectical negation" of Consciousness III.

Like the work previously discussed, *The Real Majority* also had a sizable initial impact, but in this case the impact has been longer lived, the book amounting, in important respects, to the intellectual cornerstone of the neoconservative movement. A second sharp contrast is that while *The Greening of America* is virtually devoid of systematic data, *The Real Majority* is heavily laden with poll results, census information, and tabulations of national survey data; indeed, some presentation of factual materials can be found on every fourth or fifth page.[7] Thus, in contrast to Reich, Scammon and Wattenberg deserve credit for presenting a rich array of evidence on their topics, and for hewing closely to this evidence in their interpretive narrative.

Perhaps reflecting the relative sensitivities of the two books to the existing evidence on the American population, the contrast between them in theme could scarcely be sharper. To be sure, Scammon and Wattenberg also detect some important changes in the values and outlooks of the American population; they note various trends and developments that, in their view, "seem to herald the clear emergence of a new and major voting issue in America" (Scammon and Wattenberg, p. 40), an issue which, incidentally, is said to be displacing the more traditional Economic issues as the major factor in voting

[7]*The Real Majority* is one of a continuing series of works by the authors, all equally data-laden (e.g., Wattenberg, *The Real America*, 1974). Scammon and Wattenberg thus enjoy the distinction of being "popularizers" who, nonetheless, display an impressive awareness of the existing evidence on their topics, and who employ this evidence to sharp and obvious advantage. Perhaps unsurprisingly, many, although not all, of their themes are supported in the data analysis we present in later chapters. Concerning their "access" to the relevant empirical materials, it is worth noting that Scammon was director of the United States Bureau of the Census from 1961 to 1965, and was later director of the Elections Research Bureau in Washington.

Since publication of *The Real Majority*, Scammon and Wattenberg have been key figures in the initiation and subsequent growth and success of a bimonthly magazine, *Public Opinion*, a leading journal in the neoconservative movement. *Public Opinion* runs interpretive articles and summaries of poll results, and thus gives, in essence, an every-other-month update on the state of majority thinking in the country.

There has also been a rather sizable academic link-in to the *Real Majority* themes, notably in the work of the political scientist Everett Carll Ladd, Jr. See especially, his article, "Liberalism Upside Down" (1976–77), or the book-length treatment, *Transformations of the American Party System* (1978).

Another popular work appearing at about the same time as *The Real Majority*, and arguing some of the same themes, is Kevin Phillips' *The Emerging Republican Majority* (1969).

behavior.[8] But this "New Issue," of course, is not Consciousness III or any of its variants, but rather its precise antithesis: it is, in the authors' words, the "Social Issue," a reaction *against* virtually everything that Reich, Roszak, and others celebrate—most particularly a reaction against the counterculture and its values. Thus, while Reich and other critics see the counterculture itself as the wave of tomorrow, Scammon-Wattenberg's world view posits that reaction against the counterculture and all it stands for is what the future *really* holds in store.

The contents of the value changes asserted by Scammon and Wattenberg are quite explicit. From the Depression on, Americans have, as they say, "voted basically along the lines of bread-and-butter economic issues." But recently this has changed. "Suddenly, some time in the 1960's, 'crime' and 'race' and 'lawlessness' and 'civil rights' became the most important domestic issues in America" (Scammon and Wattenberg, p. 39).[9] It is not, we note, uncontrolled technology, or commercialism, or inauthenticity, or self-actualization, but the "social issue," they argue, that is central to the new political agenda in American society.

Scammon and Wattenberg elaborate the elements of the Social Issue in great detail. First is crime and the anxieties it produces. Crime rates were continually increasing in the 1960's and early 1970's, and much fear and anxiety resulted. Very few people are progressive in thinking about crime; most want it stopped as quickly as possible by whatever means seem necessary. (They also note—a marvelous irony—that "a great deal of the 'crime wave' can be attributed to a sharp increase in the numbers of young

---

[8]Thus, in an indirect way, Scammon and Wattenberg also posit some decline in the importance of "materialistic" values in American political life, at least insofar as they affect voting choices. The economic issue, they remark, is "still potent," but in addition, "Americans are apparently beginning to array themselves politically along the axes of certain social situations as well" (p. 20).

The Scammon-Wattenberg distinction between the economic issue and the social issue calls to mind a similar distinction, drawn thirty years ago by S. M. Lipset, between "status" politics and "class" politics. In Lipset's analysis, class politics is the political struggle over the distribution of income, and is thus closely akin to the economic issue; the nature of mass political preference favors progressive or liberal governments when class politics predominate. Status politics, in contrast, involve resentments over the loss of status, and as such, tend to favor conservative, restorativist, or even reactionary governments. The similarity to social issues is obvious. Lipset's paper, "The Sources of the 'Radical Right,'" was first published in 1955; it was reprinted in a more accessible source in 1963.

[9]Their conclusions about the most important domestic issues are assuredly not idle speculation. The depiction is based on a presentation of results from thirty-four Gallup polls conducted between 1958 and 1970 (pp. 37–39), and on an initial reading, their conclusions seem beyond challenge or reproach. A more detailed analysis, however, based not on the Scammon-Wattenberg presentation but on a review of the original Gallup data, shows that at least part of their depiction is a serious distortion of the evidence. This analysis is undertaken in the following chapter.

people in recent years" [Scammon and Wattenberg, p. 40]—a point Reich does not discuss.

The second element of the social issue is race—not race in the progressive "We Shall Overcome," sense, but race in the "Negroes are getting too much, too fast, with too much turmoil" sense (Scammon and Wattenberg, p. 35). The race riots of the middle and late 1960's were, in the Scammon and Wattenberg world view, particularly decisive. "Violence, disorder, and looting," as they put it, could only result in backlash.[10] "The summers of 1968 and 1969 were quieter, but the electoral damage had been done. The electoral nerve had been rubbed raw. Voters were frightened and angry" (p. 42).

"And then there was the 'kidlash' "—the kids, of course, being the bearers of Reich's revolution. "Among a highly publicized segment of young America, hair got long, skirts got short, foul language became ordinary, drugs became common, respect for elders became limited, the invasion and sacking of offices of college administrators became the initiation rite—and adults became fearful and upset. Again" (Scammon and Wattenberg, p. 42).

"A fourth element," they continue, "might simply be called values. Pornography blossomed with legal sanction; sexual codes became more permissive; priests were getting married; sex education was taught in the schools" (Scammon and Wattenberg, p. 42). The values at issue here are obviously similar to Yankelovitch's "New Morality" (see earlier); the point being claimed by Scammon and Wattenberg is that for the large majority, they represent a New Immorality—not something to be embraced, but something to be resisted.

There are, Scammon and Wattenberg believe, two final elements in the social issue mix. First is the very serious loss of popular respect for "the man who works hard, pays his taxes, rears his children" (Scammon and Wattenberg, p. 43)—in short, the relentless denigration of the bearers of Consciousnesses I and II by the proponents of Consciousness III. And "finally, to this already combustible mixture, a new highly flammable element was added: the Vietnam protest movement. Suddenly, American boys and girls were seen burning American flags on television; clergymen were pouring containers of blood on draft records; the President was jeered" (p. 43).

Here, in Scammon and Wattenberg's words, is how it all adds up:

> The Social Issue was in full flower. It may be defined as a set of public attitudes concerning the more personally frightening aspects of disruptive social change. Crime frightens. Young people, when they invade the dean's office, or destroy themselves with drugs, or destroy a corporate office with a bomb, frighten. Pornography, nudity, promiscuity are perceived to tear away the underpinnings of a moral code, and this, too, is frightening. Dissent that involves street riots frightens.

[10]Concern over the "white backlash" was a staple in liberal and left discussions from about 1966 (when George Wallace first emerged as a serious national politician) up through the early 1970's, but has more or less faded as a concern since, presumably because the postulated "threat" never appeared.

> Put together, it spelled out great change. It was change that some few Americans perceived as beneficial, but measurably larger numbers did not. Most voters felt they gained little from crime, or integration, or wild kids, or new values, or dissent. Of many of these new facets of American life they were downright fearful. These voters became the core of an antidissent dissent, feeling the breath of the Social Issue hot and uncomfortable on their necks (Scammon and Wattenberg, p. 43).

Scammon and Wattenberg, no less than Reich, thus acknowledge that the new values have hit the scene, and that "the young" are their major proponents. In their view, however, the key fact of American political life is not the presence or spread of these values but the "fearful" reaction against them. Reich looks to Consciousness III as the mechanism for liberating the society from the atrophying conventions of the past; Scammon and Wattenberg, in contrast, find that it is an insult—a frightening insult—to those conventions and to the people whose lives have been built upon them. It is, in their view, the backlash of the real majority, not the frontlash of a Green America, that will define the American political future.

Note too: like Reich's Green America, Scammon and Wattenberg's real majority also seethes with anger and discontent; the real majority is "fearful," "upset," "angry," "combustible," "frightened," the social issue breathing "hot and uncomfortable on their necks." The majority is angry, however, not because they have come to believe that life is "inauthentic," but because its authenticity has been called into question by "wild kids and new values."

Most of the commentators arguing the coming of Consciousness III in one form or another do, of course, acknowledge the possibility of some resistance, some backlash, at least over the short run. Their most charitable interpretation of The Real Majority thesis would thus be that it describes the short-term future, that the social issue is a temporary resistance destined, eventually, to wither away. If the Reichian depiction of youth is correct, then certainly Conciousness III would seem to have time on its side. In 1970, when these books were published, one half the people in America were twenty-five years old or under. If the real majority is concentrated among the middle-aged and older, then the days of its hegemony are assuredly numbered; and if Consciousness III is the consciousness of the young, then its eventual ascendancy is irresistible. A consciousness borne only among the old suffers losses daily and in time must become decimated; the consciousness of the young and very young, in contrast, will survive for many decades. Is the real majority, then, not simply the last desperate gasp of a world view passing quickly and inevitably from the scene?

Scammon and Wattenberg take up these issues in their chapters 4 and 5; the key phrase for both chapters is "Demography is Destiny." Their presentation begins with a recognition of two essential facts. First, the electorate of the future has, for the most part, already been born and so much of its demography is already known. Since the voting age for national elections is now officially set at 18 years, then every voter in the election of 1984 will have already been born by at least 1966, and every voter in the election of the year 2000 will be born by at least 1982. Barring major catastrophes, then, the age distribution of the electorate for the rest of the century is already known in some detail. Its distribution by sex and race is also known. Other aspects of its demography are less certain, not being strictly determined at birth, but we nonetheless have a fairly good idea about how much education the electorate of the future will have received, the structure of occupations open to them, their probable distribution across regions and cities, even their probable religious and ethnic identities. And secondly, the demographic characteristics of the electorate of the future will, if not perfectly determine the politics of that future, at least have some influence upon them. As Scammon and Wattenberg say, "demographic circumstances influence attitudes, which in turn influence elections" (Scammon and Wattenberg, p. 46).

What, then, does the demography of the coming electorate reveal about its likely politics? Although, as later chapters make clear, there are reasons to be skeptical about some elements of the Scammon-Wattenberg world view, it should be recognized that many of the points they make in this discussion are truly incisive. For example, they note that while the median age of the American population in 1968 was roughly 25 years, the median age of persons who voted in the 1968 election was 47 years. The maturation of the baby boom, they recognize, will cause the median age of the electorate to drop—but not by very much. "This will lower the median voting age by only a year or two" (p. 47). And eventually, of course, the baby boom will itself pass the median age of the electorate as a whole, after which time that median age will necessarily go up. The "graying of America" is, in short, definitely inevitable, whether its "greening" is or not.

Scammon and Wattenberg make two additional and valuable points about the politics of today's youth. First, as has been noted by every study of electoral behavior since the classic *Voting* study of the 1948 election (Berelson, Lazarsfeld, and McPhee, 1954), young voters are far less likely to turn out for an election than older voters. Their numbers, small to begin with, are further eroded by their differential tendency not to vote. Second, while there are some groups in society who think and vote as a bloc (blacks, for instance), the young are not among them, Reich notwithstanding. Instead, they are, just as the rest of the population, widely dispersed across the ideological spectrum.[11]

Consider, for example, the matter of Vietnam, recognized by all observers as *the* young people's issue of the era in question. In October 1968—a mere

[11] Another research commonplace that dates at least to the *Voting* study is that the single best predictor of a person's party preference is the party preference of his or her father, which indicates a definite intergenerational transmission of political preference. More recent studies continue to show a substantial overlap between parental and offspring politics. Parents, in other words, teach their politics to their children, a process known in the academic literature as political socialization. The net effect of the socialization process, as should be obvious, is toward continuity and stability in politics across generations—a fact often ignored in discussions of "the young people of today."

two months after the "Siege of Chicago" and the horrors of the Democratic convention there—Gallup asked a national sample to rate themselves as hawks or doves. Among the under-30's in the sample, 45% said they were hawks, 43% said they were doves, and 12% had not yet formed an opinion on the issue. Among the under-30's in 1968, then, there was nearly a perfect split, even on Vietnam. Perhaps even more remarkably, the proportion of under-30's who identified themselves as hawks was slightly *higher* than the corresponding proportion of the over-50 population (40%); in 1968, young people were *more* hawkish on Vietnam than older people.

Moreover, this 1968 Gallup finding is no bizarre anomaly or one-shot freak finding. Young people were also more hawkish than older people on Korea in 1952 and on Vietnam as early as 1964 (Hamilton, 1968a); they were more hawkish on Vietnam from the onset of American involvement in the conflict in 1964 all the way through the termination of American involvement in the early 1970's (Hamilton and Wright, 1975a; Chapter Five). Indeed, Hazel Erskine (1972) reviewed the available poll data for every United States war in the twentieth century and reported that young people have *always* been more prowar than the old. Warmongering, we hasten to point out, is definitely *not* identified by Reich as an element of Consciousness III, although the survey data show it to be a definite part of the thinking of the young people of today.[12]

To be sure, if the "young people of today" are more progressive or liberated, and their politics remain progressive and liberated as they age, then the politics of tomorrow will, of necessity, be more progressive than the politics of the present. "Advocates of the New Politics have used this fact," Scammon and Wattenberg note, "to support their contention that in the years to come their influence and numbers will swell" (Scammon and Wattenberg, p. 51). In the face of this argument, Scammon and Wattenberg make four related points. First, "it is not only the radical or activist youth who will be aging. The pro-Wallace youth, the Nixon youth, and the pro-Humphrey youth will be aging too." If, as in the Vietnam case, the distribution of outlooks among the young is very similar to the distributions among middle-aged and old, then the process of cohort succession, although itself inevitable, will clearly not usher in much by way of change. Second, the young people of today will, in all probability, be more educated and more affluent than the generations that have preceded them. However, education

---

[12]Some of the social critics, Theodore Roszak in particular, recognize that the counterculture, strictly speaking, was a minority phenomenon even among the young. "At this point," Roszak writes, "the counterculture I speak of embraces only a strict minority of the young and a handful of their adult mentors" (Roszak, p. xii). Even Reich notes that his "revolution" began "with a few individuals." These admissions, however, serve mainly as stylistic entries into the main point—that the minority is rapidly growing, that it is the undeniable and irresistable wave of the future. Still, one might ask, if Consciousness III and the counterculture were persuasive or attractive to only a minority of their natural constituency, the young, then by what miracle would they become the dominating world view of a very unnatural constituency, namely, the rest of the society?

and affluence are typically associated with conservative rather than liberal ideologies and world views.[13] That this has been true of the past, or course, does not guarantee that it will remain true in the future; it just makes it a good bet. Third, while the proportion of Americans partaking of the presumed liberations wrought by college education has been increasing steadily in the postwar era, holding a college degree remains a relatively rare accomplishment. As of the 1968 election, Scammon and Wattenberg point out, only one American in four had ever even *attended* an institution of higher learning, and only about one-half that number—one in eight—had actually earned a degree. Among the current cohorts, these numbers are somewhat higher, but not by much; the best available projections are that the proportion of adults in the United States holding a college degree will not rise much above 15%, or at the outside 20%, between today and the year 2000.[14] The young, in short, are distinctively a minority, and will remain so; the college-educated young are an even smaller minority, and are also destined to remain so. It is perhaps obvious but nonetheless worth remembering that in a society where 20% have earned a college degree, 80% have not. And, in the usual run of things, it is the outlooks, feelings, and consciousness of the 80% that will impinge most heavily on the course of the future.

The real majority depicted by Scammon and Wattenberg is, in their phrase, "unyoung, unpoor, and unblack"; it is white, middle-aged, middle-class, and middle-thinking—and not only is the majority all these things, it will remain all these things as far into the future as the present state of the demographic

---

[13]"The poorer strata everywhere are more liberal or leftist on economic issues; they favor more welfare state measures, higher wages, graduated income taxes, support of trade-unions, and so forth" (Lipset, 1960, p. 92). For more recent evidence on the economic liberalism of the "poorer strata," see Hamilton, (1972, Chapter 5). Lipset further claims that "when liberalism is defined in non-economic terms . . . the correlation is reversed" (p. 92). His thesis is thus that the poorer strata are more liberal on economic issues but less liberal on social issues than the more affluent or well-to-do. As regards specifically the issue of race, a detailed review and critique of available studies has challenged Lipset's argument on all major points (see Hamilton, 1972, Chapter 11; also, Hamilton, 1975, Chapter 4). For another view on the whole matter, one arguing an inversion of the traditional pattern of lower-strata leftism, see Ladd, 1976–77 and 1978.

[14]Given all the speculation on the democratization of education and the educated society (see, e.g., "The Theory of Post-Industrialism," below), Scammon and Wattenberg are to be praised for picking up the relatively small proportions for whom advanced education beyond high school is a reality. On the same point, see Hamilton and Wright (1975b); Wright (1979), or Freeman (1976).

One often hears it said that, these days, half or more of the eligible population goes on to college, and this claim is hard to square with the points and projections made above, in the text. The 50% to college claim is based on a misleading presentation of evidence. The figure cited is a false percentage based on a ratio of total college enrollments to the population age 18–21. Some of the people enrolled in college, however, are 17 or younger, and many, of course, are older than 21, as in the case of most graduate students. If one transforms that ratio into a percentage, the result will be a high but spurious enrollment figure.

art allows us to project. This, the authors also note, does *not* mean that the real majority is anti-young, anti-poor, or anti-black. What it does mean is that the unyoung, unpoor, unblack majority commands sufficient numbers now and for the foreseeable future to veto or at least inhibit change in any direction unacceptable to them. If the Scammon-Wattenberg account is accurate, then one of the "unacceptable directions" is societal change along the lines depicted by Reich. In their account, it is not the *coming* of Consciousness III but its *going*—its crushing defeat at the hands of the real majority—that will mark the politics of tomorrow.

THE WORKPLACE CRITICS

We turn now to a third set of themes and perspectives that rose to prominence in the 1970's as an account of the American condition. These focused rather more specifically on the world of work. The key theme in this literature, one anticipated in our discussion of Reich, is that for most Americans "work is mindless, boring, exhausting, servile, and hateful."

There have always, no doubt, been critics of work conditions, at least since the expulsion from Eden. In modern times, beginning with the condemnation of the "dark satanic mills," that criticism has been focused on the onerous and repetitive labors required of blue-collar workers in shops and factories. In recent decades, however, with the rise of the white-collar ranks, one finds the same lines of criticism applied to the routine work of salaried or white-collar employees.[15]

For most of the modern era, book-length treatments of the subject of objectionable work have appeared only infrequently. In most of the recent decades, one finds only a handful of contributions addressed to a general or concerned public (that is, to an audience extending beyond the ranks of the "narrow" academic specialists in the field). In the 1950's, for example, there was Charles R. Walker's *Steeltown: An Industrial Case History of the Conflict between Progress and Security* (1950). Two years later, Walker, together with Robert H. Guest, brought out *The Man on the Assembly Line* (1952). Alvin Gouldner's *Wildcat Strike* appeared in 1954. Ely Chinoy's volume, *Automobile Workers and the American Dream*, gained much attention on its publication in 1955. Georges Friedmann's *Industrial Society* appeared in the same year.

The 1960's also saw a rather sparse crop of books dealing with work and workers. The most notable among these were: Robert Blauner's *Alienation and Freedom: The Factory Worker and His Industry* (1964); Arthur Shostak's

[15]For a classic statement about work through the ages, see Tilgher, 1930.

A peculiar selectivity has characterized the treatments of work, at least in the writing of critical intellectuals. The routines of modern factory work are condemned. The routines of farm work are not, nor are the routines of guild labor. The work required of men, women, and children in the factories was and is condemned. The routine labors of the household, especially those involved in "women's work," until recently at least were not. Some other instances of selectivity are discussed in Chapter 6.

and William Gomberg's collection of commissioned articles published as
Blue-Collar World: Studies of the American Worker (1964); Arthur Kornhauser's *Mental Health of the Industrial Worker* (1965); and, toward the
end of the decade, Shostak's *Blue-Collar Life* (1969). There were others, but
by and large, the attention paid the subject of work was limited and sporadic.
In the early months of the 1970's, one would have had little reason to
anticipate the tidal wave of interest in the topic that was to appear over the
next few years.[16]

The first faint glimmer of such interest appeared in a rather unexpected
location. A front-page *New York Times* account, under the headline, "U.S.
Urged to Aid Blue-Collar Man" (Rosenthal, 1970), reported the existence of
a confidential report to the President entitled "The Problem of the Blue-Collar Worker." It contained the thinking of a panel of experts headed by
George P. Shultz, the Secretary of Labor. The report itself was drafted by
Jerome M. Rosow, the Assistant Secretary of Labor for Policy Development
and Research.

Blue-collar workers, the report argued, were falling behind economically
and were being caught in a "social squeeze." This was happening at a time
when their work and their lives were being "badly denigrated." It was felt
they were "overripe for a political response to the pressing needs they feel
so keenly." Accordingly, the report presented an eleven-point program for
these "lower middle income families," calling for training programs, adult
education to upgrade job skills, more effective guidance and job placement,
tax subsidies to pay day-care costs for working mothers, vest pocket parks
and improved transportation in urban areas, and, to counter the scorn that
was evident in some circles, a system of national awards for outstanding
craftsmen and the issue of a postage stamp series honoring the various skilled
trades.

The panel had its origins in the summer of 1969. President Nixon had

---

[16]The listing in the previous paragraphs is not meant to be exhaustive. Numerous
articles on work appeared in the publications of the left (e.g., those of B. J. Widick
and Frank Marquart in *Dissent*). The writer Harvey Swados brought out an important
article entitled "The Myth of the Happy Worker" (1957b) and also a collection of
short stories entitled *On the Line* (1957a).

Blue-collar workers were not neglected in the 1950's and 1960's. The attention,
however, was focused on other aspects of working-class life, specifically on life-styles
and politics. This refers to the sizable literature on the "affluence and the worker"
theme (see, for example, Kornhauser, Sheppard, and Mayer, 1965; Berger, 1960;
Hamilton, 1965, 1967; and Goldthorpe, Lockwood, Bechofer, and Platt, 1968a, b;
and 1969).

An even larger literature continued to deal with workers and work satisfaction, but
this was not aimed toward a general educated audience. It was directed to the
audience of specialists, particularly those interested in labor-management relations.
The wave of "work dissatisfaction" writings gained its audience in spite of the
contrary evidence contained in this specialized literature (see below, "The Empirical
Study of Work"). The problems posed by this segregation of the popular and
specialized literatures are discussed at greater length in later chapters.

circulated a magazine article dealing with blue-collar problems, attaching a handwritten note that read: "This is very disturbing. What can we do about it?" In addition to those already named, the panel included John N. Mitchell, the Attorney General; Donald Rumsfeld, the Director of the Office of Economic Opportunity; John Ehrlichman; Daniel P. Moynihan; Harry Dent; and a number of other White House aides. One panel member emphasized that their response should not be interpreted "as just a play for the hard hats. . . ."

(As it happens, the article circulated by Nixon was, according to one of the principals, Jerome Rosow, a piece written by Pete Hamill, appearing in New York, entitled "The Revolt of the White Lower-Middle Class." This piece is discussed in its own right, in some detail, later in this chapter.)

There appears to have been little significant follow-up stemming from this report, which was released officially just before the 1970 elections. (It was then treated as no more than a "working paper"—none of its recommendations received official endorsement.) Rosow published a brief statement in the Washington Post in August of that year ("The Working Man DOES Need Help . . ."). He was to play an important role in the following years in generating further concern.[17]

Probably the most important stimulus, the work ultimately setting the tidal wave in motion, was an article by Judson Gooding that appeared in Fortune in July 1970. Entitled "Blue-Collar Blues on the Assembly Line," it provided all the themes of the subsequent movement as well as the catchy slogan. The phrase "blue-collar blues" was destined to appear in scores of subsequent publications.

Where previous writing on blue-collar working conditions had been concerned with all workers, regardless of age, this article was very much focused on the young. Those coming into the plants at that time, so it was

[17]The political aims of the Administration effort were emphasized much more heavily in a Wall Street Journal account (Karmin, 1970). The U.S. News and World Report account was headlined "Nixon's Plan to Win the Blue-Collar Vote" (July 20, 1970, p. 18). Considerable attention was given the report, e.g., in The New Republic editorial (July 18, 1970, p. 9), a Saturday Review editorial (July 25, 1970, p. 18 by Peter Schrag) and, after release of the original report on August 1, 1970, the Washington Post had a discussion with Hermann P. Miller versus Jerome Rosow, on August 16 and 23, 1970, respectively. Much of the reception given the report was rather skeptical. Schrag, for example, pointed out that the recommendations "fail to mention the war . . ." A Wall Street Journal editorial (July 17, 1970) expressed doubt about the direction of the group's efforts. Alienation for blue-collar workers and others, they said, would only begin to ease "as the Government succeeds at its major tasks in the U.S. right now: Ending inflation, withdrawing from Indochina, and doing whatever is possible to cool off rising divisive passions."

Copies of the responses to the memorandum were generously provided to us by Jerome Rosow (in a letter of 5 January 1981). He writes also that some of the recommendations did become law, mentioning specifically child-care tax reform, pension reform, voluntary educational reform, and expanded trust loans for college students.

said, were very different from their predecessors, the point being stated and repeated with half a dozen variations in Gooding's first paragraphs. These were:

> . . . the new young men . . . a fractious new work force . . . managers were trying to build cars by the old methods with new workers they don't understand and often don't much like. . . . The central fact about the new workers is that they are young and bring into the plants with them the new perspectives of American youth in 1970. . . . The new attitudes cut across racial lines. Both young blacks and young whites have higher expectations of the jobs they fill and the wages they receive, and for the lives they will lead. They are restless, changeable, mobile, demanding, all traits that make for impermanence—and for difficult adjustment to an assembly line.

The correlates of this new outlook were also spelled out by Gooding, these being indicated already in the article's subheading: " . . . they vent their feelings through absenteeism, high turnover, shoddy work, and even sabotage."[18] Absenteeism, it was said, had "doubled over the past ten years at General Motors and at Ford," the sharpest increase having occurred in the last year, that is, in 1969. Tardiness, another measure of disaffection, had also increased. The quit rate at Ford in 1969 was 25.2%. Still other evidence of the new worker orientations was found in the increased dissension within the plants—"more arguments with foremen, more complaints about discipline and overtime, more grievances." There was the obvious likelihood of serious labor unrest. Gooding reported that "the younger workers, in their present temper, would probably like nothing better than to down tools for a rousing great strike."

In explaining the attitudes of the new generation of workers, Gooding stresses that they "both know more and expect more." Many of them had "never experienced economic want or fear—or even insecurity. In the back of their minds is the knowledge that public policy will not allow them to starve, whatever may happen." Later commentators were to put an even heavier stress on their "knowing more," the point being that they had more years of education and that this education, again reflecting recent changes, had a new and different character, one stressing independence, autonomy, and self-development as opposed to acceptance and submission.

Gooding's claims, coming as they did at a time when "angry and rebellious" young persons were very much in evidence in the civil rights movement, urban uprisings, and campus demonstrations, seemed highly plausible, the logic of the argument being attested to by events in cities and

---

[18]Serious evidence on sabotage, of course, is difficult to come by. In Gooding's account, as in the others that were to follow, one finds a handful of illustrative cases only: "In some plants worker discontent has reached such a degree that there has been overt sabotage. Screws have been left in brake drums, tool handles welded into fender compartments (to cause mysterious, unfindable, and eternal rattles), paint scratched, and upholstery cut" (Gooding, 1970a, p. 70).

on campuses throughout the nation. A major clash, the new generation versus the established industrial system, was clearly in the offing.

Another reason for the ready acceptance of this position was the timing of its appearance. Most of the major works in this tradition, as will be seen immediately, appeared in 1972 and 1973. The portrait of dissatisfaction and rebellion in the workplace thus came only a few years after the accounts provided by Reich, Roszak, Toffler, and other critics writing in the late 1960's. The discussion of those works (and the printing of later editions) extended well into the 1970's, so that these two "critical" positions overlapped very much in time. The arguments of the workplace critics, specifically those dealing with the new generation, had already appeared in the writings of the social critics. The latter had also anticipated the new and sweeping hostilities to the demands of the workplace. Effectively, what the workplace critics were doing was narrowing the focus of the critique and providing some evidence in support of their claims. Otherwise, the continuity and overlap are very striking, so much so that the position of this second wave of critics could easily appear under the heading: "Con III in the Workplace."

Gooding followed the initial article with two others. The second of the series, "It Pays to Wake Up the Blue-Collar Worker," appeared in September 1970 and was devoted to job enrichment programs, presenting them as the solution to the problem of blue-collar blues. Job enrichment reduced turnover, lowered absenteeism, improved production and morale and, ultimately, improved profits. The article reviewed the experience of a number of firms, estimating that approximately two score were then making use of some variety of job-enrichment procedures. The third article, "The Fraying White Collar," appeared in December. It, in effect, applied the previous themes to the white-collar labor force. They too, were "products of the youth culture" and were being swept by the same restlessness as blue-collar workers.

There was little *immediate* reaction to the Gooding pieces. They stimulated some concern, but little else followed. Later on, however, the "blue-collar blues" article was to gain considerable attention, providing the leading slogan of the movement. The second article with its focus on job enrichment was destined to provide the leading solution for the problems of blue-collar workers, at least outside Marxist circles. For them, of course, no solutions for workers' problems are to be found within capitalist society.

Three noteworthy books on work and workers appeared in 1971. Kenneth Lasson brought out *The Workers: Portraits of Nine American Job Holders* (a publication of Ralph Nader's center). A summary portrait was provided by Patricia and Brendon Sexton, *Blue Collars and Hard Hats: The Working Class and the Future of American Politics*. There was also a collection of articles edited by Sar Levitan, *Blue-Collar Workers: A Symposium on Middle America*, to which Jerome Rosow was a contributor, with an article (based on the famous memorandum) on "The Problems of Lower-Middle-Income

Workers" ("Millions of full-time workers [find] themselves in a three-way squeeze . . . paychecks don't stretch across their basic needs; they are unhappy on the job and can't break out; they find their total life pattern unrewarding," p. 76.) Rosow also contributed a set of proposals, some fifteen "Directions for Action," these paralleling the recommendations of the presidential panel. (The postage-stamp proposal, however, was omitted.)

President Nixon made a number of contributions to the buildup of attention in 1971, the first of them in an address to the Republican Governors' Conference in April, then in his Labor Day speech, and again, three days later, in a presentation before a joint session of Congress. In his Labor Day address Nixon declared that "the most important part of the quality of life is the quality of work, and the new need for job satisfaction is the key to the quality of work."[19]

In March 1972, a strike broke out in the General Motors' Vega plant in Lordstown, Ohio. This unit, which possessed the most advanced technology in the industry, had been located in the American heartland so as to draw on a labor force untouched by unions or by the industry's previous acrimonious history of labor-management relations. The work force in the plant was young and new to the industry, thus providing near-experimental conditions for assessment of the new worker hypothesis. This strike, described in scores of accounts, offered decisive proof of the case. The name Lordstown took its place alongside the catch phrase "blue-collar blues" as a staple in any discussion of the topic.

A relatively large number of book-length volumes dealing with work appeared in 1972, two of them having more than run-of-the-mill significance. A special issue of *Dissent* magazine was devoted to "The World of the Blue Collar Worker," which later appeared as a paperback book (Howe, 1972). And Judson Gooding brought out a book on the topic entitled *The Job Revolution*.

A volume that was to have considerable impact was Harold L. Sheppard and Neal Q. Herrick's *Where Have All the Robots Gone?* This was an engagé social science version of the "work problem," one based on national, regional, and local surveys. Sponsored by the W. E. Upjohn Institute for Employment Research, this volume contained all the themes enunciated in Gooding's original articles. But this time those claims were backed up with systematic evidence, at least so it appeared. The claims were also accompanied with strong declarations of urgency, these indicating the calamity that would befall us if changes in the organization of work were not promptly forthcoming. Additional words of alarm were provided in a Foreword by Harvey Swados and an Introduction by Michael Maccoby. Chapter 11 of the

---

[19]For Nixon's Williamsburg address, see the *New York Times*, April 20, 1971, p. 30. The Labor Day address is reported in the *Times* of September 7, 1971, pp. 1, 14. The speech to the Congress appears in the *Times* of September 10, 1971, p. 20. For Labor Day, 1970, incidentally, Nixon had invited seventy-five labor leaders and their wives to a White House dinner.

work, entitled "Search for Solutions," was written by Fred K. Foulkes, the author of a book on job enrichment programs (1969).[20]

Closely linked to the Sheppard-Herrick volume was a document entitled *New Directions in the World of Work* (Price, 1972), this being a summary account of a conference in Williamsburg, Virginia, in April 1972. The conference was sponsored by the Upjohn Institute as part of a grant from the Ford Foundation.[21]

Another significant happening occurred in 1972—the convening of Senator Edward M. Kennedy's Subcommittee on Employment, Manpower, and Poverty, this to discuss the problems of "Worker Alienation." Hearings on the matter were held in July, constituting, in Kennedy's words, "the first time a congressional committee has focused specifically on worker alienation" (United States' Senate, 1972, p. 91). In most respects, the materials presented at those hearings were merely previews of the more detailed government report published in the following year, *Work in America,* about which we have more to say later. Witnesses testifying at the hearings included: Gary Brynner, President of the UAW Local 1112 (the Lordstown local); James Wright, affiliated with the National Center for Urban Ethnic Affairs and a coauthor of *Work in America;* Dr. John French from the Survey Research Center at the University of Michigan; Dr. Harold Sheppard from the Upjohn

---

[20]Harold L. Sheppard had long been active in the area of work and its discontents. The Friedmann book (1955), which contained many of the themes of the 1970's work literature, was translated under his supervision. He edited the volume and wrote an Introduction.

[21]A surprisingly large amount of the workplace criticism under review here was underwritten directly by the Ford Foundation. According to the Foundation's Annual Reports, works supported in whole or in part by Foundation money include: Sar Levitan, *Blue-Collar Workers* (1971), Irving Howe, *The World of the Blue Collar Worker* (1972, this as noted originally appearing as a special edition of *Dissent*), Sheppard and Herrick, *Where Have All the Robots Gone?* (1972), Sar Levitan and William Johnston, *Work is Here to Stay, Alas* (1973), American Jewish Committee, *Not Yet a Ms: The Working Class Woman in America* (1973), Jerome Rosow, *The Worker and the Job: Coping with Change* (1974), Nancy Seifer, *Absent from the Majority: Working Class Women in America* (1973), Solomon Barkin, *Worker Militancy and Its Consequences, 1965–1975* (1975), Louis Davis and Albert Cherns, *The Quality of Working Life:* Volumes I and II (1975), Paul Goodman, *Assessing Organizational Change: The Rushton Quality of Work Experiment* (1979), Clark Kerr and Jerome Rosow, *Work in America: The Decade Ahead* (1979), Bernard Lefkowitz, *Break-time: Living without Work in a 9 to 5 World* (1979), and Robert Schrank, *American Workers Abroad* (1979).

The preceding lists only book-length volumes or reports shown in the *Annual Reports of the Foundation;* papers, articles, chapters in books, and so on are not included. Further, it lists only publications focused specifically on the working class and omits the many Foundation-supported studies of ethnicity, income maintenance experiments, education, housing, community, and other related topics. The list also does not include Foundation grants, workshops, and other activities in the area, all of which were extensive. Some sense of the scope of Foundation activity can be found in the bibliography of Robert Goldmann, *A Work Experiment: Six Americans in a Swedish Plant* (1976).

Institute and his coauthor on *Where Have All the Robots Gone?*, Dr. Neal Herrick; Basil Whiting and Robert Schrank from the Ford Foundation; Irving Bluestone of the UAW; and others. The general tenor of the hearings may be seen in Kennedy's opening remarks. "Too many young workers," he says, "are finding their jobs a place of confinement and frustration. (. . .) [O]ur lack of concern is producing a class of angry and rebellious workers. (. . .) And we have also learned that millions of Americans are alienated because they see their jobs as dead ends, monotonous and depressing and without value" (p. 8). The published proceedings from these hearings amount to 354 pages of attestation to essentially this same set of themes.

The first volume written from an unquestionably Marxist perspective appeared in 1973; it was the "bold and pathbreaking" achievement of Stanley Aronowitz, *False Promises: The Shaping of American Working Class Consciousness*. The book, not too surprisingly, opens with a chapter devoted to Lordstown. Another critical work, also focusing on Lordstown, was written by Emma Rothschild, *Paradise Lost: The Decline of the Auto-Industrial Age*. And still another putting forth the "critical" claims of this new genre was a Congressional Quarterly publication edited by Hoyt Gimlin, *Editorial Research Reports on the American Work Ethic*. Sar Levitan and William B. Johnston brought out a small volume reviewing all major issues in the area; it had a significantly new tone, one indicated already in the title, *Work Is Here to Stay, Alas*. Early in the text, all the major claims of the "deteriorating work ethic" school are rejected (although at this point, no specific supporting evidence is cited). This volume was "prepared under a grant from the Ford Foundation."

The most important contribution of 1973, the one carrying the most weight in declarations of the work dissatisfaction claims, was the report of a Special Task Force to the Secretary of Health, Education, and Welfare. It was entitled *Work in America* (O'Toole).[22] Like the panel report of Jerome M. Rosow, this too, it will be noted, had its origins in the Nixon administration (the volume contains a foreword by HEW Secretary Elliot L. Richardson). It shows many similarities to the Sheppard-Herrick work, which is not too surprising since it was prepared under the auspices of the Upjohn Institute, those two researchers being members of the Special Task Force.

The work, understandably, had a special cachet. It was not the writing of an individual scholar or free-lance critic. In effect, the United States government was giving credence to all that had come before. A small army of scholars was involved in preparing position papers for the task force. Some

[22]To avoid possible confusion, the James Wright listed among the ten coauthors of *Work of America* and who attended the Kennedy hearings is not the same James Wright who is coauthor of this volume.

Some writings by one of the present authors (RH) appeared among the previously cited works. These are: an article on skilled workers (on the affluence and worker theme) in Shostak and Gomberg, one on the attitudes of white workers toward blacks (in the *Dissent* volume), and another on the same theme in the Sar Levitan collection.

of these were published the following year in the volume *Work and the Quality of Life*, edited by James O'Toole, the chairman of the task force.

Work in America began, as we have noted, as a Task Force Report, but with its publication in paperback by MIT Press in 1973, it enjoyed remarkably greater success than the average government committee report. Like the Reich volume, it has had considerable sales as a textbook in college and university courses, and it is one of the very few government reports that one can find cited with evident approval even in Marxian literature. Indeed, the work stands in relation to the ongoing struggle to humanize the workplace much as *The Real Majority* stands in relation to the neoconservative movement, as the central text that contains and documents the canonical truths.

The concern with work continued into 1974. The American Assembly, a private national public affairs forum, devoted their 1973 Arden House meeting to "The Changing World of Work." The background papers for this Assembly, edited by Jerome M. Rosow, were published in 1974 under the title *The Worker and the Job: Coping with Change*. Many of these articles showed a refreshing individuality, which is to say they showed independent thought and research, some casting doubts on the sweeping work dissatisfaction claims. On the first page, Rosow injects a key bit of relevant evidence and therewith sharply reduces the sweep of the previous assertions. "In 1973, 77 percent expressed work satisfaction," he announced, "but 23 percent were either dissatisfied or expressed no opinion. The 11 percent who admitted that they were dissatisfied equals about 11 million people!" The American Assembly program, incidentally, was also supported by The Ford Foundation.

Somewhat less well known is the collection brought out by Roy P. Fairfield, *Humanizing the Workplace*. Organized in terms of a left or "critical" perspective, this volume was also made possible in part by a grant from the Ford Foundation. Still another collection appearing that year was Lloyd Zimpel's *Man Against Work*.

An important original work, the second of the genre written from a Marxist perspective, also appeared that year, this being Harry Braverman's *Labor and Monopoly Capital: The Degradation of Work in the 20th Century*. Unlike most of the works listed in this review, Braverman's volume generated an interest that has continued into the 1980's.[23]

The all-time best-seller on the subject also appeared in 1974—Studs Terkel's *Working*, a collection of some 140 statements by people telling of their work experience. The book sold over 275,000 copies in the hardcover edition. A Book-of-the-Month Club selection, it was also chosen by five

---

[23]The Braverman volume is discussed briefly in the following chapter, as is the subsequent research literature that it spawned. To indicate something of its academic impact, we note that it was given the C. Wright Mills award by the Society for the Study of Social Problems, as the best book on the topic of social problems published in 1974.

other book clubs. In 1974, it came out in a paperback edition that, as was to be expected, far outdistanced the hardback sales.[24]

A parallel interest in work, not surprisingly, was shown by the magazines and newspapers of the period. The *Readers' Guide to Periodical Literature* provides a useful measure of this interest, the 1970 volume containing only four listings under "Job Satisfaction," the most important of which was the first of the Gooding articles.[25] Under that heading in 1971 were seven listings, including an article by Harold Sheppard in the *Monthly Labor Review* and, in *Vital Speeches,* an address by Jerome Rosow (given before the American Management Association Annual Conference in New York, February 9, 1971).

Newsweek was also listed (May 17, 1971), the first of the major news magazines to run a "Blue-Collar Blues" article. It contained all the stock claims of the "deteriorating work satisfaction" repertory. They reported the "epidemic of absenteeism . . . " Because of the high education levels of young workers, they said, there was also a "higher level of disappointment." The strains on the shop floor were compounded by the "contemporary brand of rebelliousness" young people brought with them to the job. The article denied that it was merely a money problem. They provided a Harold Sheppard quotation: " . . . job dissatisfaction is increasing. Today's worker won't accept the things his father did. . . . " They also had appropriate quotations from Jerome Rosow. Reference was made to alcoholism and drug usage as effects of oppressive work, and a paragraph was devoted to instances of workplace sabotage. They also had a discussion of job enrichment efforts, including a discussion of the Gaines Pet Food plant in Topeka, Kansas. The work reorganization effort in that small unit (100 employees) received considerable attention in the early 1970's, references to it being part of the standard litany.

[24]This flurry of works on work stimulated the appearance of imitative products elsewhere. Terkel's book, for example, was followed by Walter Johnson's *Working in Canada* (1975), this consisting of reports by ten workers (one of whom was the author). *The Tyranny of Work* by James Rinehart also appeared in Canada in the same year. One Canadian work deserving of special mention is that by William and Margaret Westley, *The Emerging Worker* (1971). Written prior to the rise of interest in work, it anticipated many of the themes first exposed to American audiences in the Gooding article.

[25]The 1970 volume actually covers the period from March 1970 to February 1971, the same overlap being the case also with other volumes of the *Readers' Guide.*

In the nine-year period from 1961 to 1969, the *Guide* contained an average of two listings per year under "Job Satisfaction." Many of them were "how to do it" accounts with a strong focus on the individual (e.g., "Stale in your job? Try this," "How to get out of dead-end job," "Got the itch to change jobs?" and "Should you quit your job?"). Toward the end of the decade there were some signs of a change. The number of such pieces increased (to four in 1968 and to five in 1969). Some expert contributions appeared (e.g., Argyris and Herzberg). And the focus changed to one with a collective or institutional concern, three of the articles dealing with job enrichment, with the need to make "work" (versus an individual job) worthwhile.

The 1972 *Reader's Guide* contained nineteen entries on job dissatisfaction, including one on absenteeism, another on monotony, and another on the "Blue-Collar Blues." *Newsweek* provided a comment on the Sheppard-Herrick volume entitled "Workers' Woes." In addition to the "Job Satisfaction" listings, there was, of course, a rash of Lordstown articles under "Strikes—Automotive."

Attention peaked in 1973 with twenty-eight entries. The *Readers' Digest* brought out their "Blue-Collar Blues" article in April. *Harper's* had a review of *Work in America*. *Newsweek* had one entitled "The Job Blahs: Who Wants to Work?" (March 26, 1973). The magazine cover for that issue contained a picture of Charlie Chaplin taken, of course, from *Modern Times*. The article itself reviewed all the standard themes, touching once again on job enrichment programs and the Gaines Pet Food experience. Senator Edward Kennedy had introduced a bill to get $20 million for study of the entire work question. Sheppard and Herrick are quoted on absenteeism in the auto industry, their words finding support in the HEW Task Force report.

This *Newsweek* piece then made an abrupt change of course, providing some words of skepticism. George Gallup was quoted as challenging the pessimistic claims; his polls showed the situation getting better, not worse. George B. Morris Jr., a General Motors vice president, also injected a skeptical note, saying that there was nothing to it; it was just a bunch of academicians quoting each other.[26] Leonard Woodcock, president of the United Auto Workers, thought the claims to be "elitist nonsense," something he felt degraded workers. Irving Bluestone, the UAW's vice president, thought that blue-collar blues were a problem. He also thought that "everybody's confused. . . . " The article then changed direction once again, returning to the familiar ground of Gaines Pet Food and other work change projects. The Ford Foundation, they reported, was putting $500,000 into the study of work enrichment programs.

The tide of interest was ebbing in 1974, the total number of articles listed falling to sixteen. Some of these indicated more than just a passing note of skepticism. The *Newsweek* contribution (April 29, 1974) appeared with a question mark appended to the familiar phrase, the title now being "Blue-Collar Blues?" The opening sentence declared that

> Today, worry over worker alienation has become the sociological chic of the 1970s. Hand wringing executives lament, the Wall Street Journal editorializes, doctoral candidates hypothesize and even a Senate subcommittee finds it necessary to investigate the "blue-collar blues".

[26]The entire passage is deserving of attention. Morris, General Motors's vice president in charge of industrial relations, "compares the current debate with the furor over automation a decade or so ago. 'The academics started talking about it and pretty soon they were quoting each other. They said people were on their way out, which simply wasn't true,' he says. 'Well, today the same thing is happening; there is a lot of writing being done on this subject of "alienation" by people who don't know what they are talking about.' "

No mention was made of *Newsweek's* own previous contributions to the "sociological chic of the 1970s." The article provides accounts of two studies, one reporting high levels of satisfaction by automobile workers in a General Motors plant in Baltimore, the other a report of a Department of Labor study that had found "no demonstrable change . . . " in work satisfaction. The General Motors vice president is quoted as rejecting the standard Lordstown claims, and Leonard Woodcock once again declares the whole thing to be "elitist nonsense" on the part of scholars and journalists.

Interest in the subject lingered on in liberal and left-wing journals (for example, *The Progressive* first published a "Blue-Collar Blues" article in December 1975). More articles appeared in the years at the end of the decade than at the beginning, but these had a wide and rather diverse coverage. One dealt with "The Confused American Housewife," another with job dissatisfaction and heart disease. Not giving up easily, *Business Week* published an article in 1976 entitled "Worker Unrest: Not Dead, But Playing Possum."

The falloff and dispersion of interest in work was also reflected in the later book-length treatments of the subject. Barbara Garson, author of a leading Lordstown article, brought out *All the Livelong Day: The Meaning and Demeaning of Routine Work,* the only major entry in 1975. Elliot Richardson, the sponsor of *Work in America,* produced his own analysis of the human condition in 1976 in a book called *The Creative Balance.* One chapter, entitled "Worker Discontent: Enhancing Job Satisfaction," recapitulates the main themes of the tradition, in the process "mining" many of the works already cited—Rosow, Terkel, *Work in America*—and providing yet another review of the Gaines Pet Food experience in Topeka.

Also in 1976, Richard Balzer brought out a very intelligent participant observation study, *Clockwork.* A small collection of original articles was brought out by B. J. Widick that year entitled *Auto Work and Its Discontents.* The chapter by Al Nash, "Job Satisfaction: A Critique," added to the counterliterature providing evidence against the rising discontent thesis.[27]

In 1978, an autobiographical account by Robert Schrank appeared, entitled *Ten Thousand Working Days.* It reviews a wide range of work experiences, the last of which was a job with the Ford Foundation. This job was concerned with the "Quality of Worklife."

In 1979, Jerome M. Rosow, in conjunction with Clark Kerr, brought out a volume entitled *Work in America: The Decade Ahead.* At this point Rosow was president of the Work in America Institute. In that year another Marxist work appeared, Richard M. Pfeffer's *Working for Capitali$m.*

We have reviewed books and magazine treatments of the "work dissat-

[27]We have not included studies of blue-collar families and/or neighborhoods in the review. Some works with this focus are Howell (1973), Fried (1973), Kornblum (1974), and Rubin (1976). We have also not included accounts of industrial accidents (e.g., Wallick, 1972). We do not mean to suggest that these topics are unimportant, only that they are not directly relevant to the subject under discussion.

isfaction" theme. In addition, attention was given the subject in scores of book reviews appearing in various magazines. Discussions and book reviews also appeared in newspapers throughout the land.

The most important reason for the decline of interest in the subject was that the available evidence did not accord with the predictions that had been proclaimed with such fervor. Some of those evidential problems will be considered in the next section, some in the next chapter. Some other problems, those of absenteeism, turnover, and strikes (including the Lordstown experience) are examined in Chapter 6.

The arousal of interest in work and its discontents, it will be noted, stemmed from a rather diverse collection of efforts. The initial concern, we have seen, came from within the Nixon administration, the first step having been taken by the President himself, who was moved by free-lance writer Pete Hamill's article. An assortment of scholars, intellectuals, and commentators, quite independently, took up the subject, focusing specifically on young workers and their discontents. Some events of the era lent plausibility to their analyses (or were interpreted in such a way as to provide apparent support for their claims). Work became the object of Ford Foundation attention, and that agency's monies made possible meetings to discuss the themes previously developed and aided the publication of numerous contributions on the subject (see Note 21). The *Work in America* volume, at first sight, might suggest continuity with the earlier effort of the Nixon administration. But as far as we can tell, it was an independent effort; the focus was directly on work itself, not, as with the earlier product, on worker prestige and various marginalia of working-class life. On still another front, Senator Edward Kennedy was able to generate funding for additional study and comment. The Marxist contributions, rather unexpectedly, appeared only in the later years of this brief history. Unlike the other accounts that, somewhat belatedly to be sure, proved sensitive to the presentation of contrary evidence, the Marxist accounts continue to be published and, generally, have been immune to any evidence, the basic techniques being either a wholesale dismissal of evidence or an equally sweeping neglect of evidence.

The preceding discussion gives a brief chronology and intellectual history of the products and publications of the workplace critics, and touches on all the key themes of the tradition. It does not, however, impart in any adequate way the depiction of urgency, the drama, that one finds in virtually all these accounts. So that readers unfamiliar with these works will have some sense of the general tone, we quote at length from some of the more important. First, passages from two of the more commonly cited Marxian sources:

> The transformation of working humanity into a "labor force," a "factor of production," an instrument of capital, is an incessant and unending process. The condition is repugnant to the victims, whether their pay is high or low, because it violates human conditions of work; and since the workers are not destroyed as human beings but are simply utilized in inhuman ways, their critical, intelligent, conceptual faculties, no matter how deadened or diminished, always

remain in some degree a threat to capital. (. . .) [T]he hostility of workers to the degenerated forms of work which are forced upon them continues as a subterranean stream that makes its way to the surface when employment conditions permit, or when the capitalist drive for a greater intensity of labor oversteps the bounds of physical and mental capacity. It renews itself in new generations, expresses itself in the unbounded cynicism and revulsion which large numbers of workers feel about their work, and comes to the fore repeatedly as a social issue demanding solution. (Braverman, pp. 139, 151)[28]

The condition of capitalist survival, then, is the trivialization of labor in terms of the psychic self while its significance in relation to physical needs is retained. (. . .) That is why, with few exceptions, workers expect nothing intrinsically meaningful in their labor, and satisfy their desires for craftsmanship in the so-called "private realm." (. . .) The suppressed desire for work that is satisfying, that expresses the creativity of the person, that is not a denigration of human intelligence, has become more acute in the age of automated production, where the worker is reduced to a watcher, almost an observer of the labor process. (. . .) Modern society has systematically denied the desire for intrinsic work satisfaction for the overwhelming majority of people. (Aronowitz, pp. 130–133)

And, from some of the non-Marxist sources cited above:

[S]ignificant numbers of American workers are dissatisfied with the quality of their working lives. Dull, repetitive, seemingly meaningless tasks, offering little challenge or autonomy, are causing discontent among workers at all occupational levels. This is not so much because work itself has greatly changed; indeed, one of the main problems is that work has not changed fast enough to keep up with the rapid and widescale changes in worker attitudes, aspirations, and values. (O'Toole, *Work in America*, 1973: xv–xvi)

As portrayed in a host of official studies, press findings, and industry reports, the increasingly familiar "blue collar blues" of bored, alienated, assembly-line workers have spread to a white-collar world of dull, unchallenging jobs. There is fear that worker discontent is so pervasive it may undermine the nation's social and economic structure. (Gimlin, p. 1)

The picture of satisfaction with work has revealing and complex contradictions: Poll data, for example, suggest many workers are "satisfied" with their work, but interview data uncover much work-related discontent. Blue-collarites tell me, for example, that they would never do it all over again, and many are intent on seeing to it that their children do *not* follow in their footsteps. (. . .) Overall, then, the characteristic blue-collar response to the challenge of finding satisfaction in work entails reducing one's goals so far that one can appear to be satisfied. (Shostak, 1980, p. 57)

[28]Braverman's remark about "cynicism and revulsion" with work coming to the fore as a "social issue" provides a useful occasion to point out that in Scammon and Wattenberg's analysis of the social issue, feelings about work are *never* mentioned in any connection. This is, itself, a remarkable contrast: In Braverman's account, the population seethes in anger and hatred about the dehumanization of its labor; "large numbers," he says, feel nothing less than "revulsion" about their work. Scammon and Wattenberg also chart the discontents of the day, and yet discontent about work receives not so much as a passing mention. To be sure, Braverman is discussing "the labor process," whereas Scammon and Wattenberg are discussing the politics of the "Real Majority." Still, they are both talking about *the same people*.

The average man is victimized by hard, monotonous and unrewarding labor. (. . .) The worker (blue collar and clerical) is Marx's original "alienated man." It was the estrangement of the industrial worker from the product of his labor which, Marx predicted, would generate the revolution and topple the capitalist class. While this has not come to pass in the United States, the nature of industrial work remains a source of massive discontent. (. . .) This job alienation is not limited to blue-collar workers. Except for the dirt and noise, the white collar worker is in much the same boat. (Sexton and Sexton, pp. 129–130)

THE EMPIRICAL STUDY OF WORK;
A SECOND DIALECTICAL NEGATION

Concurrent with the rise of the workplace critics and the across-the-board announcement that worker discontent had reached new and potentially insurrectionary heights, researchers were continuing to conduct empirical studies of worker alienation. *Newsweek's* comment notwithstanding, it is hardly accurate to characterize a concern with the quality of working life as the "sociological chic of the '70's." The justly famous study called *Middletown*, by Robert and Helen Lynd, was published in 1929; Chapter 7 of that book discusses the "long arm of the job." Robert Hoppock's survey study, *Job Satisfaction*, was published in 1935. In 1946, eleven years later, the literature on job satisfaction had begun to proliferate at such a rate that Hoppock initiated an annual summary of the results of published studies in the *Personnel and Guidance Journal*. Between 1946 and 1958, no less than 406 studies had been annotated. A 1957 publication by Frederick Herzberg and associates entitled, *Job Attitudes: A Review of Research and Opinion*, references more than 1500 empirical studies of job atitudes and outlooks that had been published to that date. Concerning more recent research attention given to the topic, a review of literature conducted by the American Psychological Association found that "556 reports concerning job satisfaction were published between 1967 and 1972" (Quinn, Staines, and McCullough, p. 1), and an encyclopedic review undertaken by Edwin Locke in 1973 found some 3350 articles, books, and dissertations on job satisfaction to have been published to that date. The "new" interest in work and its discontents touched off by Judson Gooding in 1970, in short, concerns subject matter that had been actively researched in more than 3000 studies spanning roughly four decades. A research literature of this size and duration scarcely qualifies as sociological chic.

Unlike the writings of the workplace critics, much of this research literature is largely inaccessible to a lay reader. It appears in out-of-the-way scholarly journals, unpublished doctoral dissertations, and technical research monographs. This fact aside, one might reasonably expect persons offering themselves as experts on the topic of work to become familiar with at least some of the research data, as it contains the best available evidence obtainable from workers themselves on their feelings about their jobs. Most of this "best available evidence" stands in flat and unmistakable contradiction to the workplace critic themes.

Since much of the detailed evidence is discussed later, we focus here on only a few of the highlights. Throughout the workplace critics' writings, one encounters the theme that work is somehow central to the whole of one's life (cf. the remark from President Nixon, "the most important part of the quality of life is the quality of work . . . "). In 1956, the sociologist Robert Dubin published an article dealing with "Industrial Workers' Worlds: A Study of 'Central Life Interests' of Industrial Workers." The methodology of the study was quite straightforward: Dubin asked a sample of factory workers to tell him what was most important in their lives. The finding: "The vast majority of the workers studied (76%) did not locate their overall central life interests in work" (Dubin, Hedley, and Taveggia, p. 6). Rather, for the vast majority, the central life interest revolved around their family, group, and community life. Since 1956, there have been nineteen replications of Dubin's study in five different countries, some done on rural workers, others on urban workers, some on industrial workers, others on white collar workers. The studies differ substantially in how central life interests are measured, as well as by year and workers studied. Over the nineteen replications plus Dubin's original, the average proportion giving work as the central life interest to them is 40% (Dubin, Hedley, and Taveggia, 1976: Table 4), which means that the interests of the majority (the remaining 60%) lie elsewhere, and apparently have for at least twenty or thirty years.[29]

One might pause at this juncture to raise a procedural question. As indicated in the previous section, there were, in the 1970's, a host of politicians, commentators, and critics who asserted, in one way or another, that work is the central facet of people's lives. Persons arguing this point range from President Richard Nixon to the Marxist Harry Braverman. In the twenty-year

[29]There is, to be sure, considerable variation around this average across the several replications. Some studies find as many as 85% claiming work as a "central life interest," others, as few as 15%. In general, the higher percentages are reported in studies of white-collar workers, and the lower percentages in studies of blue-collar or farm workers. Thus, the "centrality" of work varies across the social classes and across occupational groups, being higher in some quarters and lower in others. But this is rather a "messy" conclusion, however faithful it might be to the state of evidence on the subject.

Why is work not the central life interest of most workers? The expectation that it would be, of course, depends at least in part on the common assertion that most adults spend "half of their lives" at the workplace (e.g., Richardson, p. 232). In fact, most workers spend eighteen or more years of their lives before they ever begin working, and some period of retirement once they have stopped. In the course of a typical year at work, there are at least a few weeks of vacation. And in the course of a typical week, most workers spend roughly one-third of each of the five of seven days at work, and the remainder of the week in other activities. Adding up the years before and after one's working years, the time spent away from work during the working years, and the time spent away from work in the typical working week, the actual time spent at work for the average worker could not possibly be more than perhaps 15% of the total hours in the lifespan. And surely, what people do with their lives during the remaining 85% of their time must count for at least something.

period from the middle 1950's to the middle 1970's, there were also twenty scholarly studies asking workers themselves about the most important facets of their lives, and the response routinely reported for the majority of workers is that work is *not* their central life interest. The procedural question is this: Who is the better witness? Who is one to believe? A related, and no less important, question: Why are the politicians, commentators, and critics apparently unaware of, or insensitive to, these findings?

An even more insistent theme in the writings of the workplace critics, of course, is that most people dislike their work. Indeed, "dislike" is far too mild a characterization: the adjectives appearing in the sources cited earlier—monstrous, destructive, repugnant, inhuman, deadening, degenerated, revulsive, trivialized, denigrating, painful, dull, repetitive, meaningless, unchallenging, hateful—are among the strongest available in the English language. Now one might suppose (rightly, as it happens) that over the course of forty years and 3000 studies, someone would have thought to ask workers themselves how *they* feel about their work. In fact, such a question has been asked in hundreds of studies, and the routine finding sharply contrasts the workplace critics' theme: when people are asked point-blank whether they are satisfied with their work, the majority consistently answers "yes."

We shall have occasion to review the evidence on this finding in some detail in the following chapters. Here we only note the consistency, indeed, virtual unanimity, with which the finding has been reported.

The most comprehensive overview of the job satisfaction literature to date is a paper by Robert Kahn entitled, "The Meaning of Work" (1972).[30] The data analyzed by Kahn are "some two thousand job satisfaction studies that have been done." The studies reviewed have examined virtually every conceivable kind of worker in virtually every conceivable work and social setting; the studies have also employed a wide variety of questions to measure the key job satisfaction variable. "In spite of such differences in technique, time, and coverage, there is a certain consistency in the response patterns: few people call themselves extremely satisfied with their jobs, but still fewer report extreme dissatisfaction. The modal response is on the positive side of neutrality—'pretty satisfied.' The proportion dissatisfied ranges from 10 to 21 percent" (Kahn, 1972, p. 169).

Another scholarly review of some interest was published during the ascendancy of the workplace critics, this being the monograph by Robert Quinn and associates entitled, *Job Satisfaction: Is There a Trend?* (1974). Unlike the Kahn article, this piece is not based on a review of published job satisfaction studies, but on a reanalysis of fifteen nationally representative

[30]It is worth emphasizing that Kahn's comprehensive review of this literature appeared in 1972, right at the front end of the "tidal wave" of workplace criticism. Most of the popularizers in this area show no awareness whatever of Kahn's article. Some of the more scholarly variants do acknowledge its existence, but either ignore or seriously distort the thrust of the findings. One such treatment is discussed in the next chapter.

surveys of job satisfaction conducted between 1958 and 1973.[31] According to these surveys, the proportion of the American working population admitting job satisfaction ranged from 80% to 92%. To emphasize, these are *not* intellectuals, politicians, critics, or commentators who are speaking through the medium of the surveys reviewed by Quinn; they are national probability samples of working people themselves—people who are in a position to know, in a way that distant commentators are not, just what their work is like and what it entails.

As with many academic publications, the Quinn *et al.* review is a relatively obscure source. It was published as the United States Department of Labor Manpower Research Monograph No. 30 and can be obtained only through the Government Printing Office. And yet its central conclusion is quite remarkable, given what the workplace critics have claimed: "In spite of public speculation to the contrary, there is no conclusive evidence of a widespread, dramatic decline in job satisfaction. Reanalysis of fifteen national surveys conducted since 1958 indicates that there has not been any significant decrease in overall levels of job satisfaction over the last decade" (Quinn, Staines, and McCullough, p. 1).

Quinn's results also bear directly on another of the critics' favorite themes, that the young workers of today are especially likely to hate their work. This finding, at least, initially seems consistent with what the critics have claimed: "Young workers are less satisfied with their jobs than older workers."[32] There is, however, another part of the story that is *not* consistent with the critics' world view: " . . . but this has been true for the past 15 years. Therefore, the much-discussed large recent decline in job satisfaction of younger workers has not been substantiated" (Quinn, Staines, and McCullough, p. 1). The greater work alienation of today's youth, in short, is not some new development; in 1958, no less than now, younger workers were also less satisfied. Indeed, as Quinn concludes, "younger workers have been consistently less satisfied than their elders for the last 15 years and, probably, even earlier than that" (Quinn, Staines, and McCullough, p. 12).

The critics ascribe the work alienation of today's youth to the upwelling of new or postmaterial values, but this can scarcely be the explanation for the alienation of the working youth of 1958. Why, then, were young workers even in 1958 less satisfied with their jobs than older workers? Quinn suggests a remarkable possibility, remarkable first because of the yawning distance

[31]Of the fifteen surveys, ten were conducted prior to 1970—that is, prior to the publication of Gooding's initial piece and the subsequent explosion of concern over worker discontent. None of these national surveys is discussed or referenced by Gooding, and in the ensuing literature, their existence is either ignored or their findings are dismissed and ridiculed. On the treatment of national survey data on work by the workplace critics, see the following chapter.

[32]That younger workers are less satisfied than older workers is a commonly reported research finding; see Wright and Hamilton (1978b) for a summary and review of the relevant studies.

between it and *any* explanation for the alienation of the young that has come from the workplace critics, and, second, because of its striking plausibility: "older workers . . . are more satisfied with their jobs than younger workers simply because they have better jobs" (Quinn, Staines, and McCullough, p. 12). Why this might be true is not hard to understand. "In an achievement oriented society, the 'best' jobs are reserved for those who can perform them best. Generally, such performance depends on a worker's job experience, accrued skills, and demonstrated competence in related jobs." The idea here, in short, is that one typically starts at the bottom and works up; the higher one gets, the more satisfying the job becomes. That, of course, would be true today as well as in 1958 and would certainly not constitute some new or potentially explosive development.[33]

Still other results from the Quinn *et al.* study bear on the intellectual's "rising education" theme. This theme, recall, is that education raises expectations and instills new values; the attendant implication is that the more education one has, the less satisfied with work one will be. Quinn, however, reports no such pattern. "Among workers without a college degree," he says, "there is little relationship between educational level and job satisfaction." Whether one has eight years of formal education, or twelve years, or even a few years of college, seems, in Quinn's data, not to matter so far as satisfaction with work is concerned. But what then of the college graduates, those who have partaken completely and fully of the new values and higher aspirations that college is said to bring? Quinn's conclusion, simply, is that "those with college degrees, however, have *high* levels of job satisfaction."

The Quinn and Kahn reviews cited here are but two of a large number of scholarly papers published between 1970 and 1975 that report evidence directly contradicting the workplace critics' "hateful work" theme. Indeed, we have located twelve others, and are certain to have missed at least

[33]Two recent studies have disputed the argument that older workers are more satisfied because they have better jobs: Janson and Martin (1982), and Glenn and Weaver (1984). The Janson-Martin piece is a reanalysis of the 1973 Quality of Employment Survey. It shows that job satisfaction increases with age (Table 1), and that older workers have more challenging and more extrinsically rewarding jobs than younger workers do (Table 2), consistent with the better jobs hypothesis. Another finding that the effects of intrinsic and extrinsic rewards on job satisfaction are stronger among the young than the old (Table 3) is said to undercut the "better jobs" hypothesis, but the logic of this conclusion escapes us. We find nothing in their article that is in any sense inconsistent with the "better jobs" explanation of the age-satisfaction relationship.

The Glenn-Weaver study is an analysis of the 1972–1982 NORC General Social Survey data. Some parts of this analysis suggest that cohort effects underlie "the cross-sectional positive relationship between age and job satisfaction" (p. 11). This argument, however, does not explain why virtually the same relationship appears in the survey data from the 1950's (Quinn, Staines, and McCullough, 1974). The lesser satisfaction of the younger workers is *not* some "new" phenomenon; it has been observed in surveys for some thirty years. We see no plausible "cohort" explanation of this fact.

some.[34] Few, if any, of these publications are cited in *any* of the workplace critics' writings, and certainly none of them was sufficient to end the "work hype." The above count includes only pieces appearing during the ascendancy, the tidal wave of concern. As we have already noted, disconfirming studies had appeared for years prior to 1970, numbering in the thousands. What we apparently have here, in short, is not speculation in the absence of fact, but speculation in wholesale disregard of facts that were well documented in various specialized sources. We return to this theme, of course, in the next and later chapters.

THE THEORY OF THE POSTINDUSTRIAL SOCIETY

Several of the themes discussed previously appear in yet another world view that is relevant to our concerns, a world view that has come to be known as the theory of postindustrial society. Here we consider two prominent expositions of this view, the first being Daniel Bell's *The Coming of Post-Industrial Society* (1973); the second, Ronald Inglehart's *The Silent Revolution* (1977a).

In broad outline, the theory of postindustrialism consists of two related parts: a structural part that purports to describe structural changes in the organization and economy of the advanced capitalist societies; and a psychological part that purports to describe the necessary value conflicts and value changes that occur as a result of changing social structures. The first of these recapitulates a theme from Reich, namely, the announced arrival of the "post-scarcity society . . . when, for the first time in human history, large numbers of persons [have] to confront the use of leisure time rather than the drudgery of work" (Bell, p. 456). The second draws heavily from the hierarchy of needs theory of the psychologist Abraham Maslow. Because of the prominence of Maslow's theories in the theory of postindustrial society, a brief exposition proves useful.

Human beings, according to Maslow (1954, p. 80–92), are motivated by an assortment of needs. These are ordered into a hierarchy such that when one is satisfied, it no longer dominates (or motivates) action and another, a higher level need, takes its place. This idea, as one author put it, is "intuitively engaging." An individual is hungry and, accordingly, is moved to eat: once satisfied, he or she will be moved by some other need, the next one in the hierarchy. Maslow's hierarchy contains the following steps (the specific formulation is taken from Tausky and Parke, p. 535):

---

[34]In addition to Quinn and Kahn, the list of works includes Brooks (1972); Fein (1973); Flanagan, Strauss, and Ulman (1974); Henle (1974); Imberman (1973); Kaplan (1973); Salpukas (1974); Sirota (1974); Strauss (1974a, 1974b); and Wool (1973). These pieces appear in journals ranging from *Assembly Engineering* to *The Journal of Occupational Psychology* to the *Monthly Labor Review*. A somewhat later review, covering most of the major United States data sources and also providing some very useful comparative data, appears in de Boer (1978).

1. Physiological (hunger, thirst, sex, sleep).
2. Safety and security (protection of the physical self and life-style).
3. Belongingness and love (affection).
4. Self-esteem, esteem by others (self-approval, approval by others, prestige).
5. Self-actualization (the need to become what one is potentially, to become more of that which one is capable of becoming).

Most of human history has been characterized by scarcity; accordingly, most people at most times have been dominated by "lower-order" needs. In the context of work motivation, that means most people throughout history have been concerned with physiological needs and with safety and security. Not too surprisingly, given the dominance of those needs, money has been a prime focus of concern, being the obvious means for the satisfaction of those needs. But in modern times, with the coming of affluence, more and more people find those needs satisfied. Following the logic of the argument, that focus of concern no longer dominates and the "higher-level" needs come to have greater importance. Applied to the world of work, this means that ever larger segments of the labor force will be striving to achieve belongingness, self-esteem, and/or self-actualization. These strivings, of course, would also be evident in spheres other than work. Money will no longer be the prime motivator (increasing numbers of people have that, or enough of it for most purposes); to satisfy its employees, a firm—or for that matter, the whole society—will have to "pay off" with opportunities to achieve the higher level goals.

As indicated, the theory has an immediate intuitive appeal. Some intellectuals have built theories of "world-historical" import on its basic assumptions. The main elements of the theory, it will be noted, are contained in the first of the positions discussed here, in the writings of social critics such as Reich. The Maslow theory is at least implicit in Judson Gooding's exposition, and it is explicit in the writings of many who have argued the blue-collar blues and white-collar woes theme. Many people on the left, those in the "critical" tradition, have also found the theory appealing. It provides them with a new driving force in human events. If affluent workers meant satisfied or integrated workers, then the proletariat as a moving force would have disappeared, at least in the economically advanced nations. But this theoretical position provided them once again with an impulse, it gave them the contradiction that would, of necessity, lead to the transformation of the system. The needs in question, moreover, being rooted in the nature of things, in human psychology, constitute an eternal source of pressure against that system. It was not something that can be satisfied through distribution of an economic surplus.

Keeping these Maslovian themes in mind, the essentials of the theory of postindustrialism can be quickly stated. Owing to a large number of factors, among them rising education and concomitant increases in productivity, accelerated technological developments, increased cybernation, and so on, industrial society eventually reaches a state of such advanced affluence that the large mass of the population finds its lower-order needs satisfied. Accordingly, attention turns to the higher-order needs, especially to self-enrichment and self-actualization. In the short run, this new focus is highly conflictual: society, after all, is organized to satisfy economic or material needs, needs that have now been displaced or superseded. The crisis of early postindustrialism is thus that existing social arrangements are inadequate to satisfy these higher-order human needs: work, for example, is organized to generate economic surplus, but not opportunities to self-actualize; therefore, conflict will be present until these latter opportunities are provided. As one of the more prominent workplace critics put it, "It's not the money, it's the job."

"The end of material scarcity," then, is the first distinguishing mark of postindustrialism; the "end of physical work" is the second. Technological progress on a grand scale is the necessary driving mechanism; increasingly, the production of essential material goods—food, shelter, clothing, and all related superfluities—will be done by machines, and such human labor as remains will be labor of the mind, not the body.

The postindustrial society thus brings a massive transformation of the labor force and the nature of work. The decline of manual labor and the corresponding rise of nonmanual or white-collar labor have, in many accounts, been steady and continuous trends in American society for most of the post-World War II era; under postindustrialism, these trends continue, even accelerate.[35] The whole focus of human work shifts from the production of goods to the production of services, chief among which is the production of knowledge necessary to fuel the process of technological change. And by this criterion, of course, postindustrialism has already arrived in the United States. "The United States today is the only nation in the world in which the service sector accounts for more than half the total employment and more than half the Gross National Product. It is the first service economy, the first nation in which the major portion of the population is engaged in neither agrarian nor industrial pursuits" (Bell, p. 15).

[35]This refers, of course, to the class shift hypothesis: the manual or working class is declining in size and importance, while the nonmanual or middle class, presumably, has grown to become the majority class. This view is central to several other theories in sociology, apart from the theory of postindustrialism. See Hamilton, 1972, Chapter 2.

In general, the expansion of the white-collar ranks and the decimation of the blue-collar ranks have been misrepresented in the received accounts. Overall, the available data do show a white-collar majority in the nonfarm ranks at the present, but this mixes two distinct patterns that ought to be kept separate. Among women workers, whose proportion within the labor force has been steadily growing, white-collar work predominates, mostly because of the large numbers of women in the clerical category. Among men workers, in contrast, the majority (that is, more than 50%) continue to be employed in manual or blue-collar work (Hamilton, 1972, Chapter 4).

A related development, of course, is the continued democratization of access to education, especially higher education. A society with a sharply reduced need for manual work will obviously have little or nothing for the uneducated and untrained to do; to be a contributing and productive member of the postindustrial society will necessarily require some years of advanced college or university training. Further expansions of higher education, and access to it, will also be required in order to produce the advanced scientific and technical knowledge upon which the livelihood of the society will directly depend. "The major problem for the postindustrial society will be adequate numbers of trained persons of professional and technical caliber" (Bell, p. 232).[36]

"Services," of course, will not fill the stomach or keep the body warm; these basic human needs will exist indefinitely. But their satisfaction will no longer depend so heavily on physical human labor; the cybernation of the production of goods will become virtually complete.

The economy of postindustrialism will therefore depend directly and immediately on continued technological development, and this gives rise to another major characteristic of the postindustrial society, "the pre-eminence of the professional and technical class" (Bell, p. 15). Society will need manual laborers less and less; the computerization of the office will make many clerical and other "lower" white collar jobs obsolete; but as the need for labor along these lines declines, the need for scientific, technical, and research labor will correspondingly increase. Any society that must depend on an advanced state of technology to feed, clothe, and house its people will obviously be in great need of scientists and researchers to develop new and more advanced technologies, engineers to install them, and technicians to keep them running. Thus, in Bell's words, "the scientists and engineers . . . form the key group in the post-industrial society" (Bell, p. 17).

The theorists of postindustrialism share with Charles Reich and other social critics at least one key theme; namely, that the technology already in place, or soon to be in place, is sufficient to produce all the material goods that American society requires. "Since machines can produce enough food and shelter for all," Reich writes, "why should not man end the antagonism derived from scarcity and base his society on love for his fellow man? If machines can take care of our material wants, why should man not develop the aesthetic and spiritual side of his nature?" (Reich, p. 383). Or as Roszak says, "the economy can do abundantly without all this labor." Or as

[36]Up to the early 1970's, the idea that industrial society would face a chronic shortage of adequately trained technical and scientific workers was a common theme. Bell is one of the last intellectuals to seriously argue the point, the concern having been replaced by today's more frequent worry about overeducation. Today, in short, the problem seems to be that the society has produced more highly trained and highly educated people than it has work for. On the theme of overeducation and its cognate concept, underemployment, see Blumberg and Murtha (1977), Freeman (1976), or O'Toole (1977). We have considered many of the claims of this *genre* elsewhere; see Hamilton and Wright (1981) or Wright and Hamilton (1978a, 1979).

Inglehart, whose work will be discussed below, says, "technology [has] liberated part of mankind from bare subsistence." The "part of mankind" so liberated, of course, is the Western democracies, especially the United States. In the Third World, "clearly, the problem is one of too little technology, not too much" (Inglehart, 1977a, p. 376).[37]

The work by Ronald Inglehart just cited is the most systematic statement yet written of the theory of postmaterial society and the value changes that accompany it, and the influence of his work, especially in political science, has been considerable.[38] There are, in his view, two major developments that point toward his Silent Revolution: first, "the unprecedented prosperity experienced by Western nations during the decades following World War II," and second, "the absence of total war" (Inglehart, 1977a, p. 21–22). "In short, people are safe and they have enough to eat. These two basic facts have far-reaching implications." One of these implications is, of course, the growth of postmaterial, or Consciousness III, values. "[S]ome groups in advanced industrial society have attained a sense of economic and physical security that enables them to give top priority to the belonging and intellectual-aesthetic needs" (Inglehart, 1977a, p. 363).[39] It is these new needs that cut across all social activities; they appear in family life, in community life, in the schools, in the churches, and finally in the political sphere.

The diminution of material scarcity and the subsequent liberation of consciousness from the burden of such concerns is a development of profound importance, of course, one that is "gradually but fundamentally changing political life throughout the Western world" (Inglehart, 1977a, p. 363). One might assume that this change would be in the direction of what could be called the "de-politicization" of society. In all industrial societies, political struggle is the struggle over scarce resources and their allocation;

[37]The idea that the American economy has already freed most of the population from economic want also comes through consistently in the writings of the workplace critics. For example, "on the average, no workers have ever been as materially well-off as American workers are today" (O'Toole et al., pp. 11–12). Or, "most American workers . . . can now take for granted that tomorrow they will have meals on their tables, shirts on their backs, and roofs over their heads" (O'Toole, 1977, p. 44). Even the Marxist Aronowitz remarks, "the old goals of decent income and job security . . . have lost their force" (1973).

[38]The initial statement of Inglehart's position appeared in the American Political Science Review in 1971. A second article-length treatment containing new data and analyses and Inglehart's response to some early criticism of the initial statement appeared in 1977 in the journal, Comparative Political Studies (1977b). Material from both articles is incorporated into the book-length treatment, The Silent Revolution, which also appeared in 1977 and which is discussed at some length in the text.

[39]As might be expected given the theme being argued here, Inglehart is generally sympathetic to the works of Reich and Roszak discussed in an earlier section. "Charles Reich's The Greening of America strikes me as insightful. (. . .) [H]e had intuitive glimpses of an extremely important phenomenon" (Inglehart, 1977a, p. 83). As for Roszak, Inglehart finds him "interesting and articulate" (1977a, p. 374).

what, then, will politics be about once resources are no longer scarce? From this point of view, "post-scarcity politics" would be a contradiction in terms; there can, after all, be no serious struggle between the haves and the have nots when nearly everybody has all they reasonably require.

But this misreads the character of the political problem in postindustrialism. In Inglehart's view, the looming problem of postindustrial civilization, or at least of the period of transition to it, is the scarcity of opportunities to self-actualize. The societies that the bearers of the new, postmaterial values (the young, the affluent, the better educated) inhabit are less than perfectly suited for satisfying these new needs—to belong, to be fulfilled, to self-actualize—and so, given their obvious talents, education and sharpened mental faculties, and advanced affluence, they are, "gradually but fundamentally," changing things, re-creating society along lines more favorable to themselves. "This group has distinctive value priorities. It places less emphasis on material welfare and more on qualitative aspects of society" (Inglehart, 1977a, p. 365). And later, "our findings indicate that the relatively prosperous postmaterialists now comprise the most likely source of political dissatisfaction and protest."

Thus, the contrast between industrial and postindustrial society could scarcely be sharper. In industrial and all previous societies, labor for the purpose of satisfying the basic material needs of self and family is the essential constant of all life; food, clothing, shelter, and the productive work that makes their acquisition possible, one might say, have been the ever-present and predominating worries ever since the species first evolved on the planet. The advanced technology of postindustrialism, however, will soon liberate the species from these concerns; as the production of essential goods is automated, consciousness will be freed from the chains of materialism.

But this serves only to create new problems: in the very process of solving the predominant problem of human existence throughout history, new values and new demands are unleashed which then force their way into the political arena for resolution. The key political struggle thus no longer concerns the distribution of scarce material resources, but the distribution of scarce psychological resources; namely, opportunities to lead a creative and enriching life. No longer does one look to the working class—the have-nots in industrial society—to provide the initiative for progressive change; on the contrary, the manual workers (whose force and numbers are, in any case, rapidly diminishing) "have acquired a stake in the established order and a 'bourgeois' mentality" (Inglehart, 1977a, p. 287). Rather, the major source of "political dissatisfaction and protest" are the "relatively prosperous Post-Materialists," and their concerns, obviously, have little or nothing to do with scarce material goods, but with the "quality of life" and the opportunities to self-actualize.

In the short run, to be sure, the rise of postmaterial values poses strains and conflict for the society as a whole. The existing economy and corresponding social structure are generally well suited to produce goods and services and oversee their distribution, but the production of opportunities to self-actualize is obviously another matter. In some respects, then, the residual "dissatisfaction and protest" that Inglehart notes arise because the advanced industrial society continues to pursue a set of needs or concerns that have lost their force for a large fraction of the population.

Over the long run, however, the prognosis is considerably brighter. Sooner or later, society will catch up to the needs and values of its most affluent and most educated members, and this "catching up" represents the transition from advanced industrialism to postindustrialism. Perhaps the essential hallmark of the mature postindustrial society is thus that it will have to struggle with the quality of its citizens' lives as much as its predecessor struggled over their material well-being.

THE "LITTLE MAN'S REVOLT": A THIRD DIALECTICAL NEGATION

The image of American society and its transformation that derives from the theory of postindustrialism is contradicted on virtually every serious substantive point by one last body of literature relevant to the purposes of this volume, one written by what we will refer to as the "intellectuals of the little man's revolt." Again, this is less a coherent theoretical position than a loose collection of disparate contributions, all tending, however, to share a common theme. And the theme, to borrow a famous line from Peter Finch in *Network,* is, "I'm mad as hell, and I'm not gonna take it anymore."

Who *was* this "little man" (or, presumably, "little woman") about whom so much was written? It can be said, without serious distortion, that Little Man is the dialectical negation of Postindustrial Man in every important respect. As we have just seen, Postindustrial Man is preeminently White-Collar Man, college-trained and performing mental labors in the expanding service sector. Little Man, in contrast, is preeminently Blue-Collar Man, not likely to have progressed beyond high school, or even through high school in many cases, and still chained, despite the advanced cybernetics of postindustrialism, to one or another sort of manual work. Too, the life of Postindustrial man is one of unprecedented affluence, one so opulent, in fact, that material well-being has ceased to be an issue. Little Man, in contrast, although not impoverished, is also not affluent—and most assuredly *not* as affluent as he wishes to be. He is, in the expression of Herbert Gans, "Subaffluent," and his style of life may be, and often is, described as "modest but respectable." In social class terms, Little Man is working class, or among writers for whom that phrase is an anachronism, lower-middle class. For Little Man, self-actualization is not likely to be a high priority concern, falling well below inflation, the high cost of medical care, the need to provide an education for his children, and so on. Politically, Little Man was once described as the "forgotten American," or, another favorite phrase, the "silent majority," but he is no longer silent or forgotten. "The ignored man of the sixties is the star of the seventies. His face gleams on the covers of national magazines ... his views are aired respectfully and faithfully by David, Walter, and Frank, and ... his political opinions are scrutinized microscopically by all the major politicans" (Howe, p. 295).[40]

Little Man bears an obvious demographic resemblance to the "real majority," or in Scammon and Wattenberg's other memorable phrase, middle voter—"a forty-seven-year-old housewife from the outskirts of Dayton, Ohio, whose husband is a machinist." There is, however, one very important difference between Middle Voter and Little Man. In the Scammon-Wattenberg presentation, the economic issue has, at least temporarily, lost its force; Middle Voter's issue is the social issue in all its ramifications:

> To know that the lady in Dayton is afraid to walk the streets alone at night, to know that she has a mixed view about blacks and civil rights because before moving to the suburbs she lived in a neighborhood that became all black, to know that her brother-in-law is a policeman, to know that she does not have the money to move if her new neighborhood deteriorates, to know that she is deeply distressed that her son is going to a community junior college where LSD was found on the campus—to know all this is the beginning of contemporary political wisdom (Scammon and Wattenberg, p. 71).

It is worth noting that the only remark contained in the above passage touching, even indirectly, on the economic issue is that Middle Voter "does not have the money to move" if the new suburban neighborhood deteriorates, and if, as seems likely, "deteriorates" means "turns black," then even this concern is an indirect reflection of the more basic social issue.

For Little Man, in contrast, the economic issue is, one might say, the only issue; all other issues take on meaning and importance only through their

[40]The Howe passage is from the "Afterword" to her edited volume, *The White Majority: Between Poverty and Affluence* (1970). As the title implies, this book may be taken as a primer on "little man" themes. We touch on only a subset of the themes here, but a good "feel" for the genre as a whole may be obtained just from the titles of the chapters. The opening paper in the volume is Pete Hamill's "The Revolt of the White Lower-Middle Class" (discussed in more detail below). This is followed by a piece called "Life with Cappelli on $101 a Week." Other papers in the book include: "Working Class Youth: Alienation without an Image," "How They Get Away from It All," "White Against White: The Enduring Ethnic Conflict," "The Fear of Equality," "Respectable Bigotry," "The Wallace Whitelash," "Workers and Liberals: Closing the Gap," "Is There a New Republican Majority?" and so on. According to the dust jacket, Little Man "is the ordinary employee in an office or factory. . . . He is a family man, strapped for money, in debt, fearful about his future, his job, his neighborhood, and the security of his family. He is overburdened with taxes, and the services he depends on . . . are inadequate."

The postindustrialists would presumably grant the continuing existence of people of the sort just described, at least in the transitional phase. The question here, as elsewhere in this volume, concerns the relative proportions and the trends therein.

For the record, "David, Walter, and Frank" in the Howe passage cited in the text refer to David Brinkley, Walter Cronkite, and Frank Reynolds—at the time of publication, the evening news anchormen for NBC, CBS, and ABC television, respectively.

relationship to the economic issue. Little Man, as Middle Voter, may well have a mixed view about race, but the source of Little Man's hostility is that advances made by blacks are eroding his own relative economic position. Little Man may also be hostile toward hippies and welfare chiselers, but mainly because his tax dollars pay for the social services that keep hippies and welfare chiselers going. He is less concerned about LSD on campus than the rising cost of tuition; his major concern over crime is what it costs these days to fight it. Being "subaffluent," Little Man has some, but wants more, and deeply resents any development that will cut into his own piddling and barely adequate share. For Little Man, life is a perpetual struggle to maintain a precarious financial security in the face of long odds, and his "enemies" are all who expropriate what is rightfully his—government chief among them. The idea that he would "renounce further material gains" in exchange for an opportunity to self-actualize is, of course, a towering absurdity.

Readers of *New York* were introduced to Little Man and his concerns as early as 1969, in a once-famous article by Pete Hamill entitled, "The Revolt of the White Lower-Middle Class." As Hamill explains, the white lower-middle class of which he writes is what was once known as the working class:

> That is, they stand somewhere in the economy between the poor—most of whom are the aged, the sick, and those unemployable women and children who live on welfare—and the semi-professionals and professionals who earn their way with talents or skills acquired through education. The working class earns its living with its hands or its backs; its members do not exist on welfare payment; they do not live in abject, swinish poverty, nor in safe, remote suburban comfort. They earn between five and ten thousand dollars a year. And they can no longer make it . . . (Hamill, p. 11).

The key conditions and concerns of the class are illustrated in the following passage, attributed to "an ironworker friend named Eddie Cush":

> I'm going out of my mind. I average about eighty-five hundred a year, pretty good money. I work my ass off. But I can't make it. I come home at the end of the week, I start paying the bills, I give my wife some money for food. And there's nothing left. Maybe, if I work overtime, I get fifteen or twenty dollars to spend on myself. But most of the time there's nothin'. They take sixty-five dollars a week out of my pay. I have to come up with ninety dollars a month rent. But every time I turn around, one of the kids needs shoes or a dress or something for school. And then I pick up a paper and read about a million people on welfare in New York or spades rioting in some college or some fat welfare bitch demanding—you know, not askin', *demanding*—a credit card at Korvette's . . . I *work* for a living and *I* can't get a credit card at Korvette's . . . You know, you see that, and you want to go out and strangle someone" (Hamill, pp. 11–12; emphasis and ellipses in the original).

Another ironworker (unnamed) is quoted as follows:

> Up on the iron, if the wind blows hard or the steel gets icy or I make a wrong step, bango, forget it, I'm dead. Who feeds my wife and kids if I'm dead? Lindsay? The poverty program?(. . .)They take the money out of my paycheck

and they just turn it over to some lazy son of a bitch who won't work. I gotta carry him on my back. . . . You shouldn't have to put up with this. And I'll tell ya somethin'. There's a lotta people who just ain't gonna put up with it much longer (Hamill, p. 12).

The two passages just quoted contain all the major seeds of Little Man's revolt. First, both passages are attributed to ironworkers; that is, to manual laborers. Ironworking qualifies as skilled employment, and so the two men are somewhere toward the top of the blue-collar hierarchy. Since no one has yet designed a machine to do the work that ironworkers do, these men are not likely to be displaced by technological development. Except for Cush's comment about "working my ass off," neither man has much to say about their work *qua* work; their concerns and dissatisfactions apparently lie elsewhere. Neither man (nor Hamill himself) comments on his education background, but it seems a safe bet that neither has graduated from, or even attended, college.

Hamill's interviewing was done in working-class bars in New York City, where the cost of living is higher than virtually anywhere else in the country.[41] Cush earns an annual income of about $8500 (as of 1969). In the same year, the median annual income for all United States families was $9586 (*Statistical Abstract of the United States,* 1975, p. 395). Cush's annual income is thus some $1300 *below* the family average, in a city where the cost of living is much higher than average. And yet he describes his income as "pretty good money." Cush is clearly not rapacious or appetitive in all this. Not that he would not like more, but he sees even his well-below-average share as "pretty good."

The work these men do is physically demanding and dangerous, even fatal if they "make a wrong step." And the income they earn at it is hardly handsome. Yet neither expresses any overt dissatisfaction about his work per se (at least not in the passages quoted), and while neither mentions it, it is easy to imagine that they both take some pride in what they do—working the high steel being among the more prestigious of manual jobs. Cush remarks that overtime is how he makes a little money "to spend on myself." Given his evident financial worries, perhaps Cush's most insistent complaint about his work would be that he does not get as much overtime as he would like.

James O'Toole has written that "most American workers . . . can now take for granted that tomorrow they will have meals on their tables, shirts on their backs, and roofs over their heads" (O'Toole, p. 44). But this is not Eddie Cush's story, not by any means. He doesn't take "meals on the table" for granted; rather, he recognizes that he has to "give my wife some money for

[41]Going to working class bars and chatting with the clientele is a favorite methodology among the intellectuals of the little man's revolt; the assumption is that here one finds the working class in its true element—that is, drowning its sorrows with a shot and a beer. Not all workers drink in bars, however, and those that do (the barflies) are not representative of the class as a whole. We discuss some of the biases of the barfly methodology in the following chapter.

food" every week. The $90 per month for rent is also not taken for granted; it is something he "has to come up with." And as for shirts on the back, "every time I turn around, one of the kids needs shoes or a dress . . . " Far from taking his basic material well-being for granted, Eddie Cush seems rather insistently worried about it. The second ironworker explicitly acknowledges the dependency of his family on his income. "Who feeds my wife and kids if I'm dead?" he asks. Clearly, *he* is not taking the welfare of his family for granted; he is quite obviously anxious about it.

"They," says Eddie Cush, "take sixty-five dollars a week out of my pay." "They"—distant and alien—are, of course, government. The second ironworker touches on the same theme: "They take the money out of my paycheck and they just turn it over . . . " For both men, the burden of taxation and their animosity toward government are obvious. The taxes they have to pay strike immediately at the heart of their concerns.

Finally, consonant with the other depictions we have considered, Little Man also seethes with anger and discontent, albeit of a qualitatively different sort. Eddie Cush is ready to "strangle someone," and the second ironworker "ain't gonna put up with it much longer." "Their grievances," says Hamill, "are real and deep; their remedies could blow this city apart" (Hamill, p. 10). To the intellectuals of the little man's revolt, the future, too, will be a "great transformation" of the past, although here, the impending transformation is dark and frightening. These people, Hamill says, are "on the edge of open, sustained, and possibly violent revolt." The revolt of the little man, as with all the "revolutions" we have considered in this chapter, is *also* imminent.

The little man's revolt has been a subliminal theme among the intellectuals of the American majority for most of the past decade. Much of the initial concern was stimulated by liberal alarums over the Presidential candidacy of George Corley Wallace, preeminently *the* candidate of Little Man.[42] More recently, Proposition 13, the tax revolt, and the electoral successes of Ronald Reagan have rekindled interest. Indeed, in the weeks following the passage of Proposition 13 in California, Little Man symbolism appeared on the cover of both *Time* and *Newsweek*. In *Time's* version, it was in the *persona* of Howard Jarvis, author of the proposition, this to announce the arrival of "A New Conservatism" (19 June 1978). The *Newsweek* cover featured an assemblage of "Little People," showing clenched fists and "V for Victory" gestures, displaying posters with such sentiments as "Yes on 13," "13—Hell Yes!," and *STOP* Unlimited Taxation" (19 June 1978). Little Man, indeed, is

[42]On the appeals of Wallace to the alienated working class, see Wright (1976, Chapter 9) and Hamilton (1972, pp. 460–467; 1975, Chapter 4). In general, both the alienation theme and the social class theme receive little support; the Wallace phenomenon was *not* a distinctive alienation phenomenon, and it was also not a distinctive working class phenomenon. It was, rather, primarily a *regional* phenomenon: the Wallace vote, as is well known, was concentrated heavily in the South; outside the South, the highest proportion of Wallace votes came from persons born and raised in the South. In contrast to these regional effects, the effects of class and political alienation were minor.

"mad as hell," and like Hamill's second ironworker, he is also "not going to take it anymore." In the *Time* and *Newsweek* accounts, nothing was said about the postscarcity society. In contrast, much was said about infla- tion devouring wage gains and eroding economic security. Self-actualiz- ation went unmentioned, as did any concern over belonging or intellectu- al-aesthetic needs. The looming need, discussed on virtually every page, was for economic relief, preferably through the medium of a sharp tax cut and the imposition of strict limits on governmental spending, themes ex- ploited quite successfully in the 1980 and 1984 Reagan campaigns. No one has mistaken the tax revolt for the "dissatisfaction and protest" of "rel- atively prosperous postmaterialists."

PORTRAITS OF "THE MASSES": A CONCLUDING NOTE

In the preceding pages, we have reviewed six major positions, view- points, or *genres,* each claiming to provide some sort of account of the characteristics and trends of the American population in the 1970's. In capsule form, the key claims of each position are as follows:

The Social Critics (Reich, Roszak, Toffler): American society and culture as a whole have turned sour. Materialism is no longer the main animating force, since, for the vast majority, all plausible material needs have long since been satisfied. The new consciousness of the times is Consciousness III—a consciousness that renounces material goals in favor of love, beauty, and self-actualization, and a consciousness borne primarily among the young, the affluent, and the well-educated.

The Real Majority (Scammon and Wattenberg): The major animating force among the population is the reaction against Consciousness III. The economic issue has lost its force, having been displaced by the social issue— the backlash, the "kidlash," the affirmation of traditional values.

The Workplace Critics (Braverman, Aronowitz, *Work in America*): The work available in society is ill-suited to meet the "new needs" of an affluent and educated population; "blue-collar blues" and "white-collar woes" are the result. Job discontent is general and on the increase. In the liberal variant, these developments bespeak an immediate need to improve the quality of working life, to defuse an otherwise "potentially explosive" situation. In the radical variant, we are face-to-face with a fundamental (and irresolvable) contradiction in the structure of capitalism. In both variants, Lordstown is merely the most dramatic visible manifestation of the tensions present within the existing organization of work.

The Workplace Researchers (Kahn, Quinn): Most people are satisfied with their work, and have been for as long as research on the topic has been conducted. There has been no substantial increase in job discontent in recent years. For most people, the job is a secondary concern, having lower priority than certain other spheres of life.

The Postindustrialists (Bell, Inglehart): The United States is approaching a postscarcity economy; as such, ever larger fractions of the population are being liberated from traditional material concerns and are thus freed, or moved, to pursue the higher-ordered Maslovian goals of beauty, self-expression, and self-actualization. The key problem of postindustrial society is not material scarcity but the scarcity of opportunities for self-expression and self-enrichment. The rise of new values is again said to be concentrated among the young, the affluent, and the well-educated.

The Intellectuals of the Little Man (Hamill): Inflation and taxation have seriously eroded the economic security of the American working population; the economic issue is paramount, and all other issues are subsidiary. Here, too, the situation has reached crisis proportions, with various backlash reactions predicted.

There are, to be sure, some important similarities to be found among some of these positions. Excepting the workplace researchers, for example, all five of the remaining theses posit that society is now (or was in the 1970's) on the edge of something new and different, that the immediate future would be a great transformation of the past. (The *direction* of hypothesized change, of course, varies greatly across formulations, but all are in essential agreement that change is in the offing.) Too, all five posit some sort of value change as the cause or effect of these other changes; the outlooks, values, concerns, and priorities of the American population are in flux. (Again, the *kinds* of new values being posited vary from one position to the next.) Finally, all five posit, in one way or another, a widespread sense of discontent or disenchantment with the way things are.

These general similarities notwithstanding, the particulars of the various formulations are such as to make it seem unlikely that each is describing the same society. But, of course, they are: each of them purports to describe the American population of the 1970's. Some of them also provide substantial amounts of evidence to bolster the case, although, to be sure, several do not, these latter being more in the nature of speculations than descriptions. In any case, the depictions being offered are sufficiently contradictory from one writer to the next that some sifting and winnowing of the various claims is obviously in order.

2 THE QUESTION OF EVIDENCE

All claims to knowledge imply a method of knowing. Method, put simply, is the set of procedures followed to generate or support empirical claims. A basic principle of the sciences, whether natural or social, is that the validity of a claim is a function of the methods used to produce it. The method may be sheer intuition, guess, hearsay, generalizations from personal experience, a study based on haphazard sampling, or a high quality research effort. No claim, in short, should be taken at face value. One must ask about the method of knowing, about how the knowledge was produced.

The previous chapter reviewed an assortment of sharply divergent claims made about the American population in the 1970's, each of them based on one or another method. In some cases, the methods followed are so haphazard and casual that the "findings" can hardly be taken seriously. In others, however, the claimants appear, at least initially, to have assembled substantial amounts of credible evidence. The aim of the present chapter is to review and critique the various methods and evidence provided in those works, to show that the existing evidence is far more consistent and less ambiguous than the diversity of claims would suggest, and, correlatively, to offer a defense of the methods employed in the remainder of this volume.

As will soon become obvious, this book relies almost exclusively on national sample surveys of the sort routinely done by Gallup, Harris, or other national polling firms, or on the generally larger and more detailed surveys done by the National Opinion Research Center at the University of Chicago or by the Survey Research Center at the University of Michigan. Our reliance on the national sample survey reflects our judgment that it is the *only* method that gives empirically credible descriptions of large populations. To restate slightly, if one wishes to make statements about "most Americans" or "the American population," then there is no alternative to the sorts of national surveys employed here.

The inevitability of sample surveys as a means of knowing the outlooks and conditions of the American masses follows from a few elementary considerations. First, the sheer size of the population of interest is such that a complete enumeration is out of the question in the normal course of events.

Excepting only the once-per-decade efforts of the United States Bureau of the Census, no group or organization, much less a lone individual, can possibly hope to obtain data from each and every person in the society. Fortunately, everything one needs to know about a population can be learned by studying samples of it: one can learn all about the flavors and seasoning of a pot of soup by tasting a few spoonfuls, all about the characteristics of a person's blood by analyzing a few milliliters, and all about the American population by studying a carefully chosen sample of it.

Excepting the purely speculative, all the works reviewed in Chapter 1 are based on some sort of sample: Charles Reich's sample consists of the Yale students who happened to dine at the Stiles-Morse dining common; Pete Hamill's of the ironworkers who happened to have been drinking on a particular night at a particular bar in Queens. These are samples of the American population, no less than the Gallup data reviewed by Scammon and Wattenberg or the several surveys analyzed by Inglehart are based on samples. The issue, in short, is not whether to sample, but rather the quality of the sample that is used. Given the evident need to study samples rather than whole populations, it is obvious that complete, systematic, and nationally representative samples are preferable to partial, haphazard, or severely restricted ones.

Conducting a national sample survey is a formidable and expensive undertaking. Fortunately, there is a tradition in this and most other countries that surveys of more than passing interest are deposited in various data archives, from which they are redistributed to other interested researchers. Two of the more prominent archives are the Roper Public Opinion Research Center, now located at the University of Connecticut, and the Inter-University Consortium for Political and Social Research, located at the University of Michigan. All the survey data presented in this book were obtained from these two organizations.[1]

[1]Surveys presented and analyzed in later chapters are as follows: I. The National Opinion Research Center (NORC) *General Social Surveys*, 1972, 1973, 1974, 1975, 1976, 1977, 1978, and 1980. These surveys are based on multistage area probability samples of adults in the United States age 18 and over; institutionalized populations are excluded. Technical details of the survey design, sampling plan, exact question wordings, and marginal results can be found in *General Social Surveys, 1972–1980: Cumulative Codebook* (available through the Roper Center, Box U-164R, University of Connecticut, Storrs, CT 06268).

II. Institute for Social Research, Survey Research Center, Center for Political Studies, *The Quality of American Life, 1971* and *The Quality of American Life, 1978*. Both these are very large surveys of "quality of life" based on nationally representative probability samples of the American adult, noninstitutionalized population. The first of the series is the basis of Campbell, Converse, and Rodgers (1976), which may be consulted for additional details. Codebooks containing technical details, sample design, question wordings, and marginal results can be obtained through the Inter-University Consortium for Political and Social Research (ICPSR), P.O. Box 1248, Ann Arbor, MI 48106.

III. The ISR/SRC/CPS/ *American National Election Studies*, 1972, 1974, 1976, and

There is a vast difference between the expense of generating national survey data and the cost of having access to the resulting information. The cost of doing a competent national survey from scratch runs into hundreds of thousands of dollars, but the study codebook, the basic survey reference document showing the specific questions asked and the frequencies with which each response was chosen, can be had for the price of an ordinary novel or biography. Assuming the relevant questions had been asked, such a codebook would contain precise, high-quality evidence on what proportion of the working population was satisfied with its work, or what proportion had attended a college or university, or what proportion had materialistic values, and so on. The point, in short, is that answers to many of the questions raised in Chapter 1 are readily available in existing resources. All that is required is the inclination to look them up.

As noted in the previous chapter, the inclination to "look it up" is highly variable among the sources discussed in this book. Some of these sources (for example, Inglehart or Scammon and Wattenberg) are heavily laden with poll data and survey results and thus enjoy considerable surface credibility. It must be noted, however, that reference to the existing national survey data can serve rhetorical as well as informational purposes, and for this reason questions about the accuracy of the presentation and the faithfulness of the account are always in order. Other sources, especially those of the workplace critics, indicate some awareness that appropriate national survey data on the topic exist but dismiss the results on the grounds that the truth about such matters can only be revealed through other methods. Given our reliance on surveys, it is clearly appropriate that these arguments be considered in some detail. Finally, at least some of the sources show no awareness whatever that such data even exist, drawing exclusively on impressions and fancy or such odd lots of "information" as can be had in conversations with persons conveniently at hand. Such, indeed is the method of *The Greening of America* (and of many other works of so-called social criticism). Thus, following the order of presentation in the previous chapter, it is here that we begin.

1978. This is the biannual election study series, ongoing since 1952. Although the topical focus is more expressly political than the Quality of American Life series, the samples are similar. Codebooks for all these surveys may also be obtained from the ICPSR (address given above).

IV. The ISR/SRC/CPS/ *1969 Survey of Working Conditions, 1972–1973 Quality of Employment Survey*, and *1977 Quality of Employment Survey*. This series focuses on attitudes and experiences concerning work and is restricted to labor force participants only, but is otherwise similar in scope and sample plan to the other SRC series. Codebooks for these studies are also available through the ICPSR.

We have also drawn on materials from the Gallup, Roper, and Harris polls where appropriate, although we have done no original analyses of data from these sources.

CHARLES REICH AND THE PROBLEM OF
UNWARRANTED GENERALIZATION

Reich wrote *The Greening of America* while a professor at Yale University, and so far as can be told, the information presented in the book derives exclusively from two sources: from his own obviously fertile imagination, and from casual conversations with various Yale students. To the extent that he says anything at all about more systematic methods of inquiry, it amounts only to an expression of open contempt.

To illustrate briefly, in his chapter on Consciousness III Reich comments that "journalists, writers for opinion journals, social scientists, novelists have all tried their hand at discussing the issues of the day" (Reich, p. 267), but, "almost without exception, they have been far more superficial than writers of rock poetry." Later in the same paragraph, Reich invites a comparison of "a sociologist talking about alienation with the Beatles' *Eleanor Rigby* or *Strawberry Fields Forever.*" Taking this comment at face value, Reich's point is apparently that the collected efforts of several decades of social science research have produced less compelling evidence on the satisfactions and sorrows of the American population than the lyrics composed by four rock musicians from Liverpool.

There could be only one reason for such an absurd claim. If an entire tradition of inquiry and research can be dismissed in a single sentence, then one need not bother incorporating any of it into one's own analysis. Once liberated from the constraining influence of facts, then anything, no matter how bizarre or fanciful, can be asserted.

To the extent that Reich has independent evidence for any of his assertions, it apparently consists of what he was told by Yale students at the Stiles-Morse dining common. As to the generalizability of this evidence, little need be said. Even assuming he talked to some sort of representative cross section of Yale students, which is unlikely, there is no reason to suppose that what is true of them would be true of the population at large. Indeed, given their status as students in one of America's most prestigious and expensive universities, there is every reason to suppose otherwise. It is, of course, possible that Yale students, while obviously not representative of the American masses, do nonetheless possess useful and accurate information about them. But this, too, is unlikely. Consider instead the observations made by one Yale student, a black, who in 1968 reported:

> After I'd been here a while I realized that the whites here were much more ignorant than I could ever have believed . . . . This is supposed to be one of the best colleges in the country. But these guys live in an unreal world, a world that doesn't encompass the things that a man who is struggling in society has to deal with. They don't know half as much about us as we know about them—because they've thought so little about us for so long (quoted in the *New York Times*, 3 June 1968, p. 51).

Reich's procedures are best described as the method of free fantasy, a method that makes anything possible. At best, it is a generalization based on the atypical experiences of an absurdly biased sample.[2]

THE REAL MAJORITY AND THE DISTORTION
OF POLL RESULTS

Despite the apparent topical similarity, Scammon and Wattenberg's *The Real Majority* is a wholly different kind of book from Charles Reich's. There is, first, the sharp difference in substantive conclusion (see Chapter 1) and, more to the present point, there is an equally sharp difference in method, *The Real Majority* being packed with survey and poll results. Most of the data presentation in the volume is straightforward and unobjectionable, and the tabulations shown there contain much useful information that any credible analysis of contemporary American society should take into account. There is, however, one aspect of the presentation that proves to be seriously misleading, and this concerns the poll data cited in behalf of their "social issue" thesis.

The thesis itself was discussed in Chapter 1. It is a claim about a transformation in the agenda of human concerns, a claim that traditional bread-and-butter economic issues were losing their political force, being replaced by a set of anxieties concerning race, kids, protest, moral decay, and new values—collectively, the social issue. The evidence cited in favor of this thesis is of two sorts: first, a discussion of data from thirty-four Gallup polls spanning the period 1958–1970, and second, a series of exemplary cases that "flesh out" the poll materials and illustrate the essentials of the social issue at work.

We shall not comment on the latter, except to note that one can cite exemplary instances of virtually anything one wants to argue. Generalization from such instances is always open to question. Indeed, one of the many virtues of systematic evidence, such as the Gallup poll data, is that it shows just how widespread the "for instances" are.

The Gallup data presented by Scammon and Wattenberg are derived, for the most part, from Gallup's standard door-opener question: "What do you think is the most important problem facing this country today?" This is an open-ended question: respondents answer as they wish in their own terms,

---

[2] We mentioned in Chapter 1 a reader (Nobile, 1971) containing various critical reactions to Reich's book. While much of the reaction was unquestionably negative, very few of the critics expressed any manifest concern over Reich's method of inquiry. Some, for example, worried about the book's disturbing implications, which is an appropriate concern only if the substance of the book is thought to be accurate. One comment contained in the reader makes the same methodological point we have argued in the text: "Reich spends too much time in the Stiles dining hall where the book was written. Yale students may in large number illustrate the new life-style, but how widespread is this long hair, rock music, bell-bottomed communal culture?" (Nobile, p. 56). Contrast this cogent remark with Karl Meyer's reference to "the appalling accuracy of [Reich's] description of present day America."

rather than picking a response from a preselected set of categories. As a device for getting at what is on peoples' minds, the question obviously has much to recommend it. Their presentation of this material is shown in Table 2.1; their conclusion was quoted earlier: "Suddenly, some time in the 1960's, 'crime' and 'race' and 'lawlessness' and 'civil rights' became the most important domestic issues in America" (Scammon and Wattenberg, p. 39).

As will be seen, their presentation of the data is incomplete. Scammon and Wattenberg simply list the most frequent responses to the question, with what they take to be social issue responses highlighted in italics. The actual *percentages* who gave each response are *not* presented. To take an example, the entry for 4 August 1968 reads: "Vietnam war, *crime and lawlessness, race relations*, high cost of living." From this, one infers (correctly) that in this poll, Vietnam was most often mentioned as the most important problem, with crime and lawlessness second, race relations third, and so on. What is therefore missing is information on just what percentage people mentioned each of these things.

Adding the corresponding percentages to this material requires that one dig into the original source materials, which are contained in *The Gallup Poll*.[3] Only through this extra step does one learn, for instance, that for the poll in question, Vietnam was cited as the most important problem by 52% of the population surveyed, crime and lawlessness by 29%, race relations by 13%, and the high cost of living by 9%. That concern over Vietnam outweighed the nearest competitor by a factor of almost two to one is thus submerged in the Scammon-Wattenberg presentation.[4]

Another important lesson, also hidden, is that in this poll, the total proportion mentioning *any* social issue was 44%. (This counts, in addition to "crime and lawlessness" and "race relations," a third Gallup category labeled "general unrest"; to emphasize, it also counts multiple responses [see Note 4].) The *majority*—the remaining 56%—was more concerned about other things, chiefly the war in Vietnam. The size of the *minority* expressing social issue concerns, incidentally, is nearly constant throughout 1968. In the 26 May poll, the proportion with such concerns was 43%, and in the 8 September poll, 41%. At no point in 1968 did a majority express social issue concerns. Vietnam dominated all responses.

An opposite impression is created by the entry for 28 February 1968. Of the thirty-four polls represented, this is the only one where crime heads the list. And of the five polls shown for 1968, this is the only one where Vietnam

[3] The source employed for most of the following discussion is George Gallup, Jr., *The Gallup Poll*, Volumes II and III (1972).

[4] The Gallup interviewing procedures, incidentally, allow people to volunteer more than one response to this question, and these multiple responses are counted equally in the published tabulations. What this means is that the results represent everybody's first concern and some fraction's second concern as well; for this reason, the totals always sum to more than 100%. There seems to be no way to subtract these "second concerns" from the tallies.

Table 2.1. Scammon and Wattenberg's Presentation of Gallup Trend Data on "The Most Important Problem Facing the Nation Today"[a]

1958	
Feb. 2	Keeping out of war
Mar. 23	Unemployment
Nov. 16	Keeping out of war
1959	
Feb. 27	Keeping world peace, high cost of living, *integration struggle*
Oct. 16	Keeping out of war, high cost of living
1960	
Mar. 2	Defense "lag"
July 8	Relations with Russia
1961	
Mar. 15	Keeping out of war
1962	
Apr. 29	International tensions, high cost of living, unemployment
1963	
July 21	*Racial problems,* Russia
Oct. 2	*Racial problems*
1964	
Mar. 1	Keeping out of war
May 20	*Racial problems,* foreign affairs
June 3	*Integration,* unemployment
July 29	*Racial problems*
Aug. 21	International problems
Oct. 11	International problems
Nov. 18	Vietnam war, medical care for the aged
1965	
Apr. 16	*Civil rights*
May 9	Education, *crime*
June 11	International problems
Aug. 11	Vietnam war, *civil rights*
Oct. 13	*Civil rights,* Vietnam war
Dec. 1	Vietnam war, *civil rights*
1966	
May 27	Vietnam crisis, threat of war
Sept. 11	Vietnam war, *racial problems,* cost of living
1967	
Oct. 18	High cost of living, taxes, health problems, cost of education, Vietnam war
1968	
Feb. 28	*Crime, civil rights,* high cost of living
May 26	Vietnam war, *crime and lawlessness, race relations,* high cost of living
Aug. 4	Vietnam war, *crime and lawlessness, race relations,* high cost of living
Sept. 8	Vietnam war, *crime, civil rights,* high cost of living
Oct. 30	Vietnam war, *crime, race relations,* high cost of living
1969	
March	Vietnam war, *crime and lawlessness, race relations,* high cost of living
1970	
February	Vietnam war, high cost of living, *race relations, crime*

[a]Source: Scammon and Wattenberg, *The Real Majority* (1970, pp. 37–39).

is *not* mentioned. From this entry, then, one might infer that at least once in 1968, the social issue became even more important than Vietnam. This, however, proves not to be the case. Gallup's own discussion of the results of this poll notes: "The Vietnam war is cited most often (by 53% of the respondents), but in terms of domestic or national problems, the remainder of the responses divide as follows: crime and lawlessness, civil rights, the high cost of living." The expressed majority concern over Vietnam revealed in the 28 February poll is simply omitted from the Scammon-Wattenberg listing.[5]

There are other irregularities in the presentation. The entry for 9 May 1965 is a case in point. Attention is drawn to this entry because it contains the first mention of crime in the entire listing. A check of the sources, however, reveals that this entry is not based on the standard open-ended "most important problem" question. Rather, in the 9 May poll, *respondents were given a list of national problems by the interviewer*, then asked: "Which three of these national problems would you like to see the government devote most of its attention to in the next year or two?" The concern with crime indicated in this survey therefore cannot be compared with the concerns elicited by the open-ended question. Two additional entries are based on questions differing from the standard Gallup question. The results for 18 November 1964 are based on an item reading, "What problem would you most like to have President Johnson deal with now that he has won the election?" And the entry for 18 October 1967 is based on the question, "What do you consider to be the most urgent problem facing you and your family today?"[6]

It is worth discussing the 18 October 1967 poll in more detail. As noted, this question differs in an important way from the usual Gallup item because it asks about urgent problems facing one's *family*, not about the most important problem facing the *nation*. The distinction here is between public and private concerns, the former being, necessarily, somewhat remote, the latter having all the immediacy of every Friday's paycheck. What is the overlap between these classes of concern? The Scammon-Wattenberg discussion certainly implies an internalization or personalization of the social issue. Yet responses to the question about "urgent problems facing you and your family" are remarkably thin in social issue themes. In fact, the only social issue registered *at all* in the poll is "racial problems" (mentioned by

---

[5]In fairness, Gallup's own tabulation also omits the Vietnam percentage, it being referenced only in the accompanying text.

[6]Nowhere in the Scammon-Wattenberg text is it stated that the various entries in the table are based on different questions. They say, wrongly, that the table "concerns what the American public perceives as 'the most important problem' facing the nation" (Scammon and Wattenberg, p. 37). Unless one consulted the original sources, one would never know that several of the table entries are not strictly comparable.

4%). In contrast, the high cost of living and related economic problems was mentioned by 60%. An additional 8% mentioned "sickness and health"— the second most frequent response. The implication, one sustained by additional evidence presented below and in the following chapter, is that for the majority, the paramount *personal* concerns are economic.

Some useful contrasts can be drawn between this poll and a second poll conducted on 12 November 1967, less than one month later. The second poll (not included in the Scammon-Wattenberg presentation) contained the usual "most important problem facing the nation" question. As with virtually all polls using this question up through 1973, the consensus choice for the most important national problem was Vietnam, mentioned by 50%. One month earlier, the proportion mentioning Vietnam as their most urgent *personal* problem was only 5%. Similar disparities are seen in virtually all the results. The November poll shows 21% mentioning civil rights as a *national* problem; the October poll shows a mere 4% mentioning this as a *personal* problem. Most dramatic of all, the concern over the high cost of living, mentioned by 60% as their most urgent personal problem, was mentioned by only 16% as the leading national problem. What these data suggest, at least as of late 1967, is that the much-discussed social issue was rather sharply divorced from the everyday personal concerns of most of the American population. And those personal concerns, in contrast to the Scammon-Wattenberg account, were heavily dominated by bread-and-butter economics.

The Gallup data give an extremely useful short-term overview of the coming and going of issues on the agenda of personal and national concern. As the Scammon-Wattenberg presentation makes clear, the period through mid-1963 was dominated by foreign policy concerns—keeping the peace, relations with Russia, East-West relations, international tension, and later, Cuba and Castro. It is not likely that many people were bothered *personally* by such issues (see Chapter 3), but in terms of important national problems, these represented the consensus choices. The latest poll showing this basic pattern is for 3 April 1963 (taken on the heels of the Cuban missile crisis and not included in the Scammon-Wattenberg materials). In that poll, 63% mentioned some sort of international concern as the "most important problem facing the nation," Cuba and Russia leading the list. In the same poll, "racial problems" were mentioned by 4%, the closest thing to a social issue appearing in any of the polls taken prior to 1963.

The basic pattern, however, changed dramatically between the 3 April poll and the 21 July poll of that year. In the 21 July poll, racial problems led the list of stated national concerns, with Russia slipping into second place. The poll for 2 October 1963 demonstrates the sudden intensity of racial concerns: in that poll, racial problems were mentioned by 52%, up from only 4% just six months earlier. There is, however, very little mystery in this pattern. Between the April and July polls, four black children, all girls, were killed in the church bombing in Birmingham, Alabama—the first omen of racial violence that was to plague this country for most of the remaining decade.

The concern over race relations, civil rights, and related themes is more or less continually present in all the polls from mid-1963 through the end of the Scammon-Wattenberg presentation, but with considerable fluctuations from poll to poll in the proportions. These fluctuations follow rather closely the actual occurrences of racial problems in the society. As we have just seen, the Birmingham bombing triggered a sharp upswing in racial concern. Another upswing came in the late spring and summer of 1964, concurrent with the incidents and riots in Cleveland, Philadelphia, and Harlem. Mentions of racial concerns dropped off considerably in 1966, a relatively calm year, then increased sharply during and after the summer of 1967, which witnessed serious race riots in many large cities (the Detroit riot being perhaps the most memorable). It will be remembered that the events of the summer of 1967 occasioned the convening of the well-known Kerner Commission. What the poll results on racial concerns document, in short, is not the appearance of a "new" and potentially ominous backward mentality, a "white backlash" that will be "with us" for years to come. It shows that people became concerned with racial problems when there was clear evidence that these problems were very serious; they showed lesser concern when the visibility of the problem faded.

Also, a stated concern about race says nothing about how people might want racial problems solved. In the Gallup procedures, bigots and racial liberals could both show up in the figure for "civil rights." Many discussions of The Real Majority have assumed that the increasing racial concern was linked to growing hostility toward blacks, to the "white backlash," yet as the authors themselves mention, if only in passing, "white attitudes about civil rights for blacks were probably *liberalizing* throughout this entire period (Scammon and Wattenberg, p. 42). The word "probably" shows an unexpected hesitance about a very positive trend, especially since every *study* of public opinion concerning race has noted this liberalization.[7]

[7]Readily available poll and survey data on racial attitudes for the 1960's are reviewed in Campbell (1971), Hamilton (1972, Chapter 11), and Hamilton (1975, Chapter 4). All reviews of these data show a progressive liberalization of racial attitudes. One of the above-named sources (Campbell, 1971) draws on the SRC election series (see Note 1). Scammon and Wattenberg also present some evidence from this series; thus, their failure to research or report on the liberalization of racial attitudes in this period is not a result of their not having had access to the relevant data. Given the otherwise heavy data contents of the book and their emphasis on race as a keystone in the social issue package, this omission is all the more inexplicable.

The liberalization of the 1960's was a continuation of trends extending back even earlier, trends that were reported in the literature well before the publication of The Real Majority. The most comprehensive overview of the 1950's era data is in Hyman and Sheatsley (1964), this article appearing in Scientific American. There is also evidence that the liberalizing trend continued well into the 1970's; see Taylor, Sheatsley, and Greeley (1978); or Condran (1979).

As a popular political concern, the Vietnam war first appears in late 1964 and 1965. The poll of 13 October 1965 shows that the war was mentioned as a concern by 19%. In the 1 December poll of that year, the proportion mentioning Vietnam had risen to 37%; by 27 May 1966, to 45%; and finally, in the poll for 11 September 1966, to a majority concern, 56%. With the exception of the poll for 18 October 1967, which was based on an entirely different question, all polls from 11 September 1966 through the end of the Scammon-Wattenberg list show Vietnam as the majority choice for "most important problem" facing the nation. The persistent popular concern with the Vietnam war is treated rather lightly in the Scammon-Wattenberg account. Vietnam is acknowledged to be "more important" during this period than the social issue, yet is dismissed mainly on the grounds that the war was "nondomestic."[8] This is a difficult judgment to accept. It is of course true that the war was fought on foreign soil, yet much of the concern over Vietnam was certainly rooted in the domestic situation. Some portion of this, to be sure, would have reflected social issue concerns, for example, concern over rebellion and protest stimulated by the war. But some additional part, perhaps the largest part, would have been based in bread-and-butter economics: people were objecting to the war-related effects on living standards.[9] To the extent that this is true the Gallup data would understate the importance of economic worries. A large share of these worries, that is, would have been "hidden" in the stated concern over Vietnam. Unfortunately, Vietnam fits neatly into neither of Scammon and Wattenberg's two issue categories (economic and social), so it is simply not given extended consideration, although it was the *majority* concern for the entire period.

The looming presence of Vietnam obscures the Scammon-Wattenberg presentation in an even more fundamental sense. Sooner or later, any war is bound to disappear—first as a war, then as a popular concern. The war itself and the concerns about it are necessarily transitory; or, putting it another way, once the war disappears, mass concerns and feelings are freed and attention shifts to other things. Vietnam, especially from 1968 on, amounts to the major concern of half the population. So for as long as Vietnam was

---

[8]A second reason given for the light attention to the Vietnam concern is that "Americans were not voting primarily on a pro-Vietnam or anti-Vietnam basis despite its importance" (Scammon and Wattenberg, p. 39). In 1968, it would have been rather difficult to "vote on a Vietnam basis." Nixon avoided discussion of the issue on the grounds that such discussion would imperil the peace talks then in progress. Likewise, Humphrey avoided the war issue as long as possible, since he was heavily identified with the Johnson administration. Late in the campaign, however, Humphrey did endorse a bombing halt, and it is generally agreed that this concession to the antiwar forces accounted in large measure for his modest late-October surge. (See Hamilton, 1975, Chapter 5, and Page and Brody, 1972, for extended discussions.)

[9]Some relevant evidence on the bases of Vietnam opposition in the mass public is presented in Schuman (1972).

present, then, the underlying worries of this half are hidden from view. What this means, in effect, is that trends in concern for the remainder of the population are really only trends among that minority who, for whatever reason, was not primarily concerned about Vietnam. The routine concerns of the *majority*, the ostensible topic of the Scammon-Wattenberg book, in short, are submerged because of the stated concern over Vietnam. The best evidence on what happens to that concern once the war ends, of course, can be obtained from the polls of 1973 and beyond. This material is discussed briefly later in this chapter.

Next to race and civil rights, the rising concern with crime and lawlessness is the best evidence shown on behalf of the social issue hypothesis. Here again, however, there is less to the evidence than Scammon and Wattenberg suggest. Excepting the noncomparable entry for 9 May 1965, crime and lawlessness are first mentioned in the poll for 28 February 1968 and are present in all six subsequent polls shown in the Scammon-Wattenberg listing. Yet in terms of proportions of the population, the expressed concern with crime and lawlessness never exceeds 29%—barely more than a quarter. In the poll of 26 May 1968, for example, crime and lawlessness are mentioned by 15%. The peak figure of 29% is registered in the 4 August 1968 poll, but the proportion regularly dwindles thereafter—to 21% by 28 September and to 17% by 30 January 1969. The degree of concern with crime and lawlessness is clearly exaggerated in their presentation.

Polls subsequent to the Scammon-Wattenberg presentation, incidentally, show even further drops in the proportion mentioning "crime and lawlessness." In the poll for 18 March 1971, for example, 7% cited this as the most important national problem. The poll for January 1976 shows a nearly equivalent figure of 8%. Were the social issue somehow basic to the emerging outlooks of the American population, one would expect concerns with matters such as "crime and lawlessness" to increase once Vietnam had disappeared. They did not: rather, they dropped off substantially, being squeezed out, as we see later, by economic issues.

In sum, the Scammon-Wattenberg presentation distorts the actual poll results. *At no point in the period covered by their data were social issues the principal concern of the majority of the American population.* There was a brief period in 1968 when crime and lawlessness were the predominating concerns of about a quarter of the population, but even this minority shrinks in the later polls covered in their series. Likewise, the increasing concern over race relations, while clearly present, was linked to ongoing patterns of racial turbulence, the proportions rising as racial disturbances increased and falling otherwise, and was, in any case, accompanied by a substantial *improvement* in racial attitudes, an area that Scammon and Wattenberg did not research. The book thus provided an inaccurate account of the data available at the time of publication. The social issues claim, moreover, has been further undermined by subsequent trends and developments, as we discuss below. The concerns registered in the Gallup polls over social issues were undoubtedly real, but they were not—and are not now—the concerns of the majority.

That social issue concerns were minority rather than majority concerns is obvious as soon as one adds the Gallop percentages to their presentation. Why, then, are those percentages not reported? It is not because the authors wish to spare readers the burden of dealing with precise numerical data, since the book is filled with percentaged tabulations of poll and survey results. One therefore suspects that the percentages are omitted because to include them would have definitively undercut the principal conclusion of their work.

Opinion data for years subsequent to 1970 provide additional insights into the social issue and give some indication whether this alleged "new tide" will truly be "observable for decades to come," as Scammon and Wattenberg assert. The polls for 1971 provide a useful beginning point. Early in the year, in the 18 March poll, concern over the economy began to challenge Vietnam as the most frequently mentioned national problem. In that poll, 28% mentioned Vietnam, and 24% mentioned some concern over the economic situation. In the same poll, "crime and lawlessness" and "race relations" had dropped off to 7% each, steadily becoming less visible. In the 17 June poll of that year, a similar pattern was observed: 33% mentioned Vietnam as the most important problem, 22% mentioned the economy, and again, there were 7% each mentioning crime and race. At the end of the year, in the poll for 19 December, concern over the economy had rocketed into first place, mentioned by 41%. And the concern over Vietnam had dropped to 15%. As for the social issues, the combined proportion mentioning drugs, racial problems, crime and lawlessness, unrest in the nation, and lack of religion and morality was 28%. (We emphasize again, these percentages include multiple mentions.) Within a year of the end of the Scammon-Wattenberg presentation, the social issue tide was ebbing rapidly.

The polls for 1972 show similar patterns. In four polls taken that year, from late April to late September, the average proportion mentioning Vietnam was 28%; the proportion mentioning inflation, the high cost of living, and related economic problems was 25%. Mentions of race relations, in contrast, essentially disappeared in 1972; the Gallup tabulations, in any case, no longer contained the category. Once again, taking a whole set of social issues combined (drug abuse, crime and lawlessness, a new category labeled problems of youth, and another called moral decay), the proportion with any social issue concern averaged out to 22%, down about 6 points from the previous year and off by more than half from the peak 45% figure registered in 1968.

In 1973, the Gallup procedures changed somewhat, making direct comparisons with earlier years difficult. In the two 1973 polls, one in February, the other in September, Gallup asked respondents to name two "most important problems" facing the nation, and both responses are treated equally in the tabulations. Nonetheless, a continuation of the earlier trends is apparent. In the February poll, 59% mentioned the high cost of living as their first or second problem; this was by far the most common response. Some related economic concerns were also present: 16% mentioned unemployment, 8% mentioned poverty, and so on. These data show that something over 80% of the population in the United States in 1973 had an economic worry as their primary or secondary concern. In contrast, concern with Vietnam had all but disappeared by this point: 7% mentioned "Southeast Asia" in the February poll; in the September poll, the category was dropped. By September of 1973, some entirely new concerns had begun to emerge. The economy remained the leading worry: In September, 89% mentioned the high cost of living as their primary or secondary concern, and there was an additional 14% mentioning some other economic problem. But some new concerns were also present; for example, the energy crisis (mentioned by 8%), distrust in government (19%), and corruption in government (14%). In this same poll, counting both first and second problems equally, crime and lawlessness were mentioned by 13%, drug abuse by 10%, general unrest by 6%, and race relations by 4%—for a total of 33%. By the end of 1973, in short, economic issues were outweighing social issues by about three to one.

The dominance of economic concerns continues throughout the Gallup data of the 1970's. In the poll for 5 January 1976, for example, 47% mentioned the high cost of living as their primary concern and 23% mentioned unemployment; thus a total of 70% of the population indicated an economic issue as the "most important problem facing the nation today." The same survey showed 8% mentioning crime and 4% mentioning general "moral decay"—the *only* two social issues mentioned with sufficient frequency to warrant inclusion among Gallup's categories. By 1976, then, the ratio of economic to social issue concerns stood at roughly 6 to 1. The sharp fade-out of the social issue after the 1968–1969 peak might be contrasted with some late predictions from *The Real Majority*. "There is no evidence," the authors report, "that it [the social issue] will go away . . . To the authors it seems clear that the issue will remain" (Scammon and Wattenberg, p. 282). But the issue has not remained. The proportion of the population mentioning a social issue as a number one national problem, never a *majority* in the first place, has by now dwindled to around one-tenth.

The most straightforward conclusion to be drawn from the above materials is that Vietnam was the most pressing national problem from about 1966 through 1973, and that the state of the economy has been the most pressing problem since. The emergence in the 1960's of the social issue was, to be sure, a development of some importance. But it is seriously misleading to portray it as a majority development. In all polls covered by Scammon and Wattenberg, and in all the Gallup polls since, the majority of the population cited something other than a social issue as the most important problem facing the nation.

THE METHODS OF THE WORKPLACE CRITICS

As noted in Chapter 1, much of the debate over "work in industrial America" turns on the seemingly simple question of whether people like or dislike their work. This appears to be a simple question because the obvious way to answer it would be to ask a sample of workers directly how satisfied or dissatisfied they are with their jobs. One might debate the proper form of wording of the question, or ask it in a variety of ways. But certainly, any respectable answer to the question would have to depend in one way or another on what workers themselves had to say about their jobs.[10]

We have already emphasized that questions along these very lines have been included in surveys of the work force for approximately forty years. They were also routinely included in many of the surveys done in the 1970's. One series of surveys, on which we draw heavily in later chapters, are the General Social Surveys conducted by the National Opinion Research Center at the University of Chicago. Their version of the job satisfaction question asks, "On the whole, how satisfied are you with the work you do—would you say you are very satisfied, moderately satisfied, a little dissatisfied, or very dissatisfied?" Results for the eight surveys in the series are shown in Table 2.2.[11]

[10]There is much debate in the workplace critics' writings about how to ask a job satisfaction question. Most survey organizations use a straightforward question with four possible answers, as in the NORC version: "On the whole, how satisfied are you with the work you do—would you say you are very satisfied, moderately satisfied, a little dissatisfied, or very dissatisfied?" In some other versions, the allowable responses are: "very satisfied," "somewhat satisfied," "not too satisfied," and "not satisfied at all." In an earlier era, it was sometimes simply asked, "Are you satisfied or dissatisfied with your work?" Gallup, for example, used this latter item up through 1973, but not thereafter. (Gallup's decision to change the wording of the question is perfectly justifiable on some grounds, but has the unfortunate effect of discontinuing the longest-running time series on job satisfaction available.) When we refer in the text to the "standard job satisfaction question," we are referring to the above or to other close variants.

[11]The NORC question and its variations noted in the above footnote (10) are all relatively "flat"; that is, the question is simple, direct, and nonleading. This has not always been the case in surveys of job satisfaction. One of the earliest "quality of employment" surveys on record, done in France in 1880, asked:

> If you are paid piece rates, is the quality of the article made a pretext for fraudulent deductions from your wages?

Another item in the same survey read:

> Have you noticed that the delay in paying your wages makes it necessary for you to resort frequently to the pawnbroker, paying a high rate of interest, and depriving yourself of things which you need; or to fall into debt to shopkeepers, becoming their victim because you are their debtor?

The author of the survey from which the above questions are taken is Karl Marx. The entire questionnaire is published in Bottomore (pp. 204–212). The historical

Table 2.2. Job Satisfaction of the American Population[a]

| | Year | | | | | | | | |
	1972	1973	1974	1975	1976	1977	1978	1980	Total
Very satisfied	49	49	48	54	52	48	51	47	50
Moderately satisfied	37	38	37	33	34	39	36	36	36
A little dissatisfied	11	8	10	9	9	10	8	13	10
Very dissatisfied	3	4	5	4	4	3	5	5	4
%	100	99[b]	100	100	99[b]	100	100	101[b]	100
N	994	1141	1223	1165	1185	1262	1280	1246	9446

[a]Source: NORC General Social Surveys.
[b]Rounding error.

The lesson to be learned from this table is obvious: very small proportions of the working population indicate even "a little dissatisfaction" with their work. In all surveys, the most common response is "very satisfied," the most positive answer provided in the response categories. The very satisfied constitute one-half the work force. An additional one third to two fifths are moderately satisfied. The proportion indicating any degree of dissatisfaction never exceeds 18%. Despite the fervid declamations of the workplace critics, most people prove to be satisfied with their jobs. Note also the absence of any significant trend, despite the many claims about deterioration in work outlooks and conditions.[12]

---

record indicates, incidentally, that Marx received very few replies to this questionnaire, and no results from the survey were ever published.

The above example is instructive because much of the hostility to survey research in contemporary neo-Marxist writings is accompanied by some comment to the effect that it is "the method of bourgeois social science." Many of these present-day Marxists seem unaware that Marx himself obviously saw no philosophical problem in the use of the method. Lenin, as it happens, also tried his hand at survey research (see Fischer, p. 21). That these efforts seem amateurish in the present context only indicates how far the science of sample surveys has come since.

[12]It has often been argued that job satisfaction questions cause people to overstate their degree of satisfaction, mainly on grounds that "to demean one's job is to question one's very competence as a person" (Blauner, 1960, p. 355). Recently, the Survey Research Center and some other survey organizations have begun experimenting with alternative forms of the question; several of these alternative forms are contained, for example, in the SRC 1969 Survey of Working Conditions, results from which are discussed later. One experiment uses a seven-point rating scale to record responses, where 1 is "completely satisfied" and 7 is "completely dissatisfied." As with the more conventional forced-choice questions noted above, the results are very highly skewed toward the "completely satisfied" end (see Chapter 6). Our general conclusion in all this can be simply stated: no matter how one goes about asking the question, the answers one gets are very similar to those shown in the text in Table 2.2. The often-advanced methodological argument that a different wording of the question would give remarkably different results is not supported by any actual evidence of which we are aware.

One should not, of course, read more into this result than is actually there. It is doubtful whether the people who say they are very satisfied with their jobs look on them as yielding a Nirvana-like perfection. Even the very satisfied would no doubt change some aspects of the job if given the chance. Even with all due allowances, however, the general mood is unmistakably positive. One might, reasonably, wonder what "very satisfied" really means in this context, and one might, appropriately, ask about the comparable degree of satisfaction with the various aspects of work—the pay, the fringe benefits, the chances for promotion, and so on. (Several of these questions are addressed later in this chapter and in Chapter 6.) But it is very hard to see how one could conclude that most Americans actively *dis*like their work in the face of these results. It would, moreover, be difficult to argue a negative trend in the face of those results.

There is, furthermore, nothing unusual in the findings from the NORC surveys. Allowing for differences in question wording and for the usual sampling variability, they are in essence identical to the results obtained in every other survey of job satisfaction ever conducted in the United States. (An extensive review of some of the leading surveys is contained in Chapter 6.) All credible surveys have found large majorities satisfied with their work to some degree.

One might suppose that such consistent results would put an end to claims that most Americans dislike their work, but this has obviously not been the case. Why, then, does the claim persist, even though it is demonstrably contrary to fact?

For some, to be sure, it is a matter of ignorance, these being the intellectuals who write on a topic without consulting the appropriate evidence. But for others, there is more than ignorance at work; many of the workplace critics are perfectly aware of the mass of opposing findings, but casually dismiss them, damn them with ridicule, or distort the thrust of the results. Much of the ridicule and condemnation is methodological in character, the claim being that the truth about such matters can only be gained through other methods. What this amounts to, of course, is a claim that people themselves do not always, nor even usually, give accurate accounts of the character and quality of their lives.[13]

Many of the workplace critics understand that the method of direct reporting, of survey research, leads to conclusions that are sharply at variance with the ones they prefer. This method, in short, gives findings that

---

[13]Some would argue, in contrast, that while people *are* good sources, surveys are incapable of eliciting honest testimony. Reference is frequently made to the "demand characteristics" of the interview situation and to the presumed social undesirability of saying that one is unhappy in any way. (To indicate any degree of dissatisfaction, that is, would be to affirm one's failure as a human being.) Some studies, however, have taken independent measurements of the tendency to give socially desirable responses and report them to be, at best, only modestly correlated with various satisfaction measures (e.g., Campbell, Converse, and Rodgers, Chapter 4).

contradict their worldview. Rather than abandon the a priori conclusion, they prefer to reject the method itself, and its results.[14] To this end, they have developed an array of theory-saving devices which, considered as a whole, are remarkable both for their deviousness and for their disregard of conventional scholarly standards. Herewith, a brief excursus:

The Double Standard

One common strategy for dealing with the survey evidence is to reference it selectively, discussing only those aspects that seem consistent with the a priori conclusion and ignoring (or ridiculing) the rest. A case in point is provided by the widely acclaimed work of Harry Braverman, *Labor and Monopoly Capital: The Degradation of Work in the Twentieth Century* (1974).

Braverman's is an avowedly Marxist critique of work under capitalism. The key thesis is that capitalism, under the aegis of the theories of Frederick Winslow Taylor, controls the labor process through an increasingly precise division of labor.[15] As labor becomes more and more divided, skill is

[14]The condemnation of a method of research and observation on the grounds that it gives the "wrong" results has been chronic among the Know-Nothings of history. This was, for example, the essence of the Church's objections to Galileo's telescope. Turned to the planet Venus, the telescope revealed that Venus exhibited phases, from which Galileo correctly deduced that Venus did not revolve around the earth. Likewise, Galileo discovered moons in orbit around Jupiter, and these moons also clearly did not revolve around the earth. At the time, of course, the Church "knew" that all heavenly bodies revolved around the earth. With the same telescope, Galileo also made the first observation of sunspots, and this too was wrong because the Church knew that the sun was a perfect sphere: Galileo's discovery of blemishes on its surface thus implied that God was guilty of shoddy workmanship. For these various unholy observations, Galileo was tried by the Holy Inquisition, which banned publication of the book in which the implications of these observations were set forth, and lived the remaining ten years of his life under virtual house arrest. The facile dismissal of surveys of job satisfaction because they give the wrong result is no less preposterous. (Galileo's travails with the Church are well chronicled in the history of science; see, e.g., Ridpath, 1979; Gribbon, 1980).

[15]Taylor was a leading advocate of divided labor, close supervison, time and motion studies, and piecework incentive plans. In Braverman's account, he is written up as the evil genius of capitalism, as the key figure responsible for the perpetual degradation of labor. The "anachronism of Taylorism" is also cited in *Work in America* as the first of two major sources of dissatisfaction (the second being the "diminishing opportunities to be one's own boss"—O'Toole et al., pp. 17–23). In one recent neo-Marxist source, Taylor is even credited with "the invention of management and bureaucracy," these being the key inventions that "made it possible for capitalists to control the production process" (Clawson, pp. 30–31). In fact, many of Taylor's arguments, especially those in behalf of dividing labor, appear already in the writing of Adam Smith (1776), who was merely generalizing from some then current practices. In like vein, something very close to bureaucracy in its modern form existed in the Roman Empire and elsewhere in the ancient world.

Some capitalists have not been at all enthusiastic about Taylor's proposals. The

degraded, and the ability to apply skill to the manufacture of a product comes increasingly to rest in the hands of the overseers of the labor process—namely, the owners and managers. Most workers, naturally, resent such degradation, indeed, are "revulsed" by it in Braverman's account.

Given these themes, it is obviously necessary to argue, in the face of much opposing evidence, that most workers dislike their jobs. Thus, there "must" be something wrong in that evidence. In Braverman's case, the accumulated evidence is simply dismissed with an offhand comment about "the feeble results achieved by questionnaire-sociology" and a following remark that "this particular method of trying to know . . . is superficial, remote, and mechanistic" (Braverman, p. 29).

Several comments are in order. First, a result reported in hundreds of surveys over scores of years can hardly be considered "feeble." It is, to the contrary, among the more robust of findings in all the social sciences. Further, that surveys are "feeble, superficial, remote, and mechanistic" does not constitute an explanation of why people would say they were satisfied with their jobs when in fact they were not. Thus, in addition to being facile, the passage is also a non sequitur. As in the Reichian case, the effort here is apparently to absolve oneself of the responsibility for serious confrontation with evidence relevant to one's thesis.

Braverman's use of the double standard comes in the several pages following the above quotation, in a section on job dissatisfaction in the 1970's. These pages contain a largely approving (although condescending) account of survey findings reported in *Work in America* and a few other sources—findings, to emphasize, that were produced by the same "remote" and "superficial" methods he has already dismissed. Why, then, are *these* findings cited favorably? Only because they appear at first glance to be consistent with a conclusion to which Braverman is already committed: they seem to show, as other survey findings do not, a sizable degree of work discontent. (In fact, they do not show this at all; see below, "Reification of Non-Findings.") His practice, clearly, is to use survey results when they suit his purpose and ridicule them when they do not.

This practice is not confined to Braverman. It is, in fact, widespread among the workplace critics. Bowles and Gintis, for example, cite *Work in America* as one among "dozens of recent studies" showing results "starkly reminiscent of Marx's description of alienated labor" (Bowles and Gintis, pp. 71–72). In an earlier passage, they *also* remark "the notorious inability of questionnaires to measure actual job satisfaction" (p. 70). Of the "dozens of recent surveys," incidentally, only one, *Work in America*, is referenced. Some other aspects of the Bowles and Gintis achievement are discussed later.

owners of Bethlehem Steel rejected many of them and dismissed Taylor shortly before Charles Schwab took over the firm. Schwab then "discarded almost all of Taylor's policies." Taylor himself wrote that "he ordered our whole system thrown out." This history appears in Hessen, 1975, pp. 166-167. See also Meiksins, 1984.

Some empirical research, incidentally, has addressed various aspects of Braverman's thesis. Spenner (1979), for example, has researched the argument that the skill content of jobs is degraded under capitalism. This analysis, based on changes in the job descriptions contained in successive editions of the *Dictionary of Occupation Titles*, "suggests very little change, if any a slight upgrading, in the actual skill content of work over the last quarter-century" (Spenner, 1979, p. 973). Spenner acknowledges that the DOT data provide "a weak test" of the thesis, but further remarks that the data for a strong test do not exist (also p. 973). Other studies addressing questions raised by Braverman include Spenner, 1983; Stark, 1980; Lee, 1981; Littler and Salaman, 1982; and Penn, 1983.

Mueller *et al.* (1969) have researched the extent and impact of technological change on a cross-section of 2662 American workers for the period 1962–1967. Only 10% of the sample reported that their job had been significantly affected by changes in machine technology over that period (p. 44). Further, the respondents also overwhelmingly *liked* the machines they worked on and reported enjoying jobs that involved the use of equipment, the most frequent comment being that machines and equipment increased the challenge and interest of the work (Mueller *et al.*, pp. 120–122).

Braverman notwithstanding, impact of Taylorism per se on the thinking of the American capitalist and managerial classes appears to have been rather modest (Nelson, pp. 70–76). One of the most ardent enthusiasts for Taylorism as a method of organizing production, surprisingly, was V.I. Lenin. In considering the problems of organizing Russian industry, Lenin remarked: "The possibility of socialism will be determined by our success in combining Soviet rule and Soviet organization or management with the latest progressive measures of capitalism. We must introduce in Russia the study and teaching of the Taylor system and its systematic trial and adoption" (quoted in Fein, 1976, p. 495). Taylor's principles were in fact introduced and used more extensively in Russia than in any capitalist country. One source has more than three quarters of Soviet industrial workers in 1936 and 1953 engaged in incentive piecework, a level that declined to 60% in 1961 (Bergson, p. 110). The decline was not the result of any humanistic concern over degraded labor; according to Fein, it was because "piece work . . . had been introduced where it was inappropriate and . . . because, with changes in technology, it often ceased to be appropriate where it once had been." By way of contrast, in the period from 1948 to 1968, wage incentive coverage in the United States amounted to only a little more than one quarter of the labor force (Stelluto, 1969).

Where the "Marxism" of the 1970's and 1980's would have one believe that the organization of work under advanced capitalism is distinctively pernicious, something to be avoided at all costs, Lenin argued just the opposite. His notes from March and April 1918 indicate his thoughts about the necessary means: "raise productivity . . . learn socialism from the big organizers of capitalism, from trusts . . . Tailors (sic) system, Motion study

[these phrases in English] . . . piecework pay according to results. . . . ''
And finally, "the Soviet government plus Prussian railroad efficiency plus
American technology and organizations of trusts plus American public
school education, etc., etc., plus plus equals socialism" (from Fischer, 1964,
p. 258). Lenin's advocacy of Taylor's methods represented a change for him.
Like most people on the left and like most trade unionists, he too, prior to
World War I, had viewed Taylor's methods with much disfavor [see Bailes,
p. 50].[16]

The Hiding of Unpalatable Findings

Another of the recent studies cited favorably by Braverman and, as we see
later, by many other workplace critics is the volume by Sheppard and
Herrick entitled, *Where Have All the Robots Gone?* (1972). The subtitle of
the book is *Worker Dissatisfaction in the 70s*. Like *Work in America*, this
volume is also based on "feeble" questionnaire and survey methods, but
then, as the subtitle indicates, its findings appear to be strikingly different.
Thus, following the just-discussed double standard, this book's findings are
taken seriously by many who ordinarily dismiss the survey method. The
general tenor of the presentation is set forth in the authors' prefatory
comments. "[M]ore and more workers—and every day this is more apparent—are becoming disenchanted with the boring, repetitive tasks set by a
merciless assembly line or by bureaucracy. They [the workers] feel they have

[16]As might be anticipated, Lenin's enthusiasm for Taylor and the subsequent use
of Taylorist principles in organizing Soviet industry have posed difficulties for
present-day Marxist accounts. Clawson, for example, refers to "the painful passages
in Lenin that praise Taylorism and call on the Soviet Union to adopt it as progressive"
(Clawson, p. 65). Braverman also acknowledges the influence of Taylorism in Soviet
industrial history and then remarks, "Whatever view one takes of soviet industrial-
ization, one cannot conscientiously interpret its history, even in its earliest and most
revolutionary period, as an attempt to organize labor processes in a way fundamentally different from those of capitalism" (Braverman, p. 22). In a highly sympathetic
500-page treatment of Soviet economic affairs, Maurice Dobb provides only two
brief mentions of Taylorism. The Stakhanov movement of the 1930's, he writes,
"introduced no new principle and it is true that few of them will surprise students of
American Scientific Management. Many of them represented an extension of the
division of labour in an elementary form." He adds that this "movement to rationalise
working methods . . . arose from the initiative of individual workers themselves"
(Dobb, p. 468). A check of sixteen other biographical studies of Lenin (of various
political persuasions) revealed no mention of this enthusiasm for Taylor's methods.
The same was true of five biographical studies of Trotsky. Trotsky himself refers to
Lenin—"in planning his own work"—as "a Taylorist before the Taylor system," this
referring to Lenin's study habits. But he says nothing of Lenin's implementation of
Taylor's methods in the Soviet economy (Trotsky, p. 167). A brief biography of Taylor
contained in one edition of Lenin selections describes him as follows: " . . . an
American engineer, founder of the system of labour organisation consisting in the
maximum utilisation of the working day and the rational utilisation of the means of
production and instruments of labour. Under capitalism this system is used to
intensify the exploitation of the working masses" (Lenin, p. 781).

been herded into economic and social *cul-de-sacs*" (Sheppard and Herrick, p. xi). Later, in a more moderate vein, they summarize their key conclusion: "[T]he mainstream of American workers contains a significant number of men who are unhappy with their jobs" (p. xiv).

Evidence presented in the book derives from two separate surveys. The first consists of a sample of "nearly 400 white male blue-collar union members (in two Northern states)." Given its small size and restricted coverage, this is not an especially compelling sample, so any divergence between its findings and those of previous nationally representative surveys would cause one to question this study, not its predecessors. The second survey was conducted in 1969 by the Survey Research Center at the University of Michigan (like NORC, one of the leading survey organizations in the world) and is based on a nationally representative sample of 1533 employed persons.[17]

The 1969 Michigan survey contains a large number of questions that indicate levels of job discontent. One of them, very similar to the NORC item discussed earlier, reads as follows: "All in all, how satisfied would you say that you are with your job—very satisfied, somewhat satisfied, not too satisfied, or not satisfied at all?" Responses came out as follows (see tabulation below):

Very satisfied	46%
Somewhat satisfied	39
Not too satisfied	11
Not satisfied at all	3
	99%[a]

[a]Rounding error. N = 1528.

Allowing for the minor differences in question wording, these results are virtually identical to those reported in Table 2.2. Here, the proportion on the "positive side of neutrality," as Kahn puts it (1972, p. 169), adds up to 85%. The proportion "very satisfied" is some *15 times* the proportion "not satisfied at all." These results, quite obviously, do not contradict any previous research, but rather confirm it in all details.

There are many other questions in the 1969 survey bearing on job satisfaction, all producing essentially equivalent results. One asked, "If a good friend of yours told you (he/she) was interested in working in a job like yours for your employer, what would you tell (him/her)?" More than three-fifths (63%) would "strongly recommend" their job in this situation.

[17]The 1969 survey is known as the Survey of Working Conditions, and was the first in a series of what are now three major work surveys; the second and third, both called the Quality of Employment Surveys, were done in 1973 and 1977. Results from the 1969 survey are discussed throughout the present chapter; results from the 1973 and 1977 surveys, and from several other survey series, are presented below in Chapter 6.

(Twenty-five percent said they would "have doubts about recommending it," and the remaining 12% would advise against it.) Another item asked, "Knowing what you now know, if you had to decide all over again whether to take the job you now have, what would you decide?" The substantial majority, 64%, said they would "decide without any hesitation to take it." Similar patterns are, as we have said, obtained on literally dozens of parallel items.[18]

One might, therefore, ask how it is possible to write a book on "job *dis*satisfaction in the 1970's" when the major survey evidence on which the book is ostensibly based clearly shows, as have all other surveys, widespread satisfaction with work. Clearly, any straightforward presentation of these results, such as the tabulation given above, would undermine conclusions to which the authors are already committed. Thus, in the present case, the relevant presentation of evidence is buried deep in the back of the book, in a section entitled, "Appendix A, Statistical Tables, Table 1."

One of the columns in Appendix A, Statistical Tables, Table 1 is labeled "Negative Attitudes Towards Work." A footnote in the text (not to the table itself, incidentally) indicates that the column contains the "percentages of respondents who answered, 'not at all satisfied' or 'not too satisfied'" to the standard job satisfaction question (Sheppard and Herrick, p. 14). Direct accessing of the key evidence on which the book is presumably based, in short, is a rather formidable undertaking: one must first burrow into the Appendix, past the intimidating title, and into the table itself. One must then go back almost two hundred pages earlier in the text to find the footnote that states what the table actually contains. Having taken these steps, one could then read down the column to find the percentages of workers in various sociodemographic categories who, when directly asked, had responded to the work satisfaction question in a negative manner. Even here their presentation is rather attenuated. It fails to give the figures separately for the very and somewhat satisfieds, presenting only a *combined* figure for the two dissatisfied categories. It thus hides the respective proportions, that the "not too" and the "not at all satisfieds" stand in a ratio of 11 to 3. What purpose is served by burying evidence in this manner? The purpose seems obvious: reading down the indicated column, one finds the *highest* percentage recorded there to be 25%—registered in this case for workers under age

[18]It will be noted, of course, that all these questions reveal a dissatisfied *minority*, the size of which varies, say, between 5 and 25%, depending on how strictly one defines "dissatisfaction." In 1970, the size of the American labor force was roughly 86 million workers. Multiplying through by 5% gives some 4.3 *million* workers who are very dissatisfied with their jobs, and that, by any standard, is a significant number. But it leaves some 82 million who are *not* dissatisfied, and that too is a significant number that, by rights, ought also to be reported.

This illustrates the inherent meaninglessness of phrases such as "a significant number" or "many Americans." These phrases can mean anything from 1% to 100%, and are thus virtually without meaning unless accompanied by a statement as to just how many or how large a number.

twenty. Thus, in the *most dissatisfied* subgroup shown in the table, one quarter were dissatisfied with their work, and three quarters were not. Given a straightforward, clear, and readily accessible presentation, in short, any reader would be able to see that the findings directly contradict the conclusions presented throughout the text.

Sheppard and Herrick's discussion of the results shown in this table (contained in Chapter 1, "Pockets of Discontent") does not mention that the majority of workers surveyed said they were satisfied at some level with their work. At no point is there even a passing reference to the satisfied three quarters majority. Rather, the tenor of the discussion is along the following lines: "Worker dissatisfaction metamorphosed from a hobby horse of the 'tender-minded' to a fire-breathing dragon because workers began to translate their feelings of dissatisfaction into alienated behavior!" (Sheppard and Herrick, p. 3) This manner of presenting evidence effectively prevents all but the most diligent of readers from coming to the only reasonable conclusion warranted by the evidence: that most American workers are satisfied with their jobs.

This practice of implying things in the text that are contradicted by the tables in the Appendix occurs elsewhere in the book. Their Chapter 6 ("The Now Generation of Workers"), for example, is a discussion of job dissatisfaction among younger workers. One key theme is indicated in a major chapter subheading: "Why Are Young Workers Dissatisfied?" In the course of this discussion, attention is directed to "Appendix A, Statistical Tables, Table Four," which again shows the percentages expressing negative attitudes on the main job satisfaction question. Among the findings reported, it is stated that 24% of the under-thirty workers (blue-collar and white-collar alike, incidentally) are dissatisfied with their jobs. From this it follows directly that the strong majority of young workers are not. Again, that a large majority even of the youngest workers are basically satisfied with their work is not mentioned in the text.

The best to be said about *Where Have All the Robots Gone?* is that it is unfaithful to the evidence on which it is based, and the worst, that it is a dissimulation. Had the evidence been properly presented, the work would be entirely consonant with all prior and subsequent research on the topic. Compounding the seriousness of these distortions, the work now exists as a "scholarly" survey study to be cited and quoted—obviously uncritically—by others who wish to conclude that work is hateful and demeaning.

The title of the work was presumably chosen to suggest that American workers are no longer robotlike in their acceptance of the industrial system. In response, one can appropriately ask, Where have all the data gone? They are buried in the graveyard of the "Appendix—Statistical Tables."

Reification of Nonfindings

To reify is to treat as real something that is not. Reification of nonfindings is another principal technique for dealing with troublesome evidence. Every so often a work appears, such as *Where Have All the Robots Gone?*, that claims to contain "the" evidence that work is demeaning and hateful. Soon thereafter, routine references to such works appear in the workplace critics' writings. Repeated citations in many sources give these works credibility, such that they are then picked up and cited again in secondary and tertiary sources. Eventually, these citations are made with such certainty and authority that the actual evidence contained in the initial source is lost or forgotten. In the Sheppard-Herrick case, this amounts to the reification of a nonfinding: few of the workplace critics who cite this source seem to know that the conclusion of sweeping job dissent is directly contradicted by the book's own evidence.

To illustrate, we quote at length from a paper by the economist Richard Edwards entitled, "The Social Relations of Production at the Point of Production." (1978)

> Thus bureaucratic control has created among American workers vast discontent, dissatisfaction, resentment, frustration, and boredom with their work. We do not need to recount here the many studies measuring alienation: the famous HEW-commissioned report, *Work in America*, among other summaries, has already done that. It argued, for example, that the best index of job satisfaction or dissatisfaction is a worker's response to the question, "What type of work would you get into if you could start all over again?" A majority of both white collar and blue collar workers—and an increasing proportion of them over time—indicated that they would choose some different type of work. This overall result is consistent with a very large literature on the topic. (Edwards, p. 123)

A footnote is appended to this passage, in which exactly two studies are referenced: one is *Work in America*, the second is *Where Have All the Robots Gone?* The impression created by this passage, a false one, is that these are but two of a vast number of studies (" . . . a very large literature . . . ") that might be cited in demonstration of the point. In fact, of the vast number of empirical studies that could indeed be cited (see, for example, the references in note 34 of Chapter 1 and the accompanying discussion), these are for all practical purposes the *only two* that argue widespread worker discontent, and in the Sheppard-Herrick case, as we have just seen, the argument to this effect is sharply contradicted by the evidence presented.

What about the findings reported in *Work in America?* It is perhaps relevant to note that Sheppard and Herrick were themselves members of the Task Force that produced the *Work in America* report, so the commonality in position is understandable. Braverman's favorable reference to this work was mentioned earlier. The findings from *Work in America* mentioned in Edwards' passage are also cited by economists Samuel Bowles and Herbert Gintis in support of their contention that "only 43 percent of white collar workers and 24 percent of blue collar workers in a large representative sample say they are satisfied with their jobs" (Bowles and Gintis, p. 71).

Bowles and Gintis, it should be noted, are presumably aware that the finding, as they have stated it, runs counter to the bulk of previous evidence. Gintis is one of the coauthors of the well-known work by Christopher Jencks, *Inequality* (1972), and Chapter Eight of that book ("Inequality in Job Satisfaction") is based entirely on data from the 1969 Michigan Survey of Working Conditions. *Inequality* refers to this survey, incidentally, as "the most comprehensive national survey of job satisfaction" yet conducted (Jencks, p. 247). This survey, to emphasize, found not 24% or 43%, but 85%, who were very or at least somewhat satisfied with their work. It is therefore not unreasonable to expect that Bowles and Gintis would at least remark on the discrepancy between *Work in America* and previous findings, if not attempt to resolve it. They do not.[19]

The relevant footnote from the Bowles and Gintis passage directs attention to Table 1 in *Work in America* as the source for the 24% and 43% figures. The text surrounding that table makes it plain that the responses recorded there are *not* based on answers to a conventional job satisfaction question. Rather, the table shows the proportions who say they would voluntarily choose the same work that they were doing when asked, "What type of work would you try to get into if you could start all over again?" Thus, Bowles' and Gintis' formulation (" . . . say they are satisfied with their jobs . . . ") is an inaccurate report of the result.

Edwards' formulation at least has the advantage that the difference between this question and the more conventional question is directly acknowledged; note that the actual wording of the question is given in the passage quoted earlier. Note further Edwards' reference to the argument from *Work in America* that this "what would you do if . . . " question is "the best index of job satisfaction."

Edwards' depiction is correct: *Work in America* does contain an argument that the conventional job satisfaction question is inferior to certain other alternative indicators of attitudes about work. It is, however, *only* an argument. No supporting data for the argument are presented, and no references are cited. To illustrate, *Work in America* refers at one point to the standard Gallup item and remarks the high percentages who routinely say they are satisfied. "Does this mean that such high percentages . . . *are really satisfied* with their jobs? Most researchers say no" (O'Toole et al., p. 14).

---

[19]Quoting from the chapter in question, "The SRC survey asked workers eight questions designed to get an overall estimate of whether they liked their jobs or disliked them. These were questions such as whether the worker would recommend his present job to a friend (63% would), whether he would have any hesitation about taking the same job if he had it to do over again (27% would hesitate and 9% would not take it), whether he planned to look for a new job within the next year (30% said they might), and what he would do if he could have any job he wanted (49% would choose their present jobs)" (Jencks et al., p. 247). These are, of course, the same findings discussed earlier in the present chapter; all of them give a picture very much different from the picture depicted in the Bowles-Gintis passage. To emphasize, the passage quoted here is from a book of which Gintis is coauthor.

There is, however, no reference provided in the volume to *any* researcher who has reached this conclusion, much less a demonstration that most researchers share it. As we have said, the conventional job satisfaction question has been included in hundreds of surveys and has been written about in thousands of research reports. It is obvious that many researchers find it a useful indicator.

Indeed, the entire *Work in America* discussion of this issue is bizarre. At one point, the authors opine that the usual survey result means only that "their pay and security are satisfactory, but this does not necessarily mean that their work is intrinsically rewarding" (O'Toole *et al.*, p. 14). This is, in the first instance, an unwarranted read-in: the standard question asks whether workers are satisfied or not with their jobs, not whether the pay is good, the security acceptable, or the intrinsic rewards adequate. Their depiction of what satisfied workers are really saying is gratuitous. The question really asks, "All in all, how satisfied would you say that you are with your job?" What 46% of the sample said in response was "very satisfied," and another 39% said "somewhat satisfied."

Later questions in the 1969 Survey of Working Conditions presented workers with a list of presumably desirable job traits and asked the extent to which each was true of the worker's own job. One such was, "I have an opportunity to develop my own special abilities." About one half (46%) said this was very true of their job, and 24% said it was somewhat true. Another was, "the work is interesting," and here, 63% said it was very true, 22% said it was somewhat true. About two thirds (65%) also said it was very true that "I can see the results of my work," and another quarter felt this was somewhat true. The conclusion from these and other similar items is clearly that specific questions probing issues of intrinsic rewards elicit patterns of satisfaction similar to those routinely elicited by the standard question. *Work in America's* claim that the conventional result somehow hides much discontent over the intrinsic rewards of work appears unjustified.

Later in the discussion, *Work in America* claims that "more sophisticated measures of job satisfaction designed to probe the specific components of a job offer great contradictions to simple 'Are you satisfied?' surveys. When it asked about specific working conditions, the Michigan survey found that great numbers of 'satisfied' workers had major dissatisfactions with such factors as the quality of supervision and the chance to grow on a job" (O'Toole *et al.*, p. 15). The reference is to the question sequence discussed in the previous paragraph. Concerning "chances to grow on the job," the proportions stating this to be very or somewhat true are not noticeably smaller than the proportions claiming to be very or somewhat satisfied, as the above results clearly show. Concerning the quality of supervision, one item in the sequence was, "My supervisor is competent in doing his job." Three fifths (59%) said this was very true, 25% said it was somewhat true. The assertion that more specific questions about concrete aspects of work give higher degrees of dissatisfaction therefore does not hold. There is no contradiction in any of these results, much less a great one.

Note again the ambiguous formulation, "great numbers," in the passage. If 1% of the sample said that it was very satisfied with the job as a whole, but had some complaints about supervision or chances for personal growth, this would translate into several hundreds of thousands of workers—assuredly, "a great number."

A job is not a single undifferentiated whole: rather, it consists of a wide variety of aspects, some of which may be satisfying, others not. That even workers who are *very* satisfied with the job as a whole find specific aspects to complain about is hardly unexpected. One cannot conclude from such a result that the more general question is somehow invalid or meaningless.

Finally, concerning specifically the "What would you do if . . . " question, *Work in America* remarks, "Over the last two decades, one of the most reliable single indicators of job dissatisfaction has been the response to the question: 'What type of work would you try to get into if you could start all over again?'" (O'Toole *et al.*, p. 15) Again, no reference is appended giving a source where evidence of reliability can be found, nor have we come across one. The implication that this item has proven, over the years, to be distinctly more reliable than other indicators appears unwarranted.

Returning to the essential point, it is correct that the authors of *Work in America* argue the superiority of the "What would you do if . . . " question. But their conclusion fails on all major points, being directly contradicted by key items evidence from the Survey of Working Conditions, which, remarkably, is cited repeatedly throughout the volume and is even referred to as "a unique and monumental study."

One researcher cited in the relevant *Work in America* passages is Robert Kahn, whose essay on "The Meaning of Work" was discussed in Chapter 1. Kahn does discuss the conventional job satisfaction question at some length, and also the "What would you do if . . . " question. The former, he says, is "more direct" (Kahn, 1972, p. 183). He also acknowledges the often-heard argument that the standard question is "persistently biased toward over-reporting satisfaction and understating dissatisfaction," but emphasizes that these arguments are "speculations . . . rather than methodological research findings" (Kahn, 1972, p. 174). He notes, finally, that there has been very little research "regarding the reliability and validity of such measures." The *Work in America* presentation thus conveys the false impression that a large methodological literature on measures of job satisfaction exists, and that the conventional measure has been found wanting. As for Kahn's summary judgment on the matter, the various limitations of the standard question "do not, in my opinion, eliminate the concept of job satisfaction from serious research" (Kahn, 1972, p. 175). Later, in a section of the paper concerning recommendations, Kahn calls for a "nationwide annual measurement of over-all work satisfaction," one including "direct expression of satisfaction or dissatisfaction" (Kahn, 1972, p. 202). Kahn is thus one researcher, at least (indeed, one of the leading scholars in the field), who obviously finds something of more than passing value in the conventional "Are you satisfied . . ." measure. Kahn does discuss "two inherent deficiencies in the concept of overall job satisfaction." One is that job satisfaction is "not unitary," and the second is that "satisfaction, by any difinition, is an interactive product of the person and his environment" (Kahn, 1972, p. 175). Both are important points: the first, for example, led directly (or so it appears) to the inclusion of questions about specific aspects of work in subsequent work surveys (as discussed earlier). The second point advances a causal hypothesis about the sources of satisfaction: that it reflects the degree of "fit" between what workers expect from their job and what the job actually provides, and some research effort has also been expended along these lines (see below, "Selective Misrepresentation of Findings," for a brief discussion). Any sensible reading of the Kahn article would lead to the conclusion that he is talking about various things that should be measured *in addition to* overall job satisfaction, not that measures of overall satisfaction should be abandoned. As noted above, Kahn's recommendation is for an annual work survey that explicitly includes "direct expression of satisfaction or dissatisfaction."

Consider next a passage from James Rinehart's *The Tyranny of Work* (1975). "We are particularly suspicious of social scientists' efforts to measure alienation via fixed-alternative questions which ask people to state how satisfied they are with their jobs on a scale ranging from 'very satisfied' to 'very dissatisfied.' It is quite likely that 'satisfied' responses simply mean that individuals are satisfied *relative to the job opportunities open to them*. Given the realistic range of jobs open to a worker, his present job may be the best of a bad lot" (Rinehart, p. 18). Rinehart's reference for this passage—the *only* source cited for his stated "suspicions"—is Kahn's 1972 paper!

What, ultimately, is the *evidence* to suggest that "What would you do if . . ." is somehow a better indicator of job satisfaction than a direct question that asks workers, "Are you satisfied . . . ?" The latter option certainly seems to be more direct and straightforward, while the former seems to mix attitudes about one's present work with fantasies of alternative futures. The strong preference for the fantasy question in sources such as Edwards, Bowles and Gintis, or *Work in America* derives essentially from this: the "What would you do if . . ." question gives results that seem consistent with an a priori conclusion, whereas the more direct question does not. It is, in short, another case of the double standard. Moreover, this particular use of the double standard is disguised behind references to a methodological literature that does not exist, or in those few instances of actual literature, that does not sustain the indicated conclusion.

Returning now to the substance of the *Work in America* findings, it happens that the often-cited Table 1 is not original to the Task Force Report. The table is taken, ultimately, from Kahn's essay just discussed.[20] Neither

[20]*Work in America* cites Kahn's (1974) paper, "The Work Module," as the source

Work in America nor its subsequent enthusiasts seem to have taken Kahn's other conclusions and data very seriously, least of all the central finding that "the modal response is on the positive side of neutrality—'pretty satisfied'." In fact, workplace critics have been rather single-minded in their determination to ignore this inconvenient result.

Kahn's table undergoes one very significant transformation before appearing as Table 1 in *Work in America*: all of the original footnotes are dropped. These footnotes and Kahn's text make it plain that the table is "synthesized from several different studies" (Kahn, 1972, p. 182), that it is a compilation of results from many disparate studies. *Work in America* is thus in error when it says that the table is based on "a cross section of white-collar . . . and blue-collar workers" (O'Toole *et al.*, p. 15). Bowles and Gintis repeat this error. The most serious distortion involved in their presentation is that the summary figures of 24% and 43% are *not* based on a representative national survey of the American working population. These two specific figures, as the footnotes in Kahn's version make perfectly clear, are derived from a study of lower-middle-class and upper-working-class respondents *in the Detroit area* (Kahn, 1972, p. 182, Table 5, note b). In all, six entries in the table are derived from these Detroit data, one is based on a survey of school superintendents in Massachusetts, and the remainder are taken from a Roper survey done *in 1947* of workers in sixteen selected American industries. *There is not one nationally representative survey in the lot.* The actual sources for the data in Table 1 are not given anywhere in *Work in America*. The discussion of the table imparts the false impression that it is based on a national sample; it is routinely cited as such in most secondary accounts. The result is that figures obtained for a sample of workers in Detroit are now taken to be representative of the American work force as a whole.[21]

Finally, one might ask about the Detroit study upon which the often-cited 24% and 43% figures are based. Kahn's source for the figures is a paper by Harold Wilensky published in 1964. The original source in turn shows that the 43% figure is registered for a sample of 252 lower level white-collar workers aged 30 to 55; the 24% figure, for 293 upper level blue-collar

---

of their Table 1. This paper appears in a companion to *Work in America* entitled, *Work and the Quality of Life*, (O'Toole, 1974), which contains a collection of background papers commissioned by the Task Force on which the Task Force Report was based. *Work in America's* Table 1 appears as Table 9.1 in Kahn's paper in the companion volume (Kahn, 1974, p. 204), but appeared *originally* in Kahn's 1972 paper. The versions that appear in the two Kahn papers are identical in every respect. In particular, both contain the explanatory notes that are omitted in the *Work in America* version, as we discuss shortly in the text.

[21] Table 1, moreover, does *not* contain any trend data. It is, rather, a compilation of nineteen one-shot cross-sectional findings, none based on nationally representative evidence. Further, there is no passage anywhere in the *Work in America* text even suggesting that trends on the item have been measured. Note, in contrast, Edwards' reference to "an increasing proportion of them over time."

workers also aged 30 to 55. Both groups were interviewed in 1959 and 1960. The same paper also reports the results of a four-item measure of work alienation for these two groups. For the lower level white-collar workers, 87% gave no alienated response to any of the four items; among the upper level blue-collar workers, the comparable proportion was 82% (Wilensky, pp. 137, 147).

The limitations of this study need not be belabored. It is dated, small, restricted to a single (atypical) city, and is not even a representative sample of workers in that city (being restricted by occupational group, by age, and by sex). Further, despite these limitations, results for the direct measures of worker alienation contained in the study are broadly compatible with results from all other surveys on the topic: large majorities indicated basic satisfaction with their work. And yet, this study is the ultimate source of data for Bowles and Gintis' claim that "only 43% of white collar workers and 24% of blue collar workers in a large representative sample say they are satisfied with their jobs" (p. 71).

Selective Misrepresentation of Findings

Many of the arguments for widespread worker discontent are based on some variant of a "rising expectations" or "new needs" hypothesis. Whereas workers once expected (or better, hoped somehow to achieve) good pay and secure jobs, these materialistic or lower order needs are now said to be satiated, with the result that consciousness is freed to pursue (or even expect) higher-order goals—for example, the goal of "self-actualization." In the absence of opportunity to achieve such goals, dissatisfaction on a wide scale results.

Thus, as a partial explanation of why worker discontent is on the rise, *Work in America* reports findings from a "unique and monumental study" that showed "interesting work" to be the single most important job *desideratum* from a list of some twenty-five presumably desirable aspects of work. The desire for interesting work thus easily outstripped such staples of work motivation as "good pay" (ranked fifth) or "job security" (ranked seventh). "What workers want most," the authors conclude from these findings, "is to become masters of their immediate environment and to feel that their work and they themselves are important" (O'Toole, p. 13). This desire for interesting work is, of course, prominently featured in *Work in America*. It is the cornerstone of the edifice.

There are at least three "obvious" conclusions that can be, and often are, drawn from this result. First, that today's workers value interesting work even above good pay or job security is a clear sign that values have changed and that expectations have risen. Second, with interesting work first on the list of worker expectations, it is readily understandable why so many workers "these days" are unhappy with their jobs. Finally, if we are to solve the crisis of work discontent, the traditional motivators—pay, security, and fringe—

will be inadequate. Rather, the nature of work itself will have to be transformed. From this latter consideration have followed such workplace reforms as job enrichment, job redesign, and the several other efforts to humanize the workplace.

The "unique and monumental study" from which the finding is drawn is the 1969 Michigan Survey of Working Conditions. It will by now therefore be apparent that the use of this survey by the *Work in America* Task Force was highly selective. A small digression into the complexities of such surveys is in order here. As it happens, the major costs of doing a national survey are in getting an interviewer at the door of an at-home respondent. Once these costs are incurred, the price of additional questions on the survey itself is effectively negligible. It is therefore cost-effective to conduct long rather than short surveys: hour-long interviews are perhaps the approximate average, and interviews substantially longer than this are not uncommon.

In the course of an hour, a very large number of questions can be asked, and an immense mass of information can therefore be obtained. To illustrate, the 1969 Survey of Working Conditions contains over six hundred pieces of information about every respondent, many of them representing one or another attitude toward work. One advantage of this much information, of course, is that it allows for very precise empirical understandings of the "quality of working life." One disadvantage is that it invites selective presentations. Unless such presentations are understood in the context of the total survey, they can be highly misleading: an occasional result cited out of context, that is, can impart a very seriously distorted image of the findings of the study as a whole.

Let us consider now the result obtained in the 1969 survey on the importance of interesting work. As reported in the *Work in America* formulation, respondents were given a long list of job traits and asked to state how important each of them was. One of the traits was "the work is interesting," and the result was that 73% said this was very important to them. (The numerical result, incidentally, is not reported in *Work in America*; it is our calculation from the study codebook.) As *Work in America* indicates, this was the highest rating given to any of the presented job traits.

To a person unfamiliar with the rest of the 1969 survey results, this finding is both stunning and definitive: since most jobs clearly are *not* very interesting in some objective sense, and since interesting work is the single most important feature of a job, it follows, as night follows day, that most workers must be dissatisfied. Even the most careful reader of *Work in America* would never learn that the same survey found 85% who were very or somewhat satisfied with their jobs, because this latter result is never mentioned, the authors instead turning to *other* studies.

But why, if most workers want interesting work above all other things, do so many of them report that they are satisfied with the jobs they have? The unexamined premise, of course, is that work truly *is* uninteresting to most workers. If, in contrast, most workers found their jobs to be interesting, there would be no inconsistency in the patterning of the results. As it happens, the 1969 survey, in a later section, presented respondents with the same list of job traits, asking this time how *true* each was as a description of their job (see text, above).The result: 63% of the respondents said it was very true that the work is interesting, and another 22% said it was somewhat true. Thus, while 73% think interesting work is very important, a roughly equivalent propor- tion also believe that their work *is* interesting. This finding also goes unmentioned in *Work in America*.

The workplace critics would, of course, reject the finding that work is interesting to most people, since they "know" a contrary truth, namely, that work is boring, dull, and hateful. This is a specious argument, however, since it is the opinions of workers themselves, not those of workplace intellectuals, that are at issue. In fact, as becomes increasingly apparent, the workplace intellectuals actually know very little about work in America, since they have either ignored, rejected out of hand, or selectively misrepresented the best existing evidence on the topic.

Consider next the policy mischief that might result (indeed, has demon- strably resulted) from the *Work in America* discussion of these results. In their presentation, the most pressing need on the policy agenda of the workplace is to make jobs more interesting, to redesign and enrich them so that they address the "new needs" of the "worker of today." This is, indeed, the stated policy recommendation of the Task Force report. In the overall context of the total survey, what this amounts to is spending a lot of time, effort, and money on providing a commodity—interesting work—that most workers say they already have.

Consider, by way of contrast, the matter of good pay. In the total 1969 sample, 64% rated this as very important to them, and 26% said it was somewhat important. But only 40% said it was very true that their pay actually *was* good. (Another third said this was somewhat true.) Thus, while good pay finishes well behind interesting work on the list of important job traits, the gap between what workers want and what they get is very much wider for pay. Given a choice between job enrichment and better pay, these results make it plain that many more workers would pick the latter than the former. This, we should also note, is thoroughly consistent with evidence reviewed earlier on people's most important personal problems.

Subsequent research by White (1977) and Fein (1973) has also demon- strated important differences among categories of workers in what they consider to be important in their work. The general result is that among blue-collar workers, pay and security are rated as more important than interesting work or other self-actualizing features of the job; the desire for self-actualization is concentrated among white-collar workers. Gruenberg (1980) has also reported the relatively greater importance of extrinsic factors among most categories of blue-collar workers. These are important findings, because most of the ensuing effort to enrich jobs has been concentrated in blue-collar occupations: at any rate, "job redesign" for doctors, lawyers, or university professors has not been prominent on the critics' agenda. Thus, the policy outcomes of *Work in America* are even more mischievous than the earlier discussion suggests: the report focused much attention on what turns out to have been a nonproblem in the first place, and it focused this attention on the wrong part of the labor force. One result is that funds spent in redesigning blue-collar work are not available to increase blue-collar wages.[22]

Invocation of Untested Theories

The attention given in *Work in America* and many other sources to worker needs or expectations derives, ultimately, from theories developed in the postwar era that purport to describe the psychological processes involved in work motivation. Many of these theories derive, in one way or another, from the work of Abraham Maslow (described in the previous chapter). But a theory, an intellectual framework or construction, is one thing, supporting evidence another. And, as Tausky and Parke have put it, "There is scant evidence to substantiate the view that a need hierarchy, as described by Maslow, exists" (Tausky and Parke, p. 539). The same point has been made by Campbell and associates (p. 80): "Models which spell out hierarchies of needs, such as that proposed by Maslow, have achieved high popularity despite the paucity of systematic empirical support. Our present data, while far from conclusive, certainly fail to find much confirmation for such attractive concepts as need hierarchies in understanding the roots of feelings of satisfactions with life." A similar conclusion is drawn by Korman who states that " . . . this theoretical approach has gained great popularity in many management and psychological circles. One wonders why, however, since so far as the writer is aware, *it has only been tested once as a theory of performance in an industrial context, and that test provided little or no support*" (Korman, pg. 36, emphasis in the original: the test referred to is by Hall and Nougaim, 1968). A very useful review that covers many relevant studies is that of E. E. Lawler III (1973, pp. 34–38).[23]

[22]All the information from the Survey of Working Conditions presented in the foregoing discussion was taken directly from the marginal results published in the study codebook, a document that was certainly in the hands of the Task Force, if not of subsequent critics. No knowledge of computer technology, or of the workings of survey research, is required to unearth the basic lessons. Anyone who could read the English language and work a hand-held calculator (or, failing the latter, add and divide by hand) could generate these results if the study codebook were available to them.

[23]Lawler's work is exceptional in that it makes a careful review of studies relevant to the Maslow claims. His principal conclusions are: "There is strong evidence to support the view that unless existence needs are satisfied, people will not be concerned with higher-order needs. There is, however, very little evidence to support the view that a hierarchy exists above the security level. Thus, it probably is not safe to assume more than a two-step hierarchy with existence and security needs at the lowest level and all the higher-order needs at the next level. This line of thinking leads

Chris Argyris, another motivational theorist, sees human beings in our culture developing from passivity to activity, from dependency to independence, from shallow interests to deep interests, from accepting subordination to desiring equality or superiority to peers, and from lack of control to self-control. Frustration of these drives, the stultification of these higher-order needs, will produce a wide variety of organizational pathologies. The quest for higher pay, job security, and unionization are seen as displacements, as the products of frustration of those basic aims (Argyris: 1960, 1962, and 1973). Like Maslow, these assumptions are taken as givens, as unproven axioms, rather than as hypotheses requiring validation.

Another theorist, Frederick Herzberg, has formulated the Maslow position somewhat differently, arguing a qualitative distinction between the sources of work satisfaction and dissatisfaction; they are not, in other words, the extremes of a single continuum. The sources of satisfaction he has termed "motivators," and the sources of dissatisfaction he has called "hygienes." One can have a broad array of hygienes—good pay, job security, clean and healthy work conditions—and while that may remove dissatisfactions, it will not, by itself, create satisfaction. To achieve that, the motivators are needed: challenge, opportunity, recognition, autonomy, room for advancement of knowledge and skill (Herzberg, Mausner, and Snyderman, 1959; Herzberg, 1966, 1968). Herzberg's claims are more amenable to empirical investigation than the Maslow original or the Argyris version. Tausky and Parke report that the evidence has not been favorable to Herzberg's framework (citing Dunnette, Campbell, and Hakell, 1967; Vroom, 1964, pp. 126–129; and House and Wigdor, 1967). See also King (1970), Ewen et al. (1966), and the articles cited therein (both of these articles appear also in Gruneberg, 1976). In addition, there is an extended critique in Fein (1976, pp. 465–501), who also lists the following critical studies: Graen (1966; 1968), Graen and Hulin (1968), and Hulin and Smith (1967). The basic problem, as Fein sees it, is that "only a minority, about 15% to 20% of the worker population, responds to [Herzberg's] concepts. . . . the 80% to 85% of the work force that does not find fulfillment on the job continues not to identify [with their work] regardless of how encouraging an environment management creates in the plant" (Fein, 1976, p. 501). (See also Chapter 6 of the present volume for consideration of job enrichment efforts.)

A third specialist making use of the Maslow framework is Douglas

---

to the prediction that unless these lower-order needs are satisfied, the others will not come into play. However, which higher-order needs come into play after the lower ones are satisfied and in what order they will come into play cannot be predicted" (Lawler, 1973, p. 34). In contrast to Maslow, Lawler emphasizes the evidence on individual differences in need strength. These he sees as related to both organizational factors (for example, management level) and to personal characteristics (age, sex, and educational level). Those individual differences, he says, will determine which higher-order needs will become active once the existence needs have been satisfied (Lawler, 1973, pp. 36–38).

McGregor. One survey of managers' views on behavioral science found
McGregor to be "the behaviorist who had most influenced managers'
opinions . . . " (The study is by Rush, 1969; the quote is from Fein, 1976, pp.
465–466.) McGregor has spelled out two kinds of managerial styles, these
based on contrasting assumptions about employee motivations. The first,
called Theory X, assumes the need for carrot and stick, for various techniques of external control. The second, Theory Y, calls for self-direction.
Implementation of the latter "will not only enhance substantially [our]
materialistic achievements, but will bring us one step closer to the 'good
society'," it is reported (McGregor, 1957, p. 92; see also 1960, 1966, and
1967). But, as Fein notes, McGregor offers "no proof of this contention." He
(McGregor) does indicate that he draws "heavily on the work of . . .
Abraham Maslow . . . the most fruitful approach I know," but that, as we
have seen, provides a rather infirm foundation. Maslow himself, some years
later, declares that "I of all people should know just how shaky this
foundation is. . . . " (quoted in Fein, 1976, pg. 467). Still another review
concludes that:

> The substantial American and English literature on worker attitudes toward their
> jobs, their supervisors, and their companies has tended recently to cast doubts
> on the validity of the theses propounded by Maslow, Likert, and McGregor that,
> once workers have satisfied their primary physiological, economic, and social
> needs, they would actively seek self-expression, self-actualization, and creativity
> in the workplace (Derber, p. 133).

No review of work motivation studies would be complete without a
consideration of the famous Hawthorne Experiments (Roethlisberger and
Dickson, 1939). Based on more than a decade of investigation in the
Western Electric Company's Hawthorne works in Chicago, this research
provided a serious challenge to the assumptions of Adam Smith, Frederick
Taylor, and the views of "economic man" that had prevailed hitherto in
much of the social science literature and in much of business practice. This
research showed the importance of "friendliness among peers, cohesive
work groups, and supportive, considerate, democratic supervision [which]
replaced money as the factors . . . suggested to improve satisfaction and
productivity" (Tausky and Parke, p. 539). This approach, sometimes referred
to as the "human relations in industry" movement, was very well received
and very widely advertised.

Now, some fifty years after the studies were completed, two researchers
have obtained the original results and have submitted them to detailed
statistical analysis. Some of their principal conclusions follow:

> As pointed out by Argyle [in 1953], the Hawthorne researchers had provided "no
> quantitative evidence for the conclusion for which this experiment is famous—
> that the increase of output was due to a changed relation with supervision."
> Quantitative evaluation now does provide such evidence. However it is not
> "release from oppressive supervision" . . . but its reassertion that explains higher
> rates of production . . .

> Most of the variance in production rates during the first relay experiment could be explained by measured variables [that is, by imposition of managerial discipline, economic adversity, and quality of raw materials, these accounting for some 90 per cent of the variance in quantity and quality of output]. To assume that output changes resulted from unmeasured changes in the human relations of workers therefore seems injudicious, even though it was the assumption of the Hawthorne researchers and has been accepted and built upon by many social scientists over the past several decades.

> Quantitative analyses of the data from Hawthorne, as well as empirical studies of work groups in the decades subsequent (cf. Stogdill, 1974), unfortunately do not support a contention that improvements in human relations lead to improved economic performance . . . (Franke and Kaul, pp. 636, 638).[24]

Franke and Kaul provide a comprehensive account of all aspects of this remarkable episode of intellectual history. They review the experiments themselves, the dissemination of the results, and the subsequent history of approbation and criticism (both technical and ideological). They also provide some explanation for "this enthusiastic embrace of something scientifically unproved . . . ."[25] The conclusions of the Hawthorne studies, they suggest:

> . . . seem to have been congenial to persons who were in agreement with the prevailing economic system, but were prepared to proceed from simple materialistic notions about work motivation on to more complex social theories, which could be seen as more useful, humane, and democratic. (Franke and Kaul, p. 637)

Such theories, as we have seen, remain "congenial" to the workplace critics, even to some who are not at all in agreement with the prevailing economic system.

False Consciousness

When all the previous techniques of dismissal have been exhausted, there remains the possibility that the troublesome survey results reflect false consciousness—that the people involved are telling us they are happy with their lives when, in fact, they are not, or that they are satisfied with their work

[24]The choice, incidentally, is not one of Taylorism vs. Human Relations. Franke and Kaul conclude that "such activities as participative management, industrial democracy, and sensitivity or consideration training may have benefits transcending the criteria considered here" (Franke and Kaul, p. 638).

[25]Two other critiques of the Hawthorne studies deserve mention, these being Carey, 1967; and Parsons, 1974. With regard to Carey, however, see also the counterstatement by Shepard (1971). Parsons challenges the so-called Hawthorne effect, the claim that productivity increased as a by-product of experimenter interest and attention. He points to a rather neglected aspect of the experiment—the operatives were on piecework and received daily, or even more frequent, reports of their productivity. When these aspects of the experiment were changed, the "Hawthorne effect" disappeared. For later challenges and a reaction, see Wardwell, 1979; Schlaifer, 1980; Franke, 1980; Blumbaum, 1983.

when, in fact, they hate it. This is, to be sure, a fallback position. When the intellectuals say that people are unhappy or that people hate their work, they are making a flat declarative statement purporting to describe the actual, de facto, state of mass consciousness. The false consciousness line is only invoked once the evidence has made it clear that people actually do not say that at all—"But of course, false consciousness!" But if the falseness of peoples' consciousness were so obvious from the start, why make the initial contrary-to-fact declarative statement?

Put in more conventional terms, the argument of false consciousness involves a stipulation about the correct standards of judgments. In essence, the claim is that people *ought* to be using Standard X when in fact they are, quite mistakenly, using Standard Y. Typically, the argument favoring Standard X is not put forward or even discussed; its superiority over Standard Y is merely declared or assumed. Consciousness is then said to be false to the extent that it diverges from what one would expect *if* conditions of life were measured against the superior standard.

For obvious reasons, these superior standards tend to be very demanding ones. With respect to work in particular, the standard is some loosely defined, virtually Edenic state of unity between man and work, where work and leisure are one, where work is creative and fulfilling and self-realizing, not something alien to the self. Since all existing conditions of work fall well short of this standard, the critical intellectuals know what the right answer to the job satisfaction question *ought* to be: people ought to be highly dissatisfied.

This use of the very demanding standard is a purely analytical (logical, argumentative) technique; it allows one the easy victory of a correct logical conclusion (that is, *if* people were to use this standard, *then* they would find their work hateful). But as with all purely logical arguments, this one is compelling only to the extent that the initial premise is correct. For most people, of course, that standard of judgment will appear unrealistic and impractical for the organization of their everyday lives.

Many of the intellectuals thus formulate an erroneous conclusion. Many of them, as we have seen, declare that the majority or most people *are* dissatisfied. But what is actually being said is that if most people adopted that exacting standard as the basis for judgments about their lives, they *would* be (or *should* be) dissatisfied. But if one expressed the conclusion in this way, those intellectuals would be forced to admit that most people do not in fact adopt that demanding standard, and they might even be led to the further conclusion that it is neither practical nor appropriate for most people to do so.

A much higher level of realism is found in the average person's appreciation of the world. A comment one frequently hears about objectively unpleasant (alienating) jobs is, "Someone has to do it." The advanced intellectual has little to say with respect to such ultimate realism. There is an unspoken corollary of the ordinary person's realistic judgment, that being the implicit, "Why fight it?"

This points up another difficulty in the false consciousness argument of the critical intellectual. They have a submerged, an unsaid or unspoken, argument; it is that (i) things can be otherwise, and (ii) life will be better when organized in that other way. Once again, ordinary people are ahead of the advanced thinker. They are either denying those two claims or asking to be shown. And, not seeing any demonstration, they stubbornly persist in their conservative ways, refusing to hear the voices of their supposed liberators. For this intelligence, for their rationality in the face of an incomplete argument, they are denounced as dupes, as the narcoticized masses, as the hapless victims of someone's manipulation. One may raise some questions: Who is the dupe? Who is narcoticized? Whose consciousness is false and whose is true?

A Note on Participant Observation Studies of Work

Much of the animosity directed toward survey research by the workplace critics is accompanied by an explicit or implicit assertion that meaningful information on job satisfaction can only be obtained through intensive field observations or participant observation. Surveys are mechanistic, allowing people to respond only by choosing one of a fixed set of alternative answers, whereas field studies let people speak for themselves in their own terms. Survey procedures are rigid and inflexible, field procedures open-ended and organic. Field methods thus give rich, deep, and meaningful data, whereas survey methods produce superficial, misleading, invalid results.

Much of the stated preference for field studies in the critical literature is explained by the simple observation that many such studies claim to show widespread worker disenchantment, whereas survey studies, as we have seen, typically do not. In most cases, the claim for the superiority of field methods is not based on any *comparative* studies of the advantages or disadvantages of the two methods; rather, the claim is merely a declaration. However, there are at least a few comparative studies that speak directly to this issue, often with surprising results. One study, concerned with power and partisanship in a small community, made use of both field and survey procedures (Aggar and Goldrich, 1958). After a period of participation observation in the community, the field workers reported their sense that "There was not a single Democrat on . . . Main Street." Subsequently, a survey of Main Street was undertaken, and it turned out that half the residents identified themselves as Democrats; the sense of the field workers was seriously mistaken. In retrospect, it was easy to identify the source of the mistake: the Republicans were well organized and the Democrats had almost no formal organization. Lacking an organization, the Democrats exhibited very little partisan activity and thus never came to the attention of the field workers. Seeing no politically active Democrats on the scene, they concluded (wrongly) that none existed. This study makes it clear that the one method is not fated to yield an invalid result, whereas the results of the other method are invariably correct. In this case, the survey data corrected a very serious observational error made by the field team.

It is also *not* the case that participant observation studies of workers invariably find rampant work discontent. The author of one such study, for example, spent a number of years in the field in close and continuous association with his subjects, most of whom were construction workers. (We note in passing that most of the field work was done in a local bar where these men got together.) He reports never having heard a single man say that he "hated his work—or even disliked it. . . . As a group the men seemed to enjoy their work" (LeMasters, p. 20). The conclusion that most people are pretty satisfied with their jobs is obviously not just a *simple* function of method, then, since here is at least one study, employing the recommended alternative method, that obtained precisely the same result.

The LeMasters study is not the only in-depth, sensitive participant-observer study to report that blue-collar workers do not hate their jobs. Another, more recent study by Richard Balzer has reported similar conclusions. Balzer spent five months as a "lowest grade bench hand" in a Western Electric factory in Massachusetts. "Several friends asked how I could tolerate what they considered the boring, repetitive nature of factory work. I felt somewhat uncomfortable telling them that although I probably would have felt differently if faced with ten years of benchwork, I didn't mind it for five months. It gave a solid routine to my life and that felt comfortable. I looked forward to going to work most mornings, not because of the work, but because I had friends at work. (. . .) I enjoyed the social community of which I was a part" (Balzer, p. 331). These comments, of course, speak to Balzer's reactions to factory work, not to the reactions of the workers themselves. But on this latter topic, he also has interesting and, under the circumstances, rather unusual things to say:

> Not everyone . . . wants a challenging, enlarged or enriched job. Many people don't come to work in search of job satisfaction but because of the money. . . . Some of these workers prefer, or at least don't mind, rather routine tasks that allow them the freedom to think about other things or to be more "sociable."
>
> There are other workers who derive a sense of security from knowing the boundaries of their responsibilities, and who are not anxious to give up their routines for unknown enlarged jobs. Others find satisfaction in knowing how to do their jobs well. Although many of the tasks on the shop floor are rudimentary and look easy to learn, I found that many of them take a long time to do well. It may not take long to learn the procedures, but to be able to do it effectively takes some time and skill.
>
> Still, there are plenty of workers who don't feel this way, who feel trapped in jobs that they consider too small or too limited . . . (etc.) (Balzer, p. 326).

We quote these conclusions for several reasons. First, Balzer's observations in this one factory clearly do not suggest a pattern of welling discontent.

In fact, and of considerably greater importance, Balzer makes it plain that the workers he studied had a wide range of attitudes about the work, varying from undeniable feelings of entrapment and boredom, on the one hand, to equally undeniable feelings of positive satisfaction, on the other, and embracing pretty much everything in between. On its own, this is not a surprising finding. One would not expect any single, sweeping depiction to do adequate justice to what must, after all, be a rather complex collection of feelings and viewpoints. Balzer's study—*not* a survey at all, but a field study involving much sensitivity and depth—directly contradicts one of the critics' favorite assertions and gives a result that is broadly consistent with the corresponding survey evidence.

It is, then, clearly *not* the case that all participant observation studies find the wholesale dissatisfaction that survey methods are somehow incapable of finding; at least some participant observation studies find what virtually all surveys find. Other field studies, to be sure, do give a different result. Here, one might consider an alternative hypothesis to account for the putative disparity—namely, that the survey results are valid and the field results are not. The explanation would, in this case, focus on problems of sampling, and on the more general problem discussed earlier, the unwarranted generalization. In the field situation, sampling problems might arise in any of three ways, each of which hampers the generalizability of the results: (i) in a nonrandom selection of respondents or informants, (ii) in a nonrandom selection of the information provided by one's respondents, or (iii) in a nonrandom selection of research sites.

The first problem is illustrated by a brief journalistic study undertaken by Barbara Garson (1972). Interviewing in Lordstown, Ohio, she found widespread job dissatisfaction. A brief biographical note tells us that she was active in the Free Speech Movement at Berkeley and later "worked for a year in an antiwar GI coffeehouse in Tacoma, Washington." Her investigation, she reports, began with "hanging around the parking lot [of the Lordstown plant] between shifts." Later, inside the factory, she spotted Duane, who had been in the army while she was working in the GI coffeehouse. Duane introduced her to some friends and between them, they supplied two columns of material. Later in the week, she spent some time in an "autoworkers' commune" and there acquired material for another two columns. Ordinarily one might doubt the representative character of material drawn from such manifestly atypical sources. But this frankly and openly described unscientific survey apparently provoked no pangs of doubt for either the writer or the publisher. This account, moreover, has been frequently cited in other literature, usually without so much as a single word of doubt as to the method. A single suggestion of a frequency distribution does appear in the article, incidentally. One individual appears who seems to be of a different mind from all the angry young men portrayed throughout the article. He is described in a single paragraph on the fourth of five pages, in the course of which he is treated with some condescension. "He was a cheerful, good-natured lad, and as I say, he liked the Vega." Not all of the dehumanizing, it will be noted, occurs on GM assembly lines.

The point is that it is possible for the researcher, either wittingly or unwittingly, to select respondents in such a way as to bias the results. This problem, it will be noted, does not appear in the best survey research since there the interviewer has little latitude in the choice of whom to interview.

A second possible source of bias involves a nonrandom selection of responses. In an extended interview, say on the character of one's work, an enormous quantity of information (that is, statements) will be accumulated, only a small part of which can ordinarily be presented. It is up to the researcher to decide which statements will be reported and which will be omitted. Selection is obviously involved; it would be absurd that such selection be random. There is a clear possibility that selection would proceed according to the preconception of the researcher. "Knowing," for example, that workers dislike (or should dislike) their work, quotations can be chosen accordingly.

Both the above mentioned problems are illustrated in the enormously popular book by Studs Terkel, _Working_ (1974). Terkel was interviewed in 1980 by David Smothers, a features reporter for UPI, and the interview gives some useful insights into how a field researcher like Terkel goes about his work. In the course of the interview, we learn that the 60 to 100 interviews appearing in one of his "talk books" are a selection from up to as many as 300 interviews actually conducted. Terkel does not say just how he decides which interviews to include and which to omit. In all probability, readability and drama are the major criteria. Each interview, Terkel adds, lasts an hour to an hour and a half (interestingly, no longer on the average than the typical SRC interview). Each interview is then edited until, in Terkel's phrase, he has "the gold." As to how the original 300-odd respondents are selected, Terkel declares, "I have no technique." He thus begins with some 300 people chosen in no systematic manner, pares this initial sample down to between 60 and 100, then edits the remarks and comments of this subset until he has "the gold." The possibilities of biased selection, both among respondents and among their remarks, are clearly ever-present.[26]

[26]Some other problems with the field method are worth at least a passing comment. First, for obvious reasons involving the character of this kind of research, specifically because of the confidentiality promised to the respondents, nothing like an archive of field observations could ever possibly be created. Thus, in the normal course of things, no reanalysis or reworking of the source data is possible; one must simply trust the capability and integrity of the original researcher. The surveys analyzed in this book, in contrast, are widely available and can be acquired and reanalyzed by anybody who doubts the adequacy of our or others' analysis.

One noteworthy secondary analysis of field data does appear in the literature, this being Domhoff's (1978) reanalysis of the field data from Dahl's (1961) study of community power in New Haven, Connecticut. The conclusions derived from the reanalysis are, to put it mildly, sharply at variance with the conclusions advanced in

A closely related difficulty involves the handling of summary conclusions or judgments. Jobs, marriages, and lives are complex things, and in the course of extended interviewing, one will ordinarily pick up a wide range of statements about them—some positive, some negative, some neutral. At some point in the research process, there comes a need to reach a summary conclusion; for example, whether *in general* the respondent likes or dislikes his or her work. And at this point, the researcher has a choice: one may ask respondents themselves for these summary statements about their net satisfactions or dissatisfactions with a given area of life, or the researcher may simply infer a summary from the range of available material, then back it up with selective appropriate quotations. In this latter case, the possibility of biased selection and mistaken judgment is once again obvious.

Still a third sampling problem involves the purposive selection of sites in which to conduct the in-depth field study. Sites can be chosen so as to maximize the amount of discontent one observes. In its most obvious form, this problem manifests itself as a tendency to pick factories undergoing strikes and work stoppages, or where other troubles and difficulties have been reported, as the scene of one's research, rather than other factories in the same area making much the same kind of product, factories that are not on strike or having labor problems. To be sure, plants on strike make good copy, but they do not necessarily produce results that are representative of workers as a whole. Perhaps the clearest recent instance of this is the famous Lordstown strike in 1972, which produced dozens of journalistic accounts, most of them arguing that Lordstown was typical or characteristic of some new developments in the American working class. In the year of Lordstown, however, exactly 2.3% of the American labor force was involved in work stoppages of any sort, the *lowest* percentage recorded in any year since 1963 (U.S. Department of Labor, 1975, p. 391).

Still another difficulty concerns the choice of kinds of workers to study; here too, one can make site choices that maximize the discontent one discovers. Among blue-collar workers, for example, job dissatisfaction varies by skill level, with unskilled and semiskilled or operative workers showing the most dissatisfaction (see Chapter 6). Interestingly, many field studies of blue-collar workers focus precisely on this category of worker—on assembly-line workers, machine tenders, and so on. Many of these studies make the further assumption that these workers are somehow typical or represen-

---

the original source. Domhoff documents several instances where the remarks of informants were misreported, misinterpreted, or used out of context, or where leading questions were asked. See pp. 18-19, 33ff., 45, 47, 48, 109-110.

Another feature of field study reports that sets them off from surveys is that they present the answers people gave, but only rarely the *questions* that produced those answers. There is, in short, no way to find out if leading, biased, or directive questions were asked. In contrast, every survey codebook will contain both the questions asked and the answers they generated. Given the ultimately public nature of these things, it would be very foolish to put obviously biased or leading questions into the study, since these errors would be readily detected by secondary analysts.

tative of the labor force as a whole, although in fact semiskilled workers comprise only about one *third* of the blue-collar labor force and roughly one sixth of the total labor force.[27] Field studies of presumably less alienating blue-collar work—for example, of carpenters, electricians, and the other skilled trades—are very rare. One prominent exception, the LeMasters study of construction workers, it will be recalled, did *not* show a pattern of seething discontent.

Our point in the preceding remarks, of course, is not that field methods are somehow invalid or inherently inferior to survey methods. Most capable methodologists in the social sciences grant strengths and weaknesses to either method, a judgment that we share. There are, we are confident, certain highly important questions in the social sciences for which the survey method is inappropriate, but measurements of the state of satisfaction of the American population are not among them. Arguments favoring a different conclusion are, as we have seen, ad hoc and largely unpersuasive, and are, in any case, unaccompanied by the necessary evidence. The only presumptively telling criticism of survey research that the workplace critics have mounted is that it routinely gives results sharply at variance with the conclusions they ardently defend. This, of course, is no criticism at all: that the world proves not to be the way they have depicted it bespeaks a flaw in their conclusions, not in the methods of survey research.

THE METHODS OF THE WORKPLACE RESEARCHERS

In the previous pages we have faulted the workplace critics for not coming to grips with the findings of job satisfaction surveys. Our preference for survey evidence, however, does not mean that we think the method is faultless, or that every reported survey result should be taken at face value. We have already discussed at length some serious flaws in the Scammon-Wattenberg analysis of Gallup data, and in the next section another set of conclusions will be questioned, this in connection with the empirical work of Ronald Inglehart. In Chapter 6, some recent survey data from the workplace researchers is also critiqued. In general, fault lies not with the method—either survey or field methods—but in how the method is used or abused.

Any number of problems can and do arise in the conduct of a survey on any scale, beginning with the formulation of problems, choice of sample, wording of questions, response rate, execution of the interviews, and processing of the data, all this prior to possible errors in analysis and subsequent inferences. All practitioners in the field know and recognize these possibilities. Many of the problems can be avoided with enough advance thought

---

[27]Actually, the skew is even more biased. The United States Bureau of the Census, 1979 *Statistical Abstract of the United States* (Table 687, p. 418) shows a total of 1,164,000 assemblers out of a total labor force of 94,373,000 in 1978, which is 1.2%. Not all assemblers, in turn, work on an assembly *line*. Thus, the proportion of assembly line workers among the total work force in the United States cannot be much more than 1%.

and zealous attention to details. Indeed, the last forty years have witnessed an impressive improvement in the art and science of conducting sample surveys, something many critics fail to recognize.

Many of the critics note a *possible* or *hypothetical* problem with the method and let it go at that, content to reject the method as a whole. Interestingly, survey practitioners are usually far ahead of the critics at this point. For every possibility that the critics mention, the capable practitioner could cite a rich array of further difficulties that the critic has yet to think about. But practitioners have taken two additional steps. First, to the extent possible, they research the magnitude and nature of the problem. Once it is clear how serious the problem is, and the source of the problem has been located, one may then proceed to develop appropriate solutions. The strategy, in short, is one of progressive improvement, not wholesale rejection.

A few useful examples can be cited. In 1936, the infamous Literary Digest poll missed the actual election result by a wide margin, based on a sample of several *million*. In the past few decades, Gallup's average error in predicting election results has been less than two percentage points, based on samples of about 1500 people. This remarkable improvement in accuracy is due entirely to progressive rethinking and reworking of the science of survey sampling. In the 1960's much concern was expressed about possible "acquiescence" biases in the answers to "agree-disagree" questions. Practitioners undertook the relevant research and discovered that this was, indeed, a problem. As a result, agree-disagree questions are seldom included in present-day surveys. One final example: concern about the validity of the standard job satisfaction question dates at least to 1935, Hoppock's early study articulating many of the issues that present-day critics voice. Much of the contents of the Michigan work surveys—for example, detailed questions on specific facets of the work—was a direct response to these concerns. The result is, of course, a much more detailed portrait of work outlooks than was hitherto available.

One final problem in doing survey research lies in communicating the results. Here, the problem lies not so much with the method or with its practitioners, but with the various literary and cultural journals that seem loathe to let any sort of useful quantitative information appear within their pages. Certainly, the detailed technical account of methods and findings seldom makes for riveting reading, and few survey researchers seem graced with felicities of style. The problem of transmitting results and the ensuing "balkanization" of the American intellectual effort is discussed in more detail in the concluding chapter.

THE COMING OF POSTMATERIALISM:
ANOTHER CASE OF DISTORTED RESULTS

Earlier we reanalyzed the Gallup poll data cited by Scammon and Wattenberg in regard to their social issue thesis. Contrary to the claims

made, those data showed, rather unmistakably, that economic or materialistic worries dominate the agenda of human concern for most of the
American population, and this conclusion stands in seeming contradiction
to the conclusions advanced by Reich, Inglehart, and many others, that
postmaterial values are coming to dominate the consciousness of the modern masses. The argument by Inglehart to this effect is of particular interest:
his claims are based on a series of surveys done between 1970 and 1973 in
ten European nations and in the United States; for six of the nations, more
than one survey is available. Taken as a lot, the sheer quantity of survey data
analyzed in the book is staggering. How, then, can the apparent contradiction between his data and the Gallup data reviewed earlier be resolved?

In fact, there turns out to be no disparity at all: the lessons to be learned
from Inglehart's *evidence* are for all practical purposes identical to those
revealed in our review of the Gallup series. The postulated trend in postmaterial consciousness, in other words, is not supported by the evidence
Inglehart presents.[28]

Obviously, any empirical analysis of postmaterialism requires a measure
of postmaterial values, so we may begin by asking just how this concept is
measured in Inglehart's analysis. Conceptually, postmaterial values are said
to include "the needs for love, belonging, and esteem," and "intellectual
and aesthetic satisfaction" (Inglehart, 1977a, p. 22). It turns out, however,
that for most of the analysis, postmaterialism is inferred from responses to a
question asking people to choose two of the following four things as "most
desirable to you": maintaining order in the nation, giving the people more
say in important political decisions, fighting rising prices, and protecting
freedom of speech. The responses, "give people more say" and "protect
freedom of speech," are treated as postmaterial responses, and the respondents choosing them both are therefore the postmaterialists in the analysis.
Likewise, respondents choosing both "maintaining order" and "fighting
rising prices" are said to be the materialists, and respondents choosing one
from each category are said to be mixed.

Of the four options presented, only one—fighting rising prices—seems to
bear directly on materialistic concerns. People choosing any of the remaining three could therefore perhaps be typified as nonmaterialistic in a loose
sense, but the interpretation that they are therefore *post*materialistic seems a
bit uncertain. Maintaining order in the nation seems more a traditional or
conservative value than a materialistic one; and likewise, protecting freedom of speech is a classic libertarian concern that dates at least to the Bill
of Rights, hardly a new value unique to the presumed postmaterial era. The
measure does not directly tap love, belonging, or esteem, nor does it pick up
intellectual or aesthetic satisfaction. In other words, the measure of postmaterial values used throughout the book seems to bypass almost entirely the

[28]The following pages are freely adapted from an earlier publication (James
Wright, 1978b).

concept of postmaterial values as spelled out by Inglehart and others. There is, in short, some reason to doubt whether the survey evidence discussed in the book has *anything at all* to do with material and postmaterial values. (On the other hand, Inglehart does report modest positive correlations between this question and other, more direct, more plausible measures of the value complex at issue [Inglehart, 1977a, pp. 30–31].)[29]

The central finding, the one on which the argument of value *change* is sustained, is that the proportion of postmaterialists (defined as above) is higher in all nations among younger respondents than older ones. The possibility that youthful enthusiasm for these postmaterial values will diminish with age is considered but discounted in favor of a generational explanation that predicts these values will persist throughout the lives of the people involved: this new postmaterialism, in short, is a permanent feature on the scene. Ultimately, these generational differences are said to be linked to differing economic circumstances prevailing during the period of formative socialization for each generation: older generations were reared during times of economic trouble and war and cling to their older values; younger people, raised in the affluence of the postwar era, take security and economic well-being for granted and have turned their attention to the newer, postmaterial needs. The evidence in support of this interpretation is that the measure of postmaterialism correlates more strongly with education (taken as an indicator of one's family's economic circumstances during youth) and with other, more direct measures of social class origin than with respondents' present incomes. It is not one's present affluence, then, but the affluence of one's family during one's formative years that leads to postmaterial values.

In the technical language of research methods, what Inglehart is attempting here is to infer trends (*changes* over time) from cross-sectional data (that is, data collected just at a single time point), a hazardous inference in the best of circumstances. Inglehart *does* show that at the time of these surveys (early 1970's), young people were more prone to postmaterialism (as he measures it) than older people. The conclusion that this demonstrates value *change*, however, depends on the plausible but untested assumption that the (present) postmaterialism of youth is a *new* thing, that in the past younger people were not equally prone to the same outlooks. And since Inglehart was, to our knowledge, the first researcher to ask this question, there are no

---

[29]Marsh (1975) has also questioned the validity of Inglehart's measure. Based on British data, he reports that Inglehart's postmaterialists are more nearly "crypto-materialists." They were, to illustrate, more likely to report some dissatisfaction with their incomes than the materialists (Marsh, 1975, p. 24). Inglehart has a rejoinder (Inglehart, 1977a, pp. 136–138), arguing in essence that they derive less satisfaction from their incomes precisely because they *are* postmaterialist and have moved beyond such things. (See also Inglehart, 1977b, 1981.) A subsequent study by Marsh (1977) reports a + .22 correlation between Inglehart's original measure and Marsh's preferred alternative.

available data on how younger persons of former eras might have responded to it. The argument that the results by age show value *change* is therefore based on an assumption that cannot be directly tested.[30]

Just how widespread are postmaterial values in Inglehart's data? The general tenor of his discussion aside, the data do *not* show a substantial penetration of postmaterial thinking into the mass consciousness of the Western societies. In fact, with one exception, materialists actually out-number postmaterialists *in every age group* and *in every nation* shown, the youngest group of Belgian respondents providing the sole exception to this pattern. (These data are shown in Inglehart's Tables 2-1 and 2-2.) By our calculations, across all eleven nations for which data are available, the average proportion of people who scored as postmaterialist works out to 10.5%. The materialists are, on average, *three times* more numer-ous, averaging 34.5% across all eleven nations. (The remainder, of course, are mixed.) Even by the most liberal definitions, the proportion who scored as postmaterialist in all Western societies is no more than a small minority.

Additional evidence on the relative dominance of material and postma-terial values is presented in his Table 2-6. Here, respondents were asked to choose the two most important goals from a list of twelve possible goals. Some of these goals seem to relate much more directly to postmaterialism than those offered in the main question discussed earlier: the options in-cluded, for example, "more say on the job," "more beautiful cities," a "less impersonal society," and so on. Some of the goals identifiable as postma-terialistic fare rather well in a few nations, such as France and the Nether-lands, but the average ranking of the most popular such goal ("more say on the job") across the ten nations is *sixth*. Among the twelve offerings, first place in every nation but one (Luxembourg) went to "fight rising prices"—clearly a materialistic concern. Another materialistic concern—"economic growth"—finished second only to fighting prices, and another such goal—"a stable economy"—finished fourth overall. (Third place among all goals went to "fighting crime," and fifth to "maintaining order," both also lower-order security goals.) In short, three of the top four leading goals across ten advanced Western societies prove to be economic in character.

To say that economic concerns dominate these responses is to understate the point; for the overwhelming majority of respondents in all eleven of these so-called postindustrial societies, the leading concern is *indisputably* with their economic situation. Inglehart's data, then, obviously do not contradict

---

[30]In the same vein, it is sometimes argued that job dissatisfaction is on the rise because cross-sectional survey data show that young people are less satisfied than older people. In this case, the argument of a trend can be readily rejected because job satisfaction data from earlier eras show that, even then, young people were relatively more dissatisfied (see Quinn et al., 1974, and our discussion of this source in Chapter 1). In the Inglehart case, there are no data from earlier eras that could be used in like fashion.

anything to be learned from the Gallup data reviewed above; rather, these additional data provide a confirmation of every important detail.

Inglehart, to be sure, does not claim the transformation to postmaterialism as an accomplished political fact; the postmaterialists, he acknowledges, "are heavily outnumbered" in all nations (Inglehart, 1977a, p. 38). But he does claim it to be the wave of the future. The immense materialist majorities are found mainly among older respondents, and among the very youngest, "Postmaterialists are almost as numerous." (Even here, they are still a *minority*.) For obvious reasons, then, time favors postmaterialism, and sooner or later, something approaching a postmaterial majority might well arrive.

Assuming for the moment that the age correlation bespeaks a real trend, and further, that the postmaterial values of the young will endure, we can ask an obvious question: How rapidly will this postmaterial transformation come about? For purposes of a crude calculation, we have taken the age data reported for West Germany in Inglehart's Table 2-1. The spread in postmaterialism across generational boundaries is higher in Germany than in any of the other nations, so the rate at which materialists will be replaced by postmaterialists is somewhat exaggerated by this choice. Further, we have assumed that the proportion of postmaterialists will increase *exponentially* among incoming generations. (Thus, while the proportion postmaterialist for the youngest present West German group is 22%, we assume that in the next group it will be 36%, and in the following group 49%, and so on.) Making two further favorable assumptions, that there will be *no* erosion of postmaterialism as people age and *no* further increase in life expectancies for the older materialist group, we calculate that the postmaterial majority will arrive in West Germany sometime around the year 2015. Relaxing the exceedingly optimistic assumptions that go into this calculation pushes the postmaterial arrival into the middle of the twenty-first century, and if the growth in postmaterialism among incoming generations is only linear rather than exponential, then the arrival of the postmaterial majority is postponed nearly until the twenty-second century. In the meantime, for the remainder of this century and for a goodly portion of the next, it is clearly material or "mixed" values that will occupy the center of the political stage.

For six of the nations in the study, Inglehart's data contain a measure for 1970–1971 and another measure for 1972–1973, so it is possible to look at *actual value changes* over a two or three-year period and thus, to examine directly (vs. inferentially) the principal argument of the book. (The end point of this time period comes several months *before* the Arab oil embargo of Fall 1973 and the ensuing world economic crisis, so these developments cannot be a factor in the results.) Despite Inglehart's claim of value change in a postmaterial direction, the comparison between earlier and later data (Tables 2.1 and 2.2) reveals that in 24 of 36 possible comparisons (six nations times six age groups), the proportion that is postmaterialist actually *declines* during this period, the average loss across all 36 comparisons amounting to

1.5 percentage points. Moreover, these losses are *not* concentrated among the middle-aged and old; five of the six *youngest* groups show net losses ranging from − 2 to − 6 points, and the sixth shows no change. Inglehart says nothing about this inconvenient pattern of results until Chapter 4, where data for a third time point (1976) are also presented. The pooled results for all nations (Table 4-2) show a net *loss* in postmaterialism of four percentage points among the youngest group, a net *gain* of three points among the next youngest group, a net gain of two points among the *oldest* group, and small losses everywhere else. Over the six years, then, the data reveal virtually no movement in the direction of increasing postmaterialism, contrary to the claims of the title, subtitle, and contents of *The Silent Revolution*.

Finally, although the postmaterial proportions are very low everywhere in the data, there is some reason to suspect that even the reported figures may be seriously inflated. This suspicion is aroused by the N's shown in Table 3-1, which reports the relationship between social class and value type for seven of the nations under study. Calculating the white-collar percentage of the nonfarm labor force from these N's reveals a rather anomalous pattern. First, in the United States data, the calculated percentage is 49.2%, very close to the true value in 1972 of 49.7%. No European nation has yet substantially exceeded the United States's white-collar proportion, yet the proportions calculated from Inglehart's data are 54% in France, 56% in West Germany, 57% in Belgium, 61% in Italy, and 63% in the Netherlands. None of these values is plausible. The apparent implication is that sampling errors in these five nations have created a strong bias toward middle-class respondents—exactly the respondents who (the table shows) are most likely to embrace postmaterial values. Correcting for these apparent sampling flaws would therefore drive the postmaterialist proportion even lower. (Just how sampling bias of this magnitude could creep into these surveys cannot be determined, as there is *no* discussion anywhere in the book of the sampling procedures followed.)

In sum, although Inglehart's text suggests widespread value change moving strongly toward postmaterial outlooks, his data suggest nothing of the sort. The distribution of responses to his questions at any one time shows a sizable materialistic majority; the trend data for the early 1970's in fact show no discernible trend toward increasingly postmaterialistic outlooks. As in the Gallup poll materials reviewed earlier in this chapter, the leading concern of the majority in this and most other advanced Western nations seems to revolve tightly around economic issues.

UNWARRANTED GENERALIZATION IN ANOTHER CONTEXT: A NOTE ON "BARFLY" METHODS

As we remarked in Chapter 1, there is a sharp disparity between the depicted world of the postindustrial society and the portrait of society that emerges from the intellectuals of the "little man's revolt." The former is a world of self-actualizers searching for meaning, enrichment, and spiritual fulfillment; the latter, a world of used cars, Sears Roebuck furniture, and routine factory work, where the leading problem is stretching one's weekly pay around expenses and the ever-escalating cost of living. The centrality of economic worries in the depictions of the "little man" is certainly consistent with the national survey evidence discussed in this chapter, but for the most part is not derived from it. Rather, many of the intellectuals of the little man's revolt have their own favorite method, which is sitting in working-class bars and chatting with the clientele.

There is an evident link in the minds of many literary-political critics and many of the producers of popular culture between the working class or "the common man" and the frequenting of bars and taverns. When Archie Bunker (the archetypical little man) had all he could take of Edith, he went off to Kelsey's Bar for a beer. When Edith left the show, Archie appeared as owner of a bar, this providing the new locale for the series. Possibly the most famous scene in the movie, Joe, transpired in a working-class bar. There is, it appears, a presumption that in the bars, one finds the common man in his true element—that is, drowning his sorrows in alcohol.

Much of the popular and some of the scholarly literature on the American population derives from informal interviewing done in working-class bars and taverns. The LeMasters study mentioned earlier fits this description, and the materials for Hamill's classic "Revolt of the White Lower-Middle Class" were also obtained in this fashion. Given the predominance of what could be called "barfly methodology" in the literature on the little man's revolt, it is appropriate to conclude this chapter with some remarks on the possible biases inherent in this method.

It is worth an acknowledgment at the outset that the average American is far more likely to be found in a grubby shot-and-a-beer bar than in the Stiles-Morse dining common at Yale University—of that one may be absolutely certain. Such bars are not the typical haunts of the American intellectual class, and the intellectuals who visit such places in the hopes of discerning something about how the common man is thinking are to be praised at least for making some effort to transcend the insularity of their own milieu. This aside, the barfly method nonetheless is based on several misleading assumptions that imperil the generalizability of the results.

Implicitly, the users of this method assume that the tavern clientele is somehow typical of the larger whole (for example, of the working class or the American masses). But not everybody drinks, not even every worker, and further, many of those who do drink do not drink in bars. Now, certainly, the people who choose to drink in bars do so for some reason, and this alone means that they differ (in at least one way) from everybody else. But if they differ in at least this one way, then might they not differ in many other ways? And would it not then be misleading to make inferences about the larger whole?

Fortunately, the differences between barflies and the rest of the population need not be a matter of speculation, as there is reliable national survey evidence on the topic. In four of the seven NORC General Social Surveys conducted in the 1970's, NORC asked, "How often do you go to a bar or tavern?" Compiling the results from all four surveys, the answers are shown in the following tabulation:

Almost every day	2%
Once or twice a week/ several times a month	16
About once a month/ several times a year	20
About once a year	9
Never	53
	100%

$N = 5991.$

Going no further than this simple compilation of the marginal frequencies, we already begin to sense the limitations of barfly methods. First, slightly more than *half* the adults in the country (precisely 53%, the slender *majority*) say they *never* go to a bar or tavern. And there is close to an additional one third (precisely 29%) who go so infrequently (once a month or less) that the odds on our finding them in a bar on any given evening are very slim. If we depend on barflies for our information about what the common man is thinking, our method effectively puts more than 80% of the population beyond our reach. The feelings and outlooks of this 80% will never become known to us simply because we never get a chance to talk to them. All we can know is what the remaining 20% tell us, and even this information will be strongly biased by the tiny minority of 2% who are there almost every day.

It would be odd indeed if the barfly regulars differed in no important way from those who never frequent bars and taverns; in fact, the regulars differ from the abstainers in several ways, as some additional (although simple) analysis of the NORC survey data made clear.[31] To achieve a reasonably close approximation to Hamill's "white lower-middle class," we have restricted this additional analysis to *white men* employed in *blue-collar* (or manual) occupations.[32] These restrictions leave 1235 respondents for the

[31] We thank Ms. Beth Shapiro for her assistance in preparing this analysis.

[32] Here and elsewhere throughout this volume, we use the conventional definition of blue-collar, namely, persons employed in skilled, semiskilled, unskilled, or so-called service occupations. Service workers are sometimes (although not frequently) omitted from the definition of blue-collar; our rationale for including them is spelled out in Hamilton, 1972, p. 155. The correct placement of foremen is also a matter of some dispute; in all cases, we treat them as white-collar or nonmanual (foremen, therefore, are *not* included in Table 2-1). The rationale for this is spelled out in Hamilton, 1975, p. 40ff. In our presentation, the terms working class, manual

analysis, and this subgroup (of which working-class men) can then be further divided according to how often they frequent bars and taverns. As it happens, 19% of this subsample qualify as barflies (several times a month or more), 36% qualify as irregulars (at least once a year, but no more than once a month), and the remaining 45% are abstainers (*never* going to a bar or tavern).[33] Each of these three groups can then be further sorted according to age, religion, marital status, or any other variable measured in the survey, and the ensuing comparisons across the three groups give us good information on how barflies differ from the rest of the white male working class. Selected results from this analysis are shown in Table 2.3.

The barflies turn out to be quite distinct. The barflies, when compared to the abstainers are much *less* likely to be married (54% to 81%), three times *more* likely to be separated or divorced (13% to 4%), and some three times *more* likely never to have married at all (28% to 9%).[34] Further, among the married respondents, the barflies are *more* likely to have had a prior divorce (27% to 17%). One distinctive characteristic, then, is that barflies tend disproportionally never to have married, or to have been involved in failed marriages.[35] Consistent with their marital status, the barflies also tend to be young, with an average age of 39 years versus 52 years for the abstainers. The barflies are also religiously distinct: 48% are Protestants, compared to 74% of the abstainers.

These results suggest an unavoidable conclusion: when one hangs around white working-class bars chatting with the clientele, the people one is likely to meet are young, single or divorced, non-Protestant men. The American adult population as a whole, in contrast, is predominantly nonyoung, married, and Protestant. The problems one might face in drawing conclusions about the latter on the basis of observations of the former are obvious.

Why would young, unmarried working-class men be more likely to frequent bars in the first place? One cannot be certain of this on the basis of just these data, but at least one obvious possibility suggests itself: they are looking to meet young, unmarried women. Another possibility: being both

---

workers, and blue-collar workers are treated as synonymous, and likewise the terms middle class, white-collar, and nonmanual workers.

[33]It will thus be noted that the distribution of bar-going among white working-class men is not much different than the equivalent distribution for the total population, contrary to a common presumption.

[34]In most cases, the irregulars fall about midway between the barflies and the abstainers; for economy of presentation, the results shown for the irregulars are not discussed.

[35]This is a convenient occasion to emphasize that it is usually very difficult to sort out causes and effects in cross-sectional survey data of this sort. In this case, the problem is obvious: it may be that these men drink just because their marriages have failed, and it may be that their marriages failed just because they drink; on their own, the data reported here are consistent with either interpretation.

Table 2.3. Correlates of Attendance at Bars and Taverns Among White, Blue-Collar Men[a]

	Barflies[b]	Irregulars	Abstainers
Marital status			
Married	54	76	81
Widowed	5	2	6
Divorced	9	6	3
Separated	4	2	1
Never married	28	14	9
%	99[f]	100	100
N	233	444	555
Ever divorced?[c]			
Yes	27	14	17
No	73	86	83
%	100	100	100
N	135	345	483
Religion			
Protestant	48	57	74
Catholic	35	31	20
All other	17	11	6
%	100	99	100
N	233	444	555
Average age (years)	39	39	52
Happiness[d]			
Very happy	26	30	41
Pretty happy	60	60	48
Not too happy	14	10	11
%	100	100	100
N	232	433	551
Marital happiness[e]			
Very happy	58	66	74
Pretty happy	38	32	25
Not too happy	4	2	1
%	100	100	100
N	125	337	448

[a]Source: 1974, 1975, 1977, and 1978 NORC General Social Surveys. Table includes only white, male, blue-collar respondents. Respondents with missing data on any item are dropped from the tabulation for the item.

[b]See text for category definitions.

[c]The question reads, "Have you ever been divorced or legally separated?" (asked of married respondents only).

[d]The question reads, "Taken all together, how would you say things are these days—would you say you are very happy, pretty happy, or not too happy?"

[e]The question reads, ". . . how would you describe your marriage? Would you say that your marriage is very happy, pretty happy, or not too happy?" (asked of married respondents only).

[f]Columns sometimes fail to sum to 100% because of rounding errors.

young and disproportionately unmarried, perhaps the barflies have no other regular source of camaraderie. Or, given the evidence on their marital statuses and divorce history, perhaps they have simply failed in their efforts to sustain a normal family life and hang out in bars as a substitute. Luckily, our present argument does not depend on finding out *why* barflies differ from the rest of the white male working class; that they *are* different is adequate for our purposes.

Judging from the final two questions reported in the table, the barflies differ from the rest of the population in another important way: they seem disproportionally morose. They are, for example, fifteen percentage points *less* likely than the abstainers to report that they are very happy, and among those who are married, they are some sixteen percentage points *less* likely to say that their marriages are very happy. Perhaps this is why they frequent bars in the first place, to relieve their relative unhappiness. In any case, using working-class barflies (as Hamill does) as informants on the happiness and sorrows of the larger American population would apparently give one a rather jaundiced view.

Judging from these latter results, if one were looking to find some good material on the alienation and anger of the white lower-middle class, on the discontents of the little man, a white working-class bar would be just the thing, for that appears to be just where the angry young workers prefer to congregate. The older workers, the successfully married workers, the happier and more satisfied workers, will, of course, tend to be missed. They are not at the bars, but presumably at home with their families, and to achieve a representative portrait, that is where one would have to go to find them. If one is interested in dramatic interviews that will sustain an a priori conclusion, the barfly methodology turns out to be quite convenient. As a means of knowing the outlooks and consciousness of the population as a whole, it is evidently heavily biased.

CONCLUSION

The apparent anomaly noted at the outset of this chapter—sharply conflicting social portraiture, all said to be supported in one way or another by relevant evidence—turns out not to be anomalous at all. Beneath the assorted claims and assertions, the actual evidence available on the American population gives a very consistent portrait. To summarize a few of the key *substantive* themes, ones documented and stressed in all subsequent chapters of this work, this evidence shows a population for whom economic concerns are paramount, among whom satisfaction with work is widespread. Claimants to the contrary can be sorted into the following categories:

First are those with no evidence at all, or at best very biased and exceptional evidence, of whom Reich is the prime example. The key problem with "visionary" works of this sort is that they are free and unconstrained: they make a good read and may seem profound and insightful to an uncritical reader, but they transmit no useful information about the American masses. They are best treated as works of imagination.

Then there are those who are openly hostile to evidence, or, more commonly, hostile to evidence that runs against the fundamental axioms of their world view. Many of the workplace critics fall into this category: they readily adopt and cite, very uncritically, any study that fits into their conclusions, and either ignore, selectively misrepresent, or ridicule all others. They have adopted the vocabulary of the social sciences, referring often to many researchers or dozens of recent studies, even as they resist, or reject, the substance of the work done in these fields. Their use of this vocabulary is purely rhetorical. Their effort is to persuade, not to inform.

A third category consists of the people who make some genuine effort to gather independent evidence, and thus to transcend the limitations of their own existence, but who, in the process, rely on manifestly atypical and nonrepresentative sources. Here we would include the barfly methodologists and participant observers in general. One can, to be sure, hear much of interest in working-class bars or, for that matter, in Yale dining halls, and much of what one hears may be "corrective" to the a priori world view, and therefore useful. But there is no guarantee that what one hears is representative of the voice of the American masses.

In the final and most egregious case, the claimant possesses good, reliable, nationally representative evidence, but either hides or distorts the relevant findings in the course of the presentation. The 1969 Survey of Working Conditions used by Sheppard and Herrick, for example, was the very best evidence available at the time on the job outlooks of the American working population, and it would be foolish indeed to have written a book about work in America and not to have been aware of the existence and findings of that survey. In like fashion, the Gallup polls analyzed by Scammon and Wattenberg contain the best available evidence for the 1960's on the leading concerns of the American population, and any serious book on the real majority would be obliged to take those data into account. But in each of these cases, there is an obvious, at times rather strained, attempt to advance conclusions that are sharply undercut by the source data. In some cases, such as that of Sheppard and Herrick, the divergence between evidence and conclusion is apparent in the published tables; in other cases, the divergence is unclear only because the appropriate percentages are not reported. These, in sum, are cases of survey abuse: the surveys under discussion contain information that supports conclusions very much different from the ones being put forward.

A principal conceit of the intellectuals of this or any other age is the belief that we are now at the edge of a turning point in history, that the future will be very much different from the past. In many of the cases discussed in this chapter, this turning point involves a Great Transformation in the agenda of human concern. The actual evidence—from Gallup and from Inglehart—suggests, in sharp contrast, that the thing people worry most about these days is much the same as the predominant concern of the species ever since it evolved on the planet—namely, a concern with personal or family welfare, concern with the material conditions of existence. Any account of the human condition must obviously begin with some assessment of what people are concerned with, what matters to them most, and so the apparent dominance of economic concerns revealed in the materials reviewed here clearly warrants a more extended inquiry. That, it so happens, is the topic of the following chapter.

3 THE PERSISTENCE OF TRADITIONAL GOALS AND CONCERNS

Several of the theoretical portraits reviewed in Chapter 1 depict a transformation in the goals and concerns of the American population. In order to assess some of these depictions, it is important, at the outset, to define key terms. A brief exposition of the basic substantive findings reported should also prove useful.

By goals we are referring to people's life aims, to those things, states, or conditions they would like to achieve or maintain. The leading goal for most of the population, as will be seen, involves marriage and/or family, the focus, clearly, being the achievement (or maintenance) of some unique, highly valued social relationships. Two very closely related such goals, for most of the population, are the economic well being and good health of family members.

With the term "concern," we are referring to some sensed problem, some area in which the achievement of life goals have been less than optimal. Although a priori, one could find achievement failures in any area, the leading concerns expressed by most of the adult population of the United States, involve those instrumental goals, the economic well being and health of the family.

The intellectual orientation appearing in this and the following chapters may best be described as involving a "sociology of everyday life." This position is not to be found explicitly stated in the scholarly literature. It does not have a widely accepted name, nor is it readily identified with any prominent theorists of this or any other recent decade. Although lacking illustrious antecedents, this position has one significant advantage in that, as will be seen, it is consonant with the results of the best available surveys of the American adult population. In this respect it differs from most of the positions reviewed and criticized in the previous chapters.[1]

[1]The position is not entirely lacking in antecedents. Some elements of the position advanced here may be found in the election studies of the Columbia "school" done in the 1940's and early 1950's (see especially Berelson, Lazarsfeld, and McPhee, 1954, Chapter 6, and, for further discussion, Hamilton, 1972, Chapter 2). Other elements are found scattered here and there in works of sociology and in

Our analysis begins with the assumption that simple, ordinary, everyday, commonplace routines provide the framework for most people's lives. More specifically, most people's lives are contained within the routines provided by the family, the job, and a diverse array of free-time activities. Although for some, especially for the world's "advanced" intellectuals, the notion of a routine has negative connotations, for the general population the everyday round of activity comes to be viewed rather positively.[2]

The family is the focal point of most people's lives. Much love and affection appear within its routines. And, not too surprisingly, most people put family well ahead of all other considerations when ranking their priorities in life. The predominant concern with the family may be said to form the heart and core of the position to be developed here; it is the beginning point from which all else flows. It is in this connection, primarily, that we refer to the persistence of traditional goals and concerns. (For additional evidence on this point see Bane, 1976, and Caplow, Bahr et al., 1982.)

Any sweeping statement about the centrality of the family necessarily oversimplifies somewhat, since the family is not a constant over the life cycle. Originally, the focus would be on one's parents and siblings, then on one's spouse and children, and finally, with widowhood, the focus would be, almost exclusively, on one's children and grandchildren. At any point along the way an assortment of aunts, uncles, cousins, etc., might also be included. This shifting focus should be kept in mind in the subsequent discussion; when speaking of the family, unless otherwise indicated, we are making use of this larger, more extended meaning.

The most frequently expressed concern is one best described with the colloquial phrase, "making ends meet." It is difficult to arrive at a definitive estimate of the size of this problem, since different question wordings can produce dramatically different results. A useful baseline estimate, however, can be made through use of an open-ended question, one asking about the "most important personal problem." In the 1970's, in ordinary times, economic problems were mentioned by just over two fifths of the respondents. In a period of economic downswing, in 1974, the proportion citing economic problems rose to just over one half. To that extent, then, one may say the affluent society has arrived. If one imagined (since the appropriate data are not available) that the not-so-good old days were characterized by

---

those of social psychology. We think too that most of the elements of the position outlined in the following pages will be found in the consciousness of the average American.

The expression "sociology of everyday life" has, to be sure, been used with different meanings by several other sociologists.

[2]This point will be considered in more detail later in this chapter and in Chapter 4. For a valuable summary portrait of "domain satisfactions" by age, see Campbell, Converse, and Rodgers, pp. 152–153, or Campbell's more recent work, 1981, 39ff. Satisfaction with most areas of life increases dramatically with age; the most dramatic change, however, involves health, which, not surprisingly, tends to decline sharply with every additional decade of life.

an omnipresent mass concern with economic problems, this fluctuation between two fifths in the best years of the 1970's and roughly one half at the worst point may be counted as indicating substantial progress.

Many commentators, as we have seen, evidently assume that economic problems have declined even more sharply, some apparently adjudging the problem to be not worthy of mention. It seems likely, however, that one is dealing with a sliding scale of demands; wants show *some tendency* to escalate upward such that economic problems remain, if not a persistent mass focus, at least the most frequent source of complaint. (That tendency toward upward movement—as opposed to the claim of unbounded appetites—will be considered in Chapter 7.) Although the primary area of concern remains the same, some compelling evidence will be presented (also in Chapter 7) suggesting a change in the salience of the problem. The economic problem, it would appear, is not the burden it once was for the population as a whole.

Good health, one's own and that of one's family, is also a highly valued goal, this too being a rather traditional aspiration. In response to a direct question on the importance of being in good health and in good physical condition, this goal proved even more of a consensus choice than a happy marriage. Some, a small minority of 4%, rated a happy marriage as not at all important, but only a trivial two tenths of a percent felt the same way about health. Some people, clearly, do reject the dominant marriage-and-family syndrome (hence our use of the qualifying phrase, "for most people," in the previous discussion), but few take an otherwordly stance in regard to physical well being.

Unexpectedly little concern is indicated with respect to health. Only a small minority, for example, listed health as their number one priority in life. Health did appear, however, as the most frequently mentioned second priority, three in ten making that choice (see Table 3.1). Most people, it seems, take good health for granted. The percentages reporting a concern in this area understandably increase with age as health becomes ever more problematic. Some available data indicate that the concern with health has diminished in recent decades. The 1954 Stouffer study found one quarter of the respondents expressing some health worries. In the 1970's, a somewhat different question asking about the most important personal problem found health worries indicated by only one respondent in twelve. A more closely equivalent question, actually a series asking for a listing of three personal problems, found only one respondent in eight indicating a health worry. This might well result from the reduction in the average age of the adult population occurring between the 1950's and the 1970's. Or, possibly, it might stem from the extension of medical insurance coverage, programs that would have made the delivery of medical services more widely available.

In summary, then, we are arguing that the family (taken broadly) is the highest priority goal in most people's lives and that problems connected with family welfare are the most frequently mentioned concerns indicated by adult Americans. The choice of the family as the principal life goal, of course, is a very traditional one. And the related concern with family welfare is also eminently traditional. In respect to the family-as-goal, the vast majority of the American population appears to be little different from any other, either from those living now or from those of times past. It is likely that the "family welfare" problem has eased considerably; a large part of the population, majorities in good times, mention *no* problems in this area, and many who do report economic problems also say that they are not pressing concerns.

Another change involves the concern with health, mentions of such problems having declined considerably in recent decades. It would, how-ever, be a mistake to simply extrapolate that trend into the future, since a reversal of the pattern seems more likely. The ineluctable aging of the adult population which will occur over the next few decades makes it most likely that health anxieties will once again appear as a frequently mentioned and highly salient concern for the aging respondents themselves and, indirectly, for their children.

A job, particularly the job of the family's primary earner, has an obvious instrumental link to the family's welfare. Not too surprisingly, the income provided by that job proves to be of central importance in the evaluation of its desirability (see Chapter 6). It would be a mistake, however, despite this strong instrumental orientation, to see the job as no more than a means to an end. Most people say they would continue working even if they were relieved of the financial necessity. Thus, most people find something positive about their work—even as it is structured in "advanced capitalist society."

Leisure-time activities, to be sure, are not sharply differentiated from the family sphere. Many are shared with one or more family members, that is, in eating, watching television, playing together, or in sexual relations. Also under this heading, something frequently overlooked, are religious activities, no small matter for many Americans, as well as the more individual activities: artistic creation, hobbies, reading, and, for some, political efforts. These activities, which presumably would figure prominently among the "new" values of self-fulfillment, prove to be of primary importance for only a small minority of the nation's adults. All activities in this general area are outweighed by the dominant choice of the family as a life goal and by the closely related instrumental concerns, by the problems involved in assuring that family's welfare and betterment.

This chapter reviews evidence relevant to the claims just made about people's principal life interests and concerns. In Chapter 4, we review the evidence with respect to satisfaction or dissatisfaction in *all* major areas of life, that is, without regard to the question of priorities. Although the two foci, life goals and satisfaction (or dissatisfaction) with the achievement of those goals, involve separate analytic questions, the relationship is so close that a brief preview of those later findings proves useful.

Most people reported high levels of satisfaction with their marriage and family life, a finding that stands in marked contrast to the claims of a decline in the family, ones supported by the "indubitable" evidence of soaring divorce rates. But divorce, although on the increase, is still an exceptional experience, touching only a small minority of the population. Most people, as already indicated, also made some kind of positive assessment of their jobs. And it will come as little surprise to learn that most people liked what they did in their leisure hours. It may come as a surprise to learn that most people made very positive judgments about their neighborhoods and their local communities, despite the frequent claims about communities falling apart or in disarray. Little change was indicated in any of these assessments in the course of the decade; that is to say, there were no significant trends to indicate support for the pessimistic conclusions.

Not everyone, to be sure, was happy and satisfied. In each of the areas just mentioned, some dissatisfied minorities did appear. The characteristics of those groups will be discussed in due course, along with some consideration of the grounds for their dissatisfaction (see especially Chapter 5).

There is one important area in which dissatisfaction is now widespread— with respect to the government in Washington, D.C. This dissatisfaction, as will be seen in Chapter 8, is linked to some obvious concrete political developments.

The national surveys of the American population analyzed here, in short, yield a very different portrait of the American population, of their goals, concerns, and satisfactions, from the one we would expect based on a reading of the literature reviewed in our first chapter. Except for the work researchers and for one key proposition in the little man thesis, none of the basic positions outlined in Chapter 1 gains support in these studies. Although those positions provide a poor guide to the dominant tendencies of the American population, there were, however, some contexts in which those claims were supported. The commentators, basically, had drawn general conclusions from atypical minority experiences. Such errors indicate the need for more differentiated, more finely specified social portraiture. Since the popular judgments were not all of a piece, the broad brush techniques used by some of the commentators cannot provide an accurate picture. At the heart of such specification, obviously, is the need for attention to questions of number, of quantity.[3]

We do not wish to suggest that these current judgments about family life, job, leisure-time activities, community, and nation provide a last word, some final or definitive truth on the subject. Nor do we mean to suggest that people are always right when they make the judgments they do. It might well be that

[3]Alfred North Whitehead, the noted philosopher, observed: ". . . the world is infected with quantity. To talk sense, is to talk in quantities. It is no use saying that the nation is large,—How large? It is no use saying that radium is scarce,—How scarce? You cannot evade quantity" (Whitehead, p. 11). Some people do attempt to "evade" quantity; that is practically the hallmark of the so-called critical analysis with its claim of growing dissatisfaction or unrest. Our question: How much growth?

the ultimate disaster is just around the corner; it might be that the masses are doped up (or "narcoticized," a favorite word among critical intellectuals). They might well have a false consciousness of their condition. In the first line of analysis, however, our intent is to show what people actually say about their situation. We will, at this point in the discussion, be making a simple, straightforward exposition of some relevant evidence on the subject.

We do, nevertheless, think there is a logic or rationale to the assessments people make, which are largely a function of their previous training, of their past experience. In this sense they are very definitely situational or relative judgments. It makes sense (that is to say, it helps to understand them) if one were to see those judgments from that perspective. It certainly makes more sense than the adoption of some distant, ultimate, *sub specie aeternitatis* (in the light of eternity) standard, the kind adopted by many self-declared critical intellectuals. Most people, we think, make use of those more limited frames of analysis and assessment. The intellectuals' standards, while possessing perhaps a wonderful and compelling philosophical elegance, will be peculiarly irrelevant for those persons who never had contact with such measures, who never learned them, and who, perhaps, are not in a position to pay the costs they might entail.[4]

Given the volume of claims about people's priorities and, more specifically, about recent *changes* in life goals, it is surprising that so little effort has been expended to discover the actual distribution of their preferences. The Survey Research Center's Quality of American Life Study, conducted in 1971, is one of the few to have undertaken that task. Respondents were given a list of twelve life goals and asked to rate them in terms of their importance.

[4]It is important to keep in mind the specific question being addressed. There are three likely possibilities in this area. One can ask: What do people say? Or one can ask: What would they say if they had a clear understanding of their condition? This question assumes some mechanism or procedure for removing the effects of false consciousness. And still another possibility is: What should people by saying? These are three separate and distinct questions. Any mixing of them can only cause confusion. The claims cited in the previous chapters, those we are challenging, make literal empirical assertions; that is to say, they purport to be answering the first kind of question. Our work, as will be seen, argues, with evidence, that the critical commentators are mistaken in a number of their key assertions, about both the dominant tendencies and the trends.

Once challenged on this ground, some people shift from the first to the second kind of question—"But that is just false consciousness!" But if that is the real argument being made, it should have been put forth (and justified) in the first line of analysis rather than as a fallback position on exposure of the original claim.

As for the question of false consciousness, we prefer to keep an open mind on the subject. It might be the case that the general population is mistaken in assessing their own satisfaction with life, family, work, and community. Or, it might be the critical intellectuals who are mistaken, who, to use their term, are narcoticized. We are inclined to the latter view and, indeed, will argue that case at some length, beginning with the next paragraph of the text. The intellectual's claim of widespread popular dissatisfaction when just the opposite happens to be the case indicates some initial support for our belief.

They were then asked to indicate their first and second priorities on the list. And, finally, they were asked how much satisfaction and dissatisfaction (two questions) they gained from each of these areas of their lives.[5] The list contained all the topics discussed in the previous pages plus a range of other possibilities not yet considered. Marriage and family were there, along with good health. An interesting job was one of the possibilities, and, allowing for the expression of materialist sentiments, the list also included a large bank account as one of the life goals.

For our purposes, the first- and second-place rankings of priorities are the most useful. They tell us which goals are at the center of people's lives and which, though important, tend to be of peripheral interest. Beginning with the first-place rankings, one finds a happy marriage to be the most frequent choice, chosen by two out of five respondents (Table 3.1). The second most frequent choice, rather unexpectedly, was a good country to live in: a country with a good government, chosen by 16% of the total. Then, following closely, was the concern with a good family life—having family members you can enjoy being with. No other option was chosen by more than one respondent in twelve. The job option was a relatively infrequent choice with only 7% of the respondents putting their work above the eleven other possibilities. Only 4% chose the large bank account (see Table 3.1, bottom line).

Given our initial assumption that the family is the center of most people's lives, the finding of only 54% mentioning either marriage or the family as their first concern comes as something of a surprise. One explanation of this unexpectedly low figure appears when we consider the second-place priorities.

A large portion of those making some other first choice (for example, those choosing a good country, or an interesting job, or a good apartment or house) put either a happy marriage or a good family life as their second-place preference. Some people put the large bank account ahead of the happy marriage and some others put their hobbies ahead of marriage. In both of these latter cases, however, one is dealing with only minute fractions of the total.

[5]The specific question reported here reads as follows: Q. J2. "Now would you look back over this list and tell me which two things are *most* important of all to you personally. Just give me the letters of the two most important things." The options were: (A) A house or apartment that you like to live in, (B) A city or place where you like to live, (C) A good country to live in: A country with a good government, (D) An interesting job, (E) A large bank account, so that you don't have to worry about money, (F) Things you like to do when you are not working—hobbies and things like that, (G) Organizations you want to belong to, (H) A happy marriage, (I) A good family life—having family members you can enjoy being with, (J) Having good friends, and the right number of friends, (K) Being in good health and in good physical condition, (L) Having a strong religious faith.

The results in Table 3.1 omit those who did not respond to this question, thus reducing the N from 2164 to 1975. There were 179 respondents who did not indicate any priorities; ten indicated only a first priority.

Table 3.1. First and Second Life Goals[a]

Second goal	First goal								Total
	Happy marriage	Good country	Family	House, apartment	Job	Health	Bank account	All others	
Health	30%	17%	58%	19%	18%	—	40%	44%	30%
Religion	29	9	32	5	2	74	6	7	23
Family	36	26	—	14	17	6	21	10	22
Marriage	—	38	1	31	49	8	27	24	5
Friends	3	3	9	2	8	—	4	2	4
All other	1	7	1	29	6	11	2	13	6
	99%	100%	101%	100%	100%	99%	100%	100%	100%
N =	(791)	(306)	(285)	(148)	(142)	(97)	(82)	(124)	(1975)
	40%	16%	14%	8%	7%	5%	4%	6%	100%

[a]This table is based on the *unweighted* sample. The 1981 SRC Quality of American Life survey "picked up" slightly more women respondents than it "should" have, given the known sex ratio of the population; the recommended weights are to correct for this bias. We have run the same table on the weighted sample and get identical results, the largest difference between weighted and unweighted versions amounting to eight tenths of a percentage point.

116

Many people, understandably, reported marriage and the family as their respective first and second choices. Only a tiny number reversed that procedure, putting the good family life in the first place. Some of these cited a happy marriage as their second option, but most of them, instead, gave health (58%) or religious faith (32%) as their second choices. There is a simple explanation for this. A large number of persons making this combination of choices were widows and widowers. They, it seems, viewed marriage as something that was now behind them, as no longer a realistic choice. These persons, in short, appear to have shifted (or displaced) their interests in another direction.

Two other combinations are of special relevance in this connection. Some people gave good health and religious faith as their first and second choices. And another, somewhat smaller group, gave good friends and good health as their leading priorities. Here too, it is a question of widows and, to a lesser extent, widowers. These are persons who have suffered two fateful blows; their marriages are in the past, and they have either limited family ties or no families at all. Not all widows and widowers displace their goals in these specific directions. Many of them are to be found elsewhere in the table, among those, for example, choosing their house or apartment, their community, the country, or their job as a first priority and their health as second.[6] For some persons in the sample, then, the choice of marriage and/or family as prime personal goals was excluded by virtue of their position in the life cycle and/or by the ultimate fact of death. The actual centrality of the family, in the summary, may be seen below:

Those putting marriage or family as first priority	54%
Those putting something else first and marriage second	15%
Those putting something else first and family second	8%
Total choosing marriage and/or family as first or second priority	77%

Some people among the remaining minority could not, for reasons just indicated, make a realistic choice of marriage or family. Some of them, in short, would have chosen nonfamilial goals out of necessity, that is, for age-old reasons rooted in the human condition. And that, in turn, means

[6]In contrast to the marginal distribution for the entire sample (bottom line of Table 3.1), the priorities for widows and widowers of age 60 or more were: Happy marriage, 16%; Good country, 16%; and Family, 28% ($N = 173$). A significant amount of displacement is also found among persons 60 or over who were divorced, separated, or never married. The respective percentages for this group are: 4, 27, and 20% ($N = 55$). Not all the displacement of goals is due, however, to these elderly segments of the population. There are some other minorities, as will be seen in Chapter 5, who also reject the dominant priorities.

the number choosing nonfamilial goals for any other reason (e.g., because of old style acquisitiveness or new style self-realization) would have to be a very small part of the total.

The findings presented thus far call for some modification of our original assertion about the family as the focal point of *most people's* lives. For some people, the family can no longer be a realistic goal. And that means, effectively, that the generalization should have a qualifying conditional clause—it will be the center point among those persons for whom the family is a possible or realistic goal. Even within this restricted universe, it should be noted, one finds some people who reject the family (or rank it as a lesser priority). Some of the reasons for that rejection will be explored in Chapter 5.

Some additional observations on the ordering of priorities prove relevant to the major themes of this work. One seventh of the respondents, as already mentioned, put a good country as their first priority in life, a majority of them giving either the marriage or family options as their second. Very few people chose the good country as their second ranked concern. Those putting the country first, it would seem, formed a rather distinct set of committed patriots.

A strikingly opposite pattern appears with respect to religion ("having a strong religious faith"). Only a trivial percentage gave this as their first choice. But a sizable number, more than one in five, chose it as a second priority. There are, it would seem, few saints (or zealots) in the population. Those with religious concerns do not match the patriots in their devotion, but many clearly have a strong secondary commitment to religion as a life goal. It will be noted that all three first-place choices—marriage, country, and family—are very traditional concerns. And the leading second-place priorities are health, religion, and, once again, the family. For all the focus on new or emerging values found in the literature, these results show a remarkable dominance of traditional concerns in the minds of the general population. [7]

---

[7]This traditionalism appears in many other sources; that is to say, it is not the product of one exceptional survey. A Louis Harris poll from the late 1960's reported the following as "The things Americans want most": Green grass and trees around me, 95%; neighbors with whom I feel comfortable, 92%; a church of my faith nearby, 86%; a first-rate shopping area nearby, 84%; a kitchen with all the modern conveniences, 84%; and, good schools nearby, 81%. Although this study examined attitudes at only one point in time, the author wrote as if he had detected major value changes, this beginning with the title: "The Real Change Has Just Begun." Some responses might suggest the appearance of new values, as, for example in the case of the 62% who wanted to be "able to do what you feel like doing when you want to do it," or the 59% who wanted "a full and relaxing time in [their] leisure (non-working life)." It is in this connection that the author announces a "marked shift away from the old ethic of continued hard work and success," with people stressing instead "a desire for peace and middle-class satisfactions." But without a trend study, without a comparison point from some earlier time, one cannot establish whether or not those attitudes are in fact something new. While that focus on freedom and

Some comment on the negative findings, on those claims that do not gain support, is in order. Despite the many assertions about the enormous salience of the job, despite the claims about widespread demands for interesting work, that option—an interesting job—is given as a first-place choice by only 7% of the sample and as a second choice by a mere 2%. This pattern is, of course, consistent with the long tradition of research on central life interests that was reviewed in Chapter 1. For some, the ailing, the retired, and the aged, a job is no longer a realistic goal. There is, nevertheless, an awesome gap between what some commentators would have us believe and the judgments summarized here.

A similar modest interest, despite continuously recurring claims about American materialism, appears with respect to the large bank account. Still another much-discussed goal, that of self-realization, does not appear to generate much interest. If one takes the "things you like to do when you're not working—hobbies and things like that," as indicative of this concern, it is an option chosen by less than 2% of the population as either a first or second choice.

It is difficult to assess the fulfillment claims given the lack of precisely defined referents. The focus on "a house or apartment that you like to live in" might be counted as indicative of a new demand for self-actualization. It might, however, be indicative of more traditional concerns, such as the well being of one's family (marriage and family being frequent second-place choices), or, possibly, it might reflect traditional acquisitiveness. In any event, that concern was mentioned about as frequently as the job for the first place ranking and by four *persons* as a second option. All of these nonfamily areas, the job, the bank account, the hobbies, and the home, prove to be of very limited interest, at least as first and second priorities, to the American population. It is hardly the stuff upon which to base theories of "world-historical" import.

These assessments, it will be noted, were given at one point in time, in the summer of 1971; they cannot, therefore, provide the basis for a judgment of trends. Further, the items in question were dropped in the 1978 version of the survey. The only directly warranted conclusion is that the focus on marriage and family as central life goals was very considerable at that time. For some respondents, it will be remembered, marriage and the family are unrealistic options. The proportion making one or another or both of those choices among those for whom marriage and family are realistic options must be even greater than the 77% figure given above. This account then, to summarize briefly, indicates that as of 1971, the American adult population was very traditional in its choice of life goals.

---

leisure could suggest a desire for new life-styles, that possibility does not seem likely in view of the stress on green grass and trees, good neighbors, and an appropriate church. New life-styles seem especially unlikely in view of another result in this study: 78% agreed with the statement that "traditional values are being torn down, and that's bad." See Hooper, 1970.

In the previous pages we have examined people's main priorities, their principal goals in life. Those goals, presumably, give direction to their lives and therefore help us to understand much of their behavior. A knowledge of those goals, however, gives only a partial account of their situation or condition. A second dimension requiring our attention is the degree or extent of satisfaction they feel with respect to the achievement of those goals.

A respondent might indicate marriage and family as prime life goals, and might also indicate a high state of satisfaction with respect to both. Such might imply a Nirvana-like state of equilibrium so that, if asked, the person would have little incentive to try to change his or her condition. Even if some dissatisfaction were registered, that still might not lead to a public complaint or to a demand for political intervention, the problem being seen as a personal one, something to be worked out by the individuals directly involved. In another scenario, one might find high levels of satisfaction indicated with respect to one's marriage and/or family, but at the same time, dissatisfaction might be voiced with regard to the family's welfare; they might have difficulty making ends meet. And that could give rise to the expression of some political demands.

To get some sense of the kinds of things that could move people, we turn now to a consideration of their expressed concerns. By a concern we are referring to a felt or sensed problem.[8] Concerns, obviously, are closely related to goals, the presence of a concern ordinarily indicating some inability or impediment to the realization of a goal. In addition to giving some indication of the pressure points within a society, this discussion, as will be seen, also serves to reinforce the conclusions made with respect to the persistence of traditional goals. This discussion, moreover, provides some evidence relevant to the themes considered in the first chapter. Specifically, it tells us whether people in general are now concerned with some higher level needs, whether the social issue has replaced the concerns felt in a previous era, or whether the quality of one's work has now become the dominant problem in contemporary life. Still another possibility, one receiving little attention in those works focused on "the new," is that the more prosaic bread-and-butter concerns that have occupied most people's attention throughout human history are still the ones most frequently cited.

The ideal question for this purpose is an open-ended one, a question that leaves it for the respondent, without any clues or guidance, to fill in some kind of answer. One of the first uses of an open-ended question for this purpose appeared in an important study undertaken by Samuel A. Stouffer (1955) in the early 1950's. Early in the interview, the following question

---

[8]It is easy to assume that concerns are more or less automatically transformed into political issues. But that, as will be seen, is not necessarily the case. Some concerns are difficult to treat politically (e.g., marital discord, generational conflict). In some instances, political parties are reluctant to "pick up" felt problems and make them issues in a campaign. For discussion of the latter possibility, see Hamilton, 1972, pp. 1–21, 83–84.

was posed: "What kinds of things do you worry most about?"[9] Stouffer summarized the responses as follows:

> The big, overwhelming response to the question . . . was in terms of personal and family problems. Eighty percent of the men and women in the cross-section answered *solely* in these terms. And many of the remainder answered in the same terms but went on to express anxiety about other problems. Ten percent professed no worries about any problems.

The study was one conducted toward the end of the so-called McCarthy period. One of its most striking findings was the *lack* of concern over domestic communism. "The number of people," Stouffer reported, "who said that they were worried either about the threat of Communists in the United States or about civil liberties was, even by the most generous interpretation of occasionally ambiguous responses, *less than 1%*" The concerns expressed in newspaper headlines and editorial comment, it would seem, provided a very inadequate index to the felt concerns of the general public. Another indication of the dominance of immediate personal concerns over the distant "alarm" appeared in connection with foreign affairs issues. "Even world problems, including the shadow of war, did not evoke a spontaneous answer from more than 8%" (Stouffer, p. 59).

A more detailed examination of those personal and family problems proves useful. Stouffer indicated that:

> The largest single block of personal worries involved concern over personal business or family economic problems. A total of 43% volunteered anxieties in this general area. . . . The second largest block of answers was in terms of health, either of oneself or of members of the family. A total of 24% . . . mentioned health problems (including some who *also* mentioned family finances or other problems). As might be expected, a larger proportion of women than of men were in this category. Men were somewhat more likely than women to respond in terms of finances; women somewhat more likely than men to respond in terms of the health of the family, especially of the children (Stouffer, pp. 60, 62–63).

After this second block of answers came a rather general miscellaneous category, one referred to simply as "Other Personal Problems," those not easily classified in the categories of financial or health problems. Included here were marriage difficulties, fears for the future of one's children, in-law troubles, and so on (Stouffer, p. 64 ff.).

---

[9]A trivial detail: in the text of Stouffer's work, the question reads as follows: "What kind of things do you worry about most?" (p. 59). The actual question, as given in our text, is reproduced in Stouffer on p. 250.

The study is based on two multistage probability samples of the American adult population, one conducted by the American Institute of Public Opinion (the Gallup organization), the other by the National Opinion Research Center. Each study contained more than 2400 cases. The results were so similar in all respects that they were merged for purposes of analysis, the combined sample thus containing 4933 cases. Interviewing took place in May, June, and July 1954. For details, see Stouffer, pp. 15–19, 237–244.

Concerns about the larger issues of the day, about world affairs, as indicated, received spontaneous mentions from only one respondent in twelve. Many of these concerns were also seen in direct personal terms or in terms of their impact on the immediate family. "With a boy 15, I'm concerned about the war," and "I worry about the war, as I'm still in the age," and "I am worried about my grandson going to war." "The war" at that point, of course, was the Korean "police action." One respondent, sensing a new threat, said, "I hope Eisenhower won't let us get mixed up in Indo-China" (Stouffer, p. 67).

Another miscellaneous category, "Other Local and National Problems," brought comments from only 6% of the respondents. This category, incidentally, included the subject of Negro segregation. It is perhaps indicative of the obtuseness of the white population that so few saw segregation as a problem. It is perhaps indicative of the subjection of the black population that many of them also failed to report segregation as a problem (Stouffer, pp. 67–68).

In summary, then, this study indicated that as of 1954 there was a very strong minority focus on bread-and-butter concerns among the American population and, in second-place, a concern with health problems. The most frequent concerns then were, as reported earlier, with problems of welfare and health. It was also suggested that even if the focus were the same as (presumably) in former times, there was a general recognition that things had changed for the better. This expectation is supported by some of the quotations contained in Stouffer's work. A farm wife in Iowa, for example, mentioned economic problems as something worrying her. But, she added, "I don't really worry compared with how my folks did."[10]

[10]This reflects improvements in real living standards between the generations.

A second probe was contained in the Stouffer study, this question containing a leading clause: "Are there other problems you worry or are concerned about, especially political or world problems?" One half of the sample, 52%, had nothing to add. Many of the other responses, Stouffer reports, were perfunctory. For example, "Oh yes, I guess I would say I'm concerned about what's going on in world affairs." The number concerned with world affairs increased from an initial 8 to 30%. The concern with the "Communist threat" rose from less than one to "about 6%," and the concern with civil liberties rose from less than one to "about 2%" (Stouffer, p. 70).

Another kind of probe yielded a result that reinforces the original finding. Respondents were asked: "We are interested in what kind of things people talk about. Offhand, what problems do you remember discussing with your friends in the last week or so?" The results were summarized as follows:

> Personal and familial problems again headed the list, this time mentioned by 50% of the respondents. World problems, including war, were mentioned by 28%; problems of the local community, by 21%; "McCarthyism" (mostly references to the Army-McCarthy hearings) by 17%; economic problems, not personal, by 15%; other national problems, including politics, by 15%; Negro-white problems, including segregation, by 9%; and the problem of Communists in the United States, by 6% (Stouffer, pp. 70–71).

A second major 1950's-era study, that focused directly on the question of people's concerns, was undertaken by Hadley Cantril, the United States' interviews being conducted in August 1959. His principal findings were summarized as follows:

> In the United States, as in nearly all the countries studied, the major hopes and aspirations are those involved in maintaining and improving a decent, healthy family life (Cantril, p. 35).

Classifying the personal hopes of Americans, Cantril reported that economic, health, and family goals were the most frequently mentioned—65, 48, and 47%, respectively, mentioning those as desiderata (Cantril, p. 36). In response to a second question that probed specifically for fears and worries, he found the same factors listed, although this time with the order reversed, health worries coming first (56%), followed by economic problems (46%) and family problems (25%). The relatively small number of family mentions should not be taken to mean that the family was unimportant; the more likely possibility is that most people did not anticipate family problems in their lives.[11]

Another comparable inquiry was contained in a Survey Research Center Study of Mental Health (Gurin, Veroff, and Feld, 1960). The study, based on a national probability sample with interviewing in 1957, repeated Stouffer's question: "Everyone has some things he worries about more or less. What kinds of things do you worry about most" Of the sample, 10% said, "Nothing; never worry." The leading concern, mentioned by 43% was with economic and material problems. This was followed by health-related matters, mentioned by 32% of the sample. A third cluster, current family-related matters (not economic or health), was mentioned by 19% of the sample. Those results, it will be noted, are very similar to those found in the Stouffer study three years earlier[12]

These three studies give us a portrait of the 1950's, of the first postwar decade of affluence. All show two problems as dominant: concern with

---

Still another probe was made, this based on a checklist of topical items (see pp. 71–72).

[11] The procedure used by Cantril is rather complicated and not easily summarized. The key questions read (Cantril p. 23):

> All of us want certain things out of life. When you think about what really matters in your own life, what are your wishes and hopes for the future? In other words, if you imagine your future in the *best* possible light, what would your life look like then, if you are to be happy?

And,

> Now, taking the other side of the picture, what are your fears and worries about the future? In other words, if you imagine your future in the *worst* possible light, what would your life look like then?"

[12] These percentages were calculated from the study codebook, *Americans View Their Mental Health*, 1975, pp. 11 and ff. See also 39 ff. for additional supporting evidence.

one's domestic or household economic situation, and concern with one's own and/or one's family's health. How did the American population respond in later decades?

Evidence from the Gallup polls was reviewed in Chapter 2 in connection with our discussion of the Scammon-Wattenberg social issue thesis. Most of the questions in that series asked about the most important problem facing the nation today, but one, this from October 1967, asked about "urgent problems facing you and your family." This yielded results that were generally in line with those of the Stouffer study and the Survey Research Center mental health study, although two notable differences did appear. The high cost of living and related economic problems were given as the most serious concerns by 60% of the population, by far the most frequent response. This level was higher than that discovered in the previous studies. The second most frequent response involved problems of "sickness and health," these concerns being mentioned by 8%, a figure well below those of the previous studies. These changes, we think, reflect two realities: the inflationary pressures of the 1960's and the extension of medical insurance programs during the previous decade. In the 1960's, then, no less than in the 1950's, the paramount problem facing the largest share of the population continued to be the age-old concern with economic well-being.

What, then, of the 1970's, the announced decade of the "new"? What did the American population indicate as their principal concerns in this decade, when many commentators were arguing a "silent," or, in some cases, not-so-silent, revolution in value orientations and related concerns?

The 1972, 1974, and 1976 Survey Research Center's (SRC) presidential election studies allow an exploration of this question. Each contained a question similar to the one used by Stouffer some two decades earlier. It reads:

> We like to have people tell us, in their own words, what sort of problems they have to deal with in their daily lives, can you tell me what some of the problems are that you face these days in your own life?[13]

This question, it will be noted, differs from Stouffer's in that the focus is restricted to problems faced in one's own daily life. A second open-ended question dealing specifically with respondents' concerns about national and international affairs is also included in each survey. Those results are reported later in this chapter. Data for the three studies on the most frequently mentioned daily problems are shown in Table 3.2.

We begin with the 1972 study. Perhaps the most surprising result involves

[13]In 1972 and 1974, the interviewers probed for up to three mentions of personal problems; in 1976, for up to two mentions. Of those mentioning a problem, almost half mentioned only one problem; most of the rest indicated only two. In all cases, we have treated the first problem mentioned as the most important. (It should also be noted that the actual wording of the question changes slightly over the period covered in the table.)

those classified as having no problems, "everything's okay." Of the total, 17% responded in this manner. The remaining responses have been grouped into eleven categories that are relevant to the theoretical concerns of this work. Taking all references involving economic worries, one finds 43% within this general area. One specification is of some importance here. Most of these complaints were about inflation and the cost of living (e.g., "the cost of living is too high," "there's too much inflation," "my job doesn't pay enough"). Very few were concerned with unemployment, there being approximately nine references to inflation for every reference to unemployment. In addition, 6% of the respondents mentioned a health problem, either one of their own or that of a family member. Economic or health problems were mentioned by roughly one half of the respondents as their most serious problem.

When one recognizes that roughly one sixth of those asked had no problem at all and that one half mentioned economic or health problems, it is clear that all other problems, including work dissatisfaction, the broad area of social issues, or unrealized postmaterial values, were mentioned by no more than one third of the population. Since many of these other problems were not easily categorized, a more detailed discussion is useful to indicate

Table 3.2. Most Important Personal Problem[a]

Item	1972	1974	1976
No problems	17%	14%	18%
Economic	43	53	45
Inflation	38	49	—[b]
Unemployment	5	4	—[b]
Health	6	8	7
Government	8	4	—[c]
Family	6	6	4
Youth	4	3	—[b]
Other	2	3	—[b]
Self, life situation	5	2	10
Time pressures	4	2	—[c]
Job problems	2	4	9
Crime, personal safety	2	2	1
Discrimination	1	1	—[c]
Miscellaneous, other	7	4	6
	101%	100%	100%
N =	(1039)[d]	(2475)	(2346)

[a]Source: SRC Election Studies, 1972, 1974, 1976.
[b]No separate breakdown.
[c]Category no longer included.
[d]Question was only asked of half the sample.

just how little concern was voiced about any of those themes said to be dominant (or coming to be dominant) in the general population.

The largest category of these other complaints in 1972 involves failures of government, specifically performance failures. There was a wide variety here, the constituency being very diverse, one that could not easily be aggregated into an interest group or agency for political protest. The largest number of complaints concerned inadequacies of community services (transportation, garbage and snow removal, fire protection, and so on). Some had trouble with city officials, the police, or welfare workers. Others complained about the schools and the need for improvement there. A few touched on problems of pollution and the environment. This broad collection of complaint does not easily accord with the predictions of any of the recent theoretical statements. They too, would appear to represent traditional or continuing problems.

The next most frequently mentioned problem area involves the family. It is here that one would expect to find reactions to the youth revolt, to the immorality, permissiveness, drugs, exotic life styles, and so on, this cluster of problems being central to the social issue. Thirty-nine respondents in 1972, about 4% of the total, mentioned problems that could reasonably be included under this heading, but even this result could well be misleading, since 35 of the 39 appeared under the heading, "my kids give me a lot of trouble." This is certainly not a new problem. It is merely a recent manifestation of the strains that appear between some parents and some children in every age. Complaints about family cohesion and marital problems, mentioned by 2% of the total, would also seem to be among the timeless and ever-recurring difficulties. The entire area of family decline, it will be noted, is a concern for only a small minority of the population.

A life anxiety problem is mentioned by one respondent in twenty. This too is a broad category, with the anxieties stemming from different sources— from decisions facing the respondents, from the responsibilities they bear, and from questions about the direction of their lives. Also included here are concerns over the loss of close friends and relatives. Many of these problems would appear to be traditional rather than new. Time pressures were mentioned by about 4% of the respondents. The proportion concerned about "the rat race," obviously, is not large. Lacking some previous base point, it is impossible to say whether or not this is a growing problem. It is certainly not one that is widely felt.

For all the focus on work dissatisfactions, it is remarkable that only 2% of the total in 1972 gave any indication of a complaint that could fall into this category. The actual code reads: "Fulfillment, e.g., dull or uninteresting work or job (not financial . . .) . . . " This problem, certainly as a central priority, might best be described as a mini concern, that of a tiny fraction of the population.

Fears of rising crime and for one's personal safety form another component of the social issue. Again there is some evidence supporting the claim of a concern in this area, one expressed with such phrases as "I'm afraid to go out on the streets," "My family's not safe around here," and "There's so much crime, no one is safe anymore." Eighteen respondents, about 2% of the total, mentioned something that could be classified under this heading.

A final category, discrimination, is again not something new. While no doubt more widespread than is indicated in these responses (1% of the total), it was obviously not a dominant concern. In many instances the concern with discrimination would have been displaced by the more salient and more direct concern with the cost of living or employment. Taking the same problem from a different perspective, a concern with race or racial conflict was an important component of the social issue. But once again, the social issue, as defined by Scammon and Wattenberg, is felt by only a minuscule proportion of the population, at least as a leading personal problem.

Given the alarms sounded in the early 1970's about "white backlash," it comes as something of a surprise to discover that only one respondent among the 1039 expressed what might have been a racially based hatred, this being a person whose primary concern was that "they're getting it without working for it." The intense hostilities supposedly generated by school busing were also absent from the results. Although the study provided a category for anticipated references to busing, not one response fell into the category.

The miscellaneous category, 7% of the total, defies easy description. Of the total, 1% mentioned problems of immobility (" . . . can't get around like I used to," or "I'm stuck here"). Another 1% mentioned a desire to obtain more education or training. The rest mentioned, as the category itself suggests, a wide diversity of personal problems.

Summing up the lessons contained in the 1972 study, one finds that the support for the claims of the 1970's commentators is, at best, limited. If one begins with the family problems (as listed in Table 3.2) and assumes that *all* those mentions represent new strains, something that had not appeared before, then concern with the decay of the family, youth and the youth revolt, life anxieties, time pressures, work dissatisfactions, crime and personal safety, and race, would, all together, constitute less than 20% of the total. And those concerns would be far outweighed by the concerns of the respondents with more traditional problems, most especially those related to economics, health, and unresponsive government. This line of argument, however, is unrealistic, since many of those concerns would have appeared in one way or another in previous decades and centuries. Much of what has been classified there is certainly not new.

From this review one may note that the problems focused on in four of the positions discussed in Chapter 1 are *not* the problems most frequently mentioned by Americans at that time. The answers to the question, "What is wrong with life in America" provided by those commentators differ considerably from the answers given by Americans themselves.

The problems indicated among this miscellaneous 20%, moreover, are not easily classified as to political direction. Some of them may be read as favoring the reading of the critical theorists, that is, as comments challenging elements of the established social order. Most of them, however, appear to be more in line with the Scammon-Wattenberg argument; they would appear to run against the countercultural values; put somewhat differently, they would suggest protradition orientations on the part of those respondents (see also the last sentence of Note 7).

It would be a mistake to put too great an emphasis on some of these results. Differences in coding procedures could easily shift the ordering of the complaints, especially those mentioned by only small minorities of the respondents. Were one to reallocate the time pressures, for example, work dissatisfactions or family problems might be increased, since the time pressures, obviously, could be associated with either context. Even with this caution in mind, however, it should be noted that a recoding would not remove the centrality of economic problems. And the health problems, too, have a clarity about them that would not be seriously altered by a different classification system.[14]

It is of some interest to compare the results of Stouffer's 1954 study with that of the Survey Research Center from 1972; Stouffer, it will be remembered, reported that a total of 43% volunteered anxieties in the area of personal business or family economic problems. Bearing in mind the cautionary remark of the previous paragraph, plus the differences in question wordings and in the coding procedures, it is still, nevertheless, rather unexpected, some eighteen years later, to find the same percentage reporting economic problems. Many commentators, observing the general rise in affluence, have assumed (or read in) a corresponding shift in concerns, following the psychological assumptions of Abraham Maslow. This evidence, however, is best summarized with a conclusion of "no change." Specifically, that result says no change in the focus on economic problems; it says nothing about the saliency of the problem; that is, about the degree of seriousness.

What else can one say about the trends? In 1954, 10% of the respondents said they had no problems at all. By 1972, as indicated, the figure was up to 17%, suggesting that for some, at least, there was an easing of traditional strains; for a small minority, the problem—whatever it was—appears to have been removed altogether. That conclusion, as will be seen later, is somewhat misleading.

---

[14]This discussion does not by any means exhaust the analysis of the "malaise" theme. There is a considerable feeling of concern about how America is going (as will be seen below), but that is focused on other areas of life, ones at some distance from people's home base. In part, the results reported here stem from the use of the open-ended questions. A closed-ended (i.e., fixed response) question such as, Are you concerned about crime? Yes or no? always generates a greater expression of concern. But then one must ask about the significance, about the salience, of such offhand expressions. As will be seen (in the text below), the ordering of concerns is not substantially changed through the use of such questions.

In 1954, when Americans were asked what they worry about most, a total of 24% mentioned some health problem, either their own or that of some family member. The 1972 SRC study found only 6% expressing such worries. The declining concern with health was also evident in the 1967 Gallup poll discussed above and in the two later SRC studies. This could reflect a change in the age structure, the adult population having a lower average age in 1972 than in 1954. It might be that medical improvements affected the result; one 1954 respondent, for example, indicated a worry about "the polio season," a concern that would have largely disappeared by 1972. It is also likely that private health insurance programs and expanded public services would have reduced anxieties about health problems.[15]

The Survey Research Center's 1974 Congressional election study posed the same question used in 1972, once again allowing a detailed probe of personal problems and anxieties. At that point, it will be remembered, the nation was in the midst of a minor recession, a development that was clearly reflected in the responses, with the "No problem; everything's okay" category declining to 14% of the total. The concern with economic problems, not too surprisingly, showed a fair-sized increase, some ten percentage points in the span of only two years. This result, among other things, indicates the difficulty of our earlier trend statement based on comparison with the Stouffer result. That year, 1954, also was characterized by an economic decline; hence, the comparison with 1972 involves different points in the business cycle. The 1974 result, therefore, is somewhat more appropriate.[16]

[15]The Stouffer study interviewed persons aged 21 and over. The 1972 SRC study took those of 18 or over, persons who normally would have few health problems. The large groups, therefore, beginning with those born in 1947, would already be in the sample.

The declining concern with health is also indicated in the 1971 Quality of American Life survey. One of the questions asked was, "Are there some ways in which you think life in the U.S. is getting better?" (p. 59). The most frequent comment was one coded as "economic conditions—general: higher standard of living." The second most frequent category of responses was "improved health, longer life, fewer illnesses," and related themes. The coming of Medicare and Medicaid, no doubt, made a difference for two highly vulnerable segments of the population. The Survey Research Center's 1976 election study posed a question in this area: (Q.F10) "Are you currently covered by any health insurance such as Blue Cross, Medicare or Medicaid which pays for all or part of your medical costs?" Eighty-nine percent responded yes.

The Cantril study, it will be noted, has a very different result. We suspect this is due to the different question used, one that asked people to "imagine [their] future in the *worst* possible light . . . "

The percentages from 1972 contained in Table 3.2, incidentally, are based on a total of 1039 cases. We have removed those who "didn't know" or from whom no answer was ascertained (the DK's and NA's). A similar procedure was followed with the 1974 and 1976 studies.

[16]The Stouffer study was undertaken in late spring and early summer of 1954. The Korean War had wound down by then, and a readjustment was in process. Unem-

This result again suggests that the easy conclusion—rising living standards and a corresponding decline in the dominance of economic concerns—is not justified.

There is one further observation that deserves emphasis in this connection. Although one ordinarily thinks of a recession in terms of rising unemployment, an undoubted fact in this period, the increase in concern was overwhelmingly with problems of inflation, the concern with unemployment being essentially unchanged. The percentage mentioning unemployment as a primary problem, it will be noted, is below the actual unemployment rate at that time, a finding suggesting that some of those affected did not see joblessness as their most serious concern. This is not meant to belittle the problem; for the 4% mentioning it, unemployment was clearly a very serious concern, and 4% would mean some millions of individuals. But in terms of frequency of mentions, it will also be noted, the inflation problem very much outweighed unemployment as a public concern, this time by a ratio of twelve to one.[17]

---

ployment had risen, the 1954 average rate being 5.5% as opposed to 2.9% in 1953. The Consumer Price Index was up slightly, most of that reflecting a change in the price of housing. The prices of food, household appliances, fuels, and apparel, on the other hand, were all down slightly. As of mid-June, an opposite sign was reported; the stock market had climbed over the previous nine months to reach the highest level since 1929 (*Time*, June 14, 1954, p. 96).

The 1972 SRC/CPS election study conducted its second wave of interviews (where the question on personal problems was asked) in late 1972 and early 1973. The unemployment rates then were just over 5% (which was low relative to the experience of the previous eighteen months). Prices had risen rapidly between 1971 and 1972 and were still increasing. These increases, unlike those of 1954, touched all necessities: food, housing, apparel.

The 1974 election study was undertaken in the last months of that year and early in 1975. It had been a year of double-digit inflation, the price index rising from 133.1 in 1972 to 147.7. One might call it the Year of OPEC. While the Arab oil embargo actually began in October 1973, its major impact was felt in 1974, the index figure for fuel oil and coal going from 136.0 to 214.6. At the same time, unemployment was rising, the seasonally adjusted rate going from 5.2% in June 1974 to 8.2% in January 1975. Automobile sales were off 23% compared to 1973. The 1974–1975 recession was termed the worst since World War II.

These figures are taken from the appropriate volumes of the *Statistical Abstract of the United States* and the relevant issues of the *Monthly Labor Review*.

[17]There is a simple explanation for this paradoxical finding with regard to the unemployeds. Many of them were young single persons living at home; their financial needs, conceivably, were not great, the family taking care of their basic requirements. Some of the unemployeds were wives, some of them no doubt normally in part-time employment; because their husbands' earnings continued, they were not seriously affected.

The conclusions on these points about joblessness as presented here should be taken as hypothetical, hence the use of the word "suggesting" in the text. There is some room for slippage with respect to one observation in that the 4% mentioning an unemployment problem is based on a sample of the adult population, while the unemployment rate depends on a much smaller base—the labor force. More appropriate evidence is presented in Chapters 5 and 7.

If intellectuals had focused on those problems most immediately felt by the American population in the early 1970's, inflation would have been at the center of their attention. And a similar conclusion holds for political leaders; if they had been responsive to the most frequently mentioned concerns, they would have had to make inflation their number one priority.

The concern with health appears as the second most frequent problem, being mentioned by 8% in 1974, again a sharp decline from the level of the 1950's. The diverse array of all other problems has declined slightly over the two years. This was a period when the Vietnam war receded as a problem and when the memory of student and ghetto revolts was fading. It was also a period in which many intellectuals were anticipating the emergence of new needs. The anticipation and bold pronouncements actually came at a time when all other problems were being squeezed out by the more pressing economic concerns.

A precise comparison between the 1972 and 1974 results is not possible because of changes in the coding conventions. Still the much-touted new needs do not make any significant appearance, obviously being less of a factor in 1974 than in 1972. Many of these other problems appear to be familiar concerns found in the human condition since the expulsion from Eden.

In the 1976 study, the coding categories were changed again, once more making direct comparisons with the earlier years difficult. The percentage reporting no problems at all increased a few points over the 1974 result, up to 18%. And the concern over inflation, the high cost of living, and making ends meet showed a decline to 45% in 1976. This was, it will be noted, *still* the leading choice by far.

The other apparent trends between 1974 and 1976 appear to reflect the changes in coding procedures rather than real transformations in the under-lying agenda of concerns. The separate category of time pressure, for example, is dropped in 1976 (remarks along these lines now apparently being included under "self, life situation"). Mentions of job problems showed some increase, up to 9% in 1976. But this, too, is a misleading change, since "problems with unemployment," coded previously in a separate category, are included under "job problems" in 1976. (The other most frequently mentioned job problem in 1976 was job security, which would also tend to have a direct economic well-being component to it.) With due allowances for the changes in coding procedure and de facto economic trends over the decade, the prudent conclusion is thus that the concerns of the American population, by and large, were fairly stable throughout the 1970's.

The patterns reported here are by no means confined to the SRC election studies; they have been recorded in virtually every significant poll and survey done in the decade. Here, we touch briefly on two additional sources of evidence, the Roper and Gallup organizations.

Roper's version of the "concerns" question is different from those con-sidered thus far: it asks for a choice among fixed response categories rather than using an open-ended question. Respondents were also asked for two or three responses, and each response is treated equally in the coding of the marginals. Data for two Roper polls in 1974 are shown in Table 3.3. The results are so similar to those already discussed that no extended comment is needed. One may note that in 1974 "inflation and high prices" was the most frequently chosen category. Mention of all kinds of economic problems add to roughly 100%, although, given the multiple responses, that is not likely to mean everyone had such concerns. It is clear, nevertheless, that the economic problems far outdistance all others.

Some findings from Gallup are also of interest. (All the Gallup data are obtained in open-ended fashion.) In the poll for July 1977, Gallup asked, "What is the most important problem facing your family at this time" One fifth (21%) said there were no important problems presently confronting their families, and among the remainder, the top three responses, in order of mention, were economic/financial problems (56%), unemployment (6%), and illness (5%). The only clear difference between this and previous patterns, it will be noted, involves the larger percentage with *no* problems, a remarkable result given the themes of the more pessimistic commentators of the era. (See the *Gallup Opinion Index* issue of November 1977, No. 148, p. 7.)

We can round out our picture of the principal personal concerns of the American population in the 1970's with some findings reported in the 1978

Table 3.3. Concerns and Worries of the American Population[a]

"Here is a list of things people have told us they are concerned about today. Would you read over that list and then tell me which 2 or 3 you personally are most concerned about today?"

Item	January 1974	July 1974
Inflation and high prices	55%	57%
Money enough to live right and pay the bills	25	31
A recession and rising unemployment	15	13
Total, economic mentions	95%	101%
The way the courts are run	20	26
Other relations with foreign countries	18	8
Wrongdoing by elected government officials	40	34
Crime and lawlessness	30	36
Pollution of air and water	12	14
Drug abuse	24	26
The way young people think and act	11	14
The fuel and energy crisis	46	25
Getting into another war	7	7

[a]Source: Roper Polls 74-2 and 74-7. Columns sum to more than 100% because of multiple responses.

Quality of American Life survey. This survey does not contain an equivalent to the SRC item discussed above. It does ask, however, a relevant, parallel open-ended question: "If there is one thing you could change in your life that would make your life happier and more satisfying, what would that one thing be" Since a happier and more satisfying life is something that intellectuals and politicians alike are presumably interested in creating, and since these are, so far as we know, the only data available in any source that ask people directly what one thing it would take to achieve this end, the results are worth an extended discussion.

Given previous findings, it will come as no surprise that the leading response to this question was, "To be better off financially," chosen by 15%. This understates the importance of the economic issue because many of the other response categories are variants on "more money"— for example, "To own a home or buy a house," to "own a car," to "travel more," and so on. Some also indicated a hope for parents or other family members to be better off financially. Adding specifically these categories raises the total to just under 20%. As we shall see, some of the other choices also had a direct "more money" theme to them.

An important discrepancy exists between this figure and the 40–50% figures found in the studies reported above using open-ended questions to tap the personal problems. Our guess is that the discrepancy reveals something about salience; many of those who said their most important problem was financial did not consider it serious enough to require a change. Faced with this hypothetical, costless change question, some persons, 20–30% of the total, shifted their focus of concern elsewhere. This question actually invites a more wide-ranging definition of concerns (thus explaining some of the responses appearing below). The questions dealing with the most important problem focus more on the here and now.

Next to being better off financially, the second largest category, containing exactly 15% of the respondents, was, "Nothing, I am happy," similar to the proportions giving "no problems" as a response in the SRC and Gallup studies. There is little further one might say about these people, except to note that the depiction of seething discontent certainly does not describe them.

The third largest category, 13%, is made up of people who cited a wide range of family and marriage-related issues: general mentions of a better marriage, to have met one's spouse sooner, to have had more or fewer children, not to have gotten divorced, to have a deceased spouse back, to have had more time for one's family, and related mentions are representative of the entries one finds here.

A fourth category, mentioned by 12%, concerned more or better education. Given all the talk about democratization of education and, more recently, overeducation, it is interesting to note that one American adult in eight mentions more or better education as the single change that would most improve the quality of life. Concerning the themes of this work, it can be acknowledged that such a concern *might* reflect a sensed need for more personal fulfillment and self-actualization. But it *might* reflect the more traditional economic issue, the possible implication of this more and better education being the betterment of one's financial circumstances.

The next most frequent set of mentions concerned better health, either for oneself or one's parents or other family members. This was mentioned by 8%.

About 6% of the sample mentioned "to get a better job, have job security, be self-employed, do better in job" as the one thing that would most improve the quality of life. Again, some of these responses might be indicative of a desire for more meaningful and enriching work; others would almost certainly be indicative of a desire for better-paying work. Some other job responses were also present: there were 50 respondents who said simply "to get a job," 34 who wanted to have a more successful career, 15 who wanted a better job for some other family member, and 21 who wanted to be able to stop working, retire, not have to work. Given the claims reviewed in earlier chapters about hateful work and the vast increases in job discontent over the recent years, it is worth emphasizing that the 21 people who wanted above all else to be relieved entirely of the burdens of work amount to six tenths of 1% of the total sample.

The only other single category mentioned with any significant frequency concerned the wish to have had "a different personality, be a better person," chosen by 4%. The remaining responses are dispersed over a large number of categories: to be young again (22 respondents), to have had more or closer friendships (34 respondents), to have had a different physical appearance (35 respondents), to have more free time (66 respondents), to have had a stronger religious faith (83 respondents), to have lived somewhere else (69 respondents), and a wide assortment of others. This miscellany of hopes and concerns defies easy summary, but most seem indicative of very traditional outlooks, worries, or concerns. Some new values themes also appear. Concerning self-actualization, for example, some respondents *did* want to "be more accomplished in music, art, etc." There were 27 of these, eight tenths of 1%.

Obviously, given the differences in question wording, no tight comparison between these results and other data discussed earlier can be made, but the predominance of traditional goals and issues is again apparent. If one were concerned with improving the quality of American life, as many presumably are, then the four top priorities, in sequence, would have to be: making people better off financially, improving the quality of family life, expanding educational opportunities (or doing more to facilitate use of existing opportunities), and improving health. Changes in these four areas would address the principal concerns of more than three fifths of the population. (This assessment excludes those who said their lives needed no improvement.)

We have, to this juncture, considered only the responses of total samples to questions concerning important personal problems. The kinds of problems people face, however, do vary in significant ways according to age, race, and other background characteristics. To get a sense of this variability, the patterns of responses to the 1972 SRC survey are shown in Table 3.4 according to selected sociodemographic characteristics.

Of the variables considered, age proves to be most important, in that greater differences are associated with age than with any other factor. We note first that the proportion saying they have no problems tends to increase with age, contrary to a common assumption that life becomes more miserable in later years. In the same vein, the proportion mentioning an economic problem tends to decline with age, such problems being most frequent among persons under age 30. This is the precise opposite of what one would expect given the claims of Charles Reich and Ronald Inglehart, both of whom argue a decline in materialistic concerns among the young people of

Table 3.4. Distribution of Human Concerns[a]

	Nothing	Economic	Health	Work-related	Others	N
Total population	17	42	8	10	23	1039
By age						
<30	12	47	3	11	27	315
30–64	18	42	7	10	23	569
65+	25	32	19	6	18	161
By education						
<High	19	44	11	6	20	384
High school only	20	42	6	11	22	340
Some college	11	41	6	13	29	184
College graduate	12	41	4	14	30	131
By occupation						
White collar	15	44	4	15	22	311
Blue collar	18	48	3	11	20	279
Farm	39	39	15	8	0	13
Retired	24	37	15	6	17	99
Housewife	16	36	13	5	29	274
Student	9	38	3	12	38	34
By income ($)						
4,000	15	47	14	4	21	190
4– 8	17	45	8	9	21	252
8–12	18	45	5	9	23	265
12–20	17	41	6	14	22	204
20+	14	31	2	20	33	102
By race						
White	18	42	8	10	22	922
Non-White	11	41	7	8	33	117

[a]Source: 1972 SRC Presidential Election Study.

today. At the same time, however, it should be noted that economic problems were the modal (most frequent) response in all age categories. A final, rather obvious, relationship is the increasing concern with health associated with advancing age. These correlates of age will be discussed in more detail in Chapters 5 and 7.

Despite the widespread attention given in both academic and popular accounts to social class, differences by class (and race) are, on the whole, modest. Concerning education, two patterns are worth noting: first, mentions of health problems decline as education increases (this, no doubt, is merely a restatement of the age relationship, older people, on average, having much less formal education than younger people); second, mentions of the miscellaneous "other" category increase as education increases (the college educated, it appears, have rather unusual problems relative to the rest of the population).

There are no differences of note in the patterns of white-collar and blue-collar respondents, despite a common claim that this is the "most important line of cleavage" in modern industrial societies. Several differences of note are associated with income level. There is, to be sure, some falloff in economic mentions with increasing income, but the decline is *very* slight up to the $20,000 mark, beyond which it falls off more sharply. The most affluent "$20,000 and up" category, it will be noted, contains only one tenth of the population. In short, it takes a pretty advanced level of income to be liberated from economic problems in any significant way, a level achieved by only a small fraction of the population. References to work-related problems are *highest* among the most affluent; mentions of other problems are also highest there. These results help to place the Maslow-Inglehart conclusions: The high-income category is the only one in the entire table in which references to other problems exceed the mentions of economic difficulties.

The discussion to this point may be summarized as follows: The first serious empirical efforts to inquire into the personal concerns of the American population were undertaken in the 1950's, and three major surveys from that time showed that the economic well-being and health of the family unit were the most frequently mentioned concerns. A similar item was included in a Gallup poll from 1967. Economic problems were again found to be the more frequently cited personal concern. Mentions of health concerns, however, had fallen off considerably, an undoubted change from the 1950's. A review of data from five major national surveys conducted during the 1970's (the two Quality of American Life surveys and the three SRC election surveys) and from various Gallup and Roper polls again shows family financial worries to predominate by a large factor over all competitors. All credible evidence assembled over three decades thus indicates a remarkable continuity in the pattern of human concerns. The claims of sweeping changes, of "great transformations," are not supported in any of these results. The only change discovered is the decline in health worries. Even this change, we suspect, is one that will be reversed in time.

The responses discussed in the previous pages were given to questions asking about the respondent's *personal* concerns. That restriction omits an important sector of human experience, the concern with larger issues. The SRC studies, like the Gallup studies reviewed in Chapter 2, did make some inquiry here, asking, "What do you think are the most important problems facing this country?" Respondents were again asked to indicate up to three problems. Where more than one was mentioned, as was the case with the vast majority, they were asked which one they took to be the single most important problem.

The responses to this question did yield a wider, and different, range of concerns. The number one mention in 1972 was the Vietnam war, given by 20% of the total. The second most frequently mentioned item was inflation, chosen by 11%. Some 5% referred to the problem of narcotics, and another 4% pointed to crime as *the* problem. Civil rights was also mentioned by 4%; 4% chose unemployment.

A somewhat different picture appears if one groups the many references within general problem areas. If one, for example, adds to the inflation references all those mentioning price controls, taxation, the national economy, government spending, the gold outflow, control of business, tariffs, and so forth, and places them in a category of economic concerns, some 18% now fall into this larger (and more heterogeneous) category. Regrouping all possible crime mentions, one has 9%. All possible civil-rights mentions (including those of pro and anti forces as well as law-and-order mentions) yield a concern by 7% of the adult population.

It is clear that the war was the number one object of attention at that point, followed by those having some kind of economic concern. Much of the remaining definition of problems would indicate traditional, and rather "rightist," kinds of concerns, a result that is consonant with the Scammon and Wattenberg portrait (although, to be sure, differing sharply as to the frequencies). That kind of concern is countered by some liberal sentiment; that is, those seeing unemployment as a problem plus all those wishing some extension of welfare aids (whether to the aged, the poor, those needing housing, health care, education, and so on). Some 8% chose something within this cluster as the leading national problem.

One can find very little in these statements to attest to a significant demand for institutional change: there was scarcely any suggestion of a demand for liberation or fulfillment, in fact, there were few indications found anywhere of a demand for countercultural or postindustrial values. Likewise, addressing another line of critical thought, there was no indication of a seething concern with routine jobs or with the problem of degrading labor. Some indication of such problems might appear in the final category, "other problems," but then only nine *respondents* (of 1045) were classified there.

The responses to the same question in the 1974 study yield a pattern similar to that noted in Chapter 2 in our discussion of the Scammon and Wattenberg findings. With the disappearance of Vietnam as an issue, there was a resurgence of economic concerns, this being stimulated, of course, by some very real economic problems. The number of mentions of inflation had risen to 40%, by far the number one concern. Again, as with the personal concerns, it far outdistanced unemployment (mentioned by 5%). All other subjects received only minuscule attention; 2% were concerned with moral decay (only two individuals mentioned hippies as a problem). Not too surprisingly, in the aftermath of Agnew's resignation, Watergate, and Nixon's resignation, "honesty in government" came in for some attention, but even here, it was mentioned by only 2% of the total.

The only other point to be noted with respect to the 1974 result is that once again there were no serious indications of new demands—as has been announced by the self-declared critical theorists or by the harbingers of a new postindustrial world. Again one found a cluster of conventional or traditional economic liberal concerns; otherwise, the problems mentioned had a wide scatter and are best described as involving a conservative thrust. The principal demands at that point were for a containment of inflation, and, for some, adjustment of lingering welfare state issues. As for the rest, the demand was for improvements in the traditional social order.[18]

In final summary, then, it is clear that the family is the central focus or goal of most people's lives, and that this choice of a life goal is about as traditional as it could possibly be. The felt concerns or problems, not too surprisingly, are closely linked to the family's welfare, the most frequently mentioned problems involving economic welfare. Here too, obviously, one is dealing with very traditional concerns, ones that, in all likelihood, have been dominant for several millennia. The best case to be made for the change

[18]More recent data come from the Gallup poll (May 4–7, 1979). The question reads: "What do you think is the most important problem facing this country today?" "Inflation/high cost of living" was the number one problem, mentioned by 57% of the total. One third gave energy as the second most frequently mentioned choice. Unemployment was cited by only 5%, the same figure as with "dissatisfaction with government." "Moral decline" was mentioned by 4% and crime by a mere 2%. See *Gallup Opinion Index*, June 1979, No. 167, p. 7. Figures on the inflation-unemployment trend since November 1939 appear on p. 8. An independent confirmation of this point comes from the New York Times/CBS Poll; see Adam Clymer, "40% in Survey Say Inflation is Major Issue for 1980 Race," *New York Times*, October 18, 1979.

The historical time series derived from Gallup's "most important national problem" data has been reviewed in some detail by Smith (1980). The review covers the period from 1946 to 1976. Patterns for the late 1950's and the whole of the 1960's noted in this source are the same as those reported earlier in the discussion of Scammon and Wattenberg. The resurgence and eventual dominance of economic issues in 1973, following the end of American involvement in Vietnam, is also noted: "Finally, in 1973, economics emerged as the most important problem, and persists as such down to the present" (Smith, pp. 166–67).

hypothesis in this respect involves a likely decline in the salience or urgency of such problems.

From one perspective, these results do not appear at all surprising. In fact, one might easily respond with a "So what?" or with a "What else could one expect?" One trio of authors, for example, commenting on the Stouffer results (reviewed above) has written that:

> In retrospect the result seems obvious. Of course people are likely to worry about job, family, and health, but at the time it seemed somewhat surprising (Nie, Verba, and Petrocik, p. 15).

What is actually surprising is that this obvious result still has so little impact on either scholarly or popular analyses. Most of the authors reviewed in Chapter 1 have overlooked this result, assuming that it is *passé* and that new lines of analysis are needed to describe and explain the behavior of contemporary populations. Their recommendations, it would appear, are premature.

4 THE COMMUNAL TIES

In the previous chapter we described the principal life goals of the American adult population, indicating also the main areas of concern, that is, where some difficulties had been experienced in the achievement of those principal aims. In this chapter we begin a more systematic examination of the major areas of respondents' lives, focusing on the satisfaction or dissatisfaction experienced in each area. This rather extensive review serves a number of purposes. The statement of goals and the expressions of concern contained in the previous chapter provides, at best, rather oblique indications of satisfaction or dissatisfaction. This chapter, therefore, will summarize the findings of studies directly investigating this question. The account here will be more comprehensive than that of the foregoing chapter, since all respondents will be passing judgment on all appropriate areas of their lives rather than commenting only on their primary goals and their most pressing concerns.

This review will also allow some indication of the areas of equilibrium or tension in the society, areas in which one might expect either little change or significant pressure for change. It thus allows a detailed empirical assessment of the theories of malaise outlined in Chapter 1. Since some of the materials to be examined allow comparisons over time, we can also establish what trends, if any, are underway. This means that our analysis will go beyond a simple "point in time" statement to allow some assessment of change.

The present chapter will deal with the communal aspects of life. It begins with a consideration of marriage and the family, the central concern indicated in the previous chapter. It will consider then the immediate setting of most marriages and families, one's housing and neighborhood. Then, possibly reaching beyond the immediate family and neighborhood, we will consider the satisfaction or dissatisfaction with one's friendships. And finally, we will turn to the assessment of the respondent's community.

The satisfactions in all these areas, as will be seen, are generally very high. Since that finding is so contrary to the lines of critical commentary reviewed earlier (and against much common sense), we will also be paying some attention to questions of validity—that is, whether or not the responses can be taken as real. In the final pages of the chapter we will indicate some reasons for the disparity between the critical commentary, that which argues decline, disenchantment, and malaise, and the private judgments expressed by most individuals.

In Chapter 5, we explore some often overlooked factors linked to life satisfaction and happiness, some that might even be referred to as facts of life, such as marital status, sex, and age. Although many of these findings involve obvious facts, some of the linkages as will be seen, are rather unexpected.

In Chapters 6 and 7, we consider the satisfactions and dissatisfactions expressed with some instrumental matters—with the "means," work and income—required for the achievement of one's principal life goals. Contrary to the assertions of the workplace critics, a general satisfaction is indicated with respect to most work activities. Very few, as already shown in Chapter 2, report their work to be dull, routine, hateful, boring, and so on. It will come as little surprise to most of the nation's population, however, that a considerable amount of dissatisfaction was expressed with regard to the levels of current income.

Chapter 8 takes up some "distant" concerns; where the previous chapters center on the family, the immediate milieu, and immediate instrumental matters, this chapter takes up the larger problems, judgments about the state of the nation including both public and private institutions. As will be seen, this is an area in which widespread disenchantment has appeared. Few institutions of the society manage to escape the downward trend, the general loss of faith that began in the mid-1960's.

Most people, it will be seen, make positive summary judgments about their lives. And, apart from the important financial question, most indicated fairly high levels of satisfaction with all areas of their immediate circumstances. At the same time, however, there was unquestionably a growing sense of disenchantment, a sense of malaise felt with respect to the state of the nation. And those distant events cast a shadow over what, for most people, apart from money worries, was a generally satisfactory immediate personal existence.

Chapter 9 undertakes a summary review of the areas of stability and change, essentially indicating where the critics and commentators have or have not been supported. It should already be clear, given this preliminary review of the findings, that stability or continuity has been the case in most areas. Some areas effectively cannot change, or, at best, are subject to only modest alteration, this being perhaps most notably the case with respect to health. An ineluctable fact of life, for most people, is a steady decline in the condition of their health. There have been, unquestionably, some areas of life in which change has occurred. These will also be reported, together with some indication of the magnitude of such changes and some discussion of their likely implications.

MARRIAGE

Given the claims about marital breakdown, given the fact of divorce and separation in the society, one might expect many of the intact marriages to be on the verge of dissolution. When asked about the state of their marriage, respondents, presumably, should report considerable amounts of dissatisfaction and widespread unhappiness. The 1971 Survey Research Center's Quality of American Life study found very little support for that assumption (Campbell, Converse and Rodgers, 1976, pp. 322–336). People were asked to assess their marriage on a seven-point scale (Q. H.16), the number one indicating that they were completely satisfied and seven that they were completely dissatisfied. A sizable majority, 58% of the married respondents chose the first, that is, the completely satisfied option. Another 25% chose the second, the next most satisfied option. Few respondents ranked themselves at the opposite, dissatisfied extreme; less than 1% chose either of the two most dissatisfied options. Another 2% chose the fifth point on the scale, indicating a modest dissatisfaction, and 7% chose the neutral midpoint. Even when one combines the neutrals with the dissatisfieds as likely candidates for future divorce, the total still comes to only 10%. That is to say, nine out of ten marrieds expressed some degree of satisfaction with their marriage, that distribution being heavily skewed as indicated, with most declaring themselves completely satisfied.

An identical question was asked in the 1978 version of the Quality of American Life study; a comparison between the two surveys thus gives some preliminary indication of the decade-long trend. The 1978 results were as follows:

Completely satisfied			Neutral			Completely dissatisfied	
1	2	3	4	5	6	7	
56%	28	7	4	2	2	1	= 100%
							(N = 2440)

As will be seen, these results are virtually identical to the 1971 results, there being no indication whatever of increasing marital unhappiness or distress in the American adult population over the 1970's.[1]

---

[1]There is a very large research literature on marital happiness and satisfactions, its extent, correlates, causes, and consequences. Some review of this literature can be found in most introductory marriage and family textbooks. (See, for example, Clayton, 1979, Chapter 16, or Adams, 1980, pp. 308–312.) A comprehensive review of the 1960's-era studies is contained in Hicks and Platt (1970). The original analysis of the marriage and family satisfaction data from the 1971 Quality of American Life survey is in Campbell, Converse, and Rodgers, 1976, Chapter 10. Equivalent data from the NORC General Social Surveys are analyzed in Glenn and Weaver (1978). Also relevant in this connection are Caplow, Bahr et al. (1982).

A frequent reaction to findings of this kind is the assumption of response bias. The respondents, so it is said, are not giving honest answers. It is psychologically difficult, one argues, for people to confess that their marriage, something so close to the center of their existence, is in trouble or in less than satisfactory condition. What one has in such responses, so it is argued, are face-saving efforts; they are socially acceptable answers as opposed to real answers.

There are some difficulties with this argument. If it were mere face-saving, it would still be difficult to account for the choice of the *extremely* satisfied option. The seven-point scale, after all, provides an out for those wishing to save face: they have a wide range of so-so options, there being the neutral point and its immediate neighbors.

There is also some problem with that conception of the socially acceptable. Divorce is certainly not the unacceptable thing it was a generation or two back. There has been an explosion of writing devoted to the subject of family breakdown, much of that work having a solicitous character and aiming to help people pick up the pieces. This is to suggest that the changed public definition of the acceptable should allow and encourage freer expression of any doubt or complaint.

Another difficulty with this ready objection is that it misses the point of many literal assertions made by various social critics. Many of them claim that there is a clear recognition and open expression of complaints and dissatisfactions with marriage. The consciousness is there, a de facto presence, and, so they say, the expression of complaint follows with no inhibition. This objection, then, might best be seen as an instant backtrack, as a retreat from the critic's argument of actual or present true consciousness.

Another closely related difficulty appears in this connection. Perhaps without intending it, this fallback position involves a rather striking denigration of the abilities, the intellectual capacities, of the average married person. The critics are claiming that the typical spouse is either incapable of recognizing his or her true condition or is psychologically incapable of expressing genuine feelings about it. The distant critic, one is supposed to assume, is more knowledgeable about the state of tens of millions of marriages than the concerned parties themselves. One might more justifiably entertain an alternative hypothesis: that it is the critics who are psychologically incapable—unwilling or unable to accept evidence challenging their favored hypotheses.

Additional evidence attesting to the validity of the basic finding—high levels of satisfaction with marriage—appears in the responses to other questions in this study. Respondents were asked: "Have you ever wished you had married someone else?" Seventy-one percent responded with a simple (and unambiguous), "No, never." The next most frequent choice, "hardly ever," was chosen by 17%, that followed by 7% who said "once in a while." Only 4% said "sometimes" and less than 1% said "yes, often." Another question in the same series asked directly about divorce: "Has the thought of getting a divorce ever crossed your mind?'' Two thirds 68% answered "no, never," and again the next most frequent choices were "hardly ever" 21% and "once in awhile" 6%. Those saying "yes, often," or "yes, sometimes," amounted to 5% of the total, most of those opting for "sometimes."[2]

The care with which this study was conducted is indicated by the method used at this point. The three questions on marital satisfaction were printed on a card that was given to the respondent (Campbell, Converse, and Rodgers, p. 322). He or she marked the answers and returned the card. This procedure recognized the likelihood of a spouse being present at the interview and the obvious possibility of biased answers. The interviewer was instructed to note whether the spouse was in fact present at this point in the interview. Our analysis of the data showed that attitudes toward the marriage were somewhat less favorable when the spouse was *not* present.

That result would suggest a response bias, that being our first reaction on seeing the evidence. But another possibility exists that should not be overlooked. That result might very accurately reflect the reality of the situation. In a less-than-satisfactory marriage, the partners would probably not spend as much time together. At the time of the interview, the spouse would be either out of the house entirely or in another room. This result, it will be noted, is a counterpart of the unhappy barfly phenomenon noted in Chapter 2.

A series of additional questions provide further substantiation for the claims made to this point. Two ask about mutual understanding between the marriage partners (Q's H11 and H12), and a third (Q. H13) asks about companionship, the frequency with which they "do things together." The results are presented in Campbell, Converse, and Rodgers, pp. 330–331. Again, general satisfaction is very much in evidence; virtually all (90%), for

---

[2]The results presented here are calculated from the figures given in the Quality of American LIfe Codebook, 1975, pp. 157–58. The Campbell, Converse, and Rodgers volume cited in the text gives results for husbands and wives separately. The differences, on the whole were relatively small. The questions read as follows:

Q. H14. (Asked if respondent is married) "Have you ever wished you had married someone else?"

Q. H15. (If R is married) "Has the thought of getting a divorce ever crossed your mind?"

Q. H16. (If R is married) "All things considered, how satisfied are you with your marriage? Which number [on card] comes closest to how satisfied or dissatisfied you feel?"

There is a consistency to the responses, the correlations of the three "global" questions ranging from .58 to .61 (Campbell, Converse, and Rodgers, p. 322). Those correlations to be sure, are far from perfect. However, it should be remembered that two of them are retrospective, asking for a review of the entire marriage (e.g., "Have you ever . . . "), while the satisfaction question asks for an assessment of its present condition. One could, obviously, have had problems or reservations in the past but have overcome them.

example, claimed that their spouse understood them either "very well" or "fairly well."

For persons currently divorced and separated, the same questions were asked about the previous relationship. Negative comments in these circumstances were much more frequent. "The most striking feature [of the data] is the highly negative language in which divorced and separated people describe their previous marriages" (Campbell, Converse, and Rodgers, p. 332). This, incidentally, suggests something of an explanation for the generally high levels of satisfaction observed in most areas of life, with one's marriage, job, neighborhood, and so on. Most people, in encountering a dissatisfying situation, do what they can to change it. Persons with hateful jobs seek a new job, and persons with unsatisfactory marriages get divorced.

One might consider some hypothetical possibilities. Those who thought about divorce often or sometimes would probably be the most likely candidates for a marital breakup. Assuming they were all to carry through, that would mean divorce in only 5% of the marriages, a level well below those reported in much of the current literature. To arrive at a 50% divorce rate, a frequently cited figure, it would be necessary to include those who thought about divorce once in a while, those who hardly ever thought of it, plus a considerable minority of those who never gave it a thought. Putting the matter in terms of the first result reviewed above, one would have to include all those who were less than completely satisfied with their marriages plus approximately one eighth of the completely satisfied group. This would require a rather formidable assumption about the quantities of false consciousness, or face-saving, or possibly obtuseness. Many, perhaps, do not yet see the disaster facing them in the years to come. If there were a serious decline in marital satisfaction associated with age, the latter hypothesis might have some plausibility. But as it happens, marital satisfaction, generally high in all age categories, increases dramatically after age fifty (Campbell, Converse, and Rodgers, p. 153), this increase apparently being linked to the children leaving the home (e.g., Glenn, 1975b; Rollins and Cannon, 1974). Another possibility, of course, is that the estimates of divorce are seriously misleading. As will be seen below, this is in fact the case.

A marital happiness question was included in seven of the National Opinion Research Center's General Social Surveys, which were conducted in the years of 1973 to 1980. The NORC findings are in substantial agreement with the Quality of American Life study results just reviewed. In this case, respondents were asked to classify their marriages as very happy, pretty happy, or not too happy (Table 4.1). Approximately two thirds of the respondents at all points in time chose the first of those options, and approximately 3%, again at all times, chose the "not too happy" option. Making all due allowances for normal sampling variability, no trend can be observed.

The results presented to this point are based on nine high-quality national studies. As indicated, they yield a conclusion that the institution of marriage is in remarkably good shape. Respondents, on the whole, do not indicate reluctance or doubt; instead, they overwhelmingly choose the most positive descriptions provided them to describe their own marriages. A broad range of additional evidence points in the same direction as those studies reviewed here (Bane, 1976, Chapter 2; Caplow, Bahr, et al., 1982, Chapter 6).

There is an obvious problem to be considered here: How can one reconcile these results with the figures showing massive rates of marital breakup? A *New York Times* account refers to "41 percent of marriages now ending in divorce," and a later editorial declares, "Today, half of all marriages break up . . . "[3] A review of relevant evidence on the point proves useful.

As may be seen in Table 4.2, throughout the 1970's there was a fairly steady decline in the proportion of the adult population that was married. And there was also, unquestionably, an increase in the percentage of those divorced and in the percentage of those never married. The separated show a very small increase over the decade, while the widows show an equally small decline. That said, it should also be noted just how much change has occurred. In the span of nine years, the married declined by six percentage points, while the percentage of those divorced increased by 2.6 points. The latter development is, without doubt, a significant quantitative change, involving millions of persons. At the same time, however, it should also be noted that the net increase over 1970 amounts to only one fortieth of the nation's adults. As of 1979, moreover, the divorced and separated together constituted roughly one twelfth of the adult population. That still left a substantial majority of the adult population, roughly five eighths of the total, living within the institution of marriage, and they, as just seen, report high levels of satisfaction with the relationship.[4]

With the combined separated and divorced constituting only one twelfth of the total, it will be seen that the magnitude of the broken marriage problem falls well short of the 41 and 50% figures mentioned above. Part of this discrepancy may be accounted for by consideration of those who remarry; approximately one sixth of the married (or widowed) population report having been divorced at least once (this information comes from the NORC General Social Surveys).[5] This finding points up a simple fact, one

[3]The account is by Jane E. Brody, "Sociologists Plumb the Secrets of Compatibility," *New York Times*, November 14, 1978, and the editorial is from the *Times* of March 1, 1979.

[4]The NORC General Social Surveys, covering the period 1972 to 1980, also show the decline in the percentage of marrieds and an increase in the percentage of never marrieds (calculated from the 1980 *Codebook*, p. 17). The NORC surveys show higher percentages of divorced and separateds than the Census surveys, their respective figures for 1978 being 8.6% and 3.1% for the NORC surveys, 5.7% and 2.6% for the Census surveys. It is not immediately clear why this should be the case.

[5]The question may exaggerate the frequency of divorce. It reads: "Have you ever been divorced or legally separated " Some may have been legally separated but then reconciled.

Table 4.1. Marital Happiness (1973–1980) NORC General Social Surveys[a]

Question:	"Taking things all together, how would you describe your marriage? Would you say that your marriage is very happy, pretty happy, or not too happy?"

	1973	1974	1975	1976	1977	1978	1980	All
Very happy	68%	69%	67%	67%	65%	65%	68%	67%
Pretty happy	30	27	30	31	31	32	29	30
Not too happy	3	3	3	2	4	3	3	3
Total percent	101	99	100	100	100	100	100	100
Total N	(1072)	(1059)	(995)	(973)	(965)	(954)	(882)	(6900)

[a]Source: Results calculated from *General Social Surveys, 1972–1980: Cumulative Codebook,* Chicago, National Opinion Research Center, 1980, p. 102. The marital happiness question was not asked in their 1972 study.

Table 4.2. Marital Status: 1970–1979 Population 18 Years and Over[a]

	1970	1971	1972	1973	1974	1975	1976	1977	1978	1979
Married	69.6	68.8	69.2	68.8	68.1	67.1	66.4	65.4	64.5	63.6
Widowed	8.9	8.8	8.4	8.5	8.3	8.3	8.1	8.0	8.0	8.1
Divorced	3.2	3.5	3.6	3.8	4.2	4.6	4.9	5.4	5.7	5.8
Separated	2.0	2.2	2.4	2.4	2.3	2.5	2.6	2.5	2.6	2.6
Never married	16.2	16.8	16.5	16.6	17.0	17.5	18.0	18.6	19.3	20.0

[a]Source: United States Bureau of the Census, *Current Population Reports,* Series P-20. "Marital Status and Living Arrangements," March 1970 through to March 1979, published yearly. U.S. Government Printing Office, Washington, D.C.

long recognized by specialists in the field. Far from being a threat to the family, most divorces constitute little more than way stations en route to the reconstitution of what, for most, is a happier marriage (Bane, 1976; Glenn and Weaver, 1977). The relatively high rate of divorce in combination with the high rate of remarriage among the divorced provides part of the explanation for the generally happy marriages; those that *were* unhappy have been dissolved (Caplow, Bahr et al., p. 135). In the old days, with more restrictive divorce laws, one would probably have found somewhat higher levels of marital dissatisfaction. The rate of separations in the past was definitely higher than the divorce rate. (See Ogburn, 1944; Kingsley Davis, 1950, p. 20; and also Norton and Glick, 1976.) The remarriage of the divorced has long been noted and documented—e.g., by Glick, 1949; Beale, 1950; Kingsley Davis, 1950, p. 19; and more recently, by Bane, 1976; Cherlin, 1978; Norton and Glick, 1976, and by Glenn and Weaver, 1977. The dramatic rise in the divorce rate accompanies an opposite dramatic fall in the rate of separation. The increasing number of divorces does not necessarily mean an increase in the number of broken marriages; many were already broken on the occasion of the separation. The changes in divorce laws merely allowed a de jure recognition of the de facto condition.

As judged by respondents' comments, the marriage following a divorce is typically happier than the previous one. Remarried respondents, as will be seen in Chapter 5, report levels of marital satisfaction that are roughly the same as those indicated by the first-marrieds. Some researchers, however, have found that remarriages are not as enduring as first marriages and that "the probability of divorce rises with each successive marriage" (Monahan, 1952). These are, we take it, both factual conclusions and, therefore, strictly speaking, not contradictory. Small differences in divorce rates (the number of divorces per year per thousand marriages), we feel, are not likely to be reflected in the marital satisfaction reports. A very useful discussion of the trends in the divorce rate over the twentieth century is found in Caplow, Bahr et al., Chapter 6. "The divorce rate has increased during the past 15 years, but the popular belief that it has skyrocketed is as unfounded in Middletown as it is elsewhere" (p. 129).

While it would be easy to assume that the increase in the percentage never married represents the appearance of a new life-style, an examination of the appropriate long-term evidence shows that this development, by itself, represents nothing more than a return to a normal level, following a very aberrant episode in the 1950's (Glick, 1977, p. 8). This return, in part, at least, was "in the cards." Due to the structure of the cohorts then coming of age, the age at first marriage was predestined to rise.[6]

Some change in values and some corresponding changes in life-styles have undoubtedly occurred in the 1970's. Few would doubt the recent increase in both the numbers and percentage of unmarried couples living together (Clayton and Voss, 1977). And one would expect, too, given the greater freedom of the 1960's and 1970's, that more homosexual couples would be found among the never marrieds than was the case in former times (when many, sensing social pressures, would have married). But also included

---

[6]The average age at first marriage has been increasing in recent years, this of course implicit in the finding of more never marrieds (United States Bureau of the Census, 1979a, p. 1). In a period of population expansion, where every cohort is larger than its predecessor, there will, in any given year, be a larger than usual number of women who must postpone marriage. In the statistically normal case, American men marry women approximately two years younger than themselves. In the period of growth, the number of males of a given age will be smaller than the number of females two years behind them, meaning that some of the latter will have to wait. Most of those women will ultimately marry, one or two years later than would ordinarily be the case, and they will be more likely to marry someone from their own birth cohort.

In a period of population decline, each succeeding age group will be smaller than its predecessor. For the men of a given age that means there will be an insufficient number of women in the normal age category (two years younger). They must either seek wives from among their own cohort or postpone marriage, awaiting the eligibility of still younger cohorts. Another possibility, of course, would be to marrry women older than themselves, but this does not appear to be a frequent occurrence. See Norton and Glick, 1976, p. 10, and Akers, 1967, for discussions of this point, a phenomenon called the "marriage squeeze."

among the never married would be the singles still living with their parents and singles on their own (without any cohabitation), two rather conventional categories. The only difference vis-à-vis former decades, then, would be one of quantity, the percentage of those adopting new life-styles being somewhat larger, and the absolute numbers, because of the large cohorts born in the 1950's and early 1960's, being considerably larger, although still a very small part of the total.[7]

Many of these never married, obviously, would best be described as not yet married. It would be a mistake, in other words, to count the entire category, or even a majority of the category, as devoted to new life-styles. One would anticipate, again should all other things be equal, that this percentage will decline over time. Beginning with 1972, birth rates and cohort sizes fall off precipitously. Assuming a steady tendency toward marriage, then, the proportions within the adult population should change, the never married declining and the married again increasing. In the longer run, the widowed are also destined to increase.

As of 1978, the broken marriages figured with the broadest and most comprehensive definition possible, represented 20.6% of the adult population (this figure coming from the 1978 NORC General Social Survey). That includes both the married and the widowed who had been divorced at least once. If one were to add the separated, the total would be 23.7% of the adult population, or, as a percentage of the ever-married, it would come to "only" 28.0%. Although the figure is high relative to any previous time in United States history, it still, nevertheless, falls far short of the figures given above. The 28.0% figure, moreover, is unrealistic, a peculiar construct, since many of those people were not then divorced, but ex-divorced. The proportion of actual divorced and separated, as shown in the NORC study, was less than one in eight (actually 11.7%). The Bureau of the Census figures for the same year, as indicated, were even lower, coming to 8.3%. Those figures, clearly, fall well short of the estimates predicting disaster for the family.

How can one account for these discrepancies?

The highest estimates given, those claiming 50%, have a very simple origin: they rest on a false percentage. In 1978, there were 2.2 million marriages and 1.1 million divorces. If one were to turn that into a percentage, it would indeed suggest that half of all marriages end in divorce. But that figure is not based on all marriages but on the much smaller base, on those marriages formed in 1978. It is very definitely not the case that 50% of *those* marriages ended in divorce. The actual rate in that year was nowhere near that figure; the United States Bureau of the Census reported a rate of 5.1 per 1,000 population, or, a somewhat more appropriate measure, 22.0 per 1,000 married women age fifteen or more (*Current Population Reports*, series P–23, No. 84, 1979b, p. 7).[8]

[7]These questions will be discussed below in the last section of this chapter.
[8]The often-cited divorce rate of 50%, in other words, is not a rate at all, but a

Some other frequently cited divorce figures range between one third and two fifths of all marriages ending in divorce. These are, in fact, estimates calculated in much the same manner as life expectancy statistics (for a statement of the procedure, see Glick and Norton, 1973, p. 311 ff.). Since one does not know for certain the life expectancy of a typical marriage, the next best procedure is to estimate it on the basis of the most recent experience. These estimates are given by age categories, since both the reported incidence and expectation of divorce vary substantially by age. The results, in the Bureau of the Census publications, are cautiously formulated statements of the probabilities. For example, in a 1976 publication, the authors state that "One third of recent first marriages may end in divorce" (United States Bureau of the Census, 1976a, p. 4). Where this statement describes the rate for the youngest age group and is an estimate of the ultimate likely result, some accounts, dropping all caution, report the one third figure as an established, already-present fact, applying it to all marriages, not just to those of a given age category.

One can also wonder about the reliability of projections based on past experience. The basic question is whether the future will be an approximate replica of the immediate past. Given the increase in the average age at first marriage, some increase in maturity would be expected and consequently some decline in the overall divorce rate. The age-specific rates might still remain the same, but the numbers in the most vulnerable category would be dramatically reduced. The numbers in the younger categories will reduce in any case during the 1980's because of the steady decline in the size of the groups coming of age, this stemming from the reduction in the birth numbers beginning in the 1960's. Again, the age-specific rates might remain the same but, in the process, the overall divorce rate would decline.

One might also question whether the age-specific rates will remain the

---

ratio—in this case, the ratio of the number of divorces in a year to the number of marriages in the same year. Such a ratio obviously should *not* be interpreted as a percentage, although it often is.

In a time when the age structure of the population is changing, ratios of this sort tend to be misleading. To illustrate, the generation of Americans born in 1947 was the largest ever to that point, and the 1947 generation was followed by about fifteen years of very large cohorts. This phenomenon is well known as the "baby boom." In the normal course of things, the 1947 generation would have started to marry in the late 1960's and, for those marriages breaking down, divorces would appear beginning in the early and middle 1970's. In absolute numbers, then, the number of divorces occurring in any year would begin to rise, necessarily, since the groups now experiencing divorce would be the large ones of the baby-boom years. At the same time, as these divorces were occurring, the later, distinctly smaller groups would be entering the prime marriage ages. Comparing marriages to divorces in a single year would therefore be misleading, since the divorces in question would be coming out of relatively large cohorts, and the marriages out of relatively smaller ones. Note that if one defines the divorce rate as the ratio of divorces to marriages in a single year, that figure is fated to rise through nothing more mysterious than the process of cohort succession.

same. The increased frequency of cohabitation may ultimately have some impact on marital stability. Many of those arrangements eventually lead to marriage, and one might assume, all other things being equal, that those relationships would be more stable than marriages formed in a traditional courtship. Then, too, there is the greater freedom of life-styles that appeared in the last decade. Many homosexuals in the 1950's were probably led, through social pressure, perhaps, into conventional marital relationships. Many of those relationships, no doubt, would have proved unstable. In the 1970's, given the easy alternatives, those marriages would not have occurred. The same would be true of those who, for the sake of their own individualism, chose the single state (as, for example, in the case of the "swinging singles"). With these groups having opted out, the remaining marriages might be more stable than those formed in previous decades. The new life-style choices, as already indicated, are not likely to constitute a large part of the whole. But even if only 1% of the nation's adults chose these life-styles, that would constitute a much larger portion of the divorce prone group among the marrieds and have nonminuscule effects on the rates.[9]

To summarize, the best available survey evidence for the American adult population shows high and stable levels of satisfaction with marriage. The data also show an unmistakable rise in the number of divorces, although this trend is exaggerated in many popular accounts. Expressed as an absolute number, the increase in divorce seems dramatic, and certainly, for the persons involved, the trauma that results is, without question, a serious problem. Expressed as a proportion of the population, however, it is apparent that divorce touches only a small percentage, and most of those it does touch end up remarrying. The widely reported "death" of the American family, in short, is *not* sustained in any of the results shown or reviewed here.

FAMILY LIFE

A question asking about satisfaction with one's family would tap a somewhat wider range of personal experience, specifically adding the area of parent–child relationships. Following a series of questions on the number of children and the quality of the relationships with the children, both the Quality of American Life studies asked for a summary assessment:

Q. J1. "All things considered, how satisfied are you with your family life— the time you spend and the things you do with members of your family?"

Again, as with the marital satisfaction question, a seven-point scale was

[9]For a useful overview discussion and data review, see Glick, 1978. This anticipated turnaround has occurred, the 1982 divorce rate, 5.1 per thousand population, being 4% below the 1981 figure of 5.3 (taken from a *New York Times* report, March 16, 1983).

used. The responses, not too surprisingly, showed very high levels of satisfaction:

Completely satisfied			Neutral			Completely dissatisfied		
1	2	3	4	5	6	7		
1971	43%	30	13	7	3	2	1	= 99% (N = 9165)
1978	37%	32	15	9	4	2	1	= 100% (N = 3639)

Some dissatisfaction did exist, amounting to roughly one respondent in sixteen making an outright negative assessment, and another, equal size segment choosing the neutral or fifty-fifty balance point. The result provided by this summary measure is consonant with a number of other questions contained within the study, some merely reinforcing the finding, some providing additional specification or detail.

A series of questions followed this initial assessment of family relationships, asking about the *importance* of various areas of the respondent's life. People were asked about their house or apartment, the city or place where they lived, about a good country (one with a good government), about an interesting job, a large bank account, hobbies and leisure-time activities, the organizations they belong to, a happy marriage, a good family life, having good friends, good health, and finally, a strong religious faith. The results, as shown in the previous chapter, showed marriage and family as the leading choices. The next series of questions asked the respondents how much satisfaction they found in each of those areas of their lives. The responses to this second family satisfaction question closely paralleled those made to the earlier question.

One of the big themes of the critical literature is the notion of widespread generational conflict. The high levels of family satisfaction indicated here raise serious doubts about that claim. A more detailed inquiry is made possible by two questions that probed this area. Married respondents with children were asked:

Q. H27.   "Compared to most children would you say your children have given you a lot of problems, quite a few problems, only a few problems, or haven't they given you any problems at all?"

The responses sharply contradict the expectation of widespread conflict. About three tenths report no problems at all and two fifths report only a few. The 1% reporting a lot of problems and the 4 or 5% reporting quite a few problems would add up to millions of parents in the population at large, which means the problem is not trivial when seen in terms of absolute numbers. In relative terms, however, it is evident that conflict is the

	No problems	Only a few	Some	Quite a few	A lot	
1971	32%	41	22	4	1	= 100%
						(N = 7062)
1978	28%	44	22	5	1	= 100%
						(N = 2610)

exceptional experience. The slight change between 1971 and 1978 hardly supplies the basis for a claim of trends, of deterioration. It should be remembered that *some* family conflict has probably existed at all points in human history.[10]

The other side of the parent–child relationship appears in various youth studies asking children about their relationships with parents. Probably the most important of those undertaken in recent years is that done by Kent Jennings and his associates (see Jennings and Niemi, 1974). In the spring of 1965, they interviewed a national probability sample of twelfth graders chosen from ninety-seven high schools. Children living with their fathers (or with a stepfather) were asked: "How close would you say you are to your father—very close, pretty close, or not very close?" The results were: very close, 39.6%; pretty close, 47.1%; and not very close, 13.3%. Those living with a mother or stepmother were asked: "How close would you say you are to your mother?" The results in this case were: very close, 59.9%; pretty close, 35.7%; and not very close, 4.3%."[11]

The National Opinion Research Center's General Social Surveys provide confirmation of this high family satisfaction conclusion. They also allow assessment of trends over the decade of the 1970's. The NORC posed questions about a number of areas of life, the respondents being asked to indicate "how much satisfaction [they received] from that area." Here, too, seven response categories were provided, ranging from none to a very great deal, the question being taken from the Quality of American Life study (Table 4.3).

[10]Most respondents, in response to a second question, found being a father or mother had always or nearly always been enjoyable, and few had ever wished to be relieved of their parental responsibilities. See Campbell, Converse, and Rodgers p. 343, for further details.

[11]These figures are calculated from the Codebook for Jennings' "The Student-Parent Socialization Study" (obtained through the Inter-university Consortium for Political and Social Research of the University of Michigan, Ann Arbor, Michigan).

Although various popular sources continue to treat family conflict as a widespread, serious, and growing problem, the available research studies have always indicated it to be an exceptional experience. See Elkin and Westley, 1955; and Westley and Elkin, 1957. For more general reviews, see Bengtson, 1970, and Bandura and Walters, 1959. A useful and critical summary statement appears in Bandura, 1964.

The basic NORC results are very close to those just reviewed, the 1973 findings being a near-perfect match to the finding from the Quality of American Life survey. We also emphasize that, with the usual allowances for sampling variability, no significant trend for the decade is indicated. All the yearly results are within ±3 percentage points of the overall average.

The NORC General Social Surveys also contained a series of questions on sociability, these asking about the frequency of various kinds of social contacts. Included were questions about the frequency of contacts with parents, with brothers and sisters, and with relatives (otherwise unspecified). For those convinced of the corrosive effects of the mass society, these results will come as something of a surprise.

Of those with living parents, fewer than one respondent in nine reported no contact whatsoever (the question asks about spending "a social evening with . . . " the parents, relatives, and so on). At the opposite extreme, 5% see their parents almost every day, and 22% spend social evenings with them once or twice a week. That daily contact is not surprising, since some of the respondents—about 7%—are single persons still living with their parents (see Table 5.1, Chapter 5). For the remainder, however, the contact obviously involves visiting. Most specialists in marriage and family would not find this result a surprise, it being one of the commonplace findings of the

Table 4.3. Satisfaction from Family Life: 1973–1980 NORC General Social Surveys[a]

Question:	"For each area of life I am going to name, tell me the number that shows how much satisfaction you get from that area." Your family life.							
	1973	1974	1975	1976	1977	1978	1980	All
A very great deal	43%	43%	44%	39%	42%	39%	44%	42%
A great deal	31	34	33	38	33	36	34	34
Quite a bit	10	11	10	11	12	11	10	11
A fair amount	9	7	7	6	7	7	6	7
Some	3	2	2	3	3	3	2	3
A little	2	2	2	2	1	2	2	2
None	2	1	2	2	2	2	2	2
Total percent	100	100	100	101	100	100	100	101
Total N	(1493)	(1480)	(1482)	(1490)	(1521)	(1516)	(1459)	(10,441)

[a]Source: Same as Table 4.1, p. 148. This question was taken from the Survey Research Center: Quality of American Life study, Question J.3. This is a variant on the SRC's seven-point satisfaction question presented in our text, that being Question J.1.

field. Most of the effort of those specialists involves refutation of the most recent restatements of mass society verities.[12] The volume of publication in the social sciences is such, however, that many specialists must neglect fields peripheral to their principal interests, which leads to some "balkanization" of scholarly concerns. Some social scientists, and many popularizers, as a consequence, are unfamiliar with the research demonstrating the persistence of family ties and easily accept the frequently repeated claims of family breakdown.

A similar pattern appears with respect to social evenings with brothers and sisters. Approximately the same numbers have daily contact with siblings as with parents, no doubt because they are still living at home. And about the same percentage report no contact. For the rest, much contact was indicated, almost one half reporting frequencies ranging from several times a month to several times a year. A third question, on contacts with relatives, is rather open-ended in its reference. The respondents, however, clearly interpreted the question to include kin outside the immediate family, since the frequency of contact is higher than for the immediate relatives. These results all cast considerable doubt on the argument of fragmentation or breakdown found in the mass society formulations. For a large part of the American population, the family is obviously a very important and continuing reality. Instead of isolated nuclear families, the more frequent experience has a large part of one's leisure time being spent within the bounds of the family.[13]

Mass society theorists have given considerable attention to the role of occupational and geographic mobility in the corrosion of family, friendship, and community relationships. Such moves, said to be determined by the requirements of impersonal corporations, are portrayed as frequent and growing in number. While undoubtedly some mobility has its origins in corporate requirements (with many persons, of course, actively seeking such preferment), that determinant, on the whole, is of relatively minor importance. It also touches a rather narrow segment of the nation's population, some parts of the upper middle class.

The most important single source of mobility is one linked to the life cycle; that is, the move out of the parental household, which affects nearly

[12]Talcott Parsons, the eminent social theorist, for example, argued the family breakdown thesis in some speculative essays appearing in the 1950's. This stimulated the production of a number of empirical studies that either refuted or seriously qualified the original claims. See Sussman, 1959; Blumberg and Bell, 1959; Litwak, 1960a; Litwak, 1960b; Sussman and Burchinal, 1962; and Adams, 1968.

[13]One study of urban working-class families found that approximately "two-fifths of the husbands and wives in the sample had no intimate friends outside the family and kin groups" (Dotson, 1951). Some children are separated from parents by hundreds or thousands of miles. Unfortunately, we cannot test the effect of this factor with the available studies. This is to suggest that some of the infrequent contact is to be explained as a result of distance and the costs of transportation rather than as a result of indifference or lack of affection.

all members of the society. Those moves, of course, are most frequent among people in their twenties. The United States Bureau of the Census figures show 61% of those age 20 to 24 in 1978 having changed residence since 1975. The figure is even higher, 66%, for those age 25 to 29 (*Current Population Reports*, Series P–20, No. 331, 1978). This move constitutes the big break in most people's lives. For most, it actually involves a series of moves rather than a one-time effort. As we indicate below, the first move out of the parental household, typically, is to the least attractive housing option one will ever experience. But with better jobs and improvements in income, that will be followed by a series of moves to better settings. Where the mass society theorists talk of our mobile *society*, the frequency of moves falls continuously with age, from that 66% high to a 12% low among those age 75 and over.

It would be a mistake to think of these moves as ones that would necessarily break or attenuate the ties with family and friends (as in the Chicago-to-Dallas or the Indianapolis-to-Denver moves). Most of this residential movement occurs within the local community; for most people, then, the link with friends could be maintained with a brief walk or short automobile trip. The Census reports that between 1947 and 1976 more than three of every five moves occurred within the same county. They did discover a slight decline in that period, the early figures being in the high sixties, the later ones in the low sixties (*Current Population Reports*, Series P–20, No. 235, 1972, and No. 305, 1977). We suspect the most frequent out-of-county move would be to an adjacent county.

One ought to remember also the effects of special generations. The large baby boom generations of the 1950's would be in their twenties in the 1970's, and thus would be at their point of peak mobility. Given their numbers, they would make a substantial contribution to the figures on mobile Americans; in fact, their numbers have done much to establish the conclusion of increasing mobility. But in the coming decade, their contribution will drop significantly with their move ahead in the life cycle. And they will be replaced by much smaller groups coming into their years of peak mobility. For this reason, one should expect decreasing mobility in the coming decades.

Another major theme of the mass society literature involves the disappearance of the extended family, the phenomenon of three generations living under one roof. The three-generation family, it is said, was typical in the old days but has now all but disappeared from the scene. This provides yet another proof of the family breakdown thesis. It also shows the callousness and indifference of the mass society's citizenry, a favorite theme of the newspaper "sob story."

While many three-generation families were to be found in the past, there is good reason to doubt the typicality of that experience. With a relatively high age at first marriage and a relatively short life expectancy, it is obvious that the three-generation family would be both very exceptional and, where present, of very short duration. One study of a French-Canadian community in the mid-1930's, a setting in which the extended family was unquestionably valued, found that on average the firstborn grandchild spent a total of seven years under the same roof with the grandfather. The three-generation span involving the grandmother would obviously have been somewhat greater. The 1930's, however, brings us well into modern times with the longer life expectancies. Were one to push back a few decades, the duration of such three-generation family units must have been very brief; in the majority of the cases, it was probably never achieved.[14]

There is another reason for doubting the frequency of the three-generation household. Given the large family size typical of earlier times and the practice of children moving out when establishing their own family, it is clear that, ordinarily, the grandparent(s) would be present in only one of those households. If grandparents in days of yore had ten children who survived to adulthood, married, and had children, it is clear that only one of the ten could be a three-generation unit. What this means then is that the mass society theorists have "constructed" a nonexistent or rare "ideal" against which to measure contemporary experience.[15]

[14]See Miner, 1963, p. 81. The average ages at key points in the life cycle have been calculated by Paul Glick and his associates for 1890 (as reported in Schulz, 1976, p. 113). At that time, the average male married at age 26 and normally became a parent at age 27. If that pattern had been constant over generations, one would predict the following options: If that child were a girl, she would have married at age 22, when her father was 49 years old, and again the first child—the grandchild of the original parent—would appear a year later. On average, it would appear that that grandchild could have contact with the grandfather for approximately seven years. The later-born grandchildren, obviously, would have even briefer contact with the grandfather. If the first child born to that average male were a boy, he would normally marry when the father was 55, the first grandchild again typically appearing a year later. With a life expectancy of 57 years, the possibility of three generations living under one roof in this case would obviously be very limited. Although the three generations claims have typically focused on the grandfather, there is greater chance of such development in the case of a grandmother, particularly if her first child were female.

Some direct evidence of the prevalence of extended families is available for Los Angeles in 1850 (Laslett, 1975). Of the total families in the analysis, 19% were classified as extended families (Laslett, Table 1). And even this figure is higher than that recorded elsewhere in the old days (Laslett, 1972, p. 85). See also Levy, 1965.

[15]This procedure involves what may be referred to as the "prose parallel" to the baseline problem in statistics. In the latter case, one chooses an atypical base point so as to allow the proof of some claim about trends (see Holsti, 1973). Most people are very much en garde when it comes to statistical presentations, having been trained in the belief that one can prove anything with statistics. But the exact same procedure is used by mass society theorists, only in most such instances they have no base-point statistics, no evidence, and in most cases, no source. Ordinarily, all one has is an "imaginative reconstruction" of the past, what might be called a good-old-days hypothesis. Against that base line, one presents some contemporary statistic showing a decline. The lesson, then, is that one can also prove anything *without*

It is perhaps of some interest to note the results of one NORC question (1978, Q. 120) probing directly into the issue of the three-generation household. It asked: "As you know, many older people share a home with their grown children. Do you think this is generally a good idea or a bad idea?" As of 1978, roughly one half (48.6%) of the respondents considered it a bad idea. At the same time, one third of the population considered it a good idea, the rest saying that "it depends." The NORC had asked the question three times previously, beginning in 1973. In this short span, the percentage feeling the arrangement would be a bad idea had declined from 57.9—that is, by roughly nine points. The question was first used, in a slightly different version, in a study undertaken in March 1960, that sample consisting of heads of spending units. At that point, 72.0% took an unfavorable view of "older people living with their children" (Morgan et al., 1962, p. 159).

It would be a mistake to see this opposition to sharing a home as reflecting the outlooks of indifferent or ungrateful children. The question, it will be noted, was put to the entire sample, including "many older people." Morgan and his associates (p. 160) found that opposition to the three-generation household actually *increased* with age. Retired persons were strongly opposed, 77% of them taking a dim view of the possibility.

Little need be said by way of summary. Where the social critics portray marriage and the family as two institutions in serious trouble, both in process of rapid dissolution and about to be replaced by new and freer forms, respondents themselves offer a radically different picture. They indicate, on the whole, that both their marital and family relationships are in rather good condition. In fact, as compared to the dire predictions offered by the critics, one could conclude that both are in remarkably good condition. This is not to gainsay that serious problems do appear on the margins, but then,.that is not likely to be anything new, some problems having been found with both institutions at all times and in all places. Where marriages have been dissolved, moreover, some new and different form has not evolved; most frequently, this has led to the reestablishment of a new version of the same form, that is, a conventional marriage relationship. Apart from this basic misrepresentation of frequency distributions, we have also seen that some elements of this criticism are based on "mythic" assumptions, that is to say on a constructed (a fabricated or made up) past, against which the critics then present their facts about the desolate present. But, for example, as in the case of the three-generation household of the days of yore, the base line for their trend statements depends on rather exceptional (that is, infrequent or unusual) experience.

---

statistics—and that it is more easily done without statistics. See also Hamilton, 1973, for some examples and discussion.

THE IMMEDIATE MILIEU

In this section we will consider the satisfaction or dissatisfaction expressed with respect to some key features of the immediate environment. An obvious first consideration, after the family itself, would be the respondent's house or apartment. We will then consider the assessment of the neighborhood (the immediately surrounding area). Next, we turn to the question of friendships, to the ties that would ordinarily extend beyond the neighborhood. Finally, we turn to an assessment of the larger community.

The considerations entering into these assessments would, of course, vary enormously. In the case of the home, one is dealing with a physical facility (to which, of course, there may be some considerable psychological attachment). The assessment of the neighborhood would probably involve consideration of both physical characteristics and personal ties. The assessment of friendships would involve, almost exclusively, a personal and affectional concern. The judgment of the community, however, would be a very complex one, touching on physical facilities, public services, and, no doubt, personal involvements. It is not our aim to discover the particular referents in each of these judgments; it is, rather, to indicate the level of satisfaction or dissatisfaction found in each area. The task, in brief, is to assess the validity of the sweeping claims found in the literature, particularly in the self-announced critical literatures of the mass society and Marxian traditions. The first area of inquiry, housing, allows us to deal with a claim of inadequate facilities. The other foci allow consideration of the many claims of societal breakdown, those arguing that isolation and loneliness are the obvious correlates of urban mass society.

Housing

Given the insistent complaint, given the sweeping condemnation found in the critical literature, one might expect widespread and intense dissatisfaction to be expressed with respect to housing. But the evidence from the 1971 Quality of American Life study shows a high level of satisfaction to be the typical case. A seven-point scale was used again, ranging from "completely satisfied" to "completely dissatisfied." The completely satisfied option was the most frequent choice, that being followed by the next highest level of satisfaction.[16]

These findings do not preclude the existence of some dissatisfaction, of some evident problem. Just over 10% of the population were dissatisfied with their housing, 3% being completely dissatisfied. And roughly one eighth were neutral about the state of their housing. In 1970, there were just over 63 million households in the United States. So the small percentages

[16]The question read as follows: Q. B11: "Considering all the things we have talked about, how satisfied or dissatisfied are you with this (house/apartment)? Which number comes closest to how satisfied or dissatisfied you feel?" A variant wording (and variant results) appeared later in the study; see the following note for details.

Satisfaction with Housing								
Completely satisfied			Neutral			Completely dissatisfied		
1	2	3	4	5	6	7		
36%	26	14	13	5	3	3	= 100%	
							(N = 9507)	

shown above translate, literally, into millions of unsatisfying household living arrangements. Our findings, in short, do not deny the existence of a problem here, but they do indicate the proportions involved.

We have some rather compelling evidence in this instance, showing the effects of question wording. The Survey Research Center's 1972 election study included a question on housing: (Q. S5A) "How do you feel about your house/apartment? " In this case, the seven-point format was retained, but brief descriptions were appended, the words "delighted" and "terrible" defining the extremes. Those terms, it would appear, led the respondents to avoid the extremes and instead to choose the more moderate options. This is shown in the following tabulation on satisfaction with housing based on the 1972 SRC Election Study (note: only one half of the sample was asked):

Delighted	Pleased	Mostly satisfied	Mixed (about equally satisfied and dissatisfied)	Mostly dis-satisfied	Unhappy	Terrible	
10%	34	36	12	5	2	1 = 100%	
						(N = 1107)	

While a dramatic shift from the 1971 question (and one that may be more in accord with most people's overall conception of the actual state of housing in the United States), the major change, it should be noted, was to relocate people within the "satisfied" range of the distribution, the overall percentages falling there being 76 and 80% in the two studies. Put somewhat differently, it suggests that most people who would describe themselves as completely satisfied with their housing would not say they were delighted with it. Many of them, it would seem, had they been given the second question, would have described themselves merely as pleased with their housing. And some choosing the second category in response to the 1971 question would have chosen the mostly satisfied option had they been faced with the later question. It will also be noted, at the other end of the distribution, that some who were completely dissatisfied did not mean to say their housing was terrible. The best conclusion we can draw is that large majorities, somewhere between three quarters and four fifths, express some degree of overall satisfaction with their housing. The "pleased" or "mostly satisfied" response probably expresses their feelings more accurately than does the phrase "completely satisfied."[17]

The Quality of American Life Study posed a number of detailed questions about the respondent's housing, some touching on physical characteristics, some on costs. The responses to these questions are generally consonant with the finding of general satisfaction with housing. Asked about the amount of room, 71% declared it to be about right, as against 21% judging it too small. Seventy-eight percent reported the structure to be well built, as against 18% reporting the opposite. Asked if the heating in winter was adequate, 58% described it as very good and another 28% said fairly good. On the other side of the ledger, 8% reported that the heating was not very good, and 3% said it was not good at all.

About one third of the respondents were renters. At that point, before the tight housing situation of the late 1970's, one half of them described their housing costs (rent plus utilities) as moderate. One might expect most of the rest to say that their rents were high, but the actual distribution was rather normal: 8% said the costs were very low and 14% saw them as low; 20% reported them as high and 8% said very high. Of the owners, 60% found their costs to be moderate. Among the remaining owners, one did find a skewed distribution, with 24% saying the costs were high and another 6% saying very high (Campbell, Converse, and Rodgers, p. 250).[18]

---

[17]Still another wording of the housing satisfaction question appears later in the 1971 Survey Research Center's Quality of American Life study. It asks:

Q. J3(A1) "How much satisfaction do you get from 'your house or apartment?'"

The descriptions of the seven options and the results follow:

A very great deal	A great deal	Quite a bit	A fair amount	Some	A little	None
25%	34	20	12	4	3	2 = 100% (N = 9434)

Here too, there appears to be some shifting, depending on the specific description. But once again, if we see the "fair amount" option as equal to the neutral point of the first-discussed question, the overall results are similar to those found with the other two questions. In this case, 79% located themselves in the satisfied range and 9% in the dissatisfied range.

[18]One tends to think of renting and owning as the two comprehensive options. Some respondents, however, about 1% of the total, were listed as living with their parents, and no information was gathered about their housing status. An additional 5% of the respondents were placed in a "neither owns nor rents" category. Some of these were farm laborers and some were persons "for whom housing is part of compensation (janitors, gardeners, nurses, and so on)." About 2% of the respondents were persons "for whom housing is a gift, paid for by someone outside the family

Age was a major correlate of satisfaction or dissatisfaction with housing, young persons, in general, making the most negative judgments (Campbell, Converse, and Rodgers, p. 152). The assessments, however, were more favorable in each of the subsequent age groups up to the "80 and over" category. The explanation seems simple. On leaving the parental family, one's income is typically rather low. One's financial resources, in the normal case, are the smallest they will ever be in the course of the adult career. As a consequence, the choice of housing and neighborhood is severely limited, and most of the available opportunities do not prove to be very satisfactory. This is to say that for a considerable part of the population, the housing problem is something linked to one's position in the life cycle rather than to some basic or permanent condition.[19]

It is useful, when thinking about housing and housing satisfaction, to have some idea of the types of dwelling units being considered. A sizable majority, 68%, of the nation's noninstitutional population, lived in detached single-family dwelling units at the time of the study, this being what might be called the basic American housing type. The next most frequent type was the detached two-family unit (the side-by-side arrangement or the upstairs-downstairs variety), in which 8% of the respondents lived. Some lived in row houses, a frequent style in the eastern seaboard cities, in Boston, New York, Philadelphia, Baltimore, and Washington. Some 7% lived in low-rise apartment structures. For all the concern expressed over the impersonal and aesthetically unattractive high-rise apartment buildings, we find that less than 4% of the respondents were housed in such structures. The high visibility of the giant apartment building in the urban landscape easily leads to mistaken judgments of the frequency of distribution. As it happens, a larger percentage of the nation's population was found living in trailers (the respective figures being 3.6 and 4.3%). Some of those mobile homes could be found in trailer parks, but many others were scattered throughout the countryside, many of them on individually owned plots of land. Not looming quite so large in either the urban or rural geography, it is easy for one to underestimate the frequency of this variety of housing.[20]

---

unit, owned by relative, pays no rent, or only taxes." From the Quality of American Life Codebook, p. 50.

[19]While for many people the housing problem is linked to position in the life cycle, for others, obviously, it is a more persistent fact of life. While 11% overall were dissatisfied with their housing and 13% were neutral, the respective figures among blacks were 20 and 24% (Campbell, Converse, and Rodgers, p. 459).

After the initial housing satisfaction question, people were asked if they wished to stay where they were or if they would like to move. Those choosing the latter option were asked what was "the main thing that keeps you from moving right now " By far, the most frequent reason given was financial (e.g., "cannot afford desired housing"). Some reported difficulty "in finding a suitable place." There was only minuscule mention made of discrimination (Codebook, pp. 55–57). This finding supports the major conclusion of the previous chapter—that "it's the money!"

[20]These results were calculated from the figures given in the study Codebook, p.

Campbell, Converse and Rodgers report that the respondents living in detached single-family homes "are more satisfied with their dwelling units than are those . . . in other types of structures" (pp. 253–254). Surprisingly, they find that the "next most satisfied respondents are the 4 percent who live in trailers." One line of conventional wisdom gains support in their finding that the "least satisfied, by a considerable margin, are the residents of apartment houses." They do, however, offer some additional words of explanation, indicating that:

> . . . a major proportion of these differences in the average level of housing satisfaction of residents of different types of structures can be explained by other differences among the dwelling units, such as their size and whether they are owned or rented by the respondents. In other words, there is no clear indication that the structure type per se is an important determinant of housing satisfaction.

Unfortunately, the NORC General Social Surveys did not contain questions on satisfaction with housing, so we cannot provide a detailed, year-by-year portrait of any possible trends. The 1978 Quality of American Life survey, however, does contain exact replicas of many of the questions discussed above. Again, respondents were asked for an overall assessment of satisfaction with their housing, answers being given on the seven-point scale ranging from "completely satisfied" to "completely dissatisfied." Results were as follows:

Completely satisfied			Neutral			Completely dissatisfied	
1	2	3	4	5	6	7	
38%	27	14	12	5	3	2	= 101%
							(N = 3658)

These figures are virtually identical to those shown earlier for the 1971 survey. We thus conclude that there has been no significant trend in housing satisfaction over the course of the 1970's: the levels, rather, are high and basically stable.[21]

---

227. The 1978 Quality of American Life study finds a larger portion in single-family dwelling units—73.5%. Fewer lived in double units, more in trailers. See 1978 Codebook, pp. 306–307.

[21] The same conclusion—no significant trend—is supported by comparing 1971 and 1978 results of the other indicators of housing satisfaction shown in the text. For example, concerning the wish to move, 71% of the 1978 respondents said they were satisfied to stay where they were; the corresponding 1971 figure was 72%.

The Gallup polls provide another source of trend data on the matter. Gallup's question is simply, "Are you satisfied or dissatisfied with your housing?" The question was asked nine times between 1963 and 1973. (After 1973, Gallup dropped the simple "satisfied/dissatisfied" response format, as noted in Chapter 2, so the Gallup series discontinues at that point.) Data are as follows: Percent satisfied with housing 1963, 74% (3668); 1965, 73% (3527); September 1966, 76% (3532); September 1967, 80% (3532); March 1969, 79% (1502); April 1969, 80% (1607);

Neighborhoods

Satisfaction with neighborhoods was also very high, nearly half describing themselves as completely satisfied.[22] For those anticipating widespread urban, small town, and/or rural decay, this will come as an unexpected finding. Some additional responses, however, point in the same direction and, as will be seen, we have an independent confirming assessment in this case provided by the interviewers. Later, after reviewing the assessments of friendships and community, we will return to consideration of the plausibility of these findings.

The 1971 Quality of American Life study asked a series of questions about the immediate neighborhood. The first of these asked about "the kinds of things you would like to have near where you live," that is, about the convenience of access to people, jobs, or facilities. Forty-two percent described their neighborhood location as very convenient, and the same percentage reported it as convenient enough. Thirteen percent thought it not very convenient, and 3% said it was not convenient at all. Two fifths of the respondents (41%) described the houses in the neighborhood, overall, as very well kept up, while one half (48%) said they were at least fairly well kept. The image of widespread dilapidation, which might be called the view from the South Bronx, was shared by 8% who said not very well and another 3% who said not well at all.

	Satisfaction with Neighborhood							
	Completely satisfied			Neutral			Completely dissatisfied	
	1	2	3	4	5	6	7	
1971	46%	21	13	11	4	2	3	= 100% (N = 9539)
1978	40%	26	14	12	5	2	2	= 101% (N = 3167)

One question in the series touched directly on the law-and-order issue, or, to use Scammon and Wattenberg's expression, on the social issue. This

August 1971, 77% (1505); January 1973, 77% (1508); and September 1973, 76% (1503).

While levels of satisfaction are high everywhere, these data do show a slight trend, with housing satisfaction peaking between 1966 and 1969 and declining somewhat thereafter. This, we think, may reflect the movement of young people (the baby-boom generation) into the housing market for the first time in the late 1960's. As noted in the text, young people are, for obvious reasons, less satisfied on average with their housing, which would tend to explain the small declines shown above in the early 1970's.

[22]The question: Q. A22—"And what about this particular neighborhood in (name city or county)? All things considered, how satisfied or dissatisfied are you with this neighborhood as a place to live? Which number comes closest to how satisfied or dissatisfied you feel?" It is Question A16 in the 1978 study.

asked if "it is safe to go out walking around here [in respondent's neigh-borhood] at night?" Of those with opinions, 72% answered with an unqualified yes , that it was safe. At the same time, however, over one half the respondents, 56% of the total, thought it very important to lock their doors when leaving the house or apartment (our calculation from 1971 codebook, pp. 45–46).

These results, it will be noted, are broadly consonant with the overall positive assessments made of the neighborhoods. The only negative majority judgment came in response to the question on locking doors, and that would seem a modest precautionary measure as opposed to a serious condemna-tion of the neighborhood. There are, at the same time, some areas, unques-tionably, in which serious problems were reported. If one quarter of the population feels it is unsafe to walk in the neighborhood at night, that is certainly an enormous problem, one affecting some fifty-five million persons (assuming they also speak for their children). Some of those judgments, of course, might be unrealistic; the fears, in other words, may be exaggerated. That definition of things, however, provides the subjective reality one lives with. In the first line of analysis, that definition, not the objective circum-stances out on the streets, provides the framework for the quality of one's life.

Those expressing dissatisfaction with their neighborhoods form only a minority of the total population. This finding, clearly, has implications for any discussion of Scammon and Wattenberg's real majority; most people describe their immediate environment in generally positive terms. In most instances, the very positive judgment alone outweighed all negative assess-ments. The assessments of the neighborhoods, like the judgments made about housing characteristics, were strongly related to age, with the young expressing by far the most negative sentiments (Campbell, Converse, and Rodgers, p. 152). This age linkage suggests that a simple commonplace episode in the life cycle—leaving home and starting out on one's own—is of greater moment than all of the supposed impacts of the mass society. The generally positive assessments again pose serious problems for the typical mass society claims.

The investigators reinterviewed nearly 300 respondents several months later, this restudy, in part at least, being designed to validate some of the original responses. In this connection, the interviewers were asked to make their own judgments of the neighborhoods on each of twelve dimensions. Their assessments were then correlated with the respondents' judgments. For more or less obvious reasons, these assessments were focused on the objective features of the neighborhoods, such as the amount of traffic, the number of trees, the number of children, and so forth. Relative to most social science correlations, the coefficients were generally high, the respective figures for traffic, trees, and children, for example, being .67, .61, and .59. Less agreement was found with respect to noise, attractiveness, and the upkeep of dwellings (.48, .43, and .42). The lowest correlations involved areas of more subjective evaluation, matters that would be difficult for the interviewer to assess, this being the case with a question on how good the neighborhood was as a place to live (.38), a question on "how pleasant" (.37), and another on "how friendly" (.33) it was (Campbell, Converse, and Rodgers, p. 247).

The basic lesson to be gained from this restudy is one that confirms the original results. All of these correlations were positive, most of them rather strongly so. And much of the unexplained variance in this case could readily be attributed to measurement error; the interviewers, even in a somewhat long interview, would scarcely be in a position to make accurate assessments about some of the less tangible features of the local areas.

Returning to the figures at the beginning of this discussion, it will be noted that the portion of those completely satisfied with their neighborhoods fell by some six percentage points between 1971 and 1978, most of those falling to the next degree of satisfaction, suggesting some kind of deterioration in the period. Some other questions in the 1978 study permit a limited exploration of this problem, allowing the exclusion of some ready hypotheses. The percentages describing the housing in the neighborhood as very well or fairly well kept up are roughly the same at both points, showing a slight improvement if anything. The percentages saying it was very important to lock doors when going out were identical at both times. The percentages saying it was safe to go out walking there at night actually increased between 1971 and 1978, from 72 to 78%. As will be seen later in this chapter, there is good reason to accept this result.

While we cannot pinpoint the reason for the modest decline in neighborhood satisfaction, these findings suggest that one can exclude the "neighborhood decay" and "crime in the streets" hypotheses. It might be a function of changes in demographic composition together with specific life cycle problems, those associated with leaving the parental home. One alternative hypothesis would be that of "noise in the street." During this period rock music came increasingly to be "shared"—quite gratuitously— with one's neighbors. Another hypothesis deserving consideration would be that of canine excrement on the streets, on sidewalks, and on lawns.

Friendships

A third area to be considered in this discussion of the immediate milieu of the respondent involves friendships. Apart from a straightforward descriptive concern, this topic also has some relevance for the mass society argument and its contemporary reworkings (as, for example, in Alvin Toffler, 1971, pp. 107ff. and 119 ff.). Claiming that the population moves with ever greater frequency, it follows that social contacts are of ever shorter duration. The term friend comes to be applied to someone who, in times past, would have been called a passing acquaintance. We are not in a position to assess some of the more detailed questions raised in this specific line of argument. We can, however, say something about the satisfaction and dissatisfactions associated with those friendships, since the questions ask for something more than ephemeral contacts. As will be seen, here, too, the reality is more complex than the easy assumptions of the social critics (and, more generally, of mass society theorists) would suggest.

First a question about quantity. The Quality of American Life study asked:

Q. H1. " . . . what about your friendships: Would you say that you have a good many very good friends that you could count on if you had any sort of trouble, an average number, or not too many very good friends?"

It will be noted that the question sets a rather demanding standard. To exclude the passing acquaintances, it asks about very good friends, those one could count on in time of need. Of the sample, 38% said they had a good many such friends, and another 43% said they had an average number. Only one fifth (19%) said they did not have many such dependable friends upon whom they could rely. There is, of course, some possibility of over-estimation here, of response bias. And there is also a problem of the inexact standard, the reference point, that average number, being one set by the respondent. At best, therefore, the response provides a relative measure, whether the respondent sees him or herself at, above, or below some norm.

The next question in the series asked about making more friends, in effect asking about satisfaction or dissatisfaction with that quantitative achievement:

Q. H2. "How interested would you say you are in meeting new people and making friends? Would you say you are very interested, somewhat interested, or not very interested?"

Just under half, 46%, said they were very interested, 43% said somewhat interested, and 11% were not very interested. One might imagine a simple relationship with the previous question; those with many friends would be satisfied with their achievement, while those without friends, presumably, would express themselves as very interested. The actual relationship was just the reverse; those with a good many friends expressed the greatest interest in making even more, that being the case with 64% of the gregarious respondents. Among those reporting fewer friends than average, only 30% were very interested in meeting and making more (recalculated from Campbell, Converse, and Rodgers, p. 358). This latter group, who incidentally did express considerable dissatisfaction with the quality of their friendships, would be the isolated and lonely men and women of modern society. They constitute 6% of the entire sample. The persistent focus on isolation and loneliness would seem a misplaced emphasis, at least as far as typicality is concerned.

The question on satisfaction with one's friendships also had a broad and comprehensive focus. It read:

Q. H3. "All things considered, how satisfied are you with your friendships—with the time you can spend with friends, the things you do together, the number of friends you have, as well as the particular people who are your friends? Which number comes closest to how you feel?"

	Completely satisfied			Neutral			Completely dissatisfied	
	1	*2*	*3*	*4*	*5*	*6*	*7*	
1971	37%	30	15	12	4	1	1	= 100% (N = 9505)
1978	30%	35	17	11	5	2	1	= 101% (N = 3644)

The results show essentially the same pattern reported previously in regard to marriage, family, housing, and neighborhood, the levels of satisfaction expressed being very high. The percentage expressing any degree of dissatisfaction, 6% of the total, is well below the percentage saying they did not have many friends.[23] As indicated, most of this group apparently do not value friendships, even an average number of them, very highly. These results once again present a serious challenge to the mass society portrayals of contemporary life.

One way in which the isolation and loneliness aspect of that theory could be saved would be by an assumption of massive false consciousness—most of the two thirds indicating high levels of satisfaction with their friendships could be "mistaken" in their judgments. Another possibility would be that the judgment is a relative one; they are actually settling for very little (e.g., calling a shallow relationship a completely satisfactory one). This possibility cannot be assessed with the data at hand. Still another possibility, of course, is that of true consciousness, the possibility that the respondents know what they are talking about.

Some evidence favoring the true consciousness hypothesis appears in the NORC General Social Surveys. A series of sociability questions was asked there, some of them (those asking about a social evening with parents, with brothers and sisters, and with relatives) having already been reviewed. Respondents were also asked about the frequency of social evenings with "someone who lives in your neighborhood" and also with "friends who live outside the neighborhood." The former contacts, although it is not explicitly

[23]Another question on satisfaction in this area appears later in the questionnaire, this one with different descriptions of the seven options (see Note 17 above for a parallel problem with respect to housing). The distributions shift somewhat, especially among the "satisfied" respondents but, as with previous results in other areas, the overall proportions of satisfieds, dissatisfieds, and neutrals remain much the same. The question reads: Q. J3(J1)—"How much satisfaction do you get from— 'your friendships?'"

Table 4.4. Frequency of Social Contacts: 1978 NORC General Social Survey

Spends a social evening with	Frequency of contact							N
	Almost every day	1–2 times a week	Several times a month	Once a month	Several times a year	Once a year	Never	
Parents[a]	5%	22	17	12	21	12	11	= 100% (975)
Brother/Sister[a]	5	15	14	12	24	18	11	= 99 (1355)
Relatives	7	29	19	14	19	8	4	= 100 (1526)
Neighbors	6	24	11	12	13	9	25	= 100 (1522)
Friends outside neighborhood	2	19	21	16	21	9	12	= 100 (1526)

[a]Percentages for those having living parents or siblings.

stated, would probably involve at least some component of friendship, especially where they were very frequent.

In 1978, three tenths of the respondents said they had social evenings with neighbors at least once or twice a week, some of them reporting such contacts almost every day (Table 4.4). At the opposite extreme, 25% reported never having such contacts, and another 22% said they occurred only infrequently, ranging from several times to only once a year. As for friends outside the neighborhood, 21% reported such contact at least once or twice a week, and the same percentage reported social evenings occurring several times a month. This time, at the opposite extreme, there were some 12% reporting no such contacts, and another 30% saying they were infrequent events.

These friendly contacts are not as frequent as the links to family members and relatives. At the same time, even on the basis of these marginal distributions, it is clear that the typical situation is far from one of isolation. (It should also be remembered that some people choose an isolated existence.) When one recognizes that the two categories of contact discussed here are separate and nonoverlapping, it follows that some cumulation would be the case. Social evenings would be spent with neighbors and with friends outside the local area. Adding also the contacts with parents, brothers and sisters, and relatives (some of whom, of course, could also be close friends), it is clear that a large percentage of the respondents are very much integrated in kin-plus-friendship networks. The portrait one gets from these

Table 4.5. Satisfaction from Friendships: 1973–1980 NORC General Social Surveys[a]

Question: *"For each area of life I am going to name, tell me the number that shows how much satisfaction you get from that area."* Your friendships.

	1973	1974	1975	1976	1977	1978	1980	All
A very great deal	33%	32%	29%	29%	30%	27%	34%	31%
A great deal	37	41	42	40	39	41	42	40
Quite a bit	14	14	15	16	15	17	13	15
A fair amount	11	8	9	10	10	10	8	9
Some	3	3	3	3	3	3	2	3
A little	2	2	2	2	2	2	1	2
None	1	1	1	1	1	1	1	1
Total percent	101	101	101	101	100	100	101	101
Total N	(1495)	(1484)	(1484)	(1492)	(1525)	(1526)	(1467)	(10473)

[a]Source: Same as Table 4.1. This question was taken from the Quality of American Life study, Question J.3. It is a variant on their seven-point satisfaction study discussed in the text.

studies, in short, is very much the opposite of the picture offered by mass society theorists.

The NORC studies allow an independent check on the Survey Research Center group's finding with respect to satisfaction with friendships. Those studies also allow us to say something about the trends during the 1970's. A seven-point scale taken from the Quality of American Life study was used, it being the second of the two utilized (see Note 23). The overall results, compared with the 1971 SRC results, are very similar.

The NORC results, as shown in Table 4.5, amount to seven independent confirmations of the conclusion drawn from the SRC study; namely, that people show generally high levels of satisfaction with their friendships. Looking at the trend over these years, one does find a modest decline in the level of satisfaction expressed through 1978, with a return in 1980 to the earlier standard. It is thus possible that there was some small trend toward declining satisfaction in the middle of the decade. That shift, however, is entirely from the most positive category, from "a very great deal" of satisfaction into one of the adjacent categories, that is, "a great deal" or "quite a bit." And even this slight decline reverses in 1980. The most prudent conclusion would thus again be one of relative stability and continuity.

THE COMMUNITY

In this area, too, the Quality of American Life studies found generally high levels of satisfaction. The results follow:[24]

	Completely satisfied			Neutral			Completely dissatisfied	
	1	2	3	4	5	6	7	
1971	38%	22	15	16	5	2	2	= 100% (N = 9510)
1978	34%	26	17	15	5	1	1	= 99% (N = 3665)

Respondents were asked to assess a range of community facilities, the streets, the public schools, garbage collection, parks and playgrounds, and

[24]This was the first of the satisfaction questions in the study, and it, therefore, contains some explanation of the method to be used. The question reads:

Q. A21. "Here is a card that I want you to use to tell me how satisfied you are with (name city or county) as a place to live in. This is how we will use it. If you are completely satisfied with (name city or county) as a place to live, you would say 'one.' If you are completely dissatisfied, you would say 'seven.' If you are neither completely satisfied nor completely dissatisfied, you would put yourself somewhere from two to six; for example, four means that you are neutral, or just as satisfied as you are dissatisfied." (Interviewer hands card to respondent)

There was, as with many of the previous questions, a second satisfaction question

so on. In some cases, segments of the sample were omitted, since for them the question was not appropriate. This was the case with the parks and playgrounds question for those living in rural areas. The garbage collection question was also omitted for those in rural areas. The question on the adequacy of public transportation was omitted in areas where no public transport existed.

On the whole, the assessments (based this time on a five-point scale) of these attributes were rather positive (Campbell, Converse, and Rodgers, p. 223). The greatest appreciation appeared with respect to garbage collection, 56% describing service as very good and another 28% saying it was fairly good. The least satisfaction with facilities appeared with respect to parks and playgrounds. Some 30% chose the categories "not very good" or "not good at all." Even here, however, the majority was on the positive side, the "very good" and "fairly good" answers, respectively, being 30 and 33%. These assessments, then, would be consonant with the overall evaluations of the communities. Since they involve hard or tangible facts, it is difficult to believe that the overall assessments would reflect any serious response bias or false consciousness.

At the same time, there are unquestionably considerable problem areas. If 11% find the garbage collection in their community to be inadequate (a figure based on the four fifths who were asked the question), that is a very sizable problem which certainly ought to occupy the attention of public authorities. A similar conclusion is warranted with respect to the reports of inadequate police protection (made by 16% of the sample) or those expressing some degree of dissatisfaction with the streets in their area (20% of the total).

One area appeared in which majority dissatisfaction was reported. This did not involve complaint about some local service or facility; it involved the means to pay for those services—namely, local taxes. One fifth reported that the local taxes were very high and another 39% said they were high. Just over one third (36%) found the taxes to be moderate, and only trivial percentages reported them to be low (4%) or very low (1%). This finding, it will be noted, ties in with and supports the conclusion of the previous chapter, the point about the centrality of economic concerns. That concern with local taxes will come as no surprise to the average citizen (either in 1971 or in the early 1980's). It is remarkable that some of the leading social commentators have overlooked this subject.

The second of the Survey Research Center's community satisfaction questions (see Note 24) was used by the NORC for their General Social

with a somewhat different format. Again, rather than expressing complete satisfaction, many chose the second or third options when asked this second question. The question reads: Q. J3(B1). "How much satisfaction do you get from—'the city or place you live in?'"

Surveys in the years 1973 to 1980. Somewhat less satisfaction was indicated in the first of these studies than in the 1971 SRC work, the choice of the three most positive categories being ten points lower than in the earlier study. It seem unlikely that this represents an actual change; one possibility is that their samples were different. This represents no problems for our consideration of the 1973 to 1980 trends; the NORC sampling procedure was the same throughout the decade.

From 1973, the first year the NORC asked the question, through to 1978, there was a steady if modest falloff in the percentage expressing a very great deal of satisfaction with their community (Table 4.6). The difference here is one of the largest yet reported, amounting to six percentage points. But once again, the 1980 results returns to the early 1970's-era standard. Like the other changes reported earlier in this chapter, the falloff through 1978 represents a shift to a lesser degree of satisfaction, to "a great deal" or "quite a bit," rather than a shift to a neutral or a generally dissatisfied judgment. The proportion of respondents choosing one or another of the three least satisfied options was roughly constant in all years, at about one respondent in seven.

The foregoing review of family and communal satisfactions and dissatisfactions has revealed the following: a majority of adult Americans expressed satisfaction with respect to marriages, families, housing, neighborhoods, friendships, and communities.

These results present a serious challenge to the claims stemming from the

Table 4.6. Satisfaction from Community: 1973–1980 NORC General Social Surveys[a]

Question: "For each area of life I am going to name, tell me the number that shows how much satisfaction you get from that area." The city or place you live in.

	1973	1974	1975	1976	1977	1978	1980	All
A very great deal	23%	20%	21%	20%	19%	17%	24%	20%
A great deal	24	27	30	30	28	30	31	28
Quite a bit	17	17	15	17	17	19	15	17
A fair amount	22	23	20	21	22	20	18	21
Some	6	7	6	7	6	7	6	6
A little	5	4	5	4	6	5	4	5
None	3	2	3	2	2	3	2	2
Total percent	100	100	100	101	100	101	100	101
Total N	(1502)	(1483)	(1483)	(1493)	(1525)	(1525)	(1462)	(10473)

[a]Source: Same as Table 4.1. This question was taken from the Quality of American Life study, Question J.3 (B.1).

mass society tradition and particularly to the contemporary variants, the formulations of the social critics Reich, Roszak, and Toffler. Where they declare a widespread and openly expressed dissatisfaction to be the dominant current fact, the evidence reported here shows the openly expressed dissatisfaction to be very limited. Extreme dissatisfaction, of the kind they claim to be general, was actually expressed by no more than 3% of those interviewed, that high level appearing in regard to housing and neighborhoods. As for the other areas studied, that same extreme level of dissatisfaction was expressed by only 1 or 2% of the total. The critics' claims of social dissolution prove to be almost diametrically opposite to what is actually reported. Rather than isolation, anxiety, and dissatisfaction being dominant, the evidence reviewed here shows social connectedness to be dominant. And satisfaction with all these principal areas of life is also a prevailing fact.[25]

Dissatisfaction, to be sure, is not limited to 1, 2, or even 3% of the adult population; that represents only the most extreme report. In the case of community dissatisfaction, depending on the question, we found some 9 to 14% expressing some degree of dissatisfaction. A somewhat larger portion of the population, between 12 and roughly 20%, took a neutral or middling position. That, too, representing an averaging of pluses and minuses, points to some sources of dissatisfaction. But even the combination of the outright dissatisfied categories with this neutral or middling one failed to produce so much as one instance of majority dissatisfaction in the six major areas reviewed.

The original presentation of the Quality of American Life study's findings showed that, in some part at least, those dissatisfactions were linked to a commonplace event in the normal life cycle—leaving the parental home. This event, ordinarily, means a drastic reduction in comfort and convenience. The housing and the neighborhood one is able to afford are typically much less attractive than those known previously. Where the move takes one to a distant community, it also means a break with friends and, accordingly, a period in which dissatisfactions in this area would be higher than usual. But the impact of this "structural" source of personal strain is neither vast nor long-lasting. For many, for those who move elsewhere in the local community, there is never any serious disruption of social ties, which is evidenced by the remarkably high frequency of contacts with parents, brothers and sisters, and other relatives. For those who do make major moves, the immediate task of their lives is one of settling in, of reestablishing social contacts. Most appear to do so successfully.

[25]This is speaking of commentators who claim an actual awareness or recognition, who say people have a clear and present consciousness of their dissatisfaction with current conditions. Another mass society variant holds the masses to be narcotized; although really very unhappy, they have been moved, by the mass media or by mass consumption, to think they are in fact happy and/or satisfied. Possibly the most influential statement was provided by Herbert Marcuse, 1964.

One characteristic of community life did manage to generate majority dissatisfaction. This was the matter of local taxes, a majority describing them as high or very high. This somewhat commonplace finding supports the principal conclusion of the previous chapter, the point about the centrality of economic concerns. The finding is of more than passing interest when one considers its neglect in the work of the social critics and, perhaps even more pointedly, the general neglect of such economic problems in the works of the postindustrialists. They have created, or rather, have imagined, problems where they did not exist. And they have neglected problems where they do exist. There are, for example, no references to taxes or to the cost of living in the index of Toffler's work, suggesting that this is one area of "shock" that will not be a part of our future. As a portrayal of people's actual feelings, as accounts of the problems they face, such commentaries evidently leave much to be desired.

Some of these results, especially those involving housing, neighborhoods, and communities, do pose something of a problem in that they appear to contradict "common sense." Those who have traveled widely throughout the United States will remember vast areas of urban territory containing what is obviously dilapidated and deteriorating housing (that is something immediately visible from the streets; one never knows what might be hidden behind an aging but elegant facade). And then, too, on the back roads and in the villages one finds much rural dilapidation, that combined with large numbers of trailer homes. All this is interspersed with various aesthetic horrors, the most striking of which is the garish suburban highway with its gas stations, fast-food outlets, motels, shopping centers, new and used car lots, automobile body shops, and automobile graveyards.[26] Given such obvious facts, plus the known facts of poor road repair, limited recreation space, high crime rates, and inadequate municipal services, it seems very problematic that so many people should describe themselves as completely satisfied, or, in response to the second Quality of American Life question, that so many should report getting a very great deal or even a great deal of satisfaction from their communities.

Some explanation for this paradox appears when we examine the responses given in the different kinds of community. The original publication of the Quality of Life study findings provided a breakdown of community satisfactions by size of community (Campbell, Converse, and Rodgers, p. 234). This showed a rather distinctive pattern: markedly lower satisfaction with respect to eight of nine measures in the largest cities.[27] The largest cities

[26]For those who have not traveled widely, the work of Peter Blake (1964) may be of some use.

[27]The ninth measure, the one where large cities were favorably rated, involved the adequacy of public transportation. For a detailed portrait of public attitudes with regard to American cities, see United States Department of Housing and Urban Development, 1978. Also of considerable interest in this regard are the works of Claude S. Fischer (1973a, 1973b, 1975a, 1975b, 1975c). As early as 1973, Fischer

in this discussion are the central cities of the twelve largest standard metropolitan statistical areas as of 1960. Specifically, it refers to New York, Chicago, Los Angeles, Philadelphia, Detroit, Boston, San Francisco, Pittsburgh, St. Louis, Cleveland, Baltimore, and Washington.

Possibly the most significant fact about those cities, taken collectively, is that they have suffered considerable losses of population in recent decades. Chicago, which had a population of 3,621,000 persons in 1950, fell to 3,550,000 in 1960 and fell again to 3,367,000 in 1970. What had been a gradual loss up to that point became a hemorrhage in the 1970's, the 1977 estimate for that city being 3,063,000. But Chicago's loss was modest when contrasted with that of some of the older cities. The respective figures for Cleveland on those same dates (in 1000s) are 915, 876, 751, and 609. For St. Louis we have 857, 750, 622, and 518 (from the *Statistical Abstract, 1979*, pp. 24–26). The cities were being turned inside out during this period, the central cities being emptied and the spaces surrounding them coming to be filled.

Some other characteristics of the twelve largest cities deserve special attention, the 1978 Quality of American Life study showing them to be distinctive in a number of ways. Only a minority of the adult population in those locations, two out of five, were married. Roughly one half the population there consists of single, separated, and divorced persons, the remaining one tenth being widowed (Table 4.7).

The twelve largest are also very different in the racial and ethnic composition. Blacks are overrepresented by a factor of three as compared to their overall proportion in the population. The same degree of overrepresentation occurs in the case of Hispanic and Asian populations. That triple overrepresentation means that the non-Hispanic white population is substantially underrepresented; in fact, they form only a modest 55% majority in these cities as compared to their 80–90% levels elsewhere. That average, of course, hides a considerable amount of variation, blacks in Washington, for example, numbering over 70% in 1970 as opposed to 16% in Boston.

The Campbell *et al.* findings are confirmed once again in the 1978 study, the levels of satisfaction with community and neighborhood being lowest in the twelve largest cities. In general, an inverse relationship is found between community size and satisfaction; in both instances, satisfaction in the largest cities runs at roughly half that of the outlying country. One other finding of note involves the judgments of interpersonal trust. Those in the largest cities

---

noted "a small trend for the largest metropolises to be disproportionately places of malaise" (Fischer, 1973b, p. 221). He also indicated the most obvious individual solution to this malaise, "to leave those areas in pursuit of the ideal home in the ideal smaller community" (pp. 223-234). See also Marans and Rodgers, 1975.

Table 4.7. Marital Status, Race-Ethnicity, and Attitudes by Size of Community[a]

	Size of community					
	12 largest[b] cities	Other large central cities	Suburbs of the 12	Suburbs of other large cities	Adjacent areas —all cities	Outlying areas
Marital status						
Married[c]	40%	55%	61%	65%	65%	58%
Single	29	17	18	15	11	13
Separated, divorced	21	14	12	12	9	12
Widowed	9	14	10	8	14	15
N =	(289)	(687)	(558)	(701)	(913)	(542)
Race-Ethnicity						
White	54%	79%	89%	88%	94%	89%
Black	34	17	5	6	4	9
Hispanic	9	3	3	4	2	1
Completely satisfied with						
Community	24%	33%	29%	36%	39%	45%
Neighborhood	25	36	31	38	50	55
Interpersonal trust						
Can't be too careful	67%	53%	49%	51%	51%	54%
People look out for selves	58	41	41	41	41	39
People take advantage	47	33	31	31	31	29

[a]Source: SRC Quality of American Life Study, 1978.
[b]See text for listing.
[c]Included here are those cohabiting, 0.6% of the total. They, too, are overrepresented in the large cities, where they form 1.7% of the total.

are distinctly more suspicious of people in general.[28] In this case, no serious difference between the other community-size categories was found.

A question of interpretation must be raised here: Does that dissatisfaction with the large cities stem from some distinctive features of those cities? Or is it perhaps due to the various penalties associated with race? An examination of community satisfaction for the white population only showed the same city-size effect, those in the largest cities having lower satisfaction than was the case with whites elsewhere. On the whole, there were only very small differences in the responses of whites and blacks (together with Hispanics) in response to this question. In the twelve largest cities, 23% of the whites indicated complete satisfaction with their community; 24% of the blacks and Hispanics indicated the same degree of satisfaction. The same city-size effect appeared within both of those population segments with respect to the neighborhood satisfaction question. Here the whites did express more satisfaction than blacks and Hispanics, which no doubt reflects the patterns of urban segregation within those cities.

These findings provide some clues as to the sources of the outlooks of the various critical schools. Were one to inquire about the centers of production of the nation's culture, one would be led to these twelve cities, or, more specifically, to a subset of the twelve. The nation's leading intellectuals, by and large, are very disproportionately concentrated in New York City (or, more precisely, in a few neighborhoods of Manhattan). Virtually all major network television programming comes out of New York and Los Angeles. The content of most mass circulation magazines originates in New York City. (At one point, early in its history, *Time* magazine shifted its editorial offices to Cleveland; it proved a serious error, one that was quickly rectified.) The leading prestige newspapers of the nation are located in New York and Washington. Two other prestige newspapers appear in St. Louis and Los Angeles.

Our suggestion is that the world view put forth by these producers of culture reflects their immediate circumstances. Their portrait is one of decline, that being a fairly accurate picture of the cities closest to their experience. They portray cities rent with racial and ethnic divisions, that, too, roughly reflecting the character of their cities. They discover large numbers of singles, of separated and divorced in contemporary America; they also find large numbers of widows living in troubled circumstances. And that, too, is an approximate portrait of their milieu. The problem, of

[28]The questions contained in Table 4.7 read:

Q. K3. "Generally speaking, would you say that most people can be trusted or that you can't be too careful in dealing with people?"

Q. K4. "Would you say that most of the time, people try to be helpful, or that they are mostly just looking out for themselves?"

Q. K5. "Do you think that most people would try to take advantage of you if they got the chance or would they try to be fair?"

course, is with the generalization, the extension of those findings to other settings within the nation. In 1971, only about 11% of the population lived in the central cities of the twelve largest SMSA's, and by 1978, the figure was down to 8%. Portraiture based on these twelve largest cities thus misses the circumstances and experiences of roughly nine tenths of the American population.

The evidence from the two Quality of American Life studies make clear that big city experience is by no means typical of what appears elsewhere. The 1978 study, moreover, indicates just how partial that experience is. The twelve largest cities contain less than one twelfth of the nation's population and are involved in a depopulation process that is still continuing. Basically, it means that people, those who are able to, have chosen to leave those unpleasant urban circumstances in favor of more attractive alternatives. And although the critic may focus on the desolate urban landscape, that landscape describes an ever smaller part of the contemporary human experience. Given the migration, it should come as no special surprise that overall satisfaction with home, neighborhood, and community have held up through the decade.

Few people, of course, would like or appreciate what has happened to the major cities. But then, lacking any obvious feasible program for urban improvement, the sole option remaining for most people living there is abandonment. Awesome problems are left behind, and no one in his or her right mind would belittle their seriousness. What is missing from the discussion is serious analysis and serious discussion of remedies.

The foregoing points clearly to residence in central cities, especially one of the twelve largest, as a major source of discontent in contemporary American society. In the next chapter, we consider some of the others.

5 | SOURCES OF DISCONTENT

Our discussion to this point has been somewhat global in character. Addressing the sweeping claims put forth by various schools of criticism, we have presented evidence showing the responses of the entire adult population (or, more precisely, of cross-sectional samples of that population). While a satisfactory procedure for some purposes, for "broad brush" portraiture, that method does, nevertheless, pose some difficulties by virtue of its absence of detail and lack of specification.

In the previous chapter, we presented evidence showing fairly broad levels of satisfaction with most aspects of the immediate social milieu—with marriage and family life, one's friends, house, neighborhood, and community. Despite the ever-recurring announcements of a developing malaise, no substantial increases in dissatisfaction appeared in any of these areas over the course of the 1970's. Still, in all areas, at least some degree of dissatisfaction did exist, and it is certainly worth asking where these pockets of discontent are located and what factors account for them.

At the close of the previous chapter, we indicated that one prosaic factor, living in a large central city, was linked in a very direct and plausible way with particular areas of dissatisfaction, especially dissatisfaction with place, neighborhood, and housing. In the various critical accounts of the human condition, little is typically said about city size, since it is hard to imagine this source of discontent as a basis for class consciousness or political mobilization. Our intention in the present chapter is to show that much of the remaining malaise is also rooted in personal factors that do not pose much possibility for concerted class action, namely, marital status and age. Our point is thus to show that many of the portraits of the American masses, such as those reviewed in the early chapters, not only exaggerate the levels of discontent, but misstate the sources of the discontent that does exist. In the process they also distort the unwitting reader's understanding of the likely social and political consequences.

Dissatisfaction is the presumed consequence of some thwarting of life goals and aspirations. It follows that any account of the sources of discontent has to begin with a consideration of life goals, as was done in Chapter 3.

people, we indicated, give marriage the highest possible ranking on their scale of individual priorities. But some, a fair-sized minority, rejected marriage entirely as necessary for "the good life." It is useful to have some understanding of this dissenting minority.

Most people also ranked the family as a central focus of their lives, second only to marriage, the principal bond of most families. The specific character of that interest varies, depending on the respondent's status within the family. A son or daughter, a husband or wife, a surviving widow or widower, will all relate to the family in different ways. Many of the outlooks, many of the assessments and evaluations with which we are concerned, are linked to these statuses. The significance of a job or a given level of income will differ, depending on one's sex, marital status, and age. Ten thousand dollars of annual income, for example, would mean very different things to a single person living at home, to a married head of a family, or to a retired widow. For this reason, it is important to examine people's interests, concerns, and satisfactions in relationship to these three variables. That is the task of the present chapter.

The analyses presented here show clearly that much dissatisfaction is linked to life cycle, age, and especially various marital disruptions. Certain other obvious but commonly overlooked factors, such as the physical attractiveness of a person, are also demonstrably important in accounting for happiness and life satisfaction. In contrast, many of the factors that figure prominently in the critical accounts—like social class—prove to be rather trivial.

The largest segment of the adult population, of course, consists of married people (husbands and wives), who make up nearly 70% of the total. The next largest segment consists of single persons, some of whom, the majority, were living at home with their parents; the rest were out on their own. (We have focused here on the Survey Research Center's Quality of American Life study [1971] because it, unlike the NORC studies, allows us to separate the singles at home from those on their own.[1]) The third largest segment consists of the

---

[1] It should be mentioned that most survey samples exclude institutional populations—persons living in households on military reservations plus those in large rooming houses, residential clubs, transient accommodations, barracks for workers, accommodations for inmates of institutions, and general hospitals (Campbell, Converse, and Rodgers, p. 511). It is useful to have some idea of the numbers and kinds of persons thereby excluded. As of April 1970, the United States had a resident population of 203,211,926 persons (United States Bureau of the Census, *Statistical Abstract*: 1977, p. 5, Table 1, Note 3). At that time there was an institutional population of 5,786,000 persons (Ibid. p. 47). Most of these persons would be age 18 or over, the principal segments being (in 1000's): college dormitories, 1765; military barracks, 1005; homes for the aged and dependent, 928; mental hospitals, 934; rooming and boarding houses, 330; and correctional institutions, 328. It is only when one comes to homes and schools for the mentally handicapped, 202, that one might find significant numbers of nonadults. Training schools for juvenile delinquents contained 66,000 persons. Lacking a better estimate, we might guess that 5,250,000

widows and widowers, the families broken by death. And finally, one has the families in which the husband and wife are separated or have divorced. The distribution of the adult population in the early 1970's by sex and marital status may be seen in the first line of Table 5.1.[2]

The number of married males and females should be approximately the same in any well-chosen sample. The disparity here, the respective 32 and 36% figures, represents an undersampling of husbands who, being more frequently out of the house, are not reached by the SRC interviewers. Among the singles at home, males outnumber females by a small margin, due to the earlier age of marriage for women. Among the singles on their own, the pattern is reversed, this apparently because of the differing male-female survival rates, it being "in the cards" in a monogamous society that there be more never married women than men (reflected in the age distributions in the table).

The separated category should contain roughly equal numbers of males and females, but, as may be seen, this is not the case; females outnumber males five to two. This result, which appears in all surveys, is tied, we think, to age, race, and method. The separated are disproportionately young and black. And young black males tend to be underrepresented in surveys and in United States census results. Exclusion of the institutional populations may also have had some effect here. It could be that some husbands in this

---

of the institutionalized populations were adults, 4% of the 1970 adult population of 135,177,000 persons.

We do not examine the attitudes of institutionalized populations anywhere in the present work. A useful investigation in one such setting is provided by Charles R. Tittle (1972). In line with most observations of this group, he does find that "incarceration has a negative impact on self-evaluation." He raises questions about the causes of this development and, among other things, presents data challenging "the general idea that an institutional experience necessarily has a pervasive effect on the self" (Tittle, p. 76).

[2]Most of the results in this chapter are drawn from the Survey Research Center's Quality of American Life study (July-August, 1971). That study has undersampled male respondents, and the researchers have developed a weighting procedure to adjust this fact. We have not used the weights because, in this chapter, we examine males and females separately (that is, we are not interested in values for the entire sample at this point). As compared to the Bureau of the Census's 1971 Current Population Reports, the principal differences are an underrepresentation of singles, especially single men (they report 9.4% as compared to our total of 6%), and an imbalance among the married (the Census reports 34.3 and 34.4%, respectively, for males and females). Were we to use the weights, we would have percentage base figures that would be considerably larger than the real figures. At the same time, the percentages themselves would remain unchanged.

All analyses reported in this chapter have also been run on the 1978 Quality of American Life study, and where possible, on the combined NORC General Social Surveys. There were some modest differences between the 1978 Quality of American Life results and the 1971 results reported here, all of them, however, matters of small details.

Table 5.1. Background Characteristics, Financial Circumstances, Satisfaction with Life and Happiness by Marital Status and Sex: SRC Quality of American Life Study, 1971

	Single-at home		Married		Single-on own		Separated		Divorced		Widowed		
	M	F	M	F	M	F	M	F	M	F	M	F	
	4%	3%	32%	36%	2%	3%	1%	4%	2%	4%	2%	10%	= 101%
	(75)	(66)	(689)	(773)	(50)	(69)	(20)	(49)	(34)	(80)	(37)	(222)	= 2164
Respondent's relationship to head of family:													
Is head	—	—	99	1	100	100	90	88	88	94	92	92	
Wife	—	—	—	98	—	—	—	2	—	—	—	—	
Child, stepchild[b]	87	80	*a	*a	—	—	10	6	6	3	—	1	
All other[b]	13	20	*a	1	—	—	—	4	6	3	8	7	
Age													
18–29	88	83	24	25	38	39	21	31	6	25	3	1	
30–49	9	8	40	45	40	22	37	49	24	48	5	6	
50–64	3	5	24	22	18	19	32	16	38	19	19	29	
65 or more	—	5	12	9	4	20	11	4	32	9	73	64	
Principal activity													
At work	68	56	84	38	78	65	65	69	52	73	30	26	
Housewife	—	5	—	59	—	7	—	20	—	18	—	56	
Unemployed	15	8	1	1	8	3	5	8	3	6	3	2	
Retired	—	2	12	2	4	15	25	2	35	3	62	14	
Student	17	29	2	*a	4	7	—	—	—	1	—	—	

Family income ($)												
4,999 or less	25	18	16	16	42	46	45	63	56	53	64	73
5,000– 9,999	22	27	36	30	27	42	20	23	31	42	25	18
10,000–13,999	18	25	24	26	17	7	15	4	3	4	3	4
14,000–19,999	21	13	15	17	13	5	10	8	3	1	8	4
20,000 or more	15	17	10	11	2	—	10	2	6	—	—	1
N =	(68)	(60)	(677)	(729)	(48)	(67)	(20)	(48)	(32)	(77)	(36)	(211)
Money worries												
All of the time	—	6	8	7	8	12	5	33	3	17	8	6
Most of the time	3	11	9	9	8	12	15	18	15	23	14	9
Some of the time	12	15	20	18	20	15	20	20	15	18	5	14
Just now and then	10	9	13	15	10	10	5	10	6	6	11	11
No	75	59	50	51	54	52	55	18	62	37	62	60
N =	(73)	(66)	(689)	(773)	(50)	(68)	(20)	(49)	(34)	(79)	(37)	(222)
Satisfaction with living standard												
1 Completely satisfied	25	21	26	32	14	17	15	16	32	11	38	40
2	25	29	25	28	28	29	30	8	21	13	19	26
3	27	17	22	16	26	20	20	16	18	25	16	12
4 Neutral	8	15	15	14	10	15	15	27	13	19	16	10
5	4	5	7	5	12	7	10	8	9	19	3	4
6	3	9	4	3	4	4	5	6	—	11	8	5
7 Completely dissatisfied	8	5	2	2	6	7	5	18	3	1	—	2
N =	(75)	(66)	(689)	(771)	(50)	(69)	(20)	(49)	(34)	(79)	(37)	(221)

185

continued

Table 5.1. (Continued)

	Single-at home M	Single-at home F	Married M	Married F	Single-on own M	Single-on own F	Separated M	Separated F	Divorced M	Divorced F	Widowed M	Widowed F		
	4% (75)	3% (66)	32% (689)	36% (773)	2% (50)	3% (69)	1% (20)	4% (49)	2% (34)	4% (80)	2% (37)	10% (222)	= 101% = 2164	
Satisfaction with life														
1 Completely satisfied	12	8	22	26	12	16	5	10	18	8	38	25		
2	33	55	45	42	31	33	35	29	26	21	12	31		
3	30	17	20	19	27	17	20	8	26	35	24	21		
4 Neutral	15	12	9	9	16	19	25	27	15	20	18	15		
5	3	6	2	3	8	9	15	8	12	10	—	3		
6	7	3	2	1	4	9	—	14	3	5	6	1		
7 Completely dissatisfied	—	—	1	*a	2	—	—	4	—	1	3	3		
N =	(69)	(66)	(679)	(768)	(49)	(69)	(20)	(49)	(34)	(80)	(34)	(217)		
How happy														
Very happy	15	25	32	37	23	12	37	13	12	13	19	18		
Pretty happy	73	68	61	57	60	72	26	54	74	73	58	66		
Not too happy	12	8	7	6	17	16	37	33	15	15	22	16		
N =	(74)	(65)	(685)	(771)	(48)	(68)	(19)	(48)	(34)	(80)	(36)	(219)		

aLess than 0.5%.
bIncludes a wide variety of other possible relationships to head; for example, parent of head, sibling of head, grandparent or grandchild of head, and so on. See the Quality of American Life codebook, p. 20, for detail.

186

category were in correctional institutions or mental hospitals, and thus were not included in the sample.

The divorced category may appear to be unexpectedly small, especially in view of the claims of soaring divorce rates. This category, too, shows a lopsided distribution, with more than twice as many women as men. The misrepresentation of the frequency of divorce was considered in the previous chapter. (A parallel to the present finding appears in Table 4.2, those results based on the Current Population Surveys of the Bureau of the Census.) The explanation of the sex imbalance here is simple: many divorced persons remarry, but the chances for a man are greater than for a woman, for reasons discussed later. The same methodological problem—inaccessible males—is also no doubt a factor. Finally, the widowed category shows an extremely lopsided distribution, the heavy excess of women being a function of the age at first marriage and the differences in life expectancy.[3]

Most single persons living at home are children of the head of the house, and most, not surprisingly, are under age thirty. A majority of both the males and females were employed, although a fair-sized minority were students. One finding of greater than average import is the presence of significant unemployment in this category, particularly in the case of the males. The singles-at-home form 7% of the adult population but contain 29% of the unemployed. It would, of course, be a mistake to minimize the employment problems faced by this group. Nonetheless, living at home in the parental household, they no doubt have access to resources going well beyond those provided by unemployment compensation. This may, indeed, account for the anomaly noted in Chapter 3, where, at one point, the proportion of persons mentioning unemployment as their most serious personal problem was less than the then-current unemployment rate. (See also Flaim and Gellner, 1972.)

[3]The NORC studies asked married respondents if they had been previously divorced. Of the married males and females, 15 and 13%, respectively reported a previous marriage. Combining those numbers with those of the currently divorced, one finds that 71% of the ever-divorced males had remarried, as against 60% of the equivalent females. A comparison within age categories should yield even sharper differences.

There are, we suspect, a number of reasons why remarriage rates are higher among divorced males than divorced females, a matter for discussion later in this chapter.

In recent years, the median age of the groom in first marriages has been approximately two years greater than that of the bride. In 1975, for example, the respective figures were 22.7 and 20.8 years. A 23-year-old white male in 1975 had a life expectancy of 48.7 additional years. A 21-year-old white female could expect to live an additional 57.7 years. Thus, the groom could expect to live to 72 years, the bride to 79 years. The last nine years of the bride's life, in this typical case, would be spent as a widow. It is these two disparities that account for the huge surplus of widows over widowers. The disparity in life expectancies between males and females is approximately one year greater among blacks. The disparity in the ages of the partners is approximately one year greater in marriages where the bride is remarrying (United States Bureau of the Census *Statistical Abstract . . . 1977*: pp. 66 and 74).

One might easily assume that the single men and women were alike with respect to other background characteristics; that, however, is not the case. The disparity in unemployment and student status reflects another difference in background; the single males at home are more likely to come from blue-collar families. The daughters of blue-collar families tend to marry early; the daughters of white-collar families, especially those of the upper middle class, tend instead to go to college, and later, to be on their own prior to marriage.[4]

The pattern among the married may be described very simply. A sizable majority of the married men are in the labor force, more than four fifths of the total being thus engaged. A parallel examination of the NORC studies shows the overwhelming majority to be employed full-time. A fair-sized minority, about one in eight, were retired. A majority of the married women, about three out of five, were listed as housewives (this was the first half of the 1970's, it will be remembered). Three in eight were in the labor force, roughly two thirds in full-time and one third in part-time work.

The separated males and females show an age pattern that approximates that of the married. There is some disparity, however, in that the males have a higher average age (higher, that is, than the equivalent married and much higher than the separated females). This disparity, we think, is again due to method, reflecting the unavailability or inaccessibility of young separated males. The equivalent married men, after all, are likely to be at home when the interviewer calls.

Separated women are likely to be in the labor force, and are much more likely to be full-time employees than are the married women.[5]

There is a marked asymmetry in the age structures of the male and female divorced. Because of the "rising divorce rates," one tends to think of the divorced as consisting of mostly young populations. But surprisingly, one third of the divorced males are age 65 or more, and another three eighths are between ages 50 and 64. It is the divorced women, by contrast, who are young, a substantial majority being under 50. The accessibility factor is no doubt operating here again, as among the other segments of the "not currently married." But in this case, we think that much of the difference is

[4]The best available discussion and data on the age at marriage is in Carter and Glick, Chapter 4; see especially p. 93 ff.

[5]It will be noted that many of the columns in Table 5.1 are based on rather small bases; as a result, some of the figures shown there differ from more adequate evidence, such as that provided by the Current Population Survey or the United States Census. As of March 1978 (several years after the data in Table 5.1 were produced), the Statistical Abstract reported a labor force participation rate of 56.8% among separated women (versus the 69% figure shown in our table), and a rate of 74% for divorced women (versus 73% shown in our table). Of the separated women in the labor force, 82.3% were engaged in full-time work; among divorced women, the figure was 88%. As in our table, married women were less likely to be in the labor force, and among those in the labor force, less likely to be in full-time jobs. (See Statistical Abstract of the United States, 1979, p. 400, Table No. 661.)

real. Most divorced persons remarry. But the older divorced men present in the sample, we suspect, constitute something of a residual group, those who, for one reason or another, were "left over" after this "second round" of marital choices. Some evidence attesting to this conclusion is presented below.

Like the separated women, a substantial majority of divorced women also appear in the labor force, and they, too, are employed full-time in disproportionate numbers (see also Note 5). While separation and divorce clearly constitute a major digression from the normal or preferred life course, the consequences of that digression are much more serious for women than for men. Forced out of the home and into full-time employment they, as will be seen, face the most formidable strains of any of the categories in the table.

Widowers and widows, as one would expect, are relatively elderly, majorities of both being age 65 and over. Five of eight widowers are retired. Just under a third, however, are still employed, many of them being below the normal retirement age. Reflecting no doubt their high average age, approximately one in four of those still employed work only part-time.

A striking pattern of sex differentiation appears in this context; widowers retire but widows continue on as housewives (or, in the NORC studies, continue "keeping house"). The same pattern appears in the case of the older married.[6] In part, at least, this difference must be purely conceptual, that is, not reflecting practical realities; many retired widowers living on their own would obviously also be keeping house. One does not ordinarily retire from housekeeping; the labors involved are needed to the very end.

The distribution of total family income may be easily summarized. The married together with the singles living at home report the highest average family incomes. The other categories, the singles on their own, the separated, the divorced, and the widowed, all report rather low incomes. The differences by sex in the first two categories are necessarily very small, the family income being treated as a shared possession. The differences by sex are the greatest in the other categories, with women consistently having the lower incomes.

There is, necessarily, some ambiguity in the income data as to what is reported and what is not. In the case of the divorced, for example, one might consider the question of child-support payments. For tax purposes, child-support payments are not reported as income by the recipient and are not taken as deductions by the donor. Nonetheless, such payments reduce disposable income on one side (typically, although not invariably, the male side) and increase it on the other, and such matters may well reduce some of the sex differences in "real" income among the divorced.[7]

---

[6]Looking at the marrieds who are age 65 or over, one finds 79% of the males listed as retired. Only 13% of the equivalent women are retired, 80% of them being listed as housewives.

[7]There is some exaggeration in the popular literature when it comes to the numbers receiving financial support from previous husbands. There is also consid-

The presentation in Table 5.1 only inadequately captures the inequities involved, since there are wide variations in the needs of the various segments. The most serious problems appear with regard to the separated and divorced women, many of whom are heads of multiperson family units. The poorest categories of all are the widowers and widows, but, as will be seen, their circumstances are not so straitened as first appears: most of them are single persons, and the needs and demands at that stage of the life cycle are quite different from those of the separated and divorced.

A report of expressed financial concerns appears next in Table 5.1. Least likely to indicate any such worries are the single males living at home. The greatest anxieties were reported by the separated women, roughly half of whom said they worried either all or most of the time. They were closely followed by divorced women, two fifths of whom reported financial pressures, although, to be sure, these were not of the same urgency as among the separated. Separated and divorced males, in contrast, were much less likely to report pressing financial concerns, their figures, respectively, being 20 and 18%. These males, it should be remembered, are not the precise counterparts of the females in the table. That is one reason for the difference in the responses. Then, too, the women, in most cases, have been granted custody of the children.[8] There may have been serious inequities in the assignment of income by the courts (not all of that, to be sure, being to the benefit of the male partner). In many instances, clearly, a husband who just disappears can produce serious inequity without benefit of any court.

One might anticipate that the widowed, many of whom are living on small retirement incomes, would express the most serious concerns about the inadequacy of their finances. They, however, prove to be among the least likely to express such worries. They are, in fact, very much like the at-home singles (and the divorced men), in that fair-sized *majorities* indicate no

---

erable exaggeration with respect to the amounts involved. A United States Census publication reports as follows:

> Both the likelihood that a woman with children will receive child support and the amount she receives may vary widely, depending on her characteristics. For example, 42% of currently divorced mothers with at least one child present in their homes received child support payments, compared to 26% of re-married mothers, 18% of separated mothers, and only 4% of never-married mothers. Mean amounts received ranged from $3180 (for separated mothers) to $1500 (for never-married mothers) [per year].

With respect to alimony payments, they report that: "Out of the 4.5 million divorced or separated women, only 4 per cent reported that they had received alimony in 1975. . . . The mean amount of alimony received by women was about $4,120 in 1975." From United States Bureau of the Census, *Current Population Reports,* Series P-23, No. 84, 1979b, pp. 4-5.

[8]The NORC composite file shows immense disparities in this regard. Seventy-four percent of the separated women ($N = 152$) have children present in their households, as against 24% of the equivalent men ($N = 77$). Among the divorced, the respective figures are 57% and 16% ($Ns = 233$ and 150).

financial worries whatsoever. Where an examination of the income figures alone would suggest desperation-level poverty to be typical in these categories, that inference is clearly deceptive. The small income supports a single person at a late stage in the life cycle. Major consumption expenditures (the purchase of a house and of major home furnishings) were completed years ago, and the current needs, in most cases, would be rather modest. This conclusion is reinforced by the results of the subsequent question asking about satisfaction with one's living standard, this being explicitly defined as "the things people have—housing, car, furniture, recreation and the like. . . . " The widowed had the highest level of satisfaction of all groups, exceeding that of the married and the singles living at home.[9]

Two questions in the Quality of American Life study probed for respondent's overall assessments of their lives, one asking about satisfaction, the other about happiness. Although having the same general intent, some significant differences in the responses appear, the former apparently picking up a sense of accomplishment or fulfillment, the latter touching more on the quality or tone of one's current existence (see Campbell, Converse, and Rodgers, pp. 24-37). Most of these results, given the foregoing presentation, will occasion little surprise.

The satisfaction question (Q. J4) reads: "We have talked about various parts of your life, now I want to ask you about your life as a whole. How satisfied are you with your life as a whole these days?" Respondents were asked to choose a number from a card ranging from one to seven, with the extremes labeled "completely satisfied" and "completely dissatisfied" and with the midpoint labeled "neutral." The married fell very disproportionately to the satisfied side of the scale, more than one fifth choosing the completely satisfied option, more than two fifths choosing the next degree of satisfaction, and still another fifth taking the third option. This left approxi-

[9]This same result appeared in the 1978 Quality of American Life study.

The questions read as follows: Q. G14: "Do you ever worry that your total family income will not be enough to meet your family's expenses and bills?" Q. G14(A): (IF YES) "Would you say that you have worries like this all of the time, most of the time, some of the time, or just now and then?" And, Q. G15: "The things people have—housing, car, furniture, recreation, and the like—make up their standard of living. Some people are satisfied with their standard of living, others feel it is not as high as they would like. How satisfied are you with your standard of living?" As noted, widows are among the least likely to indicate financial worries and among the most satisfied with respect to their material standard of living, despite their generally lower incomes. As suggested in the text, this might reflect only that one's need for income declines at that stage of the life cycle. Another possibility is some erosion of expectations, such that aging widows come to be satisfied with less. Still a third possibility is that many have substantial financial resources that provide an economic buffer and keep day-to-day economic worries to a minimum, e.g., capital assets from life insurance settlements, or from personal savings. Such assets would tend to reduce one's worry about paying the bills, even if the yearly income per se were relatively modest.

mately one respondent in twelve expressing neutrality about his or her life, and an even smaller group indicating dissatisfaction. Most of the latter was only modest dissatisfaction.

The singles, both those living at home and those on their own, expressed below average degrees of satisfaction. For both groups, neutrality and dissatisfaction were relatively more frequent, although still forming only modest minorities. The least satisfying lives by far were reported by separated and divorced women. Of those separated from their husbands, 26% reported dissatisfaction, and a similar percentage assessed their lives as neutral.

The patterns found among the widowers and widows showed some unexpected complexities. Among the small number of widowers, one finds the highest percentage of completely satisfied persons of any category in the table (a finding that also appears in the 1978 study). The widows, too, have an above-average percentage expressing that same degree of satisfaction, although the level is not by any means as striking as in the case of the widowers. For others, however, there does appear to be some greater sadness as compared to those with intact marriages, the level of neutral responses being nearly double that of the married group, and the very lowest level of satisfaction being somewhat more frequent. Some widowed do report dissatisfaction, although the percentages may seem unexpectedly small. Unlike most other groups, where the expressed dissatisfaction tends to be only moderate, the dissatisfied widowers and widows tend to choose the more extreme options.[10]

The study also contains a "happiness" question (Q. K13). This reads: "Taking all things together, how would you say things are these days— would you say that you're very happy, pretty happy or not too happy these days?" Overall, about three in ten said very happy, six said pretty happy, and only one in ten said not too happy.[11] The results by marital status may be

[10]A plausible explanation for the pattern noted in the text is that the highly dissatisfied widows and widowers are only recently widowed, and thus, still caught in the throes of bereavement. Since the distress associated with becoming widowed abates over time, one would expect those widowed the longest to report the most life satisfaction and those most recently widowed to report the least; this might account for the bimodal pattern shown in the table. On the matter of bereavement, useful works include Lopata, 1979; and Walker, MacBride, and Vachon, 1977.

[11]The percentage saying they are very happy is somewhat larger than the percentage saying they are completely satisfied with their lives as a whole (29% versus 22%), which means, necessarily, that one can be very happy and yet not completely satisfied. The standards for happiness, that is, appear to be somewhat lower than the standards for complete satisfaction.

The happiness question is common in surveys of the quality of life, it being included in the NORC surveys as well as many others. "Advanced" critics resist taking the questions seriously, its mere appearance in such surveys attesting, in their viewpoint, to the silliness of the whole survey enterprise. This is a remarkable position. It assumes either (i) that happiness is somehow not important as a "com- modity" to be maximized in life, or (ii) that there is some better way of finding out how happy people are than by asking them directly. Concerning the first, the

easily summarized: apart from a small number of exuberant separated males (who also appear in the 1978 study), the married are outstanding in reporting high levels of happiness. On the whole, they indicate a very happy existence nearly twice as often as other adults. Married women are somewhat more likely to report this euphoric state than are married men. Most other groups cluster disproportionately in the middling "pretty happy" catgegory. The separated differ here, roughly one third of them choosing the "not very happy" response. Among most other groups, approximately one person in six made the same choice. On balance, it seems, the best guarantee of happiness is the marital state. Even that is not a sure thing, it should be noted, since a majority of the married, approximately three in five, have missed complete bliss and report themselves as only pretty happy, and some, a small minority, say they are not too happy.[12]

The principal difference between the responses to the two satisfaction and happiness questions appears with respect to the widowed. They indicated

---

conclusions of Jonathan Freedman, author of a book entitled *Happy People* (1978), may stand as the final word on the matter: "For most people happiness is what life is all about. Our goals, aspirations, dreams and fantasies revolve around happiness. Almost every decision we make is in terms of what we think will bring us the most happiness. Everything else that is important to us—love, faith, success, friendship, sex, recognition—is a means to the end of achieving happiness" (Freedman, p. 3). And concerning the second, Freedman is again worth quoting: "Not everyone who is happy is smiling or laughing; not everyone who is unhappy is crying or scowling. We simply cannot tell with any accuracy just by looking at someone how happy he is; and there is no other way for outsiders to tell. (. . .) Happiness is a personal feeling, known fully only by the person experiencing it. (. . .) Since only the person can know how happy he or she is, the only way to find out is to ask" (Freedman, p. 8).

[12]One group is, so to speak, lost within our categories—the unmarried mothers. They form less than 1% of the total, most of them being counted here as singles at home or singles on their own. Their circumstances are, on the whole, even less attractive than those of the separated and divorced. As Campbell puts it (1981, p. 201), their portrayal of their own lives is "remorselessly negative." They are the "least willing of all the life-cycle groups to say they are very happy, some one in twenty. . . . They are similar to separated and divorced women in reporting feelings of strain; feeling tied down, worried about having a nervous breakdown. . . . In virtually every domain of life, they are among the least satisfied." The effects of marital status on happiness and life satisfaction—that married people are relatively more happy, and the divorced and separated relatively less so—is widely reported in the scholarly literature. See, for example, Glenn (1975a); Glenn and Weaver (1979); Clemente and Sauer (1976); or Spreitzer, Snyder, and Larson (1975). The effect is also reported in two book-length treatments, these being Campbell, Converse, and Rodgers, (Chapter 10) and Bradburn (Chapter 9). All the above-referenced studies are based on conventional happiness and life satisfaction questions. Similar results are also reported with other measures of psychic distress or mental illness. Warheit, Holzer III, Bell, and Arey (1976) report that being separated was significantly related to stressful scores on the Health Opinion Survey, "a widely used psychiatric assessment instrument" (p. 459). There is also evidence that being married is negatively correlated with length of psychiatric hospitalization (Gove and Fain, 1975).

remarkably high levels of satisfaction but report below-average levels of happiness. One can clearly have a sense of accomplishment or achievement gained in the course of a lifetime, one that could yield considerable over-all satisfaction. Given, however, the loss of one's spouse and a continuing loss of friends and acquaintances, as well as some deterioration in the quality of one's health, a choice of the very happy option becomes ever less appropriate.

The primacy of marriage as a determinant of life satisfaction and happiness should come as no surprise, given the findings reported in Chapter 3, where we saw a very strong focus on marriage and family life as goals. There was, it will be remembered, a considerable emphasis within the general population on a happy marriage, this being chosen by some 40% of the sample as their first preference among the twelve listed goals. For some, we suggested, a happy marriage was no longer a realistic goal. In the case of the older widowed segment, a good family life appeared as a frequent substitute choice. Some, we noted, had made another first-place choice and put the happy marriage in second place. Some important specifications of the overall result appear in Table 5.2.

By far, the greatest emphasis on a happy marriage was placed by the marrieds themselves. Forty-four percent of the married men made that choice, and 56% of the equivalent women put marriage in first place. At the opposite extreme, only 4% of the single males on their own and only 6% of the divorced males gave marriage as their first choice. In every comparison of the sexes, women indicated the greater interest in marriage, the sharpest contrast appearing among the still-at-home singles, the respective male–female percentages being 13 and 35.

Table 5.2. First-ranked Life Goal by Marital Status and Sex: SRC Quality of American Life, 1971

	Single-at home		Married		Single-on own		Sepa-rated		Divorced		Widowed	
	M	F	M	F	M	F	M	F	M	F	M	F
First-ranked goal												
Happy marriage	13	35	44	56	4	20	22	28	6	18	15	17
Good family life	15	15	9	14	7	12	—	19	13	26	24	29
Good country	18	8	18	13	20	8	28	14	25	22	12	15
House, apartment	9	7	6	6	18	15	11	19	13	8	18	9
Job	22	15	11	2	27	12	—	2	13	6	6	3
N =	(67)	(60)	(652)	(710)	(45)	(61)	(18)	(43)	(32)	(72)	(34)	(191)

A closely linked focus, actually the third-ranked goal, was a good family life. This showed a result similar to the marriage pattern, with women in all comparisons reporting the greater interest. Marriage and family together were chosen as first preferences by 53% of the married men and 70% of the equivalent women. Among the singles still at home, the most likely candidates for future marriage, the respective figures were 38 and 50%. Among the males on their own, one finds a very low 11% for males and only 31% for females. While separated and divorced women express considerable interest in marriage and the family (46 and 45%, respectively), it is hardly an exaggeration to say that the equivalent males seem, for the most part, to have rejected those goals, the percentages here being 22 and 19%. The implications of these disparate interests will be considered at some length later in the chapter.

It will be remembered that the most frequently mentioned goals apart from marriage and family were a good country, one's house or apartment, and an interesting job. These other goals were chosen disproportionately by the nonmarried, particularly by the single, the separated, and the divorced, and most especially by the males in those categories. The job and country ratings of the at-home single males, 22 and 18%, respectively, outweighed their choices of marriage and family. Among the single males on their own, the disproportion was even more pronounced (27 and 20%, with another 18% giving housing as their first priority).

A more direct indication of attitudes toward marriage appears in the responses to a forthright question on the subject [Q. J2(H)]: "How important is a happy marriage?" Only 4% of the total sample reject this goal outright, saying it is not at all important. The disparities here are extremely sharp; only one married person in a thousand (0.1%) subscribed to this view, as opposed to 41% of the divorced men. Another 10% of the latter saw marriage as only somewhat important (in contrast to 2% overall). Relatively large numbers of the other nonmarried groups also rejected marriage, but this proves deceptive because of strong age linkage. Of single men under age 30, 64% rated a happy marriage as important. Among the equivalent singles ages 30 to 64, that percentage fell dramatically to 29%. Although there was some decline with age among the single females, it was by no means as sharp (from 75 to 59%). The disparity of interest between the sexes of those ages 30 to 64 for three key subgroups are shown in Table 5.3.

It might be that those persons discounting marriage were opposed to the institution from the outset. Or, alternatively, they may have changed their orientation and adjusted as their lives unfolded. Some may have discovered that they were such strong individualists (or so irascible) that marriage was not for them. Some may have been rejected by all possible partners and have adjusted—that is, adopted other goals—for that reason. For some, the denigration of the importance of marriage may only be 'face-saving" that rationalizes previous marital failures. Many homosexuals, no doubt, would also be found among those rejecting marriage. Some of them would have

Table 5.3. Importance of Happy Marriage for Singles, Separated, and Divorced, Ages 30–64, by Sex: SRC Quality of American Life Study, 1971

	Single[a]		Separated		Divorced	
	Male	Female	Male	Female	Male	Female
Extremely important	29%	59%	46%	68%	26%	53%
Very important	18	9	18	11	11	21
Quite important	11	—	9	4	5	9
Somewhat important	18	14	9	4	16	9
Not at all important	25	18	18	14	42	9
N =	(28)	(22)	(11)	(28)	(19)	(47)

[a]Includes singles on their own exclusively; singles living at home are excluded.

never married. Some others, especially those among the separated and divorced, may have married only to discover their propensities after the fact, or, alternatively, only as an act of social conformity (Ross, 1971).

A brief summary is in order. The discussion to this point has been organized on the assumption that marriage, for most people, is the central event in the normal pattern of life. This is more than just a statistical statement describing the most frequent case, it also reflects preferences, most people very much wishing to have a happy marriage at the center of their lives. The married, accordingly, prove to be the most satisfied and, in general, the happiest segment of the entire population.

Most persons are likely to find the above conclusion rather commonplace. The finding is unexpected only when seen from some conventional intellectual perspectives. From the perspective of the social critics, the happy marriage is no more than an appearance; it is a facade behind which one finds seething hatreds and occasional angry outbursts (this in combination with either occasional or frequent extramarital affairs). Another reading, a frequent literary representation, has the happy marriage linked to subnormal intelligence; the partners are portrayed as too insensitive to know any better. The workplace critics follow another tack; they see alienation from *work* as the central fact in the human condition, their accounts either neglecting marriage entirely or treating it as a secondary or "dependent" fact.

A review of the steps in the "normal" life pattern is useful, along with some consideration of the major digressions from it. The singles at home, those still in the bosom of the family, are singularly blessed in that they are remarkably free of money worries. They share the collective benefits at a point when most families are at peak earning power (see the discussion in Chapter 7). It is not surprising, therefore, that they also express high levels of satisfaction with their living standards. Despite the material comforts, however, the levels of life satisfaction fall well short of the levels among the married, as do the reports of personal happiness. The unease or concern manifested at this point is to be expected, since these singles still face two of the most significant decisions of their lives, those involving marriage and career. Although neither choice is in any way ultimate, from the perspective of the young adults such decisions do loom large and take on enormous importance. A final point to note in connection with their lesser life satisfaction is that they are, overwhelmingly, still dependent on others, mainly parents, for their sustenance and well-being; the urge to become independent is possibly a factor here.

The singles on their own are a more diverse group than those still at home, as clearly indicated by the broader age range found among them. Many are just starting out and in poor circumstances financially (either absolutely or relatively, that is, in terms of their hopes and aspirations). Many are, as we have seen, anticipating marriage, or at least hoping for it. But others have turned away from that option because of homosexual proclivities, strong individualism and the sensed difficulties in living together, other interests that have taken precedence, or possibly, because they themselves had been rejected. On the whole, they differ little from the married in terms of expressed financial worries and are only slightly less satisfied with their living standards. The singles on their own, however, do report less satisfaction with their lives than the married, and, of course, they fall well below the married in reported happiness.

What might well be called *the* disaster in life occurs with the breakup of a marriage, the most serious problems being reported by the separated, most especially by separated women. For many broken families, a constant level of income must now be stretched to support two households. In many instances, the wife must manage a household, care for the dependent children, and at the same time enter the labor force in either a full- or part-time capacity. In some cases, the simple disappearance of a husband causes a complete disaster in the home. Separated women are twice as likely as the next contenders, divorced women, to report money worries all the time. Their distinctiveness vis-à-vis separated males, however, could be a result of the survey method, those in the most straitened circumstances simply not being available for interviews. The age difference certainly points in this direction, suggesting that young separated males are not represented in the sample in appropriate numbers. The predominance of men age fifty and over responding to the survey would mean that many had had time to make adjustments, to recover from the worst aspects of the disaster. Given these conditions, given, that is, the combination of both the emotional and financial disasters, the levels of life satisfaction are low, the lowest of all groups under consideration. The levels of reported happiness are also the lowest of all the groups.[13]

[13]The number of cases, particularly of the males here, is extremely small. We have checked these patterns with the consolidated NORC studies (1972-1976) for which the number of male and female cases, respectively, are 77 and 151. The patterns indicated there are very close to those found in the Quality of American Life study. The separated report the lowest levels of satisfaction with their financial situations;

The divorced have moved at least one step further in the process of marital breakup, and, accordingly, many of them have had more time for adjustment. The disaster, although still serious, is somewhat less formidable than among the separated (as indicated, for example, by the extent of their money worries and the expressions of dissatisfaction with living standards). The divorced males appear to have achieved the best adjustments. Although having very low average incomes, they seem to have accepted their situation, in that few report serious financial worries (three out of five report none at all) and most report a remarkably high level of satisfaction with their living standards. They also report a comparatively high level of satisfaction with life, although they do indicate only middling levels of happiness. This group, as noted, is somewhat older; apart from the widowed, they are older than any of the others, and many, it will be remembered, are retired. Unlike the majority of the divorced, who later remarried, most of these men appear to have rejected marriage (having turned to other things) or to have been rejected by likely partners (thus forcing a shift of interest to other things). For many of the divorced women, by comparison, the disaster is still very much present and manifested in everyday experience.[14]

The foregoing discussion, and most other discussions, of the separated and the divorced tend to treat these as homogeneous categories, all persons contained therein having similar experiences, problems, and so on. In fact, there may be sharp differences that result from the underlying dynamics of the divorce, and a consequent asymmetry in the pain and suffering involved.

---

they are most likely to report their incomes as below average; and they are most likely to report being not too happy. In all these respects women gave more negative reports than the men, and in all respects, the separated gave more negative assessments than the divorced. In the 1971 Quality of American Life study, 37% of the separated males reported themselves as being very happy. The 1978 Quality of American Life study has the same finding, in this case 34% of the separated males saying very happy. The NORC composite, using the same question, has only 20% giving that response. We have no ready explanation for the disparity.

[14]Although we have referred to separation and divorce as *the* disaster, the overwhelming majority of persons in this situation viewed the previous marriage as something worse, as even more of a disaster.

Again, the findings were checked with the consolidated NORC studies (1972-1976). They are a close match for the Quality of American Life studies as far as financial situations are concerned. There are some differences indicated with respect to the happiness question, males and females saying they are not too happy amounting to 30 and 24% (as opposed to the 15 and 15% reported in Table 5.1). There was no life satisfaction question contained in the NORC studies.

Of special interest in this connection are the works of R. Stein (1970) and Grossman (1978). Also of some interest is Estes and Wilensky (1978).

We think there is reason to discount some aspects of the 1971 study's portrait of the divorced males (based on 34 cases). The SRC's 1978 study (based on 112 cases) shows a different age distribution, only 10% being 65 or over (versus the 32% figure from 1971). A much higher percentage of employeds were found, the respective figures for 1971 and 1978 being 52 and 83%. At the same time, as we have indicated, the responses to the attitudinal questions proved to be remarkably similar.

For some marriages, to be sure, separation and ultimately divorce are the end stages of a progressively deteriorating relationship, the process recognized by both parties and the breakup mutually agreed to. Many marriages, however, do not end in quite this way. As Campbell, Converse, and Rodgers have put it, "With some frequency marriages are brusquely terminated by one dissatisfied partner, with the other not feeling any strong dissatisfaction with the relationship until the news is broken" (p. 101, N. 1). For those who initiate the brusque termination, separation and divorce are presumably positive steps, an affirmation that frees them from an undesirable state. For those left behind, the breakup is a very negative step—a negation of life works and life goals. Thus, among the separated and the divorced, one would expect some sharp differences in the consequent suffering, depending on whether the party is the terminator or the terminatee.

To the extent that brusque terminations result from involvements with some other party, it would normally be the male who is in a position to meet, befriend, and become sociable with other parties; the women, in contrast, being predominantly in the home, would have more limited opportunities in this regard. It is plausible, in other words, that separated and divorced men tend disproportionately to be terminators and women terminatees, and thus these differential tendencies are one possible explanation of the sex differences shown in our tables concerning happiness and life satisfaction among the separated and divorced.

The widowed provide a rather unexpected combination of results. Having very little in the way of current incomes, many, in fact, at the poverty level, one would expect appropriate expressions of worry and concern (if not outrage). But high proportions of the widowed express no financial worries at all (three out of five), and very high proportions express satisfaction with their living standards. As we have seen, they express relatively high levels of life satisfaction, approximating those found among the marrieds. We do, however, find this distinctive pattern of life satisfaction combined with an undistinctive level of happiness. Their satisfaction and happiness, it seems, are relative. In contrast to the separated and divorced, most of the widowed make their judgments by reference to a "full life" that now lies, for the most part, behind them. The separated and divorced, by contrast, have had the good life interrupted at a point where normally satisfactions are on the upgrade (see Campbell, Converse, and Rodgers, p. 152, and Table 5.8 below). Those widowed early in life, it will be noted, are like the separated and divorced in experiencing a disaster early in the normal life course; it is in their case that one finds the most pronounced life dissatisfaction and unhappiness (Table 5.4.).[15]

[15]The number of widowers, of course, is much smaller, but for what it is worth, we find the same pattern here. The percentage not too happy among those age 64 or under was 40% ($N = 110$), among those age 65 to 74, 27% ($N = 15$), and among those age 75 and over, zero ($N = 11$).
Except in response to the happiness question (where no clear pattern appeared),

Table 5.4. Financial Worries, Life Satisfaction, and Happiness of Widows, by Age: SRC Quality of American Life Study, 1971

	Age of widows				
	18–44	45–54	55–64	65–74	75 or over
Some money worries reported:	100%	65%	41%	36%	28%
N =	(8)	(29)	(44)	(73)	(68)
Life satisfactions —neutral or negative	38	31	28	20	17
N =	(8)	(29)	(43)	(72)	(65)
Happiness—not too happy	29	21	23	11	15
N =	(7)	(29)	(44)	(72)	(67)

Marital status also has a distinctive link to judgments about interpersonal relations. Basically, the married and the widowed tend to be trusting; other groups tend to be distrustful. Since the number of males in some of the categories is very small, we have restricted the following discussion to the females in the sample.

Three questions present dichotomous options: people can be trusted versus one can't be too careful, people try to be helpful versus people look out for themselves, and people try to be fair versus they take advantage. In all three instances, the married and widowed are least likely to give distrustful responses (Table 5.5). (The replication of Table 5.5 in the 1978 Quality of American Life survey sustained these findings, with one exception: in 1978, the proportion of widowed women saying that one can't be too careful was a rather high 62%, as against the 46% figure shown in the 1971 data.) The most distrustful in all cases are the separated, followed by the divorced. The singles on their own also have above average levels of suspicion. The single women still at home tend to be above average, although only by small margins.

It is important to note that one has only a correlation here, one fact being associated with the other. Without a longitudinal study it would be impossible to determine the cause. It might be that people react to the breakdown of a marriage by developing a suspicious, defensive attitude, something clearly suggested by the high levels of distrust found among the separated.

---

similar results were found in the 1978 study. Another question contained there asked (Q. M9): "Considering everything, would you say that up to now you have had all the happiness a person can reasonably expect in life or have you had less than your share or more than your share?" Using the same age categories as in Table 5.4, we have the following percentages indicating less than their share: 47% (15); 37% (35); 28% (80); 20% (114); and 17% (102). (Here too, recency of bereavement may be a factor in the results; cf. Note 10)

Table 5.5. Interpersonal Distrust by Marital Status: Women Only, SRC Quality of American Life Study, 1971

Interpersonal distrust[a]	Women by marital status					
	Singles at home	Married	Singles on own	Separated	Divorced	Widowed
Can't be too careful	51%	46%	59%	67%	62%	46%
N =	(66)	(773)	(69)	(49)	(80)	(221)
People look out for themselves	47	34	51	65	52	31
N =	(66)	(770)	(69)	(49)	(80)	(220)
Most people take advantage	35	27	40	47	45	23
N =	(66)	(764)	(68)	(49)	(80)	(217)

[a]See Chapter 4, Note 28, for question wordings.

Or it might be that suspicious and defensive persons are more divorce prone than others. Both possibilities, of course, could be operating simultaneously. The victims of cheating husbands or wives are thrown into new company on the occasion of divorce, company made up disproportionately of other divorced persons who also have their defenses up. Generalizing from that new experience, one could easily conclude that people are out for themselves.

A parallel to this linkage appears among the marrieds. Those who are highly satisfied with their marriages tend to be trusting; those who are highly dissatisfied tend to be distrustful. Taking those in the highest two categories of marital satisfaction, 46% say one can't be too careful ($N = 1195$). Among those in the two most dissatisfied categories, the figure is 79% ($N = 14$).

There are no significant differences between males in their first marriage and those who have remarried as far as marital satisfaction is concerned. Among females, however, there is a small difference, 80% ($N = 639$) of the first-marriage women being highly satisfied (two highest categories) as against 71% ($N = 86$) of those who have remarried. Some of the suspicion of the divorced appears to carry over into the new marriage. The percentages saying one can't be too careful are: first married, 44% (646); remarried, 62% (86); separated, 67% (49); divorced, 56% (135). A similar but less pronounced pattern appears among the males.[16]

[16]The interviewer's ratings of physical appearance are also related to these attitudes of suspicion, the plain and the homely, in all instances, being the most defensive. Taking the entire sample of males and females, about one half of the strikingly handsome or beautiful respondents (49%, $N = 59$) say one can't be too careful, as against 73% ($N = 45$) of the homely. Those saying people would take advantage amount to 22 and 55%.

These distrustful attitudes are more frequent in the working-class than in the

Although one cannot establish the cause, the association is clear. Singles on their own, separated, and divorced persons are more suspicious than other groups in the population. Any clustering of those populations, as, for example, in the singles bars, would yield a sample that is not typical of the larger universe. This is to suggest that generalizations based on the experience of such samples ought to be viewed with some skepticism; they are typical only of these exceptional population segments, as discussed in Chapter 2.

Most of these summary observations concerning the importance of marital status would, no doubt, strike the average American citizen as obvious. They become new, important, or unexpected only when seen from the perspectives provided by "advanced" intellectuals. Where the social critics, for example, see the principal causes of human suffering as rooted in the structure of society, in its rigid and inflexible institutions, arguing the need to either change or abandon them, large majorities of the participants themselves see their happiness and life satisfaction as rooted in the stability of those same institutions, particularly in those of marriage and the family.

The workplace critics also see unhappiness—in this case referred to as the "alienation of modern man"—having structural roots, this being found in "alienated" work. But that, too, seems a misfocus, a misdirection of attention. It focuses on a secondary and, to a large extent, an instrumental concern, and neglects the primary expressed life goal of most of the population.

The social critics, moreover, greatly exaggerate the extent of family breakdown, neglecting also to point out that much of the breakdown is followed by the formation of a subsequent marriage. As indicated in Chapter 4, they also make serious misrepresentations about the existing consciousness of the masses. There it was reported that substantial satisfaction was found with many aspects of people's immediate lives. Here we have introduced consideration of two summary measures, assessments of life satisfaction and judgments of personal happiness. Where those of a critical persuasion describe the human condition as a vale of tears, most of the people supposedly being described see their condition as one yielding considerable satisfaction and at least a passably happy existence.

The above findings point to a very different source of unhappiness, one rooted in the facts of demography and personal preferences. Were one interested in ministering to the sufferings of the *least* satisfied segment of the American adult population, as many apparently are, the focus would have to be on divorced and separated women. Given the stated importance of

---

middle-class ranks. The differences in the tone of everyday life are indicated by the following percentages of women who say that others will take advantage—middle-class married, 18%; working-class married, 37%; middle-class separated and divorced, 40%; working-class separated and divorced 58%. For the question wordings, see Chapter 4, Note 28.

marriage among this group (see Table 5.3), the nature of one's ministrations would, of necessity, have to focus on helping them get remarried. The above results, and others to be discussed in the following chapter, make it clear, for example, that remarriage assistance might do more to improve the quality of American life than job enrichment or job redesign.[17]

Given these observations, any sensible account of the sources of strain and discontent in modern American society would have to consider, sooner or later, the barriers to remarriage among divorced and separated women. Many of these barriers, as we shall see, are matters about which little can be done. There is, first of all, the general sex imbalance within the adult population, the excess of women increasing in every older group. Under the prevailing monogamic arrangements, therefore, if all the nonmarried were interested in marrying, some women would be predestined to disappointment. The chances of marriage (or remarriage) for women are further reduced by virtue of the interest factor, greater percentages of nonmarried males rating a happy marriage as only somewhat or not at all important. Some sense of the problem may be gained from the raw figures upon which Table 5.3 is based. Taking the singles, separated, and divorced who assess marriage as very important, one finds more than three women for each similarly interested man.

Still other factors appear to stand in the way of those wishing to marry or remarry, these best described as involving elements of social convention. The Survey Research Center's interviewers were asked to make an estimate of the respondent's physical appearance. The divorced and separated women were, on balance, judged as more attractive than the equivalent men. The interviewers were also asked to make rule-of-thumb judgments of the respondent's intelligence. The women, once again, were given the more favorable ratings. While not sharply differentiated, thinking merely in terms of probabilities, women would be forced to marry down (that is, to marry less attractive or less intelligent men than themselves). While physical appear-

---

[17]Lest there be some serious misreading of the point, let us emphasize: The disproportionate unhappiness of divorced and separated women is what the women *themselves* report. The importance of marriage in achieving a happy life is also *their* answer to the relevant question. We are not suggesting that these things "should" be true in some ultimate sense, only that the people involved report them as features of their own consciousness and condition. (One might, of course, dismiss these reports as indications of the falseness of women's consciousnesses or as evidence of their domination by patriarchal society, their ready acceptance of alien and oppressive male values. One could then address their problems in terms wholly foreign to their own way of thinking, and in the process, denigrate their ability to think for themselves and report accurately about the nature of their own lives.)

There are many aspects of divorce that cannot be addressed in this brief discussion. Some of them are treated, with evidence, in Glenn, Hoppe, and Weiner, 1974; Bumpass and Rindfuss, 1979; and Mueller and Pope, 1980. Also useful, but in a more speculative vein, is the work of Cherlin, 1978.

ance might not pose an insurmountable obstacle (Casanova, it is said, was not a physically attractive man), any serious difference in intellectual capabilities could pose problems for a happy marriage.

There is also a problem of age disparities among the eligible populations, in that a large number of the separated and divorced men are older (most of these indicating a very pronounced rejection of marriage), while a majority of the interested divorced and separated women were under age fifty. There are, to be sure, some fugitive males who were not captured in this sample. Many of them would also be among the eligible population. They may have been out on the town, looking for a potential mate, while the eligible women were at home being interviewed by a representative from the Survey Research Center (most of whom, incidentally, are women).

Some other possible sources of incompatibility were not tapped in this particular study (such as height or weight). One factor that was measured, although one of uncertain importance, is class, the eligible women tending to be in middle-class occupations, the men in working-class occupations (see Glenn, Hoppe, and Weiner, 1974).

It is almost impossible to add up the significance of all those potential incompatibilities. The major lesson, it would seem, is that the marital chances or opportunities for the age 30-and-over singles are dramatically reduced compared to the chances at, say, age 18 or 20. And the chances for women in the older age categories are the most dramatically reduced, given the substantial lack of interest on the part of their male peers.

Both the social and the workplace critics imply that they have solutions to the problems of the human condition. Their solutions, typically, are structural in character. For a quantum leap in aggregate human happiness, all that is required are some appropriate changes in the structure of society. But these findings indicate that the most clearly aggrieved persons in society are victims of a very different kind of structural problem, one which, given the sheer facts of demography and the stubborn human preferences involved, admits of no easy structural solution. Given the distinctive structural parameters involved, the solutions—finding appropriate mates—are largely individual or personal. One would, accordingly, be hard put to devise an appropriate program of affirmative action.

While on the topic of fate, it is useful to explore one other such element— physical appearance. A curious disparity exists between the values discussed and expressed in daily life and those found in many social science texts. Ordinary people spend a lot of time evaluating people in terms of their looks and, moreover, acting on those assessments. A good-looking woman, it is reported, is more frequently asked out on dates and gets more invitations to dance at parties. Yet it is a rare sociology text that explicitly discusses (let alone researches) the role of good (or bad) looks in determining preferment of any kind (as, for example, in the case of social mobility). Processes of discrimination that begin at a very early age and that continue, rather systematically, throughout lifetimes, are, with peculiar obtuseness, ignored by many members of the academic community, at least in their writing.[18]

Divorced and separated women, as we have seen, on the whole, are the most distressed groups of those shown in the previous tables. Nevertheless, here as elsewhere, some internal variation is found, which, as evidenced in Table 5.6, is linked to physical appearance. Those assessed by the interviewers as having better-than-average appearance reported: more satisfaction with life, greater assurance that things would work out as planned, greater control over their own lives, less fear of a nervous breakdown, a greater sense of having had a fair opportunity in life, greater enjoyment in life than most, and finally, more happiness (by a small margin). The least distinctiveness appears in the latter connection, providing another instance of a satisfaction-happiness disparity. All these levels of well-being, of course, are substantially lower than for equivalent married people. The point, however, should be clear, namely, that appearance is a factor of some evident importance in the determination of life assessments.[19]

[18]The subject of physical appearance has not been entirely neglected. See, for example, Aronson, 1980, pp. 250-255, for a review of some relevant social psychological literature, and the sources cited therein. A number of recent studies have also considered the effects of good looks on the mobility of women through marriage. (See Elder, 1969; Murstein, 1972; Taylor and Glenn, 1976; and Udry, 1977.) The effects are modest in all instances. All studies indicate the complexity, the variability, of the relationship in different contexts. Another important source is Campbell, 1981, pp. 211-213, 218-219. Campbell suggests a modest overall contribution of physical attractiveness to life satisfaction. We suspect that the effect is highly specific and differentiated, counting for much among unmarried women who wish to be married than among those already married. This is, to be sure, an inadequately explored research topic. One consideration suggested by the Quality of American Life data is that the interviewers' judgments of physical appearance and intelligence were positively related.

Most of the work done on physical attraction and its consequences has been done by social psychologists; given the academic division of labor, little of this work has filtered over into sociology, and even less into the work of critical intellectuals. Considering the evident importance of physical attraction in the organization of everyday interactions and affairs, the neglect of this phenomenon outside social psychology is all the more lamentable.

[19]Interviewers were also asked to make judgments of the respondents' apparent sincerity; that is, whether their answers appeared completely sincere (80%), usually sincere (18%), or whether they often seemed to be insincere (2%). These assessments were systematically related to the estimates of physical appearance. There were five degrees of appearance, ranging from handsome to homely (the categories having been collapsed in Table 5.5 because of the small numbers at the extremes). Taking the entire sample, one found 85% of the handsome reported as giving completely sincere answers, against 64% of the homely. Or, put differently, the perceived less-than-sincere answers increased from 15 to 36%. A similar result appeared with regard to the interviewer's estimates of intelligence, the less-than-sincere responses going from 6% in the very high intelligence category to 41% among the very low. One cannot say with any certainty what lies behind these results. One tends to think of homeliness merely as an unfortunate fact. There are, clearly, additional "hidden

Table 5.6. Physical Appearance and Quality of Life: Separated and Divorced Women, SRC Quality of American Life Study, 1971

	Interviewer's judgment of respondent's appearance		
	Better than average	Average	Less than average
Life satisfaction[a]	46%	29%	23%
Things will work out	46	36	20
Can run own life	87	59	50
No fear of nervous breakdown	90	71	63
Has enjoyed life more than most	36	18	10
Is "very happy"	15	12	10
N's =	(39)	(56–58)	(29–30)

[a]Highest two levels (of seven).

Like some of the other factors discussed above, one's physical appearance is, in the first line of analysis, determined by fate, by the facts of heredity. One can, of course, subsequently do much with whatever raw materials fate has provided. Homeliness, that is, can be overcome to some extent by dress, grooming, cosmetics, orthodontia, cosmetic surgery, and so on (all of these being growth industries over the past decades). These points notwithstanding, it is evident that homeliness detracts from the quality of a person's life; a less-than-satisfactory physical appearance, in short, is a significant source of discontent. The possible policy implications of this fact have been given little or no attention by serious scholars. (The free market economy, in contrast, has shown itself to be extremely sensitive to these needs.) An interesting possibility occurs in this connection: that more could be done to improve the quality of American life by efforts to improve personal appearance than, say, by redesigning jobs or by the creation of opportunities for self-actualization.

Much of contemporary social analysis, influenced in one way or another by the Marxist framework, has come to focus on something called class. For better or worse, much of that discussion has been concerned with the distinction between manual and nonmanual workers (or, some frequently used alternative terms, between blue-collar and white-collar ranks, or between working and middle classes), assuming this distinction to be the most significant of all the possibilities. But such analysis has been unrewarding in that the differences between these two segments, in most instances, have

---

injuries" associated with the visible fact. The desired and rewarded physical traits, it would seem, contribute to the building of ego strength. The lack of those traits would appear to stimulate personal uncertainty and, for some at least, dissimulation as a mechanism for coping. (The findings in Table 5.6, incidentally, were confirmed in the Survey Research Center's 1978 Quality of American Life study.)

proven rather small.[20] Most discussions of class, accordingly, have been devoted to explaining why this powerful factor has had so little effect.

The same result, that there are small differences related to class, appears in our analysis of the Quality of American Life study. The percentages of married males in white- and blue-collar jobs who were very satisfied with their jobs, for example, were 32 and 33% respectively, actually a slight reversal of normal expectation (for more detail see Table 6.3). Equivalent figures for employed married women were in the expected direction, 45 and 40%, but clearly the difference, again, is very small.[21] Fifty-four percent of the married male white-collar workers said they never had money worries; among equivalent blue-collar workers the figure was 44%. A somewhat larger difference appeared with respect to satisfaction with living standards, those choosing one of the two highest categories (out of seven, it will be remembered) being 58 and 40%. Such differences, on the whole, will surprise no one. Except for a school of commentators that flourished in the 1950's, no one has seriously argued that class differences have disappeared.[22] Most of that discussion focused on the size of the differences and the trends, radical critics saying they were large and increasing, moderates claiming they were small and decreasing.

But while the class difference argument progresses another phenomenon of growing importance has appeared on the scene: the increase in the numbers of separated and divorced persons. Although 71% of the married middle-class women express satisfaction with living standards, only 25% of the separated and divorced women in middle-class jobs report a comparable level of satisfaction. Such findings clearly require that more attention be given to the emerging class of the separated and divorced.

The findings in this area can best be summarized by looking at the life satisfaction and happiness of women by class and marital status. (The number of cases of separated and divorced men, especially when divided by class, is too small to warrant attention. They are also, as we have seen, a special residual class, one that in great measure has had time to work out

[20]For examples of this conceptual focus, see Lipset and Bendix (1959, especially p. 14 ff.); Alford (1963); and Lipset (1960); or, more recently, Giddens (1973, especially Chapter 6) or Parkin (1971, p. 25 and throughout). Much of the work in this tradition merely assumes that the blue-collar/white-collar distinction is crucial, that is, without providing serious supporting evidence. For criticism, evidence, and reformulation, see Hamilton, 1972: Chapter 5; and 1975; Chapters 2 and 3. An important empirical review is that of Glenn and Alston, 1968. See also the discussion in Chapter 7.

[21]This brief presentation cannot do justice to a rather complex question. Following an established social science convention, married women have been classified according to the husband's occupation. That means some of the working-class wives were in manual and some were in non-manual occupations. A more detailed examination, however, still showed no large differences.

[22]For citations, discussion, and evidence on the "affluence and the worker" theme (or, in another formulation, the "blurring of class lines" theme), see Hamilton, 1965, and 1967 pp. 4, 70.

Table 5.7. Life Satisfaction, Happiness, and Satisfaction of Ambitions, by Class and Marital Status: Women Only, SRC Quality of American Life Study, 1971

	Middle class		Working class	
	Married	Separated, divorced	Married	Separated, divorced
Life satisfaction (top two categories)	75%	31%	64%	42%
N =	(308)	(52)	(297)	(36)
Very happy	46	18	32	8
N =	(309)	(51)	(297)	(36)
Have satisfied ambitions	70	37	60	36
N =	(304)	(51)	(294)	(36)

some kind of satisfactory adjustment to their situation.) With respect to both life satisfaction and happiness, the class differences prove to be rather small. The differences related to marital status, in contrast, prove to be fairly sizeable (see Table 5.7). One other summary measure, a question asking if people have achieved their ambitions in life, yields a similar result. The best case for the class factor here is a ten percentage point difference between the manual and the nonmanual married. Again, it is separation and divorce within both classes that yield the disastrous effects. For what it may be worth, the effects of separation and divorce prove to be somewhat greater for the middle-class segment.[23]

Clearly, the emphasis on class differences has been misplaced. That much-discussed structural factor, which in many accounts is said to have world historical import, proves to be less important in accounting for differences in happiness and life satisfaction than the more prosaic matter of marital status. While some commentators and researchers have spent time and effort dealing with the elusive hidden injuries of class, some rather

[23]The question of satisfaction of ambitions (Q. K10) reads: "Up to now, have you been able to satisfy most of your ambitions in life or have you had to settle for less than you had hoped for?"

All or part of the differences in life satisfaction and happiness associated with marital status could, conceivably, be a function of race. Blacks constitute 11% of the sample, but form 16% of the divorced population and 42% of the separated. Since blacks, on the whole, have less favorable life circumstances, it could be that the previous results stem from race-related deprivations rather than the broken marriages. But that does not prove to be the case. Again taking only the women, one finds a significant falloff of life satisfaction and happiness among those with broken marriages among both whites and blacks. In all comparisons, blacks report less favorable circumstances, but the race differences are small in comparison to those linked to marital status. Of the married white women, 69% report high levels of life satisfaction, as do 58% of the equivalent blacks. Among divorced white women, the figure is 32%; among divorced black women, it is only 14%.

obvious, easily perceived grievances have been given very little attention, especially in the case of the so-called critical literature. One does not have to search far for an explanation of this omission. It is difficult, if not impossible, to formulate those grievances into an argument that allows a sweeping condemnation of the existing social order. Unlike the Marxist argument, it would be difficult to generate a collective or class conscious-ness based on these grievances, because the solutions sought are so emi-nently personal, or, put somewhat differently, so dependent on the individ-uals involved.

Another unalterable fact of life deserving attention is the matter of age. One might easily anticipate a general decline of life satisfaction with increasing age. If not a continuous fall, one would, at least, expect a sharp decline in the reported quality of life in the years following retirement. One's income, after all, is sharply reduced, and, so one hears, those on fixed incomes are very much subject to the ravages of inflation. Then, too, with a continuous erosion of health and vitality, it seems likely that most satisfac-tions in life would undergo an ineluctable decline.

Many of the relationships with age, however, prove to be strong and positive, with satisfaction levels increasing into the age 75 and over group (Table 5.8). This was the case with marital satisfaction, which went from 49% completely satisfied in the 25 to 34 age category to 83% in the 75 plus category.[24] There was also a pronounced upswing in family satisfaction, the peak again being reached in the oldest group. The number of persons gainfully employed after age 65 sharply reduces with normal retirement. But, for what it may be worth, here, too, a very sharp relationship exists, complete job satisfaction going from 23% in the youngest group to over 75% in the oldest ones. It seems likely, however, as will be seen in Chapter 6, that a strong element of self-selection is involved here, those still working at age 75, for example, being persons who are both free to continue (no forced retirement) and who clearly like their work.

Older people, it is said, are tied down. They do not have the money for travel or distant visits. Moreover, they suffer from physical frailty or inca-pacity, coming more and more to be restricted to home and neighborhood. Despite what is said, the percentages of those saying they are very free increase with age, although, to be sure, the tendency is both modest and irregular. The highest percentages of very free persons (or at least of those under that illusion) are those age 65 and over. The highest percentages of

[24]Some of these relationships are not completely linear. Marital satisfaction, as discussed in Chapter 4, begins with a high, tapers off slightly with the coming of children, and then shows a steep climb after age 40. A similar pattern is found with respect to money worries. The figures given for the satisfaction questions are for those completely satisfied. The low figures among the young should not be interpreted as meaning dissatisfaction; in most instances, they choose the second degree of satis-faction among the seven options. The results in Table 5.8, of course, closely parallel those in Campbell, Converse and Rodgers, pp. 152-153.

Table 5.8. Satisfactions and Economic Condition, by Age: SRC Quality of American Life Study, 1971

	Age						
	18–24	25–34	35–44	45–54	55–64	65–74	75 or over
Marital satisfaction[a]	56%	49%	52%	58%	67%	73%	83%
N =	(181)	(346)	(298)	(271)	(201)	(112)	(41)
Family satisfaction	38	38	35	48	51	53	56
N =	(327)	(428)	(357)	(345)	(281)	(218)	(118)
Job satisfaction	22	31	36	42	44	80	75
N =	(209)	(291)	(255)	(249)	(180)	(39)	(8)
Feels "very free"	42	49	51	46	52	55	58
N =	(332)	(436)	(363)	(364)	(292)	(234)	(131)
Satisfaction with life in United States	19	28	31	37	42	56	51
N =	(332)	(437)	(362)	(363)	(294)	(234)	(129)
Income—less than $5000 in 1970[b]	29	10	11	22	27	61	75
N =	(333)	(439)	(367)	(365)	(294)	(235)	(131)
Money worries —None	52	44	45	51	58	62	70
N =	(333)	(439)	(366)	(365)	(293)	(234)	(131)
Satisfaction with standard of living	19	21	25	27	36	46	48
N =	(333)	(438)	(366)	(365)	(294)	(235)	(129)
Life satisfaction	15	17	19	21	27	32	34
N =	(325)	(437)	(365)	(363)	(290)	(228)	(126)
Satisfaction with health	59	52	48	38	38	31	34
N =	(325)	(432)	(358)	(354)	(285)	(224)	(126)
Very happy	30	32	29	26	30	28	21
N =	(332)	(435)	(364)	(365)	(290)	(233)	(128)

[a]In all cases we have taken the per cent "completely satisfied." See note 24 for additional details.

[b]Total family income before taxes.

those saying not very or not at all free are those age 34 or under.[25] On a related theme, satisfaction with life in the United States, one again finds a strong positive relationship with age, complete satisfaction going from 19% in the youngest group to 51% in the oldest. This result does not signify a vast Reichian rejection of life in the United States by the young; it merely indicates lower levels of satisfaction, a majority choosing the second or third level (that is, apart from the one fifth expressing complete satisfaction). Only one in ten expressed dissatisfaction, most of them indicating only a modest level of complaint.

Income levels, unquestionably, fall sharply with retirement, the decline at age 65 being eminently clear in these data. Only 10% of the respondents in the 25- to 34-year-old category reported a total pretax family (or household unit) income of less than $5000 (in 1970). Such incomes were reported by 75% of the respondents age 75 or over. One might anticipate reports of serious financial problems here, but, as seen in the discussion of the widowed populations, just the opposite is the case. The percentages reporting no money worries increase with age, going from 44% among the 25-to-34 group to 70% among those 75 or over.

One obvious possibility is that older persons have reduced their expectations and demands so as to bring them into line with their drastically reduced revenues. Another possibility is that their financial requirements would be reduced in any case. Older persons eat less than the more active young. They have less wear-and-tear on clothes, hence less need for replacement. The mortgage has been paid off and household goods long since paid for. Then, too, as the family size declines to two persons—and later to one—many people move to smaller dwelling units, something that also increases the amount of disposable income. That portion of the retirement income received from Social Security is indexed to keep up with inflation, and one growing cost, medical care, comes to be covered, at least in part, by Medicare.

[25]The question, Q. C5, reads: "Some people say that there isn't as much freedom in this country as there ought to be. How about you—how free do you feel to live the kind of life you want to—very free, free enough, not very free, or not free at all?"

It would be easy to see this finding as supporting the arguments of the social critics. But, first of all, most of those under age 35 who expressed doubts about the extent of their freedom were saying "not very" (12%), and only 3% said "not at all," the total, obviously, being a rather small 15%. Given the conventional training in the social-critical tradition, one might easily conclude that these young persons were complaining about families, schools, universities, and places of employment, about rigid and confining institutions restricting their spontaneity, creativity, and so on. Most of the responses, however, indicate another target of complaint; namely, the government. The coding category is described as follows: "Laws; government bureaucracy; red tape; need for license; other governmental regulations; taxes." The suggestion, in short, is that the complaint was more clearly linked with a conservative Republican critique than with that of Charles Reich.

Not all explanation is of this salutary character. Some of the elderly would be in institutions and thus not in the sample (which, it will be remembered, contains only noninstutionalized populations). This is a consideration that would affect all the results in Table 5.8; those persons with the most serious health problems (and the greatest reason for general dissatisfaction) would have been excluded from the view of this (and most other) samples.[26] Some of the satisfaction of the elderly is doubtlessly relative; compared to what could be happening, compared to what they have seen in the lives of their age peers, the reaction in many cases might reflect a sense of welcome relief that things are proceeding as well as they have.

Satisfaction with life as a whole, one of our two principal summary measures, also varies directly with age, the percentage completely satisfied increasing from 15% in the youngest category to 34% in the oldest. Again, it should be noted that no sweeping disenchantment is indicated among the young, only a less complete satisfaction, 48% choosing the second most positive category and another 20% choosing the third among the seven options. Very few in any age category chose the negative options.

None of the responses discussed thus far indicate a decline in satisfaction with increasing age. There is, however, one measure that does cut across this picture of *rising* satisfactions, one that moves unambiguously in an opposite direction—satisfaction with health. While many aspects of life come to be judged as better and better, this central feature of it, the beginning point of an individual's life quality, inexorably deteriorates.

The percentages reporting themselves as very happy do not change significantly in the economically active cohorts. The young are not strikingly happier than the rest, the middle-aged or preretired are not strikingly less happy. Only a modest falloff appears among those age 75 and over.[27] This

---

[26]Here again one finds a distinctive indifference to number. A simple question: what percentage of the population age 65 or over lives in homes for the aged and dependent? The answer, as indicated by the 1970 census, was 4%. This increases, of course, with age, but even in the 75 or over group it is still only 8.1%, and among those aged 85 to 100 years, the proportion remains less than one in five (actually 17.7%). These are our calculations based on United States Bureau of the Census, *1970 Census of Population, General Population Characteristics, United States Summary*, Table 53, p. 1-276, and, by the same organization, *Census of Population: 1970, Subject Reports*, Final Report PC (2)-4E, "Persons in Institutions and Other Group Quarters," Table 6, p. 11. Medicare and Medicaid have gone a long way toward reducing the financial burdens of the elderly. One recent account summarizes as follows: "In 1977, Medicare and Medicaid accounted for 61% of the $41 billion expended to meet the health needs of the elderly. . . ." From Davidson and Marmor, 1980, p. 11. See also Jonas, 1977; and Wilson and Neuhauser, 1976. There can also be no doubt, as Davidson and Marmor note, that many problems remain to be solved.

[27]These findings have also been substantiated in the 1978 study. One minor point, the modest falloff in the happiness of the 75-and-over category, was not confirmed. The 1978 study showed no evident relationship between age and happiness, the "very happy" figures all being within the range of 29% plus or minus three, with no

is not correlated with an increase in the "not too happy" responses, only with an increase in the wistful "pretty happy" choices. As indicated earlier, there is a tendency for the older groups to express greater life satisfaction in conjunction with only moderate personal happiness. Given that the former involves a retrospective assessment and the latter is more a judgment of contemporary conditions, the disparity is not, strictly speaking, a contradiction.

The decline of health with advancing age is, of course, an obvious fact. It is, nevertheless, one that is regularly omitted from most of the so-called critical analyses. In most such analyses, one might note, there is an aversion to the somatic bases of human existence. One need only think of the Marxian framework to recognize the rare attention given to the facts of life and death. Some of these critics do offer one rather limited view of such problems in the area of industrial accidents, workplace environmental hazards, and the pollution of soil, streams, and atmosphere with industrial wastes. But they give very little attention to the major killers, heart disease and cancer. The explanation for the restricted focus is easily seen. Industrial accidents can be blamed on the operations of advanced capitalism, the argument, potentially at least, being one that could aid in the mobilization of an outraged clientele. Heart disease and cancer provide no such easy imputation of blame *or* do they provide similar possibilities for class action.[28]

The decline of health with advancing age is another of those problems having no *easy* structural solution. The basic mechanisms for improving health, it will be noted, involve bureaucracy and technology. For the first, one would expand the reach of health organizations, both those dealing with preventative medicine and those providing for the delivery of medical treatment. The second involves the development and use of appropriate medicines and health-related machinery. It would ordinarily involve, for example, the more efficient use of computer technology, both to search for the meaning of unusual symptoms and for the location of the best available information on cures. The solutions proposed in much of the critical literature, however, would negate both of these options; that literature recommends a sweeping rejection of both bureaucracy and technology.

The United States census of 1870 found 5.9% of the adult population (those age 20 or over) in the 65 or more age category. In 1970, the equivalent figure was 15.9%. Increases also occurred in the 55 to 64 age category (from

---

clear trend associated with age. On the general issue of age and happiness, the work by Witt, Lowe, Peek, and Curry (1980) is of some interest.

[28]The argument is selective in still another way. The linkage of industrial accidents and advanced capitalism is implicitly comparative. One should consider the following questions: Are these pathologies absent from early capitalism? Are they absent from noncapitalist economies (for example from socialist economies)? With what frequency are those pathologies found elsewhere? Is it more, less, or the same as in "advanced capitalism?" As typically formulated, such arguments are incomplete, or, as many Marxists would put it, they are one sided.

8.5 to 14.7%), and, to a lesser extent, in the 45 to 54 age category (from 15.2 to 18.4%). Given the differences in life expectancy, one would envision a rather poor standard of health among the 50-to-55-year-olds of 1870. It seems likely that their health conditions would have approximated those of the 70-to-75-year-olds of 1970. Moreover, worry or concern about health at that earlier point would have been considerably more widespread in the population, extending to all ages and class levels. Even the richest persons in the economically advanced nations at that time stood helpless in the face of what are now commonplace medical problems. Prince Albert, the husband of Queen Victoria, died of typhoid in 1861, a problem that nowadays would be solved through brief treatment with antibiotics. Even as late as 1931, Britten Hadden, a cofounder of *Time* magazine, died of an infection that a decade or so later would have been no more than a routine medical matter.

With death such a continuous presence, it seems likely that the general reports of happiness would have been somewhat lower at that time. With the older age at first marriage and the larger average family size, the likelihood of achieving adulthood with both parents still living would be much smaller than at present, which, of course, means that the frequency of orphans and single-parent families would be higher than today. It seems likely that the problems attending broken families evidenced in our data would have been present then also, in, if anything, much more aggravated form.[29] Moreover, those families in the nineteenth century were broken in an irreversible way by death, unlike the broken families of the present. For the children of divorce, it will be noted, the most frequent ultimate outcome is *two* families rather than a single and rather desolate broken unit. In addition to the loss of parents, it should be remembered, it would be rare for a child in former times to reach adulthood without having experienced the loss of brothers and sisters along the way.

This matter of what is actually related to life satisfaction and what is not deserves a more detailed and extended inquiry. As we have just discussed, the notion of class figures prominently in most of the critical-theoretical accounts of the human condition. Two other often noted structural variables are race and gender. Indeed, it is commonly claimed that race, gender, and social class are the principal lines of structural cleavage in the advanced capitalist society. In contrast, attention given to the other factors discussed in this chapter—to marital status, life cycle, physical attractiveness, and so on—is very slight.

----

[29]It ought to be remembered that at least some family re-formation occurred then, as many widows and widowers would marry. In the Plymouth colony, "about one-third of all men and one-quarter of all women who lived full lifetimes remarried after the death of a spouse. . . . Even as late as the 1920's, more brides and grooms were remarrying after widowhood than after divorce . . . " (Cherlin: p. 637). In those cases, as with the children of divorce, two families would be merged, creating the familiar problems of incompatible family traditions, jealousies, and questions about the authority of the new parent.

To give some sense of the relative importance of these various factors in determining life satisfaction, we have undertaken a multiple regression analysis of the overall life satisfaction question contained in the 1978 study. The details of the statistical techniques need not concern us here; in brief, it is a technique that allows one to look at the operation of a large number of factors simultaneously. Included in the analysis are all of the variables discussed in this chapter—marital status, age, and physical attraction. We also included some other personal variables: the interviewer's rating of respondent's intelligence, and responses to a question asking, "Do you have any particular problems with your health?" Picking up a theme from the last chapter, we have also included a variable for whether the respondent lives in the central city of one of the twelve largest cities in the United States. Finally, the analysis included race, gender, and three measures of social class: whether the household head was employed in a white-collar occupation, the respondent's number of years of education completed, and total family income.

The analysis can be quickly summarized. First, all the variables in the analysis collectively account for only 6.5% of the variance in life satisfaction. Another way to phrase this result it that there is quite a bit of satisfaction with life among even the most dissatisfied groups, which is obvious in all the tabular presentations made in this chapter. The question of present interest is which of the variables in the analysis contributes most to the explanation, and here the results were as follows: Race was *not* significantly related to life satisfaction. Gender was *not* significantly related to life satisfaction. Head's occupation, respondent's education, and total family income were *not* significantly related to life satisfaction. *Every other variable included in the analysis made a statistically significant independent contribution.*[30]

[30]These findings might strike some people as bizarre. Similar findings are, nonetheless, reported in the literature. It has been established rather definitely that income is either uncorrelated, or at best weakly correlated, with various measures of life satisfaction (see Duncan, 1975). Glenn and Weaver (1981a) show small, positive effects for education; positive effects for both education and income are also reported in Bradburn (Table 3.3). Campbell, Converse, and Rodgers (Chapter 4), in contrast, report small declines in satisfaction as education increases. If there is an effect for education at all, it must be relatively weak and is, in any case, inconsistent in sign across studies. On the whole, there is relatively little research to support the contention that measures of social standing or class are sharply related to happiness or life satisfaction.

A few other studies have attempted, as we have done, to look at comparative effects of various factors on life satisfaction. Glenn and Weaver (1979) have performed multiple regression analyses similar to ours on data from the NORC surveys. "The estimated positive effect of being married is statistically significant and is stronger for both sexes than the estimated effect of any other predictor variable" (Glenn and Weaver, p. 964). Other variables considered were children in the household, age, church attendance, family income, and occupational prestige. Another multi-variate analysis of the NORC data (Clemente and Sauer, 1976) again found marital status to be a better predictor than any measure of social status.

To the advanced critical thinker of our time, it may be difficult to believe, for example, that physical appearance contributes more to an understanding of who is and who is not satisfied with life than race, gender, and social class combined. This is, nonetheless, true. The same can be said of health, intelligence, marital status, and age. The persistent focus on structural factors as an account of life satisfaction is obviously misplaced.[31]

The lessons of this chapter should be eminently clear by now. A considerable part of the pain, sorrow, or, if one will, of the alienation found in contemporary United States is a result of broken family arrangements, personal appearance, and age.

If people, for one reason or another, fall out of the marital relationship, if the relationship that provides physical and emotional sustenance is dissolved, the partners will clearly experience considerable alienation. The sorrow involved here has a uniquely personal origin. Two individuals, Harry Jones and his wife, Sally, simply do not hit it off; they separate and eventually divorce. It is difficult to see their specific problem in anything but personal terms. Some events in this world, we are suggesting, have very personal sources, contrary to the sentiments or preferences of the generalizing sciences.[32]

Some of these sorrows, moreover, have somatic, physical causes. Soci-

[31]The results reported in this chapter, and those reported at the close of Chapter 4, also have implications for a commonly voiced (though seldom researched) methodological objection to quality of life surveys: that the answers do not indicate real levels of life satisfaction, only a desire of individuals not to demean their own existence, to save face under conditions that are, in some objective sense, generally miserable. If this were a valid objection, one would be very hard-pressed to account for some of these results. Why, for example, would small town and rural residents be compelled to save face while residents of the major central cities happily confess the discontents of their life situation? Why would married people need to save face, whereas the divorced and separated do not? Why would persons judged physically attractive avoid negative assessments of their happiness and life satisfaction, while the physically unattractive readily admit them? All this amounts to a very serious complication in the face-saving argument. The alternative explanation of these patterns is vastly more parsimonious: the responses are generally valid, indicate genuine levels of satisfaction and dissatisfaction, and vary in straightforward, plausible, and predictable ways with the factors discussed here.

[32]Some of the personal factors discussed in this chapter have structural components, to be sure. The number of divorced people, to illustrate, will usually be influenced by the ease with which divorce can be obtained and by the social approval or disapproval that accompanies the condition of divorce. Likewise, it has long been suspected that the eligibility requirements for Aid to Families with Dependent Children (AFDC) and other social welfare programs encourage marital dissolution among the poor; this, for example, is often cited as part of the explanation of the high rates of separation among the black population. Relatively homely people with advanced incomes will often to be able to overcome their handicap quite readily; poor homely people will have less opportunity in this regard, and so on. Admitting the obvious influence of these structural factors in no way diminishes our essential point, that much of the misery present in the human condition results from private or personal factors that admit of no easy or obvious structural solution.

ologists and social critics, unfortunately, have been generally indifferent to the question of physical appearance, in part, at least, because of this preference for the larger structural explanations. Physical appearance (or rather, people's judgments of physical appearance) plays a considerable role in the life chances of some of the groups we have been discussing. Among the single, separated, and divorced women a strong interest is expressed in marriage. For them, given the prevalent courtship rules, they must adopt a passive role, awaiting initiatives from eligible males. The number of such initiatives varies depending on the woman's physical attractiveness (among other things). The good-looking women, as we have seen, indicate in a variety of ways that they have been the beneficiaries of the accidents of genetics. One might give some thought to the structural changes that would be required to correct such manifest injustice.

The linkage of the life quality measures with age are somewhat more complex. Although one might anticipate general declines with the increase of age, that, on a whole, is not the case. Most measures of satisfaction show rather pronounced increases with age, but there are some important exceptions: reported happiness shows little relationship to age, and, of undoubted importance, satisfaction with health moves inexorably in a downward direction. Apart from the latter two measures, then, one may conclude that for many people youth is a source of malaise, of disenchantment, of alienation. And this, too, is a factor with no obvious structural solution. The principal solution for this sensed malaise, for most people, is to achieve satisfactory marriage and family relationships, and then to wait!

6 WORK: SATISFACTIONS AND DISCONTENTS

A sudden upsurge of interest in the subject of work occurred in the early 1970's, the history of that episode appearing in Chapter 1. The principal conclusions offered by many of those commentators were that work satisfaction was declining and that the resultant anger and hostility constituted an explosive potential, a threat to the core institutions of society. The claims put forth faced an immediate evidential problem in that a considerable amount of evidence stood in direct opposition to them. Such claims could be supported only through a very selective treatment of the available evidence, combined with a wholesale dismissal of the rest. Several of these efforts were reviewed in Chapter 2.

Additional findings of relevance to the work question were reported in Chapter 3. The evidence presented there showed that marriage and family were the dominant priorities for most of the adult population. An interesting job was given a number one ranking by only 7% of the respondents in a 1971 cross section of adult Americans. Even fewer, less than 2% of the total, mentioned a job as their second-place priority. In terms of centrality as a first place goal, an interesting job was outdistanced by concerns for marriage, country, and family. As a second-place goal, it was outdistanced by concerns for health, religion, and, again, family and marriage. It will be noted that these findings are generally consistent with the central life interest studies reviewed in Chapter 1.

The dominant goals question, to be sure, misses many dimensions of the complex of attitudes surrounding one's job. Although few people rate interesting work as a high priority life goal, they might still experience considerable dissatisfaction with their work, as the critics maintain, and that might affect other areas of their lives. But some other evidence contained in Chapter 3 challenges such an interpretation. Only 2% of the total sample in 1971 mentioned their jobs as a source of personal problems. And in 1974, with somewhat different coding, spontaneous mentions of the job as a source of concern amounted to, at best, only 4% of the total. These results came at a time when the alarms sounded by the workplace critics were at their peak, in the era of Lordstown. The expressed concern with financial problems, it may also be noted, far outweighed indications of concern with the job. While the general populace was declaring the primacy of money problems, workplace critics dismissed those statements and instead affirmed their own special view of the world. "It's not the money, it's the job!" was a favored slogan of the era.

In addition to the open-ended questions (those asking for a spontaneous expression of problems or concerns), a more direct inquiry is possible through use of closed-ended (or fixed response) questions that probe for work satisfaction or dissatisfaction. One such set of results was presented in a previous chapter (in Table 2.2). The NORC's General Social Surveys, it will be remembered, showed that approximately one half of all employed persons (including those doing housework) were very satisfied with the work they did, and another one third were moderately satisfied. As for the trend assertions, the claim that attitudes toward work were deteriorating is also directly challenged by the NORC data. The best conclusion is one of no change, the satisfaction levels being high throughout the decade.

The most compelling evidence of a decline in work satisfaction, on the surface at least, appeared in a Gallup series. Beginning in 1949, Gallup asked the following question: "On the whole, would you say you are satisfied or dissatisfied with the work you do?" The level of satisfaction had been more or less stable from 1963 to 1969, but then, in the course of 4 years, it fell ten percentage points. Given the predictions appearing in nearly all mass media sources at that time, it appeared to be no more than an obvious confirmation.

Workplace critics rarely cite this Gallup evidence. To do so would put them in a rather difficult position, for a number of reasons. If they were to accept this as valid evidence, they would be obligated to reckon with the rest of the survey data; it would be difficult to justify the selective usage. Then, too, were one to make use of the Gallup results, it would be necessary to admit an extremely high level of work satisfaction. Gallup reports more than 80% satisfaction at all points between July 1963 and December 1971. Even with the decline of January 1973, satisfaction was still at a rather high level, 77%, as opposed to only 11% dissatisfied (the rest having no opinion). One other embarrassing difficulty involves an even earlier trend. The movement from 1949 through to the early 1960's was one of significant increase in work satisfaction (from 67 to 85%), which would contradict the assumption of a continuous deterioration of the quality of work under the conditions of advanced capitalism.

Still other difficulties were apparent from the outset. Satisfaction among whites declined by eight percentage points between 1969 and 1975. But that did not mean an equivalent increase in dissatisfaction. The latter did increase from 6 to 10%, but the rest of the change involved those with no opinion, they too showing a 4% increase. The greatest change over the 4-year period involved the black population. Blacks, for obvious reasons, had always reported significantly less job satisfaction than whites. But they had reported a significant increase in satisfaction between 1965 and 1969 (going from 48 to 76%). Then there was a precipitous fall to 53% in 1973. That, again, did not mean an equivalent rise in dissatisfaction. The no opinion responses jumped by 19%, compared with a mere 4% increase in reported work dissatisfaction. Gallup, incidentally, warns against making too much of this result, the number of blacks in these samples being rather small (approximately 150 persons).

Gallup's data did show the greatest increase in dissatisfaction among the young, among those under age 30. Gallup, however, making explicit reference to the *Work in America* report and the *Newsweek* alarmism, cast doubt on their claims, pointing first to the persistent high overall level of satisfaction and second to the principal reason given for dissatisfaction—poor wages. He saw the sudden upswing in dissatisfaction as linked to the sudden onset of inflation.[1] That, too, would not sit well with the arguments of the workplace critics.

The Gallup question was put to all persons in the samples, to the employed, unemployed, housewives, students, retired, and so on. One later reanalysis showed that "the closer [one came] to include only those who work for pay, the smaller the 'decline' in job satisfaction over the last several years" (Quinn, Mangione, and Mandilovitch, 1973, p. 39). In still another refinement, in an attempt to control for changes in the composition of the labor force over this period, Quinn and his associates restricted the analysis to males age 21–65, the overwhelming majority of whom were, of course, in the labor force. They found 89% satisfied in the first of the eight studies, dating from July 1963. The seven other studies showed the same high levels of satisfaction; none varying more than three percentage points from that original figure (Quinn et al., p. 5). The respective percentages from August and December 1971 and from January 1973 were 88, 86, and 88%. Again, as with the NORC series, the basic conclusion is one of high satisfaction and no change.

A third series was developed by Quinn and his associates, consisting of seven national surveys, four by the Survey Research Center of the University of Michigan, two by the National Opinion Research Center, and one by the University of California's Survey Research Center. This set of studies covers the period 1958 to 1973, and makes two presentations, giving data first for all workers, and then, separately, for men age 21 through 65. This series also indicates high levels of satisfaction at all times, 81% being the lowest "satisfied" figure. As for the trend, the evidence from this series again contradicts the claims of the workplace critics, the level being in the low eighties in 1958 and 1962, but then climbing to the 90% level in a 1964 study and remaining there to 1973.

The fourth and more recent series involves the two Quality of American

---

[1]All the information contained in the previous paragraphs is taken from the *Gallup Opinion Index*, No. 94, April 1972, pp. 2-4, 23, and 34-37.

Life studies done by the Center for Political Studies of the University of Michigan (Campbell, Converse, and Rodgers, 1976; Campbell, 1981). The two studies, dated 1971 and 1978, found high and stable levels of satisfaction. "No careful study," Campbell reports, "that undertook to describe the nation's work force has ever failed to find an impressive majority who say they are satisfied with their jobs. In 1978, four out of five employed men [said] they were satisfied in some degree with their jobs. One out of three described themselves as 'completely satisfied' " (Campbell, 1981, p. 117).

We have reviewed four national survey series focusing on the years relevant to the claims of the workplace critics. These are: the NORC series (covering the years 1972–1980), the Gallup series (1949–1973, with special analyses covering 1963–1973), the research centers' series (covering 1958 to 1973), and the two studies in the Quality of American Life series (1971 and 1978). *None of them supports the claims of the critics; none of them shows low levels of job satisfaction; none shows a significant decline in satisfaction.* The two indications of change in the four series go in directions opposite to those claimed, Gallup showing an increase in satisfaction between 1949 and 1963, the research centers' series showing an increase between 1958 and 1964.[2] These findings, it will be noted, are based on data provided by some of the leading research organizations in the United States. They constitute the best survey evidence available. Some other evidence— contradictory evidence—will be considered in the following pages.

Many workplace critics are aware of at least some of this survey evidence. But when the lessons contained there are pointed out, as indicated earlier, they dismiss it, in effect claiming a response bias. Two principal lines of argument are put forth in this connection. The first makes reference to the superficiality of the interview situation, claiming that those answers are casual, nonmeaningful, or socially acceptable. A second alternative holds that people can not admit that their work is less than satisfying; to do so would involve self-condemnation, something most people, presumably, find difficult or impossible.

[2]One earlier trend study also found an increase in satisfaction. It made use of the literature summaries of the *Personnel and Guidance Journal*. This publication provides an annual review of job satisfaction studies, the results necessarily being erratic and piecemeal, reflecting a potpourri of samples and questions. But, given the absence of any serious comprehensive attempts at the time, the report certainly deserves some attention, or, at the very least, deserves a mention. A United States Department of Labor publication, *Manpower Report of the President* (1968a), summarized those studies in the following words: "A fairly notable decrease in job dissatisfaction since 1946-47 seems to be indicated by this one study—a compilation of the findings of independent research studies. From a post-World War II high of 21 percent, the median percent dissatisfied gradually diminished to 12 percent in 1953 and has since remained at about 12 to 13 percent" (p. 48). The last figures given were for 1964–1965. The findings of these three series, it will be noted, provide a direct challenge to the claims of Harry Braverman, who argued the "degradation" of work in the twentieth century, i.e., *continuous* erosion of job outlooks with the development of industrial capitalism.

Such arguments, however, stand in contradiction to other claims made by these same critics. They have argued the presence of a new generation, one that is unwilling to accept the old work routines. Because of their different education and experience, they, unlike their predecessors, are psychologically free to express their dissatisfaction and, more importantly, are willing and able to act upon those feelings to bring about change. That is, after all, the point of the repeated stress on absenteeism, turnover, strike activity, and sabotage. Judson Gooding, back at the beginning of "the movement," reported an increase in arguments with foremen, more complaints about discipline and overtime, more grievances, and so on. The critics argue the existence of new and explosive hostilities, on the one hand, but, on the other, in the face of challenging survey evidence, claim that the respondents are intimidated by the interview situation. One is supposed to believe that workers are prepared to challenge foremen and management but are helpless and tongue-tied in the face of a Gallup or SRC interviewer.

The point may be put still another way. It might be the case that workers, in 1963 say, were accepting and conformist. It might also be the case that a major change occurred in the late 1960's and early 1970's, that a new generation came into being. It is difficult to believe that *no sign* of this new development would be found in the surveys of the period and that the reported job satisfaction would continue unchanged at a very high level.

There is, of course, another possibility—that no significant change in outlooks occurred during this period. This suggests an alternative hypothesis: that the evidence reviewed here reflects the underlying reality—no change in attitudes toward work.

Three trend analyses appearing late in the 1970's claimed to provide evidence supporting the workplace critics. The first to be discussed (Cooper, Morgan, Foley, and Kaplan, 1979) appears under a subheading that announced: "Survey data over 25 years indicate that there has been a major shift in the attitudes and values of the U.S. work force." "A consensus is emerging," one learns in the lead paragraph, about a "shift in the attitudes and values" of the labor force, this shift being "accompanied by increased dissatisfaction with many aspects of work." The authors fault the available evidence on the point, describing the research as "isolated case studies or personal reminiscences." There is, they say, "little documentation of actual increases in dissatisfaction over time." And thus, they conclude, " . . . the core question, 'Is this shift in attitudes and resultant dissatisfaction a myth or is it a reality?' remains to be answered."

A footnote lists some of "the recent work in this area," work that is said to support their points about the consensus and the state of the evidence. Six studies are referred to, among them the Sheppard and Herrick volume, Terkel's *Working*, and the O'Toole Task Force report, *Work in America*. Widick's collection (1976) is also listed, although the articles contained there are rather skeptical about the claims that Cooper *et al.* revive once again, late in the decade. Absent from the list are the sources we have just reviewed. The work of Quinn and associates, *Job Satisfaction: Is There a Trend?* (1974), is not mentioned. Nor has reference been made to the easily available National Opinion Research Center series. None of the works that challenged the consensus among the workplace critics has been cited, although, as of January 1979, they had long been available (see Note 33 of Chapter 1 for a listing).

The authors' methodological and substantive achievement is stated briefly in their second paragraph: " . . . we present a new synthesis of employee attitude data gathered over a 25-year period that show that employee values *are* changing and that dissatisfaction *is* increasing. . . . " Their survey methodology is described as follows:

> The findings presented in this article reflect the opinions of approximately 175,000 employees in 159 of the companies for whom Opinion Research Corporation has conducted employee attitude surveys since 1950. The results are based on 51,000 of these employees during the 1950s, 48,000 during the 1960s, and 76,000 since 1970. The companies are in a wide array of industries and range in size from less than 500 employees to more than 200,000. The size of the data base, the variety of companies studied, and the survey methodology all combine to lend a great deal of confidence in the representativeness and significance of the findings (Cooper, Morgan, Foley, and Kaplan, p. 118).

No other information is presented to attest to the representativeness of their samples. No assurance is given that the samples are comparable from period to period. Does the sample reflect the appearance of new clients and the disappearance of old ones? If not a constant base, the results could reflect nothing more than the fluctuating character of the sample. The argument of size, by itself, is no argument for representativeness; size, it will be remembered, was central to the *Literary Digest* method in 1936. Without some additional information affirming that the samples are representative, there can be no proper assessment of the significance of the findings. Even if one assumed the adequacy of the sample, an unquestionable requirement for the researchers is to account for the disparity between their findings and those just reviewed. At the very least, there is a need for some mention of those other divergent findings.[3]

It does not seem likely that the ORC sample is representative either of all American firms or all American workers. In the first instance, one might

---

[3]In response to a letter of inquiry, William A. Schiemann, ORC's vice president for employee relations research, indicated (in a letter, 18 March 1981) that "some firms have been repeatedly measured, but the majority have been assessed serially." This apparently means that the base of firms from which the employee sample is taken itself shifts over time. In other words, the samples are not comparable over time which in turn means that inferences about trends are not justified.

We also asked whether ORC had made any comparisons between characteristics of their sample and known characteristics of the American labor force as a whole. Schiemann expressed doubt "that there are any national norms for the entire labor force on these questions." Appropriate comparative data are, of course, widely available in many sources, among them the *Statistical Abstract of the United States.*

reasonably suppose that large corporate enterprises are sharply overrepresented, since such firms would usually be the ones with resources for and interests in retaining a research firm to conduct inhouse employee relations research. One might also suppose that firms with the greatest interest in having such research done would be those experiencing morale problems or other labor difficulties, which would further undercut the representativeness of the results. An ORC representative, William Schiemann, confirmed that "our data base is a sample of clients over the past 30 years" (letter, 14 May 1981).

Concerning representativeness, Schiemann affirmed that "with the large data base we have, a representative national normative set could easily be constructed." Two points are worth a mention in this connection. First, this seems to be an explicit acknowledgment that the data set on which the published findings are based is not "a representative national normative set." Second, the idea that such could be constructed from the ORC data bespeaks a very fundamental misunderstanding of probability sampling theory. The statistical generalizability of a sample is a strict function of the methods by which the sample was chosen, assuredly *not* a function of the kinds of people who ultimately appear in that sample.

Several problems also appear in connection with the presentation of their findings. The major conclusion of the piece is that " . . . employee values are changing and that dissatisfaction is increasing. This is not a myth; it is an emerging reality. As such, it provides a major challenge for management in the 1980s." The data presented in the article, however, say nothing whatsoever about values. Their thirteen exhibits show how employees (actually, managers, clerical employees, and hourly employees) rate various features of their work, including an overall assessment of it. Fluctuations in these assessments are indicated, but nothing is presented showing that values or standards have changed.

The authors state that "all parts of the work force are beginning to overtly articulate their needs for achievement, recognition, and job challenge," but no evidence supporting this claim is presented. Curiously, their Exhibit IX— Rating of company on chance to get ahead (opportunity for advancement)— shows effectively no change for any of the three groups over the quarter century studied. The differences shown involve, at best, minichanges, ones of a few percentage points (the actual figures are not provided). Those results, it should be noted, involve an estimate of chances for promotion within the firm; the question does not ask about the respondent's need for that kind of achievement. All their measures have this characteristic: they ask for assessments of job features, not for an articulation of needs, wants, or values.

Even those assessments do not show the patterns so unambiguously asserted. Considerable differentiation is found in the results, the patterns being much more complicated than is suggested by the authors' summary conclusions. One, the previously mentioned assessment of chances for promotion, shows no change. Some questions showed irregular increases in satisfaction (in judgments about the ability of managers and the quality of supervision). Some measures do show substantial declines—but those declines came two decades ago, between the 1950's and early 1960's, the pattern since being one of stability. This was the case in regard to the respect shown employees, the responsiveness to employee problems, the fairness in dealing with employees, and the provision of job security. On one dimension, pay rates, all three groups reported a decline in satisfaction in the late 1960's. And all three reported considerable *improvement* in satisfaction with pay in the late 1970's[4]

One measure of special importance involves overall work satisfaction: "How do you like your job—the kind of work you do?" Managers reported high levels of satisfaction, approximately 90%, at all times. The clerical employees were high (at around 80%) and stable through the early 1970's. It was only in 1975–1977 that some decline was registered, this involving a fall of roughly 12–14 percentage points to (approximately) 65%. Some decline appeared among the hourly employees beginning in the late 1960's. The percentage liking their job very much or a good deal fell by approximately ten percentage points, to roughly 60%. Before placing too much faith in the latter findings, it would be wise to remember the uncertain character of the samples involved.

Some findings from the Opinion Research Corporation series were reported in the third of Judson Gooding's articles in *Fortune* (1970c). Declines in "job satisfaction," it was reported, had occurred "in several crucial areas" since 1965. Although the account says "job satisfaction," the greatest decline reported at that time was in satisfaction, with pay rates (a matter of some 45 percentage points), this gaining some confirmation also in Cooper *et al.*'s 1979 publication. The overall assessment of the job in the late 1960's, however, showed *no serious decline for any of the three groups, managers, clerical employees, or hourly employees* (see their Exhibit IV). The evidence of greatest relevance to the subject then under discussion had been omitted.[5]

---

[4]That pattern, reported in their Exhibit VI (Cooper *et al*, p. 120), does not accord with the findings of the National Opinion Research Center's General Social Surveys. For those results (based on national surveys of all adults), see the next chapter. The finding of increased financial satisfaction in the late 1970's, in a period of sustained inflation, will come as a surprise to many readers. The authors do offer some words of explanation; part of the reason, they declare, "is undoubtedly a failure on the part of many employees to differentiate between what they are paid (nominal wages) and their purchasing power (real wages). . . . Employees may not initially realize that raises are primarily inflation adjustments and that purchasing power has not increased." This assumes a rather extraordinary obtuseness on the part of "many employees."

[5]The Opinion Research Corporation occasionally releases findings to the press, one of those reports appearing in the *New York Times* (August 14, 1977) via the Associated Press. "Job discontent Found Rising among Workers," the headline announced, followed by a lead that declared, "More American workers in a recent survey are dissatisfied with their jobs now than at any other time in the last 25

In summary, little of substance can be concluded from the ORC trend findings. The samples of employees, derived from ORC client firms, are demonstrably *not* representative samples of the work force. The reported findings are themselves much more differentiated than the authors' sweeping conclusions would suggest. The published report makes very selective use of the available evidence. The most compelling evidence of declines in satisfaction comes in connection with pay rates rather than conditions of work. Finally, and perhaps of greatest import, the conclusions, as formulated by the authors, are contradicted by the four major national probability survey series reviewed above. The ORC report revives some of the work-hype themes that were prevalent earlier in the decade, but it does not present any persuasive confirming evidence.

A second study that reports declining job satisfaction in the 1970's is that of Staines and Quinn (1979). Unlike the ORC data, which are obviously nonrepresentative, the Staines-Quinn findings are based on a comparison of results from two massive Quality of Employment surveys done by the Survey Research Center at Michigan, the first in 1972–1973 and the second in 1977. The evidence on declining satisfaction is of two sorts: there is, first, some modest falloff indicated in the standard job satisfaction question, amounting to five percentage points in the proportion very satisfied. Specifically, the very satisfied proportion dropped from 52 to 47%, most of these moving into the "somewhat satisfied" category (which increased from 38 to 42%). These trends, it will be noted, while on the edge of statistical significance, are hardly of world historical import. Also, parallel survey data for the same two years, taken from the NORC series (see Table 2.2), do *not* show an equivalent decline (the proportion very satisfied being 49% in 1973 and 48% in 1977). Staines and Quinn, incidentally, do not acknowledge the NORC series in their article, and thus do not attempt to resolve the apparent inconsistency.

The second source of evidence on declining job satisfaction is a much more precipitous decline in various "facet-specific" measures, which focus on specific aspects of work (for example, its challenge, extrinsic rewards, relations with coworkers, and so on) and are comprised of a large number of component items. These were discussed in Chapter 2 ("Selective Misrepresentation of Findings"), and were referred to there as the "How True" items. Altogether, there are six facet-specific dimensions in the Quinn-Staines results: one of them shows some improvement over the four years

---

years. . . . " The levels of dissatisfaction, or more specially, given their question as reported above in the present text, the levels of *dislike*, are higher than those found by other researchers. The article states, for example, that 32% of "current clerical employees" are unhappy with the work they do. The merged NORC studies (1972 to 1978) showed that 18.1% (N = 188) of full-time male clerical employees were dissatisfied with their work. The equivalent figure for females was 12.0% (N = 565). A similar finding appears with respect to the dissatisfaction of blue-collar workers, the job dislike found by the ORC being more than twice the level of the job dissatisfaction found by the NORC. This could, of course, be a function of the different questions used. Or it could be a result of differences in the samples.

(relations with co-workers), but the remaining five show definite declines. It can be noted in passing that these component items ask workers for assessments of objective features of the work, not specifically for workers' satisfactions with those features.

The Staines-Quinn findings have been considered in some detail elsewhere (Chelte, Wright, and Tausky, 1982); thus, only a brief summary is in order here. All in all, the announced decline is an implausible finding for six reasons: (1) It is inconsistent with most empirically credible prior studies of trends in job satisfaction, one of the most important of which, incidentally, was written by Quinn himself. (The earlier work is cited in the 1979 study, as is the conclusion of "no change." In this connection, the authors offer the speculation that the "Are you satisfied . . . ?" question is too crude and insensitive to detect real change.) (2) The sharpest evidence favoring the conclusion of decline is that based on the "how true" items. Many of the item-specific trends seem curious and implausible. (One, for example, is a ten-point drop in "having enough time to get the job done," which would suggest a massive and hitherto unremarked speedup of American industry in the span of four years!) (3) The drop in overall job satisfaction shown in the article is not replicated in the two other major survey series of the era, the NORC series and the Quality of American Life series, as reviewed above. (4) The two Quality of American Life surveys contain exact replicas of several of the "how true" items. All comparisons between the 1973 and 1977 results based on the Quinn-Staines employment surveys show sharp declines on each component item. In the 1971–1978 comparisons from the Quality of American Life series, in contrast, *none* of the identical items shows a statistically significant decline. (5) In the original article, three hypotheses are offered to account for the decline. Two of these hypotheses are ruled out by the Staines-Quinn evidence itself, and the third—one concerning rising expectations—is inconsistent with direct data on expectations taken from the NORC surveys. (6) Finally, the employment series also contains a life satisfaction question, and this too shows a decline parallel to that shown for job satisfaction. This decline is also *not* replicated in the other survey series of the era (see Chapters 4 and 5).

A comparison of the 1977 employment survey results with other surveys of roughly the same era thus makes it plain that the former survey somehow picked up proportionally more unhappy and dissatisfied respondents than the other surveys did. How or why this might have occurred is unclear. (An inquiry to Quinn failed to produce a response.) What is clear is that until some explanation for these disparities is forthcoming, the trend conclusions based on the 1977 employment survey must be heavily discounted.

The third study reporting a decline in work satisfaction is that of Paul J. Andrisani (1978). It is based on four national samples, each containing approximately 5000 respondents who have been repeatedly interviewed over a ten-year period to ascertain their labor force experience (job changes, satisfactions-dissatisfactions, likes-dislikes, and so on). At the outset, four age and sex segments were sampled, men age 45–59, women age 30–44, young men age 14–24, and the equivalent young women. Blacks were intentionally oversampled (by a ratio of roughly 3 to 1), thus allowing examination of differences by race. Most presentations of the data thus show results for eight age, sex, and race segments. These studies, the National Longitudinal Surveys (NLS), are also frequently referred to as "the Parnes' data," after Herbert Parnes, the person who planned and carried out the study.

The overall levels of satisfaction found in these studies are broadly comparable to those reported in other serious studies of the subject. "Relatively few workers," Andrisani reports, "explicitly expressed dissatisfaction with their jobs. Fewer than 15% of the workers within any of the eight age-sex-race groups reported that they disliked their jobs either somewhat or very much at any survey date during the 1966–72 period" (Andrisani, p. 90). For whites, the modal response to their four-option job assessment question was, "like it very much" (this group, for convenience, is referred to throughout as highly satisfied). Those showing this high satisfaction ranged from 47% to 67%. The next most frequent response, of course, was "somewhat satisfied," that category alone far outweighing the dissatisfieds in every comparison. Blacks, on the whole, were less satisfied. In most instances, however, "highly satisfied" was still the modal response. It was among the younger black men, at three time points, that "somewhat satisfied" proved most frequent (ranging from 47% to 52%), followed by the "highly satisfied" response.

Andrisani's most important finding, for our purpose, involves the trend analysis. "Job satisfaction," he states, "declined during the 1966–72 period within nearly all of the eight age-sex-race groups. Among those employed throughout the entire period . . . the proportion of workers highly satisfied with their jobs dropped from 5 to 13 percentage points within seven of the eight groups. Virtually all of the decline was from highly satisfied to somewhat satisfied. . . . " The declines in job satisfaction, it is reported, were "more pronounced in the latter half of the 1966–72 period than in the former" (Andrisani, pp. 90–91).

A third finding, also of some importance for our purpose, involves the location of these changes. "Contrary to the popular notion of 'blue-collar blues,' " Andrisani reports, "the downward trends in job satisfaction are least consistent and meaningful among white-collar workers, craftsmen, service workers, farmers, and farm managers." Only for white middle-aged men was there a decline in job satisfaction among operatives or laborers.

This locational problem appeared already in the initial presentation by age, sex, and race. The most consistent decline in the percentage of highly satisfieds was found among the white males age 45–59 in 1966 (the largest of the eight segments), the 1966–1971 change amounting to 10.5 percentage points. Among the equivalent black males, the decline amounted to only one point. For young white males, the distribution was constant from 1966 to 1969, and then a 4.5 percentage point decline was registered in 1970.

Among young black males, an *increase* in satisfaction was registered (five points). The largest and most consistent decline among the women was found among the middle-aged white segment (8.7 points). Otherwise, the differences were smaller, and, again, the greatest shift was in the early 1970's (Andrisani, pp. 54–55).

Andrisani's findings, in short, show formal agreement with the claims of the workplace critics in establishing a decline in work satisfaction. In substance, however, they provide no support whatsoever for those claims. Where the critics predict massive dissatisfaction, he finds, along with all other serious work on the subject, massive satisfaction. Where they predict emerging work *dis*satisfaction, his findings show merely a decline in the degree of satisfaction. Where they predict rising dissatisfaction among young workers, his findings show the principal change among the older workers (with young black males actually showing increasing satisfaction). Where they predict rising dissatisfaction among those in repetitive blue-collar jobs, he finds the principal changes elsewhere.

Andrisani refers to the Quinn, Staines, and McCullough analysis (1974) which, it will be remembered, showed that after appropriate corrections were made, no trend was evidenced in the Gallup data. He feels that the trend shown in the NLS data may be hidden in the Gallup data by virtue of an "aggregation bias," the two degrees of satisfaction of the NLS results being contained within the single Gallup category. This possibility may be explored using the two most relevant Survey Research Center studies, the Survey of Working Conditions (1969–1970) and the Quality of Employment Survey (1972–1973), both of which contain four-option work satisfaction questions. They also span the period where Andrisani's data show the more pronounced trend.

The SRC studies, however, do not show that pattern. Overall, the percentage very satisfied increased from 46 to 52%. The somewhat satisfied portion was more or less constant (39 and 38%), and, obviously, the dissatisfieds declined somewhat. No such shift among the satisfieds, it will be noted, appeared later in the decade (as shown in NORC data of Table 2.2).

We think there are grounds for accepting the SRC result over that of the NLS. Our principal reason is that after the initial investigation, the later surveys were no longer random. If we take, for example, the older white males, we find a considerable attenuation of the original sample, to 93.8% in 1967, then to 84.6% in 1969, and finally, to 76.9% in 1971. Some of these losses, of course, would be early retirees (who, judging from other studies, would be generally unhappy with their work). Others, we think the larger portion, were persons not reached in later interviews, and many of them, we think, would have been upwardly mobile. They would, we feel, have made a significant geographical move, and would be likely to report high job satisfaction. This is to suggest that with some system these individuals have "removed themselves" from the sample, thus yielding this result of somewhat reduced satisfaction. The pattern, it will be noted, is similar to that obtained, at a later point in time, in the Staines-Quinn panel study. Some additional support for this hypothesis appears in the detailed trend results. The decline was greatest among white males in the white-collar ranks, who, presumably, have the greatest possibilities for movement into significantly better jobs.

Concerning the critics' claim of rising workplace discontent in the decade of the 1970's, then, the following summary is in order: The four major time-series available on the topic show no significant trend. Each is based on successive national probability cross sections of the American population. Two additional time-series (the Michigan employment series, 1973 and 1977, and the Parnes data) show small declines in the proportion very satisfied and corresponding small increases in the proportion somewhat satisfied. Both these series are based on panel studies rather than successive cross sections, and for this reason, even the small trends reported may be confounded with the differential attrition of satisfied workers out of the samples. One final "series," the ORC series, shows generally inconclusive results and is based on a manifestly nonrepresentative sample. The conclusion to be derived from all this is fairly obvious: there is no credible evidence available in any of the major survey series to support the claims of rising work discontent.

The most recent study of trends in attitudes about work, to our knowledge, is that of Glenn and Weaver (1982). In 1955, Gallup asked a national sample two work-related questions: (1) Do you enjoy your work so much that you have a hard time putting it aside? (2) Generally speaking, which do you enjoy *more*—the hours you are on your job, or the hours when you are *not* on your job? Both questions were then asked again in a 1980 survey. "The 1980 data show substantially lower reported enjoyment of work than do the 1955 data" (Glenn and Weaver, p. 463), a finding that remained even after compositional changes in the demography of the work force were held constant. In light of the other data series reviewed in this chapter, it is hard to know what to make of the Glenn and Weaver result. Contrary to the other series (each of them based, to be sure, on substantially different questions), this one study does show an unmistakable decline in highly positive feelings toward work. Perhaps what has been detected here is a shift in attitude *within* the highly satisfied group, which (these days) contains proportionally fewer outright "workaholics" than it did twenty-five years ago. (One can obviously be very satisfied with a job and still enjoy the hours off the job more.) A second possibility, mentioned by Glenn and Weaver, is an increase in the intrinsic enjoyability of leisure time pursuits (versus a decrease in the enjoyability of work). Glenn and Weaver also speculate (p. 468) that the change may be linked to the decline of the farm population since 1955. Those currently in farm occupations had, by considerable margins, the most positive work attitudes.

Another question of relevance to the issue of work, another indicator of satisfaction and possible trends, appears in the NORC series. It asks respondents if they would continue working were they to come by enough money to live comfortably for the rest of their lives. Approximately two thirds said they would continue working. Although some modest changes were evident, the results do not show any serious antiwork trend in the 1970's (Table 6.1). One might anticipate that the one third who would stop working were younger respondents, those who have abandoned the traditional work ethic. But, as will be shown, even that expectation is not supported.

Similar "work-if-rich" questions were asked in still other studies, specifically in those undertaken by the Survey Research Center of the University of Michigan. The results from six studies follow (percentage who would continue to work): 1953, 80%; 1957, 78%; 1969–1970, 67%; 1971, 69%; 1972–1973, 66%; and 1978, 75%.[6] The first of these results, the 80% figure, reflects a difference in the sample, it being restricted to men (who, as will be seen, are more likely to say they would continue working). The figures for the three studies from 1969–1970 to 1972–1973 are all at the same level, indicating no trend occurring at that time. The 1978 figure, it will be noted, is nine points over the 1972–1973 result. This study and the 1980 NORC study show significant increases in the percentages who would *continue* working. The only change consonant with the critics' argument would be that occurring between 1957 and 1969–1970, amounting to eleven percentage points. But all other things are not equal in that comparison. There was a considerable increase in the percentage of women in the labor force,

[6]These results are taken from Morse and Weiss, 1955, p. 192, and from the Survey Research Center codebooks. There are slight differences in the questions used. The studies and wordings follow:

1953 Morse and Weiss, 1955, p. 192: "If by some chance you inherited enough money to live comfortably without working, do you think you would work anyway or not?"

1957 Americans View Their Mental Health, Q. 60 (to male respondents): "If you didn't have to work to make a living, do you think you would work anyway?"

1969–1970 Survey of Working Conditions, Q. 137: "If you were to get enough money to live as comfortably as you'd like for the rest of your life without having to work, would you continue to work?"

1971 Quality of American Life, Q. F20: "If you were to get enough money to live as comfortably as you'd like for the rest of your life, would you continue to work?"

The latter question was repeated in the 1972–1973 Quality of Employment Survey and again in the 1978 Quality of American Life study.

Table 6.1. Work Motivation (NORC General Social Surveys: 1973–1980)

Work motivation:[a]	Total	Year				
		1973	1974	1976[b]	1977	1980
Would continue to work	70%	69%	65%	69%	70%	77%
Would stop working	30	31	35	31	30	23
N =	(4203)	(819)	(821)	(746)	(940)	(877)

[a]The question reads: "If you were to get enough money to live as comfortably as you would like for the rest of your life, would you continue to work or would you stop working?"

[b]In the 1976 survey those "unemployed, laid off, or looking for work" were not asked this question.

and there were also some important changes in the age structure of the employed population. These matters are explored in more detail below.[7]

These findings indicate that, for most employed persons, work serves more than just an instrumental purpose. If the most obvious immediate aim of work, an adequate income, were assured, most of those interviewed say they would still continue with some kind of employment. The Morse and Weiss (1955) study asked a useful follow-up question (p. 194): "Suppose you didn't work, what would you miss most?" The most frequent response involved the social contacts, 31% referring to "the people I know through or at work, the friends, contacts." Twenty-five percent said they would miss the "feeling of doing something, [they] would be restless." One eighth mentioned the work itself; the "kind of work I do" was the thing they would miss the most. And 9% mentioned a sense of "doing something important, worthwhile, [a] feeling of self-respect."

The 1957 SRC study, "Americans View Their Mental Health," also asked

[7]One might, of course, argue that the work-if-rich question is abstract or purely hypothetical and thus inadequate as a measure of what people would actually do if wealth were somehow showered upon them. One study has investigated this question through interviews with a small sample (N = 54) of state lottery winners (Kaplan, 1978). As it happens, all but fourteen of these winners did quit their jobs (pp. 70–71), which seems to sharply disconfirm the work-if-rich findings. However, it appears that many of those who did quit later returned to work. (The study does not give the precise percentage or number who did.) On p. 115, Kaplan mentions "boredom and monotony" as the primary reason. (Some, it appears, also wanted to return to work but, owing to the rise in unemployment, found there was no work for them to return to.) None of the results is presented with a control for age; there is some evidence from a small Connecticut study that lottery players are somewhat older on average than the rest of the population (Abrahamson, 1980, p. 51), and age is also correlated with responses to the work-if-rich question (see text, below). If most of these winners were age 50 and up, the initial labor-force dropout would be perfectly consistent with the work-if-rich questions, as the proportion saying they would stop working increases as one approaches retirement age. (It is also plausible, although unresearched, that people who are dissatisfied with their work and anxious to leave it for a life of leisure differentially tend to play the lottery in the first place.)

a follow-up question: "What would be your reasons for going on working?" The most frequent response categories were:

Work fills in otherwise empty time: I'd be bored if I didn't work; I don't know what else to do; it keeps me occupied; I like to keep busy.	50%
Emotional upset if didn't work: I'd go crazy if I didn't work; I'd be at my wits' end if I didn't work; I wouldn't know what to do with myself.	12
Likes to work (general: no answer why)	10
Affiliation-related ego satisfactions: likes the chance of being with people, helping people, friendships on the job.	7
Working keeps you healthy; feel better when you work.	7
	(N = 950)

Still another coding of responses to this question appeared in the 1972–1973 Quality of Employment study. Those saying they would continue to work were asked for their reasons. The categories and percentages follow:

Avoid boredom; want activity: "Couldn't stand just doing nothing"; "Wouldn't like sitting around the house all day"; "Want to be stimulated, kept on my toes"; "Need the excitement"; "Keeping busy keeps you healthy."	64%
Work supplies direction in respondent's life: Provides a focus to all of R's activities; R would feel useless; purposeless without work; Keeps R oriented in the world; "I'd be lost"; Time schedule.	21
"Likes" to work (in general), no answer why.	13
Rates some particular specific liked aspect of work: R likes what he/she is presently doing; any specific likes aspect of job (except people or financial reasons).	11
Work is important, valuable, helps others.	5
	(N = 1413)

The percentages total more than 100 because multiple answers were possible.

The previous summary of comments given by workers themselves on why they would continue working even if they did not have to can be usefully contrasted with some passages from the critical literature. We have, for example, Bowles and Gintis (1976) arguing, "It is a major indictment of our social system that most people view their jobs as, at best, a painful necessity" (p. 71). Most people—some two thirds to three quarters of them—state explicitly that they would continue to work even if the "painful necessity" of securing an income were removed. The critics claim that people hate their work in part because it is boring. Most of those who would continue working say they would be bored without it.

The workplace critics, as repeatedly noted, have placed particular emphasis on the orientations of young workers. It is the young who are said to manifest the distinctively high levels of dissatisfaction. They are the ones who have adopted new and different values, who have abandoned the traditional work ethic. Support for those conclusions should be evident in data showing the work satisfaction and work-if-rich questions by age. Those data, taken from the composite General Social Surveys of the NORC from 1972 to 1978, are presented in Table 6.2.

The young, both males and females, are, in fact, the least satisfied with their work of all the age categories. The levels of satisfaction increase in linear fashion through to the age 65-and-over category, the relationship on the whole being a rather strong one. Although the young show the lowest

Table 6.2. Work Satisfaction and Work-If-Rich By Age and Sex: Combined NORC 1972–1978

	Age						
	18–24	25–34	35–44	45–54	55–64	65 or more	Total
Work satisfaction							
Males							
Very satisfied	38%	46%	54%	53%	63%	77%	51%
Moderately satisfied	41	40	34	39	30	17	36
A little dissatisfied	16	10	9	7	4	5	10
Very dissatisfied	5	4	3	2	3	—	3
N =	(366)	(844)	(683)	(650)	(443)	(75)	(3061)
Females							
Very satisfied	36%	49%	55%	59%	65%	69%	53%
Moderately satisfied	44	36	34	35	29	29	35
A little dissatisfied	15	12	8	5	5	3	9
Very dissatisfied	5	3	2	1	1	—	3
N =	(265)	(463)	(336)	(313)	(239)	(35)	(1651)
Would continue to work							
Males	80%	79%	78%	70%	58%	59%	74%
N =	(215)	(448)	(376)	(349)	(241)	(44)	(1673)
Females	69%	70%	60%	56%	49%	61%	61%
N =	(142)	(256)	(198)	(176)	(148)	(23)	(943)

levels of satisfaction, the picture, nevertheless, is not one of raging *dissattisfaction*, since solid majorities fall on the satisfied side of the distribution. Their distinctive feature is that they are only moderately, as opposed to very, satisfied. There is, to be sure, more outright dissatisfaction among the younger groups, but that amounts to only one fifth of the total, and most of them, three out of four, are only a little dissatisfied. One might conclude that the critics are right about the direction of the relationship but are mistaken about the extent of rebellion in the younger age categories.

The workplace critics, as we have seen, argue that this rebellion is something new; it represents a distinct break with previous experience. But Quinn and his associates, as was pointed out in Chapter 1, present evidence challenging that claim. In their 1974 summary of recent studies, they conclude that " . . . the much-discussed large recent decline in job satisfaction of younger workers has not been substantiated. . . . *Younger workers have been consistently less satisfied than their elders for the last 15 years and, probably, even earlier than that"* (Quinn, Staines, and McCullough, pp. 1, 12, emphasis in the original).[8]

Commentators aware of this traditional age relationship have put forth a "wearing down" hypothesis. The older workers, supposedly, have had their youthful aspirations eroded by some obdurate realities. They now ask less of their jobs and thus are more easily satisfied. But Quinn and his associates provide another, even more plausible hypothesis. "Older workers, especially in the case of men, are more satisfied with their jobs than younger workers simply because they have better jobs" (p. 12). There is no mystery about this linkage. People who are just starting out, in all times and ages, are ordinarily given the least attractive jobs the society has to offer.

The wearing down hypothesis, although frequently invoked, is only infrequently assessed. It would be difficult to follow a sample of young workers from, say, age 20–30, showing their job preferences before and after erosion, but one can approach the question with cross-sectional data. If a valid hypothesis, the younger workers in any sample should have higher or more demanding values than their older peers. The three studies that have examined the various possibilities found no support for the wearing down hypothesis; everything pointed to the better jobs alternative (Wright and Hamilton, 1978b; Taveggia and Ross, 1978; Glenn, Taylor, and Weaver, 1977).

Part of the age-satisfaction relationship shown in Table 6.2 is artifactual.

---

[8]See also Vollmer and Kinney, 1955; and Saleh and Otis, 1964. For a more general review see Herzberg, Mausner, Peterson, and Capwell, 1957.

We have also checked the age-work satisfaction relationship in two of the SRC studies (in the 1957 Mental Health study and the 1969–1970 Survey of Working Conditions). The same basic relationship and distributions were found in three comparisons (males, 1957; males and females, 1969–1970). There was no clear relationship with age among the females in the 1957 study. Data for the 1972–1973 Quality of Employment study are reported in Wright and Hamilton (1978).

Those who are age 65 and over and still in the labor force are, to a large extent, self-selected. They are disproportionately self-employed, persons who can choose to continue working, who, in other words, are not automatically retired. While some of those continuing to work may be doing so by force of economic circumstance, many apparently are doing so because they enjoy their work, something reflected in their satisfaction and in their responses to the work-if-rich question.[9]

The claim of a new work ethic, one widely shared among the young, is dramatically challenged by the results of the work-if-rich question, also shown in Table 6.2. The pattern is diametrically opposite to the one so frequently proclaimed. The highest levels of work motivation are found among the young. The level falls off slightly among the middle-aged. And it is among the older segments of the population that one finds a serious decline in work motivation. It is clearly the older age groups who are abandoning the traditional work ethic. Put somewhat differently, and probably more realistically, they would choose to retire earlier than is currently the custom.

Overall, women are somewhat less likely to prefer continuing with work than are men, some of them apparently being reluctant members of the labor force. In the age 55-to-64 category, only one half would continue working if they were well off financially; this is the lowest level of work motivation of any segment in the table. That self-selection factor, it will be noted, appears once again among the small number in the age 65-and-over category.[10]

[9]We examined the work-if-rich responses in relationship to age in the same two SRC studies reported in the previous footnote. The same basic pattern appeared for both sexes in the 1969–1970 study. There was, however, no clear pattern associated with age among males in the Mental Health study; roughly 85% of all male segments would continue working if rich. For the females, the pattern was generally *positive* with age. We have no explanation for the two exceptions found in this study. The patterns observed in the 1978 Quality of American Life study are broadly comparable to those discussed in the text.

[10]Self-employment varies directly with age, as might be expected, a very sharp increase occurring among those age 65 and over. The Mental Health study (1957) found that approximately one fifth of the full-time employed males aged 35 to 64 were self-employed. Among the age 65 and over respondents, the figure was 47%. The 1969–1970 Survey of Working Conditions showed the same pattern, the figure for older males (47%) being identical with that of the earlier study. Self-employment is much less frequent among women, but the same increase with age is found. In this case, the figure for the older group was 29%. In all surveys we have examined, the self-employed report distinctly high levels of job satisfaction.

Concerning the sex differences in work motivation, the available studies of women's labor force participation strongly suggest that most women work primarily because of economic needs or desires of the family unit. "A number of sample surveys have asked wives why they are working, why they had been working, or why they recently started working. Invariably, considerably more than half of the women respond in economic terms" (Sweet, 1973, p. 6). The largest and possibly best of these surveys found nearly four fifths of the working women giving predominantly economic reasons (Sweet, Table 1-1). There is little to suggest "grinding poverty" as

One may carry the exploration a step farther. The work-if-rich question was first used in a 1953 study (reported in Morse and Weiss, 1955). Based on a national sample of employed males, it found that 80% would continue to work if rich. Taking the comparable males from the combined NORC studies of the 1970's, the equivalent figure is 74%, which would mean a decline in work motivation of six percentage points. Examination of the result by age categories showed some modest and inconsistent fluctuations in the age 35-to-64 categories. The largest decline—23 points—was in the 65-and-over category, but there one faced a problem of small base numbers at both times. The second largest decline appears among the young, the 1953 figure (for 21- to 34-year-olds) being 90% as opposed to 79% in 1972–1978 (for the combined 18- to 34-year-olds) who would continue working. If that were a genuine finding (and not due to small numbers, the 1953 percentage being based on 106 cases), it would mean that approximately one additional young man in ten had fallen away from the traditional work ethic over the two-decade span. One young man in ten, it will be noted, had already abandoned the traditional work ethic in 1953.[11]

If that is a genuine finding, it would, of course, suggest at least some support for the arguments of the workplace critics. Two important qualifications, however, should be noted, one concerning the amount of change and one concerning the emphasis. The rate of change among the young would be one half of 1% per year, which is not of the magnitude or rapidity some have alleged. The attention paid to the fifth who, presumably, have abandoned the traditional work ethic is certainly justified and legitimate. At the same time, it would be a mistake to overlook the four fifths who indicate their continued loyalty to that ethic.

Another reason for skepticism about (or, at least, for emendation of) the declining work ethic claim appears when one examines the female side of the labor force. The tendency among young women goes in the opposite direction from that of men: the percentages who would continue working increase from 51% (N = 74) in 1957, to 54% (N = 151 in 1969–1970, and to 70% (N = 398) in 1972–1978. While young men, presumably, were seeking freedom from their labor force involvements, young women, with increasing frequency, were welcoming the opportunity to

_____
the principal motivating factor; rather, the desire is for improvement in the overall family living standard.

[11]One can examine the pattern for the young workers over more than two decades through the use of five studies (Morse and Weiss, 1955, from the 1953 study; Mental Health, 1957; Working Conditions, 1969–1970; the combined General Social Surveys, 1972–1978; and the 1978 Quality of American Life Survey.) The respective percentages who would continue working if rich are: 90% (106); 85% (289); 81% (305); 79% (663); and 85% (513). Results are for *full-time employed males* age 21–34, except for the General Social Surveys and the 1978 Quality of American Life study, where it is for those 18–34. No consistent differences appeared between the younger and older segments of the 18–34 category.

to work.[12] For many women, full-time employment represents liberation from the stultifying regime of housework. While the workplace critics see more and more people attempting to escape the restraints of work (by which is meant gainful employment outside the home), many women have chosen that kind of activity with some evident enthusiasm. Some women prefer the routines of housework, and many are obviously free to continue with that kind of employment. The expanding opportunities within the labor force would thus have the consequence of reducing one source of dissatisfaction within the society—forced commitment of the remaining women to household routines.

In regard to the "stultifying regime" of housework itself some numbers may again be useful. The Quality of American Life study (1971) asked working women about their attitude toward housework. The question (Q. F22) reads: "Different people feel differently about taking care of a home. I don't mean taking care of children, but things like cooking, sewing, and keeping house. Some women look on these as just a job that has to be done; other women really enjoy them. How do you feel about this?" Fifty percent of the respondents indicated "unqualified liking: I like it; I enjoy it." Only 9% indicated unqualified dislike. About one eighth (13%) avoided the likes-dislikes dichotomy entirely, saying it is something that has to be done, and one tenth gave ambivalent responses. Most of the remainder indicated qualified liking, disliking only some feature or features or disliking it only sometimes.

The same question was asked of housewives (Q. F44), the result being an even more skewed distribution. Unqualified liking was expressed by 59%, with only 3% indicating an unqualified dislike. About one in ten took the

---

[12]There is a problem (see Note 9) with the 1957 study. We do not think it affects the points made in the text, since the distinctiveness of the study appears among the older groups (who, as contrasted with those in the other studies, show unusually high levels of work commitment). We are inclined to think that some fluke of method has produced that result.

In 1957, 1969–1970, and the combined 1972 to 1978 studies, women constituted 20, 31, and 36%, respectively, of the full-time employeds. (In the 1978 Quality of American Life survey, it was 40%.) The percentages of women who would continue working if rich showed no clear pattern of change, the respective figures being 59, 54, and 61%. It is on the male side of the labor force that some change is found, figures being 84, 75, and 74% (The 84% figure, the base figure for the only substantial change, stems from the 1957 study discussed above.) Most of that change occurs in the older age segments. If that is, in fact, a change, and not the result of method error, it still would not support the argument of the workplace critics, since its location is so markedly different from the one they predict. It should be remembered, too, that an opposite pattern of change is found in the 1953 to 1957 comparison.

An analysis of the 1978 Quality of American Life study suggests that even the small changes indicated above are either spurious or have been reversed. Among full-time employed males in 1978, 78% would work if rich, a modest reversal of the trend for full-time males noted above; among employed women, this figure was 71% registered in the combined NORC surveys shown in Table 6.2.

"facts of life" option, and about one in twelve were ambivalent; most of the remainder expressed qualified liking.

For all the discussion of household routines (and the suggestion of oppressiveness, of a boring round of activity), it will surprise some to learn that when asked to rank themselves on a seven-point scale (Q. F46), most housewives said they were satisfied being a homemaker. Just over half, 52%, chose one extreme position, completely satisfied, as opposed to only 1% who chose the opposite extreme. Although more than two out of three housewives had had a full-time job at some time in the past, a fair-sized majority, 59%, said no when asked (Q. F48) if they had ever wanted a career (not just a short-term job). These data suggest that there are more reluctant members of the labor force than reluctant housewives. For further discussion of the questions touched on here, see Wright, 1978a.

Another line of critical comment may be addressed with some of these same data. Many commentators, particularly those on the left, have argued that the increased employment of women in recent decades stems from economic need; with growing inflation, the earnings of wives become a necessity. Many women, in short, are forced out of their preferred traditional roles because of economic pressures. That might be the situation in the case of those who would stop working if relieved of financial concerns; such was the preference of two out of five full-time employed women. Those women tend to be in the older, presumably more traditional age categories (see Table 6.2). At the same time, it should be noted, a majority say they would continue working even if relieved of all financial burdens, which is to say they are not being forced to work.

In the previous pages we have reviewed the trends in work satisfaction or dissatisfaction and examined the patterns by age and sex. Another important dimension to explore, obviously, is the relationship with occupation. While the critics are mistaken in their overall portrait of discontent in the labor force, various pockets of dissent might exist, ones that could pose a serious disruptive potential. The most obvious location of such dissent would be in the blue-collar ranks, particularly among the semiskilled and unskilled workers, along with those in low-paid and unattractive service occupations. That pattern is indicated in the Morse and Weiss article. Their study, it will be remembered, was based on a national sample of employed men and made use of a straightforward work satisfaction question along with a work-if-rich question. They also posed a follow-up question, asking if the respondent would continue in the same kind of work.

Among the middle class males, they report, 86% would continue to work-if-rich, and 61% would continue in the same kind of work. Among the blue-collar workers, "only" 76% said they would continue working. A significant difference did appear in this connection, however, since only about one third of them would continue in the same line of work. The most frequently mentioned alternative, the authors report, was to go into business for themselves.

Although the differences shown in the Morse and Weiss article are in the direction that most people would anticipate, some comment is required about the magnitudes involved. While some commentators have portrayed white-collar jobs as involving a rat race, most middle-class males, over four fifths in the three subcategories provided, would continue to work, and majorities in each would continue in the same kind of work. Only among the managers did significant minority disaffection appear, 45% of them saying they would prefer some other kind of employment. That result, however, is subject to some question, since it is based on only twenty-two respondents.

All four blue-collar subcategories had majorities preferring some other work. Not too surprisingly, the skilled workers reported the highest levels of content among the blue-collar workers. Four fifths of them would continue working, and two fifths would continue in the same line of work. In response to the question about satisfaction with their current work, one third of those skilled (32%) said they were very satisfied, and 57% said they were satisfied.

Perhaps even more surprising were the responses of the operatives, this category including the machine operators and assembly line workers, groups that have figured prominently in the writings of the workplace critics. Three out of four said they would continue to work even if their financial needs were adequately covered. One third would even continue in the same type of work. Asked about their satisfaction with their present jobs, one quarter said they were very satisfied and three fifths said satisfied. The pro-con responses were combined with the dissatisfieds in the Morse-Weiss presentation, the total less-than-satisfied segment amounting to only 15%. The pro-con and dissatisfied percentages were somewhat higher for the two other relevant working-class categories, 21% among the unskilled and 31% among the service workers. The remarkable point to be noted, however, is that large majorities in all three categories reported some net balance of satisfaction with their jobs. The image of monolithic dissatisfaction, of disenchantment and/or hostility to the job, was not supported, even among those with jobs that objectively were the least attractive among the available options. That was the portrait yielded in a 1953 study.

The combined NORC General Social Surveys allow a much expanded version of the Morse-Weiss portrait. One may examine the attitudes of full- and part-time workers, both male and female. Because of the large numbers involved, one may examine some detailed subcategories. The studies also contain information on satisfaction with housework. And, finally, it is possible to make some limited assessment of the trends since 1953. The first task will be to compare the pattern of satisfaction/dissatisfaction found among full-time employed males in the 1970's.

The basic results, shown in Table 6.3, are broadly similar to those discovered two decades earlier. In this case, the highest level of job satisfaction was reported by the managers and administrators, who were closely followed by the professionals and sales workers. The preeminent position of the managers and administrators found here strongly suggests that the

Table 6.3. Work Satisfaction and Continuing to Work by Occupation and Sex (Combined NORC Studies: 1972–1978)

	Total	Nonmanual occupation				Manual occupation					
		Professional, technical	Manager, administr.	Sales	Clerical	Craftsmen	Operators	Transport operators	Unskilled	Service	Farm
Work satisfaction and continuing to work (full-time employed persons)											
Males											
Very satisfied	51%	59%	65%	57%	42%	52%	35%	37%	39%	48%	58%
Moderately satisfied	36	31	27	33	40	38	48	44	42	37	36
Dissatisfied	12	10	8	9	18	10	17	19	19	15	7
N =	(3043)	(531)	(440)	(190)	(188)	(714)	(349)	(163)	(153)	(208)	(106)
Females											
Very satisfied	53%	65%	70%	40%	52%	55%	36%			49%	
Moderately satisfied	35	26	23	44	36	23	49			38	
Dissatisfied	12	9	7	16	12	23	15			13	
N =	(1645)	(316)	(136)	(55)	(565)	(31)	(251)	(11)	(15)	(264)	(1)
If enough money, would continue to work											
Males	74%	79%	78%	77%	69%	68%	69%	72%	74%	73%	85%
N =	(1660)	(296)	(240)	(99)	(95)	(378)	(215)	(81)	(88)	(107)	(61)
Females	61%	76%	65%	62%	57%		47%			64%	
N =	(938)	(178)	(72)	(37)	(325)	(14)	(142)	(8)	(12)	(149)	(1)
Percentages across											
Male		17	15	6	6	23	12	5	5	7	4
Female		19	8	3	34	2	15	1	1	16	—

disaffection of the managers in the Morse-Weiss study was an exceptional or fluke finding probably linked to the small case base in their sample. Majorities in all three of these categories indicated that they were *very* satisfied with their jobs, the next most frequent choice being moderate satisfaction. Despite the often-heard talk of stress and strain in the executive role, of the rat race and the consequent ulcers and heart attacks, few, less than one in ten, expressed themselves in a way that would be consonant with that conclusion. Most of those expressing dissatisfaction indicated that the problems were of a moderate character; fewer than 2% said they were very dissatisfied.

The finding with respect to the sales workers may initially come as a surprise, many social scientists treating the category as lower middle class, having poorly paid retail clerks in mind. But on the male side of the labor force, the category contains highly paid, relatively high status occupations (for example, advertising agents, insurance agents, brokers, underwriters, real estate agents and brokers, stock and bond salesmen). It is the male *clerical* workers who are likely to be lower middle class, as indicated by the lower level of work satisfaction they report.[13]

In the blue-collar ranks, it is the craftsmen, not too surprisingly, who reported the highest level of job satisfaction.[14] On the whole, they expressed greater satisfaction with their work than did the clerical employees. A rather sharp division separates the skilled from the next three working-class categories, the operators (two categories thereof) and unskilled having the lowest levels of satisfaction of all major occupational groups. It is, however, important to note the actual distributions; while satisfaction is lower than elsewhere, between 35 and 40% reported that they were very satisfied with their jobs. Another 40–50% said they were moderately satisfied, these being the only categories in which this was the modal response. As for outright dissatisfaction, fewer than one worker in five chose those options, most of them, roughly two out of three, declaring only moderate dissatisfaction. Given the unqualified formulations and the utter certainty of the workplace critics' conclusions, it will, no doubt, come as a surprise to discover that only

---

[13]We have checked these results with two other studies, Americans View Their Mental Health and the Survey of Working Conditions. Although there are some inconsistencies and, of course, the usual small differences in percentages, there is a general consonance with the findings of the General Social Survey results as reported in the text.

[14]Fifteen percent of the skilled workers were foremen, and they reported somewhat higher levels of satisfaction, 57% being very satisfied. But with the foreman removed, the picture was not substantially changed. None of the three figures for craftsmen in Table 6.3 changed by more than one percentage point.

The two studies (mentioned in Note 13) show a similar pattern, although the gap between the skilled and the other blue-collar categories was not as great.

A useful table providing "Summary Descriptions of Adjustment Patterns Peculiar to Various Occupational Groups" appears in Gurin, Veroff, and Feld, 1960, pp. 224-226.

about 5% of the workers in these categories declare themselves to be *very* dissatisfied. The same basic pattern also appeared in some of the subcategories (among assemblers, sewers and stitchers, and a miscellaneous category of machine operators).

The results for the service workers are rather unexpected; they have a pattern similar to the skilled workers. They have a higher proportion of very satisfieds than is found among the clerical employees. Part of this result stems from the heterogeneity of the category. A large number of janitors are contained there (among whom satisfaction is *relatively* low, 22% indicating dissatisfaction), but there are also an even larger number of waiters and an equivalent number of cooks.

The farm populations, finally, express an extremely high level of job satisfaction, the overall pattern being similar to that found in the three high-status nonmanual categories.

Turning to full-time employed women, also shown in Table 6.3, one finds some general similarities and some sharp differences. The first point deserving attention involves the very significant differences in the kinds of jobs performed. Only a minority of the men, 44%, were engaged in nonmanual occupations. By comparison, one finds a majority, close to two thirds, of the women engaged in middle-class occupations.[15] Over one half of these middle-class women are found in a single category—the clerical employees. While men appear in significant numbers in all ten categories shown in this table, three of those categories contained less than 1% of the employed women, and a fourth, the crafts category, contained less than 2% of their total (taking the figures before rounding off). Stated differently, 92% of the full-time employed women were found in five of those ten categories.

Looking at the satisfactions indicated, one finds very high levels among the professionals and the managers—higher than for equivalent males (despite their holding lower prestige and lower paid positions than the equivalent males). Significant differences appear with respect to the sales employees, their level of satisfaction being much lower than that of the professionals and managers and also lower than that of the males in sales occupations. For

[15]Many commentators have claimed that the United States, along with other economically advanced societies, has a middle-class majority. That conclusion is based on the presence of a majority in nonmanual occupations. But, as indicated here, the middle-class majority exists only on the female side of the labor force, the males still having a fair-sized blue-collar majority. This means that many of those middle-class women come from working-class families, from families with a husband employed in a blue-collar occupation. Rather than a majority of the *families* being white-collar or middle-class, this means that most are still blue-collar. And it means that in many of those families, wives (and/or daughters) go off during the day to work in offices. It would probably be a mistake to think that they work in a middle-class milieu and that middle-class values rub off on them. Most of them probably work in and around working-class neighborhoods; most of their co-workers are probably people like themselves, persons of working-class backgrounds. For a more detailed discussion of this point, see Hamilton, 1972, Chapter 4.

this group, moderate satisfaction was the most frequent case, the pattern being similar to that of semiskilled and unskilled blue-collar workers. The explanation, already suggested, is that they have the lower-middle-class jobs; that is, the poorly paid jobs, those in the retail trades with only limited opportunities for advancement.

Women in the clerical occupations, on the whole, show a middling level of job satisfaction as compared with other employed women. The percentage very satisfied, it should be noted, is ten points above the figure for equivalent males. That no doubt reflects sex-related differences in training and in resulting aspirations. Because of those differences, males in that category tend to be unenthusiastic, falling below the average for all males. Another even more pronounced culturally induced result will be considered shortly.

The patterns found among the women in blue-collar occupations may be easily summarized: they closely approximate the patterns of equivalent men. The small numbers of skilled women show a middling level of satisfaction, which, at the same time, is the highest of all the blue-collar categories. The operators show the lowest level of satisfaction, with moderate satisfaction again being the modal case. And the service workers once again, as with the men, show middling levels of satisfaction. This category is also a rather heterogeneous one. It contains a large number of maids, two fifths of whom are very satisfied with their work, only one fifth expressing dissatisfaction. There is a large number of nursing aids and orderlies, 54% of whom said they were very satisfied with their work. Their pattern of responses, curiously, was almost identical to that of registered nurses.

The results for the work-if-rich question may be simply summarized. The percentage of men who would continue working if rich tends to be high across the entire occupational spectrum. There is a small class-related difference, but the gap between manuals and nonmanuals is, on the whole, less than ten percentage points. Women, as noted, are somewhat less likely to wish for continued employment (at least in the labor force), the respective male and female responses amounting to 74 and 61%. Among the women professionals one finds a level of work commitment close to that of equivalent males. But for all other categories the women show less work motivation. Despite their higher level of job satisfaction, more than two fifths of women clerical employees would withdraw from the labor force. That category, it will be noted, contains one third of all employed women. The greatest difference occurs with the female operators; less than one half of them would continue working if freed of the necessity.

A large part of the work dissatisfaction literature is focused on the dissatisfactions of male workers, the angry young blue-collar male being the prototypical case of the new worker. These results show that a larger proportion of women are reluctant workers. The most reluctant of all are those in the factories, those engaged in routine assembly tasks and, presumably, in light manufacturing operations. Given the choice, they would quit work and, apparently, return to their homes.

One group not contained in the previous table, even though at work, are those not *gainfully* employed—specifically, those keeping house. The overwhelming majority are housewives (or homemakers) who, on the whole, show high levels of work satisfaction, roughly one half describing themselves as very satisfied. Their responses, in short, are little different from those with full-time labor force commitments (Table 6.4). Although some have claimed intense dissatisfaction with the routines of housework, that is a very exceptional experience, only one in twenty reporting themselves as very dissatisfied.

In this connection, one finds a second reaction linked to culturally defined roles. This large sample contains a small number of house-husbands; they constitute 1.2% of those occupying the homemaker role. Making all due allowance for the small number of cases ($N = 26$), the level of dissatisfaction registered, 46%, more than twice the level registered by any other segment of the male population, is very striking. Of those disliking the role, the majority, seven of twelve persons, said they were *very* dissatisfied. This is the only segment of the population where that degree of intense dissatisfaction was found.

Not much attention will be given to the part-time employed, since they, for obvious reasons, have not figured prominently in the accounts of most workplace critics. The part-time males form only a relatively small part of the total and show somewhat lower levels of work satisfaction than the equivalent full-time workers. This group, on the whole, is younger than the full-timers. The explanation for their dissatisfaction seems relatively simple; like young persons in general, they have less attractive jobs.

The part-time women workers form a much larger segment, constituting more than one quarter of all employed women. Much of the increase of

Table 6.4. Work Satisfaction and Continuing to Work by Work Status and Sex (Combined NORC Studies: 1972–1978)

Work status	Male			Female		
	Full-time	Part-time	House-work	Full-time	Part-time	House-work
Work satisfaction						
Very satisfied	51%	46%	27%	53%	48%	49%
Moderately satisfied	36	33	27	35	40	36
Dissatisfied	12	21	46	12	12	15
$N =$	(3043)	(252)	(26)	(1645)	(616)	(2184)
If enough money would continue to work	75%	73%	—[a]	61%	66%	—[a]
$N =$	(1660)	(138)		(938)	(319)	

[a]Not asked of homemakers.

women's labor force participation in recent decades has involved this category rather than those with full-time commitments. They are not sharply differentiated in satisfaction or commitment from either the full-time employed women or the homemakers. It seems likely that, for them, unlike the equivalent men, part-time employment is their preferred long-term option (Logan, O'Reilly III, and Roberts, 1973).

Some further observations are in order with respect to the work-if-rich question. Which segments of the population would stop working if rich? Part of the answer has already been provided: it is older persons just short of retirement, those in the less attractive blue-collar jobs, and women, especially those in semiskilled jobs.

Many commentators have seen education as instrumental in creating the new work ethic. Overall, given these results, that hypothesis is not supported, since it is the young, those in the better jobs, and men who have the higher educational levels. A more specific test, an examination of the pattern by age, sex, and education, also failed to support that hypothesis. Among the young men, the college-educated (those with some college and those with a degree) had the greatest commitment to work. The differences vis-à-vis less educated age and sex peers were not large, since all groups had high levels of commitment. Among the younger women, the college graduates had the highest level of work commitment of any group in the sample, 88%. In this case, there was a sharp relationship with education, two fifths of those with less than high school training wishing to quit work. In the categories of older men and women, the college-educated showed the strongest preference for continued work, and those with less than a high school education preferred to quit. Among the older (age 45–64 years), less-educated men, for example, two fifths would stop working. Among the women, a majority, 53%, would do so. In contrast, only 23% of the men with college degrees would quit, as would 39% of the equivalent women. On balance, it is difficult to see education as antithetical to the work ethic. This evidence suggests it may play a supportive role in maintaining that ethic.[16]

Work satisfaction is another factor associated with job commitment responses. Not too surprisingly, those who do not like their jobs are more likely to say they would quit working if rich. The patterns are not uniform for all subgroups, however, men and women responding somewhat differently, and the responses also vary with age. Among the young men (ages 25 to 34), the wish to quit varies systematically with work dissatisfaction, the percentages who would quit going from 14% among the very satisfied to 43% among the very dissatisfied. Before jumping to world historical conclusions, it should be noted that only 5% of this category were very dissatisfied with their work. In the next age category, those 35–44, that

[16]For a study exploring the relationship of education and job attitudes among male blue-collar workers, one that, again, finds no support for the workplace critics' claims, see Wright and Hamilton, 1979, and for a replication, Hamilton and Wright, 1981.

association largely disappears, all segments, regardless of satisfaction level, showing relatively high work commitment. Among the older men the relationship appears again, this time very strong, ranging from 27 to 63% at the extremes. Here, too, however, it should be noted that very few, only 3%, express extreme dissatisfaction with their jobs.[17]

Among the women, those who are very satisfied with their work say they would continue working. The percentages who would quit are relatively high in all other groups, from those only moderately satisfied to those very dissatisfied. Among those ages 35 to 44, for example, only 29% of the very satisfied would quit, as opposed to 63% of the others. In an older category, ages 45–54, the respective figures are 39 and 61%. These results would appear to reflect both different options available to women and the differences in prior training and resultant aspirations.

Marital status plays an important role among the young women. Among those age 18–24, 47% of the married say they would quit work if rich, as opposed to only 19% among the singles. Even among the 25- to 34-year-olds, there is still a fair-sized difference, the respective figures being 32 and 20%. The differences in outlook appear in the specific job desiderata indicated. Fifty-six percent of the young married gave money a first- or second-place ranking (among five considerations), while 37% of the singles gave such answers. The singles place greater emphasis on promotion chances, 42% putting that in first place, while only 25% of the young marrieds did so. Many young married women, clearly, are reluctant members of the labor force. They are there for the money.

Much of the effort of the workplace critics is based on claims about the "new." New outlooks, new motivational patterns, they say, are eroding the old, the traditional, the established. The evidence we have reviewed to this point shows very little support for that position. For the most part, we have found stability or continuity of the old patterns, particularly with respect to

---

[17]Some relevant findings appear in a study of British workers. Reviewing previous studies, Jacobson (1972) reports, "Almost universally, the major reasons given by low-level industrial workers for wanting to give up employment are ill health, declining physical capacity and unsuitable or heavy work. Thus, a favourable orientation to retirement appears to indicate little more than a sought-after release from an unpleasant situation. Reasons given by those who are not willing to retire are often similarly negative in their connotation; fears from financial difficulties, loneliness, meaningless leisure and supposedly detrimental effects of retirement on health loom large, rather than a positive attachment to work" (Jacobson, p. 193). In Jacobson's study of 145 male semiskilled British factory operatives age 55 to 64, the men were classified on the basis of a set of objective characteristics into those with jobs having light, moderate, and heavy strain. Very strong relationships were found, with those suffering heavy strain willing to retire at the pensionable age and preferring also early retirement. They described their health as fair or poor and reported their belief that retirement would have positive effects on their health. Those having jobs with light strain anticipated that retirement would have negative effects on their health. Also of some relevance is the article by Powell (1973) dealing with the retirement prospects of coal miners. See Reno (1971) for data on the United States.

the traditional work ethic. Even when looking at those specific pockets of work disaffection, at those groups who work only because they have to, we find continuities with traditional patterns rather than evidence of the predicted new development. Those who are close to retirement would quit; married women would quit; those in the least attractive jobs would quit. Even here, those statements should be interpreted relatively, as tendencies rather than as absolute or categoric judgments. Those who are manifestly dissatisfied with their work, especially the preretirees and the married women, are not likely to pose any serious threat to the institutions of the nation; their's is not an explosive potential. Their removal from those positions, their withdrawal from the labor force, is not likely to have any earthshaking implications either. By vacating those positions, they make them available for someone else. Some of those jobs, particularly those currently held by young women, are never likely to be very attractive labor force options. Many others, those held by persons just short of retirement, are, on the whole, more attractive. When the latter jobs are vacated, through retirement, it means a step up for some other workers.

One major new development has occurred in recent years, one which does involve a serious break with traditional ways. Many women have abandoned full-time housekeeping and now show a commitment to jobs in the paid labor force. At the same time, however, this development goes very much against the predictions of the workplace critics; for the younger groups it means a net increase in work force commitment rather than a withdrawal of effort. Although some of that new work effort is motivated by financial goals, many of those new workers say they would continue even if their financial needs were satisfied.

The questions reviewed thus far, for the most part, have focused on the respondents' general or overall work satisfaction or dissatisfaction. It is also useful to examine those questions dealing with the specifics of the job. Given the more concrete character of those specifics, a different picture might result, one less susceptible to either psychological needs or social acceptibility biases. Such questions also allow, clearly, a much richer and more detailed portrait of work in America than is possible with the general satisfaction questions. A major difficulty, however, arises from the sheer magnitude of the task, scores of relevant questions being contained in the best of the studies as compared to only two or three general satisfaction questions. For this reason, the following review must necessarily be severely restricted; it covers only a small part of the available materials. We have focused on the 1972–1973 Quality of Employment survey, principally because it was done at the height of the workplace critics' activity when, presumably, dissent was at its peak.

In one series, respondents were given cards describing different aspects of a person's work (for example, "Travel to and from work is convenient"). They were then asked to indicate the degree to which this was true of their own jobs. The seven statements listed in Table 6.5 under "Job Characteris-

Table 6.5. Specific Work Characteristics (SRC Quality of Employment Survey, 1972–1973)

	How true is this of your job?				
	Not at all true	A little true	Some- what true	Very true	N = = 100%[a]
Job characteristics					
Q. 178(D)—I have an opportunity to develop my own special abilities	11%	19%	27%	43%	2122
Q. 178(G)—I am not asked to do excessive amounts of work	12	17	37	34	2101
Q. 178(H)—The work is interesting	6	12	22	60	2131
Q. 178(K)—I am given a lot of freedom to decide how I do my own work	8	12	31	49	2127
Q. 278(L)—I am given a chance to do the things I do best	13	17	30	40	2114
Q. 178(T)—I can see the results of my work	3	9	25	64	2129
Q. 178(V)—I have enough time to get the job done	5	14	40	41	2128
Supervision					
Q. 178(W)—My supervisor is very concerned about the welfare of those under him	9	17	34	40	1851
Q. 178(DD)—My supervisor is friendly	4	10	27	59	1862
Q. 178(EE)—My supervisor is helpful to me in getting my job done	7	14	29	51	1859
Relations with co-workers					
Q. 178(A)—I am given a lot of chances to make friends	5	16	28	51	2127
Q. 178(C)—The people I work with are friendly and helpful	2	8	36	54	2112
Q. 178(BB)—The people I work with take a personal interest in me	8	20	38	33	2096

[a]Due to rounding errors, these do not always add up to exactly 100%.

tics'' yielded results that sharply contradict the critics' assertions. Most said it was either very true or somewhat true that their jobs allowed them to develop their own abilities and gave them a chance to do the things they did best. Three fifths said very true that the work is interesting, and another one fifth said somewhat true. Half reported a lot of freedom in deciding how to do their work, and another three tenths said it was somewhat true of their work. In contrast to a major claim about the division of labor, nearly two thirds said very true to the statement that they could see the results of their work.

Even in regard to questions dealing with the amount and pace of the work, the critics are, to say the least, not generally supported. Given the statement, "I am not asked to do excessive amounts of work," one in three said very true and more than a third said somewhat true. One respondent in eight gave the answer that would be appropriate to support the critics' assertions; that is, the statement was not at all true of their jobs. Approximately one in six said it was a little true of theirs. Another statement focused on the work pace, this reading, "I have enough time to get the job done." Here only 5% supported the critics with an outright rejection of the claim. Only one in seven answered "a little true." By comparison, two fifths said it was very true.

In assessing the above results, it should be remembered that these are the marginal distributions. They contain the responses of all gainfully employed persons, male and female, full- and part-time, employers and employees, those at all levels of organizational hierarchies. Not all of those indicating excessive work or the lack of time for their work would be blue-collar workers. Some would be owners, some executives and middle-level managers; some would be professionals and some would be clerical workers.

A trio of statements about supervision follows. In this case, the number of respondents is somewhat smaller, the self-employed, those persons without supervisors, having been excluded. Given the frequent image of the tough productivity-oriented foreman, the unfeeling agent of a profit-maximizing capitalist bureaucracy, the results, again, are unexpected. Most respondents described their supervisors as friendly, helpful in getting the job done, and concerned with the welfare of those under them.

A third set of statements describes relations with co-workers. Given the near-automatic use of the word impersonal to describe bureaucracy, the principal setting for contemporary work (presumably), these results, too, are rather unexpected. Half the respondents gave unqualified assent to the statements that their jobs allowed them a lot of chances to make friends and that their co-workers were friendly and helpful. At the same time, however, co-workers, on the whole, were not typically counted among one's closest friends; although the relationships were warm, co-workers were not likely to take a personal interest in the respondent (although even here, one third said the statement was very true and another three eighths said somewhat true). One would not expect the human relations in industry to be among the warmest of possible contacts, since, after all, many if not most of the relationships formed at work would depend on chance or fluke circumstances. While people generally prove friendly and helpful, such relationships would not easily move to the next stage, that of deep personal involvement.[18]

Some further comments, some specification of these specifications, are in order. As indicated, a large number of questions of this kind are available, and only a small part of the total can be reviewed in any detail. There are some ways, however, in which the questions and responses contained in Table 6.5 prove at least somewhat misleading. Returning to the questions on amount and pace of work, we may contrast those results with the responses to two parallel questions asked earlier in the study. Question 28E asks: "How much does your job require you to work very hard?" Here 39% said "a lot," and another 38% said "somewhat." That might seem like a contradiction to the modal responses given to Question 178(G). Strictly speaking, however, they are not opposed. Most people appear to be saying they have to work hard but not excessively so. In addition, one in eight, it will be remembered, did indicate excessive demands; they, presumably, would also fall among those saying their job requires them to work very hard. Neither of those patterns would be contradictory.

Question 28B asks: "How much does your job require you to work very fast?" Here, 38% responded "a lot," and another 37% said "somewhat." A substantial majority, in other words, expressed either a serious or at least moderate concern with the pace of their work. How does that square with the majority report that they had enough time to get the job done? Is that a contradiction? Again, strictly speaking, we think not. Many were saying that they have to work fast but they have enough time for the task or tasks assigned. In fact, of the 75% who said that they had to work very fast ("somewhat" or "a lot"), a large majority, 78% ($N = 1077$), also said that the time allowed was adequate (indicating "somewhat" or "very true" to the question of whether they had enough time). To be sure, some were saying, as the critics indicate, that they have to work fast *and* that they do not have enough time. The critics' claim, in this case, however, is based on a small portion of the total experience. The most generous possible reading of the cross-tabulation finds 15% to fit this category. The extreme case, those indicating a lot of very fast work and saying "not at all true" to the question about enough time, amounts to 3% of the sample.

Two questions, one coming right after the other, appear to stand in flagrant contradiction, so much so as to cast doubt on the credibility of many of those responses. The first (28I) asks how much the job allows the respondent "to do a variety of different things," that being followed by one (28J) asking if the respondent is required to "do things that are very repetitive (do things over and over)." In both cases the modal response was "a lot." But again, one must ask if the contradiction is real or only apparent. One can, without any contradiction, say "a lot" to both questions; that is, the

[18]This is a point that has long been recognized in the appropriate literature. See Dubin (1956) for an early presentation of evidence and discussion.

job may both "allow" variety and "require" repetition. The appropriate questions then become: how much of each is allowed? Rather than pre-judging the issue, moreover, one should ask to what extent each is desired? Or, another way of putting it, is the respondent satisfied with the mix?

The other questions in this series do not provide even apparent contra-dictions. Respondents say they have many occasions to learn new things (28A) and that they have much freedom in the conduct of their work (28G). There is a rough balance in the responses to a question asking if the job requires creativity. Again, before judging this one, it would be wise to inquire about the extent to which creativity is a desired feature of the job.

Most of the self-announced critical writers declare that work, in contemporary capitalist societies, is unfree. In the bureaucracies of the advanced capitalist countries, jobs are narrowly defined, and the worker is simply *told* what to do and how to do it. It is against this authoritarian form that the enlarged and enriched jobs and the participative styles have been advocated and developed (or that some form of socialism is recommended). Such declarations are frequently heard and, so it would appear, frequently accepted (at least they often pass without serious expression of doubt or dissent). From the above results it is clear that this portrait is very much in error.

The Quality of Employment survey contains another range of questions dealing with this topic of worker autonomy and/or participation in decision-making. Question 28G asks: "How much does your job allow you to make a lot of decisions on your own?" Again, the most frequent response was "a lot" (47%), followed by "somewhat" (25%). Even a question on participa-tion in larger decision-making efforts—[Does job] "allow you to take part in making decisions that affect you?" (28L)—found a majority saying "a lot" (36%) or "somewhat" (29%). Wage and salaried employees were asked specifically about their participation: "In the last year have you made any suggestions to your supervisor on how work methods or procedures could be improved on jour job?" (Q. 33). Sixty-seven percent said yes, they had made such suggestions. A subsequent question asked if the suggestion had been followed. Of those making suggestions, 58% said yes, and another 17% said the matter was still being considered (it was too soon to know).

Also of interest in this connection are the results of a large comparative study, the renowned study by Almond and Verba (1963), that in 1959 and 1960 put some relevant questions to cross-sectional samples in five nations. Employed persons who had someone in authority over them in their day-to-day work were asked the following questions:

> We'd like to find out how decisions are made on your job. When decisions are made affecting your own work, do those in authority over you ever consult you about them? Do they *usually* consult you, do they *sometimes* consult you, does this happen *rarely,* or are you *never* consulted?

> If a decision were made affecting your own work that you disagreed with strongly, what would you do—would you feel *free* to complain, would you feel

uneasy about complaining, or is it better to accept the decision and not complain?

Have you ever actually complained about such a decision?

In response to the first of these questions, nearly four fifths of the employees in the United States said they are usually or sometimes consulted. More than four fifths said they would feel free to complain about a decision with which they strongly disagreed. More than three out of five reported having in fact protested such decisions. The actual responses, in short, are sharply opposed to the claims provided by the workplace critics (Almond and Verba, pp. 342–343).

There are two additional questions in the sequence that are of some interest. These results were not reported in Almond and Verba. Following the question about sensed freedom to complain, the survey asked, "If you did complain, would it do any good?" Given the common critical depiction of intransigent management, we would anticipate a lot of "no" answers. In fact, among the American respondents, a large majority—69%—said yes. This was also the majority response in every other country except Italy (where only 37% said yes).

The final question in the sequence read, "The way things are, do you think that those who run the place where you work take your interests and needs into account when they make decisions or do they ignore your interests?" More than three quarters of the American respondents (78%) felt that management took their needs and interests into account, and similar high percentages were reported for the other countries. Here again, the gap between the critics' claims and the responses given by workers themselves could scarcely be sharper.

Those claims face difficulties in still another direction. The highest levels of reported consultation, of sensed freedom to protest, and of actual protest were found in the United States and in the United Kingdom (the latter levels being somewhat higher). The Federal Republic of Germany was intermediate in all three comparisons. And the least consultation, the least sense of freedom, and the least actual protest came in Italy and Mexico. If one assumed that the United States had the most "fully developed" industrial bureaucracies, in Max Weber's sense of the term, and that those of Italy and Mexico were the least developed, it would mean that consultation and freedom of protest both *increase* with the degree of bureaucratization.

Almond and Verba also presented some results by occupational level. In general, consultation and felt freedom to protest varied directly with occupational status. In the United States, for example, among the lower level blue-collar workers, 69% were usually or sometimes consulted, as opposed to 87% of the professional and managerial employees. In Germany, only half of the equivalent blue-collar workers reported such consultation. In Mexico, the figure was 48%; in Italy, 40%. In Italy, only 38% said they felt free to protest job decisions. These were the most pronounced authoritarian settings in any of the five nations and four occupational levels. Positive majorities are reported in all other contexts (Almond and Verba, p. 344). The Almond-Verba findings, it will be noted, were in the public domain two decades before the workplace critics issued their a priori denials.

It is useful, after this brief review of specifics, to return to the general measures of job satisfaction contained in the 1973 employment survey. Not too surprisingly, the standard four-option satisfaction question shows high levels of approval. A sizable majority also say they would recommend their job to a close friend. And an even larger majority, if they had to decide all over again, would take the same job without hesitation. People were also asked how often they did extra work that was not required of them. The most frequent response was "often," and that was followed by "sometimes" (Table 6.6). It is hard to imagine all those people doing *extra* work if it were "mindless, exhausting, boring, servile, and hateful. . . ."

Given the disparity between the findings reported here and the expectation of widespread dissatisfaction with work, especially with the more routine and repetitive jobs, some further exploration to resolve the paradox

Table 6.6. Work Satisfaction: Some Additional Indicators (SRC Quality of Employment Survey, 1972–1973)

Q. 179—All in all, how satisfied would you say you are with your job?	Very satisfied	52%
	Somewhat satisfied	38
	Not too satisfied	8
	Not at all satisfied	2
	N =	2153
Q. 180—If a good friend of yours told you he/she was interested in working in a job like yours for your employer, what would you tell him/her? Would you . . .	Strongly recommend this job	64%
	Have doubts about recommending it	27
	Strongly advise against this sort of job	9
	N =	2107
Q. 181—Knowing what you know now, if you had to decide all over again whether to take the job you now have, what would you decide? Would you . . .	Decide without any hesitation to take the same job	70%
	Have some second thoughts	25
	Decide definitely not to take the same job	6
	N =	2143
Q. 32—How often do you do some extra work for your job which isn't required of you? Would you say you do this . . .	Often	42%
	Sometimes	38
	Rarely	12
	Never	8
	N =	2149

seems an obvious necessity. For this purpose we review some studies of factory work, particularly those dealing with simple and repetitive tasks. As will be seen, some unexpected or hidden lessons appear.

One early classic dealing with automobile workers was by Walker and Guest, *The Man on the Assembly Line* (1952). The analysis was based on interviews with 180 production workers in a plant having "one of the most modern automobile assembly lines in the world" (p. 3). The study, begun in the summer of 1949, is unusual in that it contains statistical analysis together with a large number of individual quotations. One hears the voices of the men themselves commenting on various aspects of their work.

Many of these quotations could easily be used to support critical conclusions. Some, indeed, have been used for just that purpose. Consider, for example, the following:

> The bad thing about assembly lines is that the line keeps moving. If you have a little trouble with a job, you can't take the time to do it right.

> The line speed is too great. . . . There's an awful lot of tension.

> The work isn't hard, it's the never-ending pace. . . . The guys yell "hurrah" whenever the line breaks down . . . you can hear it all over the plant (Walker and Guest, p. 51).

This latter quotation appeared frequently in the critical literature of the 1950's. All these quotations, it will be noted, focus on pace rather than monotony. Some workers made explicit distinction between the two factors.

> It's not the monotony, it's the rush, rush, rush.

> The line speed is too fast . . . . The work isn't monotonous.

> It's very interesting because I see all the different kinds of jobs around me (Walker and Guest, p. 52).

There were many, however, who made an opposite assessment, who found the monotony to be the most oppressive feature of the job.

> I dislike repetition. One of the main things wrong with this job is that there is no figuring for yourself; no chance to use my brain. It's a grind doing the same thing over and over. There is no skill necessary.

> I'd like to do more things. That's the trouble with the line. Monotony. You repeat the same thing day in, day out.

> It's not a matter of pace. It's the monotony. It's not good for you to get so bored. I do the same thing day after day; just an everlasting grind.

> The job gets so sickening—day in and day out plugging in ignition wires. I get through with one motor, turn around, and there's another motor staring me in the face. It's sickening.

The authors also point out, however, that a minority "liked the challenge and excitement of keeping up with the line. . . ."

> I do my job well. I get some satisfaction from keeping up with a rapid-fire job. On days when the cars come off slowly, I sometimes get bored.
>
> I get satisfaction from doing my job right and keeping up with the line.
>
> There's too much rush for the manpower to get quality. It makes you feel good, though, when the line is going like hell and you step in and catch it up.

There was also a minority who preferred "doing the same thing over and over. . . ."

> I like the routine. You can get in the swing of it.
>
> I repeat the same thing day in and day out. I like it—I can do it fast.
>
> I like to repeat the same thing, and every car is different anyway. So my job is interesting enough. (Walker and Guest, p. 55)

The first three sets of quotations provide ample evidence of job hatred among assembly-line workers; it would be no problem at all to work up a telling case against the assembly line using these comments. At the same time, however, even in this brief review, one discovers complexities that are overlooked in the wholesale condemnations provided by the workplace critics. Where they condemn pace and monotony, the workers themselves distinguish between the two and make differentiated evaluations of these components. Then, too, a minority report a preference for pace and/or routine. But then, for instances are one thing, systematic evidence another.

The authors, as indicated, did provide systematic evidence. A direct question on job preferences yielded a very lopsided distribution, 85% wishing to perform different operations, 8% preferring repetitive work, and 7% saying it made no difference. A second question asked about the character of their actual jobs: "Would you say your job was very interesting, fairly interesting, not too interesting, or not at all interesting?" (Walker and Guest, p. 53). Given the "trained expectation" that dislike would be the dominant response, it comes as a surprise to discover that almost half (49%, $N = 180$) described their work as very or fairly interesting. It might be noted, in passing, that even in the Walker–Guest volume, this finding appears only in the raw figures in the margin of a table (p. 54). The percentage does not appear, nor is there any comment made about this specific result. The finding also suggests that the disparity between worker interest (that is, the preference for variety) and actual job content is not as wide as the original finding would suggest; it is not as if the 85% were doomed to frustration.

Some words of explanation are in order. Although one tends to equate automobile work with the assembly line, the actual situation is somewhat more complicated. Just under half the workers in this plant (47.8%) were on the main assembly line. Another 15.5% were on moving belt subassembly lines. Approximately one fifth (21.1%) were doing subassembly work, although not on a moving line. Most of the rest were repairmen and utility men. It should be clear that even on the main line, some limited variety would be possible; not all would be single-task jobs. Consonant with the expressed interest in variety, one finds the level of interest increasing substantially with the number of tasks performed. However, one third of those performing a single task, it should be noted, assessed that work positively; they saw it as something other than a "deadening" routine.[19]

One may summarize as follows: first, the kinds of jobs present in this automobile assembly plant were more diverse than one would expect, given the assertions contained in the critical literature. Second, the orientations toward this work, even including the routine single-task job, are more diverse than one has been led to believe. The most unexpected finding in this study is that almost half found their work either very or fairly interesting. This point is overlooked in the Walker-Guest text itself and, not too surprisingly, in the various critical writings that have drawn on this text. Third, it is *probable* that this level of job interest was lower than that of blue-collar workers generally (and obviously, of the entire labor force) at that time. The critics appear to be justified at least in a relative sense; jobs in the automobile industry, particularly those on the line, are less attractive than those elsewhere in the labor force. The critics are mistaken, however, at least as far as this study is concerned, in their judgment of the frequencies. Where the critics suggest a wall of opposition to the job, this study found unexpected quantities of interest.

What about those who are dissatisfied? Why do those workers hating the pace and/or monotony of the line keep at it? There is little mystery about this question; another of the Walker-Guest findings shows that the median earnings in the automobile plant were nearly 50% above those the workers received in their previous employment (p. 83).

Another study allowing some insight into the question of alienating work was undertaken many years ago by Elmo Roper for *Fortune* magazine (1947). It was later reanalyzed by Robert Blauner, whose findings appeared in an influential book, *Alienation and Freedom* (1964). The original study, according to Roper, was a "pretty carefully controlled quota sample" of 3000 workers, providing a cross section of sixteen factory industries. It is useful, once again, to focus on the automobile workers, their work environment, as Blauner notes, having "the most alienating consequences" of all. Automobile plants, as a result, he states, have been "the favorite research laboratory for the sociologist of the manual worker." Blauner, however, makes clear that the automobile worker is by no means typical. "If the most

[19]The percentages reporting that their work was very or fairly interesting, for those performing 1, 2 to 5, and 5 or more operations, respectively, were: 33% (57): 44% (64): and 69% (59) (recalculated from Walker and Guest, p. 54). The overlapping categories, incidentally, appear in the original. For a useful statement of the logic of the assembly line, its advantages and disadvantages, see Deming, 1977.

alienated workers," he says, "are viewed as typical workers, it is no wonder that there is a persistent tendency to view manual workers in general as alienated. Yet assembly line workers in all industries probably constitute no more than 5 per cent of the entire labor force. And comparisons of the job attitudes of automobile workers with factory employees in other industries suggest that their level of alienation is not typical" (Blauner, 1964, p. 5). The heart of Blauner's book, accordingly, consists of a comparison of printers, textile workers, automobile workers, and chemical workers. The result, simply put, is that automobile workers have the worst conditions of all.

That said, it is useful to explore the matter in more detail, specifically, to examine the distribution of attitudes within the industry. The most appropriate question for this purpose concerns workers' descriptions of their jobs: "Which one of these statements comes closest to describing how you feel about your present job? (a) My job is interesting nearly all the time; (b) While my job is interesting most of the time, there are some dull stretches now and then; (c) There are a few times when my job is interesting, but most of it is pretty dull and monotonous; (d) My job is completely dull and monotonous; there is nothing interesting about it." (All results and question wordings are taken from Blauner, 1964, pp. 199–204). One might easily assume that most persons working in the industry would choose this last option. In fact, however, only 18% made that choice. One third said their jobs were interesting nearly all the time, and another one third said their jobs were interesting most of the time. Only one third, obviously, made a negative judgment, about one half of them saying the job was pretty dull, and the rest, as indicated, rating it completely dull ($N = 174$). Even here, in the a fortiori case of oppressive work, one finds a majority making a positive assessment of their jobs.

Some of Blauner's other findings have relevance for the persistently repeated critical claims. On the narrow division of labor and the consequent deadening routine, we have the following: "Is [your job] too simple to bring out your best abilities, or not?" The automobile industry was third on this list (after sawmills and planing; stone, clay, and glass). Only 35% of the automobile workers found their jobs too simple for them; a majority, 58%, rejected that description. Those convinced of the unconscionable speed of the line will be surprised by the response to a question on this theme: "Does [your job] make you work too fast most of the time or not?" Only one worker in three found the work pace too fast. That figure, to be sure, is higher than in any other industry (in printing it was 10%, in oil refining, 6%). It was approximately the same as was found in textiles and apparel manufacture, the respective figures there being 32 and 31%. The "don't know" responses, an "insignificant proportion of all responses" have been removed in Blauner's tabulations, meaning that two thirds of the automobile workers who gave answers did not feel they had to work "too fast. . . ."

To probe the exhausting demands of the job, one has the following question: "Does [your job] leave you too tired at the end of the day, or not?"

Again about one third (34%) of the automobile workers said yes. In this connection one ought to note the role of the union, of the United Auto Workers. One writer stated, "There is general agreement in the industry that the UAW has slowed down the assembly lines from the pre-union days" (Northrup, 1955, p. 39).

On the question of personal job control or discretion, one again discovers an unexpected result. Of the automobile workers, 47% felt their job "really" gave them a "chance to try out ideas" of their own. The automobile industry was well down on the list in this respect (printing, 79%; chemicals, 64%) but was still ahead of five other fields, ones that have not come in for any serious attention in this regard.

How did workers feel about the company—is it "about as good a place as there is to work, or do you think there are other places that are better?" Of the respondents, 62%, a relatively low figure compared to other industries, felt their company was as good a place as any. Job instability was high (although that was a concern expressed by only a small [21%] minority in this study). Fifty weeks of work per year was relatively infrequent; still, according to data cited by Blauner, it was the majority experience.

The best single datum for the workplace critics comes in response to a "do it over again" question. "If you could go back to the age of 15 and start life over again, would you choose a different trade or occupation?" Three fifths (actually 59%) of all factory workers would have chosen a different occupation. For the automobile industry, the figure was 69%, just below the leather, sawmills and planing, and oil refining industries. Some critics are quick to translate such results into a fundamental dissatisfaction with work. The results of the previous questions, however, make it clear that the dissatisfaction is not fundamental by any stretch of the imagination. Even people in attractive jobs, ones they like and appreciate, could easily, when asked this hypothetical (and abstract) question, think of something else they might have preferred. The nostalgia-choice question is probably always destined to find high percentages willing to consider some other path.

One of Blauner's tables provides some explanation for the apparent paradox of the prevous findings. He sorted workers into four skill categories: unskilled, low-skilled, medium-skilled, and skilled. The first of these groups consisted of workers requiring less than one month's training, most of them, no doubt, having jobs on the assembly line. Of the jobs in the automobile industry, 48% had this very low skill requirement (as against 32% for all factory work). Returning to the first question considered above, concerning whether the work was interesting or dull, one finds a very high percentage of the unskilled workers in the automobile industry rating their jobs as dull or monotonous either all or most of the time. Their figure, 61%, was above that of equivalent workers in the next industry (sawmills and planing, 50%) and well above the overall figure of 38% for the unskilled. There was a sharp division within the automobile industry between the unskilled and all others, the equivalent figures for the other three skill grades listed above being 27,

16, and 6%, respectively. These categories do not stand out at all in comparison with their peers in other industries. The peculiar center of work dissatisfaction, then, is not the industry per se, but that minority working at the very lowest skill levels. Even here, it should be noted, a significant segment, two out of five, did *not* assess their work as dull or monotonous. Asked if their work was too simple, 46% agreed; but that means, obviously, just over half disagreed, even though the skill requirement was very modest. Of the unskilled automobile workers, 44% felt too tired at the end of the day; which again, means that a majority did not feel physically exhausted (Blauner, 1964, p. 104).

Some readers might be inclined to view these results with incredulity. One should recognize, however, that a process of self-selection is likely to be operating. The persons most adverse to the routine and boring tasks would normally bid up to other jobs as opportunities arose, and thus would remove themselves from the most alienating conditions. Others, those who actually prefered simple and uncomplicated job tasks, would (one assumes) be content to stay put. Then, too, what would be challenging, diverse, and interesting to a workplace intellectual is not necessarily what would challenge or excite unskilled workers in the automobile industry. To one of modest intellectual resources, the pace, challenge, and complexity of assembly work may be more than adequate. One might also ask about the appropriate comparison standards. Compared to the labors of the intellectual life, assembly work seems almost unimaginably routine and boring. Few workers would use such a demanding standard in assessing the conditions of their own work. Compared to realistic and available alternatives (for example, sweeping floors, driving a cab, or whatever), work on the automotive assembly line might well appear challenging indeed. There is, moreover, a strong incentive when the going wage is half again the pay to be earned in alternative occupations.

Another study of automobile workers deals with the much-discussed question of job enlargement (Kennedy and O'Neill, 1958). It focused on four adjacent departments: the first "assembled the body, [the second] painted it, a third applied the trim and a fourth assembled the chassis and then assembled it to the body." For convenience, they were referred to as Departments A, B, C, and D. The organization of the departments was the same in all cases, with each foreman's section of the line having some 20 to 30 assembly workers and one or two utility men. The study interviewed all the utility men and a 20% random sample of the assembly operators.

The basic comparison is of such dazzling simplicity that one wonders why it has not been done many times before and since. One also wonders why the results have not been in the forefront of the discussion over the "degradation of labor." The key comparison is between the assembly operators and the utility men. The former perform the much-discussed routine tasks—the "complete time cycle for each task was between one and two minutes." The tasks were either identical for each make and model of car or were only negligibly different. "Each assembly operator's job was highly repetitive, routine, de-skilled, mechanically paced, and such that the end result of his efforts contributed only an infinitesimal part of the total process of assembling a complete car." The utility men, in contrast, relieved the assembly workers for routine or emergency breaks. They trained new workers and also completed or corrected inadequate work. They performed "a wide number of these same routine tasks—as many as 20 or 30. . . . "

Although one might anticipate dramatic differences in work satisfaction between the holders of these single- and multitask jobs, the basic finding for Departments A and B was of "no significant difference." This conclusion was based on overall scale scores and their two components, the first concerned with "the more general aspects of the work situation (pride in work group, relations with other units, confidence in the company and satisfaction with the job itself)," and the second involving those aspects of the job concerned with the immediate supervisor.

The situations in Departments C and D were somewhat different. There, some efforts had been made (or were being made) to "enrich" the work. It was decided "to train experienced assembly operators on several jobs in addition to their regularly assigned job so that they might be rotated on jobs when the need arose. . . . " This additional training was the responsibility of the utility men. They received some special training (eleven one-hour lecture sessions over a five-week period). They then spent one-half their time in their ordinary relief work, the other one-half in this new training. To ensure that they would have sufficient time for both tasks, some assembly operators "were upgraded to the status of utility men to help in the more routine tasks of providing relief, making repairs, etc." This innovation had been completed (by two weeks) in Department C at the time of the interviewing. It was still in process in Department D. In this case, there were significant differences in scores, the utility men's results being more positive in both instances for the composite as well as the two component scores. But there, regrettably, the report of the findings ends. The authors' table, however, shows another finding: the assembly operators in departments C and D (who had learned additional tasks and who, possibly, were practicing them) had scores that were no different from those of their peers in departments A and B.

The authors then raise some important questions about the one positive result reported. There were, it will be remember, two changes involved—the expansion of job duties and, for some, a change in status. The authors, unfortunately, do not give separate results for these two segments so as to allow isolation of the specific causal factor. They also felt, judging from the results in departments A and B, that the effects "would not be expected to persist." Another possiblity mentioned is that of a Hawthorne effect—that the special attention given this group, plus the classroom training, had stimulated the heightened morale. And with those speculations the report ends.

What lessons may be drawn from this study? One is very clear and lacks any ambiguity: the difference between the responses to the routine assembly tasks and the more diverse utility men's jobs was zero. Two observations may be drawn from the second or experimental experience in departments C and D. First, the modest enlargement provided for the assembly-line workers by this innovation also had a zero effect. The second, the one clear indication of an effect, is ambiguous in two ways—we do not know the cause and we do not know if the effect was lasting. Hence, pending the appearance of the follow-up study, no firm conclusion may be drawn. A summary conclusion may be reached; namely, that this study does *not* support the claim that significant improvement of outlook would be correlated with job enlargement. There are two clear lines of evidence against the claim and only one ambiguous line that could, possibly, speak for it. One other point, a methodological one, is also clear; the authors have located an experimental setting where replication is simple, where that ambiguity could, in subsequent work, be very easily resolved.[20]

An early 1950's study of Detroit area automobile and other factory workers came up with additional findings consonant with those reported above. "The two salient conclusions," it was reported, "are that: (1) overall job feelings of automobile workers are predominantly favorable though at the same time there is enough dissatisfaction to suggest need for substantial improvement; and (2) large and important differences exist between occupational skill levels with pronouncedly more negative reactions among men on routine production jobs" (Kornhauser, 1965, p. 157). Using a five-part choice question, the least satisfaction, he reports, was among the young workers in the repetitive, semiskilled jobs, basically among those "on the line." Those satisfied, neither, and dissatisfied amounted to 37, 27, and 37% (N = 30). Among the middle-aged workers, the equivalent figures were 60, 23, and 16% (N = 73, p. 159). No ultimate liking of those jobs was indicated

---

[20]Another study deserving attention focused on voluntary intraplant job changes by nonsupervisory workers. This study, obviously, allows comparison of the characteristics of the past and present jobs, thus enabling a very concrete investigation of preferences. It is, again, like the Kennedy and O'Neill study, one of dazzling simplicity. Their findings are:

In 51 of the 71 pairs of jobs, employees transferred to jobs with increased pay; only 4 moved to lower pay. The majority of the higher paid jobs to which workers moved were more enriched, but when the job shift did not provide a pay increase, no preference was shown for the more enriched job. No statistically significant preference for less routine (more enlarged) jobs was shown either with or without increased pay" (Simonds and Orife, 1975, p. 606).

A study of assembly-line workers in a radio and television set factory in Chicago found 51% preferring smaller assembly tasks and only 12% wishing larger, more enriched work tasks. The rest were indifferent—that is, had no preference. Asked whether they preferred a mechanically paced line or one they themselves controlled (a push line), 90% preferred the former, saying it was easier or that it provided "better rhythm" (Kilbridge, 1960).

since, were they to start over, 86 and 84%, respectively, of the young and middle-aged semiskilled would choose different work. Asked whether the job was "really interesting and enjoyable," or if it were "all right but not very interesting," or if it were "dull and monotonous," the results for the young were 17, 47, and 37% ($N = 30$), respectively. Among the middle-aged workers the equivalent figures were 32, 50, and 18% ($N = 72$). While this certainly indicates far from ideal work conditions, it should be noted that even among the young, outright dissatisfaction was expressed by only three in eight. Among the middle-aged, only one in five said their work was "dull and monotonous." One might easily assume the wearing down hypothesis in the face of the different age patterns. Another alternative explanation, however, would again be self-selection, a sort-out; those finding the work completely unacceptable would quit or bid up to a better job.

A more recent study focused on workers employed in an automobile assembly plant in Baltimore in late 1968, a time, presumably, when the rebellion in the workplace was already very much in evidence. These authors say that "95% [of the workers] reported themselves as satisfied with their jobs; 71% reported no part of their work as tiring or upsetting." Taking up the blue-collar blues theme, the authors noted that "depression and its symptoms are often assumed to be ubiquitous in this population." That assumption, however, "is not borne out by worker responses to direct questions. Overwhelmingly, most workers do not report the presence of these symptoms" (Siassi, Crocetti, and Spiro, 1974, pp. 262, 263).

These authors spent considerable time in the plant and, expressing their own reactions, say they "still cannot understand why the workers do not express more dissatisfaction." They note, however, that their findings are "quite consistent" with other field surveys. One possible explanation, they suggest, is that the respondents have "masked" their feelings. Another possibility mentioned is self-selection. The workers in this plant were older, had moved about less, and had been on the job longer than most workers. The most dissatisfied, they thought, may have been "weeded out over time."

Still another study, the work of William Form (1976), provides comparable results. Form studied the General Motors' Oldsmobile plant in Lansing, Michigan, on four occasions, the last of these researches being in the mid-1960's. Those rating their jobs as "good" or "very good" were: crafts, 90%; test, inspection, repair, 72%; machine operator, 63%; and assembly line, 51%. Those reporting they were satisfied with their jobs amounted to: 92, 85, 82, and 75% (Form, p. 126).

Form concludes as follows: "The results of this study cast serious doubt on the ideology of the machine-haters. Even in the American automobile industry, where technology is allegedly most dehumanizing, workers expected satisfaction in their work. The situation differed little in the less industrial countries; the autoworkers preferred working to leisure, not out of a sense of duty or a need for sociability, but because they thought that work ordered their lives. . . . The response to technology is a much more complicated business than American scholars have believed. . . . As See-man (1971) has suggested, the speculations concerning human responses to machines, from Marx to Marcuse, need thorough reexamination" (Form, pp. 135–137).[21]

One other study deserves special attention. A. A. Imberman's 1973 analysis was based on "3,800 factory workers, black and white, men and women, in five states and in five different industries. All were involved in assembly work, producing furniture, automobile components, electronic equipment, radio and tv components, and non-electrical machinery." The principal finding was that "Blue Collar Blues are experienced by only about 20% of assembly line workers." Those results, Imberman notes, are conso-nant with those of most other serious researchers in the field: "The only thing significantly different about [this] study was the larger number of em-ployees included—nobody had covered as many as 3,800 assembly work-ers—and the geographical and industrial diversification of five different industries in five different states."

Imberman puts his conclusions even more forcibly: "from 79% to 88% of the assembly line workers whose comments we obtained firsthand *liked assembly work*. They *did not want* added responsibilities or quality require-ments, nor any significant changes in job content. In short, this large majority showed no signs of suffering from Blue Collar Blues as that condition is commonly understood" (emphases in the original).

Imberman provides a straightforward matter-of-fact explanation for these results:

> Assembly line work is regarded as a step upward by persons from disadvantaged backgrounds in the cities, and by a good number of rural and small town workers as well. Those people, both black and white, are able to acquire a limited skill quickly and come to be regarded as semi-skilled workers, which they consider to be a step up from unskilled laborers or janitors. Acquiring semi-skilled status in a society that values skill is a positive gain. We did not find many assemblers who thought their work was demeaning.

Of the five assembly-line plants studied, Imberman found the greatest frustration and discontent among the auto assembly workers compared to those in furniture, radio and tv, electronics, and textiles. The income factor is easily excluded, the industry's average wage levels being the highest in the

---

[21]Another set of findings of considerable interest involves the evaluations made of three kinds of jobs—small independent farmer, skilled factory worker, and office worker. The Oldsmobile workers gave the following responses (Form, p. 123): Most desirable occupations: farmer, 44%; factory worker, 39%; office worker, 14%. The attitudes expressed about the office job are of special interest: most respected, 39% (versus skilled factory worker, 12%); most necessary, 3% (versus farm, 59% and factory, 14%); gives most satisfaction, 5% (versus farm, 65%, and factory, 20%); most monotonous, 51% (versus farm, 9%, and factory, 34%). Office work, one is told, "ranked as more monotonous than factory work . . . especially by skilled workers" (Form, p. 122n). One might consider how many mobility studies have counted a move from blue-collar skilled jobs to white-collar clerical jobs as upward mobility.

country. He suggests four factors as decisive in this result: (1) the size of the automobile factories, which are considerably larger than those in other industries; (2) the extreme compression of the wage rates; (3) the lack of opportunity for advancement and skill development (Robert Guest found that only 6% of skilled maintenance workers had begun their careers on the line); and (4) management's failure to listen to employees.[22] These factors are clearly separate and distinct from the work process itself; the process, assembly-line work, was a constant in all five industries studied.

To summarize, assembly-line jobs within the automobile industry do appear to be among the most objectionable jobs to be found anywhere within the United States labor force. About that there can be little doubt. A number of specifications, however, need to be added to that statement. While some commentators have treated these assembly-line workers as the prototypical blue-collar workers, one principal conclusion noted by many serious commentators is that they are not typical at all; they are, in fact, a very atypical or extreme case among the blue-collar workers.

A second principal conclusion touches on the attitudes of workers within the industry and, more specifically, of those on the line. Even here, it has been shown, there is a distribution of attitudes. While the percentage of those disliking their work is highest (or among the highest) of all industries, there is still a large group present that likes, is satisfied with, or otherwise accepts the work. In the reports of Siassi et al, and of Imberman, those satisfied actually are majorities. While some commentators would have us believe that monolithic dissatisfaction is the typical reaction to such "obviously" alienating conditions, no study has shown that extreme result. The critical tradition has simply failed to report these nonconforming cases, or, as in the case of Barbara Garson, treated them as isolated and ridiculous exceptions.

This review has also indicated some of the reasons for such liking. Some people are not attracted by complex and challenging jobs. Some people prefer these uncomplicated routines; they object to the well-meaning efforts to enrich their jobs[23] Walker and Guest indicate that the pace of the work

---

[22]Imberman appears to be leaning on Blauner's discussion at this point. Evidence backing up these summary claims is found there (Blauner, 1964, pp. 109–115). Blauner presents findings from an Opinion Research Corporation study showing that auto and auto equipment workers were the least likely, of nine industries, to feel "their company takes a real interest in its employees' (p. 111). The fourth consideration discussed by Blauner, "relatively few close-knit, functional work groups," has become "management's failure to listen to employees" in Imberman's presentation. Imberman's article, it should be noted, is more a summary review of his (and others') work than a detailed exposition of his own research.

[23]One early study of routine work, the assembly of high-quality electronic products with a typical job cycle of one minute or less, found "a majority of the operators [saying] they found the job fairly or very 'interesting,' while less than 20 per cent complained that the job was monotonous or 'boring'" (Turner and Miclette, 1962, p. 216). Another, even earlier, review and presentation came up with an

was the number one complaint in the factory they studied. But some workers there (though a minority, to be sure) found that very pace to serve as a challenge. A self-selection factor no doubt operates everywhere. Those most intensely disliking the work would be the first to leave. Over time, the proportion liking it would increase.

Still another factor, one present from the beginning, from the time of Henry Ford's original Dearborn line, is that of income. Many workers are there for the financial advantage provided in this, the highest paid of all industries. The critics frequently overlook this factor in their auto-worker-as-modern-man treatments. The blue-collar worker faces a choice: high pay at onerous tasks or less pay at less onerous tasks. In a free labor market situation, that would be the normal relationship. It means these workers have chosen those jobs; it is hardly the case that they were forced into this specific job by the system. (It is, to be sure, not always a matter of free choice, the availability of work in the potentially accessible geographical area also being a prime determinant in many cases.) These workers might well indicate dissatisfaction with the intrinsic characteristics of their jobs; they would also, no doubt, indicate that the money was the reason for them being there. That might add up to a portrait of alienated workers, but in this case the alienation is self-assumed rather than forced. For some workers, as Imberman has noted, work on the line is a step up in the world; it is better than the opportunities they had had previously. It seem unlikely that such workers would experience it as alienating.

To summarize, then, the critics have failed to report the range of job attitudes found among automobile workers. They have also failed to report the complexity of motives indicated in the available literature. In short, they have, in most cases, described the repulsive objective characteristics of such work and assumed a uniform creative human personality. The *logical* conclusion is one of ineluctable conflict between jobs and men. Where other contrary evidence exists, however, evidence indicating the complexities just reviewed, such selective treatment of the facts is inexcusable. While the automobile assembly line is clearly not a jobholder's paradise, it is not the hell that critics of the Hieronymus Bosch School of Industrial Relations have portrayed it.

It is useful at this point to consider the principal solution offered by the workplace critics—job enrichment. Here too the scholarship has been rather deficient. Imberman, to begin, states that:

> *Work in America* is a comprehensive compendium of those—*only* those—academic studies that purport to find a great groundswell for job enrichment. If you tunnel beneath the language of the report, you'll find that virtually all the companies cited are rather small, and with so-called job enrichment in limited areas of production. In many of the cases given, job enrichment consists merely of added tasks, such as having the assemblers put on additional parts. . . .

important negative finding, one with considerable relevance to the claims of Maslow and later of Inglehart. As this study put it, "The relationship between intelligence and boredom is by no means established" (Smith, Patricia, 1955, p. 328).

Further, it appears that nearly all the enrichment projects described are in non-union plants, and that the employees are paid no more for their broader jobs than they were for their narrower jobs . . .

Nothing is said in the report about contrary findings by other reputable researchers. Nothing is said either about the tremendous upheaval and chaos that implementing HEW's recommendations would bring about in industry.

The best summary review of the theories underlying the job enrichment movement, of the evidence relevant to those theories, and of actual case studies, is that of Tausky and Parke (1976). The changes made in work processes, they note, go beyond the mere addition of or enrichment of tasks. Workers at the Corning Glass plant in Medfield, Massachusetts, for example, did assemble a complete hot plate and performed quality-control checks. In addition, they placed their initials on the completed products. That initialing, it is reported, allowed employees to identify with their work, but "the initials were also used to 'reference' customer complaints. It was reported that after implementation of the program, product rejects dropped from 23% to 1" (Tausky and Parke, p. 556). In the Maytag job enrichment program "each worker placed his identification number on each completed unit. . . . " They also received more pay than ordinary assembly jobs (pp. 556–557). Tausky and Parke report that in "each case" there were features that increased accountability, thus linking performance more directly than before to job security and pay.

The Gaines Dog Food experience, the most frequently cited case, is also reviewed. While the emphasis in the many glowing accounts had stressed "the challenging jobs, opportunities for personal growth, and participation in decision making," other accounts have reported several additional factors of likely relevance. Management was highly selective in their initial recruitment, taking only 70 of 600 applicants. Pay in this case was also a factor. Workers in that unit could, potentially, earn nearly 50% more than single-task workers. There was, moreover, considerable informal group pressure to be at work, since no provision was made for substitutes. A missing team member could endanger the group's earnings. One author referred to "excessive peer group pressure" in this connection (Tausky and Parke, p. 555). For more details see Schrank, 1974.

What one has, in short, is a complex set of changes. The job enrichment advocates have chosen to emphasize those features involving task complexity and autonomy, those elements fitting in with their Maslovian preconceptions. In doing so, they have neglected other salient features of the changes, notably the new control mechanisms. For other valuable critiques, see Strauss and Rosenstein, 1970; Sirota, 1973; Fein, 1974; Berg, 1976; Kaplan and Tausky, 1977; Berg, Freedman and Freeman, 1978, Chapter 15; Lawler, 1969; Goodman, 1979, 1980.

One relevant study (Weinberg, 1975) involved an arrangement whereby six American automobile workers, with the assistance of the Ford Foundation, were taken to Sweden to work in, and comment on, the redesigned jobs in the Saab-Scandia plant. During their one-month stay, they worked in engine preassembly and in final assembly of the engines. In the preassembly task, "the traditional assembly line method was used [but] job tasks [were] rotated on a weekly basis." For engine assembly, the line had been abandoned in favor of the autonomous three-member teams.

The six Americans liked the leisurely pace of the preassembly line and the idea of job rotation. At the same time, however, they did not see how the company "could function economically at this slow pace, particularly when coupled with what seemed to be frequent production breakdowns. They felt that this frequency of work stoppages would not be tolerated in Detroit."

As for the team assembly of engines, the American reactions were negative. Most felt that "the rapid pace and complexity of the work task . . . imposed psychological pressures which outweighed [the] benefits of variety in work tasks. Only one worker felt that the Saab approach was superior to Detroit." Two reported mixed reactions, liking the complex work task but having doubts as to whether that interest would persist in the long run. They also felt that "the assembly line method allowed more freedom of thought and action, in that it required less concentration."

The Americans, moreover, were reported to be "indifferent or negative to the worker participation schemes." The work council meetings seemed a mixture of a shareholders and general sales meeting. They also observed that the members of the council "did not seem to be a representative sample of workers. . . . " One final observation is deserving of some note. "There have been no attitudinal studies at Saab-Scandia to determine if the group assembly approach is more satisfactory than an assembly line method" (all quotations are from Weinberg, 1975; see also Schrank, 1978, pp. 214–218).

One of the earlier articles on job enlargement is also of some interest in this connection. It is by Robert H. Guest (1957). His account reviews some early moves in the job-enrichment direction by IBM, Sears, Roebuck, Detroit Edison, and the Colonial Insurance Company (East Orange, New Jersey), as well as several unnamed ventures. It is curious that none of these cases is among the talked about experience of the 1970's. If the efforts were so eminently successful, one wonders why they did not take off and dominate discussions in the 1960's and 1970's. There is a suggestion here that the case for job enrichment is being made by selection, through a neglect of the failures (or the indecisive cases) and an emphasis on the new successes. The work of Hackman (1974) is of some interest in this connection.

One notable failure has been studied by Champagne and Tausky (1978). This particular job enrichment program was generally a disaster for reasons described in some detail in the article, "When Job Enrichment Doesn't Pay." Because job enrichment "had been based on Herzberg's somewhat utopian theory of the motivating power of intrinsic rewards . . . management apparently hoped that somehow it would fix everything by itself and at once" (Champagne and Tausky, p. 39). Shortly after the program was terminated, an employee survey was conducted.

"Eighty-two percent of those interviewed indicated that they believed the enriched tasks had been more interesting, but a large majority (79%) also said they believed that participants should have been paid more" (p. 37). One participant is quoted as follows, "It's more mental work for less money." In this job enrichment program, in short, "enrichment" consisted of giving workers more tasks to do but no commensurate increase in pay. Champagne and Tausky comment at the end of the article, "Perhaps a more realistic approach could have been found in reinforcement theory, which recommends the use of extrinsic rewards" (p. 39).

A major difficulty with the work enrichment literature is the assumption of a uniform human psychology, the underlying assumption being that all people, at heart, are self-actualizers. But a counter-literature has developed which, at minimum, would require a recognition of relatively fixed frequency distributions, many people falling well short of that high psychic state. A 1976 study of British workers by Taveggia and Hedley found that "perceived job performance discretion is only marginally related to work satisfaction. Consonant with the growing literature which suggests that factors other than job discretion may contribute more substantially to work satisfaction . . . our data indicate that . . . discretion with regard to where one works and at what kind of job, is a stronger explanatory factor of satisfaction than whether or not one perceives discretion in the actual performance of his job" (Taveggia and Hedley, p. 364). An important review of the literature on job enrichment has led to the conclusion that, "The case of job enlargement has been drastically over-stated and overgeneralized. . . . These studies do not support the hypothesis that job size or job level is positively correlated in general with job satisfaction. Such hypotheses must be modified to take into account the location of the plant and the cultural backgrounds of the workers" (Hulin and Blood, 1968, pp. 50, 53). See also Hulin, 1971.

Some readers, no doubt, will have recognized a problem here. Why has the job enrichment movement been given so much attention? Why has it been given such credence when the evidential base was so limited? Part of the answer has to do with a "balkanized" literature. The criticisms we have been quoting appear in out-of-the-way places; we have cited from an article in Assembly Engineering, from a rather specialized handbook, and then, among others, from the Sloan Management Review, Monthly Labor Review, Pacific Sociological Review, and Psychological Bulletin. The claims of the job enrichment movement also appear in the specialized journals, but it will be remembered, they appeared in Fortune magazine as well, in the third of Judson Gooding's blue-collar blues articles. In the heyday of workplace criticism, one found a chapter of the Sheppard and Herrick book given to an exposition of the new arrangement's merits. And then the HEW Task Force report, Work in America, devoted an entire chapter (of seven) to "The Redesign of Jobs." These solutions were also given much attention, for a time at least, in the pages of some national news magazines, Newsweek leading the way. The basic problem has been summed up by George Strauss (1976, p. 46): " . . . most of the writing in this field has been devoted to describing and often extolling individual experiments rather than carefully evaluating their results. Successes are more widely publicized than failures, and, frequently, reports are written by the very consultants who introduced job restructuring—hardly unbiased observers."

The specialized literature on work is generated by university-based researchers, by researchers employed in industry, and, last but not least, by researcher-practitioners in management consulting firms. That literature contains a diversity of recommended solutions for the problem of unsatisfactory work. One consultant argues, with evidence, that pay, after all, is the problem (Weintraub, 1973). Another, the previously cited Imberman, argues, also with evidence, that communication is the problem; it is a failure to listen to worker complaints and suggestions. What has happened in this instance is that various academics and an assortment of journalists have fastened onto one of several approaches and, ignoring its demonstrated limitations, have announced it to the world as the solution to the problems of the postindustrial age.

One might wonder about liberal intellectuals and equally liberal journalists borrowing so uncritically from management consultants. One possible explanation is that the intellectuals and journalists were simply taken in by the claims of the advocates. (Among the major works of advocacy are Foulkes, 1969; Ford, 1969; Maher, 1971; Dickson, 1975; Walton, 1974). A second possibility is a bias, a predisposition toward this solution. The approach, after all, accords with the basic value commitments of good liberals everywhere. This solution provides for participation, involvement, autonomy, and humanization of the workplace. It would construct the world in a way that they, the liberal intelligentsia, would prefer to see it. Assuming that everyone else in the world possesses a close replica of their own psychologies, it would be easy for them to conclude that this was the right and proper solution. The possibility that they were merchandising someone's wares does not seem to have occurred to them.

Closely linked to the job enrichment focus is the concern with worker participation. Most accounts of such arrangements are (a) glowing and enthusiastic and (b) without any serious supporting evidence. Many of these accounts pay special attention to the developments in Yugoslavia, where worker participation has had long-standing government support, being both the law of the land and having informal backing from the regime and leading intellectuals. The one instance in which serious supporting evidence is available is in the researches of Josip Obradovic who studied developments in twenty Yugoslav factories. In 1970, he reported that:

> My findings fit no fixed pattern. Perhaps the most important finding is that participation in self-management should not be overemphasized as a source of satisfaction. Even participants ranked participation no higher than fifth in their list of desired job characteristics, and participants felt more alienated than

nonparticipants. . . . This failure of participation to generate satisfaction may be due to a variety of reasons: Dubin's thesis that work is not a central life interest, the frustrations and headaches that come from trying to administer an industrial bureaucracy, the present situation in workers' councils, factors inherent in the Yugoslav culture, etc." (Obradovic, p. 169).

Some of these findings were elaborated and reinforced in a later publication. Managers, it should be noted, may not be members of the workers' councils, although they may attend meetings and speak. Obradovic reports that:

. . . deliberations in these councils are largely dominated by high-level managers and technical experts, most of whom are members of the League of Communists and have better than average educations—with the result that the rank and file members participate less actively than theory might suggest. . . . *Rank and file workers who become council members are more alienated from their work than those who merely view its operations from afar;* those who are actually present at the proceedings recognize how limited their real power is (the emphasis has been added in both quotations—1975, p. 32).

To this point in the chapter our presentation has been based on survey evidence drawn from face-to-face interviews. Many of the workplace critics, as noted, reject these attitude studies and instead base their case on indicators of *behavior*. As one of them, James Rinehart, has put it, "We believe that behavioural responses to work are more valid indicators of subjective alienation than verbal statements" (1975, p. 18). It is necessary, therefore, that we also consider evidence of this kind.

In Chapter 1, we reviewed the writings of the workplace critics, writings that claimed and predicted a wide range of pathologies on the work front. Judson Gooding's original article, it will be remembered, stated that blue-collar workers "vent their feelings through absenteeism, high turnover, shoddy work, and even sabotage." That list, it will be noted, makes no mention of the most obvious possibility for the expression of protest; namely, strike activity. It is in another context, and there only as a strong likelihood, that he takes up this theme: "The younger workers, in their present temper, would probably like nothing better than to down tools for a rousing great strike."

Even in the later, more comprehensive HEW report, *Work in America*, unexpectedly few references to strikes appear. Among the "malignant signs" noted by the Task Force authors was "the doubling of man-days per year lost from work through strikes," a statement that avoids reference to the time span involved. They also add, "In some industries there apparently is a rise in absenteeism, sabotage, and turnover rates" (O'Toole *et al.*, p. 11). That sentence, with its qualifications—in *some* industries and *apparently*—does not suggest a compelling case. Another passing reference is made to the behavioral indicators of dissatisfaction, to the increasing "costs of absenteeism, wildcat strikes, turnover, and industrial sabotage . . . " (p. 19). The only other reference to strikes indicated in the volume's index is to still another one-liner, that "increased industrial sabotage and sudden wildcat strikes, like the one at Lordstown, portend something more fundamental than the desire for more money" (p. 38).[24]

There was, obviously, an unexpected avoidance of strike activity as an indicator of worker discontent. The reason, very simply, is that the evidence on strike activity did not provide clear and unambiguous support for the critics' claims. When one examines the United States Department of Labor figures showing "Work Stoppages, 1947 to date," one can find evidence of a "doubling of man-days per year lost" through strikes. Indeed, if one compares 1961 and 1970, it is much more than that, the number quadrupling, from 16,300,000 to 66,414,000. But if one were to take 1959 as the starting point, a slight decline is indicated, from a high of 69,000,000. What this means, in short, is that the number of days lost fluctuates considerably, and one can prove anything by selection of appropriate beginning and end points. A more appropriate strategy, of course, would be to review all years summarizing the lessons for the entire period. One does find a fairly steady increase in strike activity from 1960, reaching a peak in 1970. But then a substantial falloff occurred in 1971 (to 47,589,000), and another drop occurred in 1972 (to 27,066,000). In 1973, the year the HEW report was published, the figure was still relatively low, 27,948,000.

The latter figure does, to be sure, indicate a vast loss of person-days. But, at the same time, seen as a portion of total estimated working time, it is trivial, 28 million person-days in 1973 amounting to about .1% of the total. It should also be noted that that minuscule amount includes losses through strikes and lockouts. If one were to sort out just the wildcat strikes, spontaneous walkouts over work conditions, the percentage would amount to a microscopic, hence unimpressive, indication of work dissatisfactions.[25]

---

[24]Only the first passages, those from p. 11, are accompanied by a reference, this being to a Task Force paper written by Richard Walton entitled, "Workplace Alienation and the Need for Major Innovation." In the later collection of Task Force papers (O'Toole, 1974), there is a Walton paper (pp. 227-245) entitled, "Alienation and Innovation in the Workplace" (it first appeared, incidentally, in the *Harvard Business Review*, November-December 1972, as "How to Counter Alienation in the Plant"). The paper in the O'Toole collection provides no supporting evidence for the claims of the *Work in America* volume. There is merely one of many reiterations of the established verities (p. 228). Reference is made to absenteeism, sabotage, and turnover rates. Interestingly enough, Walton does not mention strikes, let alone a doubling of rates.

[25]The evidence from subsequent years also does not support the rising dissatisfaction claims. Days lost rose to 47,991,000 in 1974, but fell of again to the thirty millions in 1975, 1976, 1977, and 1978.

The low level of strike activity in the early 1970's could, perhaps, have been a result of the Nixon wage-and-price freeze. The freeze, which had four phases, some mandatory, some voluntary, lasted from August 15, 1971 to April 30, 1974. The level of strike activity in the postfreeze years, as just noted, was not sharply differentiated from the level of 1972 to 1974. To the best of our knowledge, the wage freeze was never mentioned by any workplace critic as something that would restrain, dampen,

The comprehensive review of the "rising job discontent" question undertaken by Harold Wool (1973, p. 41) summarizes the matter as follows:

> A sharp increase in the level of strike activity was recorded in the second half of
> the 1960s and in the early 1970s. Man-days of idleness due to strikes rose from
> 0.13 percent of estimated working time in 1961–65 to 0.26 percent in 1966–71.
> However, the incidence of strikes normally tends to increase during inflationary
> periods. Strike idleness, as a percentage of working time, was actually consid-
> erably higher during the years immediately following the end of World War II
> (1946–50) and following the outbreak of the Korean War (1952–53) than during
> the more recent period of rapid price increases.

Addressing the more specific question, that of a changed focus or a changed
character of strike activity, Wool reports that:

> . . . "bread and butter" issues, such as pay, benefits, job security, and union
> organization or security issues, have continued to account for all but a modest
> percentage of all strikes. In 1971, only 5.5 percent of strike idleness was
> attributed to plant administration or other working condition issues.[26]

Absenteeism is a second behavioral indicator that might attest to the
decline in work motivation. More and more workers, it is said, are just taking
off. Managers, accordingly, are reported to alternate between desperation
and despair as they struggle to make production quotas in the face of
enormous numbers of absent workers. Because of the new orientations,
particularly among the young, the managers are helpless, completely unable
to enforce traditional labor discipline.

---

or otherwise depress the seething anger present, particularly in the blue-collar ranks.
That possibility, in any case, focuses on the pay question, and the critics regularly
asserted that pay was not the heart of the matter.

The focus on the absolute numbers of days lost, incidentally, is doubly misleading.
It provides a large absolute number (while hiding a very modest rate); it also fails,
unlike the rate, to take into account the growth of the labor force. The roughly
equivalent absolute numbers for 1959 and 1970, those cited at the beginning of this
discussion, yield rather different percentages: 0.50 and 0.37%, respectively.

Data on strike activity are taken from the Monthly Labor Review, October 1979,
pp. 119, and February 1981, p. 123.

[26]Two other comprehensive reviews came to the same conclusions; see Flanagan,
Strauss, and Ulman, 1974, pp. 109–112; and Henle, 1974, pp. 133–135. Flanagan
et al. (p. 110) note that " . . . if large-scale, impersonal, assembly-line production
breeds discontent and strikes, then we would expect . . . strike increases to be
greatest in the industries characterized by these conditions. In fact, the reverse
occurs: in the private sector, residual strike increases were found to be largest in
construction, an industry with relatively small firms and substantial individual control
over work, while residual increases were generally small among durable goods
manufacturing industries."

Both these sources also review Federal Mediation and Conciliation Service figures
on contract rejections, another possible indicator of worker dissatisfaction. Here, too,
they find no evidence of increasing discontent (see Flanagan, Strauss, and Ulman, p.
112, and Henle, pp. 135–137).

Given all the confident claims made about increasing absenteeism, it comes as something of a surprise that Wool should begin his discussion with the statement: "In the absence of *any* direct program for statistical reporting of absenteeism trends, the Bureau of Labor Statistics has analyzed data from the Current Population Survey . . . " (Wool, p. 41, emphasis added). That observation, it will be noted, means that all of the previous assertions must have had, at best, a rather flimsy basis in fact.

The study referred to was published later in that year (Hedges, 1973), and it provided some elaboration on this basic point. The Current Population Survey, it noted, "is the *only* source of systematic national data on job absences . . . " (emphasis again added). This was the first study making use of CPS data for this purpose, and much space in the article was given to discussion of the limitations of even that data. Another point of some interest in this connection is a passing reference to an earlier feasibility study undertaken by the BLS in 1971. This involved some 500 firms, the aim being to obtain a more direct and precise measurement of absenteeism trends. They discovered that "fewer than two-fifths of all the employed worked in firms keeping records on absences." If the critics had sampled that experience at all, little or no assurance could be given that their findings were representative. If absenteeism is such a serious problem in American industry, one wonders why only a minority of firms keep records on the subject.

In this case, after the fact, there does seem to be at least some initial support for the critics' assertions. Taking full-time and part-time workers combined, there was an increase in "part of the week" absences between 1967 and 1972, the rate going from 3.9 to 4.3%. While that increase, it will be noted, may seem small, it is an increase of 10% over the 1967 figure. A second series gives the rates for entire week absences, these increasing from 2.1% in 1967 to 2.5% in 1970, and then falling slightly in 1971 and 1972 (to 2.3%).[27] A majority of the unscheduled personal absences in both series were said to be due to illness, the rest falling into a miscellaneous category. The medical reasons could, of course, hide a protest against alienating work, but might reflect nothing more than illness. The statements, some of them at least, should be taken at face value.

[27]A second publication by Hedges extends the series to 1974. The part-week rate continued to increase in 1973 to 4.4%, the peak figure, then fell to 4.2% in 1974. Minor fluctuations were indicated in the full-week rate. The best overall judgment for the period 1967–1974 would indicate a slight increase to 1970, followed by a modest decline and then stability. See Hedges, 1975.

Many commentators assume an obvious relationship between work dissatisfaction and absenteeism. One early study found the relationship among blue-collar men and white-collar men in low-skilled jobs. But they found no relationship for white-collar women or white-collar men at the higher skill levels. Specifically, the authors report that "there is no relationship between absences and attitudes toward *any* aspect of the work situation for white collar women . . . " (Metzner and Mann, 1953, p. 483, emphasis in original).

A number of more detailed findings in this study deserve some comment. The two kinds of absence (part-week and full-week) have very different constituencies. Most commentators have argued that young people were demonstrating the greatest disaffection from work. Part-week absences are, by far, most frequent among the young, the rate for 16-to-19-year-olds being 7.9% in 1972, compared with a mere 3.3% for those age 55 to 64. It is also the young who, disproportionately, give miscellaneous reasons for the absence (that is, reasons other than illness). Among the young men, a majority of those reporting part-week absences gave some miscellaneous reason; this was the only segment showing that pattern. Full-week absences, in contrast, have a diametrically opposite pattern, the rate being lowest among the young and highest among those 55 to 64. Illness seems an obvious likelihood in this case.

Most discussions of the rebellion in the workplace have, rather inexplicably, focused on male workers. But Hedge's data show that the part-week absence rates are considerably higher among the women workers, the respective figures for male and females in 1972 being 3.3 and 6.3%. In addition, some complex linkages appear with regard to marital status. Married men had a relatively low rate of 3.1% (second only to the divorced men at 2.5%). Among the males, singles had the highest part-week rate (4.6%). Married women, in contrast, had a fairly high overall rate (6.8%), Hedges indicating that frequent absence was especially pronounced among those with children under 18. Married women separated from their husbands had the highest rates of all (8.6%). They were followed by the married women (spouse present), and then by the widowed (5.8%) and divorced women (5.4%). The latter figures differ considerably from those for widowed and divorced men, 3.7 and 2.5%, respectively.

The period covered in this study was one in which the numbers of young persons and the numbers of women entering the labor force were increasing rapidly. The age and sex linkages with the part-time absence rates alone could have caused much of that 10% increase registered from 1967 to 1971.[28]

The workplace critics have also placed considerable emphasis on the automobile industry, it providing the a fortiori case of punishing work conditions. In 1967, that industry led the list of twenty manufacturing industries in full-week unscheduled absences. Despite claims of rising dissatisfaction, Hedges notes that in 1972, the "unscheduled absences by automobile workers of a week or more were not significantly higher than in

---

[28]Above-average absenteeism rates are associated with the least attractive jobs, operators and laborers leading the list in both 1967 and 1972 in part-week absences. They are followed by the service workers, with clerical employees next. Hedges notes that women are "more likely to be new hires, and more likely to be employed in the lower skilled, lower paid occupations . . . " (p. 28). Data for part-week absences were not available in the 1967 study, Hedges reports; hence, the appropriate test was not possible.

1967 and the industry dropped to second place," having been overtaken by those in rubber manufacturing.[29]

In the same period, while the automobile industry showed virtually no change, the paper industry jumped from one of the lowest rates, 2.0%, to an above-average 3.0%. The article, unfortunately, does not give the same detail for part-week absences. There is nothing in Hedges' account to indicate an alarming growth in the rates. What little growth was registered seems to have a nonalarming explanation—increasing numbers of young persons and women in the labor force, both groups, in the normal state of things, having above-average rates.

Another misplaced emphasis appears in connection with the part-week absences. Although most of the focus has been in manufacturing industries, absenteeism has been very high in the field of public administration. The rates there, in both 1967 and 1972, exceeded the overall figures for manufacturing. Hedges notes that workers in public administration "ranked among the top three industry divisions both in the incidence of full-week absence caused by illness and in the proportion who were paid, giving support to the thesis of a positive relationship between the two" (Hedges, 1973, p. 27). The biggest changes in the period, moreover, were not in manufacturing, but in trade, in finance, and in services, the percentage point increases in those fields being double those occurring in manufacturing. The education industry in particular stands out, the rate going from a below-average 3.8% in 1967 to an above-average 4.4% in 1972. All that increase, it should be noted, was reported as due to illness.

These findings indicate that the absenteeism problem is also much more complex than the critics would have one believe. Their targets are frequently misplaced (as with the emphasis on men as opposed to women, their focus on automobile manufacture as opposed to public administration and education, and in their failure to distinguish the diverse age relationships). Hedges, moreover, notes that the figures measure absence per se. Unlike the critics, who make an easy imputation of motive and significance, Hedges ends this preliminary account on a note of caution: " . . . the data are not sufficient to determine the causes of high or increasing rates of absence or, conversely, of relatively low or stable rates. Nor do they permit a measurement of

---

[29]Henle (p. 124) also reports this absence of change in the automobile industry. The president of General Motors, he says, "observed that the absenteeism rate for his firm recently dropped after more than doubling over a ten-year period." A U.S. News and World Report account ("Absent Workers—A Spreading Worry," November 27, 1972, p. 48) declares that "absenteeism among the largest firms—General Motors, Ford Motor Company and Chrysler Corporation—has doubled in the past seven years: It was 2 to 3 per cent in 1965, is 5 to 6 per cent now." Henle, in contrast, cites the Bureau of Labor Statistics (Hedges), which showed absenteeism in the automobile industry at 3.7% in 1967 and at 2.8% in 1972. Those figures probably hide an actual change; there was a rise in absenteeism in the 1960's, peaking late in the decade, and a falloff in the early 1970's (see also, p. 280 on this point).

'absenteeism' as distinguished from unavoidable absence" (Hedges, 1973, p. 29).[30]

A third behavioral indicator of work dissatisfaction involves labor turn-over or quit rates. On this question we can again cite Wool (p. 41), who reports that:

> A detailed multivariate analysis of quit rates of manufacturing workers recently completed by the Bureau of Labor Statistics indicates that year-to-year fluctua-tions in these rates over a 20-year period are largely explained by cyclical variations in job opportunities, as measured by the rate of new hires, and that there has been *no* discernible trend in the quit rate over this period.

Should there be any uncertainty about the last point, it means that *apart from* the cyclical variations, no new or added factor, one that would suggest a basic change in motivations, had been discovered.

The study referred to (Armknecht and Early, 1972) contains a chart showing the seasonally adjusted manufacturing quit rate from 1947 to 1971. It shows the very high rate in 1947 plummeting through to late 1949 and early 1950, which was a period of economic recession. The rate rose considerably in mid-1950 and remained high throughout the Korean War, plummeting again in late 1953 and in 1954. There was some recovery in the mid-1950's, and a fall again in 1957, another year of recession. A slight rise occurred in the late 1950's followed by a slight fall in 1960. The overall trend in the quit rate from 1947 to 1960 was downward, the tendency being so

---

[30]See also the later update (Hedges, 1977): "The proportion of scheduled hours lost through absence in May 1976 was the same as 3 years earlier, when such data were first collected" (p. 16). Flanagan, Strauss, and Ulman find the average work week within an industry to be a determinant of absenteeism—"an industry with an hours schedule which is 9 per cent higher than the average for manufacturing would have an absence rate which was one percentage point higher than the manufacturing average, other things equal" (p. 120). Their summary conclusion reads: " . . . the cross-sectional evidence increases our skepticism that the data on unscheduled absences indicate changes in job dissatisfaction. Not only is the overall increase in absence rates slight, but the increases which do occur are relatively large in sectors which are not characterized by monotonous, assembly-line production conditions, and the small increase that is observed appears attributable to changes in the demographic composition of the work force—particularly the increasing proportion of women" (p. 121).

A report in a West German newspaper provides data on absenteeism losses for 1979 in seven advanced industrial nations. These losses were given as a portion of the normal or contractual work year (that is, excluding vacation, holidays, overtime, or short weeks). Japan had the lowest losses, 1.9% of the total (that work year, incidentally, was also the largest of the seven, 2056 hours, some 9% greater than the next contender, the United States, with 1888 hours). The United Sates also had relatively low losses through absenteeism, 3.5% of the total. The Federal Republic of Germany and France both had losses of 8.4%. The highest figures were 12.0% for the Netherlands and 13.8% for Sweden (from the *Frankfurter Allgemeine Zeitung*, January 16, 1981).

pronounced that some commentators spoke of a developing "industrial feudalism," the nontransferability of pensions and some other fringe benefits in effect binding workers to their employers (Ross, 1958).

But the pattern of the 1960's showed an opposite tendency, the rate, for most of the decade, showing a steady increase. This was an obvious parallel to the improvement of business conditions accompanying the early years of the Vietnam war. This 1960's trend peaked in 1969 at 2.7%, a figure that, while relatively high, was still below those reported for the early 1950's, or in 1947 and 1948, or during World War II. The development in the years following 1969, of course, is crucial for the argument of the critics. But contrary to their assertions, the Bureau of Labor Statistics figures show that the quit rate fell precipitously in 1970 (to 2.1%) and again (to 1.8%) in 1972. At a time when the workplace critics were declaring an increase in labor turnover, the actual tendency was one of *decrease*. The rate climbed once again to 2.7% in 1973 (reflecting the decline in the rate of layoffs), but then, still closely reflecting general business conditions, it fell to 1.4% in 1975 (United States Department of Labor, 1968b: p. 87; and 1977; p. 100).

A methodological observation is in order. Those commentators who in 1971 and 1972 were claiming an increase in the quit rate had not taken the time and trouble to examine the most appropriate evidence on the subject. Their failure to examine that evidence means they were ignorant of the rather obvious link to recessionary cycles that is immediately evident in the figures provided by the Department of Labor.

One other point should be noted. The critics take a "blind" indicator and assign a meaning to it, i.e., work dissatisfaction (or hatred). The month-by-month figures, however, show a peak each year in August and September. The possibility of students quitting to return to school seems a strong likelihood. And, one might note, in a period when more and more people were attending universities, the impact of such quits would be ever larger.

More detail on the quit rate question is provided in Flanagan, Strauss, and Ulman (1974). For the period 1958–1972, during which there was a general increase in the rate, they found a significant variation by industry. Three industries—nonelectrical machinery, electrical equipment, and transportation equipment—showed no significant trend. These are industries which "encompass many of the large-scale assembly line operations which are alleged to be most dissatisfying" (Flanagan, Strauss, and Ulman, p. 113). Rather than simply assigning the change in the other industries to an unmeasured job dissatisfaction factor, they explored a range of other alternatives (relative average hourly earnings, hours of work, length of service, and the changed demographic composition of the work force—specifically, the increases in women, nonwhite, and younger workers). With these factors controlled, they found that the quit rate *declined* in this period. Put differently, this means "the positive trend in quits [was] an artifact of movement in the other variables" (p. 116). Those factors, moreover, explained "over 92 per cent of the variance in the quit rate [in that period], leaving relatively little scope for factors such as explicit measures of job content and job dissatisfaction . . . " (p. 118).[31]

Some other possible indicators of job satisfaction and dissatisfaction are reviewed in Henle (1974). These include the presumed impacts of alcohol and drug use, productivity, contract rejections, grievances and arbitration, changes in union leadership, and decertification elections. Three principal conclusions follow from his review: (1) In each of those areas, the measures leave much to be desired; they are weak, oblique, or confounded by other factors. (2) The situation in each of these areas is more complex and differentiated than the workplace critics would have us believe. (3) No serious (that is, clear and unambiguous) support for the critics' claims is found in any of these areas.

The blue-collar blues business began, as noted earlier, with the Gooding article of July 1970. Absenteeism, he declared, had risen sharply. "It has doubled over the past ten years at General Motors and at Ford, with the sharpest climb in the past year." A Ford Motor Company source says the doubling in the 1960's is accurate, but that the peak came in 1968, the year of the sharpest climb. Gooding also declared that "tardiness has increased. . . . " The Ford source says, "Company trend data were not collected or recorded to any extent for the 1960's, and we have no basis for confirming or disproving that tardiness increased during those years."

Gooding gives the 1969 quit rate at Ford as 25.2%. He does not give figures for any other year. The Ford source says that Gooding's figure is accurate and adds the following: "By comparison, the annual quit rate was around 20% for 1967 and 1968, just under 17% for 1970, and about 11% for 1971. Over the longer term, the 1969 experience was comparable to that of the early 1950's, but relatively high for most of the 1960's and more recent years."[32]

One final indication of young workers' outlooks, the famous Lordstown strike, requires consideration. The General Motors' Vega assembly plant

[31]For still further discussion of the determinants of quit rates, see Parsons, 1973, and Miner, Mary, 1977. Miner points up some interesting linkages between quit rates and absence rates. While the workplace critics write of the two as if they were both immediate and direct responses to job dissatisfaction, Miner points to their differing characteristics. Job absence in 1976, for example, peaked in January and February; job turnover was highest in the summer months. Absence rates were highest in the northeastern states; turnover was lowest in that region. Absence rates increased with the size of firm; turnover decreased with size.

A large firm, it should be noted, is likely to be well-paying, to have a wide range of fringe benefits, to be unionized, to provide considerable job security, and to provide more opportunities for promotion than a small one. If one is dissatisfied with a given job in a large firm, greater opportunities exist there for transfer than in a small one. The responses to a bad job will differ accordingly. In a small firm one would quit; in a large firm one would stay on, but might take a couple of days off.

[32]We thank Bryce W. Russell, Ford's manager for educational affairs, for his assistance (letter of 6 May 1981).

near Warren, Ohio, became the focus of much attention in the spring of 1972, with scores of journalists and social commentators descending on the area to study the "new" phenomenon. This plant, it will be remembered, had been located there, in the American heartland, to obtain a fresh start, to find young workers who had not been touched by the tempestuous history of labor-management relations characteristic of the industry. For many commentators, both radical and not-so-radical, the strike was seen as definitive proof of the blue-collar blues case. Here were young workers reacting to alienating work conditions; this was the new generation, those not willing to take it.

While many commentators were writing of the event as the first episode in a new historical epoch, as the first battle fought by this new rebellious generation, a few explained the strike in traditional terms. One author put it as follows: "Reduced to its simplest terms the struggle was over an old issue—speedup" (Salpukas, 1974, p. 106). A reorganization of General Motors activities was in process at this time, one extending across the company; automobile assembly plants were being taken away from the divisions (Chevrolet, Oldsmobile, Pontiac, Buick, and so on) and were being assigned to a new and tougher management group, the General Motors Assembly Division (GMAD). This change had come to Lordstown shortly before the strike occurred, and these efforts at speedup had precipitated the strike. Although most critics have mentioned the GMAD role, they have failed to report the wider impact of that division's efforts. The Wall Street Journal reviewed the matter, and in their conclusion stressed the role of the efficiency moves that triggered off a "wave of strikes that . . . disrupted 13 GM plants" (quoted in Sirota, 1973, p. 42, emphasis added). Another commentator mentions one of those other strikes, fought over similar issues, occurring in Norwood, Ohio. This, he reports, "received zero attention because it did not fit into the new conventional wisdom. The Norwood workers, you see, are older" (Brooks, 1972, p. 4). The Norwood strike was bitterly fought and lasted much longer than the three-week strike at Lordstown. It was one of the longest in General Motors history.[33]

The United Automobile Workers also circulated material to counter the Lordstown reading. One such statement reads, in part: "In the General Motors plants we have had over eighty strikes since 1956 over the issue of 'speed-up' so the problem is not new. . . . In the eye of the media Norwood lacked glamour and as a consequence received very little coverage from the typewriter brigade who were telling the world about their discovery of the assembly line. Norwood is an old plant dating back to the thirties and was involved in the regional sit-down strikes of 1936 and 1937. . . . While there were a great number of older workers on the day shift at the time of the strike in Norwood, the second shift was populated with younger workers. The

[33]For a useful insider's account, see Wright, J. Patrick, 1979. This is a report by former General Motors executive, John Z. DeLorean.

majority were from the hill country of Kentucky and Tennessee. . . . The strike at Lordstown ran for *21* days while the Norwood strike lasted 172 *days*. . . . Basically the reasons for each strike were almost identical. The Lordstown strike was 'adopted' by the media instant experts who gushed and drooled over 'the rebellion of young assembly line workers' while generally ignoring the much longer struggle at Norwood."[34]

Some additional "gushing and drooling" on the same theme occurred in June 1981, at a conference in West Germany on "Political Culture in the United States in the Seventies: Continuity and Change," organized by the University of Frankfurt's Center for the Study of North America (Christadler, 1981). Two panelists discussed the question of American workers and their attitudes. The first presentation, by Marianne Debouzy of the Universitè de Paris-Vincennes, treated the work problem as one that raged throughout the 1970's. Her presentation drew heavily on left or critical sources to make her points and completely omitted *any* reference to the contrary research and literature. None of the works cited above in our Note 34, Chapt. 1, or any of the disconfirming works cited in the present chapter, was mentioned. The Lordstown experience was cited as if it were still a meaningful reality. The specific sources cited in the presentation were Garson, Rothschild, Aronowitz, and Terkel, plus a scattering of articles from various left or critical journals. None of the contrary sources or literature on Lordstown was mentioned. Although the Lordstown strike was discussed at length, no mention was made of the Norwood strike. There was, moreover, a lack of precision with regard to the date of the Lordstown strike, it being dated, on two occasions, as occurring in 1971–1972. Only in the next to last sentence of this 25-page analysis was there any recognition that the presumed insurgency may have been defeated. There was no explanation and no further discussion of this otherwise rather enigmatic possibility.

Some words of comment on Debouzy's paper by Karl Heinz Pütz gave the largely German audience no suggestion that she had misrepresented the American reality or that there had been serious omissions in her review of the relevant literature.

The second contribution at the conference on the work theme was presented by Stanley Aronowitz, then affiliated with Columbia University. Most of his contribution, surprisingly, was devoted to explaining the sources of conservative tendencies among American workers. In his text, there is no indication that he was the author of sharply opposed predictions less than a decade earlier. His predictions of the early 1970's appearing in his much-lauded *False Promises* appear nowhere in his twenty pages of text. Some of his earlier themes, however, were picked up later in his essay, the suggestion being that wildcat strikes and refusals to work were just as significant in 1981

---

[34]The UAW comments were made available by Jerry Dale, of the UAW's Public Relations Department (letter of September 28, 1981). We very much appreciate his assistance.

as they had been earlier. But no evidence was presented on this point. No references at all were provided in this contribution.[34]

Lordstown was clearly a media event. The image and understanding of that event were created by some persons in the mass media, whose efforts might best be described as involving what has been called "groupthink," the situation wherein like-thinking individuals develop a reading of events and, through their interactions and mutually reinforcing efforts, convince each other that their reading is real (Janis, 1972). In this case, it involves little more than a *post hoc propter hoc* error. The commentators assigned a favored prior event as *the* cause of the strike. Consideration of the wider range of events, of the more extended impact of GMAD's activities, would have led the critics to another conclusion.

Groupthink was clearly operating on a wider basis throughout the entire period of the antiwork "hype." This is not to say that everyone was taken in by it. Opposite views have been cited above, and both GM and UAW spokesmen provided contrary readings, but these gained little attention in comparison to the dominant tendency in the media. That reading of events, it will be noted, was developed with a sweeping indifference to, or even in opposition to, the most relevant available systematic evidence on the subject.

We can round out our analysis of the satisfactions and discontents of work by considering two final questions: first, how work stacks up in direct comparison with the satisfactions derived from other areas of life, and second, the relative importance of satisfying work in creating a satisfying life.

A question sequence from the 1978 Quality of American Life survey is especially useful for the first purpose. Late in the interview, respondents were asked to make some final ratings of the different aspects of their lives and experiences. For this purpose, a 0-to-100-point scale was used, allowing for much differentiation. Interviewers instructed respondents thus: "Note that on this scale, 100 would mean that the situation is perfect—as good as you can imagine it being; and zero would mean it is terrible, as bad as you can imagine it being." Respondents then rated seventeen aspects of their lives on this scale.

Results are shown in Table 6.7, which shows the mean scores given each aspect of life by a representative sample of the American adult population. For convenience, the various aspects are grouped into three categories:

---

[34]In contrast, one might note the responses given with regard to two very prominent social science prediction errors, the poll predictions in the 1948 United States Presidential election and in the British general election of 1970. In both cases, leading practitioners conducted postmortem investigations to discover the sources of the error and, presumably, to learn from the experience. (See Abrams, Mark, 1970, for details on the British case.) As we discuss in our final chapter, this sort of postmortem accounting is almost never undertaken for the speculative products of critical intellectuals, least of all by themselves.

Table 6.7. Comparative Satisfaction Ratings of 17 Major Areas of Life (SRC Quality of American Life Survey: 1978)

	Average Score[a]	N
Group I		
Your marriage	89.4	2169
Your family life	85.2	3580
Your life as a whole	81.9	3602
Your friendships	81.1	3615
Yourself as a person	81.1	3597
Your health	80.4	3627
Group II		
Being a homemaker	77.0	1909
Your standard of living	76.2	3618
Life in the United States today	76.2	3598
Ways you spend your spare time	75.9	3616
This neighborhood	75.9	3623
Your (house or apartment)	75.9	3627
This community	75.8	3625
Your present job	75.5	2230
Your family's present income	70.6	3596
Group III		
The amount of education you have	66.8	3620
Your savings and investments	54.8	3572

[a]Mean on a 0-to-100 scale; see text for explanation.

those aspects with the highest (80 and up), next highest (70–80), and lowest (69 or less) mean ratings.

Given findings reported earlier in this volume, it will come as no surprise that all ratings are generally high, none averaging below the 50 mark, the midpoint of the scale. All but three of the ratings are in the range of 75 and higher, which means that most people see most aspects of their lives as being much closer to perfect than to terrible. The top finishers, the aspects of life felt to be most satisfying by most of the population, are, in descending order, marriage, family life, life as a whole, one's friendships, oneself as a person, and one's health. Marriage and family life, the top two finishers, are generally felt to be in good shape. There also appears to be little concern about inadequate opportunities to actualize or realize the true self, most people being satisfied with themselves as persons. On the whole, these six top finishers constitute a traditional package of satisfactions, most people judging their own conditions as pretty close to perfect (80 or higher on the scale).

Nine remaining areas receive average rankings in the 70's, still high but somewhat below the scores of the top finishers. Again in descending order, these are: being a homemaker (asked of women only), one's standard of living, life in the United States today, spare time activities, the neighborhood, the house or apartment, the larger community, one's job, and the family's income. Little should be made of the specific rank ordering, since the mean values are very close in all nine areas (varying from a high of 77 to a low of 71). Again, all areas covered are seen as being much closer to perfect than to terrible. It is worth a note that people on the average derive as much satisfaction from their job (mean = 75.5) as they derive from their leisure time activities (mean = 75.9).

The two final areas of life covered in this analysis show mean ratings substantially below all the others: one is the amount of education received (mean = 66.8), the other concerns savings and investments (mean = 54.8). This, it will be noted, is consistent with other data from this survey reviewed in Chapter Three. The number one and number two things people would change in order to improve their overall quality of life, we reported there, were to be better off financially and to have received more education. It will also be noted that both of these items finish well below the job as a source of satisfaction. Family income finished below the job as well, by about five points. From this and many other strands of evidence reviewed elsewhere in this and earlier chapters, one important conclusion follows. It is *not* the job. It *is* the money.

With respect to work specifically, it is apparent from these results that job discontents are not especially pronounced, as compared to most other areas; the degree of satisfaction derived from work is broadly comparable to that derived from most other areas of life.

Most people, we have reported, are generally satisfied with their jobs; some, of course, are not. One of the principal claims of the workplace critics is that the job is somehow the central feature of existence, the point from which all else flows. If this were the case, one would expect a satisfying job to contribute more to one's overall happiness than, for example, a satisfying marriage. An alternative possibility suggested by our findings in earlier chapters on the centrality of marriage as a life goal is that a satisfying marriage would make the stronger overall contribution.

Interestingly, this sort of comparative question is only rarely raised in social science research work, the problem being, as we have noted on several previous occasions, that of "balkanized" interests and research literature. To illustrate, in Chapter 5, we dealt at some length with marital status and the sorrows associated with broken marriages. In this chapter, we focused on the claims of the workplace critics and said nothing at all about marriage and family matters, for the simple reason that the critics themselves place no emphasis on this question. Within the field of sociology itself, one finds a similar segregation of life experiences. Marriage and matters related thereto are treated in marriage and the family courses; workplace conditions are treated in industrial sociology courses. Judging by citations encountered in respective texts, the former specialists seldom look into the pages of journals such as *Industrial Relations*, and the latter seldom look at the *Journal of Marriage and Family*..

Some evidence on the relative contributions of marriage and job to overall life happiness is shown in Table 6.8. These data are based only on

Table 6.8. Happiness by Job and Marital Satisfaction (SRC Quality of American Life Surveys, 1971 and 1978)

	Satisfaction with job and marriage			
	Satisfied with both	Satisfied with marriage only	Satisfied with job only	Satisfied with neither
1971				
Happiness				
Very happy	39%	25%	4%	7%
Pretty happy	59	62	78	66
Not too happy	2	13	18	28
% =	100	100	100	101
N =	652	130	54	29
	(75%)	(15%)	(6%)	(3%)
1978				
Happiness				
Very happy	40%	27%	9%	0%
Pretty happy	59	64	72	64
Not too happy	1	9	19	36
% =	100	100	100	100
N =	1045	195	80	39
	(77%)	(14%)	(6%)	(3%)

persons who are both married and employed (N's = 865 and 1359 in 1971 and 1978, respectively). The sample is then subdivided into four groups, according to the stated satisfaction with marriage and job. For purposes of this table, the satisfied are those responding 1, 2, or 3 on the relevant scale, and the dissatisfied are those responding 4 through 7 (i.e., with neutral or negative assessments). Finally, the table shows the distribution of happiness among each of these four groups.

It is clear, first of all, that the distributions shown are lopsided. Three out of four married and employed people report themselves satisfied with both job and marriage; at the opposite extreme, those neutral or dissatisfied with both, one finds only about 3% of the total. And, not too surprisingly, there are substantial differences in the reported happiness at these extremes.

The two extremes, of course, are not the most interesting cases from the point of view of the present discussion. What of those satisfied with their marriages but dissatisfied with their jobs? And what of the opposite cases, those dissatisfied with their marriages but satisfied with their jobs? The table clearly shows that, in both 1971 and 1978, the satisfaction in the more intimate sphere gives the greater life happiness. Among those satisfied with their marriage but not their job, roughly one in four are very happy and about one in ten are not too happy. Among the opposite group, those satisfied with their jobs but not their marriages, some 4–9% are very happy, and about one in five are not too happy. These results show, once again, an obvious conclusion; namely, that marriage and family matters have greater salience in the average life than does the job.

One finds, especially in the critical literature, a continual stress on the "long arm of the job," as if the job were somehow an all-pervasive fact. As an argument in support of such allegations, one frequently encounters a claim that more waking hours are spent on the job than on anything else, but that too is not the case. If one assumes 40 hours of work out of a total of 112 waking hours per week, there are, clearly, 72 wide-awake nonworking hours per week, and it seems likely that those hours would be dominated by the marital relationship. (It is, moreover, not clear why the nonwaking hours should be excluded in such calculations. Normally, one sleeps alongside one's spouse, that presence providing some intimacy, affection, security, and other positive feelings.) Then, too, it is on the whole much easier to divorce oneself from an unsatisfactory job than from an unsatisfactory marriage; certainly, it is done with much greater frequency. But we need not belabor the obvious point: given the results reported in earlier chapters and those shown in Table 6.8, the insistent focus on the job that one encounters in the critical literature is clearly misplaced[35]

Results similar to those in Table 6.8 have been reported by Glenn and

---

[35]Table 6.8 is potentially misleading in two ways: first, it includes both full-time and part-time workers, and second, it includes both males and females. A reanalysis (of the 1978 survey) focused only on full-time workers (35 hours per week or more) and run separately for men and women, showed generally similar patterns. For both sexes, those with satisfying marriages *and* satisfying jobs were the most numerous and the happiest. Likewise, those with neither happy marriages nor satisfying jobs were least numerous and least happy overall. For men, those with satisfying marriages but unsatisfying jobs were, again, somewhat more likely to report being very happy than those with satisfying jobs but unsatisfying marriages, but the difference was only about 9 percentage points (23% to 14%). Thus, among women, the effect reported in the text was considerably more pronounced. Data were as follows (full-time employed, married only):

	Both	Marriage only	Job only	Neither
Men (N = 727)				
Very happy	36	23	14	0
Pretty happy	63	65	82	78
Not too happy	1	12	4	22
N =	(561)	(115)	(28)	(23)
(%)=	77	16	4	3
Women (N = 375)				
Very happy	43	41	6	0
Pretty happy	55	53	65	40
Not too happy	2	6	29	60
N =	(282)	(49)	(34)	(10)
(%) =	75	13	9	3

Weaver (1981b). This study is based on secondary analysis of the six NORC General Social Surveys conducted between 1973 and 1978 and focuses specifically on the relative contributions of marital satisfaction, job satisfaction, and satisfaction in six other life areas to overall happiness. "Except for black men, the estimated contribution of marital happiness [to global happiness] is far greater than the estimated contribution of any of the [other] kinds of satisfaction, including satisfaction with work" (Glenn and Weaver, 1981b, p. 161). (For black men, job satisfaction slightly, but not significantly, outranked marital satisfaction as a predictor of overall happiness.)

The analyses reported in this chapter may now be summarized. (1) The best available national survey data on job satisfaction provide no credible empirical support for the depiction of rising discontent. (2) The same survey data also provide no credible empirical support for the depiction of falling commitment to the work ethic. (3) The desire to quit working is higher among older workers than among the young. (4) The higher job dissatisfaction of the young is not new, but has been observed for as long as data have been gathered and appears to reflect only the fact that older people have the better jobs. (5) Job satisfaction varies by class level, but not sharply; it also varies by skill level among blue-collar workers, but not sharply. (6) At all class levels and all skill levels within the working class, most workers make some sort of positive assessment of their work. (7) This is true even of the most alienated sector of the American economy, the auto industry. (8) The job enrichment studies have been seriously misrepresented in the literatrure. (9) The generally high levels of satisfaction revealed in overall job satisfaction questions are also found when direct questions are asked about specific aspects of work. (10) Evidence on various behavioral indicators—strikes, absenteeism, and quit rates—also does not support the depiction of rising discontent. (11) Despite all the attention given to work in America, there is no more discontent with work than with most other features of life; compared to a satisfying marriage, a satisfying job contributes relatively little to one's happiness.

There is perhaps a twelfth conclusion that should be added: the work critics offered their conclusions in the face of much readily available evidence bearing on all eleven of the above. This was possible only because they ignored most of that evidence and selectively presented and distorted the rest—all of this with the aid of grants from the Ford Foundation.

7 INCOME: THE INSTRUMENTAL CONCERN

As pointed out in Chapter 3, the most frequently mentioned personal concern of adult Americans is that of household finances, the problem of making ends meet. This was mentioned by some 43% in 1972 and by 53% of the sample in the recession year, 1974. The problem, of course, is an insufficient supply of money. This should not be seen as indicative of some crude materialism or, as St. Paul put it, of a "love of money." Rather, for most people, as far as we can tell, it reflects a simple means-end relationship, money being required for the purchase of necessities and amenities. And many people do not have enough of it.

That many people have more than enough money is a key theme of postmaterialist writers; for all practical purposes, it is the beginning point for their analysis. That many people do not have enough is a key theme of those focusing on the plight of "the little man." Some reconciliation of these two positions is in order.

The postmaterialists may well be correct in their judgment that in the economically advanced nations there is less concern with basic material problems than in any other time or place. It is evident, at the same time, that economic problems remain, in the 1970's, the most frequently mentioned personal concerns expressed by adult Americans. As indicated above, just over two fifths mentioned such problems in a relatively good year, 1972, and just over one half mentioned them in the downswing year, 1974.

One obvious possibility is that they are both right. One half the population has been relieved of the age-old economic burden to the extent that such matters are no longer seen by them as problematic. The difficulty with many such formulations, however, is the forward projection to an anticipated future condition, the location of that general or majority well-being in the immediate present. In the 1970's, the other half of the population continued to live with those economic problems in one way or another on a day-to-day basis. An important, unexplored question appears in this connection, that of salience. The mention of an economic problem does not tell us how much concern or stress it causes.

This chapter attempts to answer these questions. It will inquire as to the incidence, location, and seriousness of the economic problems that have been reported.

Money, it is frequently said, does not buy happiness. It does, however, buy many things that facilitate happiness. Money buys the family's housing, whether elegant, middling, or poor; it buys the daily foodstuffs, whether steak or beans; it provides transportation, medical care, and education for one's children. This being the case, it is remarkable indeed that so many Americans were so unconcerned with money. For the others, whether the problem was making good on a late mortgage payment or finding the down payment needed for a new yacht, laying one's hands on enough money, in one way or another, has proved a notably persistent concern.

It is remarkable how little attention most intellectuals, particularly those of the literary-political persuasion, have paid to the subject of money. Their avoidance of such matters may easily be seen in works of literature. Writings that purport to deal with human experience steadfastly avoid the most commonplace of human experiences, consideration of personal finances. Characters in fiction hardly ever examine the contents of pockets, purses, or wallets. They rarely ask those elementary questions: "Can I afford it?" or "Can I make it to payday?" Even more striking, characters in fiction seldom appear in stores buying food, clothing, furniture, or household necessities.

Readers may easily establish the truth of these claims through reflection on the contents of the novels, short stories, or poems they have read, or by consideration of the motion pictures and television dramas they have seen. In the original version of Charles Dickens' most familiar work, the reader is told Bob Cratchit's precise weekly earnings, fifteen "bob" a week. In how many other works, those read, seen, or heard, has such information been provided? Even in nonfiction, in biographical studies, whether scholarly or popular, one rarely learns more than a few sketchy details about the subject's financial status.

In our review of the leading theoretical positions of the 1970's, many, it will be remembered, viewed money problems as passé. There was a remarkable consensus of Reich, Roszak, Scammon, and Wattenberg on this point. Many workplace critics, with ritualistic insistence, declared that "It's *not* the money. . . . " And the same conclusion, of course, has been reached by many writers of the postmaterialist school.

The best available evidence from the 1970's, as we have seen, shows that avoidance of or indifference to this topic is not justified. Economic concerns remain the most pressing personal problems for a large part of the American population. The consensus among such diverse intellectuals, a consensus so at variance with this easily available evidence, indicates the presence of some extraintellectual process. Put somewhat differently, it appears that we are dealing here with a deeply ingrained intellectual taboo: money, to draw a simile, is to modern intellectuals what sex (presumably) was to the Victorians—something not to be discussed in polite company.

Freud has shown that the energies expended in repression provide a reasonable index of the strength of the original interest. Concerning the money taboo, his point is well-illustrated by the extremely hostile reception given the work of one intellectual who violated it, Norman Podhoretz (in his book, *Making It*). His work strikes an audacious chord with its argument that it is "better to be rich than to be poor."[1] The intense critical reactions to the book bear a remarkable resemblance to the outrage expressed by Victorian moralists when their sacred norms were violated.

This taboo with regard to discussions of money is one that must be violated: no account of the state of the masses could possibly be complete without an exploration of this subject matter.

The 1970's could easily be titled The Decade of Inflation, the continuous increase of prices over those ten years probably outdoing any previous decade in the nation's history. It is not surprising, therefore, that newspapers and magazines, when not proclaiming the truth of various postscarcity theories, should regularly return to the sixth of the positions outlined in our first chapter, namely, the notion of a little man's revolt. We look first at the overall picture throughout the decade, then turn to an examination of some details. The principal aims of the chapter are, first, to indicate the extent of the hurt experienced, and second, to give some precision to the portraits of the little man. One point of imprecision may be noted from the outset. One financially straitened group, separated and divorced women, are not adequately described by the "little man" catchphrase.

Data on income, on the *amounts* received, exist in great quantity in the publications of the Bureau of the Census, the Bureau of Labor Statistics, and the Treasury Department, as well as in most national surveys. Evidence from two sources on the 1977 amounts is shown in Table 7.1; equivalent tables for the other years of the decade can be found in the NORC study codebooks and in the *Statistical Abstracts of the United States*. Note that the referent in the table is to total *family* pretax income, i.e., the combined before-taxes incomes of all earners in the household.

Despite the persistent depiction of America as an affluent or middle-class society, the amounts of income at the disposal of the average household are best described as modest. The modal, or most frequent, category in both

---

[1] It is worth citing a key passage from Podhoretz. On the first page of the book (in his Preface, page xi) he openly and unashamedly announced, "It is better to be a success than a failure." Not satisfied with this outrage to "good taste" (as defined in intellectual circles), he proceeded to an exposition of a series of corollary perceptions, "each one of them," he declared, "as dizzying in its impact as the Original Revelation itself." A three-fold violation of established norms appears in the passage that followed (quoted here in its entirety):

Money, I now saw (no one, of course, had ever seen it before), was important: it was better to be rich than to be poor. Power, I now saw (moving on to higher subtleties), was desirable: it was better to give orders than to receive them. Fame, I now saw (how courageous of me not to flinch), was unqualifiedly delicious: it was better to be recognized than to be anonymous.

Table 7.1. Distribution of Household Income, 1977

	NORC 1978	CPS 1977[a]
Under $5,000	14.4%	16.5%
$5–9,999	22.2	20.3
$10–14,999	20.6	17.9
$15–19,999	15.5	15.6
$20–24,999	12.4	11.5
$25,000 +	14.9	18.1
Total	100.0%	99.9%
	(N = 1398)	(N ≃ 55,000)

[a]Source: Statistical Abstract, 1979, p. 460.

presentations is from $5000 to $10,000, with about 37% of all American families—roughly two fifths—falling below the $10,000 mark. In contrast, fewer than 20% were above the $25,000 mark; and the median family income in 1977 was about $13,600. Note that these figures are for all households and therefore do not take such things as the size of the household or the number of earners into account. There are, in other words, a large number of complexities that have to be considered before rendering some judgment on the average circumstances of a typical American household. It is apparent, in advance, however, that this average circumstance is going to fall well short of postmaterial affluence.

There is no easy translation of dollar amounts into living standards, and so it is difficult to say just what kind of life-style the income average reported here would sustain. Studies of consumer expenditures show that most families spend about one quarter of their income on housing; for the median 1977 income of $13,600, that would represent an annual housing expenditure of about $3,400, which works out to about $280 per month. The sums in question, in other words, would apparently fall somewhere below affluent.

The Bureau of Labor Statistics publishes annual "Urban Budgets for a 4-Person Family." In all, three budgets are calculated: lower, intermediate, and higher. The budgets are based on various assumptions about consumer behavior—housing, diet, and so on—and on current prices for the requisite commodities in a sample of urban areas in the United States. The intermediate budget is best described as modest but adequate. It assumes a six-room home (for four people), a two-year-old used car, no savings, and so on. According to the BLS, the sum required to sustain this intermediate life-style in 1977 was $15,353 in nonmetropolitan areas, and about $1500–$2000 higher in metropolitan areas; in 1977, the median household income in the United States was about 88% of the lower budget figure. In other words, somewhat more than half of all American households receive an annual income *at or below* what the BLS calculates is necessary for an intermediate style of life.

The income necessary for the higher budget is about $21,700 in nonmetropolitan areas, and some $25,000–$26,000 in urban areas. In 1977, the proportion of households that could afford this higher style of life would be in the range of 15%–30%. (Interestingly, one important group contained within this higher income bracket, and well able to afford the associated life-style, is the American intellectual elite. According to a study of 135 leading American intellectuals published in 1974 by Charles Kadushin, the average income of the group was well over $35,000—or considerably more than twice the average for all families in the United States.)

The *Statistical Abstract* for 1979 gives trend data on median household incomes for the decade of the 1970's (Table 750, p. 458). All figures are in constant (1977) dollars; that is, they are corrected for inflation. Much of the popular commentary in the decade stressed the erosion of conditions and living standards that resulted from inflation, this being the fuel that stoked the fires of the little man's revolt. In fact, average family incomes, once corrected for inflation, were essentially constant over the decade: $13,630 in 1970 and $13,572 in 1977. The high figure for the decade was registered in 1973: $14,335. With this exception, the average (median) annual income for all years in the decade was within a few hundred dollars of the figures given above. Week to week, that means a few dollars in either direction. In other words, most people managed to stay more or less even with inflation over the decade, witnessing neither sharp improvement nor sharp deterioration in their objective economic position.

Actually, the picture is more complicated than this: some people were no doubt hurt very badly by the inflation of the 1970's, whereas others realized genuine gains, and still others stayed more or less where they were. *In the aggregate*, this combination of patterns results in a "no change" finding. A more informative analysis would therefore need to ask which groups lost and which gained, rather than simply what happened in the aggregate.

As we have already remarked, data on income amounts can be obtained from many sources. A less frequent mode of presentation, but one more relevant to present concerns, involves subjective estimates; namely, how satisfied people are with the monies coming their way. A single individual living alone at the start of an adult career, with no spouse, children, or mortgage payments, might have found $10,000 to be a princely sum in 1970, whereas the same amount might prove grossly inadequate for an older worker with a mortgage, a spouse, and three or four children. In the first case, $10,000 might provide a very satisfying condition, and in the second case, an extremely dissatisfying one. Since it is the phenomenological assessment of the sum involved rather than the sum itself that is presumably the key to any subsequent reaction, our discussion will focus on the matter of income satisfaction.

The NORC General Social Surveys give a picture of reactions at eight points across the decade (Table 7.2). Several features of this portrait deserve attention. There is, to begin, the overall picture provided in the right column

Table 7.2. Financial Satisfaction: 1972–1980 NORC General Social Surveys

Question: "We are interested in how people are getting along financially these days. So far as you and your family are concerned, would you
say that you are pretty well satisfied, more or less satisfied, or not satisfied at all?"

	1972	1973	1974	1975	1976	1977	1978	1980	All
Pretty well satisfied	32%	31%	31%	31%	31%	34%	34%	28%	32%
More or less satisfied	45	46	46	42	46	44	42	45	44
Not satisfied at all	23	24	23	27	23	22	24	27	24
Total %	100%	101%	100%	100%	100%	100%	100%	100%	100%
N =	(1608)	(1501)	(1478)	(1479)	(1492)	(1521)	(1529)	(1462)	(12,070)

294

of the table. One third of the respondents indicated they were pretty well satisfied with their income, one quarter said they were not satisfied at all, while the remainder (44%) chose the middling, the more-or-less satisfied option. Compared to the other measures of satisfaction reviewed in previous chapters, those dealing with marriage, family, community, job, and life, this is the lowest overall level of satisfaction recorded. Although the measures are not precisely comparable, most involving seven points of differentiation as opposed to the present three, the one-quarter dissatisfaction level exceeds most outright dissatisfaction levels reported in previous chapters.[2]

A second conclusion involves the changes occurring over the decade. Although the discussions of inflation, typically, have a things-getting-worse emphasis, with stress on *growing* problems or the *deepening* crisis, and *more and more* as a frequent modifier, the basic finding in this respect is that the overall result does *not* show a significant trend, the levels of satisfaction and dissatisfaction being fairly constant over the decade. The experience, in short, is not that of runaway inflation such as occurred in Germany in 1923 or, more recently, in several Latin American countries. The constancy of the pattern may be seen in the "not satisfied at all" percentages, the figures never varying from the overall 24% figure by a margin greater than plus or minus three percentage points. That rough constancy over the decade does represent a change from the two previous decades. The 1950's and 1960's were characterized by a widespread sense of economic improvement. The 1970's, in contrast, was a decade in which, overall, things either stood still or, for many, registered some decline. Note that the stability in income satisfaction is consistent with the previously discussed stability in actual average household incomes over the decade in question.[3]

[2]Lest there be any doubt, a question on income satisfaction was included in the 1978 Quality of American Life study, which had the familiar seven-degree choice. It showed 24% expressing dissatisfaction, exactly the same figure found in the 1978 NORC study (see Campbell, 1981, p. 240). Another such question is discussed in the text.

Campbell reports even greater dissatisfaction in two areas: the amount of education one has received, and the state of personal savings (see also our discussion at the end of Chapter 6). Both these points correspond with our argument of the predominance of economic concerns. The lack of education is mentioned as the principal source of people's economic difficulties, many, rather belatedly, wishing they had more of it (32% expressed outright dissatisfaction with their educational achievement in the 1978 study, and only 20% said they were completely satisfied). There is even less satisfaction with savings, the level here being the lowest of some sixteen items reported. Young people, on the whole, have very small savings (if any), a situation that ordinarily shows steady improvement over the lifetime, the satisfaction showing a pronounced relationship with age. This appears to be another one of those "facts of life" findings, one that is recognized as such and, accordingly, has little impact as a determinant of life satisfaction.

[3]*Individual* constant-dollar incomes deteriorated considerably in the decade. The gross average weekly earnings for production or nonsupervisory employees on nonagricultural payrolls in 1967 was $90.95 (all figures are in 1967 dollars). As of 1970 those earnings had increased to $103.04. They continued to increase to 1972,

A third conclusion involves responses to the two recessions of the decade, both producing a three-point increase in dissatisfaction (see also Westcott and Bednarzik, 1981). Both appear to have had limited direct effects on reported financial satisfaction. If one contrasts 1974 and 1975, for example, the response difference, on balance, involves only 4% of the total (those persons who shifted from the more-or-less-satisfied to the not-satisfied-at-all category). The pretty-well-satisfied at that point appear to have been untouched by the changing economy. The effects of the 1980 recession, which began in the automobile industry and had a wide-ranging impact, were more widely felt, touching some of those who, previously, had described themselves as pretty well satisfied. These findings, it should be remembered, represent net results. It is not likely that only 4% of the population sensed a shift in their economic circumstances in 1975; some would have experienced improvement, while others suffered losses, so it is only *on balance* that 4% were "moved."

The same basic conclusions, with one modest difference, are also reached in the assessment of change, whether the respondent's financial situation was getting better, worse, or staying the same (Table 7.3). By itself, the responses to this question prove somewhat ambiguous. Stayed the same could mean the persistence of a more-or-less-satisfied condition; the option could be chosen by a millionaire and by someone in modest circumstances, providing an accurate description of the change in both instances. It is, nevertheless, by itself a useful question for monitoring trends across time.

Looking at the overall result, one finds approximately two fifths saying that things were getting better, two fifths saying things had remained the same, and only about one fifth saying they were getting worse. Again, there was no long-term tendency, no persistent deterioration over the decade, but rather, as before, only two modest declines associated with the years of recession. This question shows more people touched by those events than was suggested by the satisfaction question, the percentage point increases of those saying things were getting worse being roughly double the increases of those not satisfied at all.

The overall figures suggest something about the dimensions of any possible little man's revolt. At maximum, one quarter were not satisfied, and one fifth were experiencing financial deterioration. However, as will become clear in the following discussion, the picture is considerably more complicated. The best conclusion, for the moment, emphasizes both the

---

reaching $109.26, after which there was a decline. As of 1979, the figure was $100.73. In the depression year, 1980, the most substantial loss of real earnings in some decades occurred, to $95.18 (from *Monthly Labor Review*, May 1981, p. 86). At the same time, the labor force participation of second and third earners in a household increased during the decade. Again, we stress that averages such as those reported will often hide considerable variability. Some workers, blue-collar, in particular, will have suffered losses considerably greater than those reported in the above figures; other workers will have realized genuine wage gains.

Table 7.3. Financial Trend: 1972–1980 NORC General Social Surveys

Question: "During the last few years, has your financial situation been getting better, getting worse, or has it stayed the same?	1972	1973	1974	1975	1976	1977	1978	1980	All
Getting better	43%	42%	40%	35%	36%	38%	41%	34%	39%
Stayed the same	39	41	39	37	41	40	40	40	40
Getting worse	18	16	22	28	23	22	19	25	22
Total %	100%	99%	101%	100%	100%	100%	100%	99%	101%
N =	(1890)	(1462)	(1474)	(1479)	(1493)	(1517)	(1526)	(1462)	(12,003)

limited size and the relative constancy of that revolt's potential constituency. This is to say it was not a problem that was growing throughout the decade, as in a pattern of successive increments. While many were arguing the "increased magnitude" case, an opposite fact went largely unnoticed: overall, nearly *twice* as many persons reported that their financial situations were getting better, despite the persistent inflation.

Other recent studies of the reaction of families to inflation have shown similar results. A 1979 survey by the Survey Research Center asked respondents whether they had been hurt by inflation, had stayed even, or had even gotten ahead of inflation. The plurality—48%—said they had stayed even, and another 12% said they had gotten ahead. There was, to be sure, a large minority, some 37%, who had been hurt, but "the important point is that a large majority of all the respondents—60%—said they had *not* been hurt by inflation over the past six months" (Converse, Kallick, and Katona, 1980, p. 13). By way of explanation, the authors point out that "in 1979, aggregate incomes rose at about the same rate as prices," which was more or less characteristic of the entire decade. The authors also asked respondents what they did to cope with inflationary prices. "A great majority . . . said that they bought fewer items whose prices were sharply higher" (p. 14). A large majority (79%) also noted that it was a good time to avoid debt.

Much the same picture emerges in the several surveys and polls taken from both NORC and SRC organizations and analyzed by Richard Curtin (1980). This author remarks on "the apparent lack of connection between people's sense of personal satisfaction and trends in the economy" (Curtin, p. 18), and concludes in a later passage that "the onset of stagflation in the past decade has not systematically reduced the level of people's happiness or satisfaction with their incomes" (p. 19).

The major news magazines at this time were arguing a very different case—one of widespread, across-the-board suffering. *U.S. News and World Report* (December 24, 1973, pp. 16–18) spoke of the "mounting inflation" and the "soaring cost of living." Government reports, they said, "make it clear how badly the typical family budget is being strained." Their case was then made with a dozen interviews from across the nation. A later report in the same magazine (April 15, 1974, pp. 30–32) has even more alarming claims. "For family after family, soaring inflation is forcing basic—often wrenching—change. Wives are hunting for work. Husbands are moonlighting at second jobs. Nearly everyone is cutting back on food. . . . " That account, it will be noted, came out at the time the NORC's 1974 General Social Survey was being conducted. The results in Tables 7.2 and 7.3 obviously do not support their claims of massive and alarming impacts. A *Time* magazine article (November 4, 1974, p. 102) reviewed the claims and prognoses of several sociologists; all of them anticipated far-reaching transformations. This account differs from the others in one important respect. In the last paragraph, the article cites some findings from National Opinion Research Center studies. Here it was said that "the big psychological effects" of inflation were "still to come." (The figures given above for the years subsequent to 1974 show this prediction to be mistaken.) As for the reports of "financial satisfaction," the article said, "the figures were just beginning to tilt downward slightly at the end of May. . . . " And, furthermore, "Despite economic pressures, figures on 'life satisfacton' were actually up." The tail end paragraph, in effect, negated just about everything that had come before it.[4]

The results presented here also provide some answer to a question treated in passing in Chapter 3, the question of the *seriousness* of people's economic problems. It will be remembered that 43% cited some economic problem as their most important personal concern in 1972, a level that rose to 53% in 1974. Although by far the most frequently mentioned problem, there is an obvious counterpart to those figures: more than one half the population in 1972 mentioned *no* economic problem, and even in the recession year, 1974, just under one half indicated an immunity to such problems. We can only imagine what comparable studies done a century ago, in the midst of the great depression of the 1870's, would have shown. It seems unlikely that the levels of immunity would have been anywhere near as high.

That 53% figure registered in 1974 tells only part of the story; some kind of an economic problem was indicated, but we learn nothing about its seriousness (or its focus: whether it is a problem of food costs or a problem of stock market losses). A direct question on satisfaction with income was asked in that SRC same study, with seven response options ranging from "de-lighted" to a neutral point (mixed) to "terrible" at the opposite extreme. Of the respondents, 26% expressed some outright dissatisfaction with their income, a figure that is close to the NORC's 23%. The NORC study was done in the spring of 1974; the SRC study, however, was postelection, most interviews coming in November and December, and some even in January 1975. These results would accurately reflect the course of economic events, the unemployment rate being 5.0% in April 1974, but rising, particularly in

[4]The performance of the leading news magazines in these respects is frequently bizarre. In July 1979, *U.S. News and World Report* ran a piece entitled, "Two Incomes: No Sure Hedge Against Inflation" (9 July 1979, pp. 45–46). In typical fashion, this story is based on a handful of "illustrative" interviews with what are clearly portrayed as squeezed two-earner families. The first couple to appear in the article is from Chicago; their combined income is reported as $52,000 per year (in real dollars, some three to four times the average family income in the United States in 1978); they are also said to own a $270,000 home. A second couple hails from New York City; their combined incomes are reported as about $60,000. The nature of their squeeze is as follows: "Instead of taking a European trip, they decided to use discount fares for a visit to California." The wife, it is said, "frequents discount boutiques and has her clothes dry-cleaned in New Jersey, where costs are lower. She also wishes she could afford a maid. 'I hate to spend part of Sunday cleaning,' she complains." Five additional couples appear in the article; their annual combined incomes are given, respectively, as $50,000, $50,000, $100,000, $130,000, and $60,000. Less than 3% of families in the United States at that time had combined incomes in excess of $50,000.

the last months of the year, to 7.2% in December, and, again, to 8.2% in January 1975.

The seven-point scale allows us an indication of salience, a statement of the degree of hurt or grievance. Five percent of the respondents described their financial situations as terrible, 10% reported they were unhappy with their finances, another 11% said they were mostly dissatisfied, and 18% indicated mixed feelings. Altogether, that means 43% had chosen the dissatisfied or neutral categories. Considering that 53% had mentioned an economic problem as their most pressing personal concern, this means that at minimum roughly one in five of those with economic problems had declared themselves to be satisfied with their financial circumstances. The actual cross-tabulation (not shown) yielded what, at first sight at least, would appear to be a rather unexpected result. Nearly one half (46%) of those reporting economic problems indicated some degree of satisfaction with their incomes. Most of these (31%) said they were mostly satisfied, although 13% said they were pleased and 1% even reported themselves as delighted. Approximately one fifth expressed mixed feelings, and one third said they were dissatisfied. Evidently, then, the felt economic problems, for most people, were not of a grievous character. These findings tie in with a point first made in Chapter 3; namely, that financial problems, while still the leading concern, are, we suspect, of lesser salience than those experienced at previous points in the nation's history.[5]

One tends to think in simple categoric terms. People indicating economic problems (especially those naming them as their prime concerns) should indicate economic dissatisfaction. But that is only one of a number of possibilities. Certainly a person could, without contradiction, declare him- or herself mostly satisfied and simultaneously declare some financial con-

[5]Lacking systematic studies, one can only speculate about the reactions in former times. Especially useful in this connection are the works of Pessen, 1978, Chapter 5; and Miller, 1967, Chapter 6. Historical data on personal wealth from the 1860 manuscript census have been reported in Soltow (1975). The analysis is restricted to males living in ten large, northern cities in the United States. The results show slightly more than one half of the adult males with exactly *no* personal wealth. The wealth figure, moreover, is an inclusive one, including all real and personal property other than clothing. This bottom one half "had little more than clothing and petty cash" (Soltow, p. 241). Interestingly, some 70 years later, in the early 1930's, W. Lloyd Warner reported that 58% of the Yankee City population had net personal wealth amounting to less than $100, roughly the same figure as the one for 1860. Soltow calculates that in the United States in 1860, "the richest 6000 men had as much wealth as the poorest 450,000" (p. 235).

Compared to these findings, the objective economic situation of most households is obviously (in Eddie Cush's phrase) "pretty good," the lessening urgency of the economic problem being clearly consistent with the depiction of the postindustrial-ists. Whether the postulated psychological consequences have occurred, however, is another matter. Much of the American population (not all) has indeed been freed from abject economic want, but this is very different from being liberated from concern about the material conditions of one's existence.

cern as the most serious personal problem. That is simply another way of saying the problem is not a serious one. The same point applies, a fortiori, for those saying they are pleased or delighted. To illustrate, a family with a total annual income in the range of $75,000–$100,000 a year would presumably (or so one hopes!) report a great deal of satisfaction with its personal financial situation. Still, even at that income level, the family might find that it is unable to afford a maid, and it might therefore report the cost of domestic help as its most pressing concern.

A parallel development appears elsewhere in the cross-tabulation: 20% of those naming some other problem as their primary concern indicated some degree of dissatisfaction with their incomes. This also is not a contradiction. A financially straitened family with a drug-addicted child might well mention drugs or the children as their most pressing personal concern and still indicate a great deal of income dissatisfaction in response to a direct question. The most obvious instance of the logical impossibility involved those reporting no problem. Of that category (some 14% of the total sample, it will be remembered), 10% reported some degree of financial dissatisfaction, 2% even describing things as "terrible."

The SRC study allows some exploration of the substance of the problems mentioned. Sorting those indicating economic concerns by family income, one finds two types of problems frequently mentioned by those poorly paid: general money worries and general job anxieties. Under the first heading, the kinds of things coded were described thus: "I don't see how I can make ends meet; or, I just don't have enough money; or, I'm in debt; lack of money for things I want/need." Under the second heading, one has the following: "References to job security or unemployment; I'm worried about my job; or, about losing my job; or, I'm out of work; or, can't find work." The former problems are, by far, the most frequently mentioned.

These kinds of problems are markedly less frequent in the high-income categories. In their place, one finds increased references to another range of complaints, these being described as follows: "Cost of living too high; or, too much inflation; or, taxes too high; or, too much governmental waste." One significant additional reference appearing here is the "cost of college."

The principal lessons to be gained from this discussion involve the differences in salience and the diversity of economic problems. The very diversity of problems suggests that there is no sizable bloc or insurgent mass ready to move against a sluggish or unresponsive government. Put differently, the numbers that could potentially be recruited for such insurgency are considerably smaller than the 53% figure would suggest. The diversity of the problems faced would also stand in the way of any concerted effort. It is, in short, a too diverse base for any developing revolt. This theme is elaborated in Chapter 8.

An important line of inquiry follows from the foregoing discussion, the basic question being: Which groups are dissatisfied? The most obvious hypothesis in this connection would be that it is poor people, those with low

incomes. While many would anticipate a strong positive relationship between income level and financial satisfaction, some commentators, assuming the elasticity of human demands, have argued another possibility.
According to this view, fulfillment of a given financial goal would be
followed by a subsequent increase in aspirations. Given the phenomenon of
rising expectations, the quest for money, so it is argued, is one drive that
cannot be satisfied.[6]

The findings contained in Table 7.4, however, generally support the
"most obvious" hypothesis rather than this alternative. Some satiation is
clearly evidenced, most change across the categories involving a decline of
the not-satisfied category and a corresponding increase of the more-or-less
satisfied. In the highest income category, only one person in ten indicated
financial dissatisfaction. Only modest increases in the pretty-well satisfied
percentages occurred until the best-off category was reached; at that point
a quantum leap in satisfaction appeared.

Massive dissatisfaction might be expected at the lower end of the income
scale, but here one comes upon a not-so-obvious finding. Only about two
respondents in five reported outright dissatisfaction. (Approximately the
same levels of dissatisfaction, incidentally, appeared in the three lowest
income categories.) Even more surprising, perhaps, is the presence of some
23% who, at this very low level of earnings, reported themselves pretty well
satisfied. Similar results have appeared in other studies. Hamilton, for
example (1972:372), examines satisfaction with income among non-South
manual workers in 1964. Even among the most poorly paid (less than
$4000), almost one in four described themselves as pretty well satisfied and
two fifths said more or less satisfied.

Part of the explanation for these paradoxical results involves other characteristics of those in the low-income category. This category alone has a
minority of married people. It contains twice as many widowed as the next

[6]The economist Lester C. Thurow puts the matter as follows: "Man is an
acquisitive animal whose wants cannot be satiated. This is not a matter of advertising
and conditioning, but a basic fact of existence" (Thurow, 1981, p. 120; also, pp. 18,
23, 117–118).

There is a small literature on the subject: see Easterlin, 1973, 1974; and Duncan,
1975. Easterlin's basic conclusion is, "In all societies, more money for the individual
typically means more individual happiness. However, raising the incomes of all does
not increase the happiness of all."

Another finding is worth reporting. In Easterlin's review of 30 surveys from 19
developed and less developed countries, a "striking similarity" was found, both
within and among countries. Asked what they meant by happiness, the responses
were grouped into broad classes. "Usually each of three concerns," he reports, "is
mentioned at least a majority of times in personal happiness judgments—economic
matters, family considerations, and health, with economic concerns being most
frequently cited. Other considerations, such as social or political conditions, are
mentioned much less often—perhaps only one person in 10, or less" (Easterlin, 1973,
pp. 4–5).

Table 7.4. Financial Satisfaction and Financial Trend by Income: NORC General Social Survey, 1975

	Family income—1974						
	$5,999 or less	$6,000– 7,999	$8,000– 9,999	$10,000– 14,999	$15,000– 19,999	$20,000– 24,999	$25,000 or more
Financial satisfaction[a]							
Pretty well	23%	25%	28%	32%	36%	31%	57%
More or less	38	37	35	44	50	52	35
Not satisfied	38	38	40	24	15	17	9
N =	(359)	(130)	(132)	(344)	(199)	(111)	(127)
Financial trend[a]							
Better	16%	26%	28%	39%	55%	50%	59%
Same	48	40	34	33	28	30	25
Worse	36	34	38	29	17	20	16
N =	(360)	(131)	(132)	(345)	(197)	(110)	(127)

[a]Income for 1974. Satisfaction and trend reports describe reaction in the spring of 1975.

303

category; it has the largest percentages of separated, of divorced persons, and, by a small margin, of those never married. It also contains, by far, the largest portion of those 65 years of age and over (38% versus the percentage in the next highest income level, only 23%). In part, then, what appears here as the "satisfaction of the poor" is the phenomenon seen earlier as the "satisfaction of the aged" (or, in a substantially overlapping category, the satisfaction of the widowed). The separated and divorced, particularly the women, provide much of the dissatisfaction in this category, black women being very strongly represented.

Another consideration providing part of the explanation for this satisfaction of the poor is community size—the cost of living, in general, being substantially higher in the larger cities. At any given level of income, therefore, one would anticipate greater satisfaction in the small towns and rural areas. Taking married respondents with a full-time employed family head (thereby controlling for the confounding marital and employment status factors) and making a crude division into three city-size categories, we did find the expected relationship. Of those in the poorest category and living in central cities of Standard Metropolitan Statistical Areas, 9% said they were pretty well satisfied, compared to 20% of those living in nonmetropolitan counties and in rural areas. The equivalent figures in the next-poorest category were 14 and 28%. The same pattern appeared in all other categories except that of the best-off $25,000 or more; in this case, the community-size effect disappeared, the respective percentages being 59 and 60%.[7]

Using the same income categories as in Table 7.4, we also examined the relationship with satisfaction in the NORC 1978 and 1980 studies. The same general patterns appeared in both years, although the linkage, on the whole, was less pronounced than in 1975. (The three studies, it should be noted, ask about family income for the previous year.) The same quantum leap appeared in the $25,000-and-over category, although the "pretty satisfied" responses fell from 57% in 1975 to 49%, and then to 40%. One source of the decline is to be found in the changed composition of the category. In this inflationary period, more and more families entered this high-income category, the respective percentages for the three years being 9, 15, and 24%. That $25,000, clearly, does not have the same meaning at those later points. An opposite shift is found at the other end of the income scale, the percentages for the poorest category declining from 26 to 20%, and then to 17%.

We also undertook a more detailed examination of the lowest income category. In this case, to assure sufficient numbers, we combined the 1973, 1974, and 1975 NORC studies. Of those in the less-than-$6000 category, 60% were women. Again, it was the separated and divorced women who

[7]For a previous analysis of these matters using data from the SRC 1964 election study, see Hamilton, 1972, p. 372 ff. For a similar analysis based on West German experience, see Hamilton, 1968b. For another American study, see Caplovitz, 1979, Chapter 3.

reported the highest levels of financial dissatisfaction, the not-at-all-satisfied amounting to 64 and 50% (N's = 64 and 74), as against the 38% figure for all women in the low-income category. Although the separated and divorced are overrepresented here compared to the higher income categories (making up 21% of the low-income women), still, 37% were married, and another 28% were widows, the remainder, of course, being single.

The claims of still another line of current argument may be addressed with the findings of Table 7.4. Some commentators have argued that inflation has its most serious effects among middle-income groups. This argument is based on the assumption that vast amounts of welfare money have been used to assist and protect the poor (at least prior to the changes brought about by the Reagan administration). Unions, moreover, have successfully pushed for cost-of-living increases for many blue-collar workers. Those left out in the cold, accordingly, are the hardworking middle classes, who have neither these supports nor the advantages of high earnings or substantial wealth. The case, from the outset, seems loosely argued and implausible in many details. In any event, this evidence casts doubt on the thesis, the middle-income categories, on the whole, having a rather "middling" experience. With respect to both the levels of reported satisfaction and the trends over the last few years, the answer to the who is dissatisfied question is simple: it is the poorest groups in the society (although here, the extent of dissatisfaction is less than most would probably expect). In general, the higher the income level, not surprisingly, the more favorable the experience.

The middle-income strain argument is more frequently put forward by legislators and popular journalists than by academic specialists. Much of the discussion of California's Proposition 13 made use of this argument. One source, Time magazine (June 19, 1978, p. 13), offers the following: "That angry noise was the sound of a middle class tax revolt erupting. . . ." and, "Those middle-income folks at $10,000 to $30,000 are on the verge of revolt." The first statement is by a Time writer, the second by Congressman Jim Jones of Oklahoma. A related piece of some interest, "The Squeeze of the Middle Class," appeared in the New York Times Magazine (July 13, 1980); the "heroes" of this story are a young married couple living in Manhattan with a reported combined income of $60,000, who are said to be squeezed by inflation and who are showing "doubt and anxiety and even fear." One of the difficulties with the argument is a lack of precision in the specification of the term "middle income." Congressman Jones's middle group, as judged by the results of the 1978 NORC General Social Survey, would include approximately three fifths of the population and would extend very far into the upper income ranks. The "middle class" family in the Times Magazine story sits in the upper 3% of the family income distribution in the United States.

There is a "wisp" of a finding in Table 7.4 that would provide some support for a "middle-income squeeze" argument; it appears in the $8000-to-$9999 category. They have the highest percentage reporting things getting worse (again by two points). That category, however, also has the highest percentage of young persons (those age 18–34) of all income categories. Included there are many people just starting out on their careers. If just out of school in 1974, they might well have had small incomes, but that would not necessarily mean a condition of poverty. The interviewing in 1975, moreover, occurred at the worst point in that year's recession.

Only small and irregular differences appear between the lower-income categories in the 1978 study. In the 1980 study, that wisp of a finding reappears, the same category, by a hair, having the largest percentage of not-at-all satisfieds and, by a margin of seven points, the fewest in the pretty-well-satisfied category. At that point, the category could no longer be counted as middle income. Our guess is that there was a change in composition, with the two lowest categories now even more disproportionately made up of retired persons. The separated and divorced plus the young married just starting out would then, we think, be heavily represented in the $8–10,000 category.

The presentation thus far addresses the question of income dissatisfaction in general. One may also pose a more specific question: who is hurt most by a recession? For this purpose, we compared results from the NORC's 1972 and 1975 studies, the former being a prerecession point, the latter, in the spring of 1975, the point when the recession was at its worst. The overall change between those two years, as indicated in Table 7.2, is very modest. The pretty-well-satisfied segment declined by about one percentage point, and the more-or-less satisfied by about two points. The dissatisfied, obviously, increased by four points. That net result, clearly, would hide a much larger amount of aggregate shifting. Part of the answer to this new question involves race. In 1972, in relatively good times, one fifth of the whites expressed dissatisfaction with their incomes. Among the blacks at that point, one third expressed dissatisfaction. The 1975 recession had very unequal impacts; among whites, dissatisfaction increased by three percentage points, while among blacks it increased by fifteen.

Age is another factor showing a link to financial satisfaction and dissatisfaction. Young persons, as noted in Chapter 6, typically begin with the least attractive and poorest paying jobs society has to offer. In general, they also have the least job security of all categories of employed persons. These basic facts are reflected in the NORC results, in that among the younger respondents, satisfaction tends to be low and dissatisfaction relatively high (Table 7.5). A similar pattern appears among those age 35 to 44, although the causes of their dissatisfaction are likely to be quite different—no doubt related to the costs of teenage children. The levels of satisfaction then increase, in the 1972 study, to the age 55-to-64 category, followed by a slight decline, or, in the 1975 study, by continuity with the preretirement level.

The families in the age 18-to-34 category would normally have small children, with relatively modest financial burdens. Those in the next category, age 35 to 44, would have teenage children, who entail, normally,

Table 7.5. Financial Satisfaction and Financial Trend by Age: NORC General Social Surveys 1972 and 1975

		Age of respondent					
		18–34	35–44	45–54	53–64	65 or more	Total
Financial satisfaction							
1972	Pretty well	27%	28%	35%	42%	36%	32%
	More or less	44	50	45	43	44	45
	Not satisfied	29	22	20	15	20	23
	N =	(558)	(240)	(315)	(252)	(243)	(1608)
1975	Pretty well	25	20	33	43	43	31
	More or less	43	45	44	41	39	42
	Not satisfied	32	36	23	16	17	27
	N =	(548)	(249)	(235)	(193)	(252)	(1479)
Change in "not satisfied"		+3	+14	+3	+1	−3	+4
Financial trend							
1972	Better	53%	48%	41%	37%	26%	43%
	Same	31	31	41	45	53	39
	Worse	16	21	18	18	21	18
	N =	(549)	(238)	(311)	(250)	(242)	(1590)
1975	Better	43	34	34	33	21	35
	Same	29	29	39	39	57	37
	Worse	28	37	27	28	22	28
	N =	(550)	(248)	(235)	(193)	(253)	(1479)
Change—"worse"		+12	+16	+9	+10	+1	+10

considerably greater financial costs. They eat more, they require more expensive clothing, and the family housing needs are typically greatest at this point in the life cycle. Some of the older children would have started college, which constitutes a substantial financial burden. Most of the university costs, however, we think would be paid by parents in the age 45-to-54 category.

A more detailed examination of financial concerns was conducted using the larger 1978 Quality of American Life study. The most frequent report of money worries (did they ever worry about being able to pay bills?) was found among 25- to 34-year-olds (57%, $N = 844$). That level of concern fell off systematically to the age 75-and-over category, where it was a low 28% ($N = 222$). When those expressing such worries were asked about the frequency of these concerns, it was the 45- to 54-year-olds who worried most, 22% saying they worried all the time. Such continuous worry also tapers off in the older categories, amounting to only 8% among those age 75 and over. Satisfaction with income (based on a seven-point scale) again varied directly with age. Complete satisfaction was expressed by 8% of those in the age 18-to-24 category, the figures increasing systematically to 31% in the age 75-and-over group.

The comparison of the 1972 and 1975 results shows the greatest recession-linked increase of dissatisfaction among the 35- to 44-year-old category, that is, among those with teenage children. Where the overall increase in dissatisfaction was only four percentage points, the increase here amounted to 14 points. Although much public discussion has been focused on the acute problems faced by the aged (those on fixed incomes), respondents in the 65-and-over category actually report a slight improvement in 1975. That amounted to only a small three-point decline in reported dissatisfaction. The "pretty-well satisfied" reports, however, went very much against the recession-year trend, increasing by seven points. These are the third and fourth studies, it will be noted, after the Quality of American Life studies, that have found this unexpected absence of economic strain among the elderly.

We checked these results also with the 1978 and 1980 NORC studies. The age 65-and-over respondents in these studies showed, by far, the highest levels of financial satisfaction. The second recession of the decade, moreover, also had a limited impact on the elderly. While overall, dissatisfaction increased by three percentage points, it decreased slightly among the age 65-and-over populations. Some decline in the percentage of pretty-well satisfieds appeared, but roughly comparable declines occurred in all categories in 1980.

Examination of the trends during the last few years shows the reports of improvement running inversely with age (again in Table 7.5). This was especially pronounced in 1972. The least satisfied category at that time, the young, had the highest percentage of those reporting that things were getting better. If dissent or insurgency were anticipated on the basis of their reported financial dissatisfaction, such incentives would be countered by this sense that things were improving.

A directly opposite conclusion about the age-trend linkage, that older populations sensed things were getting worse, is not justified. The tendency among the older populations was to report things staying the same. The basic situation of the elderly was one of relative satisfaction with their current financial circumstances, combined with a sense that they were holding their own. Outright dissatisfaction was somewhat higher among the young in 1972; otherwise, it was rather evenly distributed across the age categories.

What happened in the recession year? A significant overall decline occurred in the percentage reporting things getting better. The largest falloffs were reported in the two younger age categories. The same basic age pattern, nevertheless, appears as in 1972, the reports of improvement varying inversely and the reports of staying the same varying directly with age. At this point, however, the sense of worsening conditions was no longer spread evenly across the board. There was a pronounced increase, the greatest change again coming in the age 35-to-44 category, those with growing teenage children. Again unexpectedly, one finds the least change among the oldest respondents, those who, for the most part, are retired. Very little sense of a worsening was reported. The change indicated was a shift from getting better to staying the same, but even this was limited.

We also checked the age-recent trends relationship with the 1978 and 1980 NORC studies. The results in both cases closely match those of the previous studies. The young have the highest percentages reporting recent improvement; the elderly have the highest percentages reporting things staying the same. Comparing the two years, overall, those reporting a worsening of their condition increased by seven percentage points. The greatest change occurred in the age 35-to-44 category, an increase of ten points. For the elderly, there was no change at all in the reports of worsening. There was an actual increase—by four points—of those reporting an improvement.

A brief summary is in order. We have sought to discover which groups in the population were experiencing financial difficulties during the inflationary decade of the 1970's. One part of the answer is easy: it is poor people, those in low-income categories. That conclusion will occasion little surprise (except possibly for those who have argued that the middle income groups are hardest hit). Even within the low-income categories, however, there is a diversity of experience, with a fair-sized minority indicating they were pretty well satisfied, and an even larger proportion saying they were more or less satisfied. Those in the low-income categories reporting dissatisfaction are blacks, young persons (two separate age categories, each with somewhat different problems), and separated and divorced persons (especially women). The 1975 recession laid on an additional set of problems. Especially hard hit in this connection were the blacks and those with teenage children.

A high level of financial dissatisfaction was also expressed by the unemployed in 1972, a finding that will occasion little surprise. Forty-four percent of them ($N = 46$) were not at all satisfied, as opposed to the overall 23% figure. In passing, one may note that 22% of the unemployed were pretty well satisfied, something that might occasion at least some surprise; the remainder chose the more-or-less category. Dissatisfaction among the unemployed jumped sharply in 1975, rising to 57% ($N = 61$); the pretty well satisfied group declined to 7%. A high level of dissatisfaction appeared within another category at this point, that being persons in school, 41% of whom ($N = 49$) were not satisfied at all. The most frequent reports of things getting worse came from those in school (45%), followed by the unemployed (44%) and those with a job but not currently working (39%, $N = 26$). The General Social Surveys are conducted in February, March, and April; that is, during the course of the school year.

A similar result appeared among unemployeds in 1978 and 1980, dissatisfaction with finances increasing from 59% ($N = 39$) to 72% ($N = 39$) in 1980. The same pattern did not appear among those in school at this time.

Some further clues helping to explain the paradoxical findings among the unemployed appear in the Quality of American Life study (1978). The unemployed did, unquestionably, report less happiness than was found in the sample as a whole. The respective percentages declaring themselves very happy were 13% and 30% (and the equivalent percentages "not too happy" were 20% and 8%). One group among the unemployed, married women (forming just over one fifth of all unemployed), stands out with a very distinctive pattern. They were only marginally different from the entire sample, 29% of them saying they were very happy. In most instances, presumably, they would have had other resources to fall back on (quite apart from unemployment insurance). Especially hard hit by unemployment were those on their own, the singles, separated, and divorced (who made up 43% of the unemployed, compared to just under one fifth of the sample). Only 9% of this group said they were very happy. Some 26% described themselves as not too happy. Again, one sees the importance of family status in the assessment of personal well-being.

A number of complexities require examination at this point, the problem stemming from the variety of factors affecting income, many of which overlap considerably. Blacks have the highest levels of separation and divorce in the population. Because of the higher birth rates, they are, on the whole, a younger population with a larger share of young singles. They are, disproportionately, residents of large cities which, as we have seen, means high living costs. And, of course, they are also, on the whole, poorly paid in comparison to whites. In an effort to control for at least the broken marriage and singles effects, we took the combined results for NORC studies 1976, 1977, and 1978, examining the income-financial satisfaction and income-financial trend patterns for the married only.

This inquiry yielded somewhat stronger relationships with current income, stronger than those found in any of the three years previously examined (the 1975, 1978, and 1980 studies). The most striking change in the reports of satisfaction was the reduction of the pretty well satisfied segment of the low-income category (to 19%). The stepwise changes from category to category were more uniform than those shown in Table 7.4, the decline of dissatisfaction, for example, being completely linear across all categories. The same increased clarity appeared in the accounts of recent financial trends, the reports of improvement increasing regularly from 18% in the poorest category to 65% in the richest. The poorest category had 41% reporting a worsening of their financial condition, a level nearly twice that of the next category. The figures then decline to 9% (those being the dissatisfied wealthy in the $25,000-and-over category).

The income we have been discussing throughout this work is pretax family income, including returns from all sources. For most families, the "sources" are the earnings of its employed members (as opposed to dividends, interest, sales of assets, and so forth, benefits that figure prominently only in the very highest income category). For most household units, apart from the retired, a very simple relationship exists: the higher the income, the greater the number of earners in the family. Although a simple and obvious point, it is one that is frequently neglected. To exclude the confounding influence of singles, separated, divorced, and widowed, for this analysis we have again taken only the married. The low-income category (as shown in the combined NORC studies of 1976, 1977, and 1978—see Table 7.6) is one in which a quarter of the units reported no earner in the previous year. Another 45% reported only a single earner. This category also had the smallest percentage of households with two or more earners. At the opposite extreme, in the $25,000-and-over category, only one unit (out of 450) reported no earner, suggesting only a single rentier was picked up among the three samples. Only about one quarter of the units in the highest income category had a single earner. At this level, one quarter of the units reported three or more earners.[8]

One might note, as something of an aside, that efforts to equalize the wealth would probably meet with an unexpected source of conservatism in this highest income category. Although this best-off sixth of the population has a disproportionate share of aggregate family income, much of it has been achieved through a disproportionate expenditure of effort. It is not as if the entire accomplishment depended on the exceptionally high earnings of the family breadwinner. Still focusing on the married in the same three NORC studies, one finds 22% of the breadwinners in the $25,000-and-over category ($N = 452$) in manual occupations. In the next highest category, the blue-collar workers made up 37% of the total ($N = 392$).

This point has important implications for analyses based on decile or quintile shares. Those discussions point out that the best-off fifth of spending units has a disproportionate share of income, amounting to just over 40% of the total in recent years. And the poorest fifth, in most recent analyses, has received only about 5% of total income. One also makes use of those figures to establish trends (e.g., the rich getting richer . . .). But there is an unexamined and unjustified ceteris paribus assumption being made, the assumption that those fifths are identical in other respects. These data suggest that the best-off fifth consists of relatively large family units, and the poorest fifth of relatively small ones. Their needs, in short, would differ considerably; moreover, the calculation of per capita earnings would show less inequality than is indicated by these uncorrected results. The trend statements, in addition, would also be unjustified; one would have to establish the constant character of the quintiles first—that apart from earnings, nothing else had changed. In a period during which a larger proportion of wives were entering

[8]We do not mean to suggest that family income is purely a function of the number of earners. The income of the main earner will, in most cases, be the decisive factor for a family. At minimum, one quarter of the families in the two highest categories are there due to one person's earnings.

The NORC income question, Q. 36, incidentally, reads: "In which of these groups did your total *family* income, from *all* sources fall last year before taxes, that is?" The respondent was handed a card containing a range of categories and was asked to choose among them.

Table 7.6. Number of Earners by Family Income Level: Married Only (NORC General Social Surveys: 1976, 1977, 1978)

Number of earners in family last year	$5,999 or less	$6,000–7,999	$8,000–9,999	$10,000–14,999	$15,000–19,999	$20,000–24,999	$25,000 or more
None	24%	13%	5%	2%	1%	0%	—[a]
One	45	48	46	40	28	25	26
Two	29	34	42	48	44	56	48
Three or more	2	5	8	10	17	19	26
N =	(235)	(179)	(185)	(576)	(478)	(390)	(450)

[a]One case.

the labor force (and during which there was an increase in the number of singles on their own, and of separated and divorced in the labor force), such constancy cannot be assumed.

Earnings, clearly, will vary with the size of the household unit. A unit with five children of employable age would, at the outset, have a better chance for high income than a family with only one or two children. And a broken family, whether through separation, divorce, or widowhood, would (all other things being equal) have limited opportunities. This link of family earnings with the number of earners has an important correlated implication. If one asks which family units are likely to have several of its members in the labor force, the answer, very simply, is families at the midpoint of the life cycle, those in which the head or main earner is in the 45-to-54 age category (of our previous age tables). That, basically, is the category in which wives are free to reenter the labor force if they so choose. It is also the point at which the children will have come of age and could take on outside employment. This means that family incomes, overall, are curvilinear with age (of the husband and wife), rising to this peak point in mid-career, then subsequently declining with the removal of children from the home (to be on their own, or to form their own families). With retirement, of course, still another decline follows.

Although this observation has long since appeared in the recesses of the technical literature, having been noted from the time of the first income statistics of the modern era, the point does not appear in the forefront of contemporary discussions. Most such discussions deal with medians or averages for occupations, races, sexes, and so on, and are indifferent to the question of age or life cycle. This indifference is also indicated in the decile or quintile presentations. These analysts treat the categories as if they had a fixed composition. But our point about the life cycle linkage means that some people enter the higher categories only for a limited period; they are predestined to be removed once again and to fall back into some lower category. Although it is easy to think of the top fifth as a solid upper-middle-class group, in fact, it contains a fair-sized minority of blue-collar families. They, together with some lower-middle-class families, are the temporaries in that category.[9]

The most extensive discussion of determinants of family economic well-being in the United States is that of James Morgan and associates, *Five Thousand American Families—Patterns of Economic Progress* (1974). This is a unique study on a number of counts. First, it is a panel survey (repeated interviews over several years with the same families), and thus gives better information on family income dynamics than can be inferred from cross-sectional data such as that under discussion here. Second, the dependent

---

[9]For previous discussion of the linkage of family income with life cycle and the number of earners, see Hamilton, 1972, pp. 371, 375 ff., and for the German parallel, Hamilton, 1968, pp. 253, 255 ff.

variable for most of the analysis is not absolute family income (as is the case with most prior studies), but rather family income *divided by* an index of income needs based on family size. Thus, the very definition of economic well-being employed in this study recognizes the crucial importance of family composition: $15,000 divided between two people, in short, is a better income than $20,000 divided among four.

Several of the analyses reported in Morgan *et al.* are relevant to this discussion. One concerns the relative inconstancy of the various income fifths. Our discussion focuses on the upper fifth and emphasizes that, for many families, being in the upper fifth would be a transitory experience. Despite the imagery of the permanent poor, the same is also true of the lower fifth. In any given year, by definition, exactly 20% of all families are in the lower income fifth. Over the five years of the Morgan study, the proportion of families in the lower fifth at least one of the five years was about twice that (35%), and the proportion of total families in the bottom fifth all five years was only 9%. Although the parallel figures for the upper-income fifth are not reported, they would presumably be similar.

A family in the bottom fifth in any of the five years is taken in Morgan's analysis to be the target population. For the total, as indicated above, the probability of being in the target population is 35%, or about one in three. Consistent with our points, this probability is sharply curvilinear with age (Morgan and associates, 1974, p. 22), being in the 60%-and-up range for families with heads under age 25 or over 65, and sharply lower (roughly 20%) in the age 35–55 category. Changes in family composition are also strongly related to target population membership: in particular, women who became widowed, separated, or divorced over the five years had a better than 50–50 chance of being in the target population (p. 24). Male-headed households have a lower probability than female-headed households; families with no children have a lower probability than families with any children. Among female-headed households with children at home (comprised mainly of divorced and separated women), the probability of being in the target population was about six in ten.

Concerning specifically the cost of children, "the presence of children increases the family's chances of being in the target population. This is to be expected, in part because the definition of target population was made from a measure of income relative to family needs. These needs will increase with additional children and they will rarely be offset by increases in family income" (p. 26).

A later analysis focused on the persistently poor, namely, on the families in the bottom income fifth for all five years of the study (9% of the total, it will be recalled). Interestingly, the probability of being persistently poor is linearly related to age, being lowest among the youngest respondents, and highest among the old (p. 29). (In contrast, as noted earlier, the probability of being in the target population is curvilinear with age.) What this means, of course, is that for young people, being in the lower income fifth is a temporary condition: their incomes and financial well-being are destined to rise, as seniority, experience, job changes, and promotions accrue, consistent with the analysis reported in the text. Race was also strongly related to the probability of being persistently poor, the probability for blacks being about three times that for whites. For both blacks and whites, "the sex of the head of the household and whether there are children at home *matter most* in determining that family's chance of being persistently poor" (p. 30, our emphasis). The effects of life-cycle factors in this analysis are transparently obvious, being roughly equivalent in magnitude to the effect of race and substantially greater than the effect, for instance, of the education of the head.

By way of summary, the authors of the study offer the following comment: "The implications of these findings are clear. Change in [family] economic status is largely the result of major events such as entry into or exit from the labor force [e.g., retirement of the head, entry into the labor force of second or third earners, and so on], change in numbers of other earners, or change in family size. These changes dwarf any results from the head's wage increases or marginal changes in his working hours" (p. 42). And later, " . . . changes in family composition and the often related changes in labor force participation [among family members] dominate the changes in a family's economic well-being" (p. 99).

One may specify the earnings patterns in further detail. For this purpose it proves useful to focus on the job of the main earner, in most instances that being the husband and father, whose earnings provide the cornerstone of the family financial enterprise. Most jobs, seen over the course of a career, begin at relatively low rates of pay. They typically show fair-sized increases in the early years but quickly reach a plateau, after which no further increases follow. This is especially the case with respect to blue-collar jobs. Union contracts ordinarily stipulate flat rates, punch press operators, for example, receiving the same wages no matter what the age or the point in the life cycle. Where that is the case, virtually the entire life cycle effect depends on additional earners. The only exception to this generalization would involve added efforts by the main earner, either in the form of overtime hours or second jobs (moonlighting) when the family's financial needs increase. This basic pattern, we think, is also found with lower-middle-class jobs. They, too, show little variation in earnings over the course of the career.

A somewhat different pattern appears with respect to most upper-middle-class careers, where a series of planned upward steps accompanied by an increase in income usually occurs. Such would be the case with corporate executives, whose career plan would be evident from the first days in the executive training program. A similar plan is found in the universities. In some careers, moreover, a lateral move allows a start on a new and different hierarchy, or career line, one leading to still higher levels of income. This would be the case with the school teacher who shifts to administration or the engineer who becomes a line manager.

The upper middle class, in short, tends to escape the early leveling of the main earner's income, the pattern found in both lower middle and working classes. The upper middle class, effectively, forms the middle and upper echelons of organizational hierarchies. They may begin at some low point in the hierarchy, sometimes even in blue-collar or lower-middle-class positions, but they will normally continue their upward moves for some twenty or so years (Hamilton, 1972, pp. 339–340). Given the pyramidal structure of most such hierarchies and the consequent restriction of opportunity at the top, it follows that many will reach their plateau at that time; that is, in mid-career. Some, however, those destined for the higher ranks, will continue their upward climb. Their incomes will increase accordingly until just before retirement.

Second and third earners have rather different import for upper-middle-class families. Given the relatively large earning of the family head, the contributions of other earners are, at most times, less crucial for the family's well-being. Moreover, since most upper- and upper-middle-class children attend a college or university, their jobs will normally be part-time or part-year, hence their absolute contributions are generally smaller than would be the case with lower-middle or working-class children. The children of the upper-middle-class family, in other words, would contribute relatively little to the mid-career earnings peak. On the other hand, should upper-middle-class wives choose gainful employment, given their training and background, they would ordinarily, other things being equal, earn more than wives in the lower-middle and working classes. The heavy financial demands posed by children in college do, as we shall see, lead to considerable labor force participation by upper-middle-class wives.

Few studies allow for a precise delineation of these two kinds of careers. Questions are routinely put with regard to the current occupation; rarely does one find information about future opportunities, whether the job offers great expectations or only more of the same. An approximation to this aim, however, may be had by sorting main earners' occupations according to occupational prestige scores.[10] For this purpose, we have taken those in nonmanual occupations with scores of 60 and above as the upper middle class, and those with scores of 59 or less as the lower middle class. Also, we have taken only the married, full-time employed, nonfarm populations. These restrictions have been made so as to eliminate a number of consid-

---

[10]Prestige scores are routinely used in studies of mobility and achievement; typically, the scores range from 10 to 89, with higher numbers indicating more prestigious occupations. Originally, prestige scores for occupations were derived from surveys that asked people to rank various occupations according to their general prestige or esteem. More recently, these scores are developed out of the average education and earnings for the present incumbents of any given occupation. Over the range of occupations where direct comparisons are possible, the correlation between the two methods is on the order of .9. (Details on these prestige scores can be found in any of the NORC codebooks.)

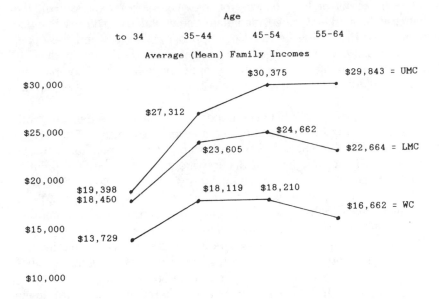

Chart 7.1. Family income by age and class. NORC General Social Survey 1975–1978, married, full-time employed non-farm respondents.

erations peripheral to the immediate point (such as the financial trials caused by separation and divorce). Wives, for this analysis, have been classified according to the husband's occupation.

The three patterns are shown in Chart 7.1. Upper-middle-class earnings show a rapid rise to the mid-point of the career. A modest falloff is indicated in the age 55-to-64 category, but this, as will be seen, hides a degree of diversity, with some continuing the upward climb and some, apparently, relaxing their effort. Both the lower-middle and working classes have more pronounced curvilinear patterns; that is to say, they both show greater declines in family incomes in the older age category. The line of differentiation between the upper middles and, effectively, the rest of the society provides the most important class division within the society.[11] This is

[11]For a previous discussion of this point, see Hamilton, 1972, Chapters 5 and 10.

A fair-sized difference, it will be noted, appears here between the lower-middle and working classes in their average earnings. That is largely a function of the way in which the lower middles have been defined. A rather high cutting point has been used, one that makes the lower-middle category almost three times the size of the upper-middle segment. Any such cutting line, of course, is arbitrary; the choice of a lower point would reduce the lower-middle-class averages and thus suggest a closer approximation to the working class with respect to life chances.

Some income overlap is to be found between most of the class categories. However, the matter of the blurring of class lines is not the point under discussion here.

speaking in terms of life chances, or, as Max Weber expressed it, the
"chance in the market." (Not evident here, something lost in these aggregate
figures, is the distinction between the upper middle class and the upper
class, those of independent wealth. That might be a more important division
but it is one involving perhaps only 1% of the population. By comparison,
the upper-middle-class masses easily constitute one fifth of the population).[12]

The income differences between upper middles and all others are moderate to large early in careers and continue to be so in the 35-to-44 age
category. But the differences widen considerably at mid-career and, because
of the smaller upper-middle-class decline, are greatest at the final point of
the active career. It seems likely that the life-style associated with the career,
the character of the major expenditures, would be different even at those
early points. Many in the upper middle class would know that large amounts
of surplus income were ahead of them and they could plan accordingly. For
the lower middle and working classes, however, the plan would not involve
ambitious spending early in the career, a mortgaging of one's future, since
there would be a clear recognition of the turnaround coming later.

One can pursue the analysis several steps further. Given the figures in the
chart, one would expect high levels of satisfaction within the upper middle
class (especially given the earlier finding of satiation effects). One would
expect less overall satisfaction in the other classes, particularly in the
working class. Moreover, one would expect sharp declines in satisfaction in
both the lower middle and working classes after the mid-career turnaround.
The actual results turn out to be different in many respects, some of these
being mere details, some rather fundamental.

The class differences in satisfaction, first of all, are not very pronounced.
Although the overall income differences are sizable, amounting to thousands
per year, the differences in satisfaction are modest. Dissatisfaction in the
upper middle class ran to 12%, as opposed to 17% in the lower middle class.
The blue-collar rank, with its markedly lower earnings, did, as one would
expect, show greater dissatisfaction, but the level here was only 25%. The
objective differences, in short, do not get translated into the "appropriate"
equivalent expressions of dissatisfaction. Another way of putting this would
be to note that the classes appear to have different frames of reference for the
interpretation of (or the assessment of) those income differences.

The level of satisfaction does increase with age, as expected, within the
upper middle class (Table 7.7). There is, however, an unexpected decline at
the point of peak earnings, which, we suspect, is linked to a somewhat
class-specific expenditure that comes at this point in the normal career—the
costs of a college education. Although a modest decline in income occurs

[12]See Weber, 1948, pp. 181–183. For a portrait of a man's rise from "mere"
upper-middle-class circumstances to the ranks of the national upper class, see
Rogow's biography of James Forrestal (1963).

Table 7.7. Financial Satisfaction and Trends by Class and Age: Combined
NORC General Social Survey: 1975–1978[a]

	Age			
Class and finances	34 or less	35–44	45–54	55–64
Satisfaction				
Upper middle class				
Pretty well	36%	49%	42%	55%
More or less	49	39	49	42
Not at all	15	12	9	3
N =	(109)	(86)	(66)	(33)
Lower middle class				
Pretty well	29%	36%	39%	47%
More or less	51	45	46	46
Not at all	20	19	15	7
N =	(323)	(228)	(199)	(124)
Working class				
Pretty well	27%	23%	41%	43%
More or less	49	48	42	44
Not at all	24	29	17	13
N =	(637)	(364)	(273)	(172)
Trends				
Upper middle class				
Better	68%	50%	44%	55%
Stayed the same	24	31	36	33
Worse	7	17	20	12
N =	(108)	(86)	(66)	(33)
Lower middle class				
Better	63%	56%	45%	57%
Stayed the same	25	29	36	31
Worse	12	15	19	12
N =	(325)	(228)	(274)	(172)
Working class				
Better	51%	38%	37%	38%
Stayed the same	33	36	41	45
Worse	16	26	22	16
N =	(638)	(363)	(274)	(172)

[a]Married, non-farm full-time employeds, wives classified by husband's occupation.

among the 55-to-64-year-olds, unexpectedly there is a substantial increase in reported satisfaction. We will have more to say on this finding after a brief review of the experience in the other classes.

Some unexpected findings appear in both the lower middle and working classes. Despite the pronounced decline of incomes in the age 55-to-64 category, these respondents show *increases* in satisfaction and *declines* in outright dissatisfaction. While, overall, the family incomes show this curvilinear pattern with age, the pattern of income satisfaction, generally, is one of linear improvement. That finding has a simple explanation. Although aggregate family income declines, per capita earnings within these families increase. It also seems likely that the amount of freely expendable earnings also increases as the mortgage payments wind down (along with any remaining payments on major household appliances, home furnishings, automobile, and so on). What at first looks like an unfortunate, a tragic outcome, a period of "hunkering down," to use a favorite Lyndon Johnson expression, turns out to be a period of some real improvement. Their circumstances are by no means as favorable as those of the upper middle class; at the same time, however, it is not a period of desolation and decline, of reduction of living standards and the quality of life.[13]

Looking at the statement of recent trends, one finds another specification of some interest and importance. Overall, we saw, there was a tendency for the reports of recent improvement to be highest among the young, and declining with age. Most of that decline, it was noted, was associated with an increase in the "stayed the same" response rather than with reports of worsening conditions. The upper-middle-class pattern shows some important variations on that trend. The reports of improvement are still highest among the young; in fact, they were the highest of all segments of the population, 68% reporting recent improvement. That percentage does decline in the next two categories, but then, in the age 55-to-64 category, reported improvement increases once again, going from 44 to 55%. Those initial changes are accompanied by an increase in the percentage reporting an actual worsening of conditions (versus a "staying the same" response), interestingly, among those whose actual incomes, as indicated in Chart 7.1, are showing considerable improvement. Note, for example, that the sense of things getting worse peaks, at 20%, in the 45- to 54-year-old segment of the upper middle class. Our guess (since it is impossible to establish the point with the data at hand) is that this results from what is probably the second largest expenditure in *these* families' lifetimes, the university education of their children. At the best schools during this period, the costs ran between $8000 and $10,000 per year, which would make a substantial dent in the finances even of someone earning $40,000 per year. If there were two or more children involved, it is clear that the financial squeeze would be considerable. In the age 55-to-64 group, however,

[13]See Glick, 1978, p. 58. One of us (RH) made the mistake, in a previous work, of taking family income figures at face value. On this basis, it was argued that the typical working-class career had "something of a tragic fate built into it. Instead of life getting 'better and better,' it improves to a point (even that being largely through the efforts of second earners), and from then on the trend is downward" (Hamilton, 1972, p. 376). But the actual reactions, as we see in Table 7.7, accord instead with the finding of Glick and the United States' Bureau of the Census researchers. In general, although incomes tend to decline in later years, income needs decline even more rapidly. On the import of family size in economic well-being, see also the Morgan study discussed in the text.

that episode would be behind them and enormous sums of freely expendable income would become available, hence the reports of
improvement.

A similar pattern appears in the lower middle class. That, we think,
reflects the same basic problems and the same dynamic. In this case,
a smaller proportion of families would be affected by the university education problem. Those with children in college would, for the
most part, be attending less prestigious and hence less costly
institutions.

In the case of the working class, the most frequent reports of recent improvement again appear in the youngest age category. After that, the reports of improvement are constant at 37–38% in the other age categories.
The more typical experience in this class is "stayed the same," the percentage giving this response showing a continuous increase and being the
modal case in the two older segments. Nowhere else in the table, it will be
noted, does this occur; for all other categories, improvement is the modal,
the most frequent experience.

Despite reports of widespread participation in university-level education,
something that supposedly involves all classes, the actual fact is quite
different. There is only a limited minority involvement on the part of
working-class children, and it is typically temporary and in less prestigious
institutions. Most frequently, that means attendance for a year of two at a
local community college or in one of the units of the state college system.
The costs of such institutions are modest. While many people would
automatically add on room-and-board costs, many working-class university
students live at home.[14]

The changing circumstances of families over the life cycle may be seen
directly by looking at the number of earners at each point (data not shown).
For all classes, there is a significant increase in the percentages of three or
more earners up to the 45-to-54 age category, after which there is an equally
significant falloff. The respective figures for the upper middle class, for

[14]For a review of some relevant studies on the working class experience in
colleges and universities, see Hamilton and Wright, 1975b, and 1981, and the
references therein cited.

Some sense of the "flows" from social classes into higher education can be had
from the 1977 NORC survey (or, for that matter, any other survey with questions on
both fathers' occupations and respondents' educations). For this purpose, we sorted
all respondents in the survey by class origins, according to whether the reported
occupation of the respondent's father was white collar (middle-class origin) or blue
collar or farm. Among those of middle-class origins, 62% have had one or more year
of schooling beyond high school, 33% of them having earned at least a B.A. degree.
Among those of working class or farm origins, 20% reported one or more years of
college, and 9% earned at least a B.A. Thus, relatively few working-class families
ever bear the cost of college education for their children. Note that the result for the
middle class reported here combines both the upper and lower segments. Among the
children of the *upper* middle class, the proportion attending college would have to
be on the order of 75% or more.

example, are 0, 16, 31, and 12%. In the working class, the involvement of wives and children in the labor force begins earlier, the respective figures there being 3, 26, 30, and 15%. Upper-middle-class families have their heaviest labor force involvement in the age 45-to-54 category, nearly four of every five families there having two or more persons in gainful employment. This suggests something of the pressure and strain imposed by the demand for the university education. Labor force participation in the older upper-middle-class segment falls off sharply, a majority of the families at that point having only a single earner. This was the only age-class segment showing that traditional pattern.

The following conclusions seem justified. The alarmist imagery of economic desperation and steadily worsening conditions during the 1970's receives no serious support in the evidence presented here. One quarter of the population reported dissatisfaction with their finances, a level that was more or less constant throughout the decade. A larger proportion, approximately one third of the total, reported that they were pretty well satisfied with their earnings, the remainder saying more or less satisfied. Similar findings appear with respect to the reports on recent trends, the most frequent declaration being that things had stayed the same. Again, despite the assertion of continually worsening conditions, the evidence shows an entirely different pattern: at all points throughout the decade, reports of improvement far outnumber the reports of things getting worse. The pattern, of course, is not constant, but is punctuated by modest de facto declines in the two recession years, 1975 and 1980.

One might well ask: If most people are at least more or less satisfied with their financial circumstances, and if more people report things getting better than getting worse, why have the media and various commentators inundated us with claims of squeeze and strain, with depictions of perpetually deteriorating (and potentially explosive) economic conditions? The answer, we feel, is simple: the truth in these matters would not make very good copy and would command little readership or attention. Imagine the story in *Time* magazine that ran, "Despite double-digit inflation and the highest unemployment rate in years, most of the American population continues to be satisfied with its personal financial situation, and more people report that their situation is improving than report the reverse."

A second factor involves the difference between numbers and percentages. If one quarter of the population reports some dissatisfaction with their income, that translates into roughly 20 *million* households, of which interviews with six or eight would typically be sufficient for an average *Time* or *US News and World Report* story. With a little diligent searching, in short, one can easily find dozens of families whose conditions, for various reasons, are strained and who are upset and anxious. Given a predisposition toward the flashy and dramatic lead, in other words, the necessary supporting material will always be readily and widely available, even when the percentages in question are small. Unless one took the trouble to inspect the relevant percentage distributions, one would never know the atypicality of the experiences being reported.

As we have already discussed, much of the media's "inflation" report-age in the 1970's focused on the supposed (and ill-defined) middle class squeeze, a rather direct variant on the revolt of the little man theme reviewed in earlier chapters. The data reviewed here show no serious support for this theme; on the contrary, dissatisfaction (and reports of worsening conditions) is most frequent in the lower-income brackets, a conclusion that should occasion little surprise. It is more surprising, perhaps, that the relationship is not more pronounced. The weakness of that linkage, basically, stems from the responses in the low-income categories where many declared themselves either pretty well or more or less satisfied. Some explanations for this "false consciousness" were provided: small household units, retired and widowed populations, and populations living in small towns and rural areas.

These findings do not in any way deny the very real financial strains experienced by millions of American families. They do emphasize, however, that strain is a relative thing. Much is written, for example, about the low incomes of the old, about the strain associated with retirement and pensions, and the difficulties of life on Social Security. In contrast, relatively little is written about the lesser income *needs* of older persons: the sharply reduced number of dependents, the consequent reduction in housing needs, in clothing and food costs, and so on. However straitened the objective circumstances of the aged might be, only a relatively small percentage pronounce themselves not at all satisfied with their financial situation. And who, in the last analysis, is in a better position to judge?[15]

Family income, we have seen, has a distinctive curvilinear relationship with age. Satisfaction with income, however, unexpectedly shows a general increase with age. The explanation for this paradox, it has been noted, is an increase in per capita income up to retirement. The patterns differ somewhat by class, the upper middle class having by far the most advantageous pattern of the three we have described.

The meaning of a high income would vary considerably from one group to another. For some families in the high income category, that result is a function of the main earner's income. For others, it results from the efforts of three or four earners. In the latter case, the accomplishment is short-lived and destined to end when the grown children set out on their own.

The meaning of low income will also vary considerably, depending on its cause. Some part of that poverty is a result of a history of slavery, discrim-

[15]We do not in any way wish to denigrate the condition of those suffering privations. One does not help those persons by propagating wildly exaggerated claims about the extent of poverty or mistaken claims about its location. Although much of this chapter reports the extent to be smaller than is generally reported, 1% of the sample, it should be remembered, represents a large number of persons. Including dependents, it would mean more than two million persons.

ination, and planned disadvantage, the effects of which persist long after the legal fact. Some are poor because of broken marriages and the breakup of normal financial arrangements. And some have low incomes because of their position in the life cycle, being either very young and just starting out on a career, or being elderly and in retirement. The former, as we have seen, report considerable improvement in their condition over the last few years. Should the age–income pattern repeat itself, they would seem destined, most of them, regardless of class, to experience considerable improvement up to at least the 35-to-44 age range. And the elderly, as we have repeatedly seen, report relatively high levels of satisfaction and rather stable trends over the last few years.

Several conclusions of practical importance follow from these findings. Solutions for the problem of poverty ought to be differentiated, depending on the source. The creation of an all-purpose safety net to guarantee a minimum income would help some people who, on the whole, do not appear to be seriously in need (those being persons at the beginning and end stages of the adult life cycle).

Monies given are also monies taken; any egalitarian move, in short, is going to involve a cost to some other group. It is easy to say that such monies should be taken from the rich (or the well-off). But if that is done blindly, without recognition of the diverse sources of well-being, such attempts may easily stimulate some unexpected results. Taking hard-earned income from well-off multiearner families of the lower middle and working classes would, no doubt, stimulate some very hostile reactions. The generous provision of welfare without an equitable tax arrangement puts many persons with basically liberal outlooks in a position of some strain. This is well exemplified in the case of California's Proposition 13, where many people found themselves voting for a measure that, on the one hand, promised to ameliorate their own position but, on the other, appeared to have very serious illiberal implications.[16] There is, of course, a more attractive alternative— more precisely designed programs with remedies appropriate to the specific problems, ones that do not shift burdens in such a way as to undermine the entire effort.

[16]California state law requires a regular reassessment of all real estate. In a period of booming property values, this meant continuous and sizable increases in valuations. Ordinarily, one might expect the local authorities to reduce tax rates accordingly, but such was not the case. Instead, many generous politicians saw those steadily increasing revenues as the basis for their exuberant plans (welfare, education, local facilities, and so on). People who, a decade earlier, had bought "ordinary" three-bedroom houses now found themselves the owners of property assessed at eight and ten times the original purchase price. Liberal professors throughout the state found themselves paying taxes on houses assessed at $250,000–$300,000, and, after some struggle of conscience, voted for Proposition 13. This did not amount to a conservative reaction; they were still liberals. It was just that they, for the first time, apparently, had faced up to the question of costs (see Musgrave, 1979; Scott, Grasmick, and Eckert, 1981). For more discussion of the matter, see Chapter 8.

Turning to another range of practical implications, one may note that, for several reasons, a revolt of the little man seems an unlikely possibility. The notion assumes dissatisfaction with household finances to be both widespread and serious. Both assumptions, we have seen, prove to be rather doubtful. The base for such a revolt, at the outset, is limited (if one takes the "not too satisfied," it is, at best, one out of four persons). But then, too, we saw that the seriousness of complaint ran the gamut from very modest concerns to very grievous ones; not all of the dissatisfied, in short, were ready for a general uprising. Another consideration that would reduce the potential for such revolt is the very diversity of the forces in question— blacks, divorced and separated women, young people, and old people are not easily aggregated into one cohesive movement. Still another difficulty facing such a coalition is posed by the temporary presence of many persons in these categories. The young are on the move—to middle age and to much improved circumstances; most of the separated and divorced, so it would appear, are anxious to change their status and, once again, to be married. Unlike the more traditional or conventional conceptions of a class, the category of "little men" does not have a permanent or even a relatively stable constituency.

Such a collection of forces could, at best, give rise to the appearance of temporary negative coalitions, relatively large numbers of persons who, for very diverse reasons, would vote against a party, or against candidates, or against specific measures. Such appears to have been the case with Proposition 13 and with some of its variants elsewhere. But those "shots" by themselves do not provide the basis for a new and different political direction. A negative coalition allows a collective veto; power, and the direction of public affairs, still remains in the hands of other forces.

8 THE LARGER CONCERNS

To this point, our principal focus has been the immediate personal concerns of the American adult population. That focus is limited, clearly, in that it overlooks any concern with larger problems, those lying beyond the immediate milieu, beyond the family, the household, the neighborhood, and the job. In this chapter, we explore the public's concerns with problems located in more distant settings.

Except for personal finances, as we have seen, generally high levels of satisfaction are reported with most aspects of the immediate milieu. As will be seen, however, considerable dissatisfaction is expressed with respect to some of the "distant" features of the society, especially with respect to the performance of the government. This constellation of concerns, satisfaction with one's immediate life and dissatisfaction with distant institutions, is nowhere indicated in the six analyses of the 1970's reviewed in our opening chapter. Before considering any theoretical implications, however, a review of evidence on this basic point is in order.

CONCERNS, OUTLOOKS, ISSUES

It is useful to begin our account of the larger concerns with a brief review of what people see as the important problems facing this country today. Evidence on the point was reviewed in Chapter 2 (in the Scammon and Wattenberg discussion) and again at the end of Chapter 3. Most credible evidence shows that from approximately 1966 through 1973, the war in Vietnam was, by consensus, the most important national problem. With the end of American involvement in that war, concern over Vietnam predictably faded, being replaced mainly by concerns over inflation, unemployment, taxes, the high cost of living, and related economic matters. All survey series through 1980 show the economic situation to be the leading national concern.

Tom Smith (1980) has reviewed 30 years of data from the Gallup series on most important national problems, covering the period 1946 through 1976. This review documents considerable over-time variability in the response to Gallup's question. Smith's summary of his findings bears quoting at length:

> Remarkable shifts have occurred in the ranking of problems over the last four decades. At the end of World War II concerns dealing with reconversion to a peacetime economy, shortages, the termination of price controls, and lingering fears of a return of the Great Depression combined to make economics the dominant problem. As the Cold War heated up in 1947 and 1948, however, more and more attention shifted to foreign affairs. This trend was briefly broken in 1949, when the passing of the immediate postwar crises and the onset of America's first postwar recession swung concern back to economics. After this hiatus, foreign affairs generally dominated the picture from 1950 to 1963, ranking first in 43 of the 45 surveys and usually commanding a plurality of from 35 to 50 percent. During this period economics remained a strong and persistent second, briefly overtaking foreign affairs during the 1954 and 1958 recessions (and coming close during the 1960–61 recession). In 1963, however, the reign of foreign affairs was challenged by the explosive eruption of the civil rights movement. Civil rights ranked as the most important problem for most of the next two years until foreign affairs, boosted by the Vietnam War, regained dominance in 1965. From 1965 until 1970 the Vietnam issue and other international problems generally topped the problem lists. The single break occurred in August 1967, when that long hot summer of riots pushed social control to first place. Over the next two and a half years (1970–1973) the situation became very fluid. The 14 available data points show foreign affairs on top 6 times, social control 5 times, and economics 3 times. Finally, in 1973, economics emerged as the most important problem, and persists as such down to the present (Smith, pp. 166–167).

The essential point to note in Smith's account is that the rise and fall of concerns on this larger agenda correspond more or less sensitively to the appearance of those developments on the national or world political scene. Economic concerns increase in periods of recession or inflation and fade at other times. The appearance of foreign affairs as public concerns corresponds directly to the outbreak of foreign crises and, with even more insistence, to the nation's involvement in military conflicts. In like fashion, as was discussed in Chapter 2, race relations and civil rights appear on the lists in more or less direct response to outbreaks of racial violence or turmoil. There is some underlying rationality in this: people focus on whichever pot is boiling most vigorously at the moment.

There is an obvious mass media role in this process; most of those distant events that appear to determine the general consensus about important national problems are matters about which the population would know little or nothing were it not for media coverage. An important implication follows: through their choices in reporting, the media have considerable influence on popular views about what are the central or urgent concerns. Their's is, indeed, an agenda setting function. Some room for error is possible in this process; a mistaken judgment, the easy (or gullible) acceptance of source material, or collective misperception could, of course, lead to a corresponding error within the general audience.[1]

In contrast to the obvious historical variability revealed in popular judgments about the most important *national* problem, our review of the evidence on most important *personal* problems showed an impressive continuity from one decade to the next. In the private realm, the most frequent response has always been some concern with the financial well-being of the individual and/or family. As we saw in the previous chapter, financial problems were not always, nor even usually, sources of extreme discontent; the problem was the enhancement of what, for most, was an already satisfactory standard of living, or, a second possibility, the protection of that standard against erosion. The financial concern itself, apart from the matter of salience, seems ever-present on the agenda of personal worries. In contrast, the same issues—the economic issues—are present as a national *concern* mainly during recessions and periods of inflation.

This contrast leads to the first major substantive conclusion to be advanced in this chapter, namely, that most people make a sharp distinction between the public and private spheres.[2] Different problem agendas appear in those spheres, and, in all likelihood, there are different assessments of urgency or salience. This means, among other things, that the comprehensive, overall, or total judgments provided by some critics (by those, for example, who affirm the alienation or powerlessness of modern man) are

---

[1]First, an episode that goes back more than half a century. Adolph Ochs, publisher of the *New York Times'*, spent an evening with the head of the *Times'* Washington bureau, Richard Oulahan. During the evening, Ochs discussed monetary problems and showed a special interest in silver. Ochs' concern so impressed Oulahan that he began to contribute stories dealing with "the silver question." Given the Oulahan authority, these stories, of course, appeared on the front page of the *Times*. Other *Times* correspondents recognized that silver was big news, that something was happening there, and they began to write stories on the subject. The *Times* office in New York, seeing the large number of silver stories now appearing, concluded that the subject was more improtant than they had previously believed. They responded by giving special attention to all subsequent stories about silver (see Rosten, 1937, pp. 233–234). Rosten reports several other instances of reporters mistakenly "sensing" policy.

The Oulahan episode amounts to making something out of nothing, but it had no special impact or consequence. A much more serious case involves the reporting of the 1968 Tet offensive in the midst of the Vietnam war. At the time, it was widely reported in the American press as a Viet Cong victory (and, of course, a defeat for the South Vietnam government and its American allies). This reading of the outcome had a great impact in changing the direction of the American commitment there. Some recent analysis, however, has argued the opposite—that the offensive ended with a serious military defeat for the Viet Cong. See Braestrup, 1977, and Lesher, 1982.

On the agenda-setting function of the mass media, see Shaw and McCombs, 1977; and Erbring, Goldenberg, and Miller, 1980.

[2]The same point has been made by others, among them Rourke, Free, and Watts (1976), Watts and Free (1978), Andrews and Withey (1976), Lipset (1979b), and Lipset and Schneider (1983).

mistaken. Many people, clearly, make a differentiated assessment, the dominant response in the 1970's being one of private satisfaction (economics again excepted) combined with a sense of dissatisfaction with the more distant, and less easily controlled, realm of national affairs.

Some sense of the importance of this distinction may be found in Chapter 2, in our discussion of Scammon and Wattenberg. There, we compared results from two polls taken only one month apart, the first asking about personal problems, the second about national problems. Those polls were done in 1967. At that time, not surprisingly, Vietnam was most often cited as the most pressing national problem, being mentioned by 52%. In contrast, the proportion mentioning Vietnam as their most important personal problem was a slender 5%. As in all other polls and surveys we have examined, the leading personal problem in 1967 was the high cost of living or some related economic concern, such matters being mentioned by roughly three out of five respondents. Only one respondent in six mentioned economic issues as the most important national problem at that time. Clearly, there is no automatic transfer of the personal problems, presumably the more pressing of the two, onto the national agenda; the choices made, for the most part, reflect different sets of determinants.

The 1976 SRC election study, which contains both the "personal problems" and the "national problems" questions, is also useful in this connection. Data for the first of those questions were presented in Chapter 3 (Table 3.2). There, we noted that the modal response was inflation, unemployment, or some related economic issue, these being mentioned as the leading personal problems by 46%. At that time, the proportion mentioning one of those economic concerns as the leading *national* problem was much higher, about 75%. The cross-tabulation of the two questions is shown in Table 8.1.

Inflation and unemployment are, far and away, the leading choices for most important national problem, *irrespective of the respondent's most important personal problem*. The most frequent mention of these matters as a national problem, to be sure, comes from those reporting personal economic problems. But that figure, 78%, is only marginally higher than those found for some of the other groups shown in Table 8.1. In no group does the proportion mentioning national economic problems fall below two thirds. These findings indicate that many people do not define national concerns in a narrow or self-interested way. The lesson is one of openness, of generous altruistic concern.

A second lesson, a peripheral one here, is a reiteration of a point made earlier concerning the distinctly secondary position of the entire package of social issues. Crime is mentioned by one respondent in twelve. The only component of that package receiving significant mention within the "all others" category is race, and that by only 1%. Even with a favorable reading of the evidence, the economic and social concerns stand in a ratio of 75 to 10.

Those people citing economics as the leading national problem in 1976

Table 8.1. The Overlap between Personal and National Concerns: SRC 1976 Election Study

Most important national problem	Most important personal problem						
	None	Family/self	Job	Economic	Health	Others	Total
Economics: inflation, unemployment	77%	69%	73%	78%	70%	67%	75%
Crime, law-and-order	8	10	6	6	10	15	8
Foreign affairs, defense	1	7	8	6	7	6	6
Government functioning	4	4	4	3	5	5	4
Social welfare	4	3	3	4	3	6	4
All others	7	6	7	3	5	2	4
$N =$	(287)	(238)	(163)	(778)	(117)	(128)	(1711)
$\% =$	17	14	9	46	7	8	101

(three out of four persons, it will be noted) formed a rather diverse constituency. Only about half of them mentioned economic questions as their leading personal problem; the remaining half touched on a wide variety of other matters or indicated no personal problems. Looking at the matter in yet another way, the people for whom some economic problem was both the leading public concern *and* the leading personal concern represented only slightly more than a third (36%) of the adult population. Roughly two fifths (39%) cited economics as the leading national problem but mentioned some other personal concern. The remaining fourth fell into two further segments: those who felt the economic issue as a personal concern but saw some other issue as the most important problem facing the nation (10%), and those— perhaps the true postmaterialists—who saw economics as neither the leading personal nor the leading national problem (15%). Thus, even at a time of presumably high overlap of public and personal concerns, the convergence of agendas was characteristic of only a little more than one third of the population.

Before proceeding with the direct line of exposition, a small digression may prevent some misinterpretation. It is easy to think in terms of simple equations: a concern (as used here) is equal to a demand, and a cluster of demands made by any large segment of the population will equal a political issue. These equations, with their assumptions of automaticity, have an atmospheric presence in democratic societies, so much so that even self-announced critical scholars sometimes accept those conclusions without evident qualms.

If by the term concern we are referring to a felt or sensed problem, it is clear that the feeling or sense, by itself, is not the same as a demand; that is, something sought as a right, as a requirement of simple justice. Some problems are (or are seen as) insoluble; some are simply lived with. Some are so large as to discourage any demand; they seem to defy any solution. As for the second equation, even though concerns may be widely or generally known (say, through public opinion polls), it is not automatic that they become political issues—for the simple reason that the major political parties may choose not to make them issues. On the local level, for example, a party of landlords is not likely to make rent control an issue, even though it would be a clear winner with an electorate made up, overwhelmingly, of tenants. In nineteenth-century United States, both major parties apparently conspired to avoid a winning issue, a response to an evident mass demand for currency inflation.

Some theories of democracy assume an ease of expression that is rather unrealistic. With basic freedoms, speech, assembly, and press, some contend that any mass concern will be expressed and make itself heard. But that overlooks the cost factors (time, effort, money) and the possibility that some listeners (political leaders) do not wish to hear, or, having heard, do not wish to respond. There is, inevitably, a class bias in the process; less privileged groups will always find it difficult to gain adequate expression of their wishes. Another line of democratic theory focuses on competing parties; if one party fails to respond to a concern (or demand), another will. The fact of competition thus forces all contending parties to pay attention to public wants. But the presumed ineluctable constraint may under some circumstances be circumvented. Through collusion, both (or all major) parties may agree not to respond to a demand, not to make it an issue. Still another argument of democratic theory assumes "anticipated reactions." Recognizing the absence of mobilizing efforts at or near the grass roots, some have argued that politicians anticipate the demands present there and react accordingly, without any significant manifest pressures from below being required. But this argument assumes both a knowledge of the mass demands and a will to respond. Both assumptions, obviously, may be put to an empirical test; some recent evidence casts doubt on both claims, at least in their extreme, necessitarian formulation.

A few recent instances provide a serious challenge to all three lines of argument. Were mass sentiment (as either concern or demand) the decisive force in the American democracy, the nation would have: (1) prayers in public schools, (2) no forced school busing, and (3) national gun registration. Solutions to the problems of the economy, to the high level of inflation, moreover, would have been the leading subject of discussion in all elections of the 1970's in the United States, as well as in most other economically advanced nations.[3]

A simple lesson is contained here: public concerns alone do not cause things to happen; they do not determine issue agendas; they do not compel reactions by democratic governments. Many concerns appear to "lie fallow." They are simply there, and could provide the basis for mobilization; but, by themselves, they are mere facts with no compelling or imminent implications.

Another possible source of misinterpretation also deserves some consideration and analysis. It would be easy to assume that the economic concerns discussed above would lead in a given political direction. In the normal course of things, liberals (or leftists) tend to see those concerns as fitting in with some version of their program; persons reporting economic problems, in short, are seen as likely recruits for a liberal (or left) constituency. In recent years, however, some alternative readings have been propounded, which assume that, because of the increased burden of welfare state costs, a

---

[3]For an earlier discussion of the concern-issue distinction, see Hamilton, 1972, pp. 83–85. For a criticism of the claim that party competition forces responsiveness, see the same source, Chapter 1. A more general theoretical statement of this position may be found in Wittman, 1973. A useful empirical study of politicians' motives and reactions to the public wishes may be found in Prewitt, 1970. For a discussion and analysis of "anticipated reactions," see Gregory, 1969; see also Eulau and Prewitt, 1973.

conservative reaction has developed.[4] Although seldom discussed, another option would be an immobilization thesis; lacking any clear and obvious linkage between the problem and the many putative solutions available, many people would be moved neither one way nor the other. An a priori conclusion, under the circumstances, is obviously unsatisfactory.

Actually, the linkage between economic concerns and political outlooks proves to be fairly weak even on issues where one might anticipate a relatively strong relationship, as with those questions concerning government guarantees of jobs and good living standards and government-subsidized medical insurance (Table 8.2). The differences between the three groups expressing some kind of economic concern (that is, for self and nation, self only, and nation only) are minuscule. Where one might expect some special liberal sentiment among the first group, presumably the most concerned of the three (as opposed, say, to those expressing only commiserative feelings), there are, for all practical purposes, no differences. Only in the fourth group, among those who mention no economic problems in either arena, does any "distinctiveness" in outlook appear; they are noticeably more *conservative* than the others.

The character of the distributions should also be noted. Only 22% of the first group classified themselves as liberal in response to a question on general political position; almost one half opposed any federal government guarantee of a job and good living standard; and even with respect to government-subsidized medical care, those in favor exceeded those opposed only by a slight margin. The expression of an economic concern, in short, does not indicate the presence of (or the basis for) a broad liberal coalition.

In summary, then, the three quarters majority who saw the leading national problem to be economic, were divided among themselves by personal involvement, by general political stance, and by positions on two specific plans for the solution of economic problems. It is not the case, clearly, that 75% of the nation's adult population were pressing the government for a specific plan, program, or even direction of activity.

The small group who did not mention economics as either a personal or a national concern were clearly not postmaterialists, at least not as conceived by Inglehart. Compared to the others, they were somewhat more conservative. This group, not surprisingly, is more affluent than the others. Their outlooks are more in line with classical assumptions about the rich (indifference, obtuseness) than with Inglehart's revisionism.

It is useful, for several reasons, to undertake a more extended examination of some of these indicators. The principal reason is to allow some assessment of trends. The 1976 data, after all, capture opinion only at a single time and might, therefore, hide a significant trend. Indeed, some commentators have

---

[4]This, for example, is the predicted reaction to the economic issue in the theory of the little man's revolt. See Chapter 1 for discussion.

Table 8.2. Personal and National Problem by Liberal-Conservative Self-Rating and Welfare State Issues: SRC Election Study–1976

	Respondent cites an economic issue as most important problem to			
	Self and nation	Self only	Nation only	Neither
Self-rating as Liberal-Con-servative[a]				
Liberal (1–3)	22%	25%	26%	20%
Moderate (4)	41	36	34	31
Conservative (5–7)	37	39	39	48
% =	100	100	99	99
N =	(445)	(118)	(476)	(186)
100% =	36%	10%	39%	15%
Guaranteed job and living standard[b]				
Favor (1–3)	28	24	28	24
Neutral (4)	26	27	20	21
Opposed (5–7)	46	49	52	55
% =	100	100	100	100
N =	(501)	(139)	(549)	(217)
Support for government-sub-sidized medical care[c]				
Favor (1–3)	45	44	43	34
Neutral (4)	14	10	14	10
Opposed (5–7)	41	45	43	55
% =	100	99	100	99
N =	(503)	(135)	(533)	(210)

[a]The question reads: "We hear a lot of talk these days about liberals and conservatives. Here is a seven-point scale on which the political views that people might hold are arranged from extremely liberal to extremely conservative. Where would you place yourself on this scale?"

[b]The question reads: "Some people feel that the government in Washington should see to it that every person has a job and a good standard of living. Suppose that these people are at one end of this scale—at point number 1. Others think the government should just let each person get ahead on his own. Suppose these people are at the other end—at point number 7. And, of course, some peole have opinions in between. Where would you place yourself on this scale?"

[c]The question reads: "There is much concern about the rapid rise in medical and hospital costs. Some feel there should be a government insurance plan which would cover all medical and hospital expenses. Others feel that medical expenses should be paid by individuals and through private insurance like Blue Cross. Where would you place yourself on this scale?"

argued just this, noting that the radicalism of the early 1970's had yielded to a rising tide of conservatism later in the decade. This was attested to, so it has been claimed, by the vote for Proposition 13 and other tax revolt referenda, by the election of a moderate Democrat, Jimmy Carter, in 1976, and then by the election of a conservative Republican, Ronald Reagan, in 1980 and 1984. Also in the 1980 election, even more telling evidence, the United States Senate gained a Republican majority for the first time since 1954.

But such indicators are open to considerable question (as was seen, for example, in our discussion of Proposition 13 in the preceding chapter). Elections prove to be, at best, ambiguous indicators of opinion. Many issues are present in a campaign, making it difficult to say what the specific causes of any voter shifting were. Even a simple question—Was it a vote for the winner, or a vote against the loser?—cannot be determined through assessment of aggregate voting results. Many electoral victories, moreover, are based on small, even minuscule shifts in voter preferences; a new tide of opinion, for example, may depend on a net shift of a percentage point or two within the total vote.[5] Such shifts become even less portentous when it is recognized that we are ordinarily focusing on *an electorate*; in the United States, typically, that means a segment that is considerably smaller than the adult citizen population. The opinions of the vast numbers of nonvoters, in short, are nowhere signaled in those results.[6] Fortunately, it is not necessary to rely on remote indicators with rather ambiguous implications, since the available survey series contain a wealth of direct information on the topic.

[5]Grover Cleveland was the first Democrat elected to the presidency since 1856. The historian Allen Nevins argued that Cleveland's election, in 1884, resulted from a vast wave of moral outrage over the Republicans' nomination of the morally tainted James G. Blaine. The historian Lee Benson went to the election figures and discovered that the wave of reaction had the smallest ripples in all of American electoral history, the shift vis-à-vis the previous election amounting to only a fraction of 1%. More precisely, the outcome was determined by a shift in one state, New York. There, it too depended on a fraction, something determined by a minuscule shift to a prohibitionist splinter party and/or by the rain on election day that lowered the turnout in heavily Republican upstate counties. (See Benson, 1957, pp. 123–146.)

When the Republicans gained the Senate majority in 1980, for the first time since 1954, this too was taken as signifying a wave of reaction. The voting evidence again suggests more of a ripple, or at best, an eddy. One victorious Republican won with 45% against two liberal opponents. Three Republicans won with 50% in straight fights; another five won with 51%, and two won with 52%. The majority, in short, was based on very slim margins *of the electors*.

[6]The electorate, in recent years, has, at maximum, amounted to only a little more than one half of the voting age population. In 1980, for example, the votes cast for president amounted to 52.6% of that total. (If one took the percentage on the basis of eligible voters, thereby excluding noncitizen populations, the figure would be somewhat higher; but "citizen population" seems an inaccessible figure for the United States census). In off-year elections, electoral participation is much lower. In 1978, for example, it was 34.9%. At that rate, approximately one fifth of the adult population could determine the outcome (United States Bureau of the Census, 1982, p. 489).

Two useful indicators of trends in mass political thinking are the self-rating as to liberalism or conservatism and party identification; trend data on both, taken from the NORC series, are shown in Table 8.3. In sharp contrast to the depictions of massive changes or rising tides, the data reveal only modest changes, ones best summarized as very small.

The self-ratings do show some limited support for the rising conservatism theme. Between 1974 (when the question first appeared in the series) and 1980, the proportion of the adult population identifying themselves as conservatives increased *by exactly four percentage points*. (Self-identified liberals showed a corresponding decline in the same period.) A trend of this small magnitude is hardly of world-historical importance and is not appropriately depicted as a rising tide. An additional "rivulet" of conservatism would seem more appropriate. It should also be noted that although much of our thinking tends to be in terms of the polar extremes—liberalism or conservatism—the most frequent choice in response to such questions has always been an in-between, moderate or middle-of-the-road position. That is the modal choice in all six studies reported in Table 8.3.

A similar Gallup series spanned the period from April 1972 to September 1980. Their question read: "People who are conservative in their political views are referred to as being right of center and people who are liberal in their political views are referred to as being left of center. Which one of the categories best describes your political position?" Respondents were handed a card containing these options: Far left, substantially left, moderately left, just slightly left of center, just lightly right of center, moderately right of center, substantially right of center, far right. The Gallup finding was an 8% decline in liberal identification accompanied by an 8% decline in conservative identification. The gain, of course, was entirely in the center categories. (These results are reported in *Public Opinion* magazine, February/March 1981, p. 20.)

It would be a mistake to see these identifications as fixed, stable, or as reflecting basic commitments. For many people, they appear to have little meaning. An alternative question used by the NORC in 1978 had the following wording: "Where would you place yourself on this scale, or haven't you thought much about this?" Sixteen percent said they had not thought much about this. The results also fluctuate considerably depending on the specific options presented. A study done for *Time* magazine by Yankelovich, Skelly, and White in 1980 asked: "Do you think of yourself as: Conservative, Moderate, Liberal, Radical?" This yielded the respective results: 44, 41, 13, and 2%.

Some sense as to *where* those categories are meaningful appears in an election study done by ABC News in 1980. The poorly educated populations tended to describe themselves as moderate. It was in the highly educated categories that the moderate choice diminished and the overwhelming majority chose either the liberal or conservative options. The respective percentages identifying as liberal, moderate, or conservative were: for those

Table 8.3. Trends in Liberal–Conservative Self Ratings and Party Identification, 1970–1980: NORC General Social Surveys and SRC Election Studies

	1970	1972	1973	1974	1975	1976	1977	1978	1980
Self-rating as[a]									
Liberal (1–3)	—	—	—	30%	30%	29%	29%	28%	26%
Moderate (4)	—	—	—	40	40	40	39	38	40
Conservative (5–7)	—	—	—	30	30	31	32	34	34
% =	—	—	—	100	100	100	100	100	100
N =	—	—	—	(1410)	(1397)	(1401)	(1453)	(1453)	(1429)
Party Identification[b]—NORC									
Strong Democrat	—	21%	16%	18%	17%	15%	18%	14%	13%
Weak Democrat	—	28	27	27	24	27	26	26	26
Independent Democratic leaning	—	10	13	15	14	14	13	13	13
Independent	—	10	10	10	14	16	12	15	17
Independent Republican leaning	—	7	10	8	8	7	9	9	8
Weak Republican	—	15	15	15	16	14	15	16	15
Strong Republican	—	8	9	8	6	6	7	7	8
% =	—	99	100	101	99	99	100	100	100
N =	—	(1538)	(1431)	(1402)	(1473)	(1491)	(1513)	(1517)	(1456)

Party identification[c]—SRC										
Strong Democrat	20%	—	15%	—	18%	—	15%	—	15%	18%
Weak Democrat	24	—	26	—	21	—	25	—	24	23
Independent, Democratic leaning	10	—	11	—	13	—	12	—	14	11
Independent	13	—	13	—	15	—	15	—	14	13
Independent, Republican leaning	8	—	11	—	9	—	10	—	10	10
Weak Republican	15	—	13	—	14	—	14	—	13	14
Strong Republican	9	—	10	—	8	—	9	—	8	9
Apolitical	1	—	1	—	3	—	1	—	3	2
N =	(1501)		(2694)		(2505)		(2850)		(2283)	(1614)

[a]The question reads: "We hear a lot of talk these days about liberals and conservatives. I'm going to show you a seven-point scale on which the *political* views that people might hold are arranged from extremely liberal—point 1—to extremely conservative—point 7. Where would you place yourself on this scale?"

[b]The question reads: "Generally speaking, do you usually think of yourself as a Republican, Democrat, Independent, or what?" Persons responding with a party label were asked to indicate the strength of their attachment; persons responding "Independent" were asked whether they leaned toward the Republican or Democratic party.

[c]Table 2.1, p. 81 of *The American National Election Studies Data Sourcebook, 1952–1978*, W. E. Miller, A. H. Miller, and E. J. Schneider, Cambridge: Harvard University Press, 1980. The 1980 data are taken from the study codebook.

of grade school education: 21, 47, and 32%; for those with postgraduate university education: 36, 23, and 41%. The liberal-conservative categories, then, appear to be those preferred by the highly educated. The use of those terms and their application to the rest of the population, therefore, would represent something of an imposition, a read-in. (All of these findings appear in the issue of *Public Opinion* cited above, pp. 20–22.)

The most frequently used party identification question (actually two questions, see Table 8.3, note b) yields a seven-point scale containing the following categories: Strong Democrat, Weak Democrat, Independent leaning to the Democrats, Independent, Independent leaning to the Republicans, Weak Republican, and Strong Republican. For many years, those Independents with leanings to one or the other party were viewed as, and frequently classified with, the "pure" Independents. But subsequent research has indicated that they are, in fact, hidden partisans. Unlike the pure Independents, who swing en masse from one party to the other, the leaners vote consistently, with heavy majorities, for the party of their leaning. In most elections, they prove even more partisan than the weak identifiers, since a larger percentage of these so-called Independents vote their party than is the case with the weakly identified.[7]

Much the same point may be made about trends in party identification as was made with regard to liberalism and conservatism—very small changes. Democratic identifiers outnumber Republican identifiers by relatively wide margins in every year shown in the table, and relative constancy is the most appropriate initial substantive conclusion. Looking at the small changes over the eight-year span, one finds a net loss of eight percentage points, the largest change observed, among the Strong Democrats. Minor fluctuations appear in the percentages of Weak Democrats, along with a similar pattern among the Independent Democrats. The latter fluctuations are so small as to cast doubt on any claim of change, an easy alternative hypothesis being normal sampling variations. One could argue, with some plausibility, a minuscule decline of the Weak Democrats accompanied by an equally minuscule increase of the independent Democrats after 1972.

Still remaining with the small differences noted within the Democratic ranks, one may observe that the largest shift occurred between 1972 and 1973, when the stock of party regulars declined by six points, that being partially offset by a three-point gain among the independent Democrats. The Independent Democrats went beyond the 10% level for the first time and remained above that figure in all subsequent studies. The General Social Surveys, it may be noted, are taken in March and April; the 1972 measure, therefore, occurred many months before the McGovern disaster, and the 1973 result was obtained only a few months thereafter. The principal source

---

[7] There has been some reluctance to recognize this fact. For evidence establishing the point—and a text still showing signs of the reluctance—see Asher, 1980, pp. 60 ff. and 92–93. This point was first brought to our attention, more than a decade ago, in an unpublished article by Roger Marz.

of this particular transformation within the Democratic ranks, we suggest, was the McGovern candidacy and campaign, which stimulated a considerable disaffection among Democrats and within the electorate generally.[8] There was, nevertheless, some continuing loss experienced by the Democrats, the combined figures for all three segments being lowest in 1978 and 1980.

It is clear from the table that these modest Democratic losses did not redound to the direct benefit of the Republicans. The proportion identifying as Republican (including Independents with Republican leanings) was, for all practical purposes, exactly the same in 1980 as it had been in 1972. No trend is indicated; in all those years, the Republican constituency ran at about 30%, plus or minus a few points.

It is thus obvious that the bulk of the Democratic loss over the decade went into the pure Independent category. Considering only the net change (the only possibility open to us), the Democrats lost eight points over the period, and the pure Independent category gained seven.[9] The size of the Republican minority, as indicated, has been rather stable in all the years shown; more precisely, it increased by one percentage point.

A parallel set of figures, also shown in Table 8.3, are drawn from the SRC election series. This series describes the decade beginning with 1970 and continuing, at two-year intervals, to 1980. The largest change noted in the NORC data, the eight-point decline of the strong Democrats, does not appear in these data. The figure was 20% in 1970 and 18% in 1980. If one began with 1972, the date of the NORC beginning, it would be necessary to report an increase, from 15 to 18%. Overall, the best conclusion here is one of no change.

Moreover, no clear confirmation of the increase of Independent Democrats is found in the SRC data. The Independent Democratic percentages were higher in the 1970's than in previous decades, but it is difficult to see this as a result of the 1972 campaign and the McGovern candidacy. The

[8]A series in the 1972 election study asked if several leading political figures "could be trusted" as president. Seven response categories were offered, ranging from "strongly agree" to "strongly disagree." The percentages choosing the two highest agreement categories (agreeing that the man could be trusted) were: Richard Nixon, 49%; George Wallace, 38%; George McGovern, 28%.

[9]Independent identifications (pure and "leaning" varieties) vary inversely with age; party identifications and strong commitments to party tend to increase with age (Campbell et al., 1960, p. 162; Nie, Verba, and Petrocik, 1976, p. 60; and Asher, 1980, p. 59). One might assume that the increase of Independents (the pure type) found in the NORC series during the 1970's was the result of changes in the age composition of the electorate, since the sizable cohorts of the "baby boom" years were making their entry at that time. Examination of the age distributions of the 1972 and 1980 samples, however, shows no support for that hypothesis. It must, therefore, be a matter of individual changes; more people than before, for some reason, have chosen to call themselves Independents (for evidence on this point, see Nie, Verba, and Petrocik, 1976, p. 365).

combined figures for all three Democratic categories were little different at the end of the decade from those at the beginning.

The Republican percentages were also unchanged throughout the decade, that being the single result precisely matching the NORC findings. The sameness of both Democratic and Republican patterns here means that the third category, the pure Independents, also showed no change. There was a slight increase of two percentage points registered here in mid-decade, but that was followed by a decline of the same magnitude later.

There is, clearly, a minor divergence between the two series. The NORC study shows a slight change within the Democratic ranks, a slight growth of the pure Independents, and no change for the Republicans. The SRC series shows no significant change anywhere. The best summary conclusion, perhaps, would be one that stressed the continuity of outlooks over the decade.[10] The changes observed were not of a magnitude that would deserve front-page treatment or some major new theoretical analysis.

Both the liberal-conservative and party identification questions have difficulties posed by their general or omnibus character. They are, in effect, shorthand summary devices for describing a presumed cluster of specific orientations. As such, they force people to overlook some of the complexity they might otherwise bring to their own analysis or self-description. There is also the problem that some people do not understand the conventional coding procedure, thus adding an element of confusion to the result.[11] To

---

[10]This conclusion may appear to contradict findings reported by Nie, Verba, and Petrocik. The difference is largely a function of time span, their focus being on the early 1950's, to the early 1970's, versus our focus on the 1970's.

In the longer time span, there is undoubtedly an increase in the proportion of Independents. Nie, Verba, and Petrocik (p. 49) show an increase from 23% in 1964 to 38% in 1974. (From 1952 to 1964, incidentally, there was effectively no change.) Our feeling is that *some* of this change represents relabeling; some strong partisans chose to call themselves Independents (perhaps the image of strong partisan is less attractive, or the position itself less palatable, than before). About one half of the growth in the Independent category is an increase in the highly partisan leaners; half is of the pure variety.

There were other significant changes indicated in the period, the decline of trust in government and an increased sense of powerlessness being two among many. The decline of trust, as will be seen, continued throughout the 1970's. There was a massive falloff of the initially very positive evaluations of the parties, most coming after 1964 (Nie, Verba, and Petrocik, p. 69). There were changes in political behavior (more split-ticket voting, for example). And there was more issue consistency indicated than in the 1950's. On the latter point, there has been some controversy, one argument being that the change was a function of method. See the work of George Bishop et al., 1978a, 1978b, 1978c, 1979; Sullivan et al., 1978, 1979; Nie and Andersen, 1974; and Nie and Rabjohn, 1979.

[11]The 1976 SRC study asked (Q. D5): "Would you say that one of the parties is more conservative than the other at the national level?" Of those who provided a substantive answer, a large majority, 72%, said yes. (Roughly one fifth, 19%, to be sure, said that they didn't know.) The follow-up question asked which was the more conservative party. Again, of those providing a substantive answer, the overwhelm-

circumvent these problems, one may undertake a more direct assessment of the underlying issue orientations. We consider first the public responses to a range of economic issues, those linked to or reflecting the dominant areas of concern. We then consider an array of social issues.

A prior note of caution is in order. The discussion of these results makes use of conventional definitions of liberalism and conservatism. We cannot stress too much that this is a convention, a loose general agreement to think about things in a given way. We do not think this ordering of things is justified by any compelling logic. One takes a hodgepodge of discrete issues, each with its own distinctive implications, and declares a liberal (or left) and conservative (or right) position in all instances. One then assumes that a consistency should follow, that people *should* adopt the "appropriate" position on all of those issues. Some groups in the society—rather influential ones—go along with this ordering of things and, for better or worse, use this classification scheme in their thinking, discussion, and writing. But this ordering principle, as will be seen, proves to be of limited value when it comes to the political outlooks of the masses. For the moment, however, we are accepting the convention, largely for heuristic purposes, to see what is to be said about the claims based on that categorization.

One cornerstone of contemporary conservative economic ideology is, without doubt, that government spending should be reduced, an idea, it is said, that became increasingly appealing to the American people over the last decade, and, furthermore, one that has become manifest in such noteworthy events as the passage of property tax limitation referenda and, on the national scene, the election of Ronald Reagan. One useful indicator of conservative economic ideology is thus the popular opinion on whether (and if so, where) government spending ought to be reduced.

There is a lengthy series from the NORC surveys bearing directly on this question (Table 8.4). The series presents respondents with a list of problem areas and asks whether we are spending "too little money on it, too much money, or about the right amount." If the population were basically conservative in economic ideology, according to conventional definition, we should find "too much" as the most common response. And if the popula-

---

ing majority, 76%, chose the Republicans as the more conservative. This implies that in the minds of a substantial majority, party labels have some ideological content, and that the concepts "liberal" and "conservative" were correctly understood by most.

As a precaution, however, one should think about the following finding: A postelection study in 1980 found that 20% of those who had identified themselves as "very liberal" voted for Ronald Reagan. Some 29% of the self-identified "very conservative" category did *not* vote for Reagan (that is, they voted for either President Carter or third-party candidate John Anderson). This is reported in *Public Opinion*, 4 (February/March 1981) 45.

Table 8.4. Attitudes About Government Spending 1973–1980: NORC General Social Surveys

"We are faced with many problems in this country, none of which can be solved easily or inexpensively. I'm going to name some of these problems, and for each one I'd like you to tell me whether you think we're spending too much money on it, too little money, or about the right amount."

Attitude	1973	1976	1980
Space exploration			
Too little	8%	9%	20%
About right	31	29	38
Too much	61	62	43
N =	1432	1459	1344
The environment			
Too little	65	57	51
About right	27	33	33
Too much	8	10	16
N =	1413	1425	1382
Improving health			
Too little	63	63	57
About right	32	32	35
Too much	5	5	8
N =	1445	1441	1407
Helping big cities			
Too little	55	48	46
About right	31	30	30
Too much	14	22	24
N =	1319	1318	1278
Fighting crime			
Too little	69	69	72
About right	26	22	22
Too much	5	8	6
N =	1405	1413	1400
Dealing with drug addiction			
Too little	70	63	65
About right	23	29	27
Too much	6	8	8
N =	1399	1390	1353
Improving education			
Too little	51	52	55
About right	39	38	34
Too much	9	10	11
N =	1434	1449	1404
Helping blacks			
Too little	35	29	26
About right	42	43	48
Too much	23	27	26
N =	1402	1392	1347

(Continued)

Table 8.4. (Continued)

Attitude	1973	1976	1980
Military, Arms, defense			
Too little	12	26	60
About right	48	45	28
Too much	40	29	12
N =	1407	1395	1370
Foreign aid			
Too little	4	3	5
About right	21	19	21
Too much	74	78	74
N =	1421	1438	1389
Welfare			
Too little	21	14	14
About right	25	23	27
Too much	54	63	59
N =	1432	1429	1401

tion is becoming more conservative, we should witness increases in the proportions saying "too much" over the decade.[12]

The actual data show us neither of these patterns. All told, eleven problem areas are reflected in the table. Even in 1980, at the presumed crest of the rising conservative tide, the majority (or, in cases where there was no majority, the plurality) response in seven of the eleven areas was that we are spending *too little*. The seven areas were the environment, health, big cities, crime, drugs, education, and the military. In one area—improving the conditions of blacks—the modal response was that current expenditures were about right, and in the remaining three areas—space exploration, foreign aid, and welfare—the modal judgment was that we were spending too much. These patterns do not by any remote stretch of the imagination suggest a widespread public demand for across-the-board cutbacks in government spending. In most areas, the demand was for more, not less, government spending.[13]

To be sure, some of the areas in which people want more to be spent have

[12]We see no reason, a priori, why one should accept the simple equation: spending is liberal; opposition thereto is conservative. When the costs of liberal programs press on liberal but nonaffluent populations, it stands to reason that they would oppose that tax burden. But that opposition per se does not mean they are not (or are no longer) liberal; it only means they think someone else should pay, someone better able to carry the burden. One should not infer a position on the issue from the position on financing. The issue preference and the question of financing are two separate questions and deserve separate investigation in all cases.

[13]Another question from the 1976 SRC study (Q. H6) asks: "The government should spend less even if it means cutting back on programs like health and education." Seventy-nine percent of those with opinions (N = 2698) disagreed with this suggestion for economizing.

a conventional conservative cast—areas such as crime, drug addiction, and the military. But other areas have a more liberal cast—environment, health, the cities, and education. Most people, three out of five, think that too much is being spent on welfare, and to the liberal intellectuals of the world, that is an ominous sign. Only one quarter, however, think too much is being spent to improve the conditions of blacks. On other welfare issues— education and health—the consensus is that too *little* is being spent. It would take a remarkably pessimistic liberal to find nothing but despair in these patterns.[14]

As for the trends over the decade, they are, with a single important exception, rather modest in size. They are not, moreover, changing in the same direction. For this purpose, let us focus on the "spending too much" response and take a ten-point change in that response as the minimum difference worth discussing. Over the eleven areas, only three show a significant change by this criterion, and of the three, only one shows an actual *increase* in the "too much" proportion: the idea that "too much" is being spent to help the big cities increased from 14 to 24% over the decade. The other two areas of substantial change are space exploration, where, reflecting actual cutbacks, the proportion thinking too much was being spent declined from 61% to 43%, and military, armaments, and defense, where the "too much" proportion declined from 40 to 12%. There are, of course, other changes indicated in the table, all falling below the ten-point criterion. (It is worth a passing mention that the antimilitarism found in the early years of the decade was clearly not a fixed or permanent attitude. With the resurrection, late in the decade, of the idea that we were falling behind the Soviets in military preparedness, the proportion feeling that too little was being spent for defense correspondingly increased. The military item shows the most dramatic changes over the decade of all questions in the sequence.)

Other areas of conservative thinking, unfortunately, were omitted in the NORC surveys. For further information, therefore, we must turn to the SRC election series. There are five items of relevance that appear more than once in the series, shown in Table 8.5. Most of these items show some trend in a conservative direction, although, again, most of the changes were very modest. The largest trend indicated is a fifteen-point increase in the proportion thinking government is getting too powerful (up from 61 to 76%). At one

[14]The feeling that too much is being spent on welfare might have some realistic basis. Welfare costs are the single largest expenditure in the federal budget, outdoing even defense spending. A standard read-in typically appears in this connection, that the opposition to welfare, and the correlated focus on "welfare cheats" signifies conservatism and opposition in principle to a worthy, decent, and humane effort. Another possibility is that cheating might well exist (aided, to be sure, by loosely written laws or administrative arrangements), and that people, in fact, are pointing to unjustified, unnecessary expenditure. The problem becomes particularly intense when, as indicated in Note 12, less affluent populations are forced to foot a share of the costs they can ill afford. That liberal commentators and press denounce them as heartless conservatives does little to either clarify or alleviate the problem.

Table 8.5. Trends in Economic Ideology, 1973–1978: SRC Election Studies

	1972	1974	1976	1980
1. Government too powerful?				
Yes	61%	*	*	76%
No	39	*	*	24
N =	(900)	*	*	(1292)
2. Government job & living standard guarantee				
Pro (1–3)	32	30	30	22
Pro/con (4)	23	25	22	24
Con (5–7)	45	45	48	55
N =	(1172)	(2058)	(2272)	(1820)
3. More progressive income tax				
Pro (1–3)	45	*	40	*
Pro/con (4)	15	*	16	*
Con (5–7)	40	*	43	*
N =	(1166)	*	(2010)	*
4. Government medical insurance?				
Pro (1–3)	46	*	44	45
Pro/con (4)	14	*	12	13
Con (5–7)	40	*	43	42
N =	(1112)	*	(2248)	(1884)
5. Government help minorities?				
Pro (1–3)	34	32	35	28
Pro/con (4)	23	24	22	25
Con (5–7)	42	43	43	47
N =	(2001)	(2114)	(2358)	(2037)

Questions were as follows:
1. Some people are afraid the government in Washington is getting too powerful for the good of the country and the individual person. Others feel that the government in Washington is not getting too strong. Do you have an opinion on this? If respondent is coded "yes" on above question: What is your feeling? Do you think the government is getting too powerful or do you think the government is not getting too strong?
2. Some people feel that the government in Washington should see to it that every person has a job and a good standard of living. Suppose that these people are at one end of this scale—at point number 1. Others think the government should just let each person get ahead on his own. Suppose that these people are at the other end—at point number 7. And, of course, some other people have opinions in between.
3. As you know, in our tax system people who earn a lot of money already have to pay higher rates of income tax than those who earn less. Some people think that those with high incomes should pay even more of their income into taxes than they do now. Others think that the rates shouldn't be different at all—that everyone should pay the same portion of their income, no matter how much they make. Where would you place yourself on this scale, or haven't you thought much about this?
4. There is much concern about the rapid rise in medical and hospital costs. Some feel there should be a government insurance plan which would cover all medical and hospital expenses. Others feel that medical expenses should be paid by individuals, and through private insurance like Blue Cross. Where would you place yourself on this scale, or haven't you thought much about it?
5. Some people feel that the government in Washington should make every possible effort to improve the social and economic position of blacks and other minority groups. Others feel that the government should not make any special effort to help minorities because they should help themselves. Where would you place yourself on this scale, or haven't you thought much about it?

time, this would have indicated an unmistakable conservative drift, but nowadays, liberals, too, worry about governmental power and its abuses, so it is not obvious that this shift should be read as indicating a conservative direction.[15] There is also a ten-point increase (from 45% to 55%) in the proportion who oppose the idea that government should guarantee everyone "a job and a good standard of living," an apparent conservative drift.[16] Changes on the other three items, however, are modest and not of much substantive importance, all of them falling in the range of five or six percentage points at most. With one possible exception, then, these data on economic outlooks do not support the rising tide of conservatism theme.[17]

Twenty items taken from the NORC's General Social Surveys dealing with major social issues current in the United States during the 1970's are shown in Table 8.6. All the major social issues are touched: crime and crime control, race and race relations, women's issues, and abortion. With a few exceptions, the items shown exhaust those available in the GSS series for which more than one measure is available—that is, those for which we have some indication of trends. The trend lesson can be quickly summarized: Of the twenty series shown, exactly *four* show changes of appreciable magnitude between the earliest and latest available measurement; they show net opinion shifts over the decade of ten percentage points or more. These data thus confirm the conclusions advanced on the basis of self-rating and party identification. For the most part, the political consciousness of the American people was stable, constant, and unchanging over the course of the 1970's, contrary to all claims of a great transformation.[18]

[15]For an earlier discussion of this government power question, one indicating some media influence, see Hamilton, 1972, pp. 97–98 and 295–297. See also Nie, Verba, and Petrocik, 1976, pp. 125–126.

[16]A majority of the American public favors a government guarantee of employment; that is, they favor provision of the means to work for a living. There is no majority favoring "a job and a good standard of living." For data and discussion, see Hamilton, 1972, pp. 92–93.

The NORC General Social Surveys contained a question asking whether "the government ought to reduce the income differences between rich and poor." The item first appeared in 1978 and was asked again in 1980. The plurality response at both times was that the government *should* attempt to reduce income differentials (47 and 44%, respectively). The more conservative idea, that the government should not, was favored by only about a third of the respondents.

[17]There was, to be sure, a conservative plurality in most years on two of the four substantive issues (job and living standard guarantees, and government aid to minorities). But there is a consistent liberal plurality on one of the four issues (government-subsidized medical insurance), and a pretty fair standoff on the last issue (a more progressive rate of income taxation).

[18]We have omitted several items from the NORC compilation that deal more or less directly with the personal (as opposed to the political) sphere, for example, attitudes about pre- and extramarital sex, homosexuality, the ideal number of children to have, and so on. We have also omitted a lengthy series on attitudes about civil liberties, which have been analyzed and reported elsewhere (James Davis,

It is also of some interest to note that the direction of the four substantial changes indicated in the table itself provides no clear pattern. In two cases, the evidence shows rising conservatism. The proportion of the adult population favoring the death penalty for persons convicted of murder increased from 57 to 72% over the decade. In like fashion, the proportion feeling that the courts are not harsh enough on criminals increased from 74 to 88%. These, to emphasize, are clearly changes in a conventional conservative direction. But the other two significant (more than ten-point) changes are clearly in a liberal direction. The proportion of the population agreeing that "blacks should not push themselves where they are not wanted" fell from 76 to 66%, and the proportion stating that they would vote for a black for president increased from 74 to 85%. Obviously, no general claim of either rising conservatism or rising liberalism would adequately describe these results. In the 1970's, the population became more conservative on two issues (those related to crime and its control), became more liberal on two others (in the area of race relations), and became neither more nor less liberal or conservative on the other sixteen issues.

The data in Table 8.6 also indicate the silliness of assertions to the effect that the American majority is basically conservative, or that it is basically liberal. There are, as it happens, immense conservative majorities on some issues (the death penalty, court treatment of criminals, legalization of marijuana, and busing), but equally immense liberal majorities on other issues (gun registration, wiretapping, interracial marriage, integrated schools, and most women's issues), and there are many issues where the split in public thinking is too close to 50–50 to allow a definite conclusion about majority sentiment. This is assuredly *not* to argue that the popular consciousness is inchoate, unstructured, or otherwise unknowable. It *is* to argue that the popular consciousness is much too complex to be adequately understood through the imposition of a simple liberalism–conservatism framework.[19]

1975). And we have omitted all questions that were not asked frequently enough to allow for an examination of trends.

The *General Social Surveys, 1972–1980 Cumulative Codebook* (published in July 1980 and available from the Roper Center) shows marginal response frequencies for every variable contained in the GSS series, however frequently it was asked, and may, therefore, be consulted for additional information about trends in these other areas.

[19]This conclusion might appear to differ substantially from an earlier report (Hamilton, 1972, p. 87 ff.). There it was stated: "Contrary to common belief, majority sentiment in the United States is solidly liberal with respect to *domestic economic issues*" (emphasis added). We feel that the present findings are generally consonant with that claim. The focus there was on *domestic economic issues*, and liberalism in that connection was defined as "a disposition to favor 'welfare-state' legislation . . . government action to aid or ensure personal or family welfare." It was also indicated that majority sentiment at that time (up to 1964) did not go beyond the liberal framework to favor, for example, government guarantees of living standards. The complexity of the present discussion results from the broader focus, from the inclusion of the wide range of social issues. In the latter area, studies have always indicated wide support for conservative positions.

Table 8.6. Opinion on Social and Political Issues, 1972–1980: NORC General Social Surveys

	1972	1973	1974	1975	1976	1977	1978	1980
Favor death penalty?[a]								
Yes	57%	63%	66%	64%	69%	71%	70%	72%
No	43	37	34	36	31	29	30	28
N =	(1484)	(1417)	(1404)	(1383)	(1426)	(1423)	(1443)	(1372)
Favor gun control?[b]								
Yes	72	75	76	76	73	73	*	71
No	28	25	24	24	27	27	*	29
N =	(1562)	(1470)	(1459)	(1450)	(1472)	(1499)	*	(1439)
Court's treatment of criminals?[c]								
Too harsh	7	5	6	4	3	4	3	3
Not harsh enough	74	81	84	85	86	88	90	88
About right	18	14	10	10	11	9	8	8
N =	(1436)	(1356)	(694)**	(1379)	(1405)	(1443)	(1448)	(1378)
Wiretapping[d]								
Approve	*	*	17	17	*	19	20	*
Disapprove	*	*	83	83	*	81	80	*
N =	*	*	(1424)	(1428)	*	(1480)	(1483)	*
Legalization of marijuana[e]								
Favor	*	19	*	21	29	*	31	26
Oppose	*	81	*	79	71	*	69	74
N =	*	(1471)	*	(1414)	(1447)	*	(1464)	(1420)
Laws against interracial marriage?[f]								
Yes	39	38	35	39	33	28	*	30
No	61	62	65	61	67	72	*	70
N =	(1309)	(1289)	(1280)	(1292)	(1330)	(1327)	*	(1427)

Object to a black for dinner?[g]								
Strongly	13	16	11	*	*	13	12	*	10
Mildly	16	15	16	*	*	15	17	*	13
Not at all	71	69	73	*	*	72	72	*	77
N =	(1318)	(1292)	(1288)	*	*	(1332)	(1333)	*	(1444)
Blacks shouldn't push[h]								
Agree	76	74	*	75	71	73	*	66
Disagree	24	26	*	25	29	27	*	34
N =	(1258)	(1299)	*	(1289)	(1331)	(1322)	*	(1428)
Whites can keep blacks out[i]								
Agree	40	*	*	*	39	42	*	31
Disagree	60	*	*	*	61	58	*	69
N =	(1253)	*	*	*	(1337)	(1309)	*	(1414)
Against open housing law?[j]								
Yes	*	65	*	65	64	*	58	57
No	*	35	*	35	36	*	42	43
N =	*	(1274)	*	(1294)	(1322)	*	(1480)	(1418)
Integrated schools[k]								
For	88	*	*	*	86	87	*	89
Against	12	*	*	*	14	13	*	11
N =	(1574)	*	*	*	(1457)	(1495)	*	(1433)
Bussing[l]								
For	20	*	21	18	16	17	21	*
Against	80	*	79	82	84	83	79	*
N =	(1544)	*	(1427)	(1417)	(1459)	(1482)	(1459)	*
Vote for a black president[m]								
Yes	74	*	83	82	*	78	85	*
No	26	*	17	18	*	22	15	*
N =	(1265)	*	(1423)	(1247)	*	(1298)	(1460)	*

(Continued)

Table 8.6. (Continued)

	1972	1973	1974	1975	1976	1977	1978	1980
Women should stay home[n]								
Agree	*	*	36	36	*	38	32	*
Disagree	*	*	64	64	*	62	68	*
N =	*	*	(1431)	(1446)	*	(1490)	(1482)	*
Approve of women in labor force[o]								
Yes	65	*	69	71	*	66	73	*
No	35	*	31	29	*	34	27	*
N =	(1577)	*	(1449)	(1462)	*	(1506)	(1509)	*
Vote for woman president?[p]								
Yes	74	*	80	80	*	79	82	*
No	26	*	20	20	*	21	18	*
N =	(1533)	*	(1433)	(1440)	*	(1484)	(1492)	*
Men better suited for politics?[q]								
Agree	*	*	47	50	*	49	44	*
Disagree	*	*	53	50	*	51	56	*
N =	*	*	(698)**	(1429)	*	(1454)	(1468)	*
Favor abortion if woman's health endangered?[r]								
Yes	87	92	92	91	91	91	91	90
No	13	8	8	9	9	9	9	10
N =	(1539)	(1496)	(1452)	(1449)	(1464)	(1488)	(1492)	(1429)
...If family cannot afford more children?[s]								
Yes	49	53	55	53	53	53	47	52
No	51	47	45	47	47	47	53	48
N =	(1507)	(1456)	(1417)	(1416)	(1434)	(1478)	(1469)	(1408)
...If she does not want more children?[t]								
Yes	40	48	47	46	46	47	40	47
No	60	52	53	54	54	53	60	53
N =	(1528)	(1453)	(1411)	(1426)	(1447)	(1462)	(1483)	(1407)

^aDo you favor or oppose the death penalty for persons convicted of murder?

^bWould you favor or oppose a law which would require a person to obtain a police permit before he or she could buy a gun?

^cIn general, do you think the courts in this area deal too harshly or not harshly enough with criminals?

^dEverything considered, would you say that, in general, you approve or disapprove of wiretapping?

^eDo you think the use of marijuana should be made legal or not?

^fDo you think there should be laws against marriages between Negroes/blacks and whites?

^gHow strongly would you object if a member of your family wanted to bring a Negro/black friend home to dinner? Would you object strongly, mildly or not at all?

Here are some opinions other people have expressed in connection with Negroes/black-white relations. Which statement on the card comes closest to how you, yourself, feel? (Agree-Disagree)

^hNegroes/blacks shouldn't push themselves where they're not wanted.

ⁱWhite people have a right to keep (Negroes/blacks) out of their neighborhoods if they want to, and Negroes/blacks should respect that right.

^jSuppose there is a community-wide vote on the general housing issue. There are two possible laws to vote on. Which law would you vote for?

(A) One law says that a homeowner can decide for himself whom to sell his house to, even if he prefers not to sell to Negroes/blacks.

(B) The second law says that a homeowner cannot refuse to sell to someone because of their race or color.

^kDo you think white students and Negro/black students should go to the same schools or to separate schools?

^lIn general, do you favor or oppose the busing of Negro/black and white school children from one district to another?

^mIf your party nominated a Negro/black for President, would you vote for him if he were qualified for the job?

ⁿ(Agree-Disagree): Women should take care of running their homes and leave running the country up to men.

^oDo you approve or disapprove of a married woman earning money in business or industry if she has a husband capable of supporting her?

^pIf your party nominated a woman for President, would you vote for her if she were qualified for the job?

^q(Agree-Disagree): Most men are better suited emotionally for politics than are most women.

(Would you favor or oppose abortion if:)

^rThe woman's own health is endangered by the pregnancy.

^sThe family has a very low income and cannot afford any more children.

^tIf she is married and does not want any more children.

*Question not asked.

**Question asked only of half the sample.

The patterns by issue area provide some indication of the complexities of political consciousness abroad in the land. Crime, for example, is declared to be a conservative's issue. The vast majority, to be sure, would prefer to see the courts toughen up on crime. A sizable majority also favors the death penalty. At the same time, there is widespread popular support for laws that would require a police permit before a person was allowed to own a gun (and gun control is sometimes said to be the acid test of liberalism. On the complexities of public thinking specifically on gun controls, see Wright, James, 1981a). And there is also overwhelming popular *opposition* to wiretapping. So even in the area of crime and its control, there are important elements of liberal sentiment.

The racial opinions are equally complex. The progressive improvement in racial attitudes of the American population has been noted by many observers (see the sources cited in Chapter 2, Note 7). For the most part, the data in Table 8.6 show a continuation of this trend. The proportion *disap*-proving of laws against interracial marriage is high throughout the decade, and increases by about nine points from 1972 to 1980. At the end of the decade, such laws were opposed by seven of ten adults. An equally large majority would not object at all if a member of their family brought a black friend home for dinner, the size of this majority increasing over the decade (from 71 to 77%). Disagreement with the idea that "white people have a right to keep Negroes out of their neighborhoods," and willingness to vote for a black Pesidential candidate, both show a nearly identical pattern: a very large, and growing, progressive majority over the whole decade.

Even here, however, some illiberal sentiments are to be noted. A substantial majority believes, for example, that "black people should not push themselves where they are not wanted." But, again, the size of this majority is declining (from 76 to 66% between 1972 and 1980); also, we have no question on whether white people should push themselves where *they* are not wanted. (In other words, this item may well tell us as much about reactions to pushiness in general as it does about racism. See also Hamilton, 1975, p. 154, for discussion of this question.) Most of the population would also favor a housing law that let homeowners decide for themselves who to sell to, "even if they prefer not to sell to blacks," even as a similar-sized majority approves of the general notion of open neighborhoods. Note, finally, that support for the fair housing law also increases (by eight percent-age points) over the decade. The conclusions to be drawn from these materials are that most people have progressive ideas on most matters related to race, and that the trend on most items (as in past decades) is toward still more progressive outlooks, but even here some exceptions deserve attention.

The two items related to schools are of particular interest in the present context. An immense majority of the population, almost 90%, endorses the concept that "white students and Negro students should go to the same schools." But nearly as large a majority—on the order of 80%—is against the busing of "black and white children from one school district to another," presumably a conservative position. Does this imply some massive inconsistency in popular political consciousness? No, it obviously does not. What it implies is only that most people endorse the concept of racially integrated schools but oppose busing across school districts as the means. These two opinions come to be inconsistent only when one imposes a conventional liberal-conservative dichotomy on those preferences.

Most of the population also endorses the progressive view with respect to most women's issues as well, and here, too, the trends, although modest, tend to be in the liberal direction. The idea that "women should take care of running their homes and leave running the country up to men" is rejected by a large and slowly increasing majority. The concept of women's labor force participation also receives widespread popular support, the size of the relevant majority increasing from about two thirds to approximately three quarters over the decade. Most people also say they would vote for a woman Presidential candidate, and the proportion who say this likewise has increased somewhat (from 74% in 1972 to 82% in 1978). Finally, there is a very thin majority that rejects the idea that men are better suited for politics than women. Of some additional interest, a detailed analysis of these items undertaken by Ferree (1974) showed that in most cases, men were somewhat *more* likely to take the progressive position than were women.

The results shown for the three abortion questions deserve some special emphasis. (There are, all together, six items in the series, of which we have shown just three for economy of presentation.)[20] There is much heated political debate these days over whether the public favors or opposes abortion. The NORC data show that the debate is entirely miscast: the public is strongly in favor of abortion *in some situations* (for example, if the fetus is defective or if the pregnancy threatens the mother's health, where the majorities favoring abortion approach 90%), splits very close to 50–50 *in other situations* (for example, if the family is poor and cannot afford any more children), and is on the whole opposed to the idea *in some other situations* (for example, if the mother simply does not want the child). In general, there is strong support for abortion for reasons of health (of either the fetus or the mother) and, unsurprisingly, if the pregnancy was the result of rape, and close to a 50–50 split in most other situations, with thin majorities opposing the notion of abortion on demand. Even here, however, the results show splits in the range of 60 to 40, so opposition to the concept is not extremely widespread.

Summarizing briefly, the available evidence indicates that concern over the domestic economy increased during the 1970's, and for most of the decade was seen as the leading national problem. That concern with the

[20]The other three items ask about approval of abortion "if there is a strong chance of serious defect in the baby" (overwhelming approval), "if she became pregnant as a result of rape" (also overwhelming approval), and "if she is not married and does not want to marry the man" (nearly a 50–50 split).

economy, however, was not accompanied by any sharp transformation in political outlooks, either on general measures such as self-rating and party affiliations, or on most specific economic issues. With the exceptions that we have noted, the economic views encountered at the end of the decade were very similar (in most cases, effectively identical) to those predominant at the beginning of the decade. Stability in outlook, rather than great change, is the only justifiable conclusion to be derived from these results. The same conclusion holds for the wide range of social issues examined here.

The major conclusions coming out of this review of issue positions, in short, are: *a general constancy of position on most issues, minichanges where any changes have been discovered, and conflicting tendencies as far as the direction of change.*

Still another conclusion derives from the same findings. A favorite mode of analysis much in use among academics and journalists is a classification in terms of liberalism and conservatism, or, in another familiar pairing, of left and right. A moment's thought, however, would reveal that many of these issues are not inherently left or right. The tough law-and-order position, so it is said, is rightist, and all good liberals (or leftists) should, therefore, oppose any such position. But for the poor, for the down-and-out, for the elderly who cannot walk the streets at night for fear of mugging, the demand for law and order makes perfect sense. It is the right and proper thing given their specific class interests (and given an understandable lack of solidarity with others sharing the same objective class position—their muggers). Put in still another way, their preferences for increased policing and for more severe punishments are, for them, liberal positions. The removal of muggers from the streets is a precondition for their liberation, for their free access to and use of public streets.

The left–right, liberal–conservative analysis, in short, constitutes no more than a convenient, simplified classification scheme, one that gives its users a very economical device for summarizing and presenting some very complicated facts. But that economical conceptual scheme does not adequately portray the reality being analyzed. Given the complexity of the findings reported here, it is clear that such usage actually amounts to a read-in. Effectively, it means that those analysts pay little or no heed to the manifest lack of fit between data and concepts.

The findings reported here point to another obvious conclusion: the general populace organizes its experience in a markedly different way. They do not lay out or "calibrate" the issues in terms of a left-right continuum; they do not organize their world in the same way as academics or journalists. This means, among other things, that one ought not impose (and measure) issue constraint in terms of that "outsider's" standard, which results in the general populace getting failing grades for inability to organize their own thoughts. But if, from the outset, they never intended to organize matters in that way, if they had their own basis for organization, one would have simply judged things by an extraneous standard, and the exercise would mean only that most people do not think in the same ways as academic intellectuals.

A further implication should also be considered. If there is no inherent logic to the conventional organization of beliefs, then what we are dealing with is a conventional linkage or ordering. The sense that Issues A, B, C, D, and so on "should" all cohere in a given way is a function of a special training; ultimately, to use Pavlov's term, we are dealing with a conditioned reflex (one reinforced, perhaps, by the routine rewards and punishments associated with small group life everywhere).

To this point in the present chapter we have dealt with the relatively simple question of political orientation, whether left or right, liberal or conservative. Two additional questions deserve attention before we turn to another theme. These are, first, the question of importance, of salience. In the discussion that follows, three indicators of salience are considered. A second question asks about the degree to which a solution for the problem is viewed as the responsibility of the government in Washington. Both questions are important for discussions of the democratic process, of the relationship of masses and government. They also have implications for a long-standing concern with the possibility of an overload of demand—that the government will be led to do more than is technically possible (Rose, 1980). In its classical formulation, public wants are portrayed as increasing without limit (especially in affluent societies). Any government, of course, operates with *relatively* scarce resources, hence the problem (or crisis); the government is forced to reject many "mass" demands, for the simple reason that it cannot comply. This thwarting of narrowly or blindly conceived public demands may then lead to a "crisis of legitimacy." It is a situation "ripe for demagogues."[21]

[21] In the classical version of the mass society theory, the problem lies with the masses. It is posed by their unbounded appetites, as stimulated and directed by everpresent demagogues. Although this model derives from the experience of ancient Greece and Rome, the imagery is also applied to contemporary experience, frequently in an exotic scientific language—as in the work of David Easton (1965, p. 57) who reports that "demands have the capacity to impose strains on a system by driving its essential variables toward their critical limits." (For an extended discussion, see James Wright, 1976, pp. 277–279.)

The classical discussions portray the established elites as basically sensible and responsible, but helpless vis-à-vis the massive threat "from below." Such portraiture overlooks elite support for the demagogues. In the 1950's, a responsible statesman, Senator Robert A. Taft, declared that "the pro-Communist policies of the State Department fully justified Joe McCarthy in his demand for an investigation" (cited in Hamilton, 1972, p. 116). For the solicitous and supportive words of Germany's conservative press with regard to Adolf Hitler prior to his taking office, see Hamilton, 1982, passim.

There is also the problem posed by elite liberal demagogues who stimulate appetites with vast promises of payoff and who enact welfare programs that, from the outset, are known to be inadequately financed. Against such elite irresponsibility, one should note the widespread responsibility found among the masses, namely, a persistent restraint placed on their own aspirations and an understanding that many things, desirable as they might be, are not financially possible.

With some presentations of public opinion data, it is easy to assume overload—because of the facile assumption that all opinion, every "for" or "against," represents a demand. But for many citizens, that expression represents an opinion and nothing more; it is a response to a question with no further implication. Such expressions could fail to be effective for two reasons. First is lack of salience (the subject being seen as having little or no importance). Second, assuming salience, is the failure of a respondent to do anything about the concern or issue. If there were no communication, say, with one's legislative representative, no organization of protest meetings, no formation of a pressure group, the demand would prove a very quiet one indeed. A closely related source of demand failure involves definitions of responsibility. At least two questions arise here: who is seen as to blame for (as causing) the problem? And, who is seen as responsible for finding a solution? Narrow definitions in either case would reduce the pressures on a government. This formal discussion points to the simple conclusion that worries about demand overload are frequently exaggerated.

We begin with a series of items taken from the 1976 SRC election study, a series designed to measure the salience of many of the issues discussed in the first part of this chapter. Respondents were given a deck of ten cards, each listing a political issue (honesty in government, high taxes, and so on). The first question in the sequence simply asked the respondent to indicate which of the ten issues "is not at all important to you." Column 1 of Table 8.7 shows the proportion of the sample indicating that each issue was, at some level, important to them. As the table shows, all these proportions are very high, none beneath 80%, and most well into the 90's. Indeed, 62% of the respondents said every one of the ten was of some importance to them; a mere 24 individuals said that none of these issues was important. Most of these major political issues, in short, were clearly of *some* importance to most people.

Owing to the narrowness in the range of variation, little need be said about the results shown in the first column. Given the points made earlier in this chapter, it will come as no great surprise that every economic issue shown in the table is felt to be of *some* import by 90% or more of the population—another indicator of the salience of the economic concern. For present purposes, the most interesting result is the very strong showing of honesty in government, chosen by 96% of all respondents (second only to inflation, which was noted by 97%). Under the circumstances, in the immediate aftermath of Watergate, it is perhaps not surprising to find honesty in government given such attention.[22]

[22]The NORC General Social Surveys have regularly asked respondents about the most desirable qualities for a child to have. A list of thirteen character traits is presented. In 1975, nearly two out of five persons chose as the "most desirable /quality/ of all," the option that the child be honest! In order of frequency, the other choices were: has good sense and sound judgment; obeys parents; is responsible; is considerate of others; has self-control; has good manners; is interested in how and

Table 8.7. Salience of Issues: SRC 1976 Election Study

Issue	Is issue of some im- portance[a] (% yes)	If *YES* Most important?	Among the top four?	Govern- ments responsi- bility[b]	"Salience"[c]
Honesty in government	96%	34%	67%	84%	.54
High taxes	95	15	69	83	.54
Inflation	97	26	77	79	.59
Energy shortage	93	4	40	67	.25
Unemployment	94	18	64	68	.41
Foreign relations	86	3	26	85	.19
Racial issues	81	2	17	46	.06
Crime and drugs	96	7	45	59	.25
Consumer protection	90	1	16	55	.08
Pollution	88	3	18	59	.09
(N = 2397)					

[a]The instructions to the interviewer read: "Hand respondent 10 playing cards. 'Now we'd like you to read through the issues on these cards and tell me the letter of any issue that is not at all important to you so we can put it aside.' Interviewer: check issues not important to respondent." Q. E7. from the 1976 SRC Codebook.

[b]% saying Washington has "a great deal."

[c]Column 1 × Column 3 × Column 4; see texts for details.

Persons who said an issue was important were asked two further series of questions about that matter. First, they were asked to indicate "how much responsibility you think the government in Washington has toward solving each problem" (the table shows the proportion responding "a great deal"). Second, they were asked to choose from the entire set of important issues, the first, second, third, and fourth most important to them. The table shows the proportions choosing each of the ten as the single most important issue to them, and the proportion who ranked each issue at least among their top four. Thus, while the results in the first column show that all ten issues are of at least some importance to most people, the second and third columns give us a more precise indication of their salience or urgency.

The surprise in these data, of course, is again the strong showing of honesty in government. It is chosen as most important by the largest fraction of the population, 34%, which is noticeably higher even than the proportion choosing inflation, 26%. And it was placed among the top four issues by 67%. The government in Washington, moreover, was seen by a large majority as having the responsibility for dealing with the problem (roughly the same sized majorities appeared with respect to foreign relations and high

why things happen; and, gets along well with others. It is only at this point, tenth on the list, that one finds the success ethic—"tries hard to succeed"—an option chosen by 2.3% of those interviewed. The ordering of priorities, moreover, was the same in the 1973 study, before the full impact of Watergate was felt, and similar results have appeared in all subsequent years. Use of the question in the pre-Nixon era (Kohn, 1969) in the early 1960's, found similar results.

taxes, appropriate targeting in all three instances). The evident concern expressed in these results for the honesty with which government was being conducted is unmistakable and deserving of more detailed inquiry.[23]

Most of the remaining results shown in the middle two columns are precisely as our previous discussion would lead one to expect. Four issues were chosen as among the four most important issues by more than half the population, and three of these were expressly economic: inflation, high taxes, and unemployment, in that order. Likewise, four issues were chosen as the single most important issue by at least 15% of the population, and three of them were these same economic issues.

The other issues shown in the table were judged as having considerably less salience. Among the issues judged most important, the *worst* showing among the three economic issues is high taxes. In contrast, the *best* showing for the six remaining issues is crime and drugs, mentioned by 7%; and energy shortages, mentioned by 4%. Most of these other issues, it will be noted, would fall into Scammon and Wattenberg's category of social issues. The lesson here is the same as that noted many times since our initial review of relevant data in Chapter 2.

The results in the fourth column of the table provide one additional complexity; there is considerable variation in whether a given issue is seen to be the national government's responsibility. Some issues are felt to be relatively important but not the federal government's responsibility; in relative terms, crime and drugs display this pattern. Others are viewed as the federal government's responsibility, but are not seen as very important; here, foreign relations provides the best example. Since these attributions of responsibility are almost certainly going to influence the character of political demands, a complete account of the popular political agenda must take them into account as well.

The general character of political demand in the United States in the middle 1970's can be most readily summarized simply by multiplying the proportions appearing in the first, third, and fourth columns of the table. The resulting multiplication would equal 1.0 for an issue that everybody felt was important, that everybody agreed was one of the four most important, and that everybody felt was definitely the federal government's responsibility. A "one," in short, would be the ultimate insistent demand, and we can take these cross products as our final indicators of issue saliency in 1976 (column five). By this standard, clearly, inflation was the number one "demand" made on Washington in the middle 1970's, closely

[23]The strong showing of the honesty issue in this series is all the more surprising because the issue does not arise in any major way in any of the open-ended most important problem questions reviewed in this and previous chapters. Still, given the appropriate prompt in the question wording, the issue comes through with considerable force. Perhaps the concern being tapped here is largely latent—that is, not something that people have on their minds as they go about their daily affairs, but, when forced to think about it, one that concerns them deeply, nonetheless.

followed by another economic issue, high taxes—and, again, honesty in government. The only other strong showing, to round out the top four, is unemployment. Thereafter, issue salience drops off rather precipitously. The relatively poor showing of crime and drugs and racial issues once again illustrates the inappropriateness of the social issue focus. Some of the other "hot" issues of the middle 1970's—energy, pollution, consumerism—also fare pretty badly in these results.

Given these and other data discussed elsewhere in this book, it is clear that any plausible account of American politics in the 1970's would necessarily have to focus on the economic issue, which we have dealt with in Chapters 3 and 7 and, to some extent, in the present chapter, and also with the honesty issue, to which we now proceed.

POLITICAL DISAFFECTION

Many commentators on the 1970's era depicted the decade as one of widespread and rising discontent. In contrast, in virtually all areas relevant to the private spheres of existence, the pattern showed the precise opposite: high degrees of satisfaction were indicated in almost all areas, and no trend toward increasing dissatisfaction was discerned. The data we have examined to this point show those claims of rising discontent to be pure fiction.

There is, however, one area of life where the tendencies were exactly as those commentators *might have* anticipated; this involves dissatisfaction with the performance of government. There had been considerable growth of political alienation in the previous years; available indicators of trust and confidence in government showed sizable downward trends.

The earliest available measures of the general complex of outlooks at issue here date to the early 1950's, and thus represent a time-series that now spans some three decades. This general complex of outlooks can be referred to in various ways: political alienation, discontent, disaffection, dissatisfaction, and so on. In each case, the referent is to some sort of belief that all is not right in Washington, that government could be more efficient, more responsive, more trustworthy—indeed, more democratic—than it actually is. There are, as we have suggested, a fairly large number of indicators of these attitudes in the available survey series, and virtually all of them showed sharp increases in the level of political disaffection in the society from roughly 1960 through the 1970's.

One of the better known trend series is that derived from the biannual national election surveys conducted by the Survey Research Center at the University of Michigan. In the 1950's, the SRC developed measurements of two key components of political alienation: (1) political *powerlessness*, the sense that people are relatively powerless to influence governmental decisions; and (2) political *distrust*, the sense that government and the people running it are dishonest, corrupt, and otherwise not to be trusted. Table 8.8 shows the SRC trend data on the nine component indicators for the period 1956 to 1980.

The proportion of the American population feeling powerless (items 1–4) increased by a modest amount during the twenty-four years in question. The trends on the political efficacy (or powerlessness) questions, on the whole, were not as sharp as with other measures. Most of the change, moreover, came in the 1960's, followed by a leveling off in the 1970's. Throughout the decade, two fifths of the respondents said they did not have "any say" about what the government did; roughly half said public officials did not "care much what people like me think," and a sizable majority, over 70% at all times, felt that politics and government were sometimes "so complicated that a person like me can't really understand what's going on." Although the highest levels recorded, *these* measures of alienation, as indicated, did not change much during the 1970's, thus negating the claim of growing disaffection in that decade.

The trends on the trust items (5–9) were considerably more pronounced and have persisted, more or less unabated, through to the most recent year in the table.[24] Four out of five felt the government wastes "a lot" of tax money, almost as many felt the government is run "by a few big interests," and three out of four felt they could trust the government in Washington to "do what is right" only some of the time (64 respondents volunteered their own response category here—"none of the time"). All these changes were considerable, the view of government serving the "big interests," for example, rising from 28% in 1964 (when first asked) to 77% in 1980. The pattern of change, moreover, was continuous, showing increases in both the 1960's and 1970's.

Trend series from sources other than the Survey Research Center show similar patterns of declining trust. Lipset and Schneider (1983) have undertaken an exhaustive compilation of relevant survey and poll materials, drawing not only on the SRC data but also on materials from Gallup, Harris, the National Opinion Research Center, the Yankelovitch polls, and selected other sources. "Many public opinion polls," they indicate, have discovered "a sharp downturn in public confidence in a wide variety of institutions," a trend that began in the late 1960's (Lipset and Schneider, p. 13; see also Ladd, 1976–1977; Erskine, 1973–74). Analysis of data from the Detroit Area Studies (Duncan, Schuman, and Duncan, 1973), from a special series of Gallup polls commissioned by Potomac Associates (Rourke, Free, and Watts, 1976), and from, indeed, virtually all available trend series, shows the emergence of political disaffection beginning in the 1960's and, in most instances, continuing to grow in the 1970's. The single exception, the SRC's powerlessness series, saw the disaffection stabilized at the high level reached in the late 1960's, no further changing occurring in the subsequent decade.[25]

[24]A modest reversal in this long-term decline of trust was registered in the SRC's 1982 study. See Miller, 1983.

[25]The NORC General Social Surveys contain a series asking about confidence in various institutions, very specifically focusing on the people running them. The question: "I am going to name some institutions in this country. As far as the *people running* these institutions are concerned, would you say you have a great deal of

The political alienation trend shown in Table 8.8 is among the most thoroughly analyzed of any subject considered in contemporary political scholarship. The more prominent reviews and commentaries are those by: Converse (1972); Citrin (1974, 1977); Cutler and Bengston (1974, 1976); House and Mason (1975, 1978); Inglehart (1977a); Janowitz (1978); Lipset and Schneider (1983); Miller (1974); Nie, Verba, and Petrocik (1976); Robinson, Michael (1976); Rourke, Free, and Watts (1976), Wright, James (1976). Later in this chapter, we review the leading explanations that have been offered. Before doing that, however, some additional comments on the trend itself, and its implications, are in order.

First, the honesty issue revealed in the 1976 data is *not* unique to that year and is *not* simply a reaction to the Nixon administration. The comparison of the 1972, 1974, and 1976 trust results shows that the erosion of confidence in government was certainly accelerated by those events, but the trend itself predates the Nixon administration by many years, having commenced sometime in the middle 1960's. These data, in other words, show something more basic and more enduring than a simple response to Watergate.

Second, as indicated, the trends in Table 8.8 (and similar trends based on comparable items in other data) have been widely reported and discussed in the scholarly literature. They are, nevertheless, rarely cited in popular sources arguing the rising alienation theme. The critics ignore not only evidence that undercuts their world view, but also evidence consistent with it. One possible explanation is the strongly antiempirical bent evident in most such writings, along with a general hostility toward quantitative information of any kind. Or the critics might simply be unaware of the findings reported elsewhere in a highly compartmentalized social science literature. Another explanation, a somewhat less charitable one, is that any acknowledgment of *these* trends would require some acknowledgment of the lack of changes in dissatisfaction in other areas, a complication that is inconvenient to an all-or-nothing world view.

The sharp disparity between the political alienation trends and the generally high and unchanging levels of satisfaction found in other areas of life, reviewed in previous chapters, warrants more discussion. We noted earlier that the disparity has turned up in a number of sources. Rourke, Free, and Watts, for example, note both the sharp falloff in confidence in American institutions, and the much more positive evaluation by large majorities concerning their personal well-being and "expectations for the future.

----

confidence, only some confidence, or hardly any confidence at all in them?" Thirty percent expressed a great deal of confidence in the people running the executive branch of the federal government in 1973. That fell to 14% in 1974 and remained there until 1977, the first year of the Carter administration, when it rose to 29%. It fell once again, however, to 13% in the following year, and remained at that level in the 1980 study. The attitudes toward those running the other institutions (e.g., major companies, organized religion, organized labor, medicine, and so on) are much less volatile.

Table 8.8. Trend Data from the Survey Research Center (University of Michigan) on Nine Indicators of Political Alienation[a]

	1956[b]	1958[c]	1960[b]	1964	1966[d]	1968	1970	1972	1974	1976	1978	1980
Political powerlessness												
1. People like me don't have any say about what the government does.												
Agree	28%		27%	30%	36%	41%	36%	40%	41%	42%	46%	40%
N =	1735[e]		1911	1541	1215	1329	1492	2673	2455	2331	2239	1381
2. Voting is the only way that people like me can have any say about how the government runs things.												
Agree	74		74	74	72	58	60	62	62	56	59	60
N =	1721		1888	1546	1225	1321	1486	2671	2427	2326	2234	1358
3. Sometimes politics and government seem so complicated that a person like me can't really understand what's going on.												
Agree	64		59	68	72	71	74	74	73	73	73	71
N =	1732		1894	1534	1234	1334	1491	2681	2463	2351	2251	1376
4. I don't think public officials care much what people like me think.												
Agree	27		25	37	38	44	49	50	52	54	53	55
N =	1700		1853	1525	1173	1310	1457	2634	2393	2283	2179	1335
Political trust												
5. Do you think people in the government waste a lot of money we pay in taxes, waste some of it, or don't waste very much of it?												
A lot		45		48		61	70	67	76	76	79	80
N =		1702		1410		1307	1484	2241	2458	2772	2236	1572

6. How much of the time do you think you can trust the government in Washington to do what is right—just about always, most of the time, or only some of the time?

Some (or none)	24	22	32	37	45	46	63	66	70	74
N =	1709	1421	1230	1308	1471	2232	2443	2763	2215	1576

7. Would you say that the government is pretty much run by a few big interests looking out for themselves, or that it is run for the benefit of all the people?

Big interests		28	38	44	55	59	73	73	73	77
N =		1383	1103	1212	1360	2070	2270	2565	2058	1457

8. Do you feel that almost all of the people running the government are smart people, or do you think that quite a few of them don't seem to know what they are doing?

Not smart	39	31		39	46	42	48	53	56	65
N =	1700	1333		1278	1437	2161	2378	2660	2077	1532

9. Do you think that quite a few of the people running the government are crooked, not very many are, or do you think that hardly any of them are crooked?

Quite a few	26	30		26	33	38	47	44	42	48
N =	1668	1380		1281	1445	2170	2412	2685	2128	1543

aSources: Data entries for 1956 through 1972 are adapted from James Wright, *The Dissent of the Governed: Alienation and Democracy in America* (New York: Academic Press), 1976, Table 7.1.

Data entries for 1974 through 1980 were computed directly from the SRC study codebooks. See *The CPS 1974 American National Election Study Codebook* and *The CPS 1976 American National Election Study Codebook* (Ann Arbor, MI: Inter-University Consortium for Political and Social Research).

bItems 5 through 9 were not asked in either the 1956 or 1960 surveys.

cItems 1 through 4 and item 7 were not asked in the 1958 survey.

dItems 5, 8, and 9 were not asked in the 1966 survey.

eN's shown in the table are the number of respondents giving a valid, nonmissing response to each item in each year. Percentages are based on just these valid responses; intermittently missing data have been omitted on an item-by-item basis.

Americans express a sharp dichotomy between views about their personal lives, which have remained uniformly positive and essentially unchanged over the years . . . , and their far more sober view of the state of the nation" (Watts and Free, 1978, p. 204). Andrews and Withey (1976) find the same dichotomy. Respondents in their 1972 national survey were asked how satisfied they were with various aspects of life in the United States, in particular, with "your job," "your own family life," "yourself," "the way our national government is operating," and "life in the United States today." Roughly two thirds pronounced themselves "delighted" or "pleased" with their jobs and family life, and roughly half had the same reaction to "yourself." But less than one third (29%) were "delighted" or "pleased" with life in the United States as a whole, and only 9% felt the same about "the way our national government is operating." A 1977 Gallup poll (discussed by Lipset, 1979b) found 60% or more of the adult population expressing high satisfaction with family life, life overall, their health, the neighborhood, and their housing; only one third (32%) felt the same about the way democracy in this country is working.

The implications of this consistent pattern are first, that political alienation is conceptually and empirically distinct from other sorts of dissatisfaction, unhappiness, or discontent. That people are unhappy with the way government is being run, clearly, tells us little or nothing about how they feel about any other aspect of their lives. Second, the alienation that does exist on the contemporary scene is rather differentiated. We are not dealing here with some sweeping, across-the-board increase in levels of discontent, but with a specific dissatisfaction having roots in the operation of government and related political institutions. This further implies that political discontent is not necessarily connected to any other form of discontent. Many who are intensely dissatisfied with government are, nonetheless, quite pleased about their jobs, marriages, and communities.

Five principal lines of explanation for the decline of satisfaction with government have been advanced: (1) increasing political alienation as part of a more general and sweeping malaise; (2) increasing political alienation as a result of the changing sociodemographic composition of the population; (3) increasing political alienation as a result of cohort succession—that is, the dying of older (less alienated) populations and their replacement by younger (more alienated) populations; (4) increasing political alienation as a function of specific political experiences and events; (5) increasing alienation as a result of changing mass media treatment of public events.[26]

[26]As food for thought, one should consider some trend data from the Federal Republic of Germany. There, the responses to the political efficacy (or powerlessness) questions showed a positive trend in the period 1959 to 1972, just the opposite of the American experience (Baker, Dalton, and Hildebrandt, 1981, p. 27 ff.). Where the United States began with almost euphoric levels of enthusiasm in the 1950's, West Germany began the same period with a heritage of extreme cynicism, one so deep that little but upward movement was possible. In 1959, for example, less than 30%

Of these five, at least the first can be immediately dismissed, since the rising tide of discontent, for all practical purposes, has been *exclusively* restricted to political life. The second explanation, that the trend reflects growth in the size of traditionally more alienated social groups, can also be dismissed. It is well known that the average education level of the population has increased steadily, as has the proportion employed in white-collar jobs and, therefore, the proportions upwardly mobile.[27] Real incomes have also risen at least into the late 1960's. Owing to the maturation of the postwar generations, the average age of the electorate has tended to decline. The general thrust of demographic change through the 1970's, then, was toward a better educated, more affluent, more middle class, and younger population. What this amounts to, however, is a relative increase in the size of social groups that are, in most studies, the *least* politically alienated (Wright, 1976, Chapters 5, 6 and 7). Demographics, in other words, would lead one to expect a *decline* in political discontent, rather than an increase.

This, of course, is only a deductive argument against the demographic explanation, but direct empirical examinations by Converse (1972) and House and Mason (1975) substantiate the conclusion. "Contrary to what Scammon and Wattenberg (1970) imply, demography is *not* destiny with regard to either political alienation or issue attitudes" (House and Mason, p. 145).

The third explanation, cohort succession, must also be ruled out. First, its plausibility rests on the assumption that current generations (the "young people of today") are more politically alienated than older generations who are being replaced, and while a few studies have reported this pattern, most report just the opposite. Most studies, indeed, report that political alienation is *lowest* among the young and tends to increase with age, which would again lead one to anticipate *declining* alienation as the result of cohort succession (Wright, 1976, pp. 143–148). Here, too, direct empirical examination of the hypothesis by Cutler and Bengston (1974, 1976) supports the present conclusion. The differences associated with age over the 1952 to 1968 period, they report, "are small and appear to be the result of the different educational compositions of the different age groups rather than indicators of the existence of clearly identifiable generational groups" (1974, p. 174). Rising political alienation characterized *all* age groups during the period, which rules out any sort of cohort or generational explanation. By the same token, rising political alienation characterized virtually all social

---

of the West Germans disagreed with the statement that "people like me have no say." That rose to 40% in 1972. Equivalent figures for the United States for 1960 and 1972, from Table 8.8, are 73 and 60%.

[27]Most such accounts exaggerate the extent of the transformation by failing to recognize that most of the change is sex-linked. Employment of nonfarm males in manual jobs declined from 69.9 to 64.2% in the first half of this century. The equivalent figures for women were 78.0 and 45.6%. For data and discussion, see Hamilton, 1972, p. 156 ff.

groups as well (House and Mason, 1975), which likewise rules out any demographic explanation.

This brings us to the fourth explanation, that the trend in political alienation has had basically political causes. Although particulars vary from analysis to analysis, most serious empirical inquiries into the causes of the alienation trends sustain this explanation.

Miller (1974) has analyzed the drop in political trust from 1964 to 1970. In his analysis, the major source of increased political distrust was dissatisfaction with government policies in the areas of racial integration and, especially, Vietnam. Thus, political trust among blacks and among whites favoring integration actually increased between 1964 and 1966, during the Johnson Administration's big civil rights push, then fell sharply in the years after 1966, when Johnson (and later Nixon) was diverted from domestic issues by the events in Vietnam. In the same vein, between 1964 and 1970, political trust declined much more sharply among *both* those who favored an immediate withdrawal from Vietnam *and* those who favored an escalation and total military victory than among those favoring a more Administration-oriented policy. The key lesson that emerges from Miller's analysis is that trust in government is highest among persons who feel that government is pursuing policies consonant with their own interests or preferences, and generally lower elsewhere. The increase in alienation is here explained by an increase in the proportion of the population who felt that government was *not* pursuing such policies.[28]

House and Mason's (1975) analysis points to a similar conclusion. Based on both efficacy and trust indicators, it is thus somewhat more broad-ranging than Miller's; the essential conclusion is that "much of the shift in alienation between 1964 and 1968 resulted from the growing discrepancy between the attitudes of the electorate and the trend of political policies and events" (1975, pp. 143–144). In the House–Mason analysis, the key political issue, of course, is Vietnam. Between 1964 and 1968, as is well known, the general drift of public opinion about Vietnam was decidedly in a dovish direction (e.g., J. Wright, 1972), but the general drift in Administration war policy assuredly was not. The growing gap between what the public wanted and what the Administration chose to deliver created rising political discontent—not just among the counterculture, or among the young or college educated, but more or less across the board. "Thus, both House and Mason and Miller argue that responses to the various alienation items, and changes in these responses, during the 1960's reflected neither a general malaise nor invalid measures, but rather were due to rising discrepancies between the policy preferences or issue-

---

[28]Citrin (1974) disputes much of Miller's analysis, but not its key conclusion. "I do not dispute Miller's finding that disagreement with government policy on important contemporary issues engenders political cynicism" (p. 984).

attitudes of the electorate and the actual course of public policy and events" (House and Mason, 1978, p. 19). Our own analysis of the trends (Wright, Chapter 7) suggests a similar pattern: most of the alienation increases came among people who (1) preferred policy directions in Vietnam other than those that the Administration was pursuing, and (2) showed some concern over deterioration in their personal financial situation.

Most of the studies just discussed take the alienation trends up through 1970 or 1972, and thus do not account for any subsequent effects due to Watergate and the related irregularities within the Nixon Administration. The sharp increases on some of the alienation items between 1972 and 1974 (for example, see items 6 and 7 in Table 8.8) make it apparent that the electorate was not immune to the lessons of those events; the proportion thinking government could be trusted only some of the time jumped nearly twenty points during the Watergate period, and the increase in the proportion seeing the government run by a few big interests was nearly as sharp. All things considered, it is hard to imagine something other than Watergate as the likely cause of the post-1972 increases. (On the Watergate experience and its effects, see the collection of essays edited by Chaffee, 1975.)

The fifth possibility must also be considered in this connection: the rise of what one might call critical media. This explanation, on the whole, has not been extensively researched, although the work of Arthur H. Miller and associates (1979) is an important first step. Through to at least the mid-1960's, most of the American media—print, film, and electronic—were strongly supportive of all existing institutions. The lessons provided there amounted to one continuous, exuberant legitimation of current arrangements and practice. The institutions of government were continuously sanctified, the men and policies of government were ordinarily justified and defended (or, at minimum, in news reports, were recounted in flat, nonevaluative narration). Fictional accounts, drama, entertainment, and so forth, followed the same guidelines, persons in authority being portrayed as honest, public-spirited, and responsible. The media codes governing content required such portrayals. Evil-doers holding high position had to be portrayed as exceptions, and were balanced by portraits of upstanding persons of equal or superior rank, the latter being shown as typical, as the rule. All crime or moral dereliction, moreover, had to be punished or repented in the course of the presentation.

That structure of controls, of course, broke down in the period of the Vietnam war. Many news-gathering agencies felt they had been taken in by government "misleads" and, as a result, adopted a much more independent stance. With a loosening of the reins, unrelenting exposé came to replace the soporific supportive statement. In the drama, thrillers, and general entertainment programs one also found a change, a 180-degree shift in value orientations, and political leaders and businessmen became the near-obligatory villains. Those persons or groups previously accorded high status in media presentations were now systematically denigrated. It is unlikely that such a shift in content would have no effects.[29]

The two factors, political performance and media tendencies, would both, no doubt, have impacts in determining mass responses. Government performance, after all, is not directly observed; it is mediated information, coming through various channels of communication. And if the latter choose, with some system, to communicate approval, or in another season, disapproval, public attitudes would presumably be moved accordingly. The findings reported by Arthur Miller and associates are consistent with this interpretation.[30]

The sources of the political alienation trends, we think, are not obscure or subtle. Vietnam, race, Watergate, and a problematic economy, we assume, were the primary causal factors. These problems occurred at a time when most media were abandoning their previous protective orientations and either allowed or encouraged and supported a freedom for investigative reporting and commentary that in most previous decades would have been unthinkable.

Many people examining the patterns shown in Table 8.8 would expect some political insurgency as a result. And yet the political history of the late 1970's has been remarkably free of dissident political movements—most of all, of movements that could reasonably be said to command a mass following. If people are so upset with the way government is working, why then, it might be asked, do they not do something about it?

The answer, we think, is contained in the analyses of the previous chapters. Many of the people who are upset with the government in Washington are, at the same time, obviously quite satisfied with most aspects of their private existences (their financial condition always being the principal exception). To mount an insurgency that would address these political grievances might simultaneously threaten the satisfactions and accomplishments achieved in the private sphere.

One need not address the question in a purely speculative way, since some of the SRC studies contain questions allowing a detailed exploration of public reactions. The first series we will review involves the "problems . . . that you face these days in your own life," those first tabulated

[29]For an account of the transformations occurring within four important news-gathering organizations, see Halberstam, 1979. For an account of the antiestablishment content of prime-time television programs (complete with interviews of writers), see Stein, 1979. For an account of television treatments of business and businessmen, see Lichter, Lichter, and Rothman, 1981.

[30]It is difficult to imagine that Eisenhower's popularity would have been sustained if the press of the 1950's had had the same critical orientation as in the 1970's. One should contrast the text of his press conferences contained in the New York Times with the write-ups appearing on the front page of the same newspaper. At the same, time it should be noted, the media are not all-powerful. The heavily negative treatment of Ronald Reagan in "soft" news coverage (Robinson, Clancey, and Grant, 1983) has not produced an equivalent negative image among the general public.

and discussed in Chapter 3. A series of follow-up questions asked how people reacted to these problems, what they think should be done with regard to the single most important problem they faced.

In 1972, a significant minority, just under one fifth of the respondents, reported no personal problems (Table 8.9). Just under two fifths, when asked how their problem should be solved, indicated that it was something they could take care of on their own or, alternatively, indicated that there was little to be done about it. A considerable portion, roughly one half of those reporting a personal problem, in other words, would undertake a personal or private solution to the problem.

Among those who would reach out for help to some other person or agency, a fair proportion still avoided governments, turning instead to specific persons or to private assistance organizations. Only one quarter of the population turned to government (a term that is broadly conceived in the question, covering all levels). Of those who turned to government, 2% found the agency to be very helpful, and another 11% found it at least somewhat helpful. Roughly one half of those who sought aid from a governmental agency found that agency to be, to some degree at least, responsive to their concerns. The bottom line for the specialist in alienation is the category of those who turned to government and found it (or "them") not at all helpful. This amounted to one respondent in eight.[31]

While enormous in terms of absolute numbers, that one in eight result falls well short of the proportions imagined by those who, alarmed by visions of "appetitive" masses, assume heavy overloads of demand, something that would exceed the capacity of any government to respond to. For most of those with personal problems, some processes appear to be operating that deflect attention away from government as the obvious agency or means to provide a solution.

Before dismissing that privatization as the obvious reflection of an individualistic heritage (or as a cunning legitimation strategy), one ought to give some thought to the possibility that the respondents know what they are talking about. Some of the problems may be modest; some evidence, reviewed earlier, suggested that was the case for at least some of those reporting a financial problem. Depending on the dimension of the problem, a private solution might well be the best, most appropriate approach. Some other problems, such as declining health with advancing age, are accurately perceived as having no obvious solution.

Those frustrated citizens, the one in eight facing a nonresponsive government, ought to be at the center of studies of the alienated citizenry. One should know the character of their demands, the extent and seriousness of their problems. For those interested in improving the human condition,

[31]Economic stress, as indicated in previous chapters, was greater in 1974. This reduced the percentage of those reporting no problems (to 14%), increased the percentage saying the government ought to be helping (to 34%), and brought an increase in the percentage saying the government was not helpful at all (to 21%).

Table 8.9. The Handling of Personal Problems (SRC 1972)

Respondent reports no problems	19%

Those remaining were asked to indicate their
    "single most important" personal problem. They
    were asked if it were:

├──►"Something you have to work out on your own"   38
          —"can take care of it" on own—28
Or,
          —"can't do much" about it   — 9

└──►"Someone . . . ought to be helping"

       \Don't know, not ascertained   4
    ├─►A person   6
    ├─►A private agency or organization   4
    ├─►The government in general or a public
             or governmental agency   26

          \Don't know, not ascertained   3
                                                                  ─────
       Government/agency is: 100%

    ├─►Very helpful   2%   N = 1072
    ├─►Somewhat helpful   11
    ├─►Not helpful at all   13

inquiry should also be made as to the sources of the nonperformance, of the failure of the governmental response. One additional observation should be noted here, at least in passing; it is unlikely that those problems aggregate in any significant way, that they have the same direction or import. It is not as if this one eighth would be leaning on the government in the same way, all sharing a common purpose. Fragmentation, diversity of concern and of perceived solution, seems a stronger likelihood.[32]

The principle substantive conclusions of this chapter may be summarized as follows:

1. From the end of American involvement in Vietnam to the present, economic issues have been the leading choice for most important problem facing the nation. In all decades, economic issues are the leading choice for most important personal problem. An implication is that in the decade of the 1970's, there was a close overlap between personal troubles and public issues.

2. Despite the widespread depiction of rising radicalism early in the decade and rising conservatism later, most credible evidence shows a

[32]One indication of that diversity appears in the answers to another question (Q. E1G) in the series: "Which political party do you think would be most likely . . . to be helpful on this /personal/ problem?" One fifth said the Republicans, one third said the Democrats, and about one half said no difference.

We have undertaken some preliminary investigations of the fragmentation hypothesis. It is more than a likelihood; it is a reality.

stability in outlooks over the decade and no sharp trends toward either political extreme.

3. The political consciousness of the American masses is far too complex to be accurately characterized as basically liberal or basically conservative. The majority is strongly liberal on some issues, strongly conservative on others, and middle-of-the-road on most.

4. Although the desire to cut government spending has been seen by many as the key to the politics of the late 1970's and early 1980's, the available data do not suggest widespread popular support for across-the-board spending cuts. The public would apparently prefer to see less spending in some areas, but more spending in others; in a few areas, the current levels of spending are judged to be about right. In the 1976 SRC survey, a sizable majority rejected the idea that spending should be cut even at the expense of health and education programs.

5. Although most of the data from this and previous chapters suggests stability rather than change in the outlooks of the American masses, one obvious and important trend over the decade was the continuing increase in disaffection with political life—a continuation of trends that can be dated at least to the mid-1960's, especially the trend in political distrust. The proportions feeling that the people in Washington are honest, capable, and trustworthy have been in more or less continual decline, declines that can be ascribed to rising dissatisfaction with the specific performance of government (rather than, say, demographic changes or some more general, across-the-board, growing alienation with the conditions of modern life). The radical potential suggested by these trends, however, is sharply undercut by the persistently high levels of satisfaction people report with most or all aspects of their personal lives. Most people, it appears, see a very sharp disjuncture between their private life and the world of public affairs.

6. Politics is not a high-priority consideration in the lives of most people: most of the population find that the day-to-day routines of life dominate, and that they have neither the time nor the interest for things political. For this reason, the radical potential is severely circumscribed. A small fraction of the population (on the order of one tenth) does not even sense that there are national problems of any urgency, and many of those who do sense such problems deny that they are touched by them in any direct way. Others who are personally affected by what they see as an important problem find that they are satisfied with present governmental performance in the area, or that the area in question is not the government's responsibility. The problems sensed by adult Americans, in short, do not lead to or flow into any clear and obvious movement of protest.

9 STABILITY AND CHANGE: ILLUSIONS AND REALITIES

The Italian philosopher, Benedetto Croce, once wrote a book which, in translation, bears the title, *What is Living and What is Dead in the Philosophy of Hegel* (1915). The title contains a simple and useful idea, the notion of a sort-out, of an assessment, of something akin to a spring housecleaning. It suggests that we keep whatever has proven useful and discard the rest. Applied to the received heritage of social theory or criticism, it suggests the need for a general review of major propositions and principal claims, asking which have gained substantial evidential support, which have gained little or none, and which have yielded equivocal findings and are thus in limbo. Such a review would simply clear away the accumulated rubbish and provide the basis for subsequent construction of a more adequate theoretical framework.

These comments, of course, are not meant to suggest that the realities of social life are somehow fixed and immutable, or that an inadequate proposition, once discovered, must forever be relegated to the intellectual trash pile. Social realities, unlike those of physics or chemistry, do change. Thus, different intellectual frameworks may be required to understand different historical epochs. The theory of the mass society, for example, might have been adequate[1] for the period of mass migration from farm to city (a social

[1] Or might not have been. On the whole, mass society theory is the least adequately supported of the dominant social theories current today. To illustrate, the theory portrays cities as centers of mass society disorganization, most accentuated in urban slum conditions. But research on the matter has shown an opposite picture. One early study of an Italian slum area in Chicago reported that social control was largely "in terms of personal relationships" (Zorbaugh, 1929, p. 177), and, "In the last analysis Little Sicily is still a mosaic of Sicilian villages" (p. 180). Subsequent investigations of Italian slum areas elsewhere also found them to be characterized by high degrees of social involvement, just the opposite of disorganization (see Firey, 1947, Chapter 5; Whyte, 1955; and Gans, 1962). Even the process of migration has been shown to be not quite the disorganizing experience many have thought. They anticipate anomie because of their read-in—the uprooting, the cutting of ties, and a lack of integration in the new setting. The actual experience for many migrants is one of chain migration; they move with the aid of and assistance of kin. They move *en*

upheaval that has happened exactly once in human history), but with the near-completion of that movement, and with the rerooting of populations in their new milieux, that theory might lose its viability. At present, one might assume, it should be abandoned, or, alternatively, recognized as a special case, with validity only for a specific historical period. Instead, such theories are often simply dressed up and recycled as new intellectual offerings.

The mass society theory provides the classic case of handed-down thinking. Some nineteenth century thinkers, Gustav LeBon, for example, made use of Greek and Roman experience to fashion an analysis of the French Revolution and of subsequent "mass" events. Others picked up the elements of the position in the twentieth century, piecing together an analysis, largely without benefit of data, to deal with fascist and communist movements (for example, Emil Lederer and Hannah Arendt). Still later, in a distinct "left" variant, one finds the work of Herbert Marcuse, at this point the aim being to explain the acquiescence of the masses.

This theory, we think, more than any other, is destined for a *retour éternel* in intellectual affairs. It is *the* basic theory underlying mass media alarmist accounts. The same is true for the book-length exposé, for those authors providing new and interesting material for educated and concerned upper-middle-class readers. Given the extraintellectual purposes motivating such productions, they will always prove immune to, or generally indifferent to, systematic evidence. The hallmark of such literature is straw-in-the-wind evidence, which is then pronounced to be symptomatic of the larger development yet to come. The Charles Reich work, of course, would be archetypical. In this case, it might be termed a mass society tale with a happy ending.

Given the mutability of social phenomena, it is apparent that the sorting out process suggested in Croce's title must be a continuous endeavor, or, in other words, that there must be an ongoing interaction between theory (or speculation) and research. In the healthy or nonpathological state, the interaction is characterized by mutual benefits. Research helps refine the theoretical or speculative statement; the refined theory in turn guides future research. The rationale for such a procedure seems obvious and was, in any case, much discussed in the sociology of the early 1950's, the works of Robert K. Merton (1957, chapters 2 and 3) and C. Wright Mills (1959, chapters 2 and 3) coming immediately to mind.

In the unhealthy or pathological state, speculation and research become divorced, with little binding them together. The extreme case is the theorist who takes pride in removing theory entirely from the realm of the empirical

---

famille, and frequently with segments of entire communities. On arrival, they can thus integrate within a social structure provided by family, friends, and former neighbors. See Breton, 1964; and MacDonald and MacDonald, 1964.

For a more general critique of the mass society position, see Hamilton, 1972, pp. 46–49, and, as applied to the German case, Hamilton, 1982, pp. 433–437 and passim.

and who thus comes to live entirely amidst mental constructions; or, on the other hand, the researcher who is satisfied with the idle presentation of correlations and results, never offering any serious indication of their meaning for the understanding of social processes.

The pathological states described above are definitely in evidence in many of the works that have been reviewed in this book. The authors of several leading works of speculation and criticism considered here seem to neither know nor care about the existence of relevant empirical materials. Likewise, many of the empirical studies we have reviewed and cited prove to be curiously indifferent to the bearing of the results on some of these larger theoretical issues. The wide and clearly lamentable separation of theory and research has become an all-too-frequent practice in both scholarly and popular (or "critical") works.

We consider in some detail later in this chapter how this pathological state of affairs comes to persist. Many of its elements are illustrated in the present-day teaching of social theory in university contexts. In many cases, the theories come to be taught in a pure or deductive form, the key propositions being treated without reference to efforts of empirical assessment. In most such courses, little or no attempt is made to undertake what Croce suggested, namely, to discern what is living and what is dead in the received theoretical heritage, in the corpus of Tocqueville, Marx, Durkheim, Weber, Mannheim, Parsons, or any of the others. The theory of the mass society may be discussed and presented as a still-viable intellectual entity, with no mention of the solid empirical evidence challenging it on most points. Frequently, Marx will be taught (and learned) as a set of conclusions to be defended, rather than as a set of possibilities to be researched. The works of Weber and Durkheim (and those of the other revered founding fathers) are taught as sacred texts to be mastered and recited, much as Catholic children are (or were) taught their catechism. The decisive features of the malady we are discussing are the refusal to reject, or even to empirically examine, a sacred theoretical claim and the evident unwillingness to declare the "death" of a favored proposition.[2]

The ultimate expression of this malady comes when theory is taken as an end in itself, rather than as a means to better understand the realities of social existence. A scholar (or "pop" intellectual) announces, say, a Marxian analysis of this or that, as if the identification with a received heritage somehow gives it special analytic merit. The effort, obviously, should be to produce a *correct* analysis of this or that, and if the correct analysis also

[2]Max Weber's *The Protestant Ethic and the Spirit of Capitalism* is, of course, a classic. The leading critique of Weber's work, that of Kurt Samuelsson (1961), has been out of print for many years. Introductory texts regularly do obeisance to the Weber text; with equal regularity, they ignore Samuelsson's critique. A similar case involves Emile Durkheim's "classic" work, *Suicide*. That study has recently been subjected to a devastating critique by Whitney Pope (1976). It remains to be seen how this critique will be treated.

happens to be a Marxian one, so much the better for that tradition. But no virtue can be claimed for a line of reasoning simply *because* it can be identified with a particular received tradition. To do so is a peculiar, though common, form of ad hominem reasoning.

In the spirit of the preceding paragraphs, then, our first task in the present chapter is to consider what is living and what is dead in the various viewpoints that were discussed in Chapters 1 and 2. A second task is to organize the various threads of findings and interpretations that have been presented into a more coherent, more adequate theoretical framework than has been provided in the received accounts. A third task is to consider how dead (or moribund) elements of those theories manage to persist, even in the face of much contrary evidence.

WHAT IS LIVING AND WHAT IS DEAD IN THE SIX ANALYSES?

Charles Reich, it will be remembered, announced that "there is a revolution coming . . . the revolution of the new generation." So little of that revolution now seems manifest that one wonders at the widespread credence so readily given his declarations when they were first revealed. One would be hard put to support his claim of a qualitatively different world in the making. Even the dynamics of change are erroneously represented. The few institutional changes achieved in the 1970's of the sort Reich announced and championed were not the result of mass demands issuing from the ranks of the new generation. Most were the product of judicial decisions, many of which were sought by persons in their middle years, the decisions themselves, typically, being made by judges who were of even more advanced age.

The youth movements that supplied the "stuff" for Reich's claims had largely disappeared by mid-decade. Even their character has been misrepresented. "Activist movements consisting largely of young persons" are not the same as "young persons being activists," as if the entire generation were in motion. The former involves a part of the category of young persons. Some of them, hundreds of thousands even, were actively involved in those movements—but others were not. The latter formulation assumes that all young persons (or at least a significant majority) were active; it makes for a much more dramatic statement: "Young people today are challenging . . . " and so on. Reich, like many others, made the easy leap, and took the part for the whole. That was followed by an extrapolation, to the assumption that all subsequent generations would follow in the same direction. Some members of the younger cohorts of the late 1960's and early 1970's were behaving differently from their predecessors; that is manifestly obvious. But the assumption of continuity, of linear development, has not proven justified. There is, after all, an easy alternative theory: a cyclical development—a period of uprising that might just as easily be followed by a period of quiescence.

Reich's portrait of alienation, hostility, and discontent, his account of "the disintegration of the social fabric," proves to be completely without support. It was not valid at the time the book was written; it has not been supported by evidence collected in the course of the decade. His claim about hatred of work, as we have seen, is also without support, both at the beginning and at the end of the decade. This is based on answers given by cross-sections of the nation's population. The only way Reich could be at all correct in his claims would be if substantial majorities of those respondents were giving false reports of their actual feelings. Even then, Reich would be mistaken in his specific formulations. He claimed a wide-awake awareness, something freely, easily, and angrily verbalized; but that kind of consciousness is not indicated in the available evidence from the period.

So to the question, "What is living?" in the work of Charles Reich, the answer is "not much." Even where he was "on to something," as with the movements made up largely of young persons, that something deserved much closer and more systematic scrutiny than Reich gave it, in order to discover its sources, dynamics, and impacts. Now, long after the fact, it is eminently clear that some different lines of analysis were, and are, in order. But like so much of social theory, the favorites of the day, when no longer viable, are simply abandoned. Little effort is made to explain or account for the misperception, for the failure.[3]

The Scammon and Wattenberg book, The Real Majority, provides the second of the positions we have described and assessed. It is, essentially, a data-based response to those who argued the existence of (or the coming of) a profound liberating transformation originating in the demands of the new generation. Although not specifically focusing on The Greening of America, these authors are clearly concerned with the Consciousness III variety of argumentation. Most of the Scammon and Wattenberg claims, as indicated, were very well founded; the book has, on the whole, provided a much better, more accurate portrait of subsequent events in the decade than did Reich's work or that of various other upbeat social commentators.

Scammon and Wattenberg's demographic portrait of the American population and its likely shape in the years to come has also proved accurate. Barring war or plague, as indicated, it could hardly be otherwise. That the majority is "unyoung, unpoor, and unblack" is a truth that will hardly be disputed. Since the mid-1970's, moreover, the cohorts coming of age have all been smaller than their predecessors; the large generations of the baby-boom years have long since been part of the adult population and, inexorably, are aging. The steady increase in the average age of the adult population is a decisive fact about the foreseeable future. The Scammon-

---

[3]Notable exceptions to this generalization are the works of Beck and Jennings, 1979, and Rothman and Lichter, 1982. Two earlier works appearing in the period of student uprising and recognizing the recurrent character of such movements were those of Feuer, 1969; and Lipset, 1971, chapters 4 and 5.

Wattenberg prediction of the "graying of America" is one that will guide us through to at least the first decades of the twenty-first century.

Scammon and Wattenberg were also correct in their more detailed comments about the younger groups. Where many commentators began with the assumption that education was one of the principal keys to the whole transformation, these authors pointed out the limited incidence of higher education among the young people of today; it touches only approximately one fifth of those in the relevant age categories. Going by surveys, as opposed to the evidence of public demonstrations, they were also able to show the sharply divided character of the young. Those with opinions, for example, split fifty–fifty into doves and hawks on the major national issue of the early 1970's. Scammon and Wattenberg also signaled the limited political impact of the younger cohorts, pointing to the extremely low levels of participation typical of young people. The champions of countercultural initiatives, in short, had mistaken the part for the whole. Effectively, they had focused on a small part of the young and educated fifth, specifically on those who were vocal and active in support of antiwar and/or countercultural initiatives, and generalized their attitudes and behavior to the entire category.

Scammon and Wattenberg's summary conclusions recounted in these paragraphs are all to be counted among the living; that is, the accurate and useful observations contained in their account of the real majority. On the other side of the ledger, however, there is the problem of the social issue, which refers to a cluster of concerns, the principal components of which were crime, race, lawlessness, and civil rights. The lawlessness problem, as distinct from crime, referred to the manifestations of contempt for traditional ways and symbols and to the destruction of property—and life—associated with the demonstrations typical of that age. Scammon and Wattenberg announced that the social issue was the majority concern; it dominated the thinking of the real majority. Given the traditionalist loyalties of that majority, it was not surprising, they argued, that reactions were very hostile to everything championed by the advocates of counterculturalism.

Our review of the evidence cited by Scammon and Wattenberg showed that at no point in the period covered by their data were Social Issues a first priority concern of the majority of the U.S. population. There was, to be sure, a larger than average concern with the issues discussed, reflecting some obvious events of the period. But in the case of crime and lawlessness, for example, the high point of mentions involved only about one quarter of the population, and only for a brief period in 1968. Even that level quickly diminished as the problem receded from public view. Concerns with the various social issue components, as we have seen, were extremely modest throughout the 1970's, as evidenced by spontaneous mentions to questions about personal and national problems. The social issue, in short, was never a *majority* concern.

There *was* general, that is, majority opposition to various elements of the counterculture, that is clear enough; but that opposition, on the whole, does not appear to have been driven by the anger and intensity Scammon and Wattenberg allege. One area of backlash, moreover, never appeared, the one relative to economic and civil rights gains by blacks. The reason for this is simple; the tendency has been very much in an opposite, that is, a positive, direction. Scammon and Wattenberg, surprisingly, mentioned this well-documented trend only in passing.

The source of Scammon and Wattenberg's difficulty is easily discerned. On a crucial point, they failed to make consistent use of their basic empirical method. Their presentation of evidence with respect to the social issue, rather unexpectedly, did not contain the relevant percentage figures, thus hiding the minority status of that combination of concerns. Readers were thus led to believe that a new issue had surfaced and, just as important, that another one, the economic issue, had been eclipsed. The social issue, in summary, is best counted as a dead claim. It is one that was not properly depicted in its original exposition. Most of the minority sentiment that surfaced in the late 1960's and provided the real basis for the claim, moreover, has since receded from the popular agenda of concerns.

The third position we have considered is that of the workplace critics. Their argument may be seen as a specialized variant of the social critics' position offered by Charles Reich and company. The workplace critics took the Reichian themes and applied them to the workplace. Given the previous events and analysis, the claims of the workplace critics had a simple and "obvious" plausibility to them. The new generation, the young and well-educated, were moving out of the educational institutions and entering the labor force. Their special outlooks and demands were going to test managers in the industrial bureaucracies. These new workers, after all, would not be satisfied with the dull routines and the rigidities of the system. They would insist on enrichment, self-direction, and participation in decision-making. The managers, like the university administrators before them, were poorly prepared for this challenge; the expectation, therefore, was one of intransigence, of nonresponse in the face of the new demands. Given the intensity of the feelings involved, it was clear that the situation contained an explosive potential.

There is little point in dwelling on the claims of this position, since they have been discussed at length in previous chapters. The basic claims must be pronounced dead. The anticipated rising never appeared. The explosive potential has not been realized. After running the material for two or three years, the mass media (and some not-quite-so-masses-oriented scholarly sources) simply abandoned the theme, leaving only the most unyielding to pick away at the mine face, still convinced that they were about to come upon a rich vein of ore.

Our review of the evidence indicated that, from the outset, no credible evidence sustained this position. All credible surveys had found large majorities satisfied to some degree with their work. That same data, moreover, failed to show any welling of dissatisfaction or antiwork sentiments. The so-called hard measures—strike activity, absenteeism, turnover—also were not supportive. Some fluctuations were to be seen in those measures, but then *some* fluctuations had always been seen, most of them easily explained in terms of routine, normal, nonexceptional factors, such as the business cycle. Most studies show lower levels of work satisfaction among young workers; this was taken as telling evidence for the basic claim. But lower work satisfaction among the young, as far as we can tell, has always been the case, for a very simple reason: their work, typically, is less attractive and less rewarding in every respect.

George B. Morris, Jr., General Motors' vice president in charge of industrial relations, caught one key aspect of the workplace critics' method with his statement that it "was just a bunch of academicians quoting each other." He could, of course, have counted politicians among the perpetrators (for example, Richard Nixon, Elliot Richardson, and Edward Kennedy), plus an assortment of Marxist commentators, plus representatives from several management consultant firms, plus, for financing and publicity, the Ford Foundation. The coalition of forces involved in the effort was truly remarkable, extending from right to left on the political spectrum, including both ardent defenders and ardent detractors of the "system."

While the *social* process involved might be characterized as a mutually-supportive misinformation system, the conclusions did not depend exclusively on interpersonal determinants. Some points of empirical contact did exist, and the use of these methods, too, requires comment. The workplace critics' method required that one either ignore the available survey findings or argue the invalidity of those findings, the claim being that they did not accurately reflect underlying sentiments. Some other methods based on participant observation procedures or in-depth interviews, it was claimed, were necessary in order to obtain valid results. But even this procedure was not followed consistently. Some proponents of the position adopted a double standard. Surveys were cited where there was at least apparent support for their claims; they were neglected or ridiculed when their claims were not supported. Some researchers using survey procedures hid the unpalatable finding; they buried it (the evidence of majority job satisfaction) in a technical appendix.

There was, as indicated, a preference for the participant observation study or for those based on in-depth interviews, the claim being that they proved more accurate, only they showed workers' true feelings. But the job dissatisfaction claim was not consistently supported in their research; some of the participant observation studies came up with exactly the same kind of findings as the representative surveys. Some of the participant observation studies, moreover, which support the critics' claims, made use of flagrantly nonrepresentative samples. The researchers had reached out to persons one would know, from the outset, were going to give the "right" answers. The author of one best-selling volume based on extended interviews, describing his method, openly acknowledged two stages of selection. Between one-fifth and one-third of the original interviews were selected for the final version, and these were edited until he had extracted "the gold." One must ask: What was the principle of selection? What was excluded in the process?

The Lordstown episode provides numerous instances of biased procedure. There was the initial bias of site selection; neglecting other instances of strike activity, this one came to be defined as the textbook case for the young worker argument. It was followed by a read-in of the going claims and a neglect of an obvious (and discussed) alternative, namely, speedup. One of the researchers, with no evident qualm, described her selection of an obviously nonrepresentative sample of workers, a worker commune, which yielded a wealth of material for her purpose. To the best of our knowledge, none of those involved in the Lordstown fabrication ever came forward to explain how or why they had gone wrong in their assessment.

The misinformation communicated in this case stemmed, in the first line of analysis, from gross malfeasance in the conduct of research. It then benefited, partly through an accident of timing, from an unusual coalition of believer-publicists, who transmitted "the lessons" to a larger audience. Many of the persons in that audience, of course, were innocent victims. They would not have known the failings of the initial research efforts. After repeatedly hearing the findings vouched for by many credible sources, they would, clearly, have found them easy to believe.

The fourth of the positions outlined, coming under the heading, "The Empirical Study of Work," involves the activities of hundreds, or more likely, thousands of researchers over the span of more than half a century. Their researches, we have shown, constitute a dialectical negation of the claims put forth by the workplace critics. Given our conclusion with respect to the latter claims, the principal findings of these many researchers must be counted as among "the living."

There is little to be added at this point. As reported in our original exposition, most of this research, our best available evidence on the subject, stands in flat and unmistakable contradiction to the workplace critics' themes. Work is not defined as the central life interest of most employed persons. Most people, as shown repeatedly, report some degree of satisfaction with their work. And if any trend is discernible, going by the longer Gallup series, it is a favorable one—that is, increased work satisfaction.

It was evidence generated out of this tradition that eventually undermined key claims of the workplace critics. Quinn, Staines, and McCullough, for example, in a comprehensive review, pointed out that younger workers *were* less satisfied with their jobs, but that this had been the case "for the past 15 years . . . and, probably, even earlier . . . " (1974, pp. 1 and 12). Where the workplace critics had been arguing the negative effects of education on work satisfaction (education being the generator of new values, higher aspirations, and so forth), Quinn and his associates brought in the finding that among those workers without a college degree, little relationship existed between educational level and job satisfaction. And those with college degrees, it was reported, had high levels of job satisfaction.

Had the critics and commentators known of (or paid attention to) the workplace research, their pronouncements would never, presumably, have seen the light of day. That their claims could take off in the face of considerable contrary evidence indicates a serious pathology in the intellectual procedures of the media and of the so-called critics.

The fifth of the positions discussed and assessed is the theory of postindustrialism, advanced in the works of Daniel Bell and Ronald Inglehart. As we saw in our earlier discussion, this theory has both a structural and a psychological component. The structural component consists of a set of claims about transformations in the structure of the advanced industrial economy—that increased automation and technological change have seriously eroded the need for physical labor, that work in postindustrial societies comes increasingly to be brain work in the expanding service sector, and thus that, more and more, advanced years of formal schooling are needed to successfully compete. The awesome productivity gains achieved through technological change have, the argument continues, freed ever larger fractions of the population from basic material want.

The psychological component of the theory derives mainly from this last point. Postulating a hierarchy of needs, with material security at the bottom and self-realization at the top, the theory argues that as the economic problem is solved, consciousness is thereby freed to pursue these higher-order goals. The consequence, in most renderings of the theory, is a continuing trend toward postmaterial outlooks, and values in conflict with more strictly materialist values inherent in the established industrial order.

Among the many proponents of this line of theorizing, none is better known or more widely cited than Ronald Inglehart, whose *Silent Revolution* (1977a) was reviewed in some detail in Chapters 1 and 2. Our review noted a series of problems in Inglehart's analysis—a less-than-ideal measure of the key concept, the inherent problems of attempting to infer trends from cross-sectional data, the utter lack of support for the trend claim in the two cases where actual trend data were avilable, and so on. Our conclusion was that Inglehart's trend claims were not established in his own data.

Given the general drift of the American economy over the decade of the 1970's and the resulting political developments, the postmaterialist argument faced still further difficulties. All available survey series, as we have seen, document the persistence of economic problems as the principal concern of the largest share of the population. To be sure, there is, we suggest, a general lessening of the urgency of these concerns, one point that can be counted among the "living" elements of the theory. But the corollary idea, that an increasing proportion of the population is now actively pursuing higher-order, self-actualization goals, seems rather doubtful.

Inglehart continues to argue the postmaterialism theme; his 1981 publication, "Post-Materialism in an Environment of Insecurity," attempts to save the theory in the face of troublesome and generally nonsupportive evidence. "Have the economic uncertainty and the deterioration of East-West détente in recent years," he asks, "produced a sharp decline in Post-Materialism? As we will see, the answer is No. Overall, there was remarkably little change in the ratio of materialists to Post-Materialists among Western publics" (1981, p. 880).

We note first the striking shift in emphasis of the argument between the 1977 book and the 1981 article. In 1977, the argument was that major changes were in the offing, that a "Silent Revolution has been occurring that is gradually but fundamentally changing political life throughout the Western world" (1977a, p. 363). The passage from the 1981 article quoted above—"remarkably little change"—sharply contradicts the claim made four years earlier. The 1981 thesis thus amounts to a fall back, a revisionist position—if postmaterialism is in fact not growing, at least it is not declining. "Contrary to what some observers have assumed, Post-Materialism has not dwindled away in the face of diminished economic and physical security" (1981, p. 881).

Little need be added on this point. The 1981 conclusion of "no change" in the decade of the 1970's is obviously consistent with our conclusions about the stability of outlooks during that period.

The 1981 article adds a series of 1979 surveys to the 1970, 1973, and 1976 materials analyzed in the book. The combined proportions postmaterialist over all nations studied were 12% in 1970, 10% in 1973, 12% in 1976, and 13% in 1979. "Remarkably little change" is an acceptable characterization of these results, although "no discernible change at all" is more accurate. Later in the text, incidentally, Inglehart remarks that the "Post-Materialists were slightly *more* numerous at the end of the 1970s than they were at the start" (1981, p. 888, emphasis in the original); the difference is a matter of exactly one percentage point.

In the most advanced of the nations studied, the United States, the proportion identified in the article as postmaterialist was 10% in all years examined (1981, tables 2 and 3). Clearly, no trends are indicated in this result. In the book, the American postmaterialist proportion at the earliest point is reported as 12% (1977a, p. 38), versus the 10% figure reported in the 1981 article. If the former figure is, in fact, the correct one, the data would therefore show a modest two-point *deterioration* of postmaterial outlooks over the decade.

The brunt of the 1981 article is to argue that postmaterialism is "a deep-rooted phenomenon" (1981, p. 890), one so basic and enduring as to be impervious to "an environment of insecurity." Even in the face of a progressive deterioration in economic conditions, the postmaterialists hold the line, clinging firmly to their new values. This, clearly, is an effort to salvage an improbable and unsustained prediction; the argument is that the predicted developments probably *would* have occurred, except for the emergence of an "environment of insecurity" that has stalled, but not ended, the inexorable processes of value change. The silent revolution, one might say, was put on hold. When the environment becomes more secure, it will move forward once again.

The problem with this line of theory saving, of course, is that, as we reported in Chapter 7 (Tables 7-2 and 7-3), most people did not experience the 1970's as a period of diminished economic and physical security. Indeed, assessments of financial well-being were remarkably stable during the decade, and *at all times*, the proportions reporting that things were getting better were larger than those who saw things getting worse. Whatever the objective economic situation, in short, the subjective understanding of that situation should not have posed any significant barrier to the predicted (as of 1977) increase in postmaterial consciousness. But that increase, as we have seen, simply did not occur. The appeal to an indefinite future remains open, of course; it may be that the changes postulated in the 1977 book are, indeed, just around the corner, and that the next survey that comes available will confirm the postmaterialism trend hypothesis. In the meantime, going with the evidence now in hand, both that of Inglehart himself and that produced by other survey organizations, we think it best to consider the hypothesis dead, or, at least, not yet living. None of the predicted trends has yet materialized.

A range of additional problems with Inglehart's analysis has been pointed out by others. Higgins' (undated) paper notes, for example, that Inglehart's use of the *ratio* of postmaterialists to materialists throughout the analysis is misleading, since it treats a 16–8% distribution as identical to one of 30–15%. Higgins also points out that the factors postulated in Inglehart's analysis to explain the rise in postmaterialism in fact account for less than 1% of the variation. A final, useful contribution from Higgins' piece concerns Inglehart's discussion of a key set of findings reported by Dalton (1977). This discussion (Inglehart, 1977a, p. 95) erroneously reports that the partial correlation of current income with postmaterialism is .30; in fact, according to Dalton's analysis, the correlation is -.30, Inglehart having somehow ignored the minus sign. What Dalton shows, in short, is that postmaterial values *decline* as present income increases, the precise opposite to what would be expected given Inglehart's thesis.

Several investigators (among them Marsh, 1975; Milkis and Baldino, 1978; and Flanagan, 1982) have raised questions similar to ours about the validity of Inglehart's original measures.

Milkis and Baldino have also argued that the value differences associated with age may be more the consequence of life-cycle factors (marriage, having children, and so on), than a consequence of cohort or generational changes. The *stipulation* of a cohort effect is, of course, central to Inglehart's thesis; only through this stipulation can it be argued that cross-sectional age differences reflect true value *changes*. The life-cycle alternative argues, in contrast, that young people are more postmaterialistic because they have yet to assume the burdens of spouse, children, mortgage, and debt, the inevitable consequence being that postmaterial values will erode as people advance through the life cycle. Were this the case, the age correlations reported by Inglehart would not be something "new and different," but rather something one would expect to see in most times and places.

The various critiques and objections contained in the works just cited are too varied, complex, and numerous to recount in detail here; the preceding touches only the highlights. Our essential point is that the Inglehart thesis proclaims value changes on a vast scale—changes that were not documented in the data originally examined and that have not been observed in data assembled since. The most recent data reported by Inglehart, obtained in a 1980 survey, show a 10% postmaterial coterie. An understanding of the outlooks and consciousness of the remaining 90%—the overwhelming majority by any standard—clearly requires a different analytic framework.

The theory of the little man's revolt, the sixth of the positions we have considered, is a fairly straightforward extension of the ever-recurring backlash claim. The proponents of this position are to be credited with recognizing the persistence of economic concerns in the lives of ordinary people. For the little man—and the less-frequently mentioned little woman—the economic issue is the central concern; all other questions take on meaning and importance only by their relationship to this central fact. The position, obviously, stands in sharp contrast to one of Scammon and Wattenberg's principal claims; it also, certainly in terms of focus and trend prediction, differs sharply from the Inglehart position.

On the other side of the ledger, as seen in Chapter 7, the extent and urgency of the problem appears to be overstated. Even in a decade of sustained inflation and persistent unemployment, most people reported themselves as at least "staying even"—most of the rest said "getting better." Most reported a middling-to-high level of satisfaction with their economic circumstances. Dissatisfaction with one's finances seems more closely linked with position in the life cycle than with absolute amounts of income at the family's disposal. Many people with very limited incomes, particularly older persons, also appear to have limited needs and, accordingly, report themselves to be satisfied with their financial condition.

As was seen in Chapter 8, there also appears to be some exaggeration with respect to the political consequences. The so-called rightist reaction, the prediction of increasing conservativism, has been at best a small trace in responses both to to liberal-conservative placement questions and to those on party identification. One would also be hard put to it to establish the point on the basis of recommendations for government spending, most liberal or welfare state variety programs continuing to gain substantial public favor.

The 1970's did, unquestionably, see a vast (and "welling") dissatisfaction with the federal government, continuing a trend that first began in the 1960's. This appears to be linked to the question of honesty in government, to a sense of wheeling and dealing and special favor in Washington. This general distrust does not, however, appear to be closely linked to the economic problems felt in the 1970's. The little man position appears, therefore, to err in its assumption of directness, of the obviousness of government as the target. The anger, as far as we can tell, does not appear to be as intense as those commentators suggest. And there also appears to be more scatter than anticipated with regard to the perceived sources of the economic problems and to conceptions of appropriate solutions.

While not a well-researched topic, the various predictions of scape-goating, the expectation of intense hostilities or, possibly, of violence directed against racial or ethnic minorities—or welfare cheat targets—have not been supported. The attitudes of both working- and middle-class whites, as noted repeatedly, have been positive for some decades. There does exist some impressionistic evidence of hostility toward "cheats," in part, no doubt, linked to the tax revolt movement. But some of that revolt, as indicated, has other sources, some reflecting justified concerns, some even being expressed by liberals.

In summary, the advocates of this position were on to something with their focus on the economic problem, but they seem to be mistaken about the extent, location, and urgency. While they predicted clear, sharply focused reactions, the actual responses seem much more diffuse, in general, lacking a clear sense of target. Most of the work coming out of this school is based on erratic samples, working class bars being the preferred research locale. The regular clientele of such establishments are, to say the least, not a cross-section of the nation, of Middle America, or of the working-class populations.

Five of the positions we have considered predict some significant changes, or at least some major pressures for change (the exception, of course, being the position of the workplace researchers). Three of the positions, those of the social critics, the workplace critics, and the postin-dustrialists, anticipate new innovative thrusts, ones that would transform major elements of the received institutional heritage. The other two positions anticipate reactive changes, mass public rejection of some recent develop-ments. This is clearly the case with those responding to the "social" issues. A more diffuse response, to be sure, occurs in the case of the little man's complaint. The changes called for in the latter instances are obviously restorative in character; they aim to reconstitute a previous, more desirable condition.

Our criticism of the five positions may be easily summarized: the claims are either not supported (as with the social critics and the workplace critics), or they involve a misreading of the extent and/or location of a real problem. The rejection of the various change hypotheses means, perforce, that sta-bility is the "living" conclusion to be drawn from our findings. Since that conclusion may, especially in advanced intellectual circles, give rise to some immediate nervousness, we hasten to provide some calming qualifications.

A sticky semantic problem arises in connection with this pair of terms, stability and change. For many advanced intellectuals, change is automatically counted as a good thing and stability as a bad thing. In many formulations, those evaluations are almost completely blind; they involve a priori judgments, ones made without any serious investigation of the correlates of either new or old arrangements. For that reason, we feel it advisable, at each point, to maintain a sharp distinction between fact and evaluation. We have indicated what we take to be the facts of change and stability. The evaluation of those findings requires separate consideration.

Another semantic problem appears in connection with the second of these terms, and involves the unexamined definition of the term stability. In most such discussions, it is taken to mean a fixed state or condition. This meaning is clearly implied in the frequently used equivalent term, the status quo. But that portrait of social affairs involves a false, nonexistent condition. In contemporary human affairs, a stable state (homeostasis) is nowhere to be found. All modern societies are characterized by a general *flow* of events, by processes of continuous movement, of change. If a handy, sloganlike summary phrase is required, one might describe the normal or ordinary social experience as a condition of stable flow (or stable flux). Most such flows are gradual, long-term processes (at least when seen from the perspective of the human life span). There are, for example, the slow, gradual changes in occupational structure, amount of formal education achieved, age structure of the population, organization and management of families, etc.

The change versus status quo formula amounts to a mislabeling, the suggestion being that the latter option actually exists, that it is a de facto condition. It thus misstates the choices facing the members of the society. The choice—at its most simplified extreme—is one of stable flow versus some intervention to achieve significant change(s) in the directions of that flow. Even this dichotomy is unrealistic—that is, false—since *any* government is going to make some interventions, undertake some adjustments in the regular flow of events. It would be a rare—and bizarre—extreme case were a government to stand by, holding to an absolute *laissez-aller* course, refusing any intervention at all. The advocates of change, in short, present a false dichotomy. The disdained and rejected option, the status quo, does not exist; the preferred option, change, is typically left undefined and hence unassessed. Put differently, this is to say that the merits of the proposed change, in the ordinary case of such advocacy, are not seriously examined.

The advocates of innovative change present their analyses in a scientific guise. The essence of the procedure is to define one's preference as a de facto, on-going development, as part of an unfolding process. The preference is portrayed as stemming from the natural flow of events; it is independent of and apart from the wishes of the analyst-commentator. The advocate can then say, in true scientific manner, that the claims merely reflect or flow from the facts. Those events, moreover, in the typical analysis of this variety, are said to be moved by large ineluctable forces; they do not result from minor, passing, or adventitious causes. Such procedure hides the choices, the options, and ultimately the personal preference, by placing "hard fact" at the forefront of the discussion. It might easily be described as crypto-positivist.

Given such definition, a simple lesson follows: like it or not, one will have to live with the predicted development. Some persons, depending on personal psychology, might even draw a further implication: they might feel disposed to "get with it." Moreover, if the case looked compelling, it might have the effect of immobilizing some normal or expected opposition; persons who would ordinarily be disposed to reject the demand for change might feel intimidated by the power of the argument and, accordingly, remain silent. Such effects might be described as social psychological consequences of the "scientized" option.[4]

A problem also exists with respect to the explanatory aspects of such accounts. Many of the small changes we have observed (or confirmed) may be accounted for in terms of rather commonplace causes, such as changes in demographic structures, recent migration patterns, or normal life-cycle developments. The finding of routine causes stands in marked contrast to the claims of the critical theorists where the stress is on some ineluctable new or exotic factors that have never before been part of the human situation. But in most instances, those exotic factors prove to be only adventitiously linked to the development in question. The actual causal connection is with the ordinary, everyday routines of human existence.

A peculiar bias appears to be operating here. There is a refusal to see, face, or think about everyday routines of human existence. One might even put this forward as a general proposition: advanced intellectuals ordinarily prefer exotic explanations to those involving everyday human routines. Given the centrality of those routines for most people's lives, for the organization of human society everywhere, the exotic body of claims thus developed will, of necessity, be rather far removed from the subject matter it purports to describe and analyze.

It is useful to outline our alternative position, which begins with those everyday routines. Its basics were first stated early in Chapter 3. The family,

---

[4]This paragraph, it should be noted, consists of unresearched hypotheses, which means, of course, that the presumed effects have never been established or measured. Given the absence of any significant shift in work attitudes during the period of the workplace critics' "public relations" success, it seems likely that the magnitude of those effects would be relatively small, perhaps restricted to the ranks of the intellectuals themselves or to those most closely following the topical claims.

Diane Ravitch reports a parallel case from an area we have not discussed; it involves critics of educational practice. In the field of educational history, she reports, the "radical historians . . . encountered little opposition; even books which, in my view, flagrantly violated the rules of evidence and logic went unchallenged. Scholars who disagreed profoundly chose to look the other way rather than engage in controversy with the radical historians. One prominent historian wrote [in response to her criticism of those works] that he agreed with what [she] had written but had been afraid to state the same things himself; another historian wrote that he now realized that his error in the 1960s was in keeping silent for fear of being shouted down" (Ravitch, 1978, p. xi).

we argued, is the center point of most people's lives, providing the context in which the routines of daily living take on meaning. Much love and affection is found within the routines of everyday family living. For some, to be sure, only a lesser quality of life is achieved, a sense of satisfaction rather than happiness, a sense of adequacy, of acceptance or acquiescence, of getting by, this too having its basis in everyday family routines. Most people, as seen in the evidence of Chapter 3, put marriage and family well ahead of any other considerations when ranking their life goals. Contrary to some persistent claims, evidence contained in Chapter 4 shows that most people derive considerable satisfaction from the routines of family living. The reverse of that, the failure of the marriage (and/or family) routine, constitutes a (possibly *the*) major source of discontent and unhappiness in the lives of those who have experienced it.[5]

Despite claims of the death of the family, the institution has proved remarkably resilient. Sooner or later, the vast majority of the population marries, and the majority of those who marry do so only once, remaining with the original spouse until parted by death. Some of these lifelong marriages, to be sure, are less than wholly satisfactory (also indicated in the data of Chapter 5). Although not explored in our research, the persistence of those less-than-happy marriages, we think, is also linked to the routines of everyday life. Benefits are derived from those routines that apparently outweigh the benefits to be gained from separation or divorce. Some of our evidence suggests that the tie in such cases is economic, a less-than-satisfactory marriage being adjudged preferable to the economic disaster that, in most cases, comes with separation. Put another way, it seems likely that the "cash nexus" is holding some of those marriages together.

Some marriages do end in separation and divorce. The percentage that fail is consistently exaggerated in most popular accounts. The best *estimates* derived from the current experience have it that about one third of all marriages will end in divorce. The overwhelming majority of those divorces are followed by subsequent remarriage. As Mary Jo Bane (1976, p. 34) put it, the rates of remarriage among the divorced make it clear that divorce is the rejection of a specific marital partner, and not a rejection of the institution itself.

Some people *have* rejected the institution of marriage, and have chosen an alternative or unconventional life-style. The most frequent of these options, the growing practice of cohabitation, turns out to be very close to conventional marriage in all respects save the legal one. Most of the other arrangements—communal living, commuter marriages, sharing of a partner, and so on—are so uncommon as to have no serious place in a discussion of the American *masses*. Most people, the vast majority, live out their lives

[5]A caveat. Our earlier observation about the assymetry involved in some marital breakups should be remembered (see pp. 198–199 above). Some leave an unsatisfactory marriage for another, better marital arrangement. The observation in the text, clearly, applies to those without that better arrangement.

within the context of a single conventional marriage. For some others, it is a matter of a limited sequence of marriages, two being the most frequent experience.

The predominant focus for most people, their wish to create and sustain a happy, or at least an acceptable, family life gives rise to the most frequently expressed concern voiced by most people at most times, a problem best described with the colloquial phrase, "making ends meet." This should not be taken as indicating any general economic or material privation in the United States. Serious areas of poverty and privation do persist, some details on this having been given in Chapters 5 and 7. Even in the 1970's, in the decade of inflation, most people managed to stay even or better, and most reported a middling to high degree of satisfaction with their economic circumstances. Still, there does appear to be a sliding scale of demands, with wants tending to escalate upward, and it follows that economic or materialistic concerns are likely to continue in first place, even at this late stage in the development of the affluent society, or, to use the current phrase, of the postmaterialist society.

The focus on family and its material well-being bespeaks a very traditional package of concerns, which we have emphasized in the title of Chapter 3. Tradition, it will be noted, is a loose synonym for handed-down routines. In the works of critical intellectuals, both tradition and routine are treated with contempt, as though, to quote Edward Shils, "tradition embodies all that is obstructive of the growth and application of science and reason to the affairs of human beings" (1981, p. 7). Convention, that great organizing principle of everyday social existence, Shils observes, "falls outside the interest of intellectual discussion. It belongs to the routine of life and is too petty to be acknowledged" (p. 4). Going unacknowledged, its force is seldom appreciated and its grip on the consciousness of the population seldom understood.

"Human beings," Shils reiterates, "at least most of them, much of the time, do not fare well in a disordered world. They need to live within the framework of a world of which they possess a chart. They need categories and rules; they need criteria of judgment" (p. 326). These frameworks, categories, and criteria of which Shils writes are the traditions and routines of everyday life; they constitute the "chart" of commonplace existence. Without them, life would be chaotic and incomprehensible to most people. If one seriously wishes to understand the consciousness and outlooks of the masses, then some appreciation of these routines and their implications is an obvious first step.

Much of the analytic misdirection provided in the works of critical intellectuals results from their failure to recognize the importance of the daily routine. Many, clearly, are openly hostile to these commonplace features of existence, and thus, in exercises of wishful thinking, they announce the impending death of the routine and its replacement with new values, new needs, new social and institutional forms. It is, thus, the leading conceit of the "advanced" intellectuals of this (and most other) decades of the modern era that we stand, even now, on the edge of a Great Transformation. The idea that things will continue much as they have been in the past, with only modest changes, is abhorrent to their way of thinking.

The dialectical opposite positions we have considered in this work all, in one way or another, derive from or focus on the exact same routines. The Scammon and Wattenberg account provides something of a defense of those basic routines. It is the unwarranted attack on them that gives rise to the supposed reaction, the concern with the social issue. The little man critique believes the basic routines to be in difficulty, mainly as a result of inadequate personal or household finances in a period of inflation. This, too, leads to something of a defensive reaction. The workplace researchers are, effectively, agnostic in their evaluation of the workplace routines. They certainly do not, on the whole, display serious alarmist sentiments, nor do they advocate any plan or program. Apart from the misplaced emphasis of the Scammon and Wattenberg work and the misplaced location of financial strains in the little man critique, it should be clear that the proroutine positions are, as empirical portraiture, far more accurate than the productions of antiroutine intellectuals. We have more to say on the contributions of these antiroutine thinkers later in this chapter.

In the previous discussion, we argued that the United States' experience in the 1970's, despite the claims and appearances, actually involved little change. The work of the media and academic touts depended on magnification of minor trends, plus the projection of those developments into the indefinite future. In some instances, also, it involved the discovery of commonplace life-cycle changes, mistaking them for new generational and thus historical changes. Some detailed diagraming of the link between the masses and the reporting about them and their condition proves useful.

One of those commonplace life-cycle changes deserves special attention. Most people are raised within the bounds of the parental family, spending approximately twenty years there; they then move out. That move is probably the most significant break in lifetime routines that is experienced prior to widowhood and the transitions associated with old age. Two major life decisions typically come at this time: one concerning a career, the other involving marriage. Both, understandably, loom large in the consciousness of persons making the transition. Although later corrigible, at this point they often take on an appearance of permanence such that an error is seen as having disastrous implications. Given that these are typically individual decisions, the anxieties produced can sometimes be immense and, if stretched over months or years, can mean an extended trauma.

These transitions follow several paths. The easiest, no doubt, involves an early job choice, one linked to or aided by a parental model or parental guidance (as, for example, the entrance into an apprenticeship program for a skilled blue-collar occupation, aided by the father's experience and knowledge of the entry points). The easiest transition to marriage would involve marriage with one's high school or neighborhood sweetheart. In such cases, there would be virtually no transition period; the move from the parental family and childhood dependence to financial independence and a new family unit would be virtually seamless, that is, without any period of uncertainty or anxiety.

Transitions can also involve some break in the desired routine or plan of life, but, at the same time, entail little or no change in the social environment. This would be the case with a high school dropout who subsequently experienced employment difficulties. That would normally postpone any marital plans and would mean an extended period of dependence in the parental household. It might also be associated with strains felt by both parents and child; but, then again, it might be associated with some understanding on the part of the parents.

Some children move out to be on their own prior to marriage. This arrangement, typically, depends on full-time employment, which is the economic basis for independence. Some new contacts would be made in the process. There would be one's co-workers, supervisors, and employers, as well as a new set of neighbors. Although providing a more variegated experience than the rather homogeneous home communities, the experience here would still be limited. Co-workers and neighbors would tend to be at the same life cycle stage and, all things being equal, would share similar life goals, marriage and economic well-being coming high on the list.

Entrance into new and markedly different circumstances would ordinarily come with entry into institutions of higher learning, where one would have a much wider range of contacts than would be the case with the offices or factories. This is especially the case with large institutions recruiting a broadly based student body. The most decisive new influences, however, would be provided by faculty members. The views of professors, in general, stand more sharply opposed to the received viewpoints of most students than any others previously experienced. Many professors prove to be advocates of "new" countercultural orientations, of the outlooks described by Inglehart and others as postindustrial. Basically, one is dealing here with the core values of western *intellectual* communities, values long antedating the appearance of the postindustrial labor force. These core values involve antimaterialism, antitraditionalism, and antiauthority sentiments. On the positive side, there is a strong championing of community and, standing in some contradiction thereto, one finds even stronger enthusiasm for the highly individualistic values of self-fulfillment. Not too surprisingly, postmaterialist values prove to be most frequent in the locations where they are most actively propagated.[6]

Within the universities, to be sure, the influences are not uniform. The lessons offered in an agricultural school, in engineering faculties, or in

[6]Inglehart, 1977a, p. 75 ff.

business schools, are quite different from those offered in the social sciences and humanities. The former tend to draw middle-of-the-road and conservative students; the professors provide largely technical lessons, and those would probably come embellished with generally moderate or conservative cultural and political values. Thus, for those students, the university experience would be one of continuity with their former experience. That would probably be the case with small, regionally based colleges, too, or with those institutions having an active religious commitment. One might easily think that the most prestigious elite universities would also be supportive of established ways. That, however, is a mistaken judgment; the faculties of those universities, on the whole, are the most liberal of the entire range of American academic institutions (Ladd and Lipset, 1975, pp. 72–80, 141 ff.).

It is in the areas of social work, the social sciences, and the humanities that one finds the heaviest concentrations of left and liberal professors.[7] It is the professors there who provide the wide discussion of value questions, who, more than others, aim to provoke the students, to criticize ideas and institutions, to "open doors." In some instances, this is done through provision of factual information, material that, in one way or another, challenges the received or traditional values. Sometimes, one finds active "missionary" efforts, systematic attempts to convince students to adopt new views, to change the course of their lives, and, ultimately, to work for change in society.[8]

Teachers have influence in still another way; they select and assign readings. These, too, like the lectures or seminars, will provide factual material plus, depending on teacher propensities, some evaluation and possibly some measure of exhortation. In addition to the face-to-face contacts, the university experience also, for most students, means many hours of effort spent reading. Given the total number of persons involved, it is not inappropriate to describe the universities as a mass medium of communication. Unlike the other mass media, unlike radio, television, newspapers, or magazines, the influence of the universities proceeds through two channels. There is the impersonal experience (hundreds of thousands reading the

[7]The respective percentages reporting left or liberal politics in the three areas mentioned here are 79, 69, and 60% (as opposed to respective conservative figures of 7, 12, and 18%, the remainder being middle-of-the-road). The figures are from Ladd and Lipset (1975, p. 80), from their survey of academics undertaken in 1969. For comparison with later cross section of the United States' adult population, see Table 8.3.

[8]Although it is frequently assumed that schools and universities in times past were agents (and defenders) of the existing social order, the historical reality is much more complicated. For a portrait of a major schoolteacher "mission," for the use of an entire school system as an agency for the propagation of new values, in this case, those of nineteenth century liberalism, see Singer, 1977. In the comparative perspective, the Prussian schools are, at least in popular accounts, held to be the most conservative, to be the extreme case. For a detailed examination of the claim and for some unexpected findings, see the important article by Kenneth Barkin (1983).

assignments), and there is the personal contact (professors backing up, reinforcing, elaborating, and developing the lessons contained in the assigned texts). This combination would, presumably, be a force with considerable impact. Given the authority of the teacher in conjunction with the array of related readings, it is not surprising that one finds significant attitude change occurring in these contexts.[9]

The extent of influence will also vary, depending on the student's background and the degree of involvement with the educational institution. In the junior (or community) college, the period of contact is not normally expected to exceed two years. Given the high rates of turnover, contact is frequently no more than one or two semesters. Dropping out, in such cases, may stem from a change in career preferences or from a lack of interest, as well as from a failure in courses. All three possibilities would mean failure to influence.

Students living at home might find themselves facing some cross pressures, some of which might even be welcomed as friendly support in opposition to the "dissonant" information conveyed by the professors. If students found themselves facing faculty missionaries, they would normally receive countering influences from moderate or conservative parents and friends in their home neighborhoods. Those most subject to faculty influence would be the students living away from home. Given the costs involved, those students, typically, would be the children of fairly affluent parents. In many cases, that would also mean conservative parents, which is generally the case with upper and upper-middle-class white Protestant families. The equivalent white Catholic families are generally liberal on all issues. Conservatism is also infrequent among upper and upper-middle-class Jews and affluent blacks. Some students, in short, do not come into a new or different milieu upon entering the universities. Some are left, radical, left-liberal, or "critical" from the outset. Some enter the conservative sectors of the universities, allowing for continuity with their previous experience. And some who are directly subject to the new lessons also face a countervailing lesson in their homes and home communities. The influenceable segment, in short, must constitute a small subset of the entire category of students.[10]

[9]The classic study showing conservative or moderate upper-middle-class students shifting to the left under the tutelege of left and liberal professors in a small, progressive liberal arts college, is that of Theodore Newcomb (1943), who did the famous Bennington study. For a later comprehensive summary review, see Feldman and Newcomb, 1969. Also of some use is the work of Howard Bowen (1977).

[10]For a discussion of the conditions allowing one to avoid or escape the dominant pressures of the milieu, see Newcomb's analysis of the deviant cases found in his original Bennington study (1958). Not all students face value conflict in the university. Many students from conservative backgrounds, for example, choose conservative fields. Many liberal students choose liberal fields of study. Ladd and Lipset, for example, show that only 23% of first- and second-year undergraduates studying agriculture describe themselves as left or liberal, versus 75% of those studying anthropology (Ladd and Lipset, p. 74). Given some choice in the school attended and

The process just described might be called a reprogramming episode. On leaving academia and reestablishing connections with everyday life, some students would experience an episode best described as deprogramming. For many of the influenced students, to be sure, the lessons learned in the universities will have lasting impact, by reason of conviction or, alternatively, as a result of continuing social or media influences. They might locate themselves in an occupational or social milieu wherein the new values find steady support and renewal. While in the universities, they would have abandoned commonplace provincial newspapers—the *Reader's Digest*, *Time*, and *Cosmopolitan*—in favor of the *New York Times* and some of the more serious intellectual journals. For others, however, the next step, after leaving the academic milieu, after this digression of two, four, or six-plus years, would involve direct sustained attention to the everyday routines of occupational and family life. The heavy reading schedules, the daily converse with Kierkegaard, Dostoevsky, Proust, Mann, Joyce, Yeats—and Charles Reich—is replaced by routines involving jobs, supermarkets, cooking, cleaning, child care, and the endless problems of household finances. Faced with these new realities, the more exotic countercultural lessons learned in the academy lose both salience and credibility. The verities of everyday life impose themselves once again with unyielding insistence.[11]

---

a free choice of field of study, there will of course be a strong tendency for a match of student and professor outlooks. Given, however, the differences in the overall distributions, there will be some net disparity, with conservative or moderate students coming to be influenced by more liberal or left professors. For a portrait of the matching within one major state university, see Longhi, 1969. For a portrait of the values associated with the religious and ethnic segments of the American population, see Greeley, 1977, *passim*; and Nie, Verba, and Petrocik, 1976, Chapter 14. The finding of greatest interest in the present context is a change they discovered among the higher status northern white Protestants. In the 1950's, few liberals were found in this extremely conservative segment of the population. In the 1970's, however, one eighth of their members fell at the extreme liberal endpoint on a liberal-conservative attitude profile (Nie, Verba, and Petrocik, pp. 262–263).

[11]See Newcomb, Koeing, Flacks, and Warwick (1967) for a follow-up study of the Bennington students some 25 years later. Some reprogramming and deprogramming appears in connection with support for independence in Québec. It is an orientation learned in the academic milieu and, for many, dropped upon entering occupational life. See Hamilton and Pinard, 1982.

For a summary review of the studies of long-term effects, see Feldman and Newcomb, 1969, Chapter 10. Discussing the Bennington results, they report that "women who had become less conservative in college remained so in about three-quarters of all cases, more than two decades later. Women who had not changed their attitudes toward public issues since college had, to a relatively great extent, moved into or in some fashion created a social environment that supported attitudes held on leaving college." (Feldman and Newcomb, p. 320). More generally, on the basis of what might best be described as early and limited studies, they report, "College-experienced changes in politico-social-economic attitudes, typically in the liberal direction, in several instances have been shown to persist, or even to be extended, after college years. We have found no instances of significant reversals of such attitudes. . . . " (p. 321). Some complications appear, depending on the area

The study of university-experience effects, it should be noted, is beset with many problems. The people who go to college may be different from their age peers (for example, more flexible, more open to new experience). The effects observed within the colleges may, to some extent, at least, be happening more generally (for example, among the entire cohort). Persistence of attitudes or subsequent changes may be university-linked—or they, too, might be more general.

The life-cycle dynamic is one of a complex of three interrelated changes that occur in the modern era. There is, in addition, a long-term increase in the size of the intellectual class, giving it at least the possibility for ever greater influence. Superimposed on this long-term growth is a cyclical development, periods of activism, uprising, and mobilization being followed by periods of quiescence, of demobilization. The cyclical phenomenon would link up with the life-cycle events, accentuating or depressing, depending on the phase, the incidence of, and the extent of the reprogramming.

At the beginning of the nineteenth century, the intellectual class in any country was minute, consisting at best of only a few hundred persons. With hardly any public education, there were no large numbers of teachers. Compared to the modern establishments, the universities were minute enterprises, most having less staff than the present-day small liberal arts college. Few newspapers existed, a typical issue, moreover, having only a few small-size pages. The implication, clearly, is that only a few full-time professional journalists were needed. The rest of the modern-day mass media were yet to appear. The intellectual class, at that point, was no more than a small coterie consisting of university staffs, a handful of journalist-publishers, and the collection of so-called free intellectuals. Byron, Shelley, and Keats were directly linked only to tiny *groupuscules*. Although their poetic works sold in the tens of thousands, indicating already considerable resonance for their "advanced" themes, that was still only a minute portion of the British population. Most of the citizenry, being illiterate, had no access to their Promethean teachings. Those who did have access, it might be noted, would have been rather well-off populations. These poets, together with their followers among the intelligentsia, shared values that, in present-day terminology, could easily be described as postmaterialist—all this when *industrial* society was in its first years of "take off."[12]

The nineteenth century saw the growth of mass public education, which, clearly, created jobs for the teachers who form the core of the intellectual

studied. The decline in religious interest observed in college years apparently reverses on leaving the university milieu. The general verdict of these authors, however, is one of persistence in attitude (p. 323).

[12]For details on the groupuscules and their political orientations, see M. H. Abrams, 1971; Honour, 1979; Jones, 1974; and Winegarten, 1974. The poet Shelley once, in a lilting phrase, referred to "the tempestuous loveliness of terror." Also useful is the work of Ian Jack, 1963.

class. Most of this development, to be sure, was in primary school education, but alongside it came the elite stream, the gymnasia, the lycées, and public high schools. The universities expanded at the same time. Following the German models, the academic enterprise was divided among ever new specializations, each department requiring new professors and staff. Newspapers grew in size and importance, which also required an increase of personnel. With the coming of mass political parties, the political press appeared, each newspaper or related journal meaning jobs for scores of intellectuals.

The twentieth century saw an explosive increase in the size of this class. Educational institutions grew everywhere, the greatest relative increases occurring at the high school and university levels. Mass circulation magazines made their appearance in the United States at the turn of the century, and, shortly thereafter, came the motion pictures, constituting the second and third of the mass media of communication. Later, in the 1920's, the fourth of the mass media, radio, made its appearance in the United States. In the 1950's, and 1960's, a massive expansion of educational institutions occurred at all levels. In most economically advanced countries, the number employed increased three- or fourfold.[13] At the same time, television, the fifth of the mass media, made its appearance, providing still another setting for support of the intellectual class. Each of these new developments, of course, caused some disarray in the affairs of previously dominant media, but after a period of adjustment, the latter again found a market and continued to expand.

The foundations, Ford, Rockefeller, and others, made a significant appearance in mid-century, giving out funds that, in great measure, went to the support of researching and/or creative members of the intellectual class. Outside the United States, vast sums are provided for public radio and television broadcasting. In addition to the technical costs, those sums also pay for the creative content, for the program material, which, in translation means additional or subsidiary income for some members of the intellectual class. The larger intellectual trade, of course, is multinational in character.

The vast quantitative growth in the numbers of the class has been accompanied by a parallel growth of infrastructure, of support arrangements to provide the economic base for the class. Millions earn assured, comfortable incomes as tenured members of school or university staffs. Large numbers have reasonably secure employment in the mass media; some of them are among the most highly paid persons in the United States (Stein, 1979). Even the free lancers have sources of support that were unheard of in former times. The combination of foundations, radio-television networks, and resale rights means support for numbers of persons that would have

[13]University faculty numbers in the United States did little more than double in this period, from 247,000 in 1950 to 551,000 in 1970. The United States, of course, began from a much higher base figure, having gone from 24,000 in 1900 to 147,000 in 1940. These figures are taken from Ladd and Lipset, 1975, p. 2.

been unthinkable even for the European nobility in the late eighteenth century. In terms of the potential for influence, it is as if millions had been given permanent or near-permanent employment as communicators, to provide cultural content, in one way or another, to some tens of millions. It is a dramatic change from the days of yore, when this group began as a mere coterie.

The growth of the intellectual class implies, of course, an even larger growth of the audience for their communications. The increase in the number of years of required schooling means that, by force of law, virtually the entire population is going to be part of this audience for most of the years of childhood and early adolescence. The increased frequency of university attendance means another large segment of the population has chosen to continue its education under the tutelage of the more advanced members of the class. It is at this intersection of events that the previously described life-cycle processes are most likely to occur. Modernization has meant ever larger portions of the population removed from their families for relatively long periods. During that time, the routines of previous experience are interrupted and replaced by new routines provided by intellectual opinion leaders or, to use another expression, by new and different community influentials.

Some people, the converted, seek to maintain the linkages after leaving the academic setting. At this time, a different set of intellectuals comes into play. While some students rejoin the audience of the mass media (as conventionally defined) after graduation, others who retain the lessons (and make the necessary efforts), follow the intellectual journals and tune into educational or public broadcasting, both radio and television. Most importantly, they continue to read intellectual books recommended by the "gate-keepers," by those intellectuals writing in the leading literary and public affairs journals.[14] These people, in short, are the lifetime converts.

The third kind of change within the intellectual milieu has a cyclical character. Throughout history, one finds times of arousal, periods during which larger than usual numbers have subscribed to countercultural values or to the values of renewal, of reform, or of restoration. But then, after the period of arousal, a period of quiescence follows, in which another tone is dominant. Intellectual circles are not at all times oppositional in outlook. In any era, moreover, one could easily discover some who were (or are) of another persuasion, who accept, defend, or justify the arrangements of the society. Some kind of dialectic is always in process, as indicated by the opposing positions outlined in our first chapter. Were we undertaking an analysis of events in the 1950's, we would necessarily have to focus on the quiescent phase of the cycle. Then, in the aftermath of World War II, with the bloodletting of Hitler's Germany and Stalin's Russia clearly in mind, one

[14]For a portrait of these gatekeepers, their backgrounds, orientations, and activities, see Kadushin, 1974; and Coser, Kadushin, and Powell, 1982.

saw what was probably the most extreme episode of intellectual quiescence in the entire modern era. Our task here is not to provide an account or explanation of the cyclical process; the aim, rather, is to indicate a recognition of this "medium-term" process, to note that more is operating than just the growth of the intellectual class and its exertion of leverage at a given point in the life cycle.[15]

It is useful to consider some details about the character of the message provided at the points of contact where advanced intellectuals and students meet. Some features of the situation itself give at least some plausibility to the oppositional lessons provided, many of which, it will be noted, stem from the mass society framework. The basic assumption of that framework, briefly, is that things are falling apart. Society is losing its cohesiveness, its integratedness, its community. Given this dissolution, it is, of course, appropriate that people should feel alienated and that all decent people should be concerned or, even more, that they should do something about this terrible state of affairs. Part of the lesson deals with the patently obvious fact that many people do not feel alienated, hence the necessity for the parallel arguments of false consciousness, of narcotizing media influences, of spellbinding legitimation tactics.

For those whose social ties have just been severed, who have, in a way, been uprooted (by the move from home to university), the argument of atomization and isolation may seem plausible. The professor might provide supporting census data showing the large proportion of the population moving in any given year (or five-year period). The conclusions that the entire society is *deraciné* and, accordingly, filled with *Angst*, may easily be taken as accurate. For those not seeing clear career lines for themselves in the immediate future, a problem that is unusually pressing for liberal arts students, the lesson of *Angst* will seem especially appropriate. But, unbeknownst to them (for the professors have not told them), their anxiety in most cases is temporary. After the episode of rootlessness comes a period in which roots are reestablished, when one works out the routines of a relatively stable adult career.[16]

Some students in the universities will not see the mass society thesis as credible, since it goes against their own past experience and does not mirror their present circumstances. Some, perhaps, might even view it as a threat to their hopes and aspirations. Those who see rather clear career paths, for

[15]For discussion of the cyclical character of dissent as manifested in the universities, see Feuer, 1969; and Lipset, 1971, chapters 4 and 5. The quiescence of the 1950's became the basis for the much-discussed end of the ideology notion. It was taken as the beginnings of a new historical epoch rather than as an extreme swing of an ever-recurring cycle. For an important initial declaration of the position plus an extended review of the later discussions and commentary, see Lipset, 1981, chapters 13 and 15.

[16]Campbell, Converse, and Rodgers, 1976, pp. 152–153. Basically, judgments of overall life satisfaction and judgments with respect to most of the various domains of life increase with age. Cutting across the general upward direction is satisfaction with health. See above, pp. 209 ff.

example, those in natural sciences, engineering, law, medicine, business, or agriculture (fields leading to stable jobs facilitating early marriage and rerooting), are not likely to regard the mass society claims as credible. They, in effect, have an easy defense against this particular media influence within their own experience. Ironically, their unwillingness to accept the claims of the mass society position would normally be ascribed to false consciousness.[17]

One might also note, in passing, the possibility of another dynamic, a process likely to reinforce the pattern of influence just outlined. Some of the students present in the universities would see academic life as an attractive opportunity, as a likely or desirable career; some others, of course, would not see it that way. Those who saw the universities as liberal, critical, or as a place for radical, challenging commentary, if they themselves shared those values, could easily see themselves as part of those institutions and might well work toward an academic career. They might even improve or correct their own views so as to conform to what they perceived to be the approved lines of thought in that milieu. Those who disagreed with that reading of things, those who did not share those values, would be likely to avoid academia, sensing (or recognizing) that their chances of success were very limited. Even if they did choose academia, a second step involving selection by those already employed in their chosen field would have to be surmounted. It would be difficult to establish discrimination at that point; nevertheless, judged in terms of result, it is clear that the selection process is far from random. (See Note 7 above for relevant figures.)

The findings and observations contained in this book have implications for some larger social science concerns. If one were to place our principal findings, which involve the centrality of marriage, family, and economic welfare, in that larger perspective, it should be clear that in the terms of one famous dichotomy—reformism versus radicalism—most people would choose the former. Given the strong bread-and-butter orientations, their preferences would be for the pragmatic, ameliorative, piecemeal changes involving adjustment of the basic social mechanism rather than for some comprehensive or radical transformation. They would, turning to another terminological pair, be "possibilists" as opposed to "maximalists."

[17]An example of this kind of cultural conflict appears in the following episode (based on our own field notes).

A group of faculty members were sitting at lunch one day. A latecomer joined them and, with evident relish, recounted an event that had occurred in his class the previous evening. The evening students, mostly adults, most of them ten to twenty years older than the full-time day students, were known for their "different" views reflecting their more diverse backgrounds and adult experiences. The class had been discussing Arthur Miller's Death of a Salesman. One man offered the following conclusion: "Willy's problem is that he was stuck with the New England territory." The assembled faculty members roared with laughter at the naïveté of the remark. They, of course, knew that Willy's problem was "the alienation of modern man" and that he would have faced exactly the same problems had he been selling in Ohio, Indiana, or Iowa.

One may consider the same point from another direction. Those who argue widespread underlying (or immanent) maximalist tendencies, those who claim that the world is so ordered as to predetermine a mass-based maximalist demand, do so on the basis of an extremely truncated presentation of data, or, more specifically, of *likely* relevant factors. The moving forces, supposedly, stems from a group's "relationship to the means of production." That focus, to be sure, is not narrowly conceived. It is not just one's relationship to a machine, to a supervisor, or even to a distant employer that is decisive. It is the entire cluster of factors that comes under the heading, "economic," including, of course, the increasingly obvious character of bourgeois class rule and the implications of that rule for the distribution of socially produced surplus.

That focus, however, omits entirely the priorities reported in the present analysis. It excludes consideration of marriage and family. It avoids entirely the consideration of emotional ties found within that complex. It also fails, obviously, to give attention to the causes of gratification or sorrow within those relationships. Avoiding such matters allows one to avoid discussion of the family (broadly speaking) as a determining factor with respect to the reformism-versus-radicalism choice. A simple calculus would probably be present in anyone's mind when weighing those alternatives— how would the radical option affect my life and the lives of my family? To opt for the radical choice would require reasonable clarity, from the outset, that it promised a decisive improvement over the status quo or over the main current directions of reform. Only in rare and special circumstances would that be the case.

A second omission in the typical maximalist scenario involves domestic economic welfare, a consideration best described with the colloquial phrase, "making ends meet." Here again is a consideration which, taken in its entirety, that is, for the entire collectivity, would lead to strong support for reformist directions in human affairs. Options would typically be assessed in terms of perceived relative advantage—that is, whether the proposed innovations would make things better or worse, or leave them the same as at present. The thing measured, in such instances, would be the welfare of the family; would the innovation improve diet, housing, neighborhood, or the family's quality of life? One is touching here on a very different area of the economy or of "economic determinism" than is usually considered under that heading. Despite the manifest centrality of domestic economic welfare in most people's lives, it is remarkable how advanced intellectual critics, those charting the course of "inevitable" crises, steadfastly refuse consideration of this central life concern. It is as if they had a fear of the grocery store, as if it were a taboo subject. Refusing to consider family affections and family finances means two remarkable efforts of reality-avoidance.[18]

[18]Among the six positions outlined in Chapter 1, these concerns surface, in a significant way, only in the Scammon and Wattenberg work and in the little man's

It takes very exceptional circumstances to make revolution seem more attractive than reform. The Russian revolution of 1917, the first of the major "successful" revolutions, provides the archetypical case. The principal ingredients were the war, the war-related food supply disaster in the cities, and the war-related appearance of massive financial support for the Bolsheviks and for national separatism movements, those monies supplied, of course, by the German government. The basic scenario is obviously very different from that purveyed in the standard Marxist liturgy.[19]

The revolution, once achieved, then became a model to guide the thought of others elsewhere (e.g., workers in all countries). The Russian experience, from an early point, however, was not auspicious. The food problem worsened under Bolshevik management, moving from disaster to catastrophe. The Duma (national legislature) was forceably disbanded in January 1918 after its first meeting; it did not have a Bolshevik majority. The first murders of members of opposition parties occurred at this point. The institution and maintainance of the new arrangement, in brief, required considerable use of force and fraud (or, as some prefer, of manipulation). These matters were, of course, reported at length (and with considerable distortion) in the conservative press everywhere. But Social Democratic leaders and journals were not indifferent to those developments. They too quickly drew negative conclusions about the new experience and actively disseminated those lessons.[20]

The rejection of household finances as a central intellectual concern appears early in the modern era in the work of Marx, who contemptuously announced that the "length of the purse" was not decisive in the determination of class. One does not have to search far for an explanation of the dismissal. Economic well-being is relative, a matter of degree. A continuum of experience does not lend itself to the Marxian dramaturgy. If the social reality consists of fine gradations of well-being, it would be difficult to argue an inevitable conflict of polar opposites, the dialectical struggle. Then, too,

---

revolt. They are certainly not central in the writings of the social critics, or of the workplace critics, or of the postmaterialists. Radical critics do, of course, refer to economic difficulties facing people; they are happy to discuss, illustrate, or otherwise document the economic strains and desperation facing many people. But that concern is rarely built into their analysis; it is normally treated as an isolated fact. Instead, they have a preference for the larger or structural arguments. In lieu of these everyday commonplace concerns, they prefer to focus on alienation, something which, by definition, makes the human condition something less than satisfactory. For an outstanding discussion, see Feuer, 1963.

[19]For discussion of the food supply, see McNeill, 1982, pp. 329–330. The question of German money and the Bolsheviks is reviewed in Carmichael, 1974; Katkov, 1956; and Zeman and Scharlau, 1965. Also of some interest is the treatment by Solzhenitsyn, 1976. The support for the Ukrainian separatist movement is discussed in Fedyshyn, 1971.

[20]A useful brief overview appears in Fuller, 1961, Chapter 10. For a more extensive discussion, see Rauch, 1972. For the reaction in German Social Democratic circles, see Lösche, 1967.

in an era of generally rising living standards, the constituency for the revolution would become ever smaller, or, put somewhat differently, the inevitable would become something less than certain.

The dominance of reformist sentiment among the masses, we think, has been a fact throughout the entire modern era (and, probably, all previous eras). The inverse point, the assumption of radical masses, we think, is largely myth (see Miliband, 1964; and Moore, 1978). Karl Marx, writing in 1850, pointed to the rising of Paris workers in June 1848 as the cornerstone of his intellectual enterprise; it was the first struggle of the revolutionary proletariat seeking to overthrow the bourgeois regime (Marx, 1951). It is remarkably clear, however, even in badly distorted versions of the event, that those workers were fighting to retain a primitive welfare-state arrangement, a crude, hastily extemporized make-work program. The rising, in short, sought to perpetuate a piecemeal reform. A prime example of bread-and-butter demands, in other words, has been falsely represented as the first effort of proletarian maximalism in the modern era (for the actual dynamics see Traugott, 1980a, b; and 1985).

The favored plans of radical activists, it should be noted, constitute a serious threat to the two primary mass concerns discussed here. Revolutionary activity and armed conflict interfere with normal, routine family relationships. There is, at the outset, some chance of arrest, incarceration, and injury. The extreme case, death on the barricades, would mean the loss of a loved one and, in the case of a breadwinner, economic disaster for the survivors. It is of some interest to note that accounts of revolutions focus, almost exclusively, on the activities of men. What were the women doing at that time? Did working-class wives encourage and support their husbands and sons when they left for the barricades? Or did they do everything they could to keep them at home? Would the affectionate ties and concern for family welfare not provide a powerful incentive for them to oppose the principal imperative of the revolutionary option—putting bodies on the line? The heroic accounts are unusually silent on this aspect of revolutionary history.

The same basic contradiction between the requirements of family and those of revolution appears in a wide range of contexts, that is, in the efforts of Communist parties in the decades following the Russian revolution. Many commentators, mistakenly, have taken the official proclamations of those parties at face value, assuming that they were (or are), in fact, parties of integration, that they were led by professional revolutionaries, by people who devoted the whole of their lives to the task. Again, in the typical account, the portraits of the workers appear with scarcely a mention of workers' wives or families. A worker giving the whole of his life to the party would obviously have little time for his family. But for most workers in most countries, one may easily assume, those accounts are seriously misleading. The obligations of family life would ordinarily stand in the way of the life and activity demanded by the party. Unless those workers were totally insensitive to their families' needs and welfare, it follows that they would have to give considerable time and effort to everyday family life and to the related bread-and-butter concerns. One indication of the latter, reported in the course of research on French workers, was the high percentage of those on the left who admitted having a garden, in all likelihood a vegetable garden (Hamilton, 1967, pp. 149–151).

Communist parties, historically, have sought to establish cells in the workplaces, most especially in the large plants of the leading industries of the nation. The idea, of course, was to have the party's revolutionaries located in the pivotal centers of the national economy. But, with remarkable insistence, workers have avoided the factory cells. When affiliating with the party, their preferences were for the neighborhood cells; the reason was very simple—activity in the neighborhood did not constitute a threat to one's livelihood, as might be the case with militancy in the factory.

A simple technical matter also stood (and stands) in the way of activism in the factory. The only time available for such effort, normally, is before or after the shift. But serious problems are posed by either option, notably those of getting there or getting home from there. Transportation (at least prior to the appearance of private vehicles) was, and still is, arranged to fit the requirements of shift work. Those who miss the bus might have to wait eight hours for the next opportunity.

Even among the Communist workers, then, the interests, needs, concerns, or requirements of marriage and family living will ordinarily take precedence over the needs of the party. Where those loyalties inevitably come into conflict, the tendency, for most people, would be to abandon the party for the sake of the family. This concern for family and family welfare is doubtlessly a principal reason for a characteristic observed in Communist parties everywhere (at least prior to taking power): high rates of turnover. It is merely another expression of the dominance of reformist over radical sentiment in the normal state of human affairs. Rather than a natural (or inevitable) tendency for workers to shift from economist to revolutionary concerns, the opposite experience is more clearly in evidence; the inevitable movement is away from the revolutionary focus. It is the revolutionary commitment that contains the inherent contradiction, that is unstable or in disequilibrium. It is the revolutionary option that faces the immanent dialectic, one pushing in another direction, toward the reformist resolution.[21]

Some people, unquestionably, make an opposite ranking of the priorities; some do put the radical interest first. They are, clearly, persons who deviate sharply from the statistical norm in the general population.[22]

---

[21] For elaboration on these points plus documentation with regard to, respectively, the French, American, and German left, see Hamilton, 1967, pp. 24–31; Hamilton, 1972, pp. 543–555; and Hamilton, 1982, pp. 287–308.

[22] A striking instance of such a deviation from the statistical norm, a case of persons putting party interests before family, appears in the experience of Peggy and Eugene Dennis. The latter was, at one time, general secretary of the American

In addition to a widespread fear of radical programs, one is also likely to find a general reaction to what might be termed the radical "style." Many radicals cultivate a manner that is intended to shock ordinary citizens; it is a style that could only work to alienate the members of the most likely constituencies. This points to still another reason for the failure of the revolution. Many advocates of change, the most visible exponents of the new direction, present themselves as rather unattractive individuals. The choice of the abrasive or alienative style, of a means that could only lead to the defeat of one's own purpose, indicates a hidden nonpolitical agenda. The so-called activists in such cases are using politics to serve their own psychological needs. It is not surprising, therefore, that the masses refuse the opportunity to work for change under those auspices. In their own behavior, the activists provide convincing grounds for doubt about the likelihood that their effort would improve the human condition.[23]

The explanations provided for the failure of "change" movements also deserve some attention. The principal reasons given, particularly by persons closely identified with those movements, may be put under the headings of force and fraud (that is, manipulation). Movements are smashed through the use of police or national guard forces and/or through infiltration by informants and agent provocateurs. The other line of argument stresses the use of cunning techniques to sustain false consciousness among the masses through the mass media, thus creating and/or sustaining the requisite attitudes of consumerism and, more generally, contributing to the narcotization of the masses. Absent from the repertory of reasons for failure is the one just given, the internal sources of failure, the poor or inept choice of tactics and strategy by those directing the movements for change. Such self-criticism is not ordinarily among the options considered in such discussions. One principal line of leftist epistemology, in fact, affirms an a priori evidential rule that forbids blame for a victim. That means the analysis of such movements will be seriously distorted; it excludes from the outset any consideration of the *internal* factors contributing to their defeat.[24]

Communist Party. They were both Communists at the time of an episode that Michael Harrington reports as follows: "When Eugene Dennis was working for the Comintern, he and his wife lived in Moscow (on those rare occasions when he was home). It was decided that it would be embarrassing to bring their Russian-speaking child with them when they returned to the United States. They were told to leave him behind—and they did." From *The New York Times Book Review*, February 12, 1978, p. 11.

[23]The alienative, hostile style appears, of course, in both the life and writings of Karl Marx. The best current work on his personal style is that of Fritz Raddatz (1975, passim) and, for a more general treatment, Bertram Wolfe (1965, p. 260 and passim). For a very useful, thought-provoking consideration of the underlying psychology and the psychological uses of political movements, see Krugman, 1953.

[24]There is, of course, a simple alternative procedure: if a victim is to blame, then he, she, or it (in the case of organizations) should be blamed. It is a simple empirical matter. The work under discussion is that of William Ryan, 1971. Radical movements

The bottom line conclusion, as already indicated, is that the radical direction in the United States (and, we think, elsewhere in the industrialized world) does not have a mass base. The various radical programs do not accord with, do not mesh with, are not consonant with, the basic values and interests of the mass of the population. Even in those instances where, in principle at least, there is mass approval for aspects of the radical initiative, as, for example, in the case of support for egalitarian measures, the specter of the most visible advocates of radical change is such as to immobilize the willing.[25]

Given the penchant of advanced intellectuals for drawing on the lessons of history, it is curious that they have missed a major one here. While regularly announcing the radical tendency, they have failed to note a persistent, one might even refer to it as inevitable, tendency on the part of all major political parties of the modern era. Barring exceptional internal controls (as, for example, in some Communist parties), the tendency is to move in a left-liberal direction, essentially toward acceptance of or support for the modern welfare state. It is the consensus position, the point of convergence for all serious contenders. Put differently, it means that all parties tend in a reformist or ameliorative direction, one that addresses the dominant welfare demands observed among the masses.[26] This tendency proceeded irresistibly within German Social Democracy, the world's best documented case. Although condemned at their 1903 party meeting (in favor of the radical or Marxist direction), revisionism continued on its ineluctable course to be adopted, somewhat belatedly, at Bad Godesberg in 1959 as the party's official program. The classical conservative parties and the right-liberal (laissez-faire) parties of Europe, too, were (or are) forced to accede to these popular or mass demands. Although long opposed to the

do face the threat and reality of state power. They do face infiltration and provocation (Chevigny, 1972; Gary Marx, 1974). They are up against some efforts of manipulation, and are undermined by their own internal failures. No intellectually responsible purpose is served by omission of the latter consideration.

[25]Support for radical causes is, in some cases at least, a product of calculated manipulative efforts. Edmund Wilson, for example, reported his discovery that the Communist Party, while publicly working to save the Scottsboro boys, actually wished them executed (from Podhoretz, 1979, p. 120). Katherine Anne Porter, while working to save Sacco and Vanzetti, discovered one Communist who was "hoping only for their deaths. . . . " This "grim little person," in a "shrill, accusing voice," demanded answers: "Saved? Who wants them saved? What earthly good would they do us alive?" (Quoted in The New York Times Book Review, August 21, 1977, p. 9).

The archetypic literary treatment of the problem is John Steinbeck's In Dubious Battle. Dostoevsky's The Possessed, of course, deals with the same theme.

[26]A semantic note. The words reformist and ameliorative are regularly used as terms of denigration. The implication is that another and markedly superior option is thereby being neglected. Such insinuation is rarely accompanied by argument, by a demonstration of the case. The same denigration comes with the phrase piecemeal change. As applied to the welfare state, however, the claim is without justification. That phrase does not accurately describe the expenditures and accomplishment of most economically advanced nations. Welfare expenditures generally far exceed the heavy costs of national defense.

welfare state, defining it as financially impossible (or destructive of morale, character, or work motivation), none of those parties has undertaken to dismantle the achievements of their left-liberal competitors.

Few parties in recent decades have ventured to advocate a program of welfare state dismantlement. A passing remark by Barry Goldwater with respect to the social security program was a source of considerable difficulty for him in his 1964 campaign. Indeed, it is this convergence on the welfare issue, this broad consensus on the part of all serious contenders, that has given rise to the fiscal crisis of the 1980's. The conservative opposition to welfare measures that was present as an effective restraining force in all countries up to the mid-1950's collapsed. Their opposition had been couched in terms of costs, of the inability to pay (sometimes expressed as reflecting principles of sound finance). The ineffectiveness of that opposition, in the 1950's and 1960's, meant that generous welfare programs became the law of the land everywhere.

Anticipating continuous economic growth and a corresponding increase in tax revenues (the key term was fiscal dividend), most such plans were inadequate in their design, the plan (or hope) being that the subsequent, necessary adjustments would be achieved with no great difficulty. Operating on the same basic assumption, the ease of future funding, coverage was extended and generous provision made for cost-of-living adjustments.

But then, in the 1970's, with either no, slow, or erratic growth and with unexpected and persistent demographic changes, the plan ran into difficulties; the fiscal dividend turned into fiscal deficits, and the various welfare insurance arrangements needed emergency supplementation. The exuberant extension of welfare plans, in short, set things up for a later reaction. While it is easy to portray this as partisan, as political, as something stemming from Reaganite or Thatcherite principles, a more complete review of western experience indicates that the effort is linked to systems rather than to parties. The Socialist Mitterand government in France and the Socialist-led Craxi government in Italy were both forced to move in exactly the same direction. Although the moves are sometimes labeled neoconservative, the generality of the experience indicates that it is due to fiscal necessity, the patently obvious need to bring payments into line with revenues, rather than a question of political ideology.[27]

[27]See also our previous discussion of Proposition 13 (in Chapter 8). Another example of economic retrenchment by a "left" government appears in the Quebec case, in the performance of the social-democratic *Parti Québécois*.

Although often alleged, the Reagan administration has not dismantled the welfare state. Nor, again, as frequently alleged, has it cut back on funding. Except for some minor programs, the funding continued to increase substantially to 1983 (the latest figures at this writing). The principal changes made have been some restrictions on eligibility. For a summary review of the Reagan performance (along with a comparison of Carter's accomplishment), see Novak, 1983.

The use of the word systems in the text should not be misread. We are not using the term to refer to some inherent crisis of capitalism. The problem is not systemic (or

The proof of this historic tendency may be seen in the exceptions, in the experience of those parties that violate the requirement of attention to the basic welfare-oriented mass demands. They suffer a penalty—defeat at the polls. This, in fact, occurs with such insistence that it might be termed an iron law. Some units of the Social Democratic party in Germany, in the 1970's, again turned in a radical direction. Through use of their superior organizational skills, groups of intellectuals were able to gain control of important local units of the party and impose their views. But those victories proved to be pyrrhic; they gained the organization but lost previous members and, more importantly, lost votes. In the process, they managed to lose such bastions as Berlin, Munich, and Frankfurt.[28] The left also made significant in roads within the Labour Party in Britain, and with the same effect—subsequent losses in by-elections and in the 1983 general election.

These dynamics—radicals alienating the party faithful—are typically omitted from the accounts of advanced intellectuals. There is, in short, a bias or tendency that is operating. It is a bias that protects the radical, the left or critical direction and its interpretation of social affairs. The processes of distortion we have been discussing may be considered in terms of the media (or outlet) needs and the needs of individuals producing media content.

The aim of commercial media, put simply, is to make money. To convey fact, information, or analysis per se is a distinctly secondary interest. Were the two needs to conflict, it is the concern with information that would be sacrificed. Put somewhat differently, the perceived demands of the market will normally take precedence over the requirements of adequate coverage (including that of veracity).[29] From among the range of valid findings, one will also, normally, find a strong tendency or bias. Given a random array of informational possibilities, the media preference will be for exciting, topical, or hot news items, for subjects likely to grab audience attention. That would mean a systematic bias in favor of the exceptional, the new, the different, the

---

structural), but one of faulty political judgment. That does not change the character of the current problem; it does indicate, however, a different etiology, and recognizes a range of possibilities for solution.

[28]For discussion of the Munich case, as portrayed by the defeated SPD Bürgermeister, see Georg Kronawetter, 1979. Kronawetter later defeated his left opponents and regained office.

[29]*Newsweek* magazine, it will be remembered, was especially active in the propagation of the antiwork hype in the early 1970's. Showing similar zeal, it is perhaps not surprising that it should have bought the rights to the bogus Hitler diaries so as to be the first to transmit their contents to the North American audience. It is easy to point to media cupidity in such cases. There was, however, no evident negative audience reaction (such as, for example, a drop in newsstand sales or discontinuance of subscriptions). *Der Stern*, the original West German purveyor of this material, suffered a very modest circulation loss, but then, just as quickly, regained its previous position. It is not what one has been led to expect of a responsible, educated, upper-middle-class citizenry. For some useful background, see the *New York Times* article, "Newsweek's Editor in Chief Resigns," January 5, 1984.

wave-of-the-future speculation—as opposed to the everyday, ordinary, commonplace events, or, for that matter, reports on basic social trends. As an analogy, one might think about reports on a river. The main channel of flow would never be judged as newsworthy, even though it is the largest single fact about the total event. Instead, it would be the ice jam, the spring flood, the broken dike, the washed out bridge, or the unsuspected pollution that would be given attention.

Extending the image to social affairs, the point is that the major flows of family life, community affairs, or work life will not ordinarily be given serious attention. The "news" that most families report very positive feelings between the marital partners and between parents and children, is not likely to be reported. It would not serve the principal interest. Even if, perchance, a story did appear reporting such findings, it is unlikely that there would be a follow-up, say a year later. One would not update the previous findings to report, for example, that most people are still married, most spouses still favorably disposed, and so on. With only moderate hyperbole, one may note that everyday life is the one subject that is not ordinarily treated in news or public interest magazines. In this respect, the so-called serious journals are no different from the scandal sheets. They both share a devotion to exceptional experience.

The same principle operates with respect to popular book-length analyses. The basic requirement for a best-seller is a focus on the new, the different, the exceptional—in short, the nonroutine development. The prediction of imminent collapse, or sweeping value changes, or inevitable social transformations, will normally gain more attention (and hence, more favor in the publishing houses) than the work arguing more of the same or, recognizing the existence of change, one noting that a 3% shift in values occurred in the course of the last decade.

The book-length accounts may focus on some narrowly defined trend (for example, the use of manipulative procedures by the new managers of elections, or the uses of electronic media to survey, keep records on, and, ultimately, control the general populace). If one wished to provide a larger theoretical grounding, the mass society theory, with its claims of uprootedness, mobility, isolation, aimlessness (or anomie), and resultant anxiety (or *Angst*), provides the best basic material for such scenarios. For the purposes of commercial publishers, the actual direction of change described or predicted is largely a matter of indifference; the requirements are size and drama, not political ideology. It could be a simple tale of everything falling apart (the Spenglerian or *Götterdämmerung* option), or it could be a higher synthesis option ("out of this will come the new transformed humanity"— the Childe Harold, Zarathustrian, or Promethean variant).[30]

---

[30]For a discussion of one major work in the mass society-cum-manipulation tradition, Joe McGinniss' *The Selling of the President: 1968*, see Hamilton, 1975, Chapter 6, "The Myth of the Electoral Technocrats."

Most of the so-called critical analyses of the media stress the purely political uses,

The second focus of this discussion involves the producers of media content. They could, of course, be the leading experts in a given field, those at the forefront of research in the area. Or they could be intermediaries, freelance writers, popularizers, or full-time journalists. For several reasons, some involving media needs, some involving the orientations of leading experts, one finds a pronounced tendency for the media to rely on intermediaries. Some explanation is in order.

A common process appears in the history of most intellectual fields. The pioneers in a given area might be described as brilliant, highly gifted amateurs. (They might also, incidentally, be persons possessing broad-based knowledge and understanding of social, cultural, and intellectual affairs). In most fields, it is this coterie of gifted individuals who first see the hitherto unsuspected linkages, who design the crude, primitive experiments, and who make the first fundamental breakthroughs that force rethinking of the received paradigms. Other bright and capable people, their immediate students, continue research and development of the new tradition, building on the original foundations. The process is then elaborated, with ever greater refinement, in each subsequent intellectual generation. At the outset, the findings in any given field are easily accessible to any intelligent citizen; they might, with no difficulty, be made available to educated citizens by the original researcher. In the course of the process of technicization, however, direct public access, for all practical purposes, is reduced to zero. This is most clearly the case with work in the natural sciences, regardless of whether we are talking about physics, geology, or nephrology.

The same process also occurs in the social sciences. The broad outlines of a problem, the first article or book on a given subject, will typically be accessible to the intelligentsia of any nation. But in short order, in any active field, the frontiers of the field will shift to a wide range of finer, detailed problems, the answers to which would be derived from a sparse documentary record, or from a small number of surveys containing only oblique indicators of the relevant variables, or findings dependent on hairbreadth differences in probabilities, a problem that might tax the abilities of the best statisticians. The technicization process, of necessity, creates a substantial gulf between the leading practitioners in a given field and the general public. This means, of course, that the latest findings will not be immediately

---

to the exclusion of the economic interests or concerns of the owners. The political and economic aims, however, are not always consonant. Publication of a consistent conservative line might easily, especially in a liberal age, mean the death of the enterprise, or at least a serious threat to the fortunes of the owners. A conservative publisher confronted with strong liberal demand will have to make concessions. Those anticipating a hard line in the face of this dilemma would do well to consider the conclusion drawn by one conservative book publisher who, in the late 1960's, said, "Well, we published that conservative shit, we might as well publish this radical shit." We thank the late William Gum for passing on the quotation.

For a comprehensive portrait of decision-making processes in the book-publishing industry, see Coser, Kadushin, and Powell, 1982.

accessible to the larger audience. It means some process of mediation becomes necessary. If a communication of findings occurs at all, it would require translation and, typically, a separate medium to bring the digested findings to the larger public.

The most obvious possibility would be that the leading experts themselves undertake this task of translation, or, to use the more frequent term, of popularization. For several reasons, however, this is not often the case. Many technical experts show no interest in a wider dissemination of their findings; they see their audience as consisting of the world's specialists, of the (possibly) one or two thousand persons working on their specific topic. Even in the face of misleading (or botched) popularizations, many experts feel no sense of obligation to make correction. The end result, of course, is an abandonment of that translation task; it is left to others, to persons who, perforce, are less competent than the experts.

A second consideration discouraging the use of the technical experts involves the previously discussed needs of the media. Given their prime consideration, given the economic determinism that moves at least the commercial media, they would not ordinarily be encouraged to stimulate contributions from the specialists in many fields. If the topic does not accord with the requirement that it be hot, topical, or in some way stimulating, there would be no incentive for such translation. If such a contribution arrived without solicitation, it would receive no reward.

A third consideration discouraging dependence on the leading experts involves the technical requirements of the media. Periodical literature, whether newspapers or magazines, along with regular radio or television news and comment programs, operate under nearly inflexible time constraints. The material has to be in by the deadline. It has to be presented while the subject is hot. But such demands, typically, do not accord with schedules in the world of scholarship. Scholarly research efforts do not ordinarily yield results at noon, say, on a given Friday when the news editor needs some appropriate copy.

A fourth consideration militating against use of the expert is also technical in character. Many results cannot be easily fitted into the brief summary format required by the media. Most findings are contingent, probabilistic, subject to alternative interpretation, and, in a fundamental way, always preliminary. The media requirement, in the ordinary run of things, is to strip away the doubts, the tentative formulations, and the qualification in favor of the bold, unambiguous, challenging conclusion.

A fifth consideration impeding the use of experts-as-transmitters, one not yet fully appreciated, is found in the requirements of union contracts. In recent decades, such contracts have contained stipulations limiting the extent of outside contributions. The aim, clearly, is to reserve the pages of newspapers for full-time, regular members of staff.

For all these reasons, there is, effectively, a major gulf separating expert sources and the transmitting media. Their conflicting interests discourage continuous working relationships. The technical specialists, typically, are not able to deliver material according to the demands of media managers. The specialists, in general, are unreliable producers who are either unwilling or unable to meet deadlines. Thus, there is a strong incentive for media managers to make use of their own agents, people who typically are not themselves experts but who can provide easy (or popular) summaries of complex materials and respond quickly to the demands imposed on them.

The previous paragraphs describe what might be termed the formal content requirements. They say nothing about the specifics of the content. In recent decades, one has seen the appearance of a left-of-center (or a left-liberal, or, as it is sometimes put, a critical) tendency. This preference, or, to use an appropriate synonym, this bias, has two independent contributing sources, the preferences of media elites and those of the generators of media content.

Media elites in recent decades have generally been left-liberal in personal orientation, and, on the whole, that tendency has been reflected in their outlets. These observations go against some fundamental points of conventional wisdom, specifically, the claims that such elites are conservative and use their media to defend their positions (both on specific issues and to provide some general system legitimation). But those claims go against the best available contemporary evidence on the attitudes of media elites. They also fail to recognize the character of much media content, particularly that contained in the major outlets (the provincial press, to be sure, remains generally conservative in orientation). That conventional wisdom has its roots in earlier experience, which is to say that it did, at one time, provide an accurate portrait. But those who still promulgate that view in the 1980's have simply failed to keep up with the times. Not recognizing the major transformation, they are now providing a largely inadequate account of some key social dynamics.[31]

Many media organizations in former decades could be characterized as having liberal or left journalists who stood in opposition to conservative

---

[31]For the orientations of media elites, see Barton, 1974; for television elites, see Lichter, Lichter, and Rothman, 1983a; for motion picture elites, see Rothman and Lichter, 1984. Also focusing on a segment of the television elite, writers of prime-time shows, is the work of Ben Stein, 1979. Stein also provides a nonstatistical review of prime-time television content. A similar portrait also appears in Michael Robinson, 1979. For a more systematic content analysis showing the negative treatment of businessmen in prime-time programming, see Lichter, Lichter, and Rothman, 1983b.

Muriel Cantor interviewed television producers and, like the previously-reported researches, found them to be strongly liberal in orientation. She does not, however, see those sentiments reflected in the material they produce, arguing a system of tight controls (Cantor, 1980, passim). Another author who fails to recognize the content change is G. William Domhoff. "The overall effect of the media efforts," he says, despite the business community's complaints, "nevertheless tends to reinforce the stability of the present corporate system" (1983, p. 108). A valuable portrait of the transformation, of the relaxation of the previous controls in four major units of the mass media, is to be found in Halberstam, 1979.

owners and managers. According to Halberstam (1979, p. 61), Henry R. Luce, the proprietor of Time, Incorporated, "often wondered aloud, [about why] all the talented writers [were] liberals." The conflict was solved by a direct or indirect exercise of power. Luce had very fixed, and mistaken, views on China and its Nationalist leadership under Chiang Kai-shek. He also had a reporter in China, Theodore H. White, who sent accounts diametrically opposed to those views. The *Time* editors in New York, the chief of whom was Whittaker Chambers, simply rewrote those stories, making them conform to the views of the publisher (Halberstam, 1979, p. 71 ff.). Norman Chandler's *Los Angeles Times* was also a tightly controlled organization (p. 117). Things at CBS News, by comparison, were handled on a more informal basis. As Halberstam put it (p. 659), "No one ever ordered anyone to kill a story at CBS, "—but the informal pressures were just as effective. Control, in some cases, was exercised through the direct order, this being most clearly the case with the Hearst enterprises. Elsewhere, however, the controls were more subtle. They rarely depended on direct orders, but instead relied on clues (the rejection of a story, the editing or rewriting of a story, its placement, whether on the front page or next to the obituaries). The key concept used in this connection is "sensing policy"—the journalist or free-lancer infers policy from the treatment of stories submitted and reacts to those clues.[32]

As indicated, some changes have occurred in the structure of controls in recent decades. The lords of the press, the founders, the authoritarian directors of newspapers and magazines, like all other mortals, eventually disappear from the scene. Their successors, in many instances, are salaried managers of a corporation (or of a division thereof), and they, unlike the original owners, do not make use of those organizations for private political purposes. Some owners (or their heirs) undergo a conversion, moving away from the solid conservatism in which they were raised, coming to a more relaxed liberal outlook. Some conversions were stimulated by the events of the civil rights movement, by the new atmosphere of the Kennedy years, or by experience in the universities during the years of uprising. Some media owners and managers, in the Johnson years, felt they had been taken in by the manipulative efforts of leading public officials, particularly with regard to the Vietnam war. They eventually abandoned their traditional supportive position and either allowed or encouraged the critical stance vis-à-vis government and incumbent leaders. Competition between the media also played some role in opening up the range of the allowable. To meet the challenge provided by the exciting, provocative, or relevant content of one's competitors, it was necessary to give freer rein to the journalists, wire editors, and editorial writers. One also was led to reach out for the work of hitherto

[32]The most frequently cited article dealing with the sensing of policy is that by Breed, 1955, which deals with a small-town daily. A more important contribution dealing with a conservative metropolitan daily is by Start, 1962. Also of use, still a valuable study, is Rosten, 1937, Chapter 10.

neglected free-lance writers, the case of Paul Goodman being the most striking example. Once the change from the bland 1950's was accomplished, it was difficult, even if desired, to reinstitute the old controls, to narrow once again the range of permissible report and comment.

This change means that the relationship, especially in major national media, is no longer one of opposed forces. For reasons of sheer technical necessity, some editorial gatekeeping continues, but the range of the allowable is considerably greater than in times past. This means that the left-liberal or critical tendency among the contributing intellectuals is now able to express itself, in some cases with the backing and support of the media elites.[33]

Our presentation here is obviously oversimplified, focusing on what we take to be a shift in the dominant tendency. It is not the case that *all* sources in previous decades were bastions of conservatism and strict censorship. The *New York Times*, from the coming of Adolph Ochs, has always been a comparatively open newspaper. Walter Duranty, for example, the *Times'* man in the Soviet Union in the early 1930's, played down the seriousness of the 1933 famine there and excused the government's efforts that had caused the problem (Carynnyk, 1983). On this occasion, the closely controlled Hearst press proved more accurate than the *Times*. It is also not the case that in recent decades *all* controls have been removed. Some controls will always exist, if only because of the space (or time) constraints, if not for the sake of intelligence or honesty.

The possible mass impacts of this changed orientation in the media should be a leading research priority. Given the liberal or critical tendency, one might anticipate a corresponding shift of mass attitudes in a liberal direction. Some dramatic shifts of attitude have in fact been reported during this period of relaxed media controls, the most notable of which has been the decline of diffuse support for the institutions and persons governing the nation (Wright, 1976, Chapter 7; Wright, 1981). A similar decline in faith or trust has been registered for almost all other institutions of the society (Lipset and Schneider, 1983).[34]

---

[33]The best portrait of these changes is provided by Halberstam, 1979, passim. The a fortiori case, discussed there at some length, involves the role of the *Washington Post* in the investigation of the Watergate affair. The owner, managers, and investigative reporters in this case were on the same side of the issue.

[34]Before drawing hard and fast conclusions, however, it would be well to recollect some nonconforming findings. The NCRC's General Social Surveys, in response to questions about political leanings, turned up a slight shift in a *conservative* direction. The Gallup studies in the 1970's found a decline of both liberal and conservative identifications, which is associated with a corresponding increase in middle-of-the-road choices (see Chapter 8 for a review). No net shift to the Democrats was registered in this period, something that might be expected if the media were having a clear and measurable impact in the predicted direction. These findings, to be sure, are extremely crude; one trend occurring at the same time as another does not establish that causality is involved. It is not established, moreover,

For many people within the intellectual ranks, the critical outlook or tendency is not data based. Their conclusions, in other words, do not stem from systematic review and analysis of evidence. The tendency, for many, exists prior to analysis and, as we have seen, is frequently accompanied by an indifference to evidence, especially to findings that challenge or bring into question key elements of their basic *Weltanschauung*. We have seen numerous examples of this data-indifference—or worse, data-denigration—in previous chapters. Many intellectuals, in short, are depending on a consensual as opposed to an evidential truth. Expressed in other terms, they are responding to processes of group dynamics rather than to processes of data collection and assessment.[35]

It was this widespread commitment to the critical tendency (combined, of course, with the distinctive methodological preference) that facilitated the takeoff of the writings of the social critics and later those of the workplace critics—despite the presence of compelling contrary evidence. Those dispositions provided a fertile field for the generation of the bold, alarmist declaration. Media owners aid and abet the generation and dissemination of the tendency, many of them, as indicated, actively seeking out useful content. And, finally, it should also be noted that a large segment of the educated upper-middle-class population provides an enthusiastic audience for such productions. Without their support as consumers of such fare, the entire mechanism would break down.[36]

---

that the changers are those who followed the media, let alone that they had followed liberal media content. One possibility is that, although the new direction was liberal or critical, segments of the audience reacted negatively to that material, rejecting the thrust of the new message. For a preliminary discussion of this entire question, see Michael Robinson, 1979.

[35]Another example of the same process: Early in the 1970's, the mass media discovered a health-care crisis. *Fortune* magazine found American medicine to be "on the brink of chaos." CBS television gave the subject two hours of prime time with reporters George Herman and Daniel Schorr detailing the problem. NBC offered a contribution on the same theme, with Edwin Newman providing their commentary. Politicians also discovered the problem. President Richard Nixon spoke of the "massive crisis" in the delivery of health care, and Senator Edward Kennedy discovered health care to be "the fastest growing failing business" in America. Commenting on this hype at the end of the decade, Harry Schwartz wrote: "American medicine was never on the edge of chaos or in danger of collapsing . . . " (*New York Times*, September 11, 1979).

[36]We are using the term "tendency" in the same manner as Frederick Engels (1969, p. 19) when he wrote of events prior to the 1848 revolution in Germany: "Poetry, novels, reviews, the drama, every literary production teemed with what was called 'tendency,' that is with more or less timid exhibitions of an anti-governmental spirit." For a collection of statements by intellectuals covering the entire modern era, statements also describing the intellectuals' tendency toward "tendency," see Lipset and Basu, 1975. For data on more recent developments covering academics, journalists, editors, and so on, see Lipset, 1979a. This adversary role of intellectuals is reflected in a library cross-reference card in the Institut für Soziologie, Ruprechts-

In these matters, as in all social affairs, one is dealing with frequency distributions. Some intellectuals, some journalists, operate in terms of group dynamics, essentially following the cues, guidelines, and approved positions provided by their friends or associates (in the language of the social sciences, by their "significant others"). Some other intellectuals, clearly, do not operate that way. For many, the positions taken appear to be a product of groupthink. But, as indicated from the time of Solomon Asch's first conformity studies, here, too, there is a frequency distribution. The majority conform, a minority do not, having the ego strength to resist group pressures and form an independent judgment.[37]

Differentiation of this kind is indicated in a natural experiment, a small group study reported by David Halberstam (1965, pp. 13–14). In September 1961, Zaïre, the former Belgian Congo, was in civil war. The United Nations' Secretary-General, Dag Hammarskjöld, was there attempting to negotiate between the contending forces. At one point, Hammarskjöld was scheduled to arrive at Ndola Airport, en route to a conference with Moise Tshombe, the leader of seccessionist Katanga. For reasons of security, Halberstam writes, the reporters were kept off the field so that:

> . . . they had to watch from behind a wire fence several hundred feet away. It was dark, and at the moment Hammarskjöld's plane was due, a plane *did* arrive. Some figures walked out on the field to greet a man getting off the plane. The figure was about the size of Hammarskjöld, and a reporter with field glasses said, 'It's Hammarskjöld.' Someone else checked with a guard . . . who confirmed the identity. A Rhodesian Ministry of Information official was also there and concurred. Then a big black car went by. There was no press conference. Back went the newspapermen to report that Hammarskjöld had arrived safely.

Most of the journalists present reported the simple fact of the Secretary-General's arrival. One reporter even provided some conversation between Hammarskjöld and Tshombe. Two reporters failed to file; they were not

---

Karls-Universität, Heidelberg which reads, "Intellektuelle—Siehe auch [See also] Elite, Opposition."

[37]For discussion of groupthink, see Janis, 1972. For a review of the conformity studies, see Hollander, 1976, Chapter 13. The situation is actually somewhat more complex than indicated here in the text. Tocqueville wrote, "There is no philosopher in the world so great but that he believes a million things on the faith of other people and accepts a great many more truths than he demonstrates." Such acceptance, he argues further, "is not only necessary but desirable" (1963, Vol. 2, p. 9). Everyone, in short, is forced to rely on persons, on faith or trust to a considerable degree. Rather than arguing the extreme relativist position—*così fan tutti* (everyone does it)—we prefer to stress the difference in typical procedure: some people trust their sources because they take the "right" position; some trust their sources because of a demonstrated responsibility in the development and treatment of evidence. The former procedure surfaces most dramatically when a source rejects the "correct" position. Max Eastman was recognized by people on the left as highly intelligent, a leading intellectual—until he wrote a book containing entirely justified criticisms of the Soviet Union. At that point, his once-enthusiastic followers dropped him; they refused to read him any longer. See Diggins, 1975, Chapter 1; and O'Neill, 1978.

convinced that the Secretary-General had arrived. In fact, the plane had crashed; Hammarskjöld was dead.

What had happened? In the face of a diffuse stimulus, most of the assembled journalists had constructed a reality and based their reactions on that construction. It is a normal, easy, reassuring response in the face of uncertainty; people do it all the time in all kinds of settings. Some people, however, have sufficient ego strength to operate independently. When the actual "finding" is lack of clarity, obscurity, and uncertainty of meaning, they are able to operate on their own; they do not accept that agreed upon interpretation. The lesson, in short, is that the response to group pressures is not universal; those determinants do not operate across the board. Put differently, the presence of those exceptions undercuts the basis for a radical epistemological relativism.[38]

If one chooses to be guided by tendency, it is best to choose wisely. In the extreme case, the choice for the advanced intellectual is one of moving against or moving with the masses. Those who, ostensibly, at least, wish the masses well, who announce their sympathy for (or identification with) people in difficult circumstances, might give serious consideration to the latter option—moving *with* the masses. As opposed to the standard a priori assumption that the masses are misled, unaware of their real interests, and hence badly in need of tutelage, one might, if only for the sake of hypothesis, give consideration to the proposition that the masses, on some fundamentals, are very well aware of their interests. In some things, they might be far ahead of the advanced intellectuals in their understanding.

One might consider the substance of some communications, of those popular expressions offered in response to proposals for radical change. Possibly the most familiar of these is the alright-in-theory-but-not-in-practice objection. That amounts to an expression of doubt as to the possibility of a net benefit to be gained from a proposed change. The appropriate tactic for any reasonable advocate would be the presentation of argument or evidence to support the claim of benefit—as opposed to the ad hominem response of

[38]The Ndola incident involved the interpretation of an obscure event; there was no preexisting preference for one or another reading. A news report from San Salvador provides an opposite instance, one where the stimulus was not at all ambiguous but where the conclusion went against a strong tendency. Six journalists, an American, a Norwegian, a Britisher, and three Germans, rented a VW bus and traveled around the countryside to get a firsthand view of the conflict. They were parked in one town when three military transports carrying government troops drove through. The inhabitants waved and applauded the soldiers. People on the street threw cigarettes, bananas, oranges, and cookies to them. A discussion among the journalists followed. One of them said, "If I hadn't seen it, I would not have believed it." The *Washington Post* reporter was asked if she would write it up as they had seen it. She said she would and that the newspaper would print it. The three Germans in the party discussed whether they dared even mention the event to the German media. The problem, as they saw it, was that it would cast doubt on their credibility. One of them, Jürgen Koch, did report the episode in the *Frankfurter Allgemeine Zeitung*, February 22, 1982.

deluded (or narcoticized) masses. Or one might consider another frequent communication—"What can you do?" Literally, that amounts to an invitation to supply direction, to provide a plan or program that has at least surface plausibility for improvement of the human condition. The refusal to provide direction or plan and, instead, to fault the questioner for pessimism (or delusion), misses the manifest point of the communication. It also amounts to blaming the victim.

It is perhaps not to be expected that ordinary citizens provide answers to the "What can you do?" question. They are not in a position, because of lack of training and requisite experience, to work out the arrangements necessary to solve the complex issues that sometimes baffle the leading experts. Solutions to problems of such complexity would normally be expected only from some groups of advanced intellectuals.

But their typical negative focus, their critical stance vis-à-vis a supposed status quo, does not, in itself, lead to a correction of imperfection. The regular assault on experts, on technology, or on bureaucracy—the most likely sources of improvement—are not likely to aid the human condition. The imperfections of a social security system, problems with the delivery of welfare services, the problem of economic development in the Third World, or the provision of food supplies in areas of famine, are all likely to depend on the development of a new, improved bureaucracy. The most likely solutions, in short, are legal and technical insofar as the planning is concerned. As for the instrumentalities, that, too, would most likely—and preferably—be some kind of bureaucracy. The need, in short, is for intelligent, capable, and humane talents working within bureaucracies. The need is for persons who are able to design and implement what, in most instances, will be bureaucratic solutions.

An intelligentsia that counsels avoidance of those institutions, that counsels hostility toward the acquisition of technical skills, that instead places the emphasis on artful presentations of criticism, is one that works to the detriment of the human condition. Apart from the possibility of psychic gratification, nothing is to be gained by neglecting (or damaging) one's own legal, technical, and social skills, those required for the solution of wide-ranging human problems. Similarly, at one remove, nothing is served by damaging the talents of students (or other audiences) who should benefit from the productions of intellectuals. Nothing is served by inadequate mappings of the social territory, by the provision of mistaken agendas of human concerns, no matter how artful they may be.

It is perhaps time for a new, improved, intellectual outlook, for a more humane and more useful tendency.

BIBLIOGRAPHY

Abrahamson, Mark
    1980   "Sudden Wealth, Gratification, and Attainment," *American Sociological Review*, 45: 49–57.
Abrams, Mark
    1970   "The Opinion Polls and the 1970 British Election," *Public Opinion Quarterly*, 34:3 (Fall), 317–324.
Abrams, M.H.
    1971   *Natural Supernaturalism: Tradition and Revolution in Romantic Literature*, New York: W.W. Norton.
Adams, Bert N.
    1968   *Kinship in an Urban Setting*, Chicago: Markham.
    1980   *The Family: A Sociological Interpretation*, Chicago: Rand McNally.
Aggar, Robert E., and Daniel Goldrich
    1958   "Community Power Structures and Partisanship," *American Sociological Review* 23 (August): 383–392.
Akers, Donald S.
    1967   "On Measuring the Marriage Squeeze," *Demography*, 4: 907–924.
Alford, Robert R.
    1963   *Party and Society: The Anglo-American Democracies*, Chicago: Rand McNally.
Almond, Gabriel A., and Sidney Verba
    1963   *The Civic Culture*, Princeton, NJ: Princeton University Press.
American Jewish Committee
    1973   *Not Yet A Ms: The Working Class Women in America*, New York: American Jewish Committee.
Andrews, Frank M., and Stephen B. Withey
    1976   *Social Indicators of Well-Being: Americans' Perception of Life Quality*, New York: Plenum Press.
Andrisani, Paul J.
    1978   "Levels and Trends in Job Satisfaction, 1966–72," In Paul J. Andrisani, ed., Work *Attitudes and Labor Market Experiences*, New York: Praeger, pp. 48–100.
Argyle, Michael
    1972   *The Social Psychology of Work*, London: Allen Lane, The Penguin Press.
Argyris, Chris
    1960   *Understanding Organizational Behavior*, Homewood, IL: Dorsey and Irwin.

1962   "The Interpretation of the Individual and the Organization," in Chris
        Argyris et al., *Social Science Approaches to Business Behavior*,
        Homewood, IL: Dorsey and Irwin.

1973   "Personality and Organization Theory Revisited," *Administrative Sci-
        ence Quarterly*, 18: 141–167.

Armknecht, Paul A., and John F. Early
1972   "Quits in Manufacturing: A Study of Their Causes," *Monthly Labor
        Review*, 95: 31–37.

Aronowitz, Stanley
1973   *False Promises: The Shaping of American Working Class Conscious-
        ness*, New York: McGraw Hill.

Aronson, Eliot
1980   *The Social Animal*, 3rd ed., San Francisco: W.H. Freeman.

Asher, Herbert
1980   *Presidential Elections and American Politics: Voters, Candidates, and
        Campaigns Since 1952* (rev. ed.), Homewood, IL: Dorsey Press.

Bailes, Kendall E.
1978   *Technology and Society under Lenin and Stalin: Origins of the Soviet
        Technical Intelligentsia, 1917–1941*, Princeton, NJ: Princeton Uni-
        versity Press.

Baker, Kendall L., Russell J. Dalton, and Kai Hildebrandt
1981   *Germany Transformed: Political Culture and the New Politics*, Cam-
        bridge, MA: Harvard University Press.

Balzer, Richard
1976   *Clockwork: Life in and Outside an American Factory*, Garden City,
        NY: Doubleday.

Bandura, Albert
1964   "The Stormy Decade: Fact or Fiction?" *Psychology in the School*, 3:
        224–231.

Bandura, Albert, and R.H. Walters
1959   *Adolescent Aggression*, New York: Ronald.

Bane, Mary Jo
1976   *Here to Stay: American Families in the Twentieth Century*, New York:
        Basic Books.

Barkin, Kenneth
1983   "Social Control and the *Volksschule* in Vormaerz Prussia," *Central
        European History*, 16: 31–52.

Barkin, Solomon
1975   *Worker Militancy and Its Consequences, 1965–75*, New York: Pr-
        aeger.

Barton, Allen H.
1974   "Consensus and Conflict among American Leaders," *Public Opinion
        Quarterly*, 38: 507–530.

Beale, Calvin L.
1950   "Increased Divorce Rates Among Separated Persons as a Factor in
        Divorce since 1940," *Social Forces*, 29: 72–74.

Beck, Paul Allen, and M. Kent Jennings
1979   "Political Periods and Political Participation," *American Political
        Science Review*, 73: 737–750.

Bell, Daniel
1973   *The Coming of Post-industrial Society: A Venture in Social Forecast-
        ing*, New York: Basic Books.

Bengtson, Vern L.
1970   "The Generation Gap: A Review and Typology of Social-Psychological Perspectives," *Youth and Society*, 2: 7–32.

Benson, Lee
1957   "Research Problems in American Political Historiography," In Mirra Komarovsky, ed., *Common Frontiers of the Social Sciences*, Glencoe, IL: The Free Press, pp. 113–183.

Berelson, Bernard F., Paul Lazarsfeld, and William McPhee
1954   *Voting: A Study of Opinion Formation in a Presidential Campaign*, Chicago: University of Chicago Press.

Berg, Ivar
1976   "Working Conditions and Managements' Interests," In B.J. Widick, ed., *Auto Work and Its Discontents*, Baltimore, MD: The Johns Hopkins University Press, pp. 96–107.

Berg, Ivar, Marcia Freedman, and Michael Freeman
1978   *Managers and Work Reform: A Limited Engagement*, New York: The Free Press.

Berger, Bennett M.
1960   *Working Class Suburb: A Study of Auto Workers in Suburbia*, Berkeley: University of California Press.

Bergson, Abram
1964   *The Economics of Soviet Planning*, New Haven, CT: Yale University Press.

Bishop, George F., Alfred J. Tuchfarber, and Robert W. Oldendick
1978a   "Change in the Structure of American Political Attitudes: The Nagging Question of Question Wording." *American Journal of Political Science*, 22: 250–269.

Bishop, George F., Robert W. Oldendick, Alfred J. Tuchfarber, and Stephen E. Bennett
1978b   "The Changing Structure of Mass Belief Systems: Fact or Artifact?" *Journal of Politics*, 40: 781–787.

Bishop, George F., Robert W. Oldendick, and Alfred J. Tuchfarber
1978c   "Effects of Question Wording and Format on Political Attitude Consistency," *Public Opinion Quarterly*, 42: 81–92.

Bishop, George F., Alfred J. Tuchfarber, Robert W. Oldendick, and Stephen E. Bennett
1979   "Questions about Question Wording: A Rejoinder to Revisiting Mass Belief Systems Revisited," *American Journal of Political Science*, 23: 187.

Blake, Peter
1964   *God's Own Junkyard: The Planned Deterioration of America's Landscape*, New York: Holt, Rinehart and Winston.

Blauner, Robert
1960   "Work Satisfaction and Industrial Trends in Modern Society," In Walter Galenson and S.M. Lipset, eds., *Labor and Trade Unionism: An Interdisciplinary Reader*, New York: Wiley, pp. 339–360.

1964   *Alienation and Freedom: The Factory Worker and His Industry*, Chicago: University of Chicago Press.

Blumbaum, Milton
1983   "The Hawthorne Experiment: A Critique and Reanalysis of the First Statistical Interpretation by Kranke and Ka ul," *Sociological Perspectives*, 26: 71–88.

Blumberg, Leonard, and Robert R. Bell
    1959   "Urban Migration and Kinship Ties," *Social Problems*, 7: 328–333.
Blumberg, Paul, and James Murtha
    1977   "College Graduates and the American Dream," *Dissent*, 24: 4 (Winter), 45–53.
Bottomore, T.B., ed.
    1956   *Karl Marx: Selected Writings in Sociology and Social Philosophy*, London: C.A. Watts & Co. Ltd. (McGraw-Hill edition published in 1964).
Bowen, Howard R.
    1977   *Investment in Learning: The Individual and Social Value of American Higher Education*, San Francisco: Jossey-Bass.
Bowles, Samuel, and Herbert Gintis
    1976   *Schooling in Capitalist America: Educational Reform and the Contradictions of Economic Life*, New York: Basic Books.
Bradburn, Norman M.
    1969   *The Structure of Psychological Well-Being*, Chicago: Aldine.
Braestrup, Peter
    1977   *Big Story: How the American Press and Television Reported and Interpreted the Crisis of Tet 1968 in Vietnam and Washington*, Boulder, CO: Westview Press.
Braverman, Harry
    1974   *Labor and Monopoly Capital: The Degradation of Work in the Twentieth Century*, New York: Monthly Review Press.
Brayfield, Arthur H., and Walter H. Crakett
    1955   "Employee Attitudes and Employee Performance," *Psychological Bulletin*, 52: 396–424.
Breed, Warren
    1955   "Social Control in the Newsroom," *Social Forces*, 33: 326–335.
Breton, Raymond
    1964   "Institutional Completeness of Ethnic Communities and the Personal Relations of Immigrants," *American Journal of Sociology*, 70: 193–205.
Brooks, Thomas R.
    1972   "Job Satisfaction: An Elusive Goal," *The American Federationist* 79 (Oct.): 1–7.
Bumpass, Larry, and Ronald R. Rindfuss
    1979   "Children's Experience of Marital Disruption," *American Journal of Sociology*, 85: 49–65.
Campbell, Angus
    1971   *White Attitudes Toward Black People*, Ann Arbor, MI: Institute for Social Research.
    1981   *The Sense of Well-Being in America: Recent Patterns and Trends*, New York: McGraw-Hill.
Campbell, Angus, Philip E. Converse, Warren Miller, and Donald Stokes
    1960   *The American Voter*, New York: Wiley.
Campbell, Angus, Philip E. Converse, and Willard R. Rodgers
    1976   *The Quality of American Life: Perception, Evaluations, and Satisfaction*, New York: Russell Sage Foundation.
Cantor, Muriel
    1980   *Prime-Time Television*, Beverly Hills, CA: Sage Publications.
Cantril, Hadley
    1965   *The Pattern of Human Concerns*, New Brunswick, N.J.: Rutgers University Press.

Caplovitz, David
    1979   *Making Ends Meet: How Families Cope with Inflation and Recession*,
            Beverly Hills, CA: Sage Publications.

Caplow, Theodore, Howard M. Bahr et al.
    1982   *Middletown Families: Fifty Years of Change and Continuity*, Minne-
            apolis, MN: University of Minnesota Press.

Carey, Alex
    1967   "The Hawthorne Studies: A Radical Criticism," *American Sociologi-
            cal Review*, 32: 403–416.

Carmichael, Joel
    1974   "German Money and Bolshevik Honour," *Encounter*, 42 (Mar.):
            81–91.

Carter, Hugh, and Paul C. Glick
    1976   *Marriage and Divorce: A Social and Economic Study* (rev. ed.),
            Cambridge, MA: Harvard University Press.

Carynnyk, Marco
    1983   "The Famine the 'Times' Couldn't Find," *Commentary*, 76 (Nov.):
            32–40.

Chaffee, S.H. (ed.)
    1975   *The Watergate Experience: Lessons for Empirical Theory, American
            Politics Quarterly*, 4 (entire issue).

Champagne, Paul J., and Curt Tausky
    1978   "When Job Enrichment Doesn't Pay," *Personnel* (Jan.–Feb.): 30–40.

Chelte, Anthony F., James Wright, and Curt Tausky
    1982   "Did Job Satisfaction Really Drop During the 1970's?" *Monthly Labor
            Review*, 105:11 (Nov.), 33–36.

Cherlin, Andrew
    1978   "Remarriage as an Incomplete Institution," *American Journal of So-
            ciology*, 84: 634–650.

Chevigny, Paul
    1972   *Cops and Rebels: A Study of Provocation*, New York: Pantheon.

Chinoy, Ely
    1955   *Automobile Workers and the American Dream*, New York: Random
            House.

Christadler, Martin, ed.
    1981   *Political Culture in the United States in the Seventies: Continuity and
            Change*, Frankfurt am Main: University of Frankfurt Center for the
            Study of North America.

Citrin, Jack
    1974   "The Political Relevance of Trust in Government," *American Political
            Science Review*, 68: 973–988.
    1977   "Political Alienation as a Social Indicator: Attitudes and Action,"
            Social Indicators Research, 4: 381–419.

Clawson, Dan
    1980   *Bureaucracy and the Labor Process: The Transformation of U.S.
            Industry 1860–1920*, New York: Monthly Review Press.

Clayton, Richard R.
    1979   *The Family, Marriage, and Social Change* (2nd ed.), Lexington, MA:
            D.C. Heath.

Clayton, Richard R., and Harwin L. Voss
    1977   "Shaking Up: Cohabitation in the 1970s," *Journal of Marriage and the
            Family*, 39: 273–283.

Clemente, Frank, and William J. Sauer
    1976   "Life Satisfaction in the United States," *Social Forces*, 54 (3):
             621–631.
Condran, John G.
    1979   "Changes in White Attitudes Toward Blacks, 1963–1977," *Public
             Opinion Quarterly*, 43 (4): 463–476.
Converse, Muriel, Maureen Kallick, and George Katona
    1980   "Learning to Live with Inflation," *Public Opinion*, 3:2 (April-May):
             12–16.
Converse, Philip E.
    1972   "Change in the American Electorate," In A. Campbell and P. Con-
             verse (eds.). *The Human Meaning of Social Change*, New York:
             Russell Sage Foundation, pp. 263–337.
Cooper, M. R., B.S. Morgan, P.M. Foley, and L.B. Kaplan
    1979   "Changing Employee Values: Deepening Discontent?" *Harvard Busi-
             ness Review*, 57: 117–125.
Coser, Lewis A., Charles Kadushin, and Walter M. Powell
    1982   *Books: The Culture and Commerce of Publishing*, New York: Basic
             Books
Croce, Benedetto
    1915   *What is Living and What is Dead in the Philosophy of Hegel*, London:
             Macmillan.
Curtin, Richard
    1980   "Facing Adversity with a Smile," *Public Opinion*, 3:2 (April–May):
             17–19.
Cutler, N.E., and V.L. Bengston
    1974   "Age and Political Alienation: Maturation, Generation, and Period
             Effects," *The Annals of the American Academy of Political and Social
             Science*, 415: 160–175.
    1976   "Alienating Events," *Society*, 13(5): 43–47.
Dahl, Robert A.
    1961   *Who Governs? Democracy and Power in an American City*, New
             Haven, CT: Yale University Press.
Dalton, Russell J.
    1977   "Was There a Revolution? A Note on Generational Versus Life Cycle
             Explanation of Value Differences," *Comparative Political Studies*, 9:
             459–474.
Davidson, Stephen M., and Theodore R. Marmor
    1980   *The Cost of Living Longer*, Lexington, MA: Lexington.
Davis, James A.
    1975   "Communism, Conformity, Cohorts, and Categories: American Tol-
             erance in 1954 and in 1972–73," *American Journal of Sociology*,
             81:491–513.
Davis, Kingsley
    1950   "Statistical Perspective on Marriage and Divorce," *Annals of the
             American Academy of Political and Social Science*, 252: 9–21.
Davis, Louis E., and Albert B. Cherns, (eds.)
    1975   *The Quality of Working Life*, Vol. I: *Problems, Prospects, and the State
             of the Art*; Vol. II: *Cases and Commentary*, New York: The Free Press.
de Boer, Connie
    1978   "The Polls: Attitudes Toward Work," *Public Opinion Quarterly*, 42
             (3): 414–423.

Deming, Donald D.
    1977   "Reevaluating the Assembly Line," *Supervisory Management*, 22:
              2–7.
Derber, Milton
    1970   "Crosscurrents in Workers Participation," *Industrial Relations*, No. 29
              (Feb.): 123–136.
Dickson, Paul
    1975   *The Future of the Workplace: The Coming Revolution in Jobs*, New
              York: Weybright and Talley.
Diggins, John P.
    1975   *Up from Communism: Conservative Odysseys in American Intellec-
              tual History*, New York: Harper & Row.
Dobb, Maurice
    1966   *Soviet Economic Development Since 1917* (rev./enlarged ed.), New
              York: International Publishers.
Domhoff, G. William
    1978   *Who Really Rules? New Haven and Community Power Reexamined*,
              Santa Monica, CA: Goodyear.
    1983   *Who Rules America Now? A View of the '80s*, Englewood Cliffs, NJ:
              Prentice-Hall.
Dotson, Floyd
    1951   "Patterns of Voluntary Association among Urban Working-Class Fam-
              ilies," *American Sociological Review*, 16: 687–693.
Dubin, Robert
    1956   "Industrial Workers' Worlds: A Study of the 'Central Life Interests' of
              Industrial Workers," *Social Problems*, 3: 131–142.
Dubin, Robert, R. Alan Hedley, and Thomas C. Taveggia
    1976   "Attachment to Work," In Robert Dubin, ed., *Handbook of Work,
              Organization and Society*, Chicago: Rand McNally, Chap. 7.
Duncan, Otis Dudley
    1975   "Does Money Buy Satisfaction?" *Social Indicators Research*, 2:
              267–274.
Duncan, Otis Dudley, Howard Schuman, and Beverly Duncan
    1973   *Social Change in a Metropolitan Community*. New York: Russell Sage
              Foundation.
Dunnette, Marvin D., John P. Campbell, and Milton D. Hakell
    1967   "Factors Contributing to Job Satisfaction and Job Dissatisfaction in Six
              Occupational Groups," *Organizational Behavior and Human Perfor-
              mance*, 2: 143–174.
Easterlin, Richard A.
    1973   "Does Money Buy Happiness?" *The Public Interest*, 30: 3–10.
    1974   "Does Economic Growth Improve the Human Lot? Some Empirical
              Evidence," In Paul A. David, ed., *Nations and Households in
              Economic Growth*, New York: Academic Press, pp. 89–125.
Easton, David
    1965   *A Systems Analysis of Political Life*, New York: Wiley.
Edwards, Richard
    1978   "The Social Relations of Production at the Point of Production,"
              Insurgent Sociologist, 8 (2–3): 109–125.
Elder, Glen H., Jr.
    1969   "Appearance and Education in Marriage Mobility," *American Socio-
              logical Review*, 34: 519–533.

Elkin, Frederick, and William A. Westley
　　1955　　"The Myth of Adolescent Culture," *American Sociological Review*,
　　　　　　20: 680–684.
Engels, Frederick
　　1969　　*Germany: Revolution and Counter-Revolution*, New York: Interna-
　　　　　　tional Publishers.
Erbring, Lutz, Edie Goldenberg, and Arthur H. Miller
　　1980　　"Front-Page News and Real-World Cues: Another Look at Agenda-
　　　　　　Setting by the Media," *American Journal of Political Science*, 24:
　　　　　　16–49.
Erskine, Hazel
　　1972　　"The Polls: Pacifism and the Generation Gap," *Public Opinion Quar-*
　　　　　　terly, 36: 616–627.
　　1973–74　"The Polls: Corruption in Government," *Public Opinion Quarterly*,
　　　　　　37(4): 628–644.
Estes, Richard J., and Harold Wilensky
　　1978　　"Life Cycle Squeeze and the Morale Curve," *Social Problems*, 25 (3):
　　　　　　277–292.
Eulau, Heinz, and Kenneth Prewitt
　　1973　　*Labyrinths of Democracy: Adaptations, Linkages, Representation, and*
　　　　　　Policies in Urban Politics, Indianapolis, IN: Bobbs-Merrill.
Ewen, Robert G., Patricia Cain Smith, Charles L. Hulin, and Edwin A. Locke
　　1966　　"An Empirical Test of the Herzberg Two-Factor Theory," *Journal of*
　　　　　　Applied Psychology, 50: 544–550.
Fairfield, Roy P., ed.
　　1974　　*Humanizing the Workplace*, Buffalo, NY: Prometheus.
Fedyshyn, Oleh S.
　　1971　　*Germany's Drive to the East and the Ukrainian Revolution,*
　　　　　　1917–1918, New Brunswick, NJ: Rutgers University Press.
Fein, Mitchell
　　1973　　"The Real Needs and Goals of Blue Collar Workers," *The Conference*
　　　　　　Board Record, 10: 26–33.
　　1974　　"Job Enrichment: A Reevaluation," *Sloan Management Review*, 15:
　　　　　　69–88.
　　1976　　"Motivation for Work," Ch. 11, In Robert Dubin, ed. *Handbook of*
　　　　　　Work, Organization, and Society, Chicago, IL: Rand McNally, pp.
　　　　　　465–530.
Feldman, Kenneth A., and Theodore M. Newcomb
　　1969　　*The Impact of College on Students*, San Francisco: Jossey-Bass.
Ferree, Myra M.
　　1974　　"A Woman for President? Changing Responses: 1958–1972," *Public*
　　　　　　Opinion Quarterly, 38: 390–399.
Feuer, Lewis S.
　　1963　　"What is Alienation? The Career of a Concept," In Maurice Stein and
　　　　　　Arthur Vidich (eds.), *Sociology on Trial*, Englewood Cliffs, NJ: Pren-
　　　　　　tice-Hall, pp. 127–147.
　　1969　　*The Conflict of Generations: The Character and Significance of Stu-*
　　　　　　dent Movements, New York: Basic Books.
Firey, Walter
　　1947　　*Land Use in Central Boston*, Cambridge, MA: Harvard University
　　　　　　Press.
Fischer, Claude S.
　　1973a　　"On Urban Alienations and Anomie: Powerlessness and Social Iso-
　　　　　　lation," *American Sociological Review*, 38: 311–326.

1973b   "Urban Malaise," *Social Forces*, 52 (2): 221–235.
1975a   "The City and Political Psychology," *American Political Science Review*, 69: 559–571.
1975b   "The Metropolitan Experience," In Amos H. Hawley and Vinant P. Rock, (eds.), *Metropolitan America in Contemporary Perspective*, New York: Sage-Halsted-Wiley, pp. 201–234.
1975c   "The Effect of Urban Life on Traditional Values," *Social Forces*, 53 (3): 420–432.

Fischer, Louis
1964   *The Life of Lenin*, New York: Harper and Row.

Flacks, Richard
1971   *Youth and Social Change*, Chicago: Markham.

Flaim, Paul O., and Christopher G. Gellner
1972   "An Analysis of Unemployment by Household Relationship," *Monthly Labor Review*, 95: 9–16.

Flanagan, Robert J., George Strauss, and Lloyd Ulman
1974   "Worker Discontent and Work Place Behavior," *Industrial Relations*, 13: 101–123.

Flanagan, Scott
1982.   "Changing Values in Advanced Industrial Societies: Inglehart's Silent Revolution from the Perspective of Japanese Findings," *Comparative Political Studies*, 14: 403–444.

Ford, Robert N.
1969   *Motivation Through Work Itself*, New York: American Management Association.

Form, William
1976   *Blue-Collar Stratification: Autoworkers in Four Countries*, Princeton, NJ: Princeton University Press.

Fortune
1947   "The American Factory Worker. What's good about his job . . . What's bad about it? What makes him satisfied with his company? What makes him happy in his type of job?" May: 5–6, 10, 12; June: 5–6, 10.

Foulkes, Fred K.
1969   *Creating More Meaningful Work*, New York: American Management Association.

Franke, Richard Herbert
1980   "Worker Productivity at Hawthorne," *American Sociological Review*, 43: 1006–1027.

Franke, Richard Herbert, and James D. Kaul
1978   "The Hawthorne Experiments: First Statistical Interpretation," *American Sociological Review*, 43: 623–643.

Freedman, Jonathan L.
1978   *Happy People*, New York: Harcourt Brace Jovanovich.

Freeman, Richard B.
1976   *The Overeducated American*, New York: Academic Press.

Fried, Marc
1973   *The World of the Urban Working Class*, Cambridge, MA: Harvard University Press.

Friedmann, Georges
1955   *Industrial Society*, Glencoe, IL: The Free Press.

Fuller, J.F.C.
1961   *The Conduct of War*, London: Eyre & Spottiswoode.

Gallup, George
    1972   *The Gallup Poll* (Vols. I and II), New York: Random House.
Gallup International, Inc.
    The Gallup Opinion Index, Appropriate Vols.
Gans, Herbert
    1962   *The Urban Villagers: Group and Class in the Life of Italian-Americans,*
            New York: The Free Press.
Garson, Barbara
    1972   "Luddites in Lordstown: It's Not the Money, It's the Job," *Harpers,* 244
            (June): 68–73.
    1975   *All the Livelong Day: The Meaning and Demeaning of Routine Work,*
            Garden City, NY: Doubleday.
Geschwender, James A.
    1977   *Class, Race, and Worker Insurgency: The League of Revolutionary
            Black Workers,* Cambridge: Cambridge University Press.
Giddens, Anthony
    1973   *The Class Structure of the Advanced Societies,* New York: Harper
            Torchbooks.
Gimlin, Hoyt (ed.)
    1973   *Editorial Research Reports on the American Work Ethic,* Washington:
            Congressional Quarterly.
Glenn, Norval D.
    1975a   "The Contribution of Marriage to the Psychological Well-Being of
            Males and Females," *Journal of Marriage and the Family,* 37 (Aug.):
            594–600.
    1975b   "Psychological Well-Being in the Postparental Stage: Some Evidence
            from National Surveys," *Journal of Marriage and the Family,* 37 (Feb.):
            105–110.
Glenn, Norval D., and Jon P. Alston
    1968   "Cultural Distances Among Occupational Categories," *American So-
            ciological Review,* 33: 365–382.
Glenn, Norval D., and Charles N. Weaver
    1977   "The Marital Happiness of Remarried Divorced Persons," *Journal of
            Marriage and the Family,* 39 (May): 331–337.
    1978   "A Multivariate, Multisurvey Study of Marital Happiness," *Journal of
            Marriage and the Family,* 40 (May): 269–282.
    1979   "A Note on Family Situation and Global Happiness," *Social Forces,*
            57 (3): 960–967.
    1981a   "Education's Effect on Psychological Well-Being," *Public Opinion
            Quarterly,* 45 (1): 22–39.
    1981b   "The Contribution of Marital Happiness to Global Happiness," *Jour-
            nal of Marriage and the Family,* 43:1, 161–168.
    1982   "Enjoyment of Work by Full-Time Workers in the U.S., 1955 and
            1980," *Public Opinion Quarterly,* 46 (4) (Winter): 459–470.
    1984   "Age, Cohort, and Reported Job Satisfaction in the United States," In
            Zena Blau, ed., *Current Perspectives on Aging and the Life Cycle,*
            Greenwich, CT: JAI Press (forthcoming).
Glenn, Norval D., Sue Keir Hoppe, and David Weiner
    1974   "Social Class Heterogamy and Marital Success: A Study of the Em-
            pirical Adequacy of a Textbook Generalization," *Social Problems,* 21:
            539–550.
Glenn, Norval D., Patricia A. Taylor, and Charles N. Weaver
    1977   "Age and Job Satisfaction among Males and Females: A Multivatiate,
            Multisurvey Study," *Journal of Applied Psychology,* 62: 189–193.

Glick, Paul C.
  1949   "First Marriages and Remarriages," *American Sociological Review*,
          14: 726–734.
  1977   "Updating the Life Cycle of the Family," *Journal of Marriage and the
          Family*, 39: 5–13.
  1978   "Social Change and the American Family," *The Social Welfare
          Forum, 1977*, New York: Columbia University Press.
Glick, Paul C. and Arthur J. Norton
  1973   "Perspectives on the Recent Upturn in Divorce and Remarriage,"
          Demography, 10: 301–314.
Glick, Paul C., and Graham B. Spanier
  1980   "Married and Unmarried Cohabitation in the United States," *Journal
          of Marriage and the Family*, 42: 19–30.
Goldmann, Robert B.
  1976   *A Work Experiment: Six Americans in a Swedish Plant*, New York:
          Ford Foundation.
Goldthorpe, John H., David Lockwood, Frank Bechhofer, and Jennifer Platt
  1968a   *The Affluent Worker: Industrial Attitudes and Behaviour*, Cambridge,
          England: University Press.
  1968b   *The Affluent Worker: Political Attitudes and Behaviour*, Cambridge,
          England: University Press.
  1969   *The Affluent Worker in the Class Structure*, Cambridge, England:
          University Press.
Gooding, Judson
  1970a   "Blue-Collar Blues on the Assembly Line," *Fortune*, July: 69ff.
  1970b   "It Pays to Wake Up the Blue-Collar Worker," *Fortune*, (Sept.), 133ff.
  1970c   "The Fraying White Collar," *Fortune*, December.
  1972   *The Job Revolution*, New York: Walker.
Goodman, Paul S.
  1979   *Assessing Organizational Change: The Rushton Quality of Work
          Experiment*, New York: Wiley.
  1980   "Quality of Work Life Projects in the 1980s," *Labor Law Journal*, 31:
          487–494.
Gouldner, Alvin
  1954   *Wildcat Strike*, Yellow Springs, OH: Antioch Press.
Gove, Walter R.
  1973   "Sex, Marital Status, and Mortality," *American Journal of Sociology*,
          79: 45–67.
Gove, Walter R., and Terry Fain
  1975   "The Length of Psychiatric Hospitalization," *Social Problems*, 22(3):
          407–419.
Graen, George B.
  1966   "Addendum to 'An Empirical Test of the Hertzberg Two-Factor The-
          ory,'" *Journal of Applied Psychology*, 50: 551–555.
  1968   "Testing Traditional and Two-Factor Hypotheses Concerning Job Sat-
          isfaction," *Journal of Applied Psychology*, 52: 366–371.
Graen, George B., and Charles L. Hulin
  1968   "Addendum to 'An Empirical Investigation of Two Implications of the
          Two-Factor Theory of Job Satisfaction,'" *Journal of Applied Psychol-
          ogy, 52: 341–342*.
Greeley, Andrew M.
  1977   *The American Catholic: A Social Portrait*, New York: Basic Books.

Gregory, Roy
    1969   "Local Elections and the 'Rule of Anticipated Reactions,'" *Political Studies*, 17: 31–47.
Gribbon, John
    1980   *The Death of the Sun*, New York: Delacourt Press.
Grossman, Allyson Sherman
    1978   "Divorced and Separated Women in the Labor Force—An Update," *Monthly Labor Review*, 101: 43–45.
Gruenberg, Barry
    1980   "The Happy Worker: An Analysis of Educational and Occupational Differences in Determinants of Job Satisfaction," *American Journal of Sociology*, 86 (2): 247–271.
Gruneberg, Michael, (ed.)
    1976   *Job Satisfaction: A Reader*, New York: Macmillan.
Guest, Robert H.
    1957   "Job Enlargement—A Revolution in Job Design," *Personnel Administration*, 20: 9–16.
Gurin, Gerald, Joseph Veroff, and Sheila Feld
    1960   *Americans View Their Mental Health*, New York: Basic Books.
Hackman, J. R.
    1974   "On the Coming Demise of Job Enrichment," Department of Administrative Sciences, Technical Report No. 9. New Haven, CT: Yale University.
Halberstam, David
    1965   *The Making of a Quagmire*, New York: Random House.
    1979   *The Powers That Be*, New York: Alfred A. Knopf.
Hall, Douglas, T., and Khalil E. Nougaim
    1968   "An Examination of Maslow's Need Hierarchy in an Organizational Setting," *Organizational Behavior and Human Performance*, 3: 12–35.
Hamill, Pete
    1970   "The Revolt of the White Lower-Middle Class," In Louise Kapp Howe, ed., *The White Majority*, 1970. The article first appeared in *New York* (a magazine) in 1969, pp. 10–22.
Hamilton, Richard F.
    1965   "Affluence and the Worker: The West German Case," *American Journal of Sociology*, 71: 144–152.
    1967   *Affluence and the French Worker*, Princeton, NJ: Princeton University Press.
    1968a   "A Research Note on the Mass Support for 'Tough' Military Initiatives," *American Sociological Review*, 33 (June): 439–45.
    1968b   "Einkommen and Klassenstruktur: Der Fall der Bundesrepublik," *Koelner Zeitschrift fuer Soziologie und Sozialpsychologie*, 20: 250–287.
    1972   *Class and Politics in the United States*, New York: Wiley.
    1973   "Nostalgia and History," *Dissent*, 20 (Winter): 93–98.
    1975   *Restraining Myths: Critical Studies of U.S. Social Structure and Politics*, New York: Sage-Halsted-Wiley.
    1982   *Who Voted for Hitler?* Princeton, NJ: Princeton University Press.
Hamilton, Richard F., and Maurice Pinard
    1982   "The Quebec Independence Movement," In Colin H. Williams, ed., *National Separatism*, Cardiff: University of Wales Press, pp. 203–233.
Hamilton, Richard F., and James D. Wright
    1975a   "The Support for 'Hard-Line' Foreign Policy," Chap. 5 in Hamilton (1975): 183–218.

1975b "Coming of Age: A Comparison of the United States and the Federal Republic of Germany," *Zeitschrift fur Soziologie*, 4 (Okt.): 335–349.

1981 "The College Educated Blue Collar Workers." In Richard and Ida Simpson (eds.), *Research in the Sociology of Work*, (Vol. I), Greenwich, CT: JAI Press, pp. 285–334.

Hedges, Janice Neipert
1973 "Absence from Work—A Look at Some National Data," *Monthly Labor Review*, 96 (July): 24–30.

1975 "Unscheduled Absence from Work—An Update," *Monthly Labor Review*, 98 (Aug.): 36–39.

1977 "Absence from Work—Measuring the Hours Lost," *Monthly Labor Review*, 100 (Oct.): 16–23.

Henle, Peter
1974 "Economic Effects: Reviewing the Evidence," In Jerome M. Rosow, ed., *The Worker and the Job: Coping with Change*, Englewood Cliffs: Prentice-Hall, Chap. 5, pp. 119–144.

Herzberg, Frederick
1966 *Work and the Nature of Man*, Cleveland, OH: World Publishing.

1968 "One More Time: How Do You Motivate Employees?" *Harvard Business Review*, 46: 53–62.

Herzberg, Frederick, Bernard Mausner, Richard O. Peterson, and Don F. Capwell
1957 *Job Attitudes: A Review of Research and Opinion*, Pittsburgh: Psychological Service of Pittsburgh.

Herzberg, Frederick, Bernard Mausner, and Barbara Bloch Synderman
1959 *The Motivation to Work*, New York: Wiley.

Hessen, Robert
1975 *Street Titan: The Life of Charles M. Schwab*, New York: Oxford University Press.

Hicks, Mary W., and Marilyn Platt
1970 "Marital Happiness and Stability: A Review of the Research in the Sixties," *Journal of Marriage and the Family*, 32 (Nov.): 553–573.

Higgins, Benjamin
n.d. "The Silent Revolution: A Critical Analysis," unpublished paper, McGill, Department of Sociology.

Hollander, Edwin P.
1976 *Principles and Methods of Social Psychology (3rd ed.)*, New York: Oxford University Press.

Holsti, Ole R.
1973 "The Base Line Problem in Statistics: Examples from Studies in American Public Policy," *Journal of Politics*, 37: 187–201.

Honour, Hugh
1979 *Romanticism*, London: Allen Lane.

Hooper, Bayard
1970 "The Real Change Has Just Begun," *Life* (Magazine) 68:1 (January 9): 102ff.

Hoppock, Robert
1935 *Job Satisfaction*. New York: Harper and Bros.

House, James S., and William M. Mason
1975 "Political Alienation in America: 1952–1968," *American Sociological Review*, 40: 123–147.

1978 "Social Indicators of Political Alienation in America," unpublished research proposal.

House, Robert J., and Lawrence A. Wigdor
1967 "Herzberg's Dual Factor Theory of Job Satisfaction and Motivation: A

Review of the Evidence and Criticism," *Personnel Psychology*, 20: 369–389.

Howe, Irving, ed.
1972   *The World of the Blue Collar Worker*, New York: Quadrangle. Based on a special issue of *Dissent*, Winter, 1972.

Howe, Louise Kapp, ed.
1970   *The White Majority: Between Poverty and Affluence*, New York: Vintage Books.

Howell, Joseph T.
1973   *Hard Living on Clay Street*, Garden City, NY: Doubleday Anchor Books.

Hulin, Charles L.
1971   "Individual Differences and Job Enrichment—The Case Against General Treatments," Ch. 9, In John R. Maher, ed., *New Perspectives in Job Enrichment*, New York: Van Nostrand Reinhold.

Hulin, Charles L., and Milton R. Blood
1968   "Job Enlargement, Individual Differences, and Worker Responses," *Psychological Bulletin*, 69: 41–55.

Hulin, Charles L., and Patricia C. Smith
1967   "An Empirical Investigation of Two Implications of the Two-Factor Theory of Job Satisfaction," *Journal of Applied Psychology*, 51: 396–402.

Hyman, Herbert H., and Paul B. Sheatsley
1964   "Attitudes toward Desegregation," *Scientific American*, 211 (July): 16–23.

Imberman, A.A.
1973   "The Blue Collar Blues—Today's Academic Hit Tune?" *Assembly Engineering* (unpaginated reprint).

Inglehart, Ronald
1971   "The Silent Revolution in Europe: Intergenerational Change in Post-Industrial Societies," *American Political Science Review*, 65: 991–1017.

1977a   *The Silent Revolution: Changing Values and Political Styles Among Western Publics*, Princeton, NJ: Princeton University Press.

1977b   "Values, Objective Needs and Subjective Satisfaction Among Western Publics," *Comparative Political Studies*, 9: 429–458.

1981   "Post-materialism in an Environment of Insecurity," *American Political Science Review* 75: 4, 880–900.

Jack, Ian
1963   *English Literature: 1815–1832*, Oxford: Clarendon Press.

Jacobson, D.
1972   "Fatigue-Producing Factors in Industrial Work and Pre-Retirement Attitudes," *Journal of Occupational Psychology*, 46: 193–200.

Janis, Irving L.
1972   *Victims of Groupthink: A Psychological Study of Foreign-Policy Decisions and Fiascoes*, Boston, MA: Houghton Mifflin.

Janowitz, Morris
1978   *The Last Half-Century: Societal Change and Politics in America*, Chicago: University of Chicago Press.

Janson, Philip, and Jack K. Martin
1982   "Job Satisfaction and Age: A Test of Two Views," *Social Forces*, 60: 1089–1102.

Jencks, Christopher, and seven others
  1972   *Inequality: A Reassessment of the Effects of Family and Schooling in
            America*, New York: Harper and Row.
Jennings, M. Kent, and Richard G. Niemi
  1974   *The Political Character of Adolescence: The Influence of Families and
            Schools*, Princeton, NJ: Princeton University Press.
Johnson, Walter (ed.)
  1975   *Working in Canada*, Montreal: Black Rose Books.
Jonas, Steven (ed.)
  1977   *Health Care Delivery in the United States*, New York: Springer.
Jones, Howard Mumford
  1974   *Revolution and Romanticism*, Cambridge, MA: Harvard University
            Press.
Kadushin, Charles
  1974   *The American Intellectual Elite*, Boston, MA: Little Brown.
Kahn, Robert L.
  1972   "The Meaning of Work," In Angus Campbell and Philip Converse,
            eds., *The Human Meaning of Social Change*, New York: Russell Sage
            Foundation, pp. 159–203.
  1974   "The Work Module," In James O'Toole, ed., *Work and the Quality of
            Life*, Cambridge, MA: MIT Press, pp. 199–226.
Kaplan, H. Roy
  1973   "How DO Workers View their Work in America?" *Monthly Labor
            Review*, 96: 46–48.
  1978   *Lottery Winners: How They Won and How Winning Changed Their
            Lives*, New York: Harper.
Kaplan, H. Roy, and Curt Tausky
  1977   "Humanism in Organizations: A Critical Appraisal," *Public Admin-
            istration Review*, 37: 171–180.
Karmin, Monroe W.
  1970   "Secret Report Tells Nixon How to Help White Working Men and
            Win Their Votes," *Wall Street Journal*, June 30, p. 32.
Katkov, George
  1956   "German Foreign Office Documents on Financial Support to the
            Bolsheviks in 1917," *International Affairs*, 32: 181–189.
Katz, Daniel
  1949   "Morale and Motivation in Industry," In Dennis, ed., *Current Trends
            in Industrial Psychology*, Pittsburgh, PA: University of Pittsburgh
            Press, pp. 145–171.
  1954   "Satisfaction and Deprivations in Industrial Life," In Arthur Korn-
            hauser, Robert Dubin, and Arthur Ross, eds., *Industrial Conflict*, New
            York: McGraw-Hill, pp. 86–106.
Kennedy, James E., and Harry E. O'Neill
  1958   "Job Content and Workers' Opinions," *Journal of Applied Psychol-
            ogy*, 42: 372–375.
Kerr, Clark, and Jerome M. Rosow (eds.)
  1979   *Work in America: The Decade Ahead*, New York: Van Nostrand
            Reinhold.
Kilbridge, M.D.
  1960   "Do Workers Prefer Larger Jobs? *Personnel*, 37: 45–48.
King, Nathan
  1970   "Clarification and Evaluation of the Two-Factor Theory of Job Satis-
            faction," *Psychological Bulletin*, 74: 18–31.

Kohn, Melvin
    1969   Class and Conformity, Homewood, IL: Dorsey Press.
Korman, Abraham K.
    1970   "Toward an Hypothesis of Work Behavior," Journal of Applied Psy-
              chology, 54.
Kornblum, William
    1974   Blue-Collar Community, Chicago: University of Chicago Press.
Kornhauser, Arthur
    1965   Mental Health of the Industrial Worker: A Detroit Study, New York:
              Wiley.
Kornhauser, Arthur, Harold L. Sheppard, and Albert J. Mayer
    1956   When Labor Votes: A Study of Auto Workers, New York: University
              Books.
Kronawetter, Georg
    1979   Mit allen Kniffen und Listen, Munich: Verlag Fritz Molden.
Krugman, Herbert E.
    1953   "The Role of Hostility in the Appeal of Communism in the United
              States," Psychiatry, 16: 253–261.
Ladd, Everett Carll, Jr.
    1976–77 "Liberalism Upside Down, The Inversion of the New Deal Order,"
              Political Science Quarterly, 91: 4 (Winter): 577–600.
    1978   Transformations of the American Party System: Political Coalitions
              from the New Deal to the 1970's (2nd ed.), New York: W.W. Norton.
Ladd, Everett Carll, Jr., and Seymour Martin Lipset
    1975   The Divided Academy: Professors and Politics, New York: McGraw-
              Hill.
Laslett, Barbara
    1975   "Household Structure on an American Frontier: Los Angeles, Calif. in
              1850," American Journal of Sociology, 81 (1): 109–128.
Laslett, Peter (ed.)
    1972   Household and Family in Past Time, Cambridge: Cambridge Univer-
              sity Press.
Lasson, Kenneth
    1971   The Workers: Portraits of Nine American Job Holders, New York:
              Grossman.
Lawler, Edward E. III
    1969   "Job Design and Employee Motivation," Personnel Psychology, 22:
              426–435.
    1973   Motivation Work Organization, Monterey, CA: Brooks/Cole.
Lee, D.J.
    1981   "Skill, Craft and Class: A Theoretical Critique and a Critical Case,"
              Sociology, 15: 56–78.
Lefkowitz, Bernard
    1979   Break-time: Living Without Work in a 9 to 5 World, New York: Haw-
              thorne Books.
LeMasters, E.E.
    1975   Blue Collar Aristocrats: Life Styles at a Working Class Tavern, Madi-
              son, WI: University of Wisconsin Press.
Lenin, V.I.
    1971   Selected Works, Moscow: Progress Publishers.
Lesher, Stephan
    1982   Media Unbound: The Impact of Television Journalism on the Public,
              Boston, MA: Houghton Mifflin.

Levitan, Sar A.
    1971   *Blue-Collar Workers: A Symposium on Middle America*, New York: McGraw-Hill.
Levitan, Sar A., and William B. Johnston
    1973   *Work is Here to Stay, Alas*, Salt Lake City, UT: Olympus.
Levy, Marion J., Jr.
    1965   "Aspects of the Analysis of Family Structure," In Ansley J. Coale *et al.*, ed., *Aspects of the Analysis of Family Structure*, Princeton, NJ: Princeton University Press, pp. 1–63.
Lichter, Linda S., S. Robert Lichter, and Stanley Rothman
    1981   *Crooks, Conmen and Clowns* (edited by Leonard Theberge), Washington, D.C.: The Media Institute.
    1983a   "Hollywood and America: The Odd Couple," *Public Opinion*, 5 (Dec./Jan.): 54–58.
    1983b   *Prime Time Crime*, Washington, D.C.: The Media Institute.
Lipset, Seymour Martin
    1960   *Political Man: The Social Bases of Politics*, Garden City, NY: Doubleday.
    1963   "The Sources of the 'Radical Right,'" In Daniel Bell, ed., *The Radical Right*, Garden City, NY: Doubleday, pp. 259–312.
    1971   *Rebellion in the University*, Boston, MA: Little Brown.
    1979a   "The New Class and the Professoriate," *Society*, 16 (Jan./Feb.): 31–38.
    1979b   "Whither *The First New Nation?*" *Tocqueville Review*, 1: 64–99.
    1981   *Political Man: The Social Bases of Politics*, expanded ed., Baltimore: The Johns Hopkins University Press.
Lipset, Seymour Martin, and Asoke Basu
    1975   "Intellectual Types and Political Roles," In Lewis Coser, ed., *The Idea of Social Structure*, New York: Harcourt, Brace, pp. 433–470.
Lipset, Seymour Martin, and Reinhard Bendix
    1959   *Social Mobility in Industrial Society*, Berkeley, CA: University of California Press.
Lipset, Seymour Martin, and William Schneider
    1983   *The Confidence Gap: Business, Labor, and Government in the Public Mind*, New York: The Free Press.
Littler, Craig R., and Graeme Salaman
    1982   "Bravermania and Beyond: Recent Theories of the Labour Process," *Sociology*, 16: 251–269.
Litwak, Eugene
    1960a   "Occupational Mobility and Extended Family Cohesion," *American Sociological Review*, 25: 9–21.
    1960b   "Geographical Mobility and Extended Family Cohesion," *American Sociological Review*, 25: 385–394.
Locke, Edwin
    1976   "The Nature and Causes of Job Satisfaction," In Marvin D. Dunnette, ed., *Handbook of Industrial and Organizational Psychology*, Chicago: Rand McNally, pp. 1297–1349.
Logan, Nancy, Charles A. O'Reilly, III, and Karlene H. Roberts
    1973   "Job Satisfaction Among Part-Time and Full-Time Employees," *Journal of Vocational Behavior*, 3: 1 (Jan.): 33–41.

Longhi, Dario Enrico
    1969   "Higher Education and Student Politics: The Wisconsin Experience,"
              Madison: Department of Sociology—University of Wisconsin, M.S.
              Thesis.
Lopata, Helena
    1979   *Women or Widows*. New York: Elsevier.
Lösche, Peter
    1967   *Der Bolschewismus im Urteil der deutschen Sozialdemokratie,*
              1903–1920, Berlin: Colloquim Verlag.
Lukas, J. Anthony
    1968   "The Negro at Integrated College: Now He's Proud of His Color,"
              New York Times, June 3: 1,51.
Lynd, Robert, and Helen Merrell
    1929   *Middletown: A Study in American Culture*. New York: Harcourt
              Brace.
MacDonald, John S., and Leatrice D. MacDonald
    1964   "Chain Migration, Ethnic Neighborhood Formation and Social Net-
              works," *Milbank Memorial Fund Quarterly*, 42: 82–97.
McGregor, Douglas Murray
    1957   "The Human Side of Enterprise," *The Management Review*, 46:
              22–28, 88–92.
    1960   *The Human Side of Enterprise*, New York: McGraw-Hill.
    1966   *Leadership and Motivation*, Cambridge, MA: The MIT Press.
    1967   *The Professional Manager*, New York: McGraw-Hill.
McNeill, William H.
    1982   *The Pursuit of Power*, Chicago, IL: University of Chicago Press.
Maher, John R., ed.
    1971   *New Perspectives in Job Enrichment*, New York: Van Nostrand Rein-
              hold.
Marans, Robert W., and Willard Rodgers
    1975   "Toward an Understanding of Community Satisfaction," In Amos H.
              Hawley and Vincent P. Rock, eds., *Metropolitan America in Contem-
              porary Perspective*, New York: Sage-Halsted-Wiley, pp. 299–352.
Marcuse, Herbert
    1964   *One Dimensional Man*, Boston, MA: Beacon Press.
Marsh, Alan
    1975   "The 'Silent Revolution,' Value Priorities, and the Quality of Life in
              Britain," *American Political Science Review*, 69: 21–30.
    1977   *Protest and Political Consciousness*, Beverly Hills, CA: Sage Publica-
              tions.
Marx, Gary T.
    1974   "Thoughts on a Neglected Category of Social Movement Participant:
              The Agent Provocateur and the Informant," *American Journal of
              Sociology*, 80: 402–442.
Marx, Karl
    1951   "The Class Struggles in France," In Karl Marx and Frederick Engels,
              Selected Works, (Vol. I), Moscow: Foreign Languages Publishing
              House, pp. 128–220.
Marx, Karl, and Frederick Engels
    1947   *The German Ideology*, New York: International Publishers.
Maslow, Abraham H.
    1954   *Motivation and Personality*, New York: Harper and Brothers.
    1965   *Eupsychian Management: A Journal*, Homewood, IL: Richard D. Irwin
              Inc., and The Dorsey Press.

Meiksins, Peter F.
    1984   "Scientific Management and Class Relations: A Dissenting View,"
              Theory and Society, 13: 177–209.
Merton, Robert K.
    1957   *Social Theory and Social Structure* (rev. ed.), Glencoe, IL: The Free
              Press.
Metzner, Helen, and Floyd Mann
    1953   "Employee Attitudes and Absences," *Personnel Psychology*, 6:
              467–485.
Miliband, Ralph
    1964   "Socialism and the Myth of the Golden Past," In Miliband and John
              Saville, eds., *The Socialist Register: 1964*, New York: Monthly Review
              Press, pp. 92–103.
Milkis, Sidney, and Thomas Boldino
    1978   "The Future of the Silent Revolution: A Reexamination of Intergen-
              erational Change in Western Europe," unpublished paper presented at
              the Mid-West Political Science Association Convention, April 21,
              1978, Chicago, IL.
Miller, Arthur H.
    1974   "Political Issues and Trust in Government: 1964–1970," *American
              Political Science Review*, 68: 951–972.
    1983   "Is Confidence Rebounding?" *Public Opinion*, 6 (June/July): 16–20.
Miller, Arthur H., Edie Goldenberg, and Lutz Erbring
    1979   "Type-Set Politics: Impact of Newspapers on Public Confidence,"
              American Political Science Review, 73: 67–84.
Miller, Douglas T.
    1967   *Jacksonian Aristocracy: Class and Democracy in New York
              1830–1860*, New York: Oxford University Press.
Miller, Herman P.
    1970   "Why Help the Blue Collar Worker?" *Washington Post*, August 16, p.
              B-1, B-5.
Miller, Warren E., Arthur H. Miller and E.G. Schneider
    1980   *The American National Election Studies Data Sourcebook,
              1952–1978*. Cambridge: Harvard University Press.
Mills, C. Wright
    1959   *The Sociological Imagination*, New York: Oxford University
              Press.
Miner, Horace
    1963   *St. Denis: A French-Canadian Parish*, Chicago: University of Chicago
              Press—Pheonix Books. Originally published in 1939.
Miner, Mary Green
    1977   "Job Absence and Turnover: A New Source of Data," *Monthly Labor
              Review*, 100: 24–31.
Monahan, Thomas P.
    1952   "How Stable are Remarriages?" *American Journal of Sociology*, 58:
              280–288.
Montagna, Paul D.
    1977   *Occupations and Society: Toward A Sociology of the Labor Market*,
              New York: Wiley.
Moore, Barrington
    1978   *Injustice: The Social Bases of Obedience and Revolt*, White Plains,
              NY: M.E. Sharpe.
Morgan, James N., Martin H. David, Wilbur J. Cohen, and Harvey E. Brazer
    1962   *Income and Welfare in the United States*, New York: McGraw-Hill.

Morgan, James N., Katherine Dickinson, Jonathan Dickinson, Jacob Benus, and Greg Duncan
　　1974　　*Five Thousand American Families—Patterns of Economic Progress* (Vol. I), Ann Arbor, MI: Institute for Social Research.
Morse, Nancy D., and Robert S. Weiss
　　1955　　"The Function and Meaning of Work and the Job," *American Sociological Review*, 20: 191–198.
Mueller, Charles W., and Hallowell Pope
　　1980　　"Divorce and Female Remarriage Mobility: Data on Marriage Matches After Divorce for White Women," *Social Forces*, 58: 726–738.
Mueller, Eva, and others
　　1969　　*Technological Advance in an Expanding Economy: It's Impact on a Cross Section of the Labor Force*, Ann Arbor, MI: Institute for Social Research.
Murstein, Bernard I.
　　1972　　"Physical Attractiveness and Marital Choice," *Journal of Personality and Social Psychology*, 22: 8–12.
Musgrave, Richard A.
　　1979　　"The Tax Revolt," *Social Science Quarterly*, 59: 697–703.
Nash, Al
　　1976　　"Job Satisfaction: A Critique." In B.J. Widick, ed., *Auto Work and Its Discontents*, Baltimore, MD: Johns Hopkins University Press.
Nathanson, Constance A.
　　1977　　"Sex, Illness, and Medical Care: A Review of Data, Theory, and Method," *Social Science and Medicine*, 11: 13–25.
Nelson, Daniel
　　1975　　*Managers and Workers: Origins of the New Factory System in the United States, 1880–1920*, Madison, WI: University of Wisconsin Press.
Newcomb, Theodore M.
　　1943　　*Personality and Social Change: Attitude Formation in a Student Community*, New York: Dryden.
　　1958　　"Attitude Development as a Function of Reference Groups: The Bennington Study," In Eleanor E. Maccoby, Theodore M. Newcomb, and Eugene L. Hartley, *Readings in Social Psychology* (3rd ed.), New York: Holt, Rinehart and Winston, pp. 265–275.
Newcomb, Theodore M., Kathryn E. Koeing, Richard Flacks, and Donald P. Warwick
　　1967　　*Persistence and Change: Bennington College and Its Students After Twenty-Five Years*, New York: Wiley.
New York Times
　　1971a　　"Nixon Seeks Welfare Role That Will Promote Dignity," April 20, p. 30.
　　1971b　　"Transcripts of the President's Labor Day Address," September 7, p. 20.
　　1971c　　"Transcripts of Nixon's Address to Congress Asking Support for His Economic Plan," September 10, p. 20.
Newsweek
　　1973a　　"Worker's Woes," January 1, p. 47.
　　1973b　　"The Job Blahs: Who Wants to Work?" March 26, p. 79–89.
　　1974　　"Blue Collar Blues?" April 29, p. 90.
Nie, Norman H., and Kristi Andersen
　　1974　　"Mass Belief Systems Revisited: Political Change and Attitude Structure," *Journal of Politics*, 36: 540–590.

Nie, Norman H., and James N. Rabjohn
  1979   "Revisiting Mass Belief Systems Revisited: Or, Doing Research is Like
            Watching a Tennis Match," *American Journal of Political Science*, 23:
            129–175.
Nie, Norman H., Sidney Verba, and John R. Petrocik
  1976   *The Changing American Voter*, Cambridge, MA: Harvard University
            Press.
Nobile, Philip, (ed.)
  1971   *The Con III Controversy: The Critics Look at "The Greening of
            America,"* New York: Pocket Books.
Northrup, Herbert R.
  1955   "The UAW's Influence on Management Decisions in the Automobile
            Industry—An Outsider's Point of View," Industrial Relations Research
            Association, *Proceedings of the Seventh Annual Meeting: 1954*,
            33–46.
Norton, Arthur J., and Paul C. Glick
  1976   "Marital Instability: Past, Present, and Future," *Journal of Social
            Issues*, 32: 5–20.
Novak, Michael
  1983   "The Rich, the Poor & the Reagan Administration," *Commentary*, 76
            (Aug.): 27–31.
Obradovic, Josip
  1970   "Participation and Work Attitudes in Yugoslavia," *Industrial Rela-
            tions*, 9: 161–169.
  1975   "Workers' Participation: Who Participates?" *Industrial Relations*, 14:
            32–44.
Obradovic, Josip, John R. P. French, Jr., and Willard L. Rodgers
  1970   "Workers' Councils in Yugoslavia: Effects on Perceived Participation
            and Satisfaction of Workers," *Human Relations*, 23: 459–471.
Ogburn, William F.
  1944   "Marital Separations," *American Journal of Sociology*, 49: 316–323.
O'Neill, William L.
  1978   *The Last Romantic: A Life of Max Eastman*, New York: Oxford Uni-
            versity Press.
O'Toole, James
  1974   *Work and the Quality of Life: Resource Papers for Work in America*,
            Cambridge, MA: MIT Press.
  1977   *Work, Learning and the American Future*, San Francisco: Jossey Bass.
O'Toole, James, and nine others
  1973   *Work in America*, Cambridge, MA: MIT Press.
Page, Benjamin I., and Richard A. Brody
  1972   "Policy Voting and the Electoral Process: The Vietnam War Issue,"
            American Political Science Review, 66 (Sept.): 979–995.
Parkin, Frank
  1971   *Class Inequality and Political Order: Social Stratification in Capitalist
            and Communist Societies*, New York: Praeger.
Parsons, Donald O.
  1973   "Quit Rates Over Time: A Search and Information," *American Eco-
            nomic Review*, 63: 390–401.
Parsons, H.M.
  1974   "What Happened at Hawthorne?" *Science*, 183: 922–932.

Penn, R.D.
  1983   "Theories of Skill and Class Structure," *Sociological Review*, 31:
            24–38.
Pessen, Edward
  1978   *Jacksonian America: Society, Personality, and Politics*, rev. ed.,
            Homewood, IL: Dorsey Press.
Pfeffer, Richard M.
  1979   *Working for Capitali$m*, New York: Columbia University Press.
Phillips, Kevin
  1969   *The Emerging Republican Majority*, New Rochelle, NY: Arlington
            House.
Podhoretz, Norman
  1967   *Making It*, New York: Random House.
  1979   *Breaking Ranks: A Political Memoir*, New York: Harper and Row.
Pope, Whitney
  1976   *Durkheim's "Suicide"—A Classic Analyzed*, Chicago: University of
            Chicago Press.
Powell, Maurice
  1973   "Age and Occupational Change Among Coal-Miners," *Journal of
            Occupational Psychology*, 47: 37–49.
Prewitt, Kenneth
  1970   "Political Ambitions, Volunteerism and Electoral Accountability,"
            American Political Science Review 64 (March): 5–17.
Price, Charleton, ed.
  1972   *New Directions in the World of Work*, Washington, D.C.: Upjohn
            Institute for Employment Research.
Quinn, Robert P., Thomas W. Mangione, and Martha Mandilovitch
  1973   "Evaluating Working Conditions in America," *Monthly Labor Review*,
            96: 32–43.
Quinn, Robert P., Graham L. Staines, and Margaret R. McCullough
  1974   *Job Satisfaction: Is There a Trend?* U.S. Department of Labor, Man-
            power Research Monograph No. 30. Washington, D.C.: U.S. Gov-
            ernment Printing Office.
Raddatz, Fritz
  1975   *Karl Marx: Eine politische Biographie*, Hamburg: Hoffman und
            Campe. There is an English language version, *Karl Marx: A Political
            Biography*, London: Weidenfeld and Nicholson, 1979.
Rauch, Georg von
  1972   *A History of Soviet Russia* (6th ed.), New York: Praeger.
Ravitch, Diane
  1978   *The Revisionists Revised: A Critique of the Radical Attack on the
            Schools*, New York: Basic Books.
Readers' Guide to Periodical Literature
  Annual   New York: The H. W. Wilson Company.
Reich, Charles A.
  1971   *The Greening of America*, New York: Bantam Books, (First published
            in 1970, in New York, by Random House.)
Reno, Virginia
  1971   "Why Men Stop Working at or Before Age 65: Findings From the
            Survey of New Beneficiaries," *Social Security Bulletin*, 34: 3–17.
Richardson, Eliot
  1976   *The Creative Balance*, New York: Holt, Rinehart and Winston.

Ridpath, Ian (ed.)
 1979   *The Illustrated Encyclopedia of Astronomy and Space*, New York: Thomas Y. Crowell.

Rinehart, James W.
 1975   *The Tyranny of Work*, Don Mills, Ontario: Longman Canada.

Robinson, H. Alan
 1959   "Job Satisfaction Researches of 1958," *Personnel and Guidance Journal*, 37: 669–673.

Robinson, H. Alan, and Ralph P. Connors
 1964   "Job Satisfaction Researches of 1962," *Personnel and Guidance Journal*, 42: 136–142.

Robinson, Michael J.
 1976   "Public Affairs Television and the Growth of Political Malaise: The Case of 'The Selling of the Pentagon,'" *American Political Science Review*, 70: 409–432.
 1979   "Prime Time Chic," *Public Opinion*. 2 (March/May): 42–48.

Robinson, Michael J., Maura Clancey, and Lisa Grant
 1983   "With Friends Like These . . . " *Public Opinion*, 6 (June/July): 2–3, 52–54.

Roethlisberger, F.J., and W.J. Dickson
 1939   *Management and the Worker*, Cambridge, MA: Harvard University Press.

Rogow, Arnold A.
 1963   *James Forrestal: A Study of Personality, Politics, and Policy*, New York: Macmillan.

Rollins, Boyd C. and Kenneth L. Cannon
 1974   "Marital Satisfaction Over the Family Life Cycle," *Journal of Marriage and the Family*, 36 (May): 271–282.

Roper Public Opinion Research Center
 1980   *General Social Surveys, 1972–1980: Cumulative Codebook*, Storrs, CT: The Roper Center Office of Archival Development and User Services.

Rose, Richard, ed.
 1980   *Challenge to Governance: Studies in Overlooked Politics*, Beverly Hills, CA: Sage Publications.

Rosenthal, Jack
 1970   "U.S. Urged to Aid Blue-Collar Man," *New York Times*, June 30, p. 1, 20.

Rosow, Jerome M.
 1970   "The Working Man DOES Need Help: Another View," *Washington Post*, August 23, p. B-3.
 1974   *The Worker and the Job: Coping with Change*, Englewood Cliffs, NJ: Prentice-Hall.

Rosow, Jerome M., and Clark Kerr
 1979   *Work in America: The Decade Ahead*, New York: Van Nostrand Reinhold.

Ross, Arthur M.
 1958   "Do We Have a New Industrial Feudalism?" *American Economic Review*, 48: 903–920.

Ross, H. Lawrence
 1971   "Modes of Adjustment of Married Homosexuals," *Social Problems*, 18: 385–393.

Rosten, Leo C.
    1937   *The Washington Correspondents*, New York: Harcourt Brace.
Roszak, Theodore
    1969   *The Making of a Counter-Culture*, Garden City, NY: Doubleday
              Anchor. (All references are to this edition. A hardbound edition was
              published by Doubleday, 1969.)
Rothman, Stanley, and Robert S. Lichter
    1982   *Radicalism: Jews, Christians and the New Left*, New York: Oxford
              University Press.
    1984   "What Are Moviemakers Made of?" *Public Opinion*, 6 (December/
              January): 14–18.
Rothschild, Emma
    1973   *Paradise Lost: The Decline of the Auto-Industrial Age*, New York:
              Random House.
Rourke, F.E., L. Free, and W. Watts
    1976   *Trust and Confidence in the American System*, Washington, D.C.:
              Potomac Associates.
Rubin, Lillian Breslow
    1976   *Worlds of Pain: Life in the Working-Class Family*, New York: Basic
              Books.
Rush, Harold M.F.
    1969   "Behavioral Science: Concepts and Management Application," Per-
              sonnel Policy Study No. 216, The National Industrial Conference
              Board Inc.
Ryan, William
    1971   *Blaming the Victim*, New York: Random House.
Saleh, Shoukry D., and Jay L. Otis
    1964   "Age and Level of Job Satisfaction," *Personnel Psychology*, 17:
              425–430.
Salpukas, Agis
    1974   "Unions: A New Role?" In Jerome M. Rosow, ed., *The Worker and
              the Job: Coping with Change*, Englewood Cliffs, NJ: Prentice-Hall,
              Chap. 4, pp. 99–118.
Samuelsson, Kurt
    1961   *Religion and Economic Action: A Critique of Max Weber*, New York:
              Basic Books. This is a translation of the Swedish language original.
Scammon, Richard M., and Ben J. Wattenberg
    1970   *The Real Majority*, New York: Coward-McCann.
Schlaifer, Robert
    1980   "The Relay Assembly Test Room: An Alternative Statistical Interpre-
              tation," *American Sociological Review*, 45: 995–1005.
Schrank, Robert
    1974   "On Ending Worker Alienation: The Gaines Pet Food Plant," In Roy
              P. Fairfield (ed.), *Humanizing the Workplace*, Buffalo, NY: Prometh-
              eus, pp. 119–140.
    1978   *Ten Thousand Working Days*, Cambridge, MA: MIT Press.
    1979   *American Workers Abroad: A Report to the Ford Foundation*, Cam-
              bridge, MA: MIT Press.
Schulz, David A.
    1976   *The Changing Family: Its Function and Future*. Englewood Cliffs, NJ:
              Prentice-Hall.
Schuman, Howard
    1972   "Two Sources of Anti-War Sentiment in America," *American Journal
              of Sociology*, 78 (Nov.): 513–535.

Scott, Wilbur J., Harold G. Grasmick, and Craig M. Eckert
    1981   "Dimensions of the Tax Revolt: Uncovering Strange Bedfellows,"
            American Politics Quarterly, 9: 71–87.
Seeman, Melvin
    1971   "The Urban Alienations: Some Dubious Theses from Marx to Mar-
            cuse," *Journal of Personality and Social Psychology*, 19: 135–143.
Seifer, Nancy
    1973   *Absent From the Majority: Working Class Women in America*, New
            York: American Jewish Committee.
Seksconski, Edward S.
    1981   "The Health Services Industry: A Decade of Expansion," *Monthly
            Labor Review*, 104 (May): 9–16.
Semple, Robert B., Jr.
    1971   "Nixon Exhorts Nation to Attain New Prosperity," *New York Times*,
            Sept. 7: 1.
Sexton, Patricia Cayo, and Brendan Sexton
    1971   *Blue Collars and Hard Hats: The Working Class and the Failure of
            American Politics*, New York: Random House.
Shaw, Donald L., and Maxwell E. McCombs
    1977   *The Emergence of American Political Issues: The Agenda-Setting
            Function of the Press*, St. Paul, MN: West Publishing.
Shepard, Jon M.
    1971   "On Alex Carey's Radical Criticism of the Hawthorne Studies," *Acad-
            emy of Management Journal*, 14: 23–32.
Sheppard, Harold L., and Neal Q. Herrick
    1972   *Where Have All the Robots Gone? Worker Dissatisfaction in the 70s*,
            New York: The Free Press.
Shils, Edward
    1981   *Tradition*, Chicago: University of Chicago Press.
Shostak, Arthur B.
    1969   *Blue-Collar Life*, New York: Random House.
    1980   *Blue-Collar Stress*, Reading, MA: Addison-Wesley.
Shostak, Arthur B., and William Gomberg
    1964   *Blue-Collar World: Studies of the American Worker*, Englewood Cliffs,
            NJ: Prentice-Hall.
Siassi, Iradj, Guido Crocetti, and Herzl R. Spiro
    1974   "Loneliness and Dissatisfaction in a Blue Collar Population," *Archives
            of General Psychiatry*, 30: 261–265.
Simonds, Rollin H., and John N. Orife
    1975   "Worker Behavior Versus Enrichment Theory," *Administrative Sci-
            ence Quarterly*, 20: 606–612.
Singer, Barnett
    1977   "From Patriots to Pacifists: The French Primary School Teachers,
            1880–1940," *Journal of Contemporary History*, 12: 413–434.
Sirota, David
    1973   "Job Enrichment—Another Management Fad?" *The Conference
            Board Record*, 10: 40–45.
    1974   "The Myth and Realities of Worker Discontent," *Wharton Quarterly*,
            Spring: 5–9.
Smith, Adam
    1937   *An Inquiry Into the Nature and Causes of the Wealth of Nations*, New
            York: P.F. Collier & Son. (First published, 1776.)

Smith, Patricia Cain
    1955   "The Prediction of Individual Differences in Susceptibility to Industrial
              Monotony," *Journal of Applied Psychology*, 39: 322–329.
Smith, Tom W.
    1980   "America's Most Important Problem—A Trend Analysis,
              1946–1976," *Public Opinion Quarterly*, 44 (2): 164–180.
Smothers, David
    1980   "Studs Terkel: Mining Interviews for the Gold," *Montreal Gazette*,
              December 24: 18.
Soltow, Lee
    1975   "The Wealth, Income, and Social Class of Men in Large Northern
              Cities of the United States in 1860," In James D. Smith, ed., *The
              Personal Distribution of Income and Wealth*, New York: Columbia
              University Press, Chap. 9, pp. 233–276.
Solzhenitsyn, Alexander
    1976   *Lenin in Zurich*, New York: Farrar, Straus, and Geroux.
Spenner, Kenneth I.
    1979   "Temporal Changes in Work Content," *American Sociological Re-
              view*, 44 (6): 968–975.
    1983   "Deciphering Prometheus: Temporal Change in the Skill Level of
              Work," *American Sociological Review*, 48: 824–837.
Spreitzer, Elmer, Eldon E. Snyder, and David Larson
    1975   "Age, Marital Status, and Labor Force Participation as Related to Life
              Satisfaction," *Sex Roles*, 1 (3): 235–247.
Staines, Graham L., and Robert P. Quinn
    1979   "American Workers Evaluate the Quality of Their Jobs," *Monthly
              Labor Review*, 102: 3–12.
Stark, David
    1980   "Class Struggle and the Transformation of the Labor Process," *Theory
              and Society*, 9: 89–130.
Start, Rodney W.
    1962   "Policy and the Pros: An Organizational Analysis of a Metropolitan
              Newspaper," *Berkeley Journal of Sociology*, 7: 11–30.
Stein, Ben
    1979   *The View from Sunset Boulevard*, New York: Basic Books.
Stein, Robert L.
    1970   "The Economic Status of Families Headed by Women," *Monthly
              Labor Review*, 93: 3–10.
Stelluto, George L.
    1969   "Report on Incentive Pay in Manufacturing Industries," *Monthly
              Labor Review*, 92: 49–53.
Stogdill, Ralph M.
    1974   *Handbook of Leadership*, New York: Free Press.
Stouffer, Samuel A.
    1955   *Communism, Conformity, and Civil Liberties*, Garden City, NY:
              Doubleday.
Strauss, George
    1974a   "Is There a Blue-Collar Revolt against Work?" In James O'Toole, ed.,
              Work and the Quality of Life: Resource Papers for Work in America,
              Cambridge, MA: MIT Press, pp. 40–69.
    1974b   "Workers: Attitudes and Adjustments," In Jerome M. Rosow, ed., *The
              Worker and the Job: Coping with Change*, Englewood CLiffs, NJ:
              Prentice-Hall, pp. 73–98.

1976 "Job Satisfaction, Motivation, and Job Redesign," In G. Strauss *et al.*, ed., *Organizational Behavior, Research and Issues*, Belmont, CA: Wadsworth, Chap. 2, pp. 19–49.

Strauss, George, and Eliezer Rosenstein
1970 "Workers Participation: A Critical View," *Industrial Relations*, 9: 197–214.

Sudman, Seymour
1976 *Applied Sampling*, New York: Academic Press.

Sudman, Seymour, and Norman Bradburn
1974 *Response Effects in Surveys*, Chicago: Aldine.

Sullivan, John L., James E. Piereson, and George E. Marcus
1978 "Ideological Constraint in the Mass Publis: A Methodological Critique and Some New Findings," *American Journal of Political Science*, 22: 233–249.

Sullivan, John L., James E. Piereson, George E. Marcus, and Stanley Feldman
1979 "The More Things Change, The More They Stay the Same: The Stability of the Mass Belief Systems," *American Journal of Political Science*, 23: 176–186.

Survey Research Center
1975 *Americans View Their Mental Health—Codebook*, Ann Arbor, MI.
1975 *The Quality of American Life—Codebook*, Ann Arbor, MI.

Sussman, Marvin B.
1959 "The Isolated Nuclear Family: Fact or Fiction?" *Social Problems*, 6: 333–340.

Sussman, Marvin B., and Lee Burchinal
1962 "Kin Family Network: Unheralded Structure in Current Conceptualization of Family Functioning," *Marriage and Family Living*, 24: 231–240.

Swados, Harvey
1957a *On the Line*, Boston, MA: Little Brown.
1957b "The Myth of the Happy Worker," *The Nation*, 185 (Apr. 17): 65–68.

Sweet, James A.
1973 *Women in the Labor Force*, New York: Seminar Press.

Tausky, Curt, and E. Lauck Parke
1976 "Job Enrichment, Need Theory and Reinforcement Theory," In Robert Dubin, ed., *Handbook of Work, Organization, and Society*, Chicago: Rand McNally, pp. 531–565.

Taveggia, Thomas C., and R. Alan Hedley
1976 "Discretion and Work Satisfaction: A Study of British Factory Workers" *Pacific Sociological Review*, 19: 351–366.

Taveggia, Thomas C., and Bruce Ross
1978 "Generational Differences in Work Orientations: Fact or Fiction?" *Pacific Sociological Review*, 22: 331–349.

Taylor, D. Garth, Paul B. Sheatsley, and Andrew M. Greeley
1978 "Attitudes toward Racial Integration," *Scientific American*, 238 (6): 42–49.

Taylor, James C.
1977 "Job Satisfaction and the Quality of Working Life: A Reassessment," *Journal of Occupational Psychology*, 50: 243–252.

Taylor, Patricia Ann, and Norval D. Glenn
1976 "The Utility of Education and Attractiveness for Females' Status Attainment Through Marriage," *American Sociological Review*, 41: 484–498.

Terkel, Studs
    1974   *Working: People Talk About What They Do All Day and How They Feel About What They Do*, New York: Pantheon.
Thurow, Lester C.
    1981   *The Zero-Sum Society: Distribution and the Possibilities for Economic Change*, New York: Basic Books.
Tilgher, Adriano
    1930   *Work: What It has Meant to Men Through the Ages*, New York: Harcourt Brace.
Tittle, Charles R.
    1972   "Institutional Living and Self-Esteem," *Social Problems*, 20: 65–77.
Tocqueville, Alexis de
    1963   *Democracy in America*, (two vols.), New York: Alfred A. Knopf. (First published, 1835.)
Toffler, Alvin
    1971   *Future Shock*, New York: Bantam Books. The book first appeared in 1970, New York: Random House.
Traugott, Mark
    1980a   "Determinants of Political Orientation: Class and Organization in the Parisian Insurrection of June 1848," *American Journal of Sociology*, 86: 32–49.
    1980b   "The Mobile Guard in the French Revolution of 1848," *Theory and Society*, 9: 683–720.
    1985   *Armies of the Poor: Determinants of Working-Class Participation in the Parisian Insurrection of June 1848*, Princeton, NJ: Princeton University Press.
Trotsky, Leon (Morris Friedberg, ed.)
    1972   *The Young Lenin*, Garden City, NY: Doubleday.
Turner, Arthur N., and A.L. Miclette
    1962   "Sources of Satisfaction in Repetitive Work," *Occupational Psychology*, 36: 215–231.
Udry, J. Richard
    1977   "The Importance of Being Beautiful: A Reexamination and Racial Comparison," *American Journal of Sociology*, 83: 154–160.
United States Bureau of the Census
    1976a   "Number, Timing, and Duration of Marriages and Divorces in the United States: June 1975," *Current Population Reports*, Series P–20, No. 297.
    1977   *Statistical Abstract of the United States*. Washington, D.C.: U.S. Government Printing Office.
    1979a   "Marital Status and Living Arrangements: March 1978," *Current Population Reports*, Series P–20, No. 338. Washington, D.C.: U.S. Government Printing Office.
    1979b   *Current Population Reports*, Series P. 23, No. 84, Washington, D.C.: U.S. Government Printing Office.
    1982   *Statistical Abstract of the United States: 1982–83*, Washington, D.C.: U.S. Government Printing Office.
United States Department of Commerce
    1975   *Statistical Abstract of the United States*, Washington, D.C.: U.S. Government Printing Office.
United States Department of Housing and Urban Development
    1978   "A Survey of Citizen Views and Concerns about Urban Life." Mimeographed report of a survey conducted by Louis Harris and Associates.

United States Department of Labor
   1968a   *Manpower Report of the President*, Washington, D.C.: U.S. Government Printing Office.
   1968b   *Handbook of Labor Statistics*, Washington, D.C.: U.S. Government Printing Office, Bulletin No. 1600.
   1975   *Handbook of Labor Statistics*. Washington, D.C.: U.S. Government Printing Office.
   1977   *Handbook of Labor Statistics*, Washington, D.C.: U.S. Government Printing Office, Bulletin No. 1966.
United States Senate
   1972   *Worker Alienation 1972*, hearings before the Subcommittee on Employment, Manpower, and Poverty (July 25 and 26), Washington, D.C.: U.S. Government Printing Office.
Vollmer, Howard M., and Jack A. Kinney
   1955   "Age, Education, and Job Satisfaction," *Personnel*, 32: 38–43.
Vroom, Victor H.
   1964   *Work and Motivation*, New York: Wiley.
Walker, Charles R.
   1950   *Steeltown: An Industrial Case History of the Conflict between Progress and Security*, New York: Harper and Row.
Walker, Charles R., and Robert H. Guest
   1952   *The Man on the Assembly Line*, Cambridge, MA: Harvard University Press.
Walker, J., and R. Marriott
   1951   "A Study of Some Attitudes to Factory Work," *Occupational Psychology*, 25: 181–191.
Walker, Kenneth H., Arlene MacBride, and Mary L.S. Vachon
   1977   "Social Support Networks and the Crisis of Bereavement," *Social Science and Medicine*, 11:1 (Jan.): 35–41.
Wall Street Journal
   1970   "Review and Outlook: Blue Collar Alienation," July 17, p. 6.
Wallick, Franklin
   1972   *The American Worker: An Endangered Species*, New York: Ballantine.
Walton, Richard E.
   1974   "Innovative Restructuring of Work" In Jerome M. Rosow, ed., *The Worker and the Job*, Englewood Cliffs, NJ: Prentice-Hall, pp. 145–176.
Wardwell, W.I.
   1979   "Critique of a Recent Professional Put-Down of the Hawthorne Research," *American Sociological Review*, 44: 858–861.
Warheit, George J., Charles E. Holzer III, Roger A. Bell, and Sandra A. Arey
   1976   "Sex, Marital Status, and Mental Health: A Reappraisal," *Social Forces*, 55 (2): 459–470.
Wattenberg, Ben J.
   1974   *The Real America*, New York: Doubleday.
   1976   *The Real America: A Surprising Examination of the State of the Union* (rev. ed.), New York: Capricorn Books.
Watts, W., and Free, L.
   1978   *State of the Nation III*, Lexington, MA: Lexington Books
Weber, Max
   1948   *From Max Weber: Essays in Sociology*, H.H. Gerth and C. Wright Mills (transl. ed.), London: Routledge and Kegan Paul.

Weinberg, Arthur S.
    1975   "Six American Workers Assess Job Redesign at Saab-Scania,"
              Monthly Labor Review, 98: 52–54.
Weintraub, Emanuel
    1973   "The Real Cause of Workers' Discontent," *New York Times*, Financial
              Section, January 21, p. 14.
Westcott, Diane N., and Robert W. Bednarzik
    1981   "Employment and Unemployment: A Report on 1980," *Monthly
              Labor Review*, 104 (February): 4–14.
Westley, William A., and Frederick Elkin
    1957   "The Protective Environment and Adolescent Socialization, *Social
              Forces*, 35: 243–249.
Westley, William A., and Margaret W. Westley
    1971   *The Emerging Worker: Equality and Conflict in the Mass-Consumption
              Society*, Montreal: McGill-Queen's University Press.
White, Bernard J.
    1977   "The Criteria for Job Satisfaction: Is Interesting Work Most Impor-
              tant?" *Monthly Labor Review*, 100: 30–35.
Whitehead, Alfred North
    1957   *The Aims of Education and Other Essays*, New York: Macmillan.
Whyte, William Foote
    1955   *Street Corner Society*, Chicago: University of Chicago Press.
Widick, B.J., ed.
    1976   *Auto Work and Its Discontents*, Baltimore, MD: Johns Hopkins Press.
Wilensky, Harold
    1964   "Varieties of Work Experience," In Henry Borow, ed., *Man in a World
              of Work*, Boston, MA: Houghton Mifflin.
Wilson, Florence A., and Duncan Neuhauser
    1976   *Health Services in the United States*, Cambridge, MA: Ballinger.
Winegarten, Renee
    1974   *Writers and Revolution: The Fatal Lure of Action*, New York: New
              Viewpoints.
Witt, David D., George D. Lowe, Charles W. Peek, and Evans W. Curry
    1980   "The Changing Association between Age and Happiness: Emerging
              Trend or Methodological Artifact?" *Social Forces*, 58 (4): 1302–1307.
Wittman, Donald A.
    1973   "Parties as Utility Maximizers," *American Political Science Review*,
              67: 490–498.
Wolfe, Bertram D.
    1965   *Marxism: One Hundred Years in the Life of a Doctrine*, New York:
              Dial Press.
Wolfe, Tom
    1975   *The Painted Word*, New York: Farrar, Straus, and Giroux.
Wool, Harold
    1973   "What's Wrong with Work in America?—A Review Essay," *Monthly
              Labor Review*, 96: 38–44.
Wright, J. Patrick
    1979   *On a Clear You Can See General Motors*, New York: Avon Books
Wright, James D.
    1972   "Life, Time, and the Fortunes of War," *Trans-Action*, 9 (2): 42–52.
    1976   *The Dissent of the Governed: Alienation and Democracy in America*,
              New York: Academic Press.
    1978a   "Are Working Women *Really* More Satisfied? Evidence From Several
              National Surveys," *Journal of Marriage and the Family*, 40: 301–313.

1978b   "The Political Consciousness of Post-Industrialism," *Contemporary Sociology*, 7 (3): 270–273.

1979   "Comment on 'Whither the First New Nation?'" *Tocqueville Review*, 1:1 (Fall): 100–113.

1981   "Political Disaffection," In Samuel Long, ed., *The Handbook of Political Behavior* (Vol. 4), New York: Plenum Publishing, pp. 1–79.

1981a   "Public Opinion and Gun Control: A Comparison of Results from Two Recent National Surveys," *Annals of the American Academy of Political and Social Science*, 455: 24–39.

Wright, James D., and Richard F. Hamilton

1978a   "Blue Collars, Cap and Gown," *Dissent*, 25:2 (Spring): 219–223.

1978b   "Work Satisfaction and Age: Some Evidence for the 'Job Change' Hypothesis," *Social Forces*, 56:4 (June): 1140–1158.

1979   "Education and Job Attitudes among Blue-Collar Workers," *Sociology of Work and Occupations*, 6: 59–83.

Wright, James D., and Peter H. Rossi

1982   "Review of D. Yankelovich, *New Rules*," *Society*, 20:1 (Nov.–Dec.): 82–85.

Wyatt, S., and R. Marriott

1956   *A Study of Attitudes to Factory Work*, London: H.M.S.O.

Yankelovitch, Daniel

1974   *The New Morality: A Profile of American Youth in the 70's*, New York: McGraw Hill.

1981   *New Rules: Searching for Self-Fulfillment in a World Turned Upside Down*, New York: Random House.

Zeman, Z.A.B., and W.B. Scharlau

1965   *The Merchant of Revolution: The Life of Alexander Israel Helphand (Parvus), 1867–1924*, London: Oxford University Press.

Zimpel, Lloyd (ed.)

1974   *Man Against Work*, New York: Eerdmans.

Zorbaugh, Harvey

1929   *The Gold Coast and the Slum*, Chicago: University of Chicago Press.

NAME INDEX*

A

Abrahamson, Mark, 233n, *421*
Abrams, Mark, 283n, *421*
Abrams, M. H., 398n, *421*
Adams, Bert N., 143n, 156n, *421*
Aggar, Robert E., 89, *421*
Agnew, Spiro T., 138
Akers, Donald S., 149n, *421*
Albert, Prince, 214
Alford, Robert R., 207n, *421*
Almond, Gabriel A., 253–255, *421*
Alsop, Stewart, 3
Alston, Jon P., 207n, *430*
American Jewish Committee, 25n, *421*
Anderson, John, 343n
Anderson, Kristi, 342n, *440*
Andrews, Frank M., 329n, 366, *421*
Andrisani, Paul J., 228–230, *421*
Arendt, Hannah, 376
Arey, Sandra, 193n, *449*
Argyle, Michael, 86, *421*
Argyris, Chris, 28n, 85, *421*
Armknecht, Paul A., 278, *422*
Aronowitz, Stanley, 2, 26, 32, 42n, 49, 282, 283, *422*
Aronson, Eliot, 205n, *422*
Asch, Solomon, 418
Asher, Herbert, 340n, 341n, *422*

B

Bahr, Howard M., 110, 143n, 147–149, *425*
Bailes, Kendall E., 71, *422*
Baker, Kendall L., 366n, 386, *422*
Balzer, Richard, 30, 90, 91, *422*
Bandura, Albert, 154n, *422*
Bane, Mary Jo, 110, 147, 148, 391, *422*
Barkin, Kenneth, 395n, *422*
Barkin, Solomon, 25n, *422*
Barton, Allen H., 414n, *422*
Basu, Asoke, 417n, *437*
Beale, Calvin L., 148, *422*
Beatles, The, 54
Bechhoffer, Frank, 20n, *431*
Beck, Paul Allen, 379n, *422*, *435*
Bednarzik, Robert W., 296, *450*
Bell, Daniel, 2, 38, 40, 41, 49, 384, *422*
Bell, Robert R., 156n, *424*
Bell, Roger A., 193n, *449*
Bendix, Reinhard, 207n, *437*
Bengston, Vern L., 154n, 363, 367, *423*, *426*
Benson, Lee, 336n, *423*
Berelson, Bernard F., 16, 109n, *423*
Berg, Ivar, 268, *423*
Berger, Bennett M., 20n, *423*

*Numbers in italics indicate the page where the complete reference is given.

453

SUBJECT INDEX